GENDER AND IDENTITY

KEY THEMES AND NEW DIRECTIONS

STEPHEN WHITEHEAD

ANISSA TALAHITE

ROY MOODLEY

OXFORD

UNIVERSITY PRESS

GENDER AND IDENTITY

OXFORD
UNIVERSITY PRESS

Oxford University Press is a department of the University of Oxford.
It furthers the University's objective of excellence in research, scholarship,
and education by publishing worldwide. Oxford is a registered trade mark of
Oxford University Press in the UK and in certain other countries.

Published in Canada by
Oxford University Press
8 Sampson Mews, Suite 204,
Don Mills, Ontario M3C 0H5 Canada

www.oupcanada.com

Library and Archives Canada Cataloguing in Publication
Whitehead, Stephen (Stephen M.)
Gender and identity : key themes and new directions / Stephen
Whitehead, Anissa Talahite & Roy Moodley.
Includes bibliographical references and index.
ISBN 978-0-19-544490-2

1. Gender identity—Social aspects. 2. Sex differences (Psychology)—Social aspects.
I. Talahite-Moodley, Anissa, 1964– II. Moodley, Roy III. Title.

HQ1075.W485 2013   305.3   C2012-906223-5

Cover image: Giorgio Majno/Photographer's Choice RF/Getty Images

Oxford University Press is committed to our environment.
This book is printed on Forest Stewardship Council® certified paper
and comes from responsible sources.

MIX
Paper from
responsible sources
FSC® C103567

Printed and bound in Canada

1 2 3 4 — 16 15 14 13

CONTENTS

INTRODUCTION

Those of us caught up in the vortex that is globalization appear to be living in an age that is obsessed with the self: the pursuit of individualism, the privileging of personhood over community, the yearning for celebrity, the desire for the "perfect" appearance. As we move deeper into the twenty-first century, so we seem to be freeing ourselves from the bonds that previously bound us to others and nourished our sense of place in the world. Now we are intent on pursuing our individual life journey rather than a family or community obligation. The displacement of settled communities and the individuals within them has been a characteristic of post-industrialization around the world for some decades now, so perhaps we should not be too surprised at the emergence of the narcissistic society. The demands of globalization have placed us all under pressure to become more entrepreneurial, individualistic, competitive, mobile, materialistic, and singular in our outlook. Our loyalties, our relationships, our trust in others, even our belief systems are no longer lasting and unchanging. In this new age, all are open to re-evaluation. We pick and mix our lifestyles and belief systems as if in a supermarket. Our community locations are chosen for their material advantages rather than their familial or emotional needs. We may well still seek solace in our associations and in our love and friendship networks, but our ultimate comfort zone appears nurtured more through our perceived material

and social status, and much less in our relationships. For increasing numbers of us, even those communities we do engage with are the virtual ones of the avatar, the so-called second lives: the playgrounds of the imagination, the ultimate example of an individualized "community" experience.

In amongst this social shift sits gender. It configures us in ways we still do not fully understand. We can see its effects on lives, on individuals, and on social systems, but we often fail to see its effects on our selves. We tend to take our gender, and sexuality, as given to us—complete, unchanging, and natural. But in so doing we invariably fail to fully appreciate just how it becomes us, how we become a gender. The irony is, then, that in our pursuit of the perfect life, the fully individualized being, we fail to recognize just how other individuals, apparently different but identical to us in many ways, reside within our minds. Other people's languages, discourses, beliefs, philosophies, and ideologies, indeed their constructions of masculinities and femininities, are in us and will, in some form or another, remain so. Our flight to individualization and the privileging of self is ultimately a flight nowhere. We remain connected to the world around us. It is in us to our very core. Indeed, as this book reveals, we do not, cannot, exist without it.

Whatever the drivers behind this growing pursuit of materialistic and narcissistic individualism, the phenomenon has come to influence research and critical inquiry across numerous, if not most, academic disciplines. If once the critical turn in sociology was concerned primarily with class, structure, and economic imperatives, the sphere has widened to include the relationship of identity to such mediating conditions. Whether involved in study and research into, for example, business and management, organizational behaviour, criminology, education, social work, health and nursing, ageing, politics, ethnicity and race, or sport and leisure, one is very likely to confront issues directly relating to the self—in particular, the social construction of gender identity.

However, the sheer range and complexity of gender identities, existing as they do across diverse and constantly shifting social landscapes, means they cannot be fully and completely explored in any one book. As other scholars in this area have noted, there are no final statements to be made on identity. No single text can say all that can be said about the self. The facets of identity are too multiple, diverse, and contingent for that (De Francisco and Palczewski, 2007; Francis and Skelton, 2001; Shepard and Walker, 2009). Nevertheless, what we offer here is a comprehensive introduction to what constitutes and contributes to gender identity. But not just an introduction into key theories of gender identity, for the book takes an extensive look at the conditions and possibilities of gender identity work across numerous contemporary social, psychological, and political sites.

Some readers may ask why we have chosen to explore the political dimensions of gender identity in such detail. Well, the social, psychological, and political are, for us, indivisible. Gender identity can never be entirely neutral. It comes to each individual already invested in numerous discourses and assumptions, which while changing and evolving over the centuries, have never lost their power or persuasiveness.

A revealing example of just how political and contested gender identity continues to be is revealed by "Storm." Storm was only four months old when s/he made the international news in May 2011. Storm's Canadian parents, Witterick and David, had publicly confirmed they were not revealing Storm's gender/sex. In an email sent to family and friends, they said, "we have decided not share Storm's sex for now—a tribute to freedom and choice in place of limitation, a stand up for what the world could become in Storm's lifetime (a more progressive place)." Their decision brought forth a mix of incredulity, support, and vitriolic condemnation, not least from within their own family. But as Witterick, insisted, "In not telling the gender of my precious baby, I am saying to the world 'Please can you just let Storm discover for him/herself what s/he wants to be'" (Poisson, 2011).

So why the polarized and, in some cases, highly critical reaction to this apparently simple but considered decision by the parents to encourage Storm "to become who s/he wants to be"? Well, as we reveal in this book, gender and sex and sexuality trouble us and make us fearful, not least of our own limitations and our possibilities. We can too easily feel threatened by those who appear different, who seem to transgress the rules of society when it comes to identity performance and representation. And the reason is that such rules are powerful influences on our actions, on our sense of self. Gender and sexuality do not come to us wholly by choice; they come invariably with impositions, expectations, and in some instances harsh social and political conditions attached. This confirms that gender is neither neutral nor benign, although it could be; the decision of Storm's parents can be seen, therefore, as a brave and worthwhile attempt to encourage such neutrality—the freedom to choose and create one's own identity.

And maybe the world is ready for more Storms, for more parents making the decision to allow their children to explore their identity possibilities and discover who they can be. We certainly hope so; indeed, it is a contention of this book that the boundaries of gender, masculinity and femininity, are already blurring, becoming less defined and more porous. As you explore gender and identity with us through this book, so you too will come to appreciate not only the diversity of the human race but also its future possibilities in a world where there is more opportunity to discover one's potential—free of gender stereotype and negative judgment based simply on one's perceived genitalia.

A FEMINIST STANDPOINT

Precisely because gender and sexuality have political affects and consequences and therefore can never be experienced in an entirely objective way, so it is impossible to write a book on gender and identity that is itself entirely neutral and without a standpoint; and our declared standpoint is as feminist scholars. Here we use the term *standpoint*, drawing on its gender studies tradition, to emphasize how people's cultural location shapes the way they know, perceive, and interpret their world and the nature of their social relationships (see Harding, 1993; Harstock, 1989; Hekman, 1996; Collins, 1990; Freedman and Marshall, 2004). As feminist scholars we are, then, not only drawing on our academic knowledge and research, but we are also informed by our individual mix of gender, racial, ethnic, and sexual subjectivities. Out of this combination of influences, however, emerges a singular aim— that is, to encourage insight, enlightenment, and understanding as to the diversity and complexity of gender identity while also challenging gender-oppressive practices and attitudes. For us, gender justice, freedom from gender stereotype, and freedom from patriarchal, racist, and oppressive social, economic, and political conditions can all usefully be aided by critically exploring

how gender identity is experienced, enabled, and evolving in society.

UNDERSTANDING GENDER

This book is not just written from a feminist standpoint; it is written at a time when the world is experiencing rapid and uncertain change. Globalization and its effects on the sexual and international division of labour, along with the Internet revolution and migratory movements around the world are transforming traditional definitions of gender. Therefore, we need to view gender not as a singular and predictable category but as a social dynamic that is continuously shifting under the combined impact of economic, technological, social, and cultural change. Gender, then, does not stand alone; it is intersected with many other variables that combine to influence our sense of identity. Categories of difference, such as class, race, ethnicity, sexuality, disability, age, and religion, are just some of the many factors intersecting with gender in today's increasingly diverse societies.

But what is gender? Well the conventional idea of gender is that it is fixed from birth and neatly corresponds to our male or female genitalia. However research shows gender identity to be anything but stable and anything but predictable. In fact, it is highly contingent. No two people are exactly the same, even twins. Each of us has a unique social profiling that gives us a sense of belonging, which we duly present as our "identity" to others. But where does this social profiling come from? How much of it is given to us at birth, and how much is a consequence of our life and social and cultural experiences?

Most sociologists and psychoanalysts now consider that biology plays little role in our adult identity social performance. We change over the course of our lives; our bodies, our minds, our very sense of who we are changes—sometimes dramatically, sometimes slowly. We might not perceive these changes in our selves, but change we do. Imagine the 18-year-old first-year female undergraduate at university, and then imagine the 35-year-old mother of two children, in a relationship, working in a demanding profession. Are these two the same female? Yes, in name, but not in many other ways. And this change has come about almost by happenstance. That is, the 18-year-old has developed into the 35-year-old virtually without knowing it. And so the 35-year-old could very likely become the 70-year-old grandmother: the same person but, again, with a very different performance of self, gender, sexuality, and, ultimately, identity. Now what if that 18-year-old first-year female undergraduate at university becomes a 35-year-old transgendered father of two children, working in a demanding profession, and later becomes a 70-year-old grandfather? Has the grandfather been the same person throughout his life journey? Hardly. But it is not only his name that will have changed; he will have undergone quite profound shifts in his sense of self. Of course, most of us do not experience such dramatic transformations, but for sure we all change. We will be aware of some of the changes we go through more than others, depending on our perceptions of ourselves, and the experiences we undergo. This is what we aim to uncover in this book: the ways in which the changes that we experience in our lives (in our childhood, schooling, leisure time, careers, intimate relationships, old age, etc.) all conspire to affect and construct our sense of a gender identity.

At this point it will be useful for you to briefly reflect on yourself, your own sense of gender and sexual identity. How has that changed for you in the past five or ten years? Perhaps you can identify some of the markers or moments of change but can you predict how you will change in the next decade? No, you cannot. There are too many possibilities, too many variables, all of which will come to influence your sense of self in some way, for example, work, relationships, travel, and family. Numerous factors outside your immediate control will inevitably come to influence who you will be in the years to come. Today, you may be in your early twenties, studying at a university in North America or Europe. But then imagine for a moment the many men and women also in universities around the world reading precisely these same words, only they will be of different ethnicities, nationalities, religions, and cultural backgrounds. What does gender identity mean for them? How does the 18-year-old woman living and studying in Mumbai perceive the world, her femininity, and her prospects? What does the 25-year-old man studying in Hong Kong think about his gender and sexuality in relationship to his cultural setting and his future life? Importantly, how different are these perceptions from those of other readers, say, in Moscow, in Johannesburg, or in Buenos Aires? How similar are they?

This is the social contingency at the heart of our gender identity. Who we become is not necessarily dependent on who we have been or who we are today. In other words, there is little predictability. At the same time, the culture within which we are born and raised does give us a sense (or at times the illusion) of knowing who we are. Indeed, our culture is tremendously important and powerful. Look, for example, at the social dress codes and languages of some businessmen or football fans. Why and how are they different, and what do these differences signal both to others and to the individual? These people may all be male, but there the commonality stops. Each draws on what sociologists describe as a differing array of discourses to give meaning not only to the world around them, but to themselves.

We all are expected to have a gender, and we all are expected to have a sex. But how we act out these terms in the social world is the important variable. As a generalized term, *gender* refers to the social performance of our sex identity (male and female) (Lorber, 1994), but how knowing is that identity performance? Butler (2004) argues that a gendered sense of self is created through repeated performances but that much of this performance operates with little self-reflection. In other words, our gender emerges without us really understanding how. Another key variable that signals the fluidity at the heart of gender is the way in which it is always subject to the "social gaze"; that is, how others see us is as important to our sense of identity as is how we see ourselves. In learning what it means to be a male or female, we must first observe the gender performances of others.

Keeping with a biological perspective, some may consider there are just two genders (masculine and feminine). But is this the case? And does that mean that only men can perform masculinity? And women, femininity? Hardly. We know that there is significant crossover between these two social performances and within each individual and across social settings (Halberstam, 1998). In the same way, the traditional assumption is that there are only two sexes: male and female. Yet the reality is there are many more sexes, the example of intersexed individuals illustrating the complexity of what constitutes sex and gender (Fausto-Sterling, 2000). So to understand gender, and sex and sexuality, we have to first be very wary of assuming a biological driver to our sense of self. Our constructions of masculinity and femininity are not hardwired into us at birth. We learn how to be a male or female as it is understood in the particular cultural and social setting in which we live and work. The Buddhist, the Christian, the Hindu, the Jew, the Muslim, the Rastafarian, or the atheist male learns how to perform his masculinity in his particular social setting, just as does the Mongolian nomad. These men are not born with their religious or cultural gender identity intact, but acquire their masculinity through learned gendered performances.

To be sure, our individual gender performances feel "natural and fixed" but just because they operate under the radar of our consciousness does not mean they are instinctual and biologically grounded in estrogen, progesterone, or testosterone, or in chromosomes XX or XY (Juschka, 2009). The gender-as-culture hypothesis (Maltz and Baker, 1982) stresses that biological differences between men and women are amplified by the social system. That is, men and women learn and subsequently acquire the gender-accepted culture of a specific society (Tamaoka, Lim, Miyaoka and Kiyama, 2010). Gender role theorists would consequently argue that these culturally specific contexts define what is socially accepted for a particular gender, that is, the roles that are seen to be for women and those roles seen to be for men (Gibbons, Hamby, and Dennis, 1997). But gender does not work on its own, it connects to other key identity facets. In this book, we adopt an interdisciplinary perspective to look at the multi-layered complexities of gender and their interrelationship with other categories, such as race, class, sexuality, age, status, power, and so forth (Juschka, 2009). As we strongly suggest, in the final reckoning there is always a synergy between self and society (Kroska, 2000). As Stets and Burke (2005) argue,

> The self influences society through the actions of individuals thereby creating groups, organizations, networks, and institutions. And, reciprocally, society influences the self through its shared language and meanings that enable a person to take the role of the other, engage in social interaction, and reflect upon oneself as an object. Because the self emerges in and is reflective of society, the sociological approach to understanding the self and its parts (identities) means that we must also understand the society in which the self is acting, and keep in mind that the self is always acting in a social context in which other selves exist. (p.128)

All this tells us that gender identity is not an inevitable consequence of our biology. Indeed, the idea that women and men are fixed as distinct biologically predictable entities appears intellectually, personally and academically incomprehensible. At the same time, we recognize just how compelling the biological answer is for many people—how easy and simple to put it all down to nature. Then we can walk away and continue as if nothing will, or could possibly, change, especially our selves. But then things do change; we change. Indeed, we see diversity and difference all around us, and for this we have no explanation. As a result, we may be tempted to ignore the new realities around us. Our obliviousness of gender and sexual diversity may allow us to believe in the constancy of our selves and of others, and may reinforce our own truth systems, but it does nothing to help us understand the human condition. The retreat to nature, whether to explain gender, sexual, class, or racial differences, is a retreat to an intellectual cul de sac; it is an ontological comfort zone and nothing more.

WHAT IS MASCULINITY AND FEMININITY?

For the very reason just stated, it is impossible, therefore, to make a definitive statement about what, precisely, are masculinities and femininities. They are what people imagine them to be in any place, culture, community, or temporal period. There is not only one masculinity that all men adhere to, any more than there is only one femininity that all women adhere to. As we explain in this book, these are very loose terms, multiple in definition and constantly shifting in meaning in response to changing social values and beliefs.

So masculinity and femininity become representative of what are considered to be the appropriate behaviour performances of males and females in particular cultural sites at a particular point in time. To be sure, it is easy for some to associate acquired physical and mental attributes such as physical strength, rationality,

logic, and emotional illiteracy with males; and passivity, emotionality, sensitivity, and nurturing, with females. But as soon as we do, we reinforce gender stereotypes; we actually play into the hands of the socio-biologists who would claim that such differences are natural and unchangeable. Clearly, they are neither. But as social markers of gender they do serve a purpose, which is to provide an ontological setting within which we can practise being men and women. And for that reason what we think of as masculine and feminine behaviour remains powerful and influential in our identity work: our being and becoming a man or woman. But we are more than mere stereotypes. Particular practices may be socially associated with men and women, but as this book clearly reveals, men do practices that are commonly understood as femininities, and women do practices that are commonly understood as masculinities—and more so in the twenty-first century than probably any time through human history.

It is better to imagine such behaviours as part of the social menu available to us at any particular time in our lives. We all partake of this menu as we are expected to by society, as we choose, or simply as it feels right to do so. Such identity work is, of course, heavily mediated by the gender and sexual prohibitions and expectations that exist in our cultural and political settings. Learning our gender identity is, then, largely a process of coming to understand and recognize such boundaries. But these boundaries are porous, not permanent, and certainly not fixed in biology. We may draw heavily on some behaviours more than others, but none of this is inevitable and predictable. As the social and cultural environment in which we live is transformed over time, so are our attitudes, practices, and expectations. Indeed, our own changing behaviour does, itself, contribute to the cycle of change around us. As Stets and Burke (2005) infer, the emergent masculinities and femininities that we now see around the world are, in some minute way, a result of our individual practices. There is no one person, no one community, no one group out there dictating, directing, controlling, and leading all this movement. There is just you and me.

ORGANIZATION OF THE BOOK

We have organized the book so as to ensure that the content, theories, and discussion are accessible to as wide a readership as possible. First, we have structured the book into four parts: Part One: Theorizing Gender Identity: Classical and Contemporary Theories; Part Two: The Politics of Gender Identity; Part Three: The Practices of Gender Identity; Part Four: New Directions in Gender Identity. We have done this so as to highlight the interrelated aspects of gender identity, and the ways in which our assumptions and behaviours impact on wider society, and how society, in turn, is changing our understanding of gender, particularly masculinities and femininities. Second, the book is organized around 11 chapters, each containing easily identifiable major themes. That way, as a student of gender studies, you can go immediately to the section of your choice, at the same time using the glossary at the end of the book to clarify any particular terms or concepts.

Each chapter begins with learning objectives for the student and instructor to follow, and concludes with a chapter summary. A further key aspect of this book are the anonymous case studies inserted at the end of each chapter. These case studies reveal real-life accounts of how individuals have experienced an aspect of their gender and/or sexual identity in particular social and cultural settings. The aim here is to move the academic discussion into the realm of the "real" for the reader. We hope that by so doing, the stories will resonate with the reader, thereby ensuring a more explicit and visible connection with the politics and practices of identity

work. To help reinforce this connection, we provide discussion questions at the end of each case study. As well, there are a number of discussion points to end each chapter, which will be helpful for students in terms of their own personal reflections on their sense of gendered self, and for tutors as seminar discussion questions.

What is the rationale behind our organization of this book? Well, from a scholarly perspective, a critical examination of any social phenomena or human condition must be firmly located within a theoretical model so that the inquiry is rooted, not in a limited and subjective judgment, but in a sophisticated and sustainable academic discourse. But there are many such models, and they are increasing in number and complexity. As a result, it is up to the individual researcher and student to select the most appropriate model for their particular study and, perhaps, from this, to develop such models even further. Of course, such selection is itself partly subjective, if not political, although we will leave that debate to others (see, for example, Ramazanoglu and Holland, 2005). Nevertheless, subjective or not, the foundation for academic inquiry is academic theory. For this reason, Part One describes and explores the key theories that have come to inform our study and understanding of gender identity, although comprehensiveness in this field is likely to remain elusive. We have attempted to cover all the primary discussions, models, and concepts, from social constructionism, psychoanalysis, post-structuralism, and postmodernism to theories of race, post-colonial theory, queer theory, and disability theory. Our purpose in outlining the diversity of ways of understanding gender and identity is twofold. First, the historical perspective (from the classical to the more recent theories) presented in Part One is intended to provide a framework within which to understand how ideas about gender and identity have evolved over time and how we have come to interpret the world the way we do today. The second objective is to provide you with a sense of the diversity of approaches and their inter-connectedness. After reading Part One, you will hopefully see the similarities between, say, feminist theory and disability theory, or post-structuralist theory and queer theory. The case studies at the end of each chapter will give you the opportunity to put these theoretical ideas into practice. It is likely that you will use more than one theoretical approach when dealing with the complexities of the individual stories outlined in these vignettes.

Identity has always had, and still has, over-arching political implications, both for the individual and the communities around them. In Part Two, we have attempted to cover most of the salient political dimensions of our ontological process of being and becoming an individual. For example, we address some of the key debates and controversies in today's society, such as the relationship between gender and multicultural-ism, the tension points between religion and sexuality, the impact of gender movements, and the role of the media. As with the rest of the book, we have sought to strike a balance between our particular standpoint and theoretical frame-works, while also being committed to exploring increasingly complex and multiple dimensions to gender identity now apparent in numerous cultural locations.

Part Three takes the reader into the realms of gender and identity as practice, although clearly practice also has political dimensions, as this will be evident from the research we draw on in order to explicate this complex gender iden-tity process. We have selected those social arenas that appear central to us in terms of identity con-struction; but also important to us as individu-als and as academics with individual histories. We focus on the changes that have happened in our day-to-day experiences, such as the ways in which we understand intimacy, the idea of love, parenting, family, work, management, edu-cation, sport, leisure, war, violence, and aging. Our objective is not simply to review the main changes that have occurred in each aspect of our lives but to assess the impact each has had on our gender identity. To achieve this aim, we have focused on the changing and at times unpredict-able relationship between the public and the pri-vate spheres of our experiences.

Finally, in Part Four, we venture into the realm of the future in terms of gender identity. Just what are the trends, indicators, and new directions in terms of how we live our lives as men and women? For sure, change is all around us, but predicting how it might proceed and what its consequences might be is much harder. Anyway, we have attempted to do just that, which is always risky in human society, so forgive us if the future turns out quite different!

ACKNOWLEDGEMENTS

We are especially grateful to the following people for their contribution to the production of this book: Nancy Reilly, Phyllis Wilson, Patricia Simoes, Eric Sinkins, and Colleen Ste. Marie from Oxford University Press; the anonymous reviewers of the first-draft manuscript; Bathseba Opini, Melody Li, and Patsy Sutherland for assistance with research and referencing; Adam Dedman, Trey Dobson, and Catherine Chen for providing additional research material; and not least all those who offered their stories for inclusion in the anonymous vignettes.

Stephen Whitehead
Anissa Talahite
Roy Moodley

Part One

Theorizing Gender Identity:
Classical and Contemporary Theories

Chapter 1
Classical Approaches and Their Critiques

▲ Who we are to ourselves and who we are to others is, inevitably, a matter of reflection.
© Alija/iStockphoto

Learning Objectives

At the end of this chapter, you will be able to:

- understand the fundamental tenets of role performance, social constructionism, and psychoanalysis.
- appreciate how these theories have evolved to provide insight into gender identity and how they differ.
- understand that gender is not biologically fixed.
- understand that masculinity and femininity are multiple and variable.
- understand how social structure informs our understanding of gender.

OVERVIEW

In this chapter we will review three classical theories that have impacted how we understand gendered roles. We consider role performance, social constructionism, and psychoanalysis to be classical theories because of their major and continuing influence on how gender identity has been understood and analyzed by generations of psychologists and sociologists. As we explain, these theoretical paradigms overlap in some places while also connecting to other major sociological theories not directly concerned with gender identity. Role performance, social constructionism, and psychoanalysis have offered us various ways of understanding how **gender** informs our sense of being in the world. While certain theorists have focused primarily on the *external* social factors that are responsible for constructing gender roles, others have chosen to examine the *internalized* psychological processes that result from gender differentiation and that, in turn, reinforce certain gender patterns. Many of the theories in this chapter have been contested, challenged, and transformed, a fact that shows the dynamic and political nature of the debates about gender identity.

gender

The social expression of our sex identity. So whereas "male" and "female" can be understood as biological identities, our gender is the cultural presentation of such sex identity in the social world, e.g., our individual balance, combination, and performance of femininity and masculinity.

TABLE 1.1   Phases in Feminist Theorizing
Stage One: First- and Second-Wave Feminism + Critical Men's Studies

First-Wave Feminism, 1950s, 1960s, 1970s		
Today: Concepts and positions have become socially mainstream although much less influential theoretically with the exception of psychoanalytical feminist research		
Liberal Feminism	Key themes are equal opportunities for women, breaking down the glass ceiling at work, equal pay for women; challenging gender stereotyping; emancipating women; emergence of the women's movement; encouraging women to enter male-dominated work environs; equal-opportunities legislation; presenting women and men as biologically different but stressing that these biological differences should not lead to discrimination against women; first critical examination of Freudian and Jungian psychoanalysis within a feminist perspective; this wave also witnesses the first men gender theorists, highlighting issues such as a male sex-role identity crisis and male gender-role strain.	Mary Wollstonecraft, Betty Friedan, Joseph Pleck, Jack Sawyer, Naomi Wolf, Gloria Steinem, Martha Nussbaum, Simone de Beauvoir, Rosbeth Moss Kanter, Dorothy Dinnerstein, Nancy Chodorow, Susan Faludi

Second-Wave Feminism, 1970s, 1980s, and 1990s		
Today: Now much less influential, although it has gone on to inform Third-Wave Feminism		
Socialist Feminism	Provides explicit and more political critique of male power, which, it is argued, is based on the materiality of women's position in society and reinforced by global capitalism and men's dominance of work, industry, commerce, and management; the emergence of socialist pro-feminist men's groups; argues that women are not intrinsically (biologically) different from men but that capitalist patriarchal power relations position women and men differently; sees patriarchy and class divisions working together to produce gender oppression (dual-systems theory).	Heidi Hartmann, Juliet Mitchell, Sylvia Walby, Alison Jagger, Barbara Ehrenreich, Rosemary Deem, Iris Young
Marxist Feminism	Places more emphasis on the capitalist class system as the cause of women's oppression; draws heavily on the writings of Marx, Engels, and Althusser; argues that capitalism produces a sexual division of labour, limiting women's freedom of opportunity and reducing women to unpaid domestic labour; seeks overthrow of capitalism as an essential condition for liberating women.	Michelle Barrett, Sheila Rowbottom, Lise Vogel, Rosemary Hennessy
Radical Feminism	Emphasizes the concept and condition of patriarchy as the universal and organized oppression of women; highlights men's sexual violence against women—rape, domestic violence, sexual harassment; also the sexualized objectification of women through prostitution and pornography; sees the patriarchal nuclear family as a key factor in women's oppression; stresses men's exploitation of women through ideological gender/sex apparatus; influences the emergence of radical pro-feminist masculinity; argues that compulsory heterosexuality is an arena for the enactment of male dominance; suggests that women can only achieve freedom through physical separation from men.	Andrea Dworkin, Shulamith Firestone, Gayle Rubin, Catherine MacKinnon, Mary Daly, Kate Millett, Monique Wittig
Standpoint Feminism	A varied and encompassing perspective that links women's subjectivities and female embodiment with feminist action; posits that women's experiences in the social arena create for them a unique way of being in and seeing the world; argues for a feminist	Sandra Harding, Nancy Hartsock, Dorothy Smith, Alison Assister, Donna Haraway, Liz Stanley,

TABLE 1.1   (continued)

epistemic community based on the commonalities of womanhood; a feminist knowledge arising from women's/feminists' experiences of male oppression and patriarchal conditions; a feminist methodological approach to research and critical inquiry; early standpoint feminists drew heavily on Marxist/materialist feminist theory; contemporary standpoint feminists more closely align with post-modern feminism and the recognition of multiple realities and subjectivities among women while maintaining the political agenda of feminism.	Caroline Ramazanoglu, Susan Hekman, Seyla Benhabib, Susan Bordo, Mary O'Brien, Patricia Hill Collins

Critical Studies of Men, 1980s, 1990s, 2000s

Today: Highly influential, continuing to inform global research into men and masculinities

Primarily developed by profeminist men politically aligned with feminist agendas and drawing on second-wave feminist theories. These male theorists maintain a subjective separation from feminism, their rationale being that men cannot be feminists because of (1) their position within the political category of men, and (2) men's masculine subjectivity, which means they cannot truly know what it is like to be and live as a woman. Draws on a range of feminist positions, but is ultimately social constructionist in its approach and perspective. Influenced by Freudian and Jungian psychoanalysis, Gramscian hegemony, and non-essentialist understandings of gender identity. Provided the first critical gender research into men's lives, including gay sexuality, work, and management, fatherhood, violence, the public-private divide, heterosexuality, schooling, sport, criminology, aging, race and ethnicity; set the foundations for the sociology of men and masculinities that followed.	Raewyn Connell, Jeff Hearn, Andrew Tolson, Kenneth Clatterbaugh, Joseph Pleck, David Morgan, Michael Kimmel, Michael Messner, John Stoltenberg, Peter Nardi, Martin Mac an Ghaill, Michael Kaufman, Donald Sabo, Harry Brod, Stephen Heath, Dale Spender, Victor Seidler, Lynne Segal, Arthur Brittan, Richard Majors, John Tosh, Tim Edwards

Key Characteristics of Phase One Feminist Theorizing

Philosophical Heritage	Enlightenment, Modernism: tendency to see men and women as unitary political categories with mostly opposing personal/political agendas and interests, although also recognizes the multiplicity of masculinity and femininity. Draws heavily on a structural understanding of gender power and seeks to weaken/overthrow male dominance through various forms of political action.

Classical Theory Linkages	Social Constructionism: Gramsci, Marx, Althusser Role Performance (including symbolic interactionism, structural functionalism; gender/sex role paradigms) Psychoanalysis: Carl Jung, Sigmund Freud
Influential Terms and Concepts	Patriarchy, sexual division of labour, hegemonic masculinity, male crisis, masculinism, public–private divide, gender order, male dominance, oppression of women, patriarchal dividend, compulsory heterosexuality, multiple masculinities, sex-gender binary, gender and sexual essentialism, gender dualism, gender and sex stereotyping, gender segregation, glass ceiling at work, phallocentrism, biological determinism, identity politics, sexual liberation, male crises, personal-political

ROLE PERFORMANCE THEORY

Role performance theory takes as its central premise the assumption that people construct their identity through social interaction with others; through the roles that people adopt or are given in society; and through their relationship to pre-given structural conditions reinforced through culture and social expectation. As we demonstrate, role performance theory has links to other classical sociological theories, such as symbolic interactionism and structural functionalism.

Specifically, **role performance** refers to the roles that society gives us and the extent to which we do or do not act out these roles. For example, teachers' roles include planning and organizing for their students' learning, learning about their students, assessing and evaluating those students, communicating with their students' parents and guardians, organizing classroom resources, and so on. We would not expect such roles to be performed by a football player or nurse. Similarly, the parental roles traditionally assigned to fathers have differed greatly from those traditionally assigned to mothers.

Whatever the theoretical tool we may incline to, there appears to be an underlying reality to gender identity that is hard to escape from. That is, whether as men, as women, or as transgendered people, we are forever engaged in some form of social, cultural, or psychological exchange that is bounded by social conventions and expectations. This exchange appears to be a constant insomuch as it exists both as a form of social interaction with others and with social organizations and communities. And, importantly, it can be seen to be present in the individual's relationship with the self. To put it another way, the self—the subject, the individual—is always situated in some type of relationship, and it can be argued that it is the demands, conditions, consequences, and circumstances of this relationship that are pivotal to identity formation. So role performances are highly influenced by society and its cultures. They are not fixed, but, as mentioned, they are to some extent imposed (Butler, 2008; Warren and

> **role performance**
> The process by which individuals are expected to display particular behaviours in society depending on their social position.

Lengel, 2005; Busby, 2000). However, each of us adopts these roles to greater or lesser degrees depending on the particular circumstances of our upbringing, education, life chances, race/ethnicity, and the myriad social interactions that inform our existence. The question remains, however, to what extent the individual can overcome the imposition of roles: Is it inevitable that we will take on the roles offered to us? And in terms of identity, how does this relate to the larger social order? Where is the individual in the social structure? In order to explore these questions in more depth we turn to this notion of the self in relationship to society.

Role Performance and Structural Functionalism

In respect of gender, the concept of the "self in relationship" has roots in the work of Talcott Parsons and his theory of **structural functionalism** (1951). Parsons attempted to synthesize the theories of Max Weber, Herbert Spencer, and Émile Durkheim to produce a multidimensional social theory formed around the Darwinian notion of society as a kind of biological organism (see, for discussion, Waters, 1994). Structural functionalism suggests that humans instinctively gravitate toward social structure and order and that this basic drive provides the means for society to function as an optimal system to the benefit of the organism as a whole. Structural functionalism assumes femininity and masculinity to be "natural" organizing principles fundamental to an ordered society. Accordingly, society requires men and women to perform different, but complementary, tasks and roles seen as appropriate to their sex, notably production for males, reproduction for females. In performing

structural functionalism

A sociological perspective that views society as a set of coherent parts that work together to create social order and equilibrium.

such gendered roles, the individual not only contributes to a functioning society but gets to have his or her gender identity validated and confirmed by an appreciative society. For Durkheim (1933; 1957), the integration of society partly resides in a *conscience collective*: a shared consciousness with its roots in foundational religious and moral values, themselves grounded in unchanging, and unchangeable, gendered principles (see, for discussion, Morrison, 2001).

What we have here is basically a conservative approach to society and the individual. After Parsons died, in 1979, structural functionalism was subjected to extensive critique by social theorists (such as Christopher Butler, 2003), not least because of the overwhelming evidence that disproved that society is so ordered and stable, or that women and men are so fixed and predictable in their gendered behaviours and roles. Gender roles are not fixed or universally agreed upon. However, while contemporary social theorists may well discount—if not largely ignore—structural functionalism, many lay people are attracted to its powerful simplicity. Structure and order are compelling, especially when we are confronted with the harsh reality of disorder, change, and uncertainty, not least in our selves. However, as we illustrate later, while this yearning for order may appear "natural," it may also appear to have its base in the very multiplicity and *un*naturalness of our identity.

While structural functionalism may not be as attractive to contemporary social theorists as it was to those in the 1950s, it has left its mark on our understanding of gender identity. The theory takes us, first, into the realm of gender and sex roles and, second, into the concept of the self as a performer. These two strands of social theory—roles and performance—emerged during the 1940s and 1950s, and they resonate with Parsons' concept of society as one that is fundamentally rational and formed around powerful social conventions that the individual benefits from adhering to, not least because to do otherwise would likely expose him or her to censure, exclusion, and marginalization. So from this paradigm we can see how gender identity can be linked to the roles that men and women are expected to perform in any given social or cultural environment. The roles exist prior to the time the individual enters into society, and they strongly inform understandings of femininity and masculinity, both of which are seen as singular, largely predictable, and naturally ordered. Such ordering is reinforced by the dualistic structure of the public (largely male) and private (typically female) spheres that appear to have informed social systems for millennia.

The exchange we referred to above can be seen within role theory in the way that the individual—woman and man—assumes her or his predestined place in a gendered society, taking on roles that both reinforce gender identity and contribute to individual well-being and social organization (for examples, Komarovsky, 1950; Linton, 1945; Mead, 1934). In this respect, individuals have a contract with society, with individuals accepting an obligation to recognize and relate to the social realities that exist outside them (Durkheim, 1933). In turn, the individual has the opportunity to gratify the basic need for recognition and acceptance by internalizing the standards, beliefs, and ideas of society and of particular institutions (Parsons, 1951). Thus, individuals are always in a state of relationship to something larger and more powerful than themselves but which, simultaneously, reinforces their sense of individuality.

There is a neatness, a synergy, to role theory, and one can see why it had such resonance through the 1950s especially. The theory suggests that society is essentially harmonious just so long as individuals, and groups, act in ways that society expects of them and that are natural for them (Lee and Newby, 1984). Should this not happen then society and individuals suffer. So it is in everybody's interests that the status

quo continues, that order is maintained, and that deviance is punished. Again, fundamental to this notion is the belief that biological differences between women and men are not only inevitable but fundamental to and supportive of social cohesion. However, if this is the case then why is it that societies and cultures change, usually in very unpredictable ways, but still thrive? How can we explain the emergence of new roles in society for men and women and the demise of traditional sex roles? Clearly we need theories that begin to explain the nuanced dynamics of social interaction, not only at a macro level but perhaps more significantly for understanding gender identity at a micro one. Symbolic interactionism is such a theory.

Role Performance and Symbolic Interactionism

Symbolic interactionism is a branch of social psychology with roots in the works of George Herbert Mead, Charles Pierce, John Dewey, William James, and Herbert Blumer; indeed, the term "symbolic interactionism" was coined by Blumer in 1937 (Dingwall et al., 2012). Symbolic interactionists assert that individuals form their identities through interaction with others. People interact socially and adjust behaviour in response to the actions of one another. They socialize as active beings and construct their social worlds, thereby forming their own social realities (Smit and Fritz, 2008; Stryker, 2008). These social realities are subjective insomuch as they are perceived and internalized by the individual, but they are also symbolic in the sense that what is performed by the individual carries

symbolic interactionism
A sociological perspective that sees the self as being constructed through face-to-face interactions with others and the use of symbols in social communication.

social mores
The customs and values of a given society.

wider social meaning and influence. Social interaction contributes not only to forming our own sense of self, but has the potential to inform the sense of self of others, too. In this respect we are in a constant process of sharing, communicating, and symbolizing our social reality to others (Blumer and Khun, 1991).

One of the foremost symbolic interactionists was Erving Goffman (1959, 1971; 1972; see Manning, 1992; Lemert and Branaman, 1997; Jacobsen, 2010, for elaboration), who takes the basic concept of role theory and restructures it with a stronger sense of the individual as a social actor, a performer of roles. For Goffman, the individual is very much engaged in *impression management* in all social situations. Goffman describes impression management as a dramaturgical technique, in which the individual is literally an actor and the social setting, literally a stage. Individuals perform and enact the roles they are required to play for the benefit of both their sense of self and the audience, which is made up of other actors who are engaged in precisely the same performance management. The roles, and the performance, vary depending on the social situation we are in at the time. This social action arises from our ability to interpret types and forms of communication and symbols, to give them meaning, and, subsequently, to act on the basis of that socially inscribed knowledge. The appearance of authenticity that we seek to achieve is absolutely key because, like the actor on the stage, each person is projecting an identity to a knowing, and potentially critical, audience. In order to do this effectively and convincingly, we must become adept at learning, above all, the appropriate language, and, following this, the actions, postures, dress, and physical arrangements that correspond to the role

of the moment. As we mature and learn more complex **social mores**, or conventions, so we become increasingly adept and sophisticated at this impression management.

The question remains, of course, where is the self in all this performance? And at this point we come back to the structure–agency dichotomy. That is, to what extent am I performing these roles knowingly and willingly? Or is there some hidden and underlying tension in my self that is only partly relieved by my constant immersion in the performance? Are these roles compulsive and pressing me into conformity, or have I the capacity to express some creative—even deviant—counter-performance against the wishes of an otherwise all-persuasive social order?

In attempting to address these questions, Lofland (1980) has argued that Goffman actually offers two models of the self. The first is the social, or "official," self, the one that performs in everyday situations. This self is largely controlled through the mechanisms of prevailing normative social standards—in other words, the social conventions that dominate whatever "theatre" the performance is being acted out in. This official self has to express and engage in multiple roles, in multiple performances, each of which he or she "impression-manages" with varying degrees of success. But behind this outer self there is another one, a "truer" self that is vulnerable to emotional and impulsive actions. While it is the outer self that is engaged in projection and performance, the inner self reflects our core individuality and personality, maybe even a repressed personality, given that it constantly has to reconcile its psychological needs for freedom of expression with the demands of generally restrictive social roles.

Consider, for example, the social pressure on a woman to be a "good mother," especially in public. As research into Ontario mothers shows, mothering contains strict moral codes that require mothers to sublimate their own needs to that of others, e.g., their children (Gazso, 2012). A woman may be feeling tired after a day spent looking after her young children and/or working in a paid job. She may be anxious about money, relationships, friendships, or work. But when she goes shopping at the supermarket and takes along her young children she must maintain the image of a "good, competent mother." She will feel the judgmental gaze of other women upon her if her children misbehave, cry, or throw a tantrum. The mother not only has to cope with the children, she has to maintain her composure and patience. This is impression management under pressure, when part of us wants to react in a certain way but must always be sensitive to how such performances are viewed by others.

While Goffman did not attend to gender specifically, his notion of role performance can be used to understand how gender operates in social situations. Is it not the case that identities of mother, husband, worker, son, daughter, lover, soldier, manager, for example, are all distinct and rooted, to a large degree, in gender stereotypes? And do not these stereotypes manifest themselves as expectations and, subsequently, roles—performances of the self—which as social actors we feel compelled to get right, that is, to be a "good" mother, a "strong" man, a "successful" worker? It would certainly seem so. While we may rail against the demands of the role and the expectations that society has of us as gendered individuals, we mostly feel compelled to continue performing, not least because in so doing we are more likely to be accepted and granted membership in organizations, in social groups, in society itself. Moreover, having the opportunity to perform to others and to project our individuality is itself highly comforting and an elementary condition of our identity work.

So on a number of counts the structural-functionalist perspective is persuasive. However, its attempt to underscore predictability as a primary component in a functioning society reveals its fundamental weakness. For is it not also apparent that gender roles, expectations, assumptions have changed dramatically since the 1950s, and continue to do so? There is, today at least, a stronger sense of multiplicity and diversity, while gender stereotypes themselves have been subjected to rigorous critique. And are we not now seeing a turn toward greater freedom of expression and away from what Goffman and Parsons understood to be very persuasive and powerful gender expectations? If so, what does this mean for our gender identity, that so-called inner self that Goffman suggests we have?

To be sure, Goffman does not align himself explicitly with feminist agendas, and his concern appears less with social change and more with understanding how the social world maintains itself. He is recognizing that there may well be more to the self than simply the actor on the stage, but he is resorting to what are fundamentally gendered Freudian understandings of the id and ego struggling to reconcile the demands of the particular social order with basic psychological needs of self-expression and innate desire (for further discussion, see Smith, 2006; Scheff, 2006; Jacobsen, 2010).

The belief that gender is a core identity of the self, founded on biological distinctions, is one constant through all the writings within theories of role performance, whether they arise from concepts of role theory or from various perspectives within symbolic interactionism. This first wave of theorizing gender identity was very much located in a paradigm that spoke of singularity, predictability, cohesion, deviance, structure. It did not speak of fluidity and disruption. Importantly, role performance had little or nothing to say about male power and patriarchal social conditions. However, the first cracks in the paradigm became visible from the late 1950s and onward when sociologists began to recognize that for all their assumptions of order, theories of role performance had to take account of massive social changes and disruption at the level of gender identity itself (for further discussion, see Plummer, 1991; Denzin, 2001; Reynolds and Herman-Kinney, 2003).

The review of structural functionalism and symbolic interactionism shows that there is no single frame or theory that can provide full explanations of social behaviour. Relating ideas across theoretical traditions becomes imperative, which leads us to our next theory, sex-role theory.

Role Performance and Sex-Role Theory

Sex roles are sets of behaviours and characteristics that are *believed* to be standard for each gender in a society. But is there only one female sex role and only one male sex role (Basow and Heckelman, 1980; Kimmel, 2000; Mangan, 2005)? Society forces people into certain roles simply by expecting that those roles are proper and enforcing them. The biological view of gender roles states that the differentiated gender roles that exist in our society are products of our evolution, and are inextricably linked with abilities predominant in one gender or the other, which are determined biologically. The roles prescribed for each sex are based on physical abilities and properties of that sex, such as intelligence, brain lateralization, and differing hormone levels (Jean, 1980; Kimmel, 2000; Tarrant, 2006).

Sociologists have critiqued the **sex-role theory** as inadequate in explaining and understanding the complexities of gender as a social

sex-role theory

A theory of gender that focuses on the physical and biological differences between men and women as the basis for understanding the different roles they perform in society.

institution (Chetwynd and Hartnett, 1977; Kimmel, 2000; Steele, 2005). For example, Kimmel (2000) argues that the idea of role minimizes the importance of gender: "Gender, like race or age, is deeper, less changeable, and infuses the more specific roles one plays; thus, a female teacher differs from a male teacher in important sociological respects (e.g. she is likely to receive less pay, status and credibility)" (Lopata and Thorne, 1978, cited in Kimmel, 2000, p. 89).

Kimmel adds that sex-role theory posits singular, normative definitions of masculinity and femininity, yet these vary across culture and with time. Additionally, other aspects of difference including race, sexual orientation, ethnicity, age, ability, religion, geography, and nationality all influence and shape gender definitions and gender roles. Societies are never static but are ever changing, and sex-role theory cannot fully explain all the differences and similarities between men and women (for further discussion, see Taylor, 2010).

What becomes apparent, then, is that we need a fuller understanding not only of how sex roles have been socially presented as biologically fixed and therefore different for women and for men, but of the issues of gender power that underpin such assumptions. We also need an understanding of how sex roles are often highly problematic for any individual to constantly attempt to perform, particularly in a way that appears "acceptable" to wider society. So rather than accept sex roles as given and essential to society, we need to question the assumptions that serve to reinforce these as paradigms of (gender) behaviour.

Female Sex-Role Paradigm

Historically, women were stereotypically considered as lesser than men. Societal values and expectations perpetuated gender-role stereotypes that mandated men to be "masculine" and women to be "feminine" (Singh and Agrawal, 2007). Stereotypes of gender roles created by different cultures have governed people's lives throughout history. The rise of the feminist movement, however, saw increased awareness of societal inequalities and bias in the female–male gender-role prescriptions. As early as the late 1940s, feminist critics such as Simone de Beauvoir, who is well known for her often quoted statement, "One is not born, but rather becomes, a woman," initiated a move away from gender essentialism (de Beauvoir, 1972 [1949], 295). Accordingly, sociological research on sex roles moved beyond the conception of **biological sex roles** to traditional sex roles of masculinity and femininity. An individual could be described as "masculine," as "feminine," or as "androgynous" (having characteristics of both men and women, or having neither strong masculine nor strong feminine characteristics). Masculinity and femininity are thus seen as separate and independent dimensions and not as opposite ends of a single bipolar continuum (Bem, 1974). Age, race, and social class further define individuals' roles, which influence how men and women interact and the attitudes and behaviours expected of each (Lindsey, 1994).

Traditional gender roles emphasize separate spheres of influence for women and men, with women inside the home and men outside the home (Duncan et al., 1997). Consequently, and for a long time in the education system and other arenas, males were described in terms of instrumentality or active ability to successfully manipulate the environment, while females were evaluated based on expressive, interpersonal, or ornamental criteria. Male sex roles were expected to translate into references to cognitive ability or cognitive styles for males along with evaluation of academic goal orientation. Female sex roles would, conversely, manifest noncognitively in references to emotional and interpersonal attributes, physical attractiveness, and sexual availability (marital status) (Parsons and Bales, 1955, cited in Henderson, Briere, and Hartsough, 1980, p. 75). However, modern views of gender roles

> **biological sex roles**
>
> The roles men and women perform based on their biology (for example, being a mother or a father).

are that men and women may engage in behaviours traditionally ascribed to either sex (Blee and Tickamyer, 1995). Women are increasingly engaging in fields presumed traditionally to be "challenging" and have achieved great success (Nizami and Ahmad, 2005). Similarly, men may engage in care work at home and tend to still remain achievement oriented in the workplace. Despite these changes, traditional assumptions of male and female sex roles still persist and are reinforced through avenues such as religion, peer influence, familial practices, and the school system.

Male Sex-Role Paradigm

In the late 1950s, social science research emerged in the US that suggested that men were struggling with the dominant male role models handed down to them by their fathers and by society generally. Men's identity, far from being comfortably ensconced in predictable patterns of behaviour and reinforced through powerful social conventions, was facing something of a crisis (Hacker, 1957; Hartley, 1959). One of the central forces in this change was the move from an industrial to a post-industrial society (Bell, 1975). The old and familiar patterns of male employment that had long served to reinforce dominant masculinity were changing. Women were becoming educated and entering the workforce in increasing numbers. Male unemployment was rising and notions of a job for life were disappearing. The male breadwinner–nuclear family model was under strain. A more forceful and confident femininity was adding to the already raised questions as to the worth and validity of traditional models of masculinity (see, for example, Ehrenreich, 1983).

These studies heralded the beginnings of a closer sociological scrutiny on men, not least encouraged by the feminist philosophies and theories emerging at this time within Western universities. Writers such as Pleck (1976), David and Brannon (1976), Fein (1978), and Pleck and Sawyer (1974) published critiques of what they saw as the inflexible and outdated male sex-role paradigm. Pleck (1981) proposed the concept of the *male sex-role strain,* which suggested that gender stereotypes defined the roles required of women and men but that men can experience the most strain and negative psychological consequences from failing to perform such roles in a way appropriate to their sex. Dominant, ideologically informed models of masculinity were increasingly seen as contributing to forms of male trauma and dysfunction as men struggled to match the expectations of the traditional male sex role with the realities of a fast changing social world. Far from contributing to an ordered and harmonious society, the male sex role was increasingly seen as problematic. Feminists were pointing out that the "functional system" described in the work of theorists such as Parsons and Durkheim was in fact sexist, patriarchal, and in many instances openly **misogynistic** (Lopata and Thorne, 1978; Gerson, 1985; Weitzman, 1984). They argued that it wasn't just the roles that were gendered; so, too, were the institutions within which these roles were required to be performed (Daly, 1978). This recognition of the price women and men paid as individuals and social actors in their continued adherence to traditional gender roles and performances began to change how sociologists saw the world. Gender went from being relatively invisible in sociology to being recognized as a primary determinant of, and potential constraint upon,

misogynistic
An attitude that consists of mistrusting, disliking, or hating women.

individual freedom, justice, equality, and opportunity (see, for discussion, Connell, 1995; Lorber, 2010; Phillips, 2010).

In the end, the powerful and compelling simplicity that makes theories of role performance so attractive is, in fact, its undoing. Societies, and individuals, are much more complicated, complex, and diverse than suggested in notions of role theory. We know from the dramatic and rapid changes of the past few decades that women and men are entirely capable of forging new and counter-intuitive roles for themselves—and then ditching them and moving on to something entirely different. Role theory cannot account for this dynamism and unpredictability in the human subject. Moreover, any attempt to slot women and men into separate categories ignores the interrelationship of masculinity and femininity. Gender is relational; our understanding of what it means to be a woman is largely defined by our understanding of what it means to be a man and vice versa. These concepts do not exist as insular and discrete models. We no longer think of femininity and masculinity in the singular but as multiple, contingent, and changeable (Connell, 1995). Any theory of gender identity must at least be able to offer some insights into diverse subjectivities, including those peoples positioned as "others" in society—for example, ethnic minorities, gays and lesbians, and transsexuals. Finally, it is always risky to base any theoretical models of society on notions of rationality and functional self-interest. Despite what we might like to believe, we are not so rational human subjects as we think.

As we noted earlier, the first wave of theorizing gender identity seemed to say it all. And then it got complicated, to the extent that many theorists now feel such simplistic theories actually say little at all. The reality is probably somewhere in between. Gender roles do exist, not least as powerful social, cultural, and organizational expectations on the individual. Work, family, and relationship behaviours are invariably informed by long-standing cultural assumptions about what it means to be a woman or a man, and gender roles are central to how such behaviours are acted out. We do perform our gender, although not as literally as Goffman suggested. What is missing from theories of role performance is, first, a cohesive and sophisticated understanding of the self and, second, a recognition that gender identity is not a tidy model handed down to us, which we then act out, but an alluring, messy, powerful, political, conflicting, and changeable dynamic that many of us struggle with all our lives.

SOCIAL CONSTRUCTIONIST THEORIES

Constructionism came about in the latter half of the twentieth century as a reaction to essentialism and has become an intellectual movement whose empirical insights are widely recognized (Burr, 2010; Gubrium and Holstein, 2007; Lock and Strong, 2010). Even though some critics have argued that constructionism is "too diverse and diffuse to define" (Lynch, 2001), Burr (2003) argues that there are some key elements that describe constructionism:

1. Recognizing that our world is culturally and historically specific
2. Recognizing that people construct their own versions of reality
3. Recognizing that language is a central influence on our thoughts and the way we see the world
4. Recognizing that there is no such thing as an objective fact

Social constructionism is about developing phenomena relative to social contexts. It argues that categories such as race, gender, and sexuality are social and cultural constructions. For example, a constructionist would consider racial difference not as a "natural," biological difference but as "the outcome of practices of (de)

social constructionism
A perspective that considers the roles we perform in society as the result of the social or cultural factors that influence our behaviour.

racialisation which position groups and subjects in more or less advantageous and discriminatory ways" (Henwood and Phoenix, 1996, p. 853). In other words, race is a category constructed by particular socio-historical conditions that posit whiteness as superior to blackness. Similarly, sexuality is, for constructionists, not pre-given or instinctual, but the result of historical and cultural factors embedded in relationships of privilege and power as demonstrated by Michel Foucault in his three volumes on the history of sexuality. The main objective of social constructionism is to demonstrate that social differences are not fixed in stone but are the result of particular historical and social practices involving hierarchical structures and relationships of power and dominance.

When considering gender, it is the political dimensions to gender identity that are the primary concern of social constructionist theorists. Unlike theories of role performance, social constructionism can be intimately and explicitly aligned with feminist agendas and issues of social justice across society. Not only is this theoretical position developed to understand the relationship between gender and social behaviour, it has a wider remit, which is to bring about changes in social policies and individual subjectivities through raising awareness of gender inequalities. Social constructionism starts from the premise that there is a clear power differential between women and men, and therefore any theories of identity must first take account of this reality. Whereas role performance never really manages to disentangle itself from essentialist, biologically informed notions of identity, social constructionism is explicit about the social basis to, and consequences of, gender (see Kimmel, 2000, and Hibberd, 2005, for elaboration).

Like all the theories under examination in this book, there will always be differing perspectives among those who otherwise might be seen to be their proponents, and this is particularly true of social constructionism. Part of the problem as already noted is the term itself—it is very broad and can, therefore, be interpreted very loosely. Social constructionist Raewyn Connell argues against the term because it does not give an adequate account of the sexed body (1995, p. 50). And we have a pro-feminist post-structuralist, Alan Petersen, aligning himself with the term because he considers it does precisely that. As Petersen recognizes, "social constructionism is

> **hegemony**
> The dominant position occupied by certain groups of people, certain ideas, and certain social norms over others.

a generic term encompassing a diverse range of shifting perspectives and projects" (1998, p. 12). Included in this wide range of perspectives are the movements and theories that have emerged in our contemporary era as the result of constructionist thinking. As we will see in the next chapter, post-structuralism and postmodernism draw heavily on the constructionist idea that identities are socially and culturally constructed and therefore multiple and variable. Furthermore, and as we will explore in Chapter 3, contemporary theories of difference based on categories of identity such as race, sexual orientation, and disability

> **juridico-discursive model of power**
> A macro perspective of power that considers a combination of state apparatuses (e.g., laws and legal system) and cultural norms to enable certain individuals and groups to dominate others.

are also largely indebted to constructionist views of identity, even though they might depart from them at times.

The Macro Perspective of Social Constructionism

From the foregoing discussion, we should note that not all social constructionism is feminist. Social constructionism, as applied within critical gender theory, rests on an understanding of gender identity as (in)formed primarily by ideology and therefore rooted in a gendered power system that men have constructed over time. This gendered power system serves men's interests directly or indirectly, for example, through what Connell terms a *patriarchal dividend* (1995). This is not a natural order based on biologically unchangeable "facts" about women and men but a socially constructed, culturally specific, **hegemonic** system, reinforced by men's control of powerful institutions and systems and their potentiality for violence. The strength of social constructionism is that it provides a comprehensive and forceful examination of gendered power. Not only does this theory enable us to understand the consequences of gendered power in the lives of individual women and men, it exposes the familial, institutional, organizational, and cultural manifestations of such power across societies.

Despite its obvious strengths, we suggest that social constructionism is best deployed as a macro (i.e., global identity) perspective, illustrative of prevailing cultural values, not a micro (i.e., individual identity) one. Social constructionism connects directly with concepts such as patriarchy, hegemony, and gender order—all concepts directly associated with and located within a **juridico-discursive model of power** (Foucault, 1980, 1983). Such a model is a liberal humanist, realist perspective that sees (gender) power as hierarchical, materially based, possessed by group or individual, and primarily coercive and prohibitive, although not necessarily imposed without resistance (see, for discussion, Whitehead, 2002; also Sawicki, 1991; Ramazanoglu, 1992; McNay, 1992). In other words, power is seen as a force that is concrete and predictable and underpinned by violence, laws, wealth, or threat. It is usually linked to larger social structures and associated cultures that people may feel compelled to adhere to. It is the power of one person over another, one society over another, one group of people over another group or individual, one gender over another gender.

However, unlike post-structuralism, which we explore later, the juridico-discursive model of power does not provide an informed and persuasive understanding of subjectivity or of the subject (individual), nor of the identity work that renders the self into existence. In short, the identity work of the individual is less apparent in social constructionist perspectives, whereas oppressive perspectives of power seen as imposed upon the individual are fundamental.

The Role of Ideology in Social Constructionist Theories

Ideology, as a concept, has played a central part in social constructionist theories. It is an elusive term to define as it is not a thing in itself, although it can become a thing inasmuch as ideas are things and therefore have material existence (Juschka, 2009). One of the key social constructionist theorists to engage with the concept of ideology was Louis Althusser (1918–90). Althusser noted that the term *ideology* was developed by Pierre Jean Georges Cabanis and Antoine Louis Claude Destutt, comte de Tracy, and their friends, who in 1796 assigned to the term an object, the (generic) theory of ideas. Karl Marx picked up the term and used it to describe a system of ideas and representations that dominate minds of peoples (Althusser, 1995, cited by Juschka, 2009, p. 3). Later Althusser took up the

term and devised a persuasive understanding of ideology, one that has maintained its currency and resonance within sociology to this day, although not without critique (see, for example, Barrett, 1991; Hall, 1985).

Althusser (1971, 1984, 2000) takes the example of the concept of God to make his point. As Althusser posits, God is the absolute subject with the power to interpellate individuals into subjects through naming them and giving them an identification, in Althusser's example within the apparatus of Christian religious ideology. Althusser is not arguing for or against the idea of God's existence, but that Christian religious ideology exists, and that this ideology is no different to any other as each ideology operates in precisely the same way. So, in this example, we have the individual subjected to the subject (apparently God, but in reality Christian religion) through the ideological apparatus of organized religion. Christian believers identify with society but in the process are required to unquestioningly accept their subjection to ideology.

Why should people concur with this act of submission? Because they are persuaded that this ideology is reality and therefore true, or, as Althusser puts it, they are given "the absolute guarantee that everything really is so, and that on condition the subjects recognize what they are and behave accordingly, everything will be all right" (2000, p. 37). People are conscious of the Christian religion; what they are not conscious of, Althusser argues, is the **ideological apparatus** that both subjects them to religion and, correspondingly, creates their identity and subjectivity as subjects (Christians). In other

ideological apparatus

The institutions (such as the school, the state, the church) that are responsible for spreading the ideas, values, and norms of a dominant social class.

words, they have a **false consciousness** about the conditions of their reality and the circumstances under which their identity was formed and is enacted. They are being, therefore, "duped" into a false reality, a way of behaving and thinking that may not always be in their best interests and that limits their potential for free expression and advancement. The ideological apparatus that creates and reinforces this condition is, in Althusser's example of organized religion, the church and those who lead it.

false consciousness

Being unaware of and unable to recognize one's own repression and subjection to ideological conditions.

So who benefits from this ideological apparatus? Not God, who is merely an enlisted tool employed to persuade and validate this religious dominance. For all we know, God may be no more than a myth. The beneficiaries are those who control, in this example, Christian religious ideology, although the point can equally be made for any religion, for the state (the social elite), for capitalism (owners of capital), and for the gender order (men). And this is the key factor in ideology and in Althusser's argument: there is always someone behind the ideology, a doer behind the deed. No ideology can exist without the conscious intent of others, namely those powerful enough to ensure its continuation. This is **Gramscian hegemony** in action, with ideological contestation being fundamental to class (and gender) dynamics (Gramsci, 1971). The doers behind the

Gramscian hegemony

The situation whereby, according to Antonio Gramsci, the ruling class uses language, culture, and ideology (such as the media) to make its dominant position look "normal" and "natural" to the larger population.

deed are those who benefit directly from the particular system of domination. Others, "cultural dopes," will be co-opted into the system to ensure its continuation, but because they are unable to see the conditions of their own subordination they remain willingly enslaved to the ideological apparatus that affects how they see and act in the world—their very sense of self.

Patriarchal Structure of Social Constructionism

Let us take the discussion into the realms of gender. A child is born, and immediately upon birth that child is identified as male through his genitalia, and upon that child is immediately imparted an ideological apparatus that names him as male/boy. The ideological apparatus of gender reinforces itself through the dominant expectations of the masculine, which will, from that time on, condition that child's subjectivity to that particular ideological apparatus.

The child eventually becomes a man but fails to recognize that this man that he has become is merely the expression of a larger ideological condition (patriarchy) that men are born into and that, throughout their life, will, in the final analysis, not only name them and identify them but dictate, or at least strongly influence, how they should behave as men. However, men also directly benefit, materially, from patriarchal ideology and the subsequent subordination of women; at the very least, they are complicit in the continuation of the gender status quo. They are born into a preexisting historical social condition that materially privileges them, for example, through greater job and career opportunities, through higher rates of pay, through greater freedom of sexual expression, through reduced child-care or domestic responsibilities, through access to positions of power and authority. Moreover, it is precisely through their position in these places of power that men continue to enforce, if not enjoy, the benefits of the patriarchal condition: examples being in the government, the police and armed forces, the judiciary, the media, indeed all those elements that sustain what Althusser describes as the *ideological state apparatus*. So whether or not individual men are enthused and active supporters of patriarchy and women's subordination, their actions, particularly their expressions of *hegemonic masculinity* (Connell, 1987), serve to ensure the continuation of patriarchy and women's subordination in some form or another.

Ideology is, then, fundamental to the concept of social constructionism, for it is seen as the underlying tool at work in this process of subjecting individuals, socializing them to dominant, powerful norms, beliefs, codes, rules, and orthodoxies. The social constructs the individual, informs the individual's very subjectivity, subjects the individual to an overarching and powerful apparatus that, in respect of feminist theory, is recognized to be a system largely deployed by men for men's benefit.

Across several key strands of feminist theory we can see Althusser's concept of ideology at work and enlisted to understand men's dominance and women's subordination, although to be sure there are differences (see Tong, 1994, for elaboration). For example, **Marxist feminism** highlights the ideology behind capitalism and the system of exchange and (class and family) power relations that serve to construct women's consciousness and so-called female nature (see, for example, Barrett, 1980; Armstrong et al., 1985; Bannerji, 1995). **Socialist feminists** maintain that the ideologically informed dual systems of patriarchy and capitalism exist as distinct forms of oppression and that through their intersection women's subordinate condition is made explicit (see, for example, Mitchell, 1971; Holmstrong, 2002). **Black feminism** and **post-colonial feminism** emphasize the role of racism and colonialism in reinforcing the capitalist and

> ### Marxist feminism
> A feminist approach that sees women's oppression as part of the larger capitalist and imperialistic inequalities that underpin society.
>
> ### socialist feminists
> Feminists who consider women's oppression as the result of both patriarchy and class inequalities.
>
> ### black feminism
> A feminist approach that focuses on the question of race and the interconnection between sexism, racism, and class domination.
>
> ### post-colonial feminism
> A feminist approach that sees women's liberation as dependent on the process of decolonization from Western forms of domination inherited from colonialism.

patriarchal ideological system that contributes to perpetuating gender, class, and race inequalities (see, for example, hooks, 1981; Mohanty, 1984; Min ha, 1989; Hill Collins, 1990; McClintock, 1995; Narayan, 1997; Bannerji, 2000; Razak, 2008). For **radical feminists**, sexuality and accompanying (heterosexualist) ideologies are at the root of women's oppression, with men using these dominant belief systems to serve their own interests (see, for example, Millett, 1970; Whittier, 1995; Lanzetta, 2005; Swarr and Nagar, 2010). **Liberal feminists** claim that women must first "cure" themselves of the ideologically informed "feminine mystique" if they are to achieve personal fulfilment and equality with men across both the public and private spheres (Friedan, 1974; Ferguson, 1986).

Social constructionism is, then, explicitly linked to the more orthodox schools of feminist thought, which seek to emphasize the

radical feminists

Feminists who consider patriarchy and sexual domination as the root causes of women's oppression.

liberal feminists

Feminists who advocate the need for more opportunities for women as individuals rather than a total transformation of the social system responsible for gender inequalities.

structuralist, patriarchal, hegemonic features of male power and the gender order. To this end, such schools of thought are forever bound up within the polarities of structure and agency. That is, to what extent can women resist such oppression, and to what extent can or will men change and challenge this system, which would appear to be historically devised in their interests?

Althusser's concept of ideology may be considered extreme and indeed has many critics, but it is persuasively devised and explicated. Althusser is making the claim for the virtual total absence and loss of agency (freedom, choice) and the subjection of the individual's very sense of self and identity to a larger, if not overwhelming, structural system. Such a system is rooted in the language of ideology and related apparatus but has the capacity to draw on a variety of conditions and forces in order to maintain itself. But this structural system, and the social constructionism that issues from it, is not a natural or biological state—it derives from the purposeful actions of men. It is, fundamentally and in feminist terms, patriarchal.

The choice then becomes, for many feminists, how to approach and critically theorize this ideological condition, and to what extent to accept or deny the notion of false consciousness, which is inherent, albeit to differing degrees, across most strands of feminist theory. For there

is a problem inherent in this analysis, which is to explain why some women (feminists, for example) are apparently able to operate outside this ideological condition, that is, not be "cultural dopes," when so many others apparently are. As McNay (1992; also 2000) argues, the more structuralistic feminist theoretical approaches must, by definition, draw heavily on a deterministic, disciplinary understanding of power. Consequently, such perspectives problematize the very possibilities of women's agency or, indeed, men's capacity to change also, for these theories "make the problematic assumption that women are simply passive victims of systems of patriarchal domination" (McNay, 1992, p. 36; see also Lloyd, 2005, for discussion). Moreover, the question must be raised as to how men have initiated this state of affairs and maintained its hegemonic legitimacy through history and across numerous cultural borders. In other words, to what extent is this a conspiracy of action by elite and powerful men, who themselves are somehow outside the condition of ideology which they apparently control? Not all men collude in such a system; many actually suffer under it. This raises questions as to how and why many women and men are able to maintain a separation from the social constructionist properties of ideology, understood in Althusserian terms as an overpowering system of identity management, which we will delve into next.

Exercising Agency and Choice in Social Constructionist Theory

One solution to this dilemma may well reside in how we actually understand the individual's capacity for exercising agency and choice, notably as resistance. In order to act, to be an actor, to exercise intentionality, and to choose, all of which are characteristics of agency, there must be power, that is, the power to differentiate, to select. Identity work is more than the overwhelming attachment of the subject to ideological language and practice; it is simultaneously the exclusion of competing possibilities:

- *I am a man; what I am not is a woman.*
- *I am gay; what I am not is straight.*
- *I am a Christian; what I am not is a Jew.*

The constitution of identity is always and inevitably invested with the power to distinguish, simply because every identity signals what it is not as much as what it is. In other words, the very "constitution of social identity is an act of power" (Laclau, 1990, p. 33), whereby the subject (individual) succeeds in affirming what he or she does not wish to be seen as, as well as what she or he purports to be.

This does not mean, however, that the individual is exercising such power from an all-knowing position, nor that the individual has recourse to some authentic, foundational knowledge and innate understanding beyond the social. What it does mean is that the individual possesses some capacity to "know" beyond the ideology but within the limits offered by their immediate cultural and social placing; such limits are not, however, forever fixed and absolute. Moreover, subjects are also likely to be aware that some aspects of this identity they perform, certainly the public presentations, are ultimately representative (although in the moment of their enaction it may well feel much more concrete than that). So we are now immersed in a fine web of identification as process, wherein we attempt to understand the constitutive properties of ideological apparatus while recognizing that, in the final analysis, no two people are exactly alike. To paraphrase the anthropologist Margaret Mead (1934), we are just like everyone else in being unique in our individuality.

Social constructionism is, then, problematic for feminist theorists especially, not least because it raises difficult questions concerning the extent to which we are ever fully in control of our identity and the circumstances that serve to make us

who we are. Yet in the past social constructionism has been, arguably, the most utilized theoretical framework for exploring gender. It is, however, used less so nowadays, at least in respect of notions of patriarchy and ideology. In its place, feminist research into gender and identity has increasingly engaged with the challenging questions laid down by philosophers such as Friedrich Nietzsche, psychoanalysts such as Jacques Lacan, and sociologists such as Michel Foucault and Gilles Deleuze, all important and influential thinkers in respect of post-structuralist thought (see, for examples, Weedon, 1991; Ramazanoglu, 1992; Grosz, 1990; McNay, 1994, 2003; Harari, 1979; Fraser, 1989; Butler, 1993).

However, while a *third wave* of theorizing is clearly apparent within feminism (see Heywood and Drake, 1997; Gillis, Howie, and Munford, 2007), one that increasingly and confidently grapples with the possibilities and contradictions of feminism from a post-structuralist position, there appears to be a reluctance to engage with these debates from a pro-feminist male position (Whitehead, 2002; Petersen, 1998). As a consequence, writings within the sociology of men and masculinity, which are mostly the products of men albeit not exclusively so, have tended to remain oriented toward the critical positions espoused by the likes of Gramsci, Althusser, and Marx, although often these associations are implicit rather than explicit (see, for examples and discussion, Whitehead, 2006).

What emerges from these writings by male pro-feminists is a clear and declared social constructionist position, one underpinned by a perception of power as primarily oppressive, hegemonic in its dynamics, and functional within a macro gender order. This gender order is one that is seen to have been, over time, constructed by men, mostly through their ability to control the means of production; family structures; political, social, and governmental agencies; the media; the judiciary; and the armed forces (Barrett, 2001; Connell, 1995; Messner and Sabo, 1990; Brittan, 1989; Hearn, 1987). Therefore, it follows that the construction of one's identity, being invested in such dominant social processes, is largely determined by these same structural factors.

Hegemonic Masculinity: A Dominant Male Performance

A key concept in these debates and writings is **hegemonic masculinity**. This concept is used to a great extent by those writers wishing to emphasize men's capacity to reinforce their ideologically underpinned and privileged position in society through enacting dominant performances of masculinity. Carrigan et al. (1987) describe hegemonic masculinity as follows:

> The ability to impose a particular definition on other kinds of masculinity is part of what we mean by "hegemony" . . . It is, rather, a question of how particular groups of men inhabit positions of power and wealth and how they legitimate and reproduce the social relations that generate their dominance. (p. 179)

For Carrigan et al. and other writers utilizing this term, hegemonic masculinity is seen

hegemonic masculinity

A form of male behaviour and expression of male identity that seeks to reinforce men's power and patriarchal values. Based on characteristics such as competition, ambition, self-reliance, physical strength, aggression, and homophobia.

total institution

An institution (e.g., the army, a prison, the police, etc.) where individuals are under the total control of an authority and subjected to a powerful organizational system and dominant singular culture.

to have strong associations with heterosexual dominance, and is reinforced through men's access to organizational and state powers. So, for example, Barrett (2001) uses the concept of hegemonic masculinity to critically examine the processes of power and dominance that operate within the US Navy, and their subsequent effect on men and women within this organization. Barrett notes that "Throughout all communities in the Navy, the image of masculinity that is perpetrated involves physical toughness, the endurance of hardships, aggressiveness, a rugged heterosexuality, unemotional logic, and a refusal to complain" (2001, p. 81).

As Barrett goes on to emphasize, the Navy recognizes that these expressions of masculinity are learned, not innate. Therefore, in order to ensure that individuals consistently uphold these masculine traits, the Navy subjects its personnel to regular testing on these very traits, which are further reinforced through rituals such as head shaving, warrior initiation rites, hazing rituals, and forms of violent discipline. The very same processes are repeated worldwide, across most armed forces and related paramilitary/police/enforcement agencies, all of which are dominated by men seen to be masculinist in their culture and organizational values (see, for example, Prokos and Padavic, 2006).

The US Navy is what Goffman (1961) describes as a **total institution** insomuch as it imposes a rigid, conforming, and authoritative regulatory discipline on its members. The power effect of this organizational cultural process is, according to Goffman, to "disinfect the identifications" of its members, removing their "identity kits" (1961, pp. 28–29), replacing them with a conception of self that mirrors and reinforces the dominant culture. However, this being the case, we can see that the US Navy is not representative of all organizational sites, although Barrett's study does powerfully expose the processes of gender socialization that surround men in such locations.

Research shows that hegemonic masculinity, as described by Barrett in respect of the US Navy but seen in many similar organizations, is not innate behaviour but rather learned (Kimmel and Messner, 1995; Messner and Sabo, 1990; Kimmel, 2000; Poynting and Donaldson, 2005). Males are not born exemplars of hegemonic masculinity (i.e., displaying a hard, competitive, aggressive, unemotional individualism); these character traits develop in them as a direct consequence of men's social experiences. Boys and men can be trained and schooled to behave this way. Indeed, as Goffman infers, they frequently are. From this we can see that hegemonic masculinity might be useful in describing how men are conditioned through a powerful patriarchal ideology to take on these dominant expressions of masculinity, which come to inform their very sense of identity as men. In essence, this is social constructionism in action.

However, the difficulty that arises from overusing the concept of patriarchy to understand gender identity processes—notably in respect of agency, difference, resistance, and diversity—similarly emerges in the many uses of the concept of hegemonic masculinity. For example, not all men perform hegemonic masculinity or perform it in precisely the same way; many actively resist it or seek to maintain a distance from it. Hegemonic masculinity suggests a desire by men to be dominant in all situations, to gravitate toward hegemonic performances of being a man so as to maintain power. This takes us down a reductionist path with men forever positioned as oppressors of women and of other men, their innate desire for dominance overwhelming other possibilities of self-expression. Hegemonic masculinity suggests a unified subject (man) comfortably engaged in this performance and at ease with the consequences. In many if not most cases, however, this is far from the truth. Moreover, at the level of the subject, identity is full of ambiguity and contradiction.

It is rarely static, it is always multiple, it is highly contingent. Furthermore, hegemonic masculinity is constantly intersected by other relationships of dominance and power. As Michael Kimmel (1994) argues, "The masculinity that defines white, middle-class, early middle-aged, heterosexual men is the masculinity that sets the standards for other men, against which other men are measured and, more often than not, found wanting" (p. 271).

For example, in a society that posits the masculine role as provider, breadwinner, and protector, men who are unemployed or from a lower income class would appear not to be "real men." Writing about the particular example of the Caribbean, where hegemonic masculinity is compounded with the history of slavery and present-day capitalism, Patricia Mohammed (2004) observes that "The idea of losing ground puts an increasing psychological pressure on men to retain notions of masculinity which perhaps were possible under different economic circumstances but are increasingly a luxury in the political economy of the contemporary world order" (p. 55). Thus, hegemonic masculinity is a concept that does not stand on its own in the sense that it constantly involves other hegemonic discourses, such as race and class (see Carby, 1998; Marriott, 2000; Walcott, 2009). Hegemonic masculinity may suggest how expressions of masculinity dominate in particular locals, but this is neither inevitable nor fixed. Finally, insomuch as hegemonic masculinity may be seen to be an exemplar of masculine performance, it is not clear what models it always relates to: "John Wayne, Leonardo DiCaprio, Mike Tyson or Pele" (Whitehead, 2002, p. 89; see also, Donaldson, 1993; Speer, 2001; Demetriou, 2001; Jefferson, 2002)?

Such criticisms of the concept of hegemonic masculinity have been acknowledged and taken up by Connell and Messerschmidt (2005). They recognize that many (pro)feminist models of gender have sought to posit men as occupying a "global dominance" over women, notably through the ideology of patriarchy and sustained through the practices of hegemonic masculinity. However, they also acknowledge that while such theorizing may alert us to aspects of male domi-

agentic
Capable of making choices and exercising free will.

nance, overuse of simplistic models of power tell us little about the complex social interactions within and between the genders. Rather, they suggest that "Our understanding of hegemonic masculinity needs to incorporate a more holistic understanding of gender hierarchy, recognizing the agency of subordinated groups and the mutual conditioning of gender dynamics and other social dynamics" (2005, p. 20).

A more holistic understanding of hegemonic masculinity would incorporate "other social dynamics," such as race and class and their interaction with gender dynamics, as in the example of Caribbean masculinities quoted above. Gender rarely stands alone, as it is part of a larger social structure involving other relations of dominance and power. Gender can take on a variety of forms and manifestations depending on the individuals involved and their responses. Furthermore, the individual is seldom completely powerless and totally at the mercy of the social forces that shape her or his identity. The debates surrounding individuals' agency to fashion their gender identities in a subtle and sophisticated manner continues to bedevil social constructionist perspectives. Tacitly, Connell and Messerschmidt acknowledge this in their attempt to retain the concept of hegemonic masculinity while also recognizing groups' and individuals' capacity to resist dominant discourses and express themselves and their identities beyond an ideologically determined structure.

This is why we suggested at the beginning of this section that social constructionism and associated terms—such as patriarchy, gender order, and hegemonic masculinity—if they are to be used at all, can only indicate the existence of macro values and perspectives. They tell us little about the micro dynamic circumstances that come to inform **agentic**, ontological processes of identity work. Speer (2001) puts it this way:

> [Hegemonic masculinity] is an abstract and decontextualised notion which does not capture the subtleties and fluidities of identity work. The concept of hegemonic masculinity, is, by its very nature, an abstract "un-capturable" yardstick, used to capture something that extends beyond local practices and actions. (p. 2)

We can recognize, then, that what Barrett describes as hegemonic masculinity in the US Navy is just that. And in this respect such empirical studies tell us much about the processes of male dominance in numerous sites, describing masculinist cultures, value systems, actions, and practices within organizations especially (see, for example, Poynting and Donaldson, 2005).

However, it is also clear from our discussion that social constructionism, at least the versions that are more prone to seeing gender identity as ideologically constructed, has weaknesses that must be addressed. To more closely understand the individual and more nuanced and complex gender identity and identification processes operating in any environment, and the ontology that informs being and becoming a gendered individual, we have to deploy more subtle theoretical tools that take us into the realms of the psyche and subjectivity. In this respect, psychoanalytical theory has played an important role in furthering our understanding of what constitutes gender identity. In particular, theories about the psycho-sexual development of the child and the unconscious processes of identification that take place in childhood have been important for feminist theorists and their attempt to define gender identity. As we will see, although there are many critiques of classical psychoanalytical theory, psychoanalytical interpretations of gender identity formation are essential in helping us understand the ways in which individuals internalize gender norms and re-enact them.

PSYCHOANALYTICAL THEORY

We have shown that structural functionalism assumes femininity and masculinity to be "natural" organizing principles fundamental to an ordered society. Following which, society requires men and women to perform different, but complementary, tasks and roles seen as appropriate to their sex, notably production for males, reproduction for females. Symbolic interactionists assert that individuals form their identities through interaction with others, implying that our identity is shaped by the world around us. Thus, gender identity is more than biology. Psychoanalytic theorists too maintain that gender is not biological but is, rather, based on the psycho-sexual development of the individual. Gender differentiations and inequities come from early childhood experiences. When children are born they find themselves muddled in varied biological processes. The first way they get to pull together this confusion is through their unconscious identifications with the people around them. As they grow older, children get to socialize and interact with others and in that process form their identities. The unconscious is therefore important in our discussion of gender identity. Bargh (2006) defines unconscious processes as those that we tend to be unaware of and that occur without our intention or consent, yet they influence us on a daily basis in profound ways.

Psychoanalytic theorists can claim to provide numerous insights into gender identity as process, experience, and construction. From the founding work of Sigmund Freud, through writers such as Carl Jung, Melanie Klein, and Jacques Lacan, and on to contemporary feminist theorists such as Nancy Chodorow, Luce Irigaray, and Judith Butler (see section below), a rich, varied, and complex range of analysis has emerged that, taken together or in part, offers illumination into the dense and complex dynamics of sexuality and gender identity.

Having made that point, we should also note that psychoanalysis and its practices have long been, and remain, highly contested, often discounted as little more than misogynistic ideology wrapped up in dense academic prose (Bart, 1977; see also Buhle, 1998) with claims that related therapies offer no respite to the afflicted only "the pretence that it is for the other's good" (Sutherland, 1995; quoted in Craib, 2001, p. 1).

Perhaps such criticisms are due in large part to Sigmund Freud, arguably the founding father of psychoanalytical theory. For although Freud's idea changed over time—from theorizing a rigid and fixed biologically informed theory of identification to one that was much more open to environmental possibilities influencing the self—outside the orthodox psychoanalytic world his ideas can be seen as outdated at best, and phallocentric and hegemonic at worst. It can also be claimed that Freud had little to say about identity, and even less to say about gender identity (Hird, 2004), and yet he remains an influential if not dominant theorist for supporters and critics alike.

Feminists such as Luce Irigaray (1977), Julia Kristeva (1986), Kate Millett (1970), Carol Gilligan (1982), and Toril Moi (2004) are just five of many who have been highly critical of Freud's work, interpreting his theories as supporting a biologically deterministic model of gender identity and framed within a **"malestream" perspective** on female sexuality (see Buhle, 1998, for overview). Indeed, one of the main criticisms of Freud is his apparent inability to understand women and femininity at any level, let alone the intellectual. As Moi (2004) puts it, "When Freud himself tries to theorize women the results are pitiful . . . If women fail to conform to the theorist's particular picture of femininity, why is this always presented as a problem for the women but not for the theory?" (pp. 842–3).

Despite these important qualifications, it is undoubtedly the case that psychoanalysis generally, and Freud's concepts and theories in particular, have had a profound impact on many areas of human understanding, knowledge, and activity, with numerous Freudian terms enjoying common usage in everyday language. In this section we provide an overview of the works of Freud, Jung, and Lacan, and related theorists, and compare these against the contemporary writings arising out of feminist psychoanalysis.

Sigmund Freud

Sigmund Freud drew heavily on Greek mythology, particularly the Oedipus and Electra narratives, to interpret and define gender identities in men and women. In adopting a biological model, Freud (1912 [1974]) presented us with what is now considered an overly simplistic way of making sense of the complexity of gender and identity, although many of his basic concepts and terminologies remain influential to this day.

According to Freud, boys develop a male identity primarily through their identification

Oedipus complex

A phrase coined by the psychoanalyst Sigmund Freud using the Greek myth to describe what he saw as an unconscious desire in young boys to sexually relate to their mothers and to kill and/or compete against their fathers.

with their fathers and a corresponding rejection of their mothers. He suggests that boys and girls become conscious of being male and female, respectively, at around three to six months, referred to by Freud as the phallic stage or phase. During this phase, boys become conscious of their body parts, especially the penis, and aware that girls do not possess this organ. Erotic pleasure is obtained from the penis for boys (unconsciously) because it is in the possessing of the penis that they can become like their fathers (different from the mother) and make a separation (detachment) from their mothers, the maternal, eternal feminine. The subsequent psychological reattachment process to the mother is what makes it possible for the child to become a boy (man). Girls, on the other hand, remain psychologically and emotionally attached to the mother in much the same way as before, the result being that the process of becoming a woman takes them on an entirely different trajectory: emergence into the feminine. This divergence and subsequent formation of appropriate masculine and feminine identifications are preceded by the development and resolution of the Oedipus complex.

Freud constructed the **Oedipus complex** as a key stage in which the development of a boy's identity is negotiated through his relation with his mother and father. In the Oedipus stage, a boy develops an intense attachment to his mother, desiring to possess her sexually while at the same time seeing his father as a rival for his mother's affections. The boy unconsciously projects his feelings onto the father, believing that his father sees him as a rival and will "castrate" or emasculate him. The boy experiences castration anxiety, which forces him to resolve the situation by identifying with his father. Through this process the boy suppresses his desire for his mother. Indeed, this suppression, according to Freud, is the actual impulse that emerges in most boys as a heterosexual orientation identity.

Attempting to resolve the Oedipus complex in this way puts boys in a position of being bisexual in their sexual orientation. In other words, boys who unconsciously position themselves not to become rivals (against the fathers) but to be the love object of their fathers continue to suppress their desire for their mothers.

For the girl, feminine identification begins when she becomes aware that she has something missing, i.e., she lacks a penis. This realization produces what Freud called "penis envy." The consequences are far reaching: the girl is wounded at a psychic level and she develops an inferiority complex, hating herself in the process. This general state of being leads her to reject her mother, whom she blames for her lack of a penis. It is through this process that she becomes a gendered individual—a woman.

Melanie Klein (1998), in reworking Freudian theory, suggests that the Oedipus complex is more a result of the child's tensions and frustrations in early development, particularly with the mother. Thus Klein makes the mother central to gender identity in both boys and girls. The development of the mental processes is then mediated through the body of the mother and related to the anatomical differences between the sexes. While Klein's model offers a shift from the dominant phallic image proffered by Freud, she nevertheless draws heavily on Freud's work, thus coming full circle to reinforce many of his phallocentric ideas on gender identity.

Klein maintains that boys very early on in childhood abandon the oral and anal preoccupation for the penis, which is associated with penetration and power. Girls, on the other hand, shift their focus from the oral to the genital and develop a receptivity for the penis, and then turn to the father as the love object. Klein argues that the early stages of the Oedipus conflict are so largely dominated by pre-genital phases of development that the genital phase, when it begins to be active, is so heavily veiled that it

is only between the third and fifth years of life that it becomes clearly recognizable. At this age the Oedipus complex and the formation of the superego reach their climax. Indeed Klein's theory is more complicated than our summary of it, and we may be doing some injustice to her work by not offering a fuller version of it.

However, we see in Melanie Klein's theory that the development of a male and female identity is very much a psycho-biological process but with far more room for the social than basic Freudian theory allows. From a Freudian perspective, one could argue that the girl's "penis envy" leads her to desire the father as a love object as a way of acquiring the penis that is denied to her. She realizes that since this is not possible, she changes, wishing instead for a child. She then enters the **Electra complex**. Her mother becomes the object of her jealousy and the girl has turned into a little woman with a love/hate relationship with her own body. Through this Freudian model it is argued that a boy's identity is available at the outset, while a girl's identity becomes possible only through her identification with the boy. In other words, the boy/male assumes, in Freud's eyes, the centred status of the object, while the girl/female assumes the problematic position of "other" or subject. As feminists have long argued, it is precisely this malestream thinking that renders much of psychoanalysis inherently flawed and certainly those theories that unproblematically assume the fixedness of the gender/sexual binary rather than recognize the binary to be a social construction underpinning mostly

Electra complex

A phrase coined by Carl Gustav Jung using the Greek myth to refer to what he saw as an unconscious desire in young girls to sexually desire their fathers and compete with their mothers.

Western societies and cultures, which in turn reinforces gender and sex stereotypes.

Feminist Interpretations of Freud

The range and depth of feminist critiques of Freudian theory is far too extensive to encapsulate here, so for reasons of brevity we offer only an overview of some of the main interpretations and feminist-inspired engagements with his work.

Nancy Chodorow (1978) has been a highly influential feminist psychoanalyst and remains so to this day. She contends that boys must learn their gender identity as being not-female or not-mother. This is so because boys and men come to deny the feminine identification that for them evokes anxiety. At the same time, the core gender identity for a girl is not problematic in the sense that it is for boys because a girl's identity is built upon, and does not contradict, her primary sense of oneness and identification with her mother.

Chodorow (1978; 1999), Dinnerstein (1976), and Eichenbaum and Orbach, (1985) adopt an **object-relations approach** to Freudian theory, but from a feminist standpoint. These theorists take women's position as primary carer and eternal mother as the starting point for women's subsequent subordination to men and, consequently, as the formation of a gendered (feminine) identity that privileges passivity, fragility, and nurturing. However, this stance is at the expense of placing women very firmly in the private, not public spheres. As Chodorow interprets it, the pre-Oedipal stage is "sexually charged for boys in a way it is not for girls," with the boy realizing that his body is male, not female; therefore, he comes to be aware that "power and prestige are to be had

---

object-relations approach

A psychoanalytical approach that focuses on the way in which individuals internalize the reality around them and create representations of objects and people in their mind.

---

through identification with men (father)" (Tong, 1994, p. 154). Chodorow maintains that gender differences must be understood in relational contexts, for example, object-relations theory. The difficulties that girls have, she argues, in establishing a feminine identity arises from identification with a negatively valued gender category and an ambivalently experienced maternal figure, whose mothering and femininity are accessible but devalued (see also Craib, 2001, for overview).

Person (1980), on the other hand, contends that there is contemporary agreement that gender differentiation is pre-phallic, observable by the end of the first year of life and immutable by the third year. The first and crucial step in psychosexual and gender differentiation arises in the early years of life, most often in agreement with parental designation of the child's sex. This self-designation, defined by the term "core gender," may have an unconscious as well as a conscious component. According to Person, the possibility of a deep connection with the mother through the body also provides the girl with opportunities to develop an androgynous orientation sexually—in other words, to construct both heterosexual and lesbian relationships in later life.

Horney (1973) questions Freud's assumption that women's bodies are inferior to men's. She suggests that psychoanalysis has regarded women as inferior because psychoanalysis is the product of a male genius and a male-dominated culture. While she accepts the idea of castration anxiety in boys and penis envy in girls, she argues that males are also envious of females because of their capacity to reproduce. Through her own work as a psychoanalyst she was able to verify this claim:

> From the biological point of view woman has in motherhood, or in the capacity for motherhood, a quite indisputable and by no means negligible physiological superiority. This is most clearly reflected in the unconscious of the male psyche

in the boy's intense envy of motherhood ... when one begins, as I did, to analyze men only after a fairly long experience of analyzing women, one receives a most surprising impression of the intensity of this envy of pregnancy, childbirth, and motherhood, as well as of the breasts and of the act of suckling. (p. 61)

This masculine envy, Horney argues, is capable of more successful sublimation that shapes our culture and society than the "penis envy" of the girl.

Another alternative to Freud's theory is Fast's proposed notion of an undifferentiated and over-inclusive earliest matrix for gender identity development. Fast (1998) suggests that boys' and girls' gender representation and identification includes both masculine and feminine traits that then informs the processes of sex and gender differentiation. In contrast to Freud's theory, she argues that boys and girls have an ambiguous sense of what it is to be male or female; initially, children have ideas of mothers with penises and fathers being able to have babies, and even when they give up notions of such bisexual completeness in themselves, they may still attribute it to others. In a matter of time, both boys and girls develop clear boundaries of who they are and of the limitations of their respective genders. Fast also redefines the ideas around the Oedipus complex in her development of a theory of gender but with a positive focus on women. She argues that a girl's relationship with her mother is not one of hatred (because she blames her mother for not having a penis) but one in which she identifies with her mother in her specifically child-bearing capacity. Fast also agrees with other feminist psychoanalysts that boys, too, experience envy for the female capacity to bear children and that this envy becomes the trigger for the boy's interest in sex difference.

Dorothy Dinnerstein (1976), following Chodorow and many other feminist theorists, accurately picks up on a key Freudian point and develops it as a contribution to feminist theory. She shows how Freud, albeit unintentionally and without self-awareness, offered feminists a means to understand gender power differentials, in particular concerning the relationship of women to mothering. While Chodorow adopts a more positive model for female mothering, emphasizing the intimacy and connectedness of the experience, Dinnerstein largely sees mothering as a source of pain and anguish for women, a condition arising out of the infant's unreliable and unpredictable association with its mother. However, both theorists see female subordination and women's subsequent position as unnamed "other" (de Beauvoir, 1954) in society as arising through the biological/social (Freudian) origins that posit the female as the eternal mother. Because of women's primacy in mothering roles, boys and girls grow up in very different ways; with boys rejecting the female and discourses of the feminine, and girls rejecting the distant unemotionality of the male and related discourses of the masculine. The only way to overcome this duality, according to Dinnerstein and Chodorow, is for dual parenting: men must assume a more intimate and involved parenting role so as to unshackle women from the conditions of their subordination.

In this way, and several decades after Chodorow and Dinnerstein put forward these arguments, we can see how such a thesis is being played out as reality in increasing numbers of families, not least through the emergence of the "househusband" in many societies.

Carl Jung

Carl Jung, as one of the major influences within psychoanalysis, has offered us some enlightened insights into gender identity and reinforced deterministic notions of masculinity and femininity as singular, fixed, and located deep within the human psyche. In terms of possibilities, the concept of androgyny, first explored by Jung (1982) is one that is pertinent to both (feminist) sociologists and psychoanalysts, not least because its implicit ambiguity suggests a revision of fixed gender/sexual identities, a serious unsettling of the sex/gender dualisms, and, consequently, political (feminist) possibilities (see Tong, 1994, for discussion). Again, as with many concepts and notions now accepted and utilized across sociology if not general society, the concept of androgyny has its roots in psychoanalytical theory.

Jung views gender identity as an evolving process where both boys and girls possess an unconscious **anima** (female essence) and **animus** (male essence). Jung's work is complex and highly problematic in terms of a contemporary feminist analysis of Jungian psychology. Using the process of archetypes (meaning cultural and mental information that come down through the course of history, culture, and social evolution), Jung suggests that the concepts of masculinity and femininity are characteristics found in both men and women, with most men acquiring more masculinity (with some exceptions, leading to feminized men, not necessarily gay), and with women acquiring feminine traits (the exception being masculinized women, not necessarily lesbian women).

Jung tends to refer to the development of gender identity as a complex process in the same way that Freud did in his writing. Jung, on the other hand, attempts to connect women and gender identity using the grand theory of psychoanalysis and personal myth—resulting in his collapsing bodily sex into psychic gender (see Susan Roland, 2002). Since the **archetypes** in the psyche are themselves fluid and multiple, Jung argues that the mind cannot be of one fixed gender. The masculinity and femininity that are acted out as material realities in society are a construction and disruption of the function of the psyche. In other words, we are never able to attain a fixed and stable gender identity because this process of being and becoming a woman or man is always subject to subconscious desires, feelings, emotions, and fears.

In short, Jung's incorporation of the psyche, particularly the role of archetypes in forming a gender and identity theory, has been complex and difficult since he advances other more essentialist ideas about gender and personality development. For example, he associates the Greek philosophical and mythological frameworks of Eros and Logos to explain the difference between male and female gender identity as mental functioning. Eros is associated with feelings, compassion, and love, which are attributed to women; Logos is associated with rationality and intellect, which in turn are attributed to men. Yet again we see the simplistic, polarized way in which these early psychoanalysts thought about gender identity. A defining feature of Jung's treatment of gender is his placing of the feminine at the centre of psychology (in many respects like Klein), while at the same time displacing women

anima

A term coined by Carl Gustav Jung to describe the female side of personality, which he believed is present in both men and women.

animus

A term coined by Carl Gustav Jung to describe the male side of personality, which he believed is present in both men and women.

archetype

A symbol or pattern that is found in cultural representations, such as in mythology, literature, folk stories, dreams, art, and religion, and is believed to be the same across cultures, across historical times, and across geographical places.

as social, material, and historical beings (Roland, 2002; Adams and Duncan, 2003).

Feminist Interpretations of Jung

By now the reader may well have spotted one of the dangers within much of psychoanalytical theory—that is, its propensity to being hijacked by essentialists, or those with a reactionary, conservative agenda. In other words, those who would wish to see a return to some functionalist gender order, with women in the home and men at work, can draw on early psychoanalytical thinking to "reinforce" their case. This is especially evident in Jungian theory and notions of masculinity. The **mythopoetic** men's movement, exemplified in the work of Robert Bly (1990), draws heavily on Jungian notions of the archetypal gendered psyche to argue that the "feminization of society" damages men as it produces within them unresolved tensions between their innate masculinity and an increasingly dominant femininity. Such dilemmas, it is argued, can only be resolved by men bonding together in "retreat zones" without contact with women, thereby "healing their grief" through a reinforcement and celebration of their "natural masculine qualities" (Guggenbuhl, 1997; see Connell, 1994, 2003, for discussion; also Whitehead, 2002, for overview).

A pro-feminist writer who has offered a substantial critique of such thinking, while also providing a more nuanced engagement between feminism and Jungian theory, is David Tacey (1997). He argues that Jungian theory can help us navigate a "middle path between the extremes of patriarchal nostalgia (Iron John) and matriarchal identification (Oedipus)" (p. 7). This route requires men to accept the paradoxical and contradictory elements of gender identification, in particular the dynamic mixture of the masculine/feminine now apparent in the postmodern age. So rather than retreat to some archetypal, mythically informed masculinity or,

> **mythopoetic**
> Literally meaning myth-making.

alternatively, rage against the patriarchal condition that has reinforced traditional masculine values and thereby produced within them a stunted emotionality and an inability to relate to loved ones, men should confront these dilemmas within themselves so as to move forward as more balanced individuals:

> At this time in history, where traditional masculinity is threatened with collapse and where ordinary men are thrown back upon themselves without any psychological knowledge or resources, it is certainly time for the "feminine" men to step forward and to show the way out of this crisis. Cissies pushed around in the schoolyard are very often the grown-up therapists and inspired lecturers who guide ordinary men to a more rich and rewarding life. (Tacey, 1977, p. 200)

Jacques Lacan

Jacques Lacan, the French psychoanalyst (born in France in 1901 in the same year that Freud published *The Interpretation of Dreams*), has more than any other psychoanalyst influenced the course of contemporary theorizing around identity. In his famous "Return to Freud," Lacan sets out a radical re-reading of many of the key concepts of psychoanalysis, such as the unconscious, repression, and infantile sexuality. According to Elliott (2002), Lacan's return to Freud is a most revolutionary insight by exploring the disruptive power of the unconscious. Indeed, Lacan, in his landmark book *Écrits: A Selection* (1977), reinterprets Freud using what is now termed post-structuralist theory. Through the process of interpreting Freudian ideas in a linguistic framework, Lacan changed the way we think about the theory of subjectivity—where the self is constructed as narcissistic misrecognition represented through the symbolic order of language. In other words, the search for self-identity is constantly mediated through language and the variable meanings that are attached to it; our individual (subjective) interpretation of language being the medium by which we come to construct a sense of self.

Following in Freud's footsteps (of maintaining a biological focus on gender), Lacan argues that the phallus as a signifier produces the (sexualized) subject, while the **socio-symbolic order** assigns masculinity and femininity as primary codes of identification. However, where Freud continues a commitment to pseudo-biological explanations for the Oedipal structure, Lacan's theorizing develops into an understanding that social, unconscious, and linguistic variables play a greater role (see, for discussion, Grosz, 1990).

socio-symbolic order
The system of social rules, norms, and representations that organize and control society.

In exploring gender identity, Lacan evolves a theory of gender subjectivity that integrates biology with psychology, in much the same way that Freud did. However, Lacan goes one step further in arguing that gender construction and sexual identity is both physical and symbolic. Lacan positions the unconscious as a critical domain for the development of gender identity. His theory suggests that maleness or femaleness begins in the unconscious, which in turn is informed through the symbolic system of language. With its identity roots in the unconscious and language representation, the gendered subject is in a state of continuous gender and sexual instability and (re)construction. The repressed material in the unconscious and the fluctuations of the social and political discourses around the individual provide a highly contingent if not potentially disruptive basis upon which to formulate and secure a sense of self.

For Lacan, the notion of the masculine or feminine provides on the one hand a signification of anatomical sexual difference giving meaning and thereby some sense of stability to the biological body. At the same time the notion of masculine or feminine acts as a signifier in the socio-symbolic order of culture and history. In other words, societies and cultures have become historically formed around gender signifiers, meanings, languages, and symbols that posit male and female as different and reinforce their separation, while also providing a powerful resource for individuals to achieve self and social validation.

However, while Lacan theorizes psychoanalytic ideas of desire, sexuality, and subjectivity in a novel way, his theories still veil the simplistic and outdated notions of Freudian understandings of gender identity. That is, the construction of gender and sexual development is assumed to rest upon possession of the penis for boys and the lack of it for girls. For the girl, the so-called penis envy actually produces Oedipal desire, causing her to reject her mother and turn to her father. Elliott (2002) puts it this way:

> For Lacan, as for Freud, the phallus is the marker of sexual difference par excellence. The phallus matches the incestuous unity of the mother/infant relation, and thereby constitutes the identity of the subject. . . . The phallus, says Lacan, is illusionary, fictitious, imaginary. The phallus exists less in the sense of biology than in fantasy, merging desire and power, omnipotence and wholeness. (p. 141)

Feminist Interpretations of Lacan

Since the publication of Juliet Mitchell's (1974) *Psychoanalysis and Feminism,* there have been numerous feminist critiques of psychoanalysis and gender. Mitchell drew on both Freud's and Lacan's ideas to argue that the phallic organization of sexuality and gender within the subject is critical to the development of gender identity and sexual difference. While attempting to critique Freud and Lacan, Mitchell inadvertently reinforces the argument that masculinity and femininity can only be achieved through the symbolic order with man as autonomous and women as the dependent other, i.e., the one who lacks (the penis) and is therefore without power but with sexual desire. She sees gender as a fixed and stable domain of identity. What Mitchell seems to ignore, however, is the turbulent and precarious terrain of the unconscious, which disrupts both foundational and repressive gender categories (Elliott, 2002).

Other feminists, such as Jacqueline Rose (1986), Julia Kristeva (1984), Luce Irigaray (1977), and Judith Butler (1990), have been highly critical of Lacan and his re-reading of Freud on sexuality and gender development. These contemporary psychoanalytic feminists have highlighted the relationship between gender and asymmetrical power relations, particularly male power, and the link to Lacan's concept of the phallus in psychoanalytic theory. Rose, for example argues that women are implicated in a system of their own domination through Lacan's phallic sexuality, while Kristeva's feminine semiotic thesis argues for political pluralism beyond a maleist paradigm underpinned by phallic symbolism. Irigaray reminds us that Lacan's symbolic order dispossesses women and marginalizes them to an undifferentiated space of being what Simone de Beauvoir (1973) terms "others" or outsiders. Butler critically interrogates Lacan by arguing that sexuality and gender-identity subjectivities and positions are fundamentally performative and therefore reside solely within culture, history, and (gender) politics. There is, in the final analysis, no foundational subjective (biologically fixed individual) that is forever and irreducibly marked by the presence or absence of a socially mediated and devised gender symbol (the phallus); indeed, any sense of such is merely the inherent process (on entrapment) of desiring to be (a gendered and sexual subject) and to which we all succumb in various ways. For Butler, the discursive subject (individual) is always in a condition of being and becoming (a woman or a man) and has the capacity to interpret and act out various performances of gender in their identity work.

While the critique of Lacan has been about his attachment to the symbolic and the phallus, feminists have at the same time been attracted to Lacan's concept of gender and sexual subjectivity in respect of its formulation through language and intersubjective meanings and processes (see Grosz, 1990). Certainly, given that Lacan has, not least through language, clearly linked sexuality and gender identity work to the cultural, the social, and the psychic, his ideas and theories remain valuable for both sociologists and psychoanalysts. Indeed, of all the founding psychoanalysts, probably Lacan stands out as the one most utilized by contemporary feminist theorists, especially those who lean toward a post-structuralist and/or postmodernist perspective on gender and sexual identities. Certainly, as the reader will note, in this book we refer to him quite extensively, integrating his concepts into numerous examinations of gender identity as both politics and as practice.

Other Psychoanalytical Theorists

Contemporary psychoanalytical theory still draws heavily on the three foundational theorists, Freud, Jung, and Lacan, although the trend is now toward recognition that it is the social, not the biological, that plays the key role in our formation of self. In other words, our cognitive functions arise not out of brains hard-wired at birth to function in an unchanging way, but from our exposure to the social world, especially our intersubjective experiences with others.

Kleeman (1971) was one of the first theorists to argue that cognitive functions play a more significant role in core gender identity formation than identification mechanisms, male genital envy, or castration anxiety. His research suggests that gender identity is a result of an intersection of the **ascription of gender** at birth, the environment, and the relationship with family, and that they each impinge on the cognitive capacities of the developing child. Thus, a person's gender identity is a composition of the socially prescribed gender of the person as well as the influences of the immediate social and cultural environments. Taken together, these all act to constitute our cognitive state and the way we function in everyday intersubjective moments. Kleeman's view of gender identity is very much the position that many psychoanalysts now appear to subscribe to, including feminist theorists.

ascription of gender
The process by which individuals are identified as male or female at birth.

In reviewing the literature, Babieri (1999) argues that from a psychoanalytic perspective, gender identity is the result of a complex development that is dialectically related to a more global developmental process of mental growth. Gender, psycho-sexual, and identity development are all intertwined. Masculinity and femininity are largely constructed by interpersonal transactions in the intersubjective field at a given time and in a particular culture. This intersubjective construction of the self and other is becoming increasingly acceptable as a model to understand the development of gender and sexual identity. In other words, the core theories of psychoanalysis have shifted from a one-person

orthodoxy
The act of conforming to an idea, doctrine, or opinion believed to be the truth.

psychology to a two-person psychology, whereby the many and varied intersubjective connections and interactions of the individual are recognized to be the primary influences on that subject's identity development.

Similarly, in respect of the sociology of men and masculinity, critical gender theorists such as Silverman (1992), Middleton (1992), and MacInnes (1998) have taken us into the realms of Freudian theory to understand the intersubjective processes surrounding masculine identity construction. In other words, they highlight the ways in which males become men and achieve reinforcement of their masculinity through their intersubjective (felt, emotive, sensitive, interpretive, and subconscious) relationships and associations with others. In so doing, they provide a persuasive materialist critique of male power and its relationship to ideological belief, patriarchal conditions, and male subjectivity.

While feminist psychoanalytic theory has been largely responsible for this shift toward recognizing the intersubjective aspects of identity work, it has failed to make serious inroads within the traditions of conventional psychoanalysis. Besides a very small number of post-Freudian feminist psychoanalysts, such as Judith Butler and Luce Irigaray, there has never been much of a dent made into the **orthodoxy** of traditional psychoanalysis. Outside of feminist psychoanalysis, writers still develop theory around the early family experience and its profound impact on gender identity, with theorists such as Tyson (1990) arguing that a woman's gender identity and her pride or shame about her body and herself as feminine have their beginnings in early childhood, in penis envy, and in the girl's "narcissistic investment" in being female.

On the plus side, we have emergent research in new areas such as transgender studies that have highlighted the need to think beyond binary (male/female) gender categories and to redefine the parameters of gender identity (see Whittle, 2002; Namaste, 2005; Valentine, 2007; Stryker, 2008). There have been other feminist psychoanalyst developments, with theorists such as Hird (2003) combining Freudian analysis and feminist and queer theory (see below) to explore gender identity in **intersexed individuals** (see also, Kessler, 1998). Furthermore, through a feminist re-reading of Freud and Lacan, Moi (2004) critiques the Freudian relationship between femininity and castration, drawing on Freud's own ideas to argue that it is the unstable but powerful social environment—not a pre-gendered or sexed biological imperative—that drives our sense of existence as a sexed/gendered being. As she writes,

> There is only one libido, which serves both the masculine and the feminine sexual function. To it we cannot assign any sex. (Freud, 1937, p. 131) [from this we can] acknowledge our spatial finitude, that is to say, our bodily, existential separation from others. Then we need to acknowledge our sexual finitude, to understand that we cannot be more than one sex . . . our desires may be infinite; our bodies certainly are not. (Moi, 2004, pp. 872–3).

Classical psychoanalysis, although riddled with contradictions and limitations, clearly has had a profound impact on contemporary theories of gender identity. Feminism in particular is largely indebted to psychoanalytical theory. Yet, as we have seen, feminism has also stretched the boundaries of psychoanalytical theory and transformed its ideological premises by giving the female subject a more agentic role. Other critics have expanded on the interactions between the environment and the psychological self in an attempt to contextualize psychoanalytical theory. For example, some re-readings of Freudian theory from a race perceptive have highlighted the ways in which constructions of

> **intersexed individuals**
>
> Individuals whose genitals are not immediately recognizable as either male (penis) or female (vagina).

"whiteness" and "blackness" interact with the Freudian's concept of gender identity formation, an area of investigation that had previously been largely overlooked by critics of psychoanalytical discourse (see for example Watson, 1995; Bergner, 2005).

What we can conclude from this overview of classical approaches to gender and identity is that theories of gender have evolved in a significant way during the course of the twentieth century, whether it is through radical shifts or continuous transformations. For example, while drawing on classical psychoanalytical theory, feminists have transformed it and adapted it to new contexts. As we will see in the next two chapters, contemporary theories such as post-structuralism, postmodernism, race theory, post-colonialism, queer theory, and disability theory continue this trend through a questioning of the traditional Western logo and its interpretative methods.

SUMMARY

As a student of gender studies you will need to utilize theory to understand what you are seeing and researching in society. Otherwise all you are doing is replicating your own subjective position—your own viewpoint. That is not the aim of academic study. The intention is to go beyond what you know and have experienced, and into the realms of, for you at least, the unknown. Of course, many people will have been there before you. You are unlikely to be learning anything that is new to the human race. But you are learning something that is new to you.

For example, you are asked to study the behaviour of children in a classroom, the group dynamics of adolescent males, women in positions of leadership, or men at a football match. These studies are all gendered in some way. But how do you interpret what you are seeing? How do you move from simply seeing to the more complex process of critically interpreting and understanding what you are seeing? Well, here you have to use theory. But which theory should you utilize? There are many of them available to you and they all have their strengths and weaknesses.

What you have to do is first understand just what these strengths and weaknesses are and then utilize the appropriate theory for your particular study. Without the theoretical model to support your analysis and discussion, you only have your experience and limited knowledge to go on. And that is not enough. There has to be more.

Chapter 1 has provided a detailed review of those classical theories that have long been influential in gender studies and that draw heavily on an appreciation of the power of the social to influence if not construct who we are and who we become. In their own particular ways, role performance, social constructionism, and traditional psychoanalytical theories, while each offering contrasting analyses, take us from notions of a functional gender system into preoccupations with gender identity as constructionist, and on to present-day psychoanalytical examinations of the intersubjective dynamics that serve to inform our gender identity.

CASE STUDY

Jennifer and Mark have been married for four years and have recently bought a three-bedroom house in downtown Montreal. Both identify as "white," although Mark's grandfather was a Métis. Mark is also a francophone and has Catholic parents. They also describe themselves as "non-religious." Jennifer and Mark could be described as middle-class professionals. Jennifer is 30 and works as a financial consultant for a large city bank. Mark is 34 and a music teacher at a private school. They have also been planning for a baby and were delighted to hear from their doctor that Jennifer is pregnant.

Jennifer is now five months into her pregnancy and is due to visit her doctor in a few days for an ultrasound scan. She is looking forward to it and hopes that she will find out the sex of her baby. So do her parents, who are already grandparents to two girls born to Jennifer's sister; they would very much like a grandson this time. Mark, on the other hand, feels that finding out the baby's sex in advance would spoil the mystery he associates with childbirth. Mark confesses that he would prefer a daughter, but what is most important to him is that the baby's sex be a surprise. Jennifer says she does not mind whether the baby is a boy or a girl but would like to know the baby's sex early because it would make the process of preparing for the baby's arrival easier. She feels it is important that they choose a name before the birth, whereas Mark would rather wait until the baby is born. He thinks that they would then be in a better position to choose a name after getting to know the baby and getting a "feel" for its personality.

Jennifer and Mark have had long discussions about choosing a name and about whether to ask the doctor to reveal their baby's sex. Both are exhausted and disappointed that they have been unable to reach an agreement. When Jennifer explains that it is her right as a mother to find out whether she is expecting a girl or a boy, Mark feels that his opinion is being discounted. This situation has caused a strain on their relationship. As the date of the ultrasound scan is approaching, they are increasingly at a loss as to how to reach a compromise.

DISCUSSION QUESTIONS

1. Is Jennifer the victim of patriarchal gendering ideology, or is she exercising choice and agency?
2. Is Mark reproducing hegemonic masculinity?
3. What reasons (whether they are culturally/socially constructed or psychological) do you think are behind Mark's fantasies of having a daughter? Jennifer's lack of preference? Her parents' desire for a grandson?
4. Compare Jennifer's and Mark's attitudes toward naming the baby.
5. Does the parents' socio-economic and cultural background have an impact on their attitude toward the unborn baby?
6. What do you think will happen when Jennifer and Mark attend their appointment at the hospital in a few days for an ultrasound scan?

QUESTIONS FOR REVIEW AND DISCUSSION

1. How are different ideologies impacting your own understanding of reality, and particularly gender roles?
2. What gender roles do you see developing in your future life?
3. Give an example of when and where you have seen hegemonic masculinity being performed by males. Was this performance of masculinity influenced by other social factors, such as class, culture, race, sexual orientation, religion, age, and (dis)ability?
4. What are the main feminist critiques of psychoanalytical theory?
5. How would you summarize the theories of Freud, Jung, and Lacan?
6. How would you theorize the househusband in terms of contemporary masculine gender identity?
7. Give examples of how your own identity role performance is different in different social and cultural contexts.
8. Why do you think hegemonic masculinity draws heavily on homophobia and misogynistic attitudes?

Chapter 2

Post-structuralist and Postmodernist Approaches to Gender Theory

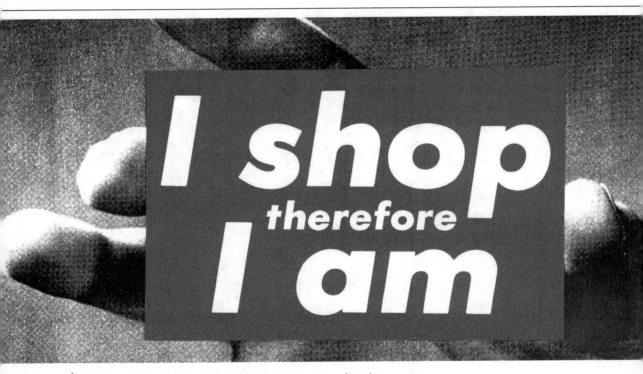

▲ We can achieve a sense of identity in many ways—even shopping.

Source: Barbara Kruger. COURTESY: MARY BOONE GALLERY, NEW YORK

Learning Objectives

At the end of this chapter, you will be able to:

- Identify the development of post-structuralist theory and postmodernist theory.
- Understand how these theories have been used to explore and define gender identity.
- Appreciate the idea of multiple identities.
- Appreciate the "contingency" at the heart of identity.
- Identify and understand the concepts of discourse, "desire to be," and "performativity."

OVERVIEW

As we have seen in the previous chapter, early feminist theorizing is characterized by a departure from notions of gender and identity as fixed and "natural" and the adoption of a social constructionist perspective highlighting the role of capitalist and patriarchal ideologies in shaping who we are. However, as we will see in this chapter, contemporary schools of thought, in particular post-structuralism and postmodernism, focus on how gender and identity are not so much constructed by external forces but emerge in the individual through a more contingent process of language and discourse. Post-structuralism and postmodernism have had a profound impact on feminist theorizing, raising important questions regarding knowledge, power, and identity—indeed, the very veracity of the feminist project itself. Both theories offer opportunities for deconstructing and challenging all power regimes, including those that support patriarchy, colonialism, heterosexism, and ableism. At the same time, as we explain below, their very emphasis on difference, multiplicity, and diversity means that they cannot easily be co-opted into a universalizing feminist project.

Post-structuralism and postmodernism emerged at a time when critical theorists, influenced especially by the work of French social philosophers such as Louis Althusser, Michel Foucault, Jacques Derrida, Roland Barthes, Simone de Beauvoir, and Jean-Paul Sartre were subjecting colonial empires and Eurocentric systems of knowledge to a radical critique. The post-structuralist and postmodern critique of the Western world view and the values inherited from the Enlightenment (rationality, objectivity, and absolute truth) also coincided with the rise of Western feminism and its critique of male power, gender inequality, and phallocentric discourse. So while early feminist theories drew heavily on notions of power as being fixed and hierarchical, reinforced through patriarchal hegemonic processes, feminist post-structuralism and postmodernism highlight the role of language, discourse, and representation to understand gender, sex, and sexuality. Their main contention is that all identities arise through language and that our sense of self is inseparable from the way we represent ourselves, our manner of speaking, and our way of interacting with others and with the world around us.

TABLE 2.1   Phases in Feminist Theorizing
Stage Two: Third-Wave Feminism + Sociology of Men and Masculinities

Third-Wave Feminism 1990s, 2000s		
Today: Highly influential		
Post-structuralist Feminism	Draws heavily on the work of Foucault, Lacan, Saussure, Derrida, and Delueze to analyze and deconstruct gender and sex as unitary, fixed identities; provides influential theories into identity and the self; highlights the (power) relationship between identity and discourse, language, signs,	Judith Butler, Luce Irigaray, Julia Kristeva, Rosi Braidotti, Hélène Cixous, Chris Weedon,

TABLE 2.1   (continued)

	symbolism, narrative, embodiment, culture, and sexuality; introduces the concept of performativity; highlights the fluid, contingent, and multiple aspects of identity; argues there is no sovereign self but that all meaning arises through the discursive subject's immersion in and response to the social arena; denies the possibility of defining *woman* or *man*; questions the notion of a unique and essential self outside of discourse (language and action); has provided the underpinning theory of gender identity now informing contemporary feminist perspectives and research.	Elizabeth Grosz, Gayatri Spivak, Joan Scott, Lois McNay, Jana Sawicki, Sylvia Gherardi, Linda Smircich, Bronwyn Davies
Postmodern Feminism	Draws on Lyotard, Rorty, Lacan, Foucault, narrative theory, and post-structuralism to challenge "grand theories" and move feminism into a global, multicultural context; highlights the diverse subjectivities, realities, conditions, and experiences of women worldwide; challenges feminist theories that are partial and universalizing, reflective only of white middle-class Western feminists; recognizes the multiplicity of meaning and epistemology; provides a theoretical place for diverse women's voices to contribute to feminism globally; adopts the post-structuralist position that there is no founding self outside of language and therefore that the political agenda of feminism is enhanced by avoiding totalization, suspect generalizations, and essentialist thinking, thereby privileging not one but many perspectives and standpoints; as with post-structuralist feminism, has come to influence feminist standpoint theory, black/post-colonial feminism, queer theory, and LGBT studies.	Linda Nicholson, Nancy Fraser, Jane Flax, Diane Elam, Lois McNay, Judith Butler, Julia Kristeva, Rosi Braidotti, Gayatri Spivak, Elizabeth Grosz
Queer Theory	Highlights how gender, sex, and sexuality are performatively enacted and therefore not embedded in some "natural" human condition; emphasizes the contingent character of gender, sex, and sexuality and how these effects, or discursive significations of self, become impersonations that pass as and are taken as real; deconstructs and unfixes the "sexed" body; offers the possibility of destabilizing normative assumptions around sex, gender, and sexuality	Judith Butler, Eve Sedgwick, Judith Halberstam, Adrienne Rich, Diana Fuss, Sara Ahmed, Lauren Berlant, David Halperin, Steven Seidman,

	through the enaction of counter-performances and representations; seeks to provide radical political (feminist) action through deconstructing and destabilizing the gender-sex binary; recognizes the interchangeable character of masculinity and femininity as discourses engaged in by both men and women; introduces the concept of female masculinity; connects strongly with sexuality studies, LGBT studies, cyber theory, queer studies, and intersectionality.	Jeffrey Weeks, Sheila Cavanagh, Patrick Califia
Post-Colonial, Third World, and Black Feminism	Stresses black/of colour/Third World women as identities and sites of political difference both within and outside feminism; power expressed in process and consequence of post-colonial "othering"; operates along the modernist-postmodernist continuum; seeks to avoid categorizations that reinforce imperialist and male-centred stereotyping; highlights previously excluded women's voices from around the world and from multiple cultural and religious arenas; refuses overarching, essentialist identity categories to black/ethnic minority/Third World women; challenges homogenizing tendencies of many Western perspectives; encompasses and seeks to affirm the multiple and diverse identities of women who have previously been at the margins of feminist politics and theory; begins to challenge the notion that gender is the single defining factor in a woman's life and that class, racial, and ethnic differences need to be taken into account also; connects strongly with intersectionality theory.	bell hooks, Gayatri Spivak, Chela Sandoval, Uma Narayan, Ien Ang, Chandra Mohanty, Heidi Mirza, Patricia Hill Collins, Anne McClintock
Intersectionality	A theoretical outcome of postmodern feminism in terms of encouraging widening the critical inquiry into women's lives while also recognizing that each life and each individual identity exists in the intersections of many aspects of self and social powers; encourages the recognition that gender intersects with, for example, race, sex, sexuality, ability, ethnicity, age, culture, and class to "produce" the individual; as discrete forms of oppression these variables combine to have a powerful impact on women's lives in ways that may not always be apparent to the individual; open to	Kimberlé Crenshaw, Patricia Hill Collins, Joya Misra, bell hooks, Leslie McCall, Irene Browne, Susanne Knudsen, Nina Lykke, Tan Lin, Marcia Texler Segal, Ngan-Ling Chow, Janet Siltanen, Andrea Doucet

TABLE 2.1   (continued)

various feminist interpretations and theoretical analysis, including those arising from first- and second-wave feminism but primarily framed around post-structuralist theories of identity and power.

Sociology of Men and Masculinities 1990s, 2000s

Today: Highly influential

Arising out of critical men's studies research, the sociology of men and masculinities offers an expanded analysis both in terms of its global reach/ inquiry and in the broader range of contemporary theories it draws on; heavily influenced by feminist post-structuralism, postmodernism, queer theory, Lacanian psychoanalysis, LGBT theories, postmodern-feminist theory, narrative theory, black/Third World/ post-colonial feminist theories, and, more recently, intersectionality; all contributors feminist or pro-feminist in standpoint; introduces the concept of the masculine subject; provides theories of masculine identity work, and highlights the contingency, fragility, and multiplicity of male identity and masculinities; draws on a Foucauldian concept of power, challenges the notion of a unitary, sovereign subject (man).	Alan Petersen, Deborah Kerfoot, David Knights, Stephen Whitehead, David Collinson, Travis Kong, Louise Archer, Bob Lingard, Bob Pease, Tony Jefferson, David Gutterman, Rachel Jewkes, bell hooks, Gary Dowsett, David Tacey, Lahoucine Ouzgane, Bryant Alexander, Hazel Carby, Peter Middleton, Kaja Silverman, Richard Collier, Victor Seidler, Lynne Segal, Susan Speer

Characteristics of Stage Two

Philosophical Heritage	Post-Enlightenment, postmodernism: Emphasizes the multiple, contingent character of identity and the self in the global age; recognizes the multiple aspects of being and becoming an individual and the diverse power effects informing a person's experience and subjectivity; dissociates from any single grand narrative or ideology; anti-foundationalist and anti-essentialist both in terms of (gender) power and identity; inclined to see the macro (social order) constructed out of the unpredictable and dynamic effects of the micro (individual action) rather than the

	reverse; different theorists position themselves at various points on the continuum between modernism and postmodernism although the overall emphasis is overwhelmingly toward postmodern multiplicity.
Classical Theory Linkages	Post-structuralism (e.g., Foucault, Saussure, Deleuze, Butler) Postmodernism (e.g., Lyotard, Baudrillard) Narrative (e.g., Ricoeur, Czarniawska, Burke) Deconstructionism (e.g., Derrida) Psychoanalysis (e.g., Lacan; de Beauvoir)
Influential Terms and Concepts	Discourse, dominant and subordinate discursive practices, performativity, narrative, deconstruction, the "other," post-colonialism, multiplicity, signifying practices, non-grounded self, anti-essentialism, othering, queering, being and becoming, discursive subject, colonialism, subjectivities, contingent selves, discursive power effects, non-normative subjects, feminist genealogy, subversive acts, sexual representations, intersectionality, multiple systems of domination, representation, reflexivity, relational power.

Notes

1. Many theorists contribute to more than one phase or wave.

2. The phases and waves influence each other and will continue to do so.

THE POST-STRUCTURALIST APPROACH TO GENDER AND IDENTITY

Post-structuralism can be seen as a response to structuralism, a school of thought that sees language, culture, and society as coherent systems that function according to a particular internal logic and particular rules. For post-structuralists, on the other hand, the reality is not a unified and self-standing system that can be explained in a single formula; instead, reality consists of multiple, and at times contradictory, facets and is very much subjective and dependent on our own interpretations.

In this section we explore what we consider to be the central, most pertinent concepts within post-structuralism, at least in respect of what they tell us about gender and identity processes. These concepts are *language, subjectivity, discourse, performativity,* and *desire.* But first, to

place post-structuralism in context, we turn to Friedrich Nietzsche (1973):

> Where does the concept *thinking* come from? Why do I believe in cause and effect? What gives me the right to speak of an "I," and even of an "I" as a cause, and finally of an "I" as a cause of thought? . . . It is falsifying the facts to say that the subject "I'" is a condition of the predicate "think." . . . "It" thinks, but that this "it" is identical with the good old "I" is at best only an assumption. (pp. 16–17)

Long before the concept of post-structuralism had ever been mooted, Nietzsche had captured its central tenet. That is, there is no doer behind the deed, at least not the doer suggested by the "I" we hold so dear. Therefore, we ought to proceed very warily with any notion that who we are is rooted in some permanent place, grounded, essential, and fixed. Similarly, we should question the extent to which this "I" that speaks to and of me (such as the "I" in the statements *I am a man* or *I am a woman*) is simply an ideological construct arising out of the sophisticated hegemonic designs of others. Within post-structuralist theory, identity is not a tussle between structure and agency, for it is seamlessly, simultaneously, and irrevocably both. Nietzsche warns us to have no faith in the coherence of the self, nor to rely on the perceived unity of any mind/body/soul interaction. Instead, he challenges us to acknowledge a simple fact: that our instinct for self-preservation is itself the driver that serves to create our illusion of self-identity.

Post-structuralist thought arises out of several distinct but complementary theoretical perspectives. The French philosopher and critic Jacques Derrida developed the concept of deconstruction, with the central premise being that language is inherently unstable in that words and phrases are subject to multiple interpretations and meanings dependent on the perspective and subjectivity of the individual. The concept of discourse offered by Michel Foucault, whose work we touched on in the last chapter, lent the idea that identity and power are not fixed and secure but always subject to movement, change, and the possibility of disruption. Gilles Deleuze and Félix Guattari's ontological work on "becoming" brought forth the notion that our identity is never settled but always in a state of being and becoming, thereby recognizing identity as a process not an outcome. Jacques Lacan posited the psychoanalytically inspired notion of the subject in language, which claims that the function of language is not to inform but to evoke a sense of identity and recognition in the speaker (see, for overview, Bailly, 2009; Sarup, 1993; Williams, 2005).

None of these male theorists writes explicitly or politically about gender, at least not from a (pro) feminist standpoint. It is not surprising, therefore, that feminist engagements with their positions and concepts have been strongly debated, if not heavily problematic. Moreover, the concerns that feminists have typically had with post-structuralism are reinforced because the theory can be seen to undermine the political project of feminism/feminists. How so? If, as post-structuralism suggests, there is no unified and cohesive subject (individual), then how can there be a unified and cohesive resistance (to male oppression) by multiple and diverse subjects (women)? (See, for discussion, Assister, 1996; Butler and Scott, 1992; Ramazanoglu, 1993; Francis, 2002; Ramazanoglu and Holland, 2005; Davies, 2000).

Yet despite the difficulties post-structuralism offers for feminist inquiry, its central tenets have taken root and, indeed, are being used increasingly by feminist researchers exploring the critical sociology of gender. Largely, this is due to the work of several key and influential feminist thinkers, for example, Judith Butler, Julia Kristeva, Luce Irigaray, Gayatri Spivak, Hélène Cixous, and Rosi Braidotti, each of whom has contributed to our understanding of the complex ways in which symbolism, language, subjectivity, and desire correspond to our felt and representative expressions of existing and acting as gendered beings (see also Lloyd, 2005).

At this point, we should mention an important aspect of sociological theory: it evolves. It is never still. Every theoretical position has a history, yet these roots can become increasingly intertwined and difficult to untangle as time progresses. For example, within all post-structuralist thought lies an indebtedness to the ideas of Freud, Althusser, Marx, Saussure, Barthes, Spinoza, Sartre, Lacan, Nietzsche, extending to the existential feminism of Simone de Beauvoir, and through to the contrasting radical feminism of Mary Daly (see, for examples, Braidotti, 2002; Hoagland and Frye, 2000; Weedon, 2003; Davies, 2000). So while each of these theorists/theories can offer a very distinct, if partial, perspective on the human condition and its interactions, they remain networked into a larger sociological analysis with its own dynamics. In many ways, to try and trace each and every connection to each and every theory/theorist is an artifice, not least because, as Derrida so tellingly notes, in the final analysis, interpretation is everything. Nevertheless, it is possible to identify certain themes common to different post-structuralist theories, such as a particular preoccupation with language and subjectivity, discourse, performativity, and a "desire to be." We will examine each of these themes in the sections that follow.

The Role of Language and Subjectivity in Post-structuralism

Within post-structuralist thought, everything starts and ends with language. Language is understood to provide us with the representations that in turn create the social and cultural landscape within which we operate and come to be held as subjects (Saussure, 1974; also Weedon, 2003; Hall, 1997). It is through language that the production and circulation of meaning takes place and that representations of "reality" are presented to us, and subsequently taken up by us as discursive signifying practices (Butler, 1990; Laclau and Mouffe, 1990). Only through language can we communicate with others and, indeed, reflect on who we are as individuals. This is a circulatory process that does not start or end in any precise place or with any particular individual but is a constant, eternal dynamic, and one that serves to validate our sense of reality and, from that, our subjectivity.

Arguably the most influential theorist in this field has been Jacques Lacan. Lacan argues that there is no subject independent of language, and that our sole means of making sense of our world, creating our own meanings and interpreting those of others (our **subjectivity** and **intersubjectivity**), is through language (Lacan, 1989; also Grigg, 2008; Cornell, 1992; Grosz, 1990). Indeed, Lacan goes so far as to suggest that an inability to learn language—and understand its reference points in

relationship to the social dynamics and conditions under which it is uttered—is indicative of psychotic behaviour. So we don't just learn words, we come to learn what Saussure (1974) calls the *signs and signifiers* within language, which serve to distinguish our individuality while also facilitating our membership within a wider community. For example, dress codes, visual presentations of our selves, bodily gestures, photography, art, cinema, music, rituals, and formal and informal displays, both public and private—these language-based symbolic practices contain a multitude of signifiers, which individually and together create both a cultural and, consequently, an individual identity. Think, for instance, of the teenage subculture "Goth." Membership of this cultural identity, which emerged in England in the 1980s and is now seen worldwide, is explicitly denoted not only by a particular dress code, hairstyle, makeup, musical genre, and literature, but also by the words and phrases that are used to convey meaning and the tone they are spoken in. Taken together they signify Goth both to others and to the individual presenting them to the outside world.

This is identity work wherein we come to learn, develop, and enhance, in quite a sophisticated fashion, the chains of signifiers that validate us in a particular social and cultural locale. Lacan recognizes that this process is never-ending and, indeed, is impossible to fully explicate. For our sense of self is not just expressed through visible and apparent signifiers of language that we may

subjectivity
Our individual understanding of the world around us and our engagement with it.

intersubjectivity
The process by which our understanding of the world is influenced by our engagement with others.

take up knowingly or not, but is also held deep within our subconscious, itself formed by language.

In effect, then, we become real, our selves become visible and apparent, in language and representation. Our subjectivity—that is, our understanding of the world around us and our engagement with it—is not formed from some inner essence but is always conditional upon the social conditions that "constitute subjects as historically and geographically, culturally specific beings" (Grosz, 1990, p. 99). However, as much as we might search for meaning, as Nietzsche warns us absolute meanings ultimately remain elusive. A key reason is that we cannot trust language; we cannot rely on the signifiers around us to "prove" what is real and what is false. Language is full of ambiguity, contingency, and temporality; it is no more fixed than the "I" that utters it.

Contingency here refers to the idea that language is open to many interpretations and meanings—there is never one single, absolute, and guaranteed understanding in any utterance—it all depends on the listener and indeed on the way a word or phrase is presented by the speaker. This contingent characteristic of language has been further exposed through the writings of Jacques Derrida, who argues that there is no pure authenticity inherent in language and in signifiers. When we interpret signifiers, and listen to and use language, we cannot be sure of their absolute meaning as all purported meanings are subject to continual **deconstruction**:

> Deconstruction is neither a theory nor a philosophy. It is neither a school nor a method. It is not even a discourse, nor an act, nor a practice. It is what happens, what is happening today, in what they call society, politics, diplomacy,

economics, historical reality, and so on and so forth. Deconstruction is the case. (Derrida, 1990; quoted in Elam, 1994: 124; see Eagleton, 1983, for overview; see also Hill, 2007; McQuillan and Willis, 2010; Pirovolakis, 2010; Silverman, 1989)

Similarly, the "I" that interprets these signifiers is itself contingent and unstable, for the "I" is formed by the very language that renders it real. Post-structuralists argue that there is no permanent presence outside the sign that constitutes that language and from which we can find an intentional meaning. Moreover, signs and signifiers indicate what is absent as much as what is present, so our subjectivity is partially formed through the recognition of what we are *not*, and what we seek a separation from, as much as through what we are. For example, by saying "I am a woman" a person implies that she is not a man. This continual process of deconstruction and multiple interpretation, what Derrida terms *difference*, renders even our sense of being in the present undeniably uncertain. For meaning is continually dynamic; it moves along a chain of signifiers, changing shape from context to context, creating "an inexhaustible complexity" (Sarup, 1993, p. 34).

For post-structuralists, language does not provide us with unity; it offers the means of *feeling* unified as individuals. The strength of language is that it is readily transmittable. The weakness is that it cannot be relied upon to be absolutely objective, truthful, factual, precise, fixed. As Emile Beneviste puts it "ultimately, human temporality with all its linguistic apparatus reveals the subjectivity inherent in the very using of language" (2000, p. 43).

However, it is precisely from within this apparent disruption to the boundaries of the self, posited by post-structuralist perspectives on language, that a feminist position emerges. Hélène Cixous (1994), for example, uses Derrida's concept of deconstruction to argue that masculine language is structured around a phallocentric,

deconstruction
A method of analysis that aims to highlight the contradictions inherent in language and reality.

logocentric order. The hierarchy of meaning that this order promotes—notably through binary oppositions such as father/mother, husband/wife, mind/body, rational/emotional—and within which one term, the masculine, is privileged, "is a fate which has been imposed upon women, of her burial . . . [under] . . . a masculine edifice which passed itself off as eternal-natural" (quoted in Weedon, 2003, p. 64). Cixous goes on to argue that women can assail and deconstruct this order, notably by developing feminine writing and language that exalts female sexuality and libido, for "by writing her self, woman will return to the body which has been more than confiscated from her" (Marks and Courtivron, 1981, p. 250).

Luce Irigaray (1985) adopts a similar approach to Cixous by arguing that female sexuality and expression have been co-opted into the patriarchal project, and that indeed they in part sustain male dominance, notably through their appropriation of the feminine, both in language and symbolically. According to Irigaray, women need to overcome this historical condition by creating a language of their own, one that both enunciates and privileges the feminine and that provides women with a feminine identity that is not rooted in a phallocentric order. Failure to achieve this aim, Irigaray argues, is to risk women's gaining so-called equality but on the terms laid down by men, with women becoming "men" rather than creating, symbolizing, and privileging their own female identity and subjectivity.

Similarly, Julia Kristeva (1986) also argues that feminine forms of signification are reduced and marginalized within dominant masculinist discourse. However, drawing heavily on Lacanian concepts of subjectivity and symbolic order and Derridian deconstruction, she suggests that the feminine in language and subjectivity is available to both women and men, and that it offers a means for subverting and disrupting the authoritarian (male-dominated) linguistic process. For Kristeva, the unspeakable,

unspoken, silenced feminine in the symbolic order of language should be articulated and used to revolutionize (women's) subjectivities. In making this case, Kristeva, unlike Irigaray and Cixous, argues that "woman" is only ever a political category, not a philosophically grounded one (see, for discussion, Elam, 1994).

All three writers have a declared standpoint, which is to change society from a masculinist, patriarchal-oriented one into a femaleist, maternalist-orientated one. Their approaches are sophisticated, nuanced, and different, although where they do overlap is in the use of language to bring about this change. Their theoretical tools are primarily Lacanian subjectivity and Derridean deconstruction. However, the question remains: to what extent can women occupy and hold some privileged **epistemological** (knowledge) place in the social? Can women be identified as an epistemic community, sustained through a feminine/feminist subjectivity, a way of living in and seeing the world that is uniquely feminine? (See Ramazanoglu and Holland, 2005, for discussion. See also Chapter 3.)

The fact that women occupy different positions in society in terms of class and race makes the idea of a unified and universal feminine subject problematic (see El Saadawi, 1997; Spivak, 1987; Mohanty, 1988). Moreover, is such an approach possible from a post-structuralist position? Indeed, a critique of theorists such as Kristeva, Irigaray, and Cixous is that while they are anxious to maintain the project of feminism, notably through exalting the feminine in language and subjectivity, each continues to acknowledge that the subject (individual) is always in process

epistemological

Pertaining to the study of the ways in which society and individuals understand the world and the nature and limitations of the knowledge they produce about it.

and, consequently, ungrounded. In this case, any hopes for a universality of (feminine) language and, accordingly, subjectivity are compromised because of continuing differences among women. Ultimately, the challenge is to recognize the political dimensions of language and subjectivity without resorting to an essentialist understanding of women and femininity, for that would serve to locate women back in the very **gendered binary** that feminist post-structuralist thought so effectively deconstructs (Weedon, 2003; Elam, 1994; Butler and Scott, 1992; Davies, 2000).

The Concept of Discourse in Post-structuralism

Clearly, recognizing the deconstructive and fragmentary meanings within language only takes us so far. We are still left with the dilemma, explicitly addressed by Cixous, Irigaray, and Kristeva, concerning the (gendered) power dynamics operating within language. That is, how do we both understand and, if possible, resist the

---

gendered binary

The way in which society divides individuals into men and women as distinct and opposite categories.

---

discourse

A Foucauldian concept that refers to both language and practice. These languages and practices, as discourses, are the means by which subjects become individuals in society. So, for Foucault, all individuals are primarily discursive subjects.

---

a priori

Describes an idea or a knowledge that already exists in our mind before we make a judgment and does not depend on experience to be validated.

---

constitutive possibilities these dynamics have for our sense of individuality and relationship to the world around us? Michel Foucault has probably done more than any other theorist to open up a way to explore this dilemma, albeit not necessarily from a (gender) political standpoint. He does so particularly effectively through his concept of **discourse**. First, however, Foucault attends to the issue of power itself:

> I . . . believe that there is no sovereign, founding subject, a universal form of subject to be found everywhere. I am very sceptical of this view of the subject . . . I believe, on the contrary, that the subject is constituted through the practices of subjection, or, in a more autonomous way, the practices of liberation, of liberty. (quoted in McNay, 1994, p. 131)

Foucault makes the point that the individual is always and ever the *expression* of power, not simply its passive recipient. Indeed, to be and become an individual, to have any sort of identity, requires the subject to exert power; no one is entirely powerless. Within post-structuralism, the discursive subject or self is prominent while notions of negative, repressive, ideologically based power are largely absent (for further examples and discussion, see Radtke and Stam, 1994; Davis, Leijenaar, and Oldersma, 1991; McNay, 1994, 2000). There is, then, little if any compatibility between the liberal humanist/Marxist concepts of ideology, and post-structuralist understandings of discourse (for discussion, see Mills, 2004; Purvis and Hunt, 1993; Hall, 1985; Peters, 2001). Theories of the former rest on an assumption of *a priori* action and intent by individuals/social groups who have a material/power investment in maintaining the status quo or acquiring hegemonic dominance over others and, moreover, can accurately predict the consequences of such actions. The latter theory recognizes that all power is ultimately invested in discourse (practice and language) and is therefore productive insomuch as it is fundamental to and dependent upon identity work, social action, and relations, but is at the same time unstable and unpredictable (Laclau, 1990; Hall, 1996; also Kerfoot and Knights, 1994). Foucault takes us beyond the structure/agency dualism that bedevils the liberal humanist concept of ideology and, correspondingly, the social constructionist perspective when he states that "Not only do individuals circulate between its threads; they are always in the position of simultaneously undergoing and exercising this power" (Foucault, 1980, p. 98).

So how, precisely, is this power effected within the social? What are its means of operation? How does it connect to subjectivity, and to the subject? In addressing these questions, Foucault (1972) takes us into his concept of discourse, which, in his analysis, means far more than merely engaging in conversation:

> Instead of gradually reducing the rather fluctuating meaning of the word 'discourse', I believe I have in fact added to its meanings: treating it sometimes as the general domain of all statements, sometimes as an individual group of statements, and sometimes as a regulated practice that accounts for a number of statements. (Foucault, 1972: 80, quoted in Mills, 2004: 6).

Examples of Foucauldian discourse theory (see O'Leary and Falzon, 2010; Wetherell, Taylor, and Yates, 2001) would be to recognize how statements that posit men as natural leaders, rational, unemotional, and the family breadwinner can be described as a dominant discourse of masculinity. Individual words and statements combine together to tell or present a "truth" about men. This discourse of masculinity has a regulatory dimension insomuch as it suggests other men and women should acknowledge its accuracy and therefore act out and, in so doing, reify this discourse through their own language and practice. A further example of Foucauldian

discourse theory would be how a mother might seek to dissuade her daughter from engaging in "tomboy" activities, encouraging her to act "like a little girl," to insist she wear "feminine" clothes, and to punish her when she acts in a way the mother perceives as masculine and therefore inappropriate for a girl. This parental approach is framed within a dominant discourse of femininity, one that posits the female as passive, quiet, demure, pretty, and "naturally" different from the male. However, as Foucault insists, while these discursive regimes of "truth" are powerful persuaders of behaviour, they do not necessarily produce a passive, dominated subject:

> We must not imagine a world of discourse divided between accepted discourse and excluded discourse, or between dominant discourse and the dominated one; but as a multiplicity of discursive elements that can come into play in various strategies. . . . Discourse transmits and produces power: it reinforces it, but also undermines and exposes it, renders it fragile and makes it possible to thwart it. (Foucault, 1984; quoted in Whitehead, 2002, p. 104)

Discourse is all around us (for discussion, see Teubert, 2010). Without it there is no gender identity, for it is the means by which the subject transforms itself into the socially recognizable individual: woman, man, or other. Discourse creates the possibility of a gender identity, not the other way around. Language is central to this process, as are its constituent elements of symbols, signs, and signifying practices. There is, then, no subject outside of discourse; every man and woman is a discursive subject. As Foucault explains:

> The individual is not to be conceived of as a sort of elementary nucleus . . . on which power comes to fasten. . . . In fact, it is already one of the prime effects of power that certain bodies, certain gestures, certain discourses, certain desires, come

to be identified and constituted as individuals. (Foucault, 1980; quoted in Mills, 2004, p. 19)

What makes us each unique is the particular formation of discourses that inform our identity, and, as Derrida notes, these are always in a state of flux. So, in the final analysis, all is discursive; every gesture, word, statement, identity, is framed within a contingent discursive field. Discourse is not, however, neutral or benign. It has power effects insomuch as it has the capacity to identify what is truth and what is not. So discourses become "historically variable ways of specifying knowledge and truth— what it is possible to speak of at a given moment" (Ramazanoglu, 1993, p. 19). Such discursive formations present themselves as a truth to the individual, and operate through discursive regulated practices existing within, for example, the state, religion, education, academic work, families, organizations, the media (Foucault, 1991). How different cultures understand and respond to different sexual, racial, and gender identities are discursive reactions, ones that purport to tell the "truth" by presenting the full "knowledge" about these conditions (van Dijk, 2008a, b; Qian, Fong, and Smith, 2008).

From a post-structuralist position, our gender identity is, then, fundamentally and only ever a discursive formation; it is not rooted in biology, nor is it imposed upon us by ideological forces. What it means to be a man or a woman is discursively laid out before the subject through language, signs, symbols, and practices. The subject (male and female) then "takes up" these discourses as "practices of self-signification" (Butler, 1990, 1993). In so doing, the individual contributes to the productive cycle of identity work fundamental to the social world. This identity work has, for Foucault, an artistic element, insomuch as the discursive subject has the capacity to resist certain discourses as well as take up others, realizing his or her own desires in the doing

(e.g., the example of the Goth, given above). Foucault describes this dynamic as "the technology of self" (Foucault, 1988).

Within post-structuralist thought, the tendency is to refer to dominant discourses rather than to ideology because, within a Foucauldian understanding of discourse, there is no possibility of any individual standing outside of discourse. So a discourse may be dominant within a particular cultural setting, but it is not imposed by individuals who are themselves somehow separate from its power effects. Moreover, the contingency of discourse renders it amenable to resistance and change. Remember: nothing is final, fixed, or determined. This is one of the main reasons that post-structuralist thought has become increasingly popular within feminist theory (see Mills, 2004). For unlike social constructionist concepts, such as patriarchy and ideology, the post-structuralist concept of discourse affirms the centrality of the subject in the social, and, from this, the possibility if not the likelihood of change and resistance to any discursively constituted power field. (An example of this would be culturally specific regulatory practices concerning how people should express their gender identity and sexuality; much as certain social groups might attempt to control and impose restrictions on human sexuality it remains impossible to do so.) Within post-structuralism, the individual is the significant element, for he/she is recognized to be the fulcrum from which the social comes into existence.

The Concept of Performativity in Post-structuralism

So far, we have explored how language and practices, as discourses, create the subjectivity necessary for all subjects to emerge into the social world and be identified as individuals. But this raises a further issue and quandary: how do individuals cope with the **ontological** uncertainty that arises from this condition? For Nietzsche's observation that there is no being behind the doing, no doer behind the deed or the action, and that the "I" therefore is merely a fiction leads us to wonder how we manage to feel so complete and unified despite the illusory foundation upon which our sense of self is constructed. Judith Butler uses this dilemma to expose the fiction of sex and gender identity and to introduce her concept of **performativity**: "There is no gender identity behind the expressions of gender; that identity is performatively constituted by the very 'expression' that are said to be its results" (Butler, 1990, p. 25).

Butler issues a warning, however, not to mislead performance with performativity (see also Parker and Sedgwick, 1995; Siray, 2009). Her concept of performativity, drawing as it does on Foucauldian, Nietzschean, and Lacanian analysis and, especially, on linguistic theories, centralizes the embodied subject:

> In no sense can it be concluded that the part of gender that is performed is therefore the "truth" of gender; performance as bounded "act" is distinguished from performativity insofar as the latter consists in a reiteration of norms which precede, constrain, and exceed the performer and in that sense cannot be taken as the fabrication of the performer's "will" or "choice"; further, what is "performed" works to conceal, if not disavow, what remains opaque, unconscious, unperformable. The reduction of performativity to performance would be a mistake. (Butler, 1993, p. 234; see also Butler, 1999, 2004; Bell, 1999)

Performativity is, then, the action of discourse upon the body and the subject, and it is the mechanism that renders individuals, and their gender identity, into "existence." As Butler puts it, "[performativity] is that discursive practice that enacts or produces that which it names" (1993, p. 13). This is not a singular act of naming, but a procession of actions, a "reiteration

ontological

Pertaining to the study of the nature and the meaning of existence.

performativity

The process by which individuals and groups draw on and repeat particular discourses (behaviour, language, dress, and other verbal or nonverbal markers) in their everyday behaviour, thereby reinforcing their sense of (gender) identity.

of a norm or set of norms" (p. 12) that have a material effect insofar as they name, form, and signify the sexed and gendered body. For Butler, there is no sexed or gendered identity that pre-exists the moment that performativity is "acted." These moments, as practices of gender signification, are when we become that which the normative rules of society consider us to be. However, the outcome, an individual's identity, is not merely the product of that person's compliance with regulatory, normative laws, for no matter how compulsory the process may appear to be it cannot foreclose all possibilities for identity expression. At this point we are back to the agentic artistry of the self posited by Foucault but largely absent within social constructionist positions (for further discussion see Salih and Butler, 2004; Davies, 2008). For example, while dominant discourses in a particular culture may historically have claimed that a "woman's place is in the home," today this is not necessarily going to stop all women in that culture from going to university, from becoming educated, from having children or not, or from getting married or not. Those women who do, knowingly or otherwise, challenge the dominant gender discourse then help create a new discourse, which is "women can choose for themselves." Going to university then becomes a performative practice requiring the person to engage with new ways of being (discourses) that are not only challenging the old gender order but serve to assist in creating a new (gender) identity.

So I am not born a man or a woman. I *become* a man or a woman through a discursively informed performative process in which I take up and repeat those gender signifiers that are available to me as a male/man or female/woman in my cultural locale. But that locale need not necessarily be fixed, and such gender signifiers are themselves ever changing. It is as a direct consequence of this dynamic, largely unpredictable performative expression of self that my gender identity comes to exist. There is nothing behind the expression, no essential essence from which my masculinity or femininity emerges. The latter, insomuch as it is mine, pre-exists my emergence into the social. I am simply taking up (masculine or feminine) discourses, repeating them through my life, while also partly re-forming them through my own performative actions. In so doing, my unique self materializes. Performativity, my engagement with these practices of self-signification, is the action by which I become male/man or female/woman. It is this action that, by concealing my illusory self, provides me with the ontological comfort and security to continue existing. Without this performativity, I am reduced to the **nihilistic** absence so powerfully posited by Nietzsche and recognized within all post-structuralist theory.

nihilistic
Considers human existence as being without inherent meaning or purpose.

subject position
The particular position or status that we acquire through the act of expressing ourselves. Individuals may use many different (discursive) subject positions depending on the social situation they are in at the time.

The Desire To Be: A Theme of Post-structuralist Thought

Who "I" am may well be, quite literally, a fiction constructed by my imagination. But it seems very real to me. For sure, one's gender identity is not something most people agonize over, every day of their lives, although clearly some do. Such individuals are invariably those who, for different reasons, are unable to settle their ontological security in respect of their gendered, socially given self. Most of us go through our everyday lives in an almost seamless fashion. However, we are not operating within a fixed, holistic gender identity but one built on ever-changing narratives and discourses (Dolan, 1993; Clarke, 2008). Deleuze and Guattari describe it this way:

> In a single day, an individual passes constantly from one language to another. By turns, he speaks as "a father must speak," then as a boss; to his beloved, he speaks in a puerile language; while falling asleep he sinks into an oneric discourse, and abruptly returns to a professional language when the telephone rings. (1980; quoted in Bogue, 1996, p. 147)

Our ability to move from language to language within and across the discursive **subject positions** (Hollway, 1984) of, for example, mother, father, daughter, son, husband, professional, or activist enables us to feel stable at our core. We don't feel insecure, at least most of the time. The driver behind our not feeling insecure is desire: our desire to exist, to relate, to produce. From a Deleuze and Guattari perspective, it is a desire rooted in the eternal quest to be and become:

> [At the level of desire] the dichotomy between essence and existence is removed; the "power of existing" is therefore an ontological desire to come into existence. Desire is not immanent to the plane of existence; desire is the immanent plane of existence. "To be" is to be coming into

a relation, to be a becoming, to produce a new effect, relation, or modification between terms that are themselves modifications. (Goodchild, 1996, p. 40)

"I" has no core; "I" is a discursive subject, a nomad, a rootless entity, a narrative construction that metamorphoses into being and becoming man or woman (Braidotti, 2002). But we cannot live out this recognition of emptiness at our core, for this would subject us to the most disturbing existential anxieties about our sense of a "self." The "I" has to believe in "me," and in "you," otherwise "I" cannot be. As Giddens puts it, "a stable sense of self-identity presupposes the other elements of ontological security—an acceptance of the reality of things and of others—but it is not directly derivable from them" (1992, p. 54).

Our desire to be is, however, gendered. For example, an adult male's gender identity is foretold before his arrival. In taking it up, he is merely following the path of countless *masculine subjects* before him (Whitehead, 2002). But to be and become this man he must learn, replicate, and assume those gendered discourses that exist around him and that speak of what a man is and does. His skill and artistry is in discerning those representations of masculinity that speak, culturally, to him, to his "I," to this manliness; this is a process that continues all his life. The masculine subject metamorphoses into a socially inscribed and validated man through the endless taking up of the practices of gender signification at its disposal. This is **masculine ontology** at work. The immanent desire to be is the power that takes this free-floating subject, "I," and materializes it into a social being. In the doing, a man's existential anxiety (fear of not existing) is diminished to the point at which it virtually disappears from his cognitive state (Whitehead, 2002; also Buchanan and Colebrook, 2000; Bogue, 1996).

masculine ontology

The desire by males/men to be recognized and accepted and to have their masculine identity validated in the social world.

Let's continue with our example of the masculine subject. As with the feminine subject, it is not bounded; it is porous. It has no shape, no pre-given form. Masculine subjects are open to the discourses and narratives that frequent the many subject positions, places they inhabit within their social world (Hollway, 1984). Some discourses and narratives they take on and replicate, some they exclude, but the vast majority invade them without their knowing. As males, their sense of self derives mostly, but not exclusively, from those masculine discourses that are available to them within their cultural setting. In the process they are also acquiring a separation from those discourses that do not confirm their ever-evolving masculine identity. Even their bodies are not wholly theirs but are, rather, inscribed with gendered discourses that render them male and therefore real and acceptable to "I" and to others (Butler, 1993; see Chapter 4). Their primary desire is to be, but this being and becoming is circumscribed by the naming of them as male at birth—in other words, this naming remains the primary basis for whatever identity emerges in adulthood. For them, as with most other males, the desire for identity is a search for a masculine ontology; a way of being in the world that grounds them as male/men, positions others similarly and as women, and thereby produces the effect of a continuous and persistent sense of unity between their mind and body—their individual identity. Their personhood is then confirmed, their self feels continuous, and their transient state feels rooted the moment they can say "I am a man."

THE POSTMODERNIST APPROACH TO GENDER THEORY

Postmodernism is a larger and more generic term than *post-structuralism* and refers to a current of ideas that emerged in the latter part of the twentieth century and transformed the ways in which sociologists, literary critics, historians, anthropologists, and cultural theorists, among others, started to understand and analyze the ways in which our identities are shaped. Postmodernism had a significant impact on theories of gender; in fact, our approach in this book is also largely influenced by postmodernist ideas. The wide range of ideas that come under the umbrella term *postmodernism* have in common a departure from the scientific **positivism** and the belief in progress inherited from the Enlightenment and carried through the modern era. Postmodernist thinkers, in this respect, reacted against modernist modes of thinking, which they saw as being still largely indebted to traditional ideas about absolute truth and unified meanings. Like post-structuralists, postmodernists challenge the idea of identity as fixed and homogeneous, and also emphasize the role of language in shaping our identity. Postmodernism found a particular echo among feminists and post-colonial theorists because

positivism

The belief that society, like the natural world, can be explained through scientific observation and experimentation.

Enlightenment project

A way of seeing the world based on ideas that emerged in seventeenth- and eighteenth-century Europe and have continued to influence Western thinking, namely the belief in rationality, logic, science, objectivity, and progress.

of its particular interest in the ways in which power relations affect the subjective nature of how humans perceive the world.

Farewell to the Enlightenment

In this book, we use postmodernism as a theoretical tool to explore and understand a particular social condition recognized to exist at this point in human history, that is, postmodernity. Postmodernity signifies a break from the assumptions and discourses of the Western-oriented **Enlightenment project** that characterized modernity. Generally, modernity is considered to have begun in European societies in the late fifteenth century, concluding in the mid-twentieth century around the 1960s, after which "it started visibly to come apart" (Lemert, 1997, p. 27). The economic, social, and cultural conditions of the latter period of Western modernity (from the late eighteenth century and onward) are especially captured in the works of German sociological theorists such as Weber, Marx, Durkheim, and Simmel. These theorists powerfully explicate the triumph of bureaucratic rationalization and industrialized capitalism, which, reinforced through religious codes, class formations, imperialism, and patriarchal values, produced the social, economic, and political systems of the modern capitalist industrial state (see Morrison, 2001).

However, at the heart of modernity was more than the capitalist project: it was an attempt to underline the inevitability of human progress and to underscore the belief that scientific-based knowledge, industrialization, and related bureaucratic systems could produce the best of all possible worlds for the maximum number of people. This ethos was sustained in the notion of a universal truth concerning the world and its people, a philosophy that claimed to speak for the *a priori* needs of a foundational, sovereign subject. This ethos was also nourished and sustained through the slave trade, colonialism, imperialism, bigoted religious ideology, and patriarchal family values. The dark side to modernity was the myth "of purity" as defined and devised by those who saw themselves as both protectors and exemplars of modernity's project (Bauman, 1997).

The myths of modernity have not entirely disappeared. We have not, for example, fully awoken from the "nightmare of modernity" as described by Terry Eagleton (1987; see also Harvey, 1991). We can see such myths continuing to work on the minds of religious radicals, especially. However, despite their undoubted power to attract, the assumptions of modernity no longer hold true in quite the way they did. As Lyotard (1984) describes it, there is now "incredulity towards all grand narratives," skepticism towards universalizing truths, and doubt about the veracity of any ideology. The legitimacy of modernity has been lost or at the very least seriously undermined. Unquestioning belief in the inevitable progression of humankind and assumptions of underlying **epistemic unity** among all or groups of peoples have turned to a questioning of what is real and true, a recognition of diversity, difference, and fragmentation in all things human. No longer do we enjoin the Marxist foretelling of the march of the proletarian toward class revolution, assume the **Hegelian dialectic of spirit** achieving its inner quest for self-knowledge, or accept the Enlightenment dream of inevitable and rational progress to reason and freedom (Nicholson and Fraser, 1999). In the postmodern age, all is subject to speculation, questioning, deconstruction, and critical evaluation.

The certainty of rational, linear progress toward a perceived utopia that modernity promised and foretold and, indeed, relied upon for justification has, in the postmodern age, given way to fluidity, difference, uncertainty, and fragmentation. There is now recognition that the subject is "dispersed into a range of plural, polymorphous

> **epistemic unity**
>
> The process by which individuals can be members of a specific social group (e.g., women), and by having a unified experience (as women) share one single way of knowing and understanding the world.

> **Hegelian dialectic of spirit**
>
> a theory developed by Georg Wilhelm Friedrich Hegel about the capacity for the human spirit to achieve self-awareness and freedom by being able to resolve contradictions and reconcile opposites.

subject-positions inscribed within language" (Sarup, 1993, p. 130). And this is the connection postmodernism has with post-structuralism—both perspectives assume an ungrounded subject and, from this, recognize the inherent contingency at the heart of all realities. In other words there is no core identity that remains fixed, absolute, and true throughout a life; there is no future that can be managed and predicted just so long as the organizational systems are functioning effectively; and there is no utopia toward which humankind can eventually arrive so long as it follows a predesignated ideological pathway.

However, postmodernism is a theory used to describe and explore the condition of a particular epoch, while post-structuralism is a theoretical analysis of identity and its relationship to power and subjectivity. From a post-structuralist perspective, there have only ever been and only ever will be ungrounded discursive subjects while the postmodern age may well evolve into something entirely different or indeed revert to a form of modernity at some point in an unknown future.

Theorizing the Postmodern Condition

While the term *postmodern* has acquired increasing currency within the social sciences, its original and probably most common usage concerns art, architecture, music, cinema, drama, and literature, where it is used to delineate a cultural movement in advanced capitalist societies toward the "playful, the self-ironizing, and even the schizoid" (Eagleton, 1987, in Harvey, 1991, p. 7; see also Millen, 1990).

Within the social sciences, postmodernist theory is used in a number of ways and by very different theorists. Lyotard is generally recognized as a the primary influence in this area, and for him the postmodern condition, which he simplifies as "an incredulity towards metanarratives," is exemplified in his concept of performativity, the commodification of knowledge, and the displacement of narrative knowledge by scientific knowledge (1994). Baudrillard (1983, for example) employs postmodernism to analyze what he sees as the contemporary displacement of reality with hyper-reality, and the concomitant breaking down of the distinction between what is "true" and what is "false." He uses the term **simulacra** to describe a state of being that is obsessed with image, spectacle, appearance, symbols, and simulation. This simulacra produces a condition where what we watch on television, for example, is more real to us than reality itself (see Harvey, 1991, for discussion). Neo-Marxist postmodernists such as Jameson (1984) see postmodernity as the inevitable "cultural logic" of advanced capitalism, where progressive cultural expressions are appropriated into the commodifying project of multinational corporations, thereby sustaining establishment/capitalist ideology. In a similar vein, Bauman (1997) welcomes the turn from the totalitarian and "cleansing" actions of modernity but warns

against the consumerist-driven, individualized desires of the self that he claims are apparent within the postmodern age.

Most theorists would acknowledge that postmodernism is complementary to poststructuralism, and this is especially so with respect to Derridean deconstructionism, and the related feminist positions of Irigaray, Kristeva, and Cixous, which we discuss later. However, the fluidity of the term has resulted in a lack of clarity, a situation further problematized by the fact that theorists from diverse standpoints now draw on the concept to underpin their perspectives or to put them into context. In an attempt at clarification, Lemert (1997) describes three types of postmodern social theory:

1. *Radical postmodernism*, exemplified in the writings of Baudrillard and Lyotard
2. *Strategic postmodernism,* seen in the works of Foucault, Derrida, Lacan, and Bauman
3. *Radical modernism*, demonstrated by Adorno, Habermas, and Jameson

A fourth dimension, one that Lemert misses, however, is *feminist postmodernism*, typified by the writings of Cixous, Irigaray, Kristeva, and Nicholson (see, for overview, Nicholson, 1990; Tong, 1994), which we will discuss next.

Postmodernism's Relationship to Feminism

Feminism's relationship to postmodernism is ambivalent. Feminism undoubtedly seeks to unravel at least one of the central strands of modernity: male dominance, masculinism, and patriarchal values, as well as the means by which these strands sustain a particular economic, cultural, and social order. As well, feminism is increasingly being used to analyze and promote cultural and sexual differences, notably by applying queer theory and postcolonial theories (see Chapter 3). From such standpoints, a feminist-postmodernist position

simulacra

Images or representations that produce a simulation of reality without bearing any relationship to it.

has been powerfully and persuasively articulated (Nicholson, 1990, 1999; Nicholson and Fraser, 1999; Flax, 1990). However, as feminists themselves acknowledge, "feminism stands on Enlightenment grounds" (Harding, 1990, p. 99), insomuch as both lay claim to universalizing truths and "the desirability and the possibility of social progress" (p. 99).

A further alignment of feminism with modernity is apparent in the notions of an **epistemic** community (of women), and assumptions of a common or related subjectivity among women, arising through their experiences as female gendered subjects (see Assiter, 1996; also Ramazanoglu and Holland, 2005, for discussion; see also Chapter 3). Consequently, postmodernism, as an incredulity towards all meta-narratives, sits uneasily with feminism's **meta-narrative**, which seeks a universal political change to an existing gender order. As Benhabib puts its,

> Postmodernism is an ally with whom feminism cannot claim identity but only partial and strategic solidarity. Postmodernism, in its infinitely sceptical and subversive attitude towards normative claims, institutional justice and political struggles, is certainly refreshing. Yet, it is also debilitating. (1997, p. 14)

As a feminist, Benhabib's wary approach toward, but desire for, a "strategic solidarity" with postmodernism is understandable. Postmodernism at the very least opens up the gateway to a less white, middle-class, Eurocentric, Americanized, dominated version of feminism (Nicholson, 1990). However, what postmodernism does is undermine all claims for political solidarity made from any single standpoint (Squires, 1993). As Wendy Brown argues, "Postmodernity unsettles feminism because it deprives us of the *moral* force that the subject, truth, and normativity coproduce in modernity" (1991, p. 78).

> **epistemic**
> Relating to knowledge and ways of knowing.

> **meta-narrative**
> A broad and overarching model or story that serves to explain the way society works. Can also be linked to the concept of ideology.

What modernity brought us, at least in respect of identity, postmodernity takes away: that is, assumptions of sameness, truth, wholeness, and reliability in the sustainability of our human condition, of any political project, of our selves. Culturally and individually, our past is disputable; our future, unknowable; our present, contingent. Postmodernism highlights this condition and articulates it in a way that resonates with many of us at this point in history. Postmodernism, crucially, enables us to not only recognize but indeed applaud diversity, not least across and within racial, ethnic, gender, and sexual identities. At the same time, it challenges us to accept that within such diversities there are also multiplicities of realities and disputes as to what counts as knowledge and truth. Postmodernism offers us a glimpse of our possibilities in a complex, globalized world of diverse subject positions and multiple discourses. However, at precisely the same moment, postmodernism closes the door on the possibility of a universal morality, at least one grounded in religious or political ideology. It removes the foundations of any core gender identity and certainly one founded upon the public (male) and private (female) domains, which proved to be the building blocks of modernity.

Postmodern Identities

The totalizing tendencies inherent in the project of modernity offered assumptions of permanence and continuity through their very application. They provided the individual with a degree of existential certainty and ontological security, not least because they required her/him to submit to authoritarian codes of behaviour, moral strictures, and cultural values, all enforced through an economic system that held the carrot of prosperity and the stick of cultural and legal sanction. However, while we can now reflect back on modernity's "totalitarian nightmare," we should ask ourselves why modernity proved so compelling for so many for such an extended period of time. What was the message contained in modernity and in the Enlightenment project, that attracted so many, and still does?

In attempting to address this question we need to refer back to some of the core ideas contained within post-structuralism, not least that of the ambiguous, contingent self—that which desires ontological grounding. We should not forget that there is comfort in structure, there is security in being dominated, and that unquestioning obedience can produce unquestioning faith. Faith, in turn, produces comfort: the ontological comfort of knowing that you have a place in and belong to a social structure reinforced by a persuasive ideology, an unwavering way of seeing reality, that claims to have a larger purpose, which is to achieve a utopian existence if not for all humanity, then at least for those who have faith. Modernity, then, worked through the human desire for ontological grounding.

At this point we can clearly see how gender identity connected to modernity and how it will have to respond to the postmodern age. Modernity was a masculine project across all cultures (see, for discussion, Dayal, 2007; Seidler, 1993; Schwartz, 2010; Tengan, 2008; Zhong, 2000). Men, maleness, and masculinity provided the tools, the justification, and the discursive context without which modernity could not have been brought into existence in quite the way it was. At the same time, modernity provided the discursive and cultural landscape upon which masculine power became reified, naturalized.

The dominant masculine discourse of modernity positioned man as a rational and reasoned provider: the patriarch, knower, leader, manager, enforcer, controller, truth giver. Man was seen as the fountain of all knowledge and experience: the archetypal scientist, doctor, priest, judge, officer, teacher, politician, and philosopher, the cultural and social icon. By contrast, postmodernity offers the possibility of positioning man as equal to woman. At the very least, postmodernism as a theory of postmodernity, through its deconstructive capabilities, questions all the inherent assumptions about men and masculinity created over centuries, which were reinforced and validated through modernity's project.

Patriarchy offers certainty, albeit at a price. Patriarchy has rarely needed to be enforced militarily or through the judiciary, although clearly it has been. Male dominance works precisely because it is oppressive and demanding of its subjects. In being oppressive, it offers "truth," certainty, order. In that respect, male dominance is no different from any totalizing ideology or dominant discourse. Modernity functioned largely by presenting itself as the optimum expression of a functional society. It was oppressive as are all modernist meta-narratives, but it suggested permanence, continuity, a "progressive" society built around the biological imperatives inherent in gender difference. Every man and woman had his or her place in the public (work-based) and private (family-based) spheres that underpinned modernity.

In many respects, our postmodern society still carries many residual aspects of modernity. However, postmodernist ideas have been useful in increasing our awareness of the myths of modernity. They take us into an altogether freer, less bounded, but more uncertain place. They have opened up the possibility of rethinking gender relations. Furthermore, in the context of multiculturalism and the global world, postmodernism offers a template to reinterpret the traditional power relations between black/white,

East/West, developed/developing nations in a less dichotomous way.

In emphasizing distinctions, differences, and diversities, both within and between the discursive regimes of male and female, postmodernism powerfully challenges any assumptions of *a priori* self, a natural gender order, or an ontologically fixed identity. Assisted by its theoretical partners—post-structuralism and psychoanalysis—postmodernism provides us with the analytical tools to understand how this identity work circulates around and inculcates the subject. It may well be that as individuals confront the existential consequences of this moment they will be attracted to the consumerist-driven, celebrity-modelled, simulacra-oriented gender identities offered in shopping malls, and plastically portrayed in the media on "reality" television and in so-called chick lit. Certainly this is the concern of many postmodernist theorists. However, one of the positions we offer in this book is to consider the self as a rather more sophisticated actor than we often give it credit for. The artistry of the self is a dimension of our possibilities as gendered subjects. This means, as Foucault stresses, that we are always potentially more than the limits of our immediate discursive surroundings.

However, whatever our possibilities as gendered beings, we must face the fact that we are now left without recourse to the certainties of the Enlightenment and modernity, even though they remain, paradoxically, part of our cultural scripts. We must, therefore, as Foucault indicated, be more artistic, if not subversive, in how we fashion this gender identity of ours. It is important that we open ourselves to doubt, to risk, and to multiplicity, and to the realization that nothing is for certain, not even the unchallenged continuity of our perceived gendered self.

Narratives of the Self

A paradox within contemporary theorizing around the self is that while theorists of all persuasions are increasingly drawn to the idea of identity as fragmented, decentred, multiple, and illusionary, the practices or discourses of individuality within society seem stronger than ever. In other words, although theorists now recognize the self to be an unstable fiction, the pursuit of individuality and self-expression appears inscribed as a right, if not a demand, in increasing numbers of societies and cultures.

This spur to "invent our selves" is not new (Rose, 1996), but it does appear to be changing, increasing in intensity, requiring a deepening reflexivity in social actors. Lash and Urry (1993) connect this emphasis on **reflexive production** with the conditions arising from post-industrialization, in particular "disorganized capitalism," which, they argue, speeds up social relations not least through the "optimum levels of information flow and knowledge acquisition" demanded of individuals in an increasingly competitive *post-traditional* society (Lash, 1995, pp. 120–1). Beck (1994) and Giddens (1992) suggest that reflexivity assumes greater importance as individuals resort to the self-construction of life narratives. They do this to ameliorate the heightened sense of ontological insecurity that arises from the breakdown or questioning of those previously assumed *trust systems* which appeared fixed in early modernity but are more vulnerable today.

Take, for example, the world of work, which we explore in depth later in the book. As we argue, paid employment is a powerful arena for our sense of identity and self, but work is today characterized by insecurity and change; no organization is totally stable, no job guaranteed for life. Working-class men could at one time have left school at 15 and gone to work in the local factory, spending a

reflexive production

The signs and meanings that are created when individuals reflect on how they relate to society and each other.

lifetime doing the same job, in the same community, with the same people. Today, those factories are either gone or they require fewer and more highly skilled labourers. The trust system that built up around male-dominated industrialism has disappeared, to be replaced by an altogether less secure work situation.

But whatever our life circumstances, the urge to reinforce and validate our sense of self is no less apparent today than it was in the age of modernity. Yet we are today facing, it would seem, incalculable and unlimited risks, a world where nothing feels stable or secure, in which case, confronting the ambivalence at the heart of our ontology can be seen to be a particularly acute condition of the late or postmodern age (Beck, Giddens, and Lash, 1995; Bauman, 1991).

The idea of our lives, our selves, and our worlds as "narratives" is key to postmodern thinking. Certainly it is possible to see a move toward the privileging of self-narrative and reflexivity across many areas of society. This is particularly true with regard to sociological discourse (Stanley, 1993; Byrne, 2003), whereby the subject as storyteller becomes, potentially, not only the heroine/hero of her/his history but by implication the architect of his or her self (Deem, 1996; David, 2002, 2003). The self then appears centred while the reflexive process that produces this effect attracts ever heightened status and currency across societies (see, for discussion, Melucci, 1996b; Giddens, 1992, 1993; Adkins, 2001). For example, this is the drive behind social networking phenomena, such as Facebook, Twitter, and blogging. By being part of these virtual communities, posting our photos, telling our stories, revealing the minutia of our lives often to nameless strangers, we are rendering ourselves valid, important, real. This is a narcissistic action but also a statement of belonging.

Once we move to a postmodernist position that recognizes the absence of any core "I"

to our self then we must attempt to understand how the "I" comes into existence for the discursive subject. We operate across various subject positions (Hollway, 1984), albeit often in contradictory fashion, and clearly we have some degree of investment in these discursive locations, not least because they serve to sustain our sense of self as a coherent unity. These "multiple realities" (Schutz, 1967) have their own "metaphysical constants" (Natanson, 1970), and the subject's skill is at "conjuring up" (Young, 1989) these immediate realities and turning them into an apparently cohesively grounded personhood and individuality. But how is this achieved? How do we go from a multiple, fragmented self, now surrounded by the real and imagined threats posited by the postmodern, post-traditional condition, to the ontologically grounded self that underpins our social presentation of our self? For, as ever, our desire is not to present our selves as unstable and incoherent but, rather, as stable, unified, and very coherent.

Theorists such as Ricoeur (1991), Harre (1979, 1983), Gergen and Gergen (1983), and Shotter and Gergen (1989) were some of the first to develop the idea of narrative (of self) as a means of explaining this existential discontinuity in our identity work. They also proffered narrative as a way of resolving the theoretical tension that exists between notions of the self as an agentic actor with choices surrounding individuality, and the self as reducible to the constructivist demands that arise from ideological and regulatory processes.

In other words, while our self is constituted in the dynamic and unpredictable effects of discourse, by re-experiencing and re-telling these discourses as "texts of everyday life" (Parker, 1994, p. 56), so we render ourselves into existence; we make ourselves feel real. Our lives become stories with us at the centre. Our relationships with others get lived out in narrative form; that is, we construct them as narratives of our past, present, and future. For example, a couple gets married and thereby engage in the narrative of romantic love and togetherness. But the wedding day can be told in any number of ways; it can have different realities for different people who attended, plus the story of that wedding can change as the couple and their relationship changes. But whoever reflects on the wedding and tells the story of the wedding day, albeit from their subjective perspective, are making it and all who attended, real: "Not only do we tell our lives as stories, but there is a significant sense in which our relationships with one another are lived out in narrative form" (Gergen and Gergen, 1988, p. 18).

However, the wedding day example being recounted by different people and very likely over many years suggests the importance of being able to deliver narratives that transcend the passing of time. By remembering an event and recounting it as a narrative, a story that we were part of, so we provide a further foundation for our existence. We existed then, so we must exist today. All this suggests linearity between who we were then and who we are today, and that linearity appears to reinforce our stable self, our fixed embodiment as individuals: "The fact that people believe they possess identities fundamentally depends on their capacity to relate fragmentary occurrences across temporal boundaries" (Gergen and Gergen, 1987, p. 20).

Our lives are temporally located, that is, they are lived out in frames of time. We are, in a very real sense, our history. But that history could have many voices, many accounts to it. The account we give of our history renders us true, if only to our selves, but also potentially to others. In voicing our history, our story, to both our self and others, so we assemble and constitute our identity into existence. Via the discourses at our disposal and taken up by us, so we enunciate and formalize our otherwise elusive self. Of course, there are limitations to this process: the limitations of our language, the limitations

of interpretation by others, and the limitations imposed upon us by the dominant discourses of our culture and social setting. As McNay puts it, "the narrative structure of self-identity is neither authentic nor ideological but an unstable mixture of fact and fabulation" (2000, p. 94).

We use stories to make sense not only of events, but of our selves. In giving an account of our selves to others and to our selves, we substantiate our individuality, give it meaning, give it colour and expression. Our repeated narrative representation is a social construction but one that we, as discursive subjects, have brought about. It is not the heroic project of the (masculine) self in which we are simultaneously agents and architects of our destiny; it is a story always in time, always undertaken reflexively, and always mitigated, to some extent, by the conditions under which it is spoken.

Theories of the self as a narrative construction not only enable us to place temporality at the heart of our existence as subjects, and untie us from the agency/structure dualism, they explain how our sense of coherence might come about. As Ricoeur (1991, 1992) argues, narrative has an ontological status in that it arises from experience as well as imagination and in so doing provides us with a framework and multiple reference points, which together serve to locate us in the social web and provide us with an understanding of its operations and our relationship to it. Our narrative renders us real, and in the process serves to reinforce both our societal identity(s) and our individuality (see also McNay, 2000, for discussion).

In respect of gender, narrative can, then, both validate and disrupt dominant notions of femininity and masculinity. Storytellers are able to fashion themselves into an appropriate, maybe flattering discursive narrative, one that serves to position them as unquestionably a representative of a gender and a sexuality. The sense of self that arises through this process retains its coherence precisely because of this validation. In this way, so we can reflexively "account" for our actions, for our performance as gendered individuals. We can reinforce our masculinity, our femininity, both to others and our selves through our stories, our narrated self. But despite the powerful effects such a process of reflecting on our history has on the subjectivity of the self, as theorists we can recognize that the subject is only ever giving a partial, if not biased, account. No one has access to all truths. We can never say that this story is the one and only account; as Rose warns us "the vocabularies that we utilize to think ourselves [into existence] do not bear the marks of their birth" (1996, p. 39). Therefore, research into gender, for example, must always be tempered by the realization that what is being presented as an objective story or narrative is subjective, and grounded, if at all, only in a complex mix of fact and fiction enlisted by the speaker. The narrative may well be real for the storyteller, but closer inspection can expose its contradictory elements and deconstructive potential (see Erben, 1998, for discussion; see also Bal, 1999).

So the self remains illusionary but is expressed as real, fixed, and essential in narrative.

In which case, when asked "Who are you?" the "I" can answer with some confidence, "This is who I am" and immediately begins the story of "me" as presented to the other, the listener, the audience, you.

SUMMARY

In this chapter we have moved into those contemporary theories of gender and identity that signal the unsettled and fluid character of the self, the "I." Post-structuralism and postmodernism have this one shared feature: the possibility, indeed the recognition, that consistency and predictability are largely absent when it comes to both assuming and performing our gender identity. The self is inevitably caught up in a social world and its associated cultural networks that are forever changing. If modernism once gave us a sense of progression toward some unifying enlightenment project of humanity, postmodernism merely gives us fragmentation and difference. At the same time, post-structuralism offers us compelling theories to understand the self as a product of discourse and language, always acting to be and become an identity—gender as a process, never a fixed outcome.

CASE STUDY

Julia is a 26-year-old single woman born in New York but now living in Los Angeles. She is at a stage in her life when her career is the most important thing. She has had boyfriends but is now on her own and has just completed a professional acting course in Los Angeles. Julia has a lot of talent. Her high school drama teacher was the first person to identify it; she advised Julia's parents to send their daughter to a high school specializing in art and drama. After graduating from school, Julia had no difficulty obtaining a scholarship to pursue her studies at a prominent acting and film school in Los Angeles. As a student, she took part in many successful stage productions and revealed her talents particularly in Shakespearian productions.

In spite of her success, Julia has recently been feeling a loss of self-confidence. Since she completed her course, she has had a number of parts in low-profile local film productions but has not been successful in getting parts in more professional productions. Although she can be very confident on stage and in front of the camera, Julia often feels insecure about herself, particularly about her physical appearance. What preoccupies her most is the fact that, in spite of the many slimming diets she has tried and regular workouts at the gym, she has not been able to attain the body she desires. She has recently been contemplating plastic surgery to remove fat around her body. She has shared her thoughts with her parents and close friends. Although they were surprised, they were all supportive except for her father, who thought that cosmetic surgery was a waste of time and money and that his daughter should concentrate on her career. Julia's mother, on the other hand, has shown complete support for her daughter and has even offered to contribute some of the money needed for the surgery. This has caused a tension between Julia's parents and between Julia and her father. At the moment Julia is not sure whether she should go ahead. On the one hand, she agrees with her father and is apprehensive about the risks of surgical intervention; on the other hand, she thinks that having a slimmer-looking body would help her regain her confidence.

DISCUSSION QUESTIONS

1. What control does Julia have over her body?
2. What are the signs and signifiers that construct Julia's sense of an identity?
3. Discuss Julia's "desire to be."
4. What discourses does Julia draw on in order to reinforce her gender identity?
5. To what extent does Julia's lifestyle exemplify (or does not exemplify) postmodernity?
6. What advice would you offer Julia if you were one of her friends?

QUESTIONS FOR REVIEW AND DISCUSSION

1. Recall what you learned in Chapter 1 and identify the main differences between classical and contemporary perspectives on gender and identity.
2. What is meant be "being and becoming" a gendered individual?
3. What are the key differences between modernity and postmodernity?
4. How does post-structuralism undermine assumptions of biological determinism in respect of our gender identity?
5. What do you consider to be the strengths and weaknesses of post-structuralist theory?
6. What discourses of identity do you perform in order to appear a particular gender?

Chapter 3
Theories of Identity and Difference

▲ *You are not a stereotype, you are a real person.*
Source: © Daniel Hoffman/Alamy

Learning Objectives

At the end of this chapter you will be able to:

- Understand the relationship between gender and other parameters of difference, such as race, sexuality, and disability.

- Identify and understand the main principles of feminist theory, theories of race and difference, post-colonial theory, queer theory, and disability theory.

- Understand and appreciate the value of intersectionality as an approach to examining gender and identity.

- Understand how processes of normalcy are embedded in questions of power and privilege.

- Approach questions related to gender and identity from a variety of interconnected theoretical perspectives.

OVERVIEW

As we discussed in Chapter 2, the second half of the twentieth century saw the emergence of theories that questioned the centrality and predominance of monolithic definitions of identity. Post-structuralist and postmodern theories transformed traditional notions of the self as a unitary, homogeneous, and coherent entity. These theories arose at a time when dichotomous definitions of identity were also being challenged by the feminist, anti-racist, and anti-colonial struggles of the 1960s. The women's movements in Europe and North America, the civil rights movement in the US, and the independence movements in Asia, Africa, and the Caribbean had the effect of challenging the master narratives of the West that posited the human subject as white, male, straight, and able-bodied. As Ania Loomba explains:

> Post-structuralists' suspicion of established truths was shared by various new social movements which also challenged the "meta-narratives" that excluded them. Anti-colonial or feminist struggles emphasized culture as a site of conflict between the oppressors and the oppressed. The decentring of the human subject was important to them because such a subject had been dominantly theorised by European imperialist discourses as male and white. They also paid attention to language as a tool of domination and as a means of constructing identity. (Loomba, 2005 [1998], pp. 39–40)

In this respect, post-structuralism offered relevant theoretical perspectives to those interested in deconstructing dominant binaries of gender, race, gender, sexuality, and (dis)ability. Feminist theorists, race theorists, postcolonial theorists, queer theorists, and disability theorists in particular have engaged with the postmodern idea of multiple identities and histories, and they have made significant contributions to the idea of difference in the context of diversity and plurality. This chapter pays particular attention to the ways in which discourses of difference based on gender, race, sexual orientation, and disability have contributed to transforming our understanding of gender difference and gender identity. We begin with a discussion of feminist theory, followed by an examination of how race and colonialism intersect with constructions of gender, before looking at queer theory and discourses of sexual diversity. We conclude our exploration of theory by looking at the ways in which the emerging field of disability theory can contribute to our understanding of gender and identity.

FEMINIST THEORY

Feminist theory covers a wide range of ideas and disciplines, some of which we have already touched on in Chapters 1 and 2 and will explore in chapters to follow. One could say that in the Western world feminist ideas go as far back as the Middle Ages, when a woman who did not conform to the social norms could be branded a witch. As Virginia Woolf has argued, women have always been present but invisible in the history of ideas (see Woolf, 1929; and Olsen, 1980). The early twentieth century saw the emergence of a feminist consciousness, spurred by the movement for gender equality, particularly in matters regarding education and the right to vote. The early feminist movement in the West was led by white, middle-class, educated women, figures such as Nellie McClung in Canada, Susan B. Anthony in the US, and Sylvia Pankhurst in Britain.

While the struggle for gender equality continued, the second half of the twentieth century saw the emergence of a more in-depth, reflective analysis that sought, for example, to examine the language, images, and representations that lay behind and reinforced gender binaries. In 1949, the publication of Simone de Beauvoir's *The Second Sex* helped lay the groundwork for the feminist theorizing of female otherness. Looking at myths of womanhood throughout the whole Western tradition, from the Greek antiquity to modern times, de Beauvoir identified patterns of binaries that have played a key role in shaping gender difference. She theorized the construction of woman as man's "other" from an existentialist perspective and emphasized the prevalence of social conditioning over biology.

The women's movements of the 1960s and 1970s led to a more distinct feminist consciousness. Psychoanalysis, as we saw in Chapter 1, played a major role in shaping discourses about gender identity and difference. Anglo-American critics such as Juliet Mitchell and Kate Millett denounced as sexist Freud's theory of penis envy, while French feminists like Julia Kristeva, Luce Irigaray, and Hélène Cixous used Freudian (and Lacanian) ideas but gave them new meaning (see Chapter 1). Feminist theorists started to investigate language as a site of difference, and many of these scholars focused their attention on women's writing (see Showalter, 1977; Toril Moi, 1985; Jacobus, 1986).

Since the 1980s, one of the main developments in feminist theory has been the growing body of writing by women of colour and women outside the Western world. The idea of "woman" as a category intersected by class, race, ethnicity, culture, sexuality, and other markers of difference has played a key role in contemporary feminist theory. Queer theorists also opened new

avenues for feminist theory by looking at how gender and sexuality intersect. Furthermore, the emergence of masculinity studies and, more recently, transgender studies has broadened the ways in which feminist theory has traditionally defined and understood gender, difference, and identity. However, aside from those theories concerned with gender, perhaps the theory that has played the most significant role in terms of examining identity is race. The intersectionality of race and gender has in fact been the preoccupation of scholars since the 1960s.

THEORIES OF RACE AND DIFFERENCE

Race and difference have been theorized by many scholars, particularly in the United States and Britain, and from a variety of disciplines. Critical race theory (CRT) developed in the US during the 1980s, inspired by the work of African-American writers such as Sojourner Truth, Frederick Douglass, and W.E.B. Du Bois. CRT focuses on the analysis of race as a political, ideological, discursive, and relational concept, particularly with regard to law and education (see Degado and Stefancic, 2001; Williams, 1997). Its first offshoot, critical race feminism, focuses on the intersection of race and gender. Its second offshoot is critical white studies, a movement that looks at the construction of white privilege. European ethnicities and cultures have traditionally been grouped into the fixed and homogenized category of "whiteness" (Bonnett, 1999, p. 202). Throughout the 1990s, and more particularly in women's studies, for white women to acknowledge their "whiteness" was seen as a self-reflective way of recognizing and understanding the position of being privileged (Charles, 1992). However, some scholars have been sceptical about this trend for they argue there are limits to the extent that such subjective reflectivity can actually bring about a true understanding of one's privileged position vis-à-vis others (see, for example, Ahmed, 2004).

Theories about race and difference clearly cover a wide range of disciplines, movements, and opinions and have helped change the ways in which race, culture, and ethnicity have traditionally been understood. While in the past some scholars have applied a genetic (racist) explanation to the concept of race, the overall position, at least now in the social sciences, is to acknowledge that race is socio-culturally, politically, and economically constructed and contested. The notion that race is not a "natural" category, that is, does not have a biological or genetic base, is now generally accepted by most writers in this field (Cornell and Harman, 2006). As a result, we now understand that race can have a variety of meanings, thus allowing for flexible, fluid, and multiple understandings of this term across space and time.

From a post-structuralist perspective, then, we can argue that race and gender are contingent categories that are a part of an individual's plurality of subjectivity. According to Warnke (2005), identities vary over time and cultural distance so that what is available as a possible identity at one time in history or in one culture is not always possible at another time or in another culture. Such contingent reflexivity challenges the fixed and essentialist ways in which people continue to be categorized and labelled in racial terms, that is, using their particular continent or country of origin, religious affiliation, racial skin tone, or ethnic dress or food as essentialist markers of fixed identity. Similarly, when reduced to a conventional Cartesian dialectic (whereby we attempt to "prove" our own existence and identity by conveniently labelling others as different), the notion of seeing the "other" in exclusively racial terms has led to the stereotyping of people and individuals, out of which arises not only misunderstandings and misinterpretations but also racist assumptions and attitudes. As Williams notes,

> The categories race, culture, black, have been problematised as a base on which to construct

analysis . . . [and] . . . leads to a reductionist's aggregation of ethnic differences . . . confuse[s] practice through oversimplification, generating stereotypes and fostering ethnocentrism. (Williams, 1999, p. 213)

At a national and state level, this oversimplified approach, which serves to identify people on the basis of fixed, essential racial categories, raises serious questions about the validity of the liberal, modernist version of the multicultural and multiracial society (see Chapter 4). Indeed, this approach can serve to conceal state ideological interventions wherein people are labelled and positioned in distinct racial groups but from a liberal discourse of diversity and difference. In other words, racial labels are applied to different people. Such individuals are then "stuck" with these labels whether they want them or not. Moreover, any question of diversity is then presented as complex, ambiguous, contradictory, and confusing. Clearly, race remains a powerful component of our identity and subjectivity, although before we can explore its conjunction with gender it is useful to trace its origins as an influential term and discourse.

History and Definitions of Race

The word *race* first appeared in the English language in 1508 when it was used to simply denote a category or class of persons. It was only in the late eighteenth century that *race* became invested with biological connotations, and not until the early nineteenth century that specific theories of racial types began to emerge in academic and other writings. Many of the ideas associated with genetics and racial differentiation during this period were founded on pseudo-scientific theories that are now discredited (see, for discussion, Alderman, 1985; Appiah, 1986; Miles, 1982; Moodley and Curling, 2006). For Appiah, race is "a socio-historical concept" (1986, p. 25):

> Race, we all assume, is, like all other concepts, constructed by metaphor and metonymy; it

stands in, metonomically, for the "Other"; it bears the weight, metaphorically, of other kinds of difference . . . Even if the concept of race *is* a structure of oppositions—white opposed to black (but also to yellow), Jew opposed to Gentile (but also to Arab)—it is a structure whose realisation is, at best, problematic and, worst, impossible. (Appiah, 1985, p. 35, original emphasis)

Popularist ideas about race and racial differences are not fixed within a trans-historical agency, nor are they contained in a cultural or historical specificity. Rather, such ideas are forever changing in relation to the discursive social, economic, cultural, and political practices that exist in any particular place or period and within which such discourses emerge and flourish. As Ferber argues,

> In representing race as a given foundation, we obscure the relations of power which constitute race as a foundation. Rather than taking race for granted, we need to begin to explore the social construction of race, and the centrality of racism and misogyny to this construction. (Ferber, 1998, p. 60)

As a response to the increasing dissatisfaction with the term *race* and with the assimilationist assumptions that arose with the contemporary focus on immigration, the concept of ethnicity found its way into political and academic discourse (Mason, 1996). Since race as a conceptual and empirical idea to locate difference was proving to be problematic, not least because of its articulation and association within a political discourse, the term *ethnicity* proved to be more appealing. While there is a tendency for scholars and researchers to use *race* and *ethnicity* interchangeably (Mason, 1996), the two terms are also regarded as separate variables that address different aspects of identity and that are infused with degrees of contestation (Cornell and Hartmann, 2006; D'Angelo and Douglas, 2008). *Ethnicity* speaks of a flexibility

and inclusiveness of all those minorities that appear positioned outside the fixed meanings of race, for example, South Asian, Chinese, and others. Yet, at the same time, combining all ethnic groups into a single category, such as South Asian, can be problematic. As Modood et al. (1997, p. 227) argue, "such categories are heterogeneous, containing ethnic groups with different cultures, religions, migration histories and geographical and socio-economic locations. Combining them leads to differences between them being ignored."

The positioning and repositioning of subjects and groups in terms of race and ethnicity have been seen as a cyclic process throughout the pre- and post-war periods. For example, in the early part of the twentieth century, the idea of ethnicity referred predominantly to Irish, Italians, and Jews although the term took on a more sinister and racialized meaning for the Jewish community. In the latter half of the last century, after the migration of West Indians, East Asians, Pakistanis, and Bangladeshis, the term revised itself to exclude, except for Jews, those white Europeans defined earlier, and focused instead on peoples from Africa, Asia, and the Caribbean (Moodley and Palmer, 2006).

In more recent times, "'ethnicity' has become the term of the hour in political science, as we grapple with its role in domestic conflict and international security" (Tilley, 1997, p. 497). This has been especially so since the early 1990s, when socio-economic and geopolitical changes in the international arena, particularly in the West, have broadened the concept of ethnicity beyond a simplistic association with ethnic minority communities. For example, the breakup of the former Yugoslavia and the subsequent Balkan wars introduced the term *ethnic cleansing* into common usage, thus questioning ethnicity as a sole non-European attachment and raising its association with many European, white minority groups. The colour white, which is often forgotten in this category, is also a part of ethnicity. According to Stewart Hall, we are all "ethnically located and our ethnic identities are crucial to our subjective sense of who we are" because "we all speak from a particular space, out of a particular history, out of a particular experience" (Hall, 1992, p. 258). Indeed, our ethnicity location is never fixed. As Adam says, "ethnic identity waxes and wanes not only in response to group members' own perceived needs, both instrumental and symbolic, but also in response to imposed identities by outsiders" (Adam, 1995, p. 463).

As we have argued throughout this book, identity is never neutral. It is invested with both political and personal dimensions that interchange, interact, and are never fully predictable. We are, in part at least, a symbol of other people's perceptions and cultural interpretations. Yet at the same time our innate desire is for grounding, permanence, predictability, association, and security. We may not be able to achieve such a sense of fixedness in our material and physical embodiment, but we certainly hope to achieve it in our sense of being an individual. Consequently, we are often torn between the need to experience ourselves existentially in the here and now and the desire to be historically, psychically, communally, and environmentally connected. Such contingent connections are powerfully constructed in ethnic and racial terms; and overlaid upon this complex and dynamic mixture is gender.

Race and Gender as Overlapping Theories of Identity

While social and cultural theories surrounding race and ethnicity have been substantively discussed and documented (see, for example, Gilroy, 1990; Hall, 1992; Law, 1996; Mason, 1996; Moodley and Palmer, 2006), scant attention has been given to race and gender as an integrated process of identity construction. Invariably, men's and women's identity developments have

been conceptualized independently of race or ethnicity, and where they have been studied in conjunction with each other, the focus has been on blacks or African-Americans in the US context (see, for discussion, Helms, 1995; hooks, 1981; Fine and Kuriloff, 2006), and on Asian and other minority groups in the UK (see, for discussion, Fine, 1994; Brah, 1996). As Henwood (1994, p. 42) argues,

> The category "women" includes within it a variety of other social positions including black/white, lesbian/heterosexual and disabled/able-body . . . Any individual woman may be the subject of multiple, perhaps contradictory, positions in wider society. Consequently identity . . . is probably best described as plural, fragmented, and with a propensity to shift contextually and over time. (cited in Malson, Marshall, and Woollett, 2002, p. 470)

When exploring race in relation to gender identity construction, we are confronted with what Solomos and Back refer to as "one of the most thorny problems in theorising about race and ethnicity . . . [that is] . . . the question of how political identities are shaped and constructed through the meanings attributed to race, ethnicity and nation" (1995, p. 16). These political dimensions of race and ethnicity in turn play a crucial role in gender identity research. For example, according to Hoffman (2006), the research on women's identity development has been to a large extent focused on white women, thereby perpetuating an unbalanced and exclusionary approach to identity development and processes. This methodology tends to perpetuate an overly simplistic, one-dimensional view of women as gendered beings, not recognizing them to be individuals who possess an ethnic or racial identity that intersects with gender to form their holistic sense of being a woman.

However, subsequent research appears to be much more inclusive in terms of incorporating a wide variety of diverse populations in its methodological approach. For example, Hoffman's (2006) study, which explored the relationships among women's gender identity constructs as well as the relationships of those constructs to ethnic identity, had fewer than half (44 per cent) of respondents identifying as white/Caucasian/Anglo/European/American. Since Hoffman's research found that "gender self-definition and gender self-acceptance were both found to be positively associated with a strong ethnic identity" (2006, p. 369), a wide range of ethnic diversity of participants in such studies would seem to be paramount. Other important variables, such as sexual orientation, age, social class, and disability, must also be taken into account. Indeed, while throughout this book we talk about gender identity development, we cannot fail to stress that gender identity should not be seen in isolation but as part of an intersecting, contested, and overlapping process within which class, race, ethnicity, age, sexual orientation, disability, and similar political dimensions and identity variables combine for the individual to create a sense of self (see also, Healey, 2009; Cornell and Hartman, 2006; D'Angelo and Douglas, 2008).

In their political constructions and usages, race and ethnicity discourses have invariably been prioritized over and above gender, a process that serves to render invisible the important interrelationship of these terms. For example, as Palmary (2006) argues, engaging with the politics of race often ignores the resistance to dominant gender constructions that takes place within families. This leaves unchallenged the "naturalization" of often colonially constructed (gender) identities, which have been labelled and categorized according to colonial meanings, interpretations, and agendas.

Such a failure to attend to the gendered nature of women's and men's identities reflects also an uncritical acceptance of the division between the public and the private spheres. As

we argue in Chapter 7, within the public/private dichotomy women are invariably positioned as politically passive; men, as politically active; women, as oriented toward the private spheres; men, toward the public. At times, though, these stereotypes can offer marginalized women (racialized or working class) a socially elevated and accepted feminine identity as primary homemaker.

Emphasizing the sensitive and political dimensions of gender and race identities, hooks (1981) suggests that the historical and systematic devaluation of black womanhood has led to a downgrading of any activity black women do. She argues that many black women have attempted, therefore, to shift the focus of attention away from their sexuality by emphasizing their commitment to motherhood. As participants in the "cult of true womanhood," black women came to be labelled hard-working and self-sacrificing, a gendered ethnic group "naturally" concerned with creating a loving, nurturing environment for their families. In support of this argument, Hill Collins (2000) argues that black women emerged from slavery firmly enshrined in the consciousness of white America as "Mammy." Created to justify the economic exploitation of house slaves and sustained to explain black women's long-standing restriction to domestic service, the "Mammy" image came to represent the normative yardstick used to evaluate all black women's behaviour and identity.

In terms of black men, hooks (2004) argues that the gender politics of slavery and white-supremacist domination of free black men became the "school" where black men from different communities, with different languages and value systems, learned "new world" patriarchal masculinity. Hooks maintains that enslaved black males were socialized by their white oppressors to believe they should endeavour to become "benevolent patriarchs," notably by seeking to attain the freedom to provide for and protect their black womenfolk. Benevolent patriarchs exercise their power without using force, and it was this notion of patriarchy that educated black men coming from slavery into freedom sought to mimic. However, a large majority of black men took as their standard the dominant model of masculinity set by white masters. Consequently, when slavery ended these black men turned to violence to dominate black women, which was a repetition of the strategies of control that white slave-masters had used. Some newly freed black men would take their wives to the barn to beat them just as the white owner had done. Clearly, by the time slavery ended patriarchal masculinity had become an accepted ideal for many if not most black men, an ideal that would be reinforced by twentieth-century norms, conditions, and values.

Any understanding of the gender identities of, for example, African-American men and women must begin with an understanding of the myths, challenges, experiences, socialization, and resiliency strategies relevant to the developmental processes of these same men and women, not least by recognizing how these processes are influenced by historic and contemporary discourses around race and ethnicity. For example, a study of black, Asian, and Latino men by Carter et al. (2005) on race and gender-role conflict found that not all "men of colour" experience gender-role conflict in identical ways; rather, significant differences exist between and within racial groups concerning gender-role conflict and racial identity. In Carter et al.'s research, black men's experience of gender-role conflict was dependent on the extent to which they idealized the dominant, traditional world view of masculinity and femininity in relation to ethnic identity. In contrast, Asian and Latino men who experienced confusion about the issue of race or who strongly identified with the values of their respective racial group were more likely to experience gender-role conflict. Enslaved

Africans did not identify themselves exclusively in terms of their race; their creation of identity in the New World took place primarily within the parameters of ethnicity, as well as gender (Nishida, 2003).

Another interesting study worthy of discussion is the one conducted by Pyke and Johnson (2003). They examine the way that second-generation Asian-American young women describe "doing" gender across ethnicity and race, and they also look at these women's assumptions about the nature of Asian and white femininities. The female respondents said they found both Asian and Asian-American cultural worlds to be patriarchal and fully resistant to change. By contrast, these same respondents perceived white Americans to be the prototypes of gender equality. Women of Asian descent were seen to be uniformly engaged in a subordinated, submissive femininity while white women were seen as universally assertive and gender egalitarian. In other words, race emerged as the primary discourse by which Pyke and Johnson's respondents gave meaning to variations in femininity: they treated gender as a racialized feature of bodies rather than as a socio-cultural product. Pyke and Johnson go on to argue that specific gender displays, such as a submissive demeanour, are required to confirm and conform to an "acceptable" Asian feminine identity in many communities and locations.

What such research tells us is that there is no neutral observer when it comes to identifying the "other" or, indeed, to naming and labelling even those nearest and dearest to us. All observations and perceptions are filtered through a political gaze, one that we invariably assume to be a "true" reality but that is, in fact, part of the larger web of socially approved and accepted discourses out there and available for our use. There are, in other words, no neat intersections of race and gender identity. All we have is an ever-changing messy mixture that continues to bedevil any attempt to impose final closure and fixed identification by sociologists, politicians, or others. As Patterson, Cameron, and Lalonde (1996) note,

> The paradoxes of identity politics might lie in a re-conceptualization of personhood to reflect the complex contributions of social location to identity and experience. This requires the recognition that identity cannot be neatly divided into a "woman" part and a "white" (or "Black") part, and corresponding assumptions surrounding these categories. (p. 237; see also Spelman, 1988)

Intersectionality

It is therefore impossible to separate out gender from the cultural contexts in which it is produced (Adu-Poku, 2001). That is, by incorporating a cross-cultural dimension to the analysis of gender and identity, theorists could usefully explore alternative conceptualizations of identity and their implications for theory, research, and practice. The cultural space is the location within which we all exist, and diverse and fluid as these spaces are, they all contain a variety of influences: not only gender but also, for example, race. In other words, the cultural location must be recognized as containing many powerful influences upon our sense of self, with gender being one of these. The very dynamic of this cultural space means that each aspect of identity intersects with another. None of us are simply man or woman; we have a race, an ethnicity, a nationality, a sexuality plus many other facets to our being. Each facet, importantly, has some influence on the other.

From this position arises the concept of the compositely presented, intersected self (see Crenshaw, 1989; Hill Collins, 2009 [1990]; Yuval-Davis, 2006; Smith, 2009). This concept became known as "intersectionality" and has, since then, been widely used as a methodology in the social sciences, particularly in studies focusing on race and gender identities.

For example, Settles (2006) examined 89 black women's racial and gender identities within an intersectional framework that emphasized their unique experiences based on the way these two identities—race and gender—intersect. Settles's qualitative analyses indicated that the intersected identity of the black women she studied was more important than the individual identities of woman and black person. Overall, the results of this study point to the fact that black women place equal importance on both their race and their gender, seeing themselves not as black people or as women but in terms of the intersected identity of "black woman." As with all intersected selves, black women appear to define themselves, to some extent, in relation to how others view them. However, they can also position themselves in opposition to the perceptions of others, such as when they perceive of themselves as strong and powerful, precisely because of their ability to overcome negative stereotypes or experiences. The intersectional framework used in Settles' research presents a way in which to consider, assess, and understand black women's lives. It provides a greater depth and quality of information than might have been gained by looking at race or gender independently.

This complexity is reiterated and highlighted by Stephens and Philips (2005) when they argue that black women's identity is a composite framing of race, gender, and sexuality. Within this cultural and socially relevant context, sexual identity is bound up with racial and gender beliefs, all of which function on multiple levels. It is the composite intersection of these potentially very diverse identities or multiple realities (Schutz, 1967) that renders the subject "woman" into existence. The level of sophistication and adaptation required in this identity work should not be underestimated. Certainly, it speaks of agency: that is, individuals with some capacity for choice in how they present themselves and how they may therefore develop a sense of identity. These agentic possibilities suggest we are not simply at the mercy of ideologically rigid external conditions. At the same time, as Acker (2006) argues, the identities of, for example, woman, black, and working class all intersect to create an "inequality regime" for the individual. Such an intersection is inevitably bound up with social and economic—material—conditions that are going to limit that person's degree of power and agency to effectively position change in their lives.

Similarly, Hill Collins (1999), Spelman (1998), and, more recently, Siltanen and Doucet (2008) all argue for recognizing the way in which intersectionality theory can be used to appreciate both the many variables informing the identity work of an individual and the power regimes that inform those variables. Numerous examples from a variety of global cultures point to the complex way in which gender is constituted through multiple intersections and convergences of gender, race, culture, class, sexualities, disabilities, age, and so on. For example, Dugger (1988), in examining black and white women in the US, argues that the historical structure of racial privilege and racial oppression has created distinct gender identities for women in these groups. If we begin with the socialization of black women as second-class citizens and then factor in issues such as social class, age, sexuality, and disability, what emerges is a complex interface between race and gender identity. And of course this complexity can be seen across cultures globally. Another example is Graham's (2004) research in South Sulawesi, Indonesia, which illustrates that gender identity is constituted through a variety of intersecting factors, including biological sex, spirituality, sense of self, behaviours, occupations, dress, sexuality, government, religious ideology, and subjectivity. These studies point to the importance of understanding the relationship between different categories of identity. As

we will see in this chapter, intersectionality has also helped post-colonial, queer, and disability theorists broaden their understanding of what constitutes a person's identity.

POST-COLONIAL THEORY

Post-colonial theory has made an important contribution to the analysis of race and gender. It has helped reveal to us the historical grounding of issues of power, social justice, and individual freedom that underpin race and gender relations in today's society. Colonialism has played an important role in shaping both the material and existential conditions of male and female lives across numerous, potentially marginalized, social, ethnic, racial, cultural, and national boundaries. Colonialism is more than Europe's power over Asia, Africa, and America and the conquest and control of land and goods from the sixteenth century onward. Colonialism also includes the historical conquests and subjugation of people and their lands through the millennia—think of the Aztec and Roman Empires, the Mongols, the Mughals, the Crusaders, the Moors in Spain, the Ottoman Empire. However, the European colonial empire is unique in that it produced socio-cultural, socio-economic, and political practices and discourses that had an impact across the globe, now manifested in twenty-first-century globalization. So post-colonialist theory has the potential to provide valuable insights into otherwise marginalized existences while also exposing the historical patterns and political influences that have served to inform how we look at male and female racialized identities in, say, China, Africa, or India—indeed, in any social/cultural space wherein men and women are exoticized, eroticized, and deemed "the other" (Prasso, 2006; Bernstein, 2009).

During the past few decades, post-colonial theory has grown steadily across many academic disciplines. The term *post-colonial* was originally introduced in English literary studies in the 1960s to refer to the literature that originated in England's former colonies. Until then, these literatures were known as "Commonwealth literatures," a label literary critics started to regard as perpetuating the supremacy of English culture and literature, while relegating other literatures in English to the margin. The term *post-colonial* was considered less ideological in that it helped historicize the literary and cultural productions from the former colonial European empires in relation to the process of colonization rather than in relation to the former colonizing power. *Post-colonial* (with or without a hyphen) has now become widespread in the social sciences and is associated with *post-colonial* theory, which we discuss later in detail. The use of the hyphen— as in *post-colonial*—suggests a chronology that emphasizes the direct relationship between colonialism and the current positioning of societies, cultures, and people regarded as now "free" to produce a version of reality that speaks to them of their particular lives, history, and culture.

On the other hand, the absence of the hyphen, as in *postcolonial*, is indicative of a non-linear relationship and suggests a critique of colonialism rather than the end of colonialism. As Ania Loomba explains,

> To begin with, the prefix "post" complicates matters because it implies an "aftermath" in two senses—temporal, as in coming after, and ideological, as in supplanting. It is the second implication which critics of the term have found contestable: if the inequities of colonial rule have not been erased, it is perhaps premature to proclaim the demise of colonialism. (2005 [1998], p. 12)

Whether nations once colonized can be regarded as post-colonial (Loomba, 2005 [1998]; McClintock, 1992) is an ongoing debate. It is particularly difficult to use the term *post-colonial* to describe settlers' colonies such as Canada and Australia, where the Aboriginal people's claims for land rights, treaty rights, and economic freedom are yet to be achieved. Indeed, many communities and subcultures have yet to experience the "post-colony" as a geopolitical, cultural, and mental space.

Given the multiple ways that post-colonialism has evolved—historically, culturally, and ideologically—it seems problematic, if not undesirable, to attempt a finite definition of *post-colonialism*; it is a highly dynamic, contested, fluid, and therefore political term. Like feminist theory, Marxist theory, and queer theory, post-colonial theory inevitably carries with it a political standpoint and perspective that may not always be accepted by those it seeks to represent. So we should be wary of positioning post-colonialism as simply a methodology by which to critically explore, say, black and white relationships within, perhaps, a gendered context that speaks to all within those cultural sites. Such a theory cannot speak for every voice nor provide a universal political standpoint across all the "post-colonized" peoples. Indeed, Loomba suggests that post-colonial studies may be "inadequate to the task of defining contemporary realities in the once colonized countries, and vague in terms of indicating a specific period of history, but may also cloud the internal social and racial differences of many societies" (2005, p. 13).

Since the events of 9/11 in 2001 and the subsequent US invasions of Afghanistan and Iraq, post-colonial studies has been situated "in relation to globalization and new imperial formations" (Loomba, 2005, p. 1), making it appear that US imperialism is now the centre of the critique that generates theory and practice of post-colonial thought and action. Furthermore, the current theoretical engagements of post-colonial studies with feminism, queer theory, disability and other social movements are taking the theory even further away from being just a socio-political critique on race, culture, and ethnicity in the modern world. Rather, these engagements are constructing newer constellations that supersede the previous hierarchies of European colonialism.

The theorizing of post-colonial studies grew out of both the structuralist and the poststructuralist movements. Post-colonial critics drew on Foucault's idea of discourse to analyze colonialism as a system of signs and representations. Post-colonial theory has its roots in literary studies, and its leading proponents—literary critics such as Edward Said, Homi Bhabha, Frantz Fanon, and Gayatri Spivak—have paid particular attention to the ways constructions of otherness pertaining to the dynamics of colonialism are embedded in literary and cultural representations.

Edward Said and Post-colonial Theory: The Impact of Colonial Discourse on Gender Studies

Edward Said is one of the first post-colonial scholars to have analyzed and theorized colonial discourse and established a theory around it, which he termed "Orientalism." He was born in Jerusalem in 1935 and left Palestine in 1947 with his family after the establishment of Israel. His early experience of exile was influential in shaping his ideas on belonging and displacement, which he recorded in *Reflections on Exile and Other Essays* (2000). His work deals with the relationship between culture and politics and more specifically with the ways in which cultural perceptions are shaped by power relations and ideology. Early in his life, Said felt a disparity between the Orient that he knew and the Orient that he saw represented in art and literature. He decided to examine this tension in depth through the work of literary writers such as Joseph Conrad, Jane Austen, and Rudyard Kipling. In *Orientalism* (1978), Said coined a new term to describe the ways in which the Western world had represented the East. Drawing on the theoretical premises established by post-structuralist critics such as Foucault and Derrida, Said contends that the representation of the Orient is an organized system of encoded images that serve to reinforce and validate the project of colonization (the East as sensual, mysterious, timeless, feminine). Thus, the East becomes the feminine "other": erotic and available for penetration by the masculine West, an aspect of his work that has a direct impact on the feminist critique of colonial discourse.

Said's concept of "Orientalism" has been criticized for its monolithic totalizing of the West's cultural practices, leaving little room for contradiction and complexity. However, most critics agree on the impact of Said's work and his concept of "Orientalism" as a way of understanding not only colonial but also post-colonial and contemporary representations of those perceived as culturally different. In *Culture and Imperialism* (1993), Said continues his critique of major literary figures and their participation in the colonial project. Said's theories have a direct relevance to the analysis of gender, particularly in terms of acknowledging the overlapping areas between representations of women and "Natives" and the commonalities between colonial and patriarchal discourses. Many critics have used Said's ideas to examine Orientalized and exoticized representations of otherness based on gender and sexuality (see, for example, Lewis, 2004 & 1996; and Boer, 2003).

Frantz Fanon and Post-colonial Theory: Resistance

Much of post-colonial theory is based on the process of resisting constructs of otherness. This idea is central to the work of Frantz Fanon, from which post-colonial theory is largely indebted. It is Homi Bhabha's (1994) new interpretation of Fanon's *Black Skin, White Masks* (1952) that places Frantz Fanon's ideas at the centre of post-colonial theory. Fanon was born in 1925 in Martinique and trained in France as a psychiatrist. His main reflection was on racism and its psychological impact. His first book-length study of race and psychology, *Black Skin, White Masks* (1952) examines the black man's position in the white world as a fundamental negation of his existence. One of Fanon's seminal ideas is the interdependence of "white" and "black" as categories. For him, the white man's centricity is based on the negation of the category "black," and the notion of blackness is constructed in relation to whiteness and superiority; that neither can exist without the other creates an existential and pathological crisis or, as he calls it, a "situational neurosis" (Fanon, 1986). Fanon took up a position as head of the Blida-Jointville mental hospital in Algeria in 1953, one year before the war for Algerian independence broke out, and became witness to a society torn by conflict and colonial violence. He recorded his observations in *A Dying Colonialism* (1959) and in *The Wretched of the Earth* (1961), much of which were based on his work with Algerian torture victims and French soldiers hospitalized at Blida-Joinville.

While Fanon tried to introduce reforms in patient care, such as desegregated wards, he came to realize that his work as a French psychiatrist in Algeria was incompatible with his anti-colonial ideas and that one could not combat the effects of racism without combating racism itself. In 1956, he left Blida-Joinville and joined the Algerian liberation movement (FLN) exiled in Tunis. While working for the FLN, Fanon wrote short pieces published posthumously in *Towards the African Revolution* (1967). Fanon died of leukemia in the fall of 1961, one year before the independence of Algeria, leaving behind a body of writing that became the foundation for post-colonial critical theory.

Fanon's description of decolonization gives women a central place. In his essay "Algeria Unveiled," published in *A Dying Colonialism* (1959), he examines the ways Algerian female revolutionaries were able to renegotiate their role within traditional culture by subverting the meaning of the veil. "Algeria Unveiled" is considered a seminal essay in the debate about the role of women in the process of decolonization. According to Fanon, the first phase of resistance against French colonialism in Algeria was characterized by a return to tradition and to what he calls "the cult of the veil," a response to the French occupier's determination to "unveil" Algeria. The second phase was marked by a subversion of tradition. The French colonizer's assumptions about the Muslim veil as a sign of female passivity was subverted and used as a tool of resistance as the veil became a coverup for female revolutionaries carrying weapons during the Algerian liberation struggle. Thus, for Fanon culture and tradition are sites where individuals can exercise agency and resistance.

Fanon's feminism has, however, been questioned by many feminist critics. Some have noted his tendency to idealize the revolutionary role of women in anti-colonial struggles and to underestimate the persistence of patriarchal culture (McClintock, 1997), at times even reinforcing patriarchal notions of gender (Bergner, 2005). Nevertheless, Fanon's analysis is not always incompatible with feminist theory (Golay, 2007). The idea of the colonized subject's capacity for infiltrating the structure of power and ideology has considerable implications for the critique of other dominant discourses, particularly patriarchal discourse. More recently, Fanon's ideas have made inroads into other theories of difference, such as disability theory (Sherry, 2007). The next section discusses Homi Bhabha's theories, which are largely indebted to Frantz Fanon's analysis of the colonial situation.

Homi Bhabha and Post-colonial Theory: Hybridity

Bhabha is known for having given post-colonial theory some of its central concepts, such as ambivalence, **hybridity**, and **mimicry**. Bhabha centres his ideas on areas left undeveloped in Fanon's critique of colonialism, particularly regarding the interdependence between the colonizer and the colonized and the resulting ambivalence and possibilities of expression outside the colonial duality. He draws on Fanon's idea of the split colonial subject and the white man's reliance on the black man's "otherness" to create a white identity to examine processes of mimicry and ambivalence at the heart of the colonial situation. For Bhabha, the colonized is for the colonizer a reflection "that splits his presence, distorts his outline, breaches his boundaries, repeats his action at a distance, disturbs and divides the very time of his being" (Bhabha, 1987, p. 119). Refuting the modernist myth of an autonomous, rational, individual self, Bhabha defines the colonial subject as both colonizer and colonized. Notions of ambivalence, "third space," and hybridity pervade Bhabha's theory and set the ground for a large part of post-colonial critical analysis. Most of his key texts are included in *Nation and Narration* (1990) and *The Location of Culture* (1994).

Although Bhabha has often been criticized for the density of his writing and what, at times, can be perceived as a lack of clear political or historical grounding in his theories, he remains a key figure in post-colonial studies. In particular, Bhabha's theory of ambivalence and mimicry has direct relevance to post-structuralist feminist ideas about constructions of femininity as dependent on male centricity. Furthermore, his notions of hybridity can be placed in dialogue with gender ambivalence and transsexual and transgendered identities. In short, Bhabha's use of post-structuralist understandings of the contingency of self and identity highlight how the colonial and post-colonial intersect in the emergence of individual subjectivity.

Gayatri Spivak and Post-colonial Theory: The Subaltern

Gayatri Spivak is a major figure of post-colonial and feminist studies and an early critic of

hybridity
The situation that results from the mixing of two or more languages, cultures, or identities.

mimicry
A process that involves imitating or reproducing an existing and usually dominant discourse, behaviour, or attitude.

Western feminism. In her article "French Feminism in an International Frame" (1987), she warns against the unproblematic reception of Western feminist ideas and the danger of eradicating differences and unequal position in favour of a homogeneous, and possibly hegemonic, definition of *gender*. Spivak's interest expands beyond post-colonial theory and into other areas, such as **subaltern** studies, comparative literature, and translation. As the first translator of Derrida's *Of Grammatology* (1967), she is often seen as having introduced deconstructivist theory to the English-speaking world. Spivak is probably best known for an article considered to be one of the founding texts of post-colonial theory: "Can the Subaltern Speak?" Drawing on Antonio Gramsci's work on the Italian peasantry, she argues that the subaltern position is what denies disadvantaged groups access to means of representing themselves and therefore defeats the possibility of a counter-discursive strategy. By doing so, Spivak challenges the idea of colonized people as homogeneous and visible to Western eyes, thus problematizing dominant academic discourse on the "other." Some critics, however, such as Benita Parry, criticize what they see as Spivak's tendency to grant dominant

subaltern
Refers to a person or a class of individuals occupying an inferior and subordinate position in society.

ideologies absolute power and her reluctance to hear subaltern voices. Spivak also introduced the notion of "strategic essentialism" into post-colonial studies, arguing that essentialism, a process usually associated with dominant colonial practices, could at times be a strategy for dominated groups to unite in order to act.

In considering these four main theorists—Said, Bhabha, Fanon, and Spivak—it is useful to view them through a continuum from (feminist) structuralism to (feminist) post-structuralism. In other words, post-colonial theory first emerges within structuralist accounts of power, colony, patriarchy, and male power, before engaging with the feminist post-structuralist concern with sex/gender identity as discursively constituted and therefore without a foundational reality. Indeed, feminism shares with post-colonialism more similarities than differences; both feminism and post-colonial theory offer critical examinations of the power relations between men and women, black and white, the global North and South, and other marginalized groups. Interrogating the (gender) binaries that serve to position women (and black and Asian peoples, for example) within the same social location as racialized minorities is a key plank in the development of post-colonial studies. Many contemporary feminist writers such as bell hooks, Nawal El Saadawi, and Trinh Minh-ha have added more specifically gender-oriented perspectives to post-colonial theory. Questions pertaining to the female and racialized "other" have attracted particular attention.

Furthermore, post-colonial theory is rapidly becoming all-embracing and inclusive of diversity. Other minoritized groups, such as gay, lesbian, deaf, and other marginalized people, are fast becoming part of this inclusiveness and intersectionality, as exemplified by Thompson's work on feminist disabilities (1997, 2002); see also Clare (1999), Dreidger et al. (1996), Hillyer

(1993), and Meekosha (1999). The rest of this chapter examines two important discourses of difference that have enabled us to further our understanding of the ways in which gender and identity are constructed: queer theory and disability studies.

QUEER THEORY

The gay and lesbian movements of the 1980s brought about an awareness of sexual diversity as an essential component of the discourse of democracy and justice and the acceptance of difference. Combating the stigma around same-sex relationships, reinforced through social responses to the AIDS epidemic, these movements sparked a discussion around questions pertaining to the social construction of sexuality. Like post-colonialism, queer theory centres on questions of representation and the role of language, discourse, and ideology in shaping constructions of "otherness." Eve Kosofsky Sedgwick's *Epistemology of the Closet* (1990) is in this respect a seminal text that laid the ground for understanding processes of denial and silencing that have shaped representations of sexuality in the Western world. Sedgwick's argument is that homoerotic desire informs a large part of Western literature, but in a silent and repressed manner. She identifies the "closet" as a particular structure in twentieth-century European and North American literary constructions of homoerotic sexuality, particularly between men. Silence, shame, guilt, and repression are for Sedgwick key aspects of the representations and discourses that have historically contributed to shape not only homosexuality but also heterosexuality. As she argues, both sexualities are dependent on each other in the sense that repressed homoerotic desire serves to reinforce the centricity and desirability of heterosexuality.

Many queer theorists, like Sedgwick, adopt the post-structuralist view of sexual desire as fluid to question essentialistic definitions of sexuality. Queer theory, in general, works to simultaneously name and yet disrupt the assumed stability that reinforces sex, gender, and sexual desire within a normative **compulsory heterosexual paradigm** (Rich, 1983; see also Jagose, 1996; Leckey and Brooks, 2010). It signals very strongly that gender identity is embedded in social and cultural norms, which, by virtue of their constant performative action by the subject, are given credence as "natural" expressions of masculinity and femininity. Queer theory stresses that our gender is simply behaviour, no more, no less. What we perform signals who we are. Therefore, queer theory suggests that if we choose to perform outside of the normative constructs of gender (e.g., by wearing drag or expressing our body in ways that appear contra to our "fixed" gender), then this is disruptive and challenging and, therefore, political. In being political, so it has the power to subvert what we've come to accept as "normal and natural" within sexual and gender identities.

At the level of everyday social discourse, the term *queer* can be, and often is, enlisted to identify, marginalize, and denigrate gay and lesbian identities and expressions. Within academic discourse, which is where for the most part *queer* as theory resides, the term can be used to identify, deconstruct, critically interrogate, and perhaps celebrate the purposely performed marginal within not just gay, bisexual, transgendered, and lesbian identities, but all "alternative" expressions of gender and sexuality, wherever and from whomever they originate.

Queer theory attempts to grapple with precisely these disruptions to "naming" while also promoting them as a way of recognizing the instability at the heart of our identity. It forces us to question the heterosexual paradigm that continues to structure if not define, to some degree, all expressions of gender and sexuality. Furthermore, queer theory requires us to accept that white, Western, heterosexual, middle-class

> **compulsory heterosexual paradigm**
> The ideas and values that are promoted by society through institutions such as the law, the media, and religion in order to impose heterosexuality as the norm.

understandings of what is "normal" in gender and identity are nothing of the sort. Such positions are subjective and therefore partial, politicized, and sectarian. What they are not, or should not become or be promoted as, is the primary point of reference for all those other identities subsequently positioned as different, unnatural, and "other" (see Jagose, 1996; Hall, 2003; Huffer, 2010; Sanlon, 2010, for discussion).

So *queer* is a powerful term for the simple reason that it stands outside heterosexuality and does so quite clearly. But is the term used as an expression of resistance to normative heterosexual assumptions and identities, or is it uttered as a form of reinforcement by virtue of identifying and, possibly, denigrating marginality? The term *queer* is, as our vignette illustrates, heavily political. It is not a neutral term. If it ever was, it certainly isn't now, at least in respect of its power to name, challenge, and identify within gender and sexual identities.

Making Gender Trouble

Queer theory provides us with a means by which we can take on and perform a central task of feminism, which is to unsettle if not overthrow political gender norms while simultaneously recognizing our own contingent self. Judith Butler, the theorist who, along with Eve Sedgwick (1990) and Gayle Rubin (1992), provided some of the earliest and most powerful conceptualizations of queer theory, describes this as an intention:

> to locate strategies of subversive repetition enabled by those constructions [of gender identity], to affirm the local possibilities of

intervention through participating in precisely those practices of repetition that constitute identity and, therefore, present the immanent possibility of contesting them. (Butler, 1990, p. 147)

Judith Butler is generally accepted to have established queer theory not only as an arm of feminist theory, but as an example of critical theory generally and one that has a political dimension rooted within, and arising from, its analysis and practice. In her book *Gender Trouble*, Butler argues that we should seek to destabilize the "natural" categories of male and female, not least by specific practices of identity performance, which in themselves signal very clearly the contingent, contextual, and **amorphous** constitution of gender:

> [by] . . . subverting and displacing those naturalized and reified notions of gender that support masculine hegemony and heterosexist power, to make *gender trouble*, not through the strategies that figure a utopian beyond, but through the mobilization, subversive confusion, and proliferation of precisely those constitutive categories that seek to keep gender in its place by posturing as the foundational illusions of identity. (Butler, 1990, pp. 33–34)

Subversion is at the heart of this analysis. Butler, as with other proponents of queer theory (see, for overview, Seidman, 1996, 2003; Jagose, 1997) argues that precisely because gender is socially constructed, so it becomes possible, through culturally "queer" or marginalized performances and languages, to disrupt and eventually give voice to different ways of being male and female. Butler is suggesting that by adopting new and challenging forms of gender expression—notably those that cause people to radically and critically reflect on and rethink so-called truths about gender and sexual identities (e.g., by adopting discursive practices: dress, body, and language styles that do not adhere to traditional gender identity)—so we can subvert and sabotage gender norms. She is alerting us to the possibilities of causing "gender trouble" precisely through repeating discursive practices that are "queer" and therefore previously understood as outside the norm. For in doing so, we reveal gender to be the performance it is and thereby undermine any assumptions as to it being a "natural" entity. The spectator is thus forced to reconsider what male and female mean, to think outside the boundaries of his or her own gender reality, and to question previously assumed truths about how to act out masculinity and femininity, and straight, gay, lesbian, and bi sexualities. This has the effect of not only displacing gender norms but of undermining the very gender binary at the core of our understandings of masculinity and femininity (see Huffer, 2010, for discussion).

Butler draws heavily on Foucauldian analysis to make her case. As with Foucault, Butler sees the subject becoming an individual through the performative action of taking up and repeating those practices of gender signification that are at the subject's disposal in the social world, such as language, dress codes, embodiment. The subject is discursive, but subordinate discourses can, Butler argues, be used as a form of resistance to dominant masculinist, heterosexual norms and, especially, the gendered binary that underpins and reinforces them as being natural. In other words, we have the capacity to act out our identity in ways that do not conform to some larger gender order, and we can, indeed, adopt a style of being that might appear strange to others but is entirely appropriate for our own sense of individuality. We can see, then, just how closely queer theory is aligned to both post-structuralism and postmodernism in its critique of **essentialism**.

amorphous
Having no definite shape, structure, or pattern.

Yet, at the same time, queer theory may indicate a way of politicizing the very act of being and becoming male and female, thereby promoting a feminist agenda. So queer theory may, unlike some versions of postmodernism and post-structuralism, offer a feminist standpoint: one rooted in a recognition that while we are discursive subjects, we also have a capacity to challenge those dominant discourses of gender that reinforce heterosexuality as compulsory behaviour and that consequently posit all "other" expressions of sexuality and gender as deviant.

Butler's writing offers some important insights that do resonate with contemporary gender identities. How we express gender and sexual identity is certainly changing and is perhaps more open to disruption and alternative performances than ever before. The breaking down of the strict public and private divide is clear evidence of such change occurring, and quite rapidly across many societies (see Chapter 4 for examples and discussion).

The Persistence of Gender Binaries

It could also be argued that, for example, a straight man dressing in drag, a straight woman deliberately growing a moustache, a lesbian adopting a skinhead look, or a gay man acting like a macho parody of Bruce Willis do little to subvert normative understandings of heterosexuality and homosexuality. Such performances are seen as marginal and therefore "unreal" for the very reason they are acted out within the heterosexual paradigm that continues to exist for most people. These performances may be increasingly tolerated and accepted, but does tolerance in itself lead to widespread social and political change? Many feminist critics suggest that it does not. They argue that subversive performances of gender identity do little or nothing to positively and materially change women's lives in the real world (for discussion, see Case, 2009;

> **essentialism**
>
> The belief that individuals, groups, or cultures are shaped by some fixed and unchanging (essential) characteristics and properties that define who or what they are.

Garber, 2001; Campbell, 2000; Richardson, McLaughlin, and Casey, 2006; Weed and Schor, 1997). Moreover, precisely because such performances are enacted at the micro level, they have little or no chance of changing macro patriarchal structures. As a result, they argue, queer theory provides us with no real tool of resistance to the hegemonic masculine and heterosexual paradigm that continues to present itself as the normative within society. Martha Nussbaum, puts it thus:

> The new feminism [led by Butler] . . . instructs its members that there is little room for large-scale change, and maybe no room at all. We are all, more or less, prisoners of the structure of power that have defined our identity as women; we can never change those structures in a large scale way, and we can never escape from them. All that we can hope to do [within queer theory] is to find spaces within structures of power in which to parody them, to poke fun at them, to transgress them in speech. (Nussbaum, 1999; quoted in Gauntlett, 2004, p. 145)

In a similar manner, Tim Edwards (1998) argues that the very diversity promoted and applauded by queer theory can, itself, do little to challenge "the assumed normality of the majority":

> Firstly, on one level diversity is not a political strategy in itself, if it is anything at all politically it's a recipe for radical individualism at the most and, more likely, fragmentation at the least. Second, diversity is an empirical reality and while societies are increasing in their complexity it is not as new as it seems. (1998, p. 479)

In effect, Edwards is making a point similar to Nussbaum's. He states clearly that individual (discursive) actions that operate outside the "norm" not only do little to challenge dominant ideologies, but they have always existed in some form or another and therefore are not so radical as Butler and other proponents of queer theory suggest. Subversive discourses and performances of gender have a long history, yet still the gender binary persists as the dominant sexual reference point for most people. Parodies of normative heterosexuality and pastiche performances of "deviant" sexuality may well open up new and potentially subversive spaces for counter discourses to flourish, but is this of itself sufficient to overturn the gender binaries? A drag artist in a nightclub elicits laughter from his/her audience precisely because the performance is understood by the audience as being outside the norm. Consequently, the norm is emphasized, this time through laughter, and therefore neither disrupted, sabotaged, nor subverted.

Another contradiction that confronts queer theorists has to do with the actions of an *a priori*, knowing subject, one that somehow exists outside of discourse. In other words, for me to adopt a political position as a discursive actor performing my gender identity at or beyond the margins of society, then I would first have to know I was doing so. Therefore, the "I" assumes a foundational quality, becoming the driver for the discursive, not the other way around. Throughout her writings, Butler recognizes that the subject is not outside of discourse but constituted through it. How, then, can I get outside of discourse in order to promote something that is ultimately a presentation of my self as a gendered subject and simultaneously subversive of that very identity? The contradiction is certainly tortuous if not unbridgeable.

Opening up Possibilities

Perhaps the role of theory is not so much to resolve contradictions but to bring them to the fore. If queer theory has not resolved the many contradictions that are embedded in the critique of heterosexist discourses and practices, it has brought them to our consciousness and opened up many possibilities for transforming our thinking about not only our sexualities but also what constitutes what we call "identity." Two possibilities are particularly significant.

First, with regard to the contra-performances of gender identity, it seems evident that small-scale, individual actions can and do elicit large-scale change. To believe otherwise would require us to discount all the evidence of change throughout history. The world and its people are not exactly the same as they were even 30 years ago, and certainly not 300 years ago. Such change has sometimes originated from the political intent of small, elitist groups. Most often, however, it has come through imperceptibly slow change by countless numbers of individuals taking on new, possibly radical discourses as forms of identity expression. Once millions of people start enacting such radical discourses, they no longer appear radical but become the norm. We make a mistake if we believe that gender change will not happen. It is happening now. That change will come as much from the micro actions of millions of individuals as it will from feminist theorists (by definition an intellectual elite) deciding it must happen but wondering and disagreeing about how to bring it about. As we write, so someone somewhere is actually doing it, but probably without intent to do so as a conscious political response to the effects of the heterosexual paradigm. So the intent doesn't actually need to be there for the effect to be political. Butler is absolutely right in her argument that it is in the doing that change happens. This then gets us around the difficulty presented by the (flawed) concept of an *a priori* knowing subject. What we cannot do is predict the precise moment of cause, effect, or direction of such change. We can no more steer it in a particular direction than politicians or any powerful figures can fully know the consequences of their decisions, actions, and policies. At the same time, this is not to discount the power of feminism to be a contributory factor to (gender) change. It clearly is. But the process of such change is too complex, too dynamic, too fluid, diverse, and unpredictable for it to be directed, managed, and steered by any individual or group.

The second possibility for transforming our thinking about our sexualities and identity concerns the way in which queer theorists might align themselves within a broader theoretical perspective recently identified as queer studies. Such connections are increasingly being made by writers such as Judith Halberstam (1998; see, also, Corber and Valocchi, 2003). Drawing on the writings of Foucault, Butler, and Rubin especially, queer studies attempt to broaden the debate to encompass critical research not only within feminism but across the social sciences and humanities while recognizing that gender and sexuality are, as Rubin puts it "two distinct arenas of social practice," with each requiring its own theory and practice (Rubin, 1984; see also Beemyn and Eliason, 1996). Corber and Valocchi observe the following:

> Queer studies scholarship . . . opens up new ways of thinking about a wide range of subcultural practices and identities . . . that previously were illegible or may have seemed incoherent insofar as they do not conform to the alignments of sex, gender, and sexuality that are normative in the subcultural contexts in which they emerge. . . . The institutional regulation of these forms of identity also suggests that on some level the dominant society recognises that there is no natural or biological relationship between sex, gender, and sexuality and that it must vigorously enforce the belief that there is. (Corber and Valocchi, 2003, p. 9)

In effect, queer scholarship asks us to broaden our scope of analysis beyond identity as theory and into practice/theory across multiple disciplines and social sites and to do the following:

- Explore and theorize how same-sex relationships thrive and flourish outside of a gay or lesbian paradigm
- Recognize the distinctions between sex, gender, and sexuality and the complex, often contradictory ways they are lived out by the subject
- Recognise that masculinity is not simply the "property of male heterosexuals" but is accessible to all subjects
- Acknowledge the agentic capacity of the subject to express his or her sexuality in ways that may well be contra to normative discourses, not least those that might otherwise signal the subject's sex and gender
- Find new ways to theorize power relations beyond the "men as oppressor, women as oppressed" dichotomy
- Render as problematic "Western notions of sexuality, subjectivity, and citizenship, rooted as they are in a concept of the nation state increasingly under pressure from globalization" (Corber and Valocchi, 2003, p. 6)

So queer studies takes us into an altogether more complex place, not only in respect of how we theorize identity but also concerning our understanding of sex, gender, and sexuality as distinct concepts operating fluidly if not randomly and across cultural, ethnic, and national boundaries. Queer studies suggests very strongly that we should not see the individual as merely a discursively gendered subject, but as a discursive subject who, through psychoanalytical and social processes, contingently occupies numerous identities, distinctively yet simultaneously. Queer theorists are increasingly looking at sexuality as dependent on other factors such as race, class, region, and nation, as demonstrated by the growing and "significant body of queer scholarship in history, anthropology, and sociology that explores how the circulation of people, commodities, media, discourses and capital across national borders has transformed the sexual politics and cultures of Western and non-Western nations alike" (Corber and Valocchi, 2003, p. 5).

This development has widened the scope of queer theory by challenging the traditional hegemony of white gay and lesbian identities (Barnard, 1999). In the past decade, critics have paid particular attention to the ways in which configurations of race and class have shaped a person's capacity to subvert normative gender and sexuality. Conversely, other critics have examined how the construction of sexuality relies on certain configurations of race and class (see Corber and Valocchi, 2003; Anzaldua, 1987; Barnard, 1999; El-Tayeb, 2011). In other words, being a man or a woman is also highly influenced by the social and racial spaces that such an individual inhabits. Our identities might simplistically be understood as corresponding to some larger sex, gender, and sexuality (normative) identification, but for the individual that emerges they are highly complex and contradictory, never simply a point of oppression but invested with some power (to be). In "disrupt[ing], comfortable, and comforting, disciplinary assumptions" (Corber and Valocchi, 2003, p. 14), queer theory not only challenges us to think outside our discursive boundaries, it has the potential to provide us with a mirror from which to gaze upon our own contradictory discursive position as sexed, gendered, racialized, and sexualized subjects.

This causes us to reflect on our sex and gender in ways that have interesting, even subversive consequences, producing, perhaps, a reflexivity with political potential as we (re)consider the "ontological puzzle" at the heart of our sense of self (Stanley, 1993). At the very least,

queer theory suggests that while there purport to be limits to our gender, sex, and sexual identities as prescribed socially, the reality is that there are more possibilities for alternative identity construction than we often imagine, indeed that are only limited by our imaginations.

DISABILITY THEORY

The key terms in disability theory have been *disability* and *impairment*. Some disability scholars make the distinction between people with disabilities and disabled people, and between impairment and disability (Titchkosky, 2007; Goodley and Lawthorm, 2005). These concepts have evolved over time and are highly fluid (Birch, 2007).

Up until the 1960s, people with disabilities were defined by their disability, for example, "handicapped people," "mentally retarded," "cripples," and so on. In the 1970s, "people first" language was adopted (Olkin, 2003), such as "people with disabilities," or "people with . . . [a named impairment]," including cerebral palsy, learning difficulties, and so on. In the 1990s there appeared to be a return to putting the disability first, for example "deaf person," "disabled people," etcetera. This arrangement of moving the disability descriptor, which functioned as an adjective, before the person converts it into a noun and thereby is a political act(ion). As Anne McGuire (2010) says,

> Disability marks the body in ambiguous ways—it appears and disappears, is noticed and is hidden—as we move through different physical and social spaces, and as we find ourselves in different political and historical moments. It's also critical to consider how disability marks different bodies in different and relational ways; systems of ableism come into contact with racialized bodies, queer bodies, classed bodies, gendered bodies, bodies that already have been touched by other (and perhaps multiple) systems of oppression. (p. 2)

And as Eliza Chandler (2010) puts it,

Imaginative expectations for disability and for what it means to be disabled vary from culture to culture, and from time to time. In my culture, and in my time, as a white child with Cerebral Palsy born into disability to middle class, married, straight parents in rural Nova Scotia, Canada in the early 80s, I was born into the expectation that disability was located in "minds, bodies, senses and emotions," with both the problem and the desire to seek *the best possible solution* located in the individual. . . . Problems demand we move from one paving block to the next without tripping on the crack, without going back, and never dwelling in the in-between. But there is always more to the story of disability than its cultural expectation of "living problems" makes of us, for even when we desire solutions for the problems disabilities can cause us we can still regard disability as that which marks our "being-in-the-world." (p. 3)

In *The Difference That Disability Makes*, Michalko (2002) describes his experience of coming into blindness, into disability as an identity. His account suggests that the events of being diagnosed with a disability as an explanation for a problem, and identifying as disabled do not necessarily occur in the same temporal moment. In other words, his words, his blindness became a "what" long before it became a "who" (Chandler, 2010; see also Michalko, 1998, 2002).

In this section we use all these terms with a critical understanding that categories are used to define for reasons of intellectual debate and discussion while at the same time we are aware that they do have profound implications for the way that people with disabilities live in our society. The second issue is one of definitions. Who is defining and who is being defined are key to making sense of the issues of power and knowledge about the disabled. For example, the World Health Organization (WHO) defines persons with disabilities as persons *with* "restrictions or inabilities to perform an activity considered normal for a human being due to a loss or abnormality of bodily structures or functions . . ." (WHO, 1980).

Clearly, people with disabilities continue to be disavowed, denied, and marginalized in cultures and societies across the globe, reaching epic proportions in some corners of the world. There appears to be no other community that is experiencing discrimination, poverty, isolation, indignity, and medicalization to such an enormous proportion as the disabled. Even disabled peoples' sexuality and sexual preferences are policed to the extent that some people with disability are managed through social policy and cultural sanctions: "Discrimination is an enduring issue for all people with disabilities. Women and girls with disabilities however, are subjected to double discrimination: sexism as well as disability bias . . . [and] . . . women and girls of color who are disabled face a third layer of bias in the form of racism" (Merle, Rubin, and Sprung, 1999, p. 1). With over 500 million people worldwide, and not counting people with psychological difficulties such as depression, the disability community is experiencing one of the most profound forms of oppression in the modern world.

Even in academic settings and scholarly publications, the issue of disability, particularly women with disabilities, has been marginalized. As Rannveig Traustadottir (2010) says, "Women with disabilities have historically been neglected by disability studies and feminist scholarship . . . traditionally used a gender-blind approach . . . not recognized the combined discrimination of gender and disability experienced by women" (p. 1). She asserts that a substantial part of the literature about women and disabilities has been written from a personal perspective; some women speak out in anger and bitterness while others celebrate achievement, strength, and happiness despite their struggles (see also Ruosso, 1988; Asche and Fine, 1988).

However, in the past two decades there has been a rise in consciousness and awareness of the issues that are confronting people with disabilities and their relationship to gender and identity. Much of this is owed to the growth of the disability movement and its more militant stand against socio-political, economic, and cultural oppression of day-to-day living. Using the human rights charter, the various disability movements have positioned themselves to seek redress in education, in social services, in the justice system, and in health care. The central plank in this struggle is not one of just basic human rights, but a fight to ensure that there are epistemological transformations occurring in the way we represent disability and the people who live with sensory, physical, or mental impairment. From material changes—such as transportation and travel accessibility, housing and employment, engagement in public discourse of governance—to evolutionary ones—such as linguistic configurations of representations of disability/ability—a shift is happening. This shift is enabling a culture of empowerment and self-determination, independence and integration, equity and social justice for people with disabilities.

Three Models of Disability

The medical, moral, and social model approach to understanding disability vary in terms of the definitions of people with disability, the moral implications of their impairment, and the kind of support systems they need. For example, the moral model approach is the oldest and still holds sway in many corners of the world where disability is seen as a defect caused by some moral relapse, sin, failure of faith, or act of Karma. To avoid the

shameful consequences of the disability, the person must seek redress through religion and engaging in spirituality and faith in god. The purpose of this engagement is greater than the self as a person with a disability. The medical model views the person as a "patient" with a defective body or a failure of the body or mental system due to genetics or personality traits. A cure is sought by modern medicine and technological advances; the body needs correcting and normalizing sometimes through invasive medical procedures. Usually non-disabled persons operate in a paternalistic way to support this perception of disability. Finally, the social model of disability put the responsibility of the difficulties on the environment, i.e., the society and political structures. People are disabled as a result of not being accommodated to full function in society, for example, deaf people are disabled because non-deaf people do not use sign language as a language of communication.

According to Koosed and Schumm (2009), "the social model of disability rejects the idea that the body is in any way disabled, and instead insists that the 'disability' experienced by different bodies is a result of socially created categories and the ways in which we construct our environments" (p. 7). Through political action and changes made to establish better accommodation and accessibility, people with disabilities will be better integrated into society. The social model incorporates the idea that people with disabilities are a minority group, with a specific culture or cultures and ought to be recognized in the same way that ethnic minorities are (Olkin, 2002). The social model of disability embraces a more comprehensive view of disability and considers bodily conditions within the broader cultural and religious milieu (Koosed and Schumm, 2009). The disability is a result of prejudicial attitudes about bodies that do not fit the socially constructed and defined "normal" body (Koosed and Schumm, 2009; Goering, 2002; Morris, 2001). Rosemarie Garland-Thomson (2005) explains the difference between the social and medical models of disability as: ". . . a cultural interpretation of human variation [social model] rather than an inherent inferiority, pathology to cure, or undesirable trait to eliminate [medical model]" (p. 1558).

How Disabilities Reinforce Gender Stereotypes

In her article "Women with Disability: The Double Discrimination," Rannveig Traustadottir (2010) explores how gender, motherhood, and sexuality remain a confounding place for women with disability, where their traditional roles as nurturers, homemakers, and lovers are not usually seen as appropriate. There are higher percentages of disabled women who never marry, divorce if they do marry, stay in abusive relationships because of economic reasons, have children removed into care, experience physical and sexual abuse, and in some cases are forced into sterilization, particularly women with mental impairment (see also Asch and Fine, 1988; Sobsey et al., 1990).

People with disabilities experience major psycho-social difficulties ranging from social isolation and low self-esteem to symptoms of stress and depression (Nosek and Hughes, 2003). In situations where women with disabilities are resilient enough not to be overcome by the social and economic barriers, they are then placed in some stereotyped category of being hyper-female and capable of doing feats and gender performances that non-disabled women are incapable of. At a more domestic level, these women are trained and are expected to be engaged in traditional gender roles related to the domestic sphere: as cooks, in makeup and hairdressing jobs, and in other sheltered occupations of a humanistic nature. This reduces their visibility as stigmatized others.

But people with disabilities are resisting this manipulation by the dominant culture. Zitzelsberger (2005) had this to say of women with physical disabilities:

> Through their lived knowledge of imposed and negotiated (in)visibility . . . [they] moved towards transforming the value and meanings of their bodies for themselves . . . and reflecting on their experiences of (in)visibility in many social contexts . . . rejected the ways they are seen through hegemonic cultural discourses about disability and difference. Through questioning the perceptions that construct their bodies in undesirable ways, the women have returned the "gaze" of dominant societies and made their own judgments on the ways they are seen. (p. 398)

The interaction of stereotypes, according to Meekosha (2004), can generate resistance that consists of embracing stereotypes. For example, some women with disabilities may not be perceived as mothers in a nurturing role (but in need of being cared for); so, as a way of resisting this perception, some disabled women adopt a very traditional female role in relation to their own children (Meekosha, 2004; Grue and Tafjord Laerum, 2002). Some disabled men, for example, create alternative masculine identities through certain occupations that do not require physical prowess or being seen in public, e.g., becoming computer experts in a basement. The disabled of both sexes may engage intensely in certain sports and physical training regimes in order to reinforce their bodily identity and ontological presence in a culture that privileges the "able bodied."

The capacity to create and recreate identities using the multiple identity matrix in terms of gender, race, class, sexual orientations, religion, and age has made it possible for many people with disability to alternate between and among various roles within which the subject can articulate a more positive sense of self.

The Intersection of Disability, Gender, and Sexuality

People with disabilities are often represented and seen at best as asexual and at worst as a monstrosity of nature. It is not uncommon to see people with disabilities as representing the worst in deviance in the media; films and TV programs portray disabled people as freaks, wizards, criminals, and so on. The visual media delight in juxtaposing the "deformed" sign of the disabled individual against a heterosexual normative template to indicate the range of human frailties and the evolution of civilization. Against a background of gender this image is then enhanced: women with disabilities are seen as disfigured, helpless, devious, corrupt, and evil while men with disabilities are seen as degenerate, wicked, crooked, twisted, immoral, and perverse. The gaze of heteronormativity has a profound impact on people with disabilities; many internalize these perceptions of themselves and in turn live to these dominant and oppressive rules. Thus for people with disabilities gender is conditional (Gerschick, 2000).

The issue that tends to put disability at the centre of any debate and that raises much controversy is whether people with disabilities should be allowed access to sex workers or to even work in this area of occupation. This question raises many interesting dilemmas regarding rights and economic support, including whether the state should pay for some people with disabilities to have free access to sex workers. The question also raises moral issues in cultures that purport to be Christian, liberal, and humanistic. To experience oneself as a sexual being is paramount in fulfilling human physical and emotional desire. In the current global cultures, body representations and mythologies are enshrined around Greek and Roman ideologies of purity, perfection, and unitary wholeness.

Consequently, many people with disabilities are disavowed and denied or are seen as negative and sexually absent, which makes the issue of sex work(ers) and disability an important one to address.

Researching Multiple Identities and Disability

While feminist scholarship has been doing a relatively good job (Einsenstein and Jardine, 1985) of engaging and interrogating the intersections of race, culture, gender, and sexuality (Connor, 2008; Grönvik and Söder, 2000; Meekosha, 2005), it has failed to theorize and analyze the complexities of disability and women's lived experiences (Spelman, 1988). Two decades on from when Spelman made this point, the situation is changing, however, with some scholars researching the intersections and overlaps of multiple identities with disability, particularly in relation to identity.

In a qualitative study by Molloy, Knight, and Woodfield (2003) investigating disability and identity, people with disability were reluctant to identify individual characteristics, such as disability or gender, as a dominant feature of their identity. But when pushed to make a choice of one of the different domains of identity—that is, gender, race, disability, sexual orientation, and class—participants chose ethnicity as the preferred identity. However, women were more likely to describe themselves in terms of gender than men were (mainly ethnic minority women). And for lesbian and gay people, sexuality formed a key component of personal identity. People chose either a social or medical model of disability, with older people using more medical explanations to describe their disability. Black Caribbean, African, and white lesbian and gay disabled people more readily described experiences of discrimination and prejudice.

TABLE 3.1   Timeline and Key Themes of Classical and Contemporary Theories of Gender Identity

Timeline	Theory	Key Figures	Key Themes
1940s–1960s	Structural Functionalism	Talcott Parsons; Émile Durkheim	Emphasizes the human desire for social order, predictability, and stability, reinforced through a collective conscience. The "naturality" of male and female sex identities are understood to correspond to a functional division of labour that demarcates the public (male) and private (female) spheres.
1950s–1970s	Symbolic Interactionism	Erving Goffman, Herbert Mead	Emphasizes human interaction as being the key factor in the development and presentation of identity. Both male and female come to understand, interpret, and perform dominant gender/sex roles as a way of projecting an "authentic" identity to others, thereby validating their sense of self.
1960s–1980s	Male Sex-Role Paradigm	Joseph Pleck, Robert Fein	Emphasizes the power of gender stereotypes to signal "appropriate" roles for men (and women) and the emotional and psychological consequences of these roles for individuals. Stresses men must find new and more emotionally productive ways of validating their sense of masculine identity or suffer a "male crisis" and "gender-role strain."
1980s–Current	Social Constructionism	R. Connell, Sylvia Walby	Emphasizes the ideologies underpinning gender inequality and patriarchal structures. Draws attention to the material consequences of male power across the public and private spheres. Critiques essentialist understandings of male and female identities and instead aims to highlight concepts such as *hegemonic masculinity, the sexual division of labour,* and *compulsory heterosexuality*.

TABLE 3.1   (continued)

Timeline	Theory	Key Figures	Key Themes
1920s–Current	Psychoanalysis	Nancy Chodorow, Simone de Beauvoir	Emphasizes the unconscious aspects of identity and the multiple ways in which we garner a sense of self through our immersion in the social world and especially familial/community influences and relationships. Depending on the theorist utilized, psychoanalysis can be considered supportive of feminist agendas or supportive of traditional gender values.
1990s–Current	Post-structuralism	Judith Butler, Julia Kristeva	Emphasizes the multiple, contingent, and fluid aspects of the self. Draws heavily on Foucauldian theory to understand the centrality of discourse (language and practice) to our sense of identity, thereby stressing that gender is not a predicted outcome but a process configured by repetitive, *performative* acts undertaken by the discursive subject (individual).
1990s–Current	Postmodernism	Linda Nicholson, Hélène Cixous	Emphasizes the demise of modernist, Enlightenment absolutes and related religious and political ideologies, and the rise of diversity, secularism, and cultural differences across societies and within gender identities. Links with post-structuralism in terms of stressing the contingent aspects of identity and the multiple ways of being in a world configured by globalizing dynamics and pressures.
1990s–Current	Queer Theory	Judith Butler, Eve Sedgwick	Emphasizes the feminist political/personal power opportunities offered by subverting the gender binary, for example through sabotaging or "queering" dominant representations of sex/sexuality.

Timeline	Theory	Key Figures	Key Themes
			Closely linked to both post-structuralism and postmodernism insomuch as it draws heavily on a discursively located, performative understanding of (gender) identity, one that is fluid and contingent.
1990s–Current	Intersectionality	Homi Bhabha, bell hooks	Emphasizes the multiple aspects of identity, and their political, historical, and culturally dynamic relationship. Drawing on post-structuralist understandings of identity as discursively enabled, gender, ethnicity, and race are understood as contingent, intersecting elements that combine to inform subjectivity and our sense of self. Identity is therefore neither neutral nor singular, but heavily invested with contrasting power dynamics, especially around *otherness*. Closely aligned with post-colonial theory, disability theory, and theories of race and difference.

SUMMARY

Theories of identity and difference are revealing not only for how they can be used as tools to unpack the hidden aspects of our daily lives, but also for how they reveal the tensions within us. Theories about race and difference and post-colonial theory resonate especially with the postmodern view of the world that sees colonialism as not only oppressive but also now out of step with the emergence of the "urban, multicultural village." Queer theory takes as its central point the possibility, if not political intent, to disrupt heterosexual normative discourses and the gender dualism that continues to suggest a fixed binary of "simply" male (masculine) and female (feminine) identities. Similarly, disability theories disturb binaries. They signal the "other" within our midst in a powerful and profound way. They unsettle us. We may be able to keep sexuality in the closet if we have to, but disability surfaces; it is visible. As such, it forces us to take note of something we are all a little frightened of—our own fragility and mortality.

One thing all these theories of difference have in common is their capacity to speak for those who would otherwise get silenced—the disenfranchised women of the South and East especially, and those disenfranchised minority women who remain largely invisible in the West and North. All the theories we have covered in this chapter contain powerful political statements about the workings of power (colonial, ethnic, cultural, national, etc.) upon our sense of (gendered) self. Intersectionality brings these theories together, and, by doing so, gives us an opportunity to gain a fuller understanding of the complex ways in which categories of identity interact.

CASE STUDY

Guy is a black man living in Vancouver. He is 35 and single. His ethnic origins are Caribbean, although if he were to trace his ancestry further back he would arrive in West Africa, probably in the region that is now Senegal.

Guy has lived in Canada all his life. He grew up in Ottawa, studied political science and media at a Toronto university, and at age 25 moved to Vancouver to take up a post as a media consultant. He recently did his PhD in media studies at a Vancouver university and is now planning to work in academia. Guy is confident, outgoing, and articulate. In that respect he is like many other black males of his generation. He likes to spend money on clothes and takes pride in his style of dress. He doesn't drive a car, preferring to use Vancouver's excellent public transport system. He has a wide circle of friends and enjoys a full and active social life.

If you spotted Guy shopping in one of Vancouver's boutique stores for men you would notice that he is attractive; women always take a second glance. However, Guy might not look twice at them. He is gay—a very open and overt gay. He has had many boyfriends, casual encounters, and one or two serious relationships. Being openly gay and black does not trouble Guy's sense of his masculinity—in every way he feels a man. It is just that he prefers men to women when it comes to relationships. However, once he moves outside his immediate circle of friends, which is a mix of gay and straight men and women of various ethnic backgrounds, he can find that straight black and white males are not always comfortable around him. It is as if being a gay black man, even in Vancouver, is not always acceptable; it seems out of kilter with the dominant heterosexual discourse that operates around black masculinity.

This is one of the main reasons why Guy rarely travels outside of Vancouver. And if he does, he tends to fly direct to Toronto, or maybe to Montreal. He has never been to the far North of Canada, the sprawling national parks of Ontario and Quebec. That is not his Canada. It is not somewhere he feels comfortable. His home is the inner city and suburbs of Vancouver. For Guy, postmodern multiculturalism means many things, not least that he can be accepted as a gay male in his home country. But his home country has many compartments, and some are more open to him than others.

DISCUSSION QUESTIONS

1. How many aspects of Guy's identity can you identify? And how do these identities intersect?

2. What is meant by "postmodern multiculturalism," and why might it help Guy perform his masculinity and sexuality without judgment from others?

3. What do you think are the main influences on Guy's masculine sense of self?

4. What does it mean to be Canadian in a globalized world?

QUESTIONS FOR REVIEW AND DISCUSSION

1. Consider to what extent your own life-style and aspirations are being determined or influenced by discourses of difference (whether they are based on race, gender, sexuality, (dis)ability, religion, age, etc.).

2. In what ways can white and black become politicized identities?

3. Discuss the ways in which the identities of gender and race combine and express themselves (positively or negatively) in your circle of friends and community.

4. Discuss the ways in which the ideas developed by queer theorists can be used to understand disability and difference.

5. What discourses of identity do you perform in order to appear a particular gender?

6. How does disability intersect with race, gender, and sexuality?

Part Two
The Politics Of Gender Identity

Chapter 4

Gender and the Politics of Belonging: Place, Nationhood, Culture, and Globalization

▲ *There is more than one way to be a woman.*
Source: © ADI WEDA/epa/Corbis

Learning Objectives

At the end of this chapter you will be able to:

- Recognize and explain the political aspects of gender identity.
- Critically examine multiculturalism as a concept that informs our world view.
- Utilize the concept of diversity to understand society and culture.
- Appreciate the influence of globalization on gender identity.
- Relate and connect the concept of place with gender identity.
- Explain the gendered character of nationhood.
- Be aware of and analyze the instability of gender identity.

OVERVIEW

Our postmodern condition has made us increasingly aware that, like identities, ways of belonging to places, cultures, and nations are multiple and changing. The multiplicity of cultures, ethnicities, and identities that characterizes our era has in turn had a profound effect on gendered notions of identity and on discourses of difference. This chapter examines the ways in which cultural, gender, and sexual identities are constructed in the context of contemporary multicultural and globalized Western societies. To do so, we will start by reflecting on the gendered meanings of place and nationhood before looking at some of the controversies about multiculturalism and gender. We will then move on to examine the impact globalization has had on gender and identity.

GENDERED MEANINGS OF PLACE AND NATIONHOOD

A fundamental understanding within any study of gender is that of inequality—between men and women, between sexualities, between individuals. At the heart of feminist theory is the recognition that the "status quo," which may be supposed to exist in complex human relations and may appear to provide some consistency and steadiness, is more often than not based on an unequal power struggle between individuals and between groups. This being so, we might wonder how any social order is maintained. For if, in the final analysis, all rests on conflict and contestation, why then does society not fall apart? How can a sense of permanence arise from a social setting based on inequality? And how are these (gender) inequalities experienced? How are they negotiated? How are they resisted and challenged?

Gendered Geographies

As this book reveals, there are many ways to address these questions. Feminists have turned their attention to community in their attempts to (1) expose and interrogate the persistence of gender inequalities in all areas of the social and (2) explore the ways in which notions of community can both sustain and challenge such conditions. That is, feminists are concerned to understand the centrality of place, locale, and space to formations of gender identity and to our particular sense of being and becoming a sexed and gendered individual. This work has given rise to a new specialism within feminist studies: feminist geographies (see, for example, McDowell, 2004; Laurie et al., 1999; Massey, 2004; Rose, 1993; Domash and Seager, 2001). As McDowell (2004) writes, "The specific aim of a feminist geography, therefore, is to investigate, make visible and challenge the relationships between gender divisions and spatial divisions, to uncover their mutual constitution and problematize their apparent naturalness" (p. 12).

McDowell argues that women and men experience space and place very differently and that this differentiation contributes to the politicization of place, space, and time. This is not due to an inherent and biological difference between the sexes but to the social and historic ordering of space and time, particularly within communities and locales. A most obvious example would be that of the public and private spheres, whereby women and men have, historically, been assigned a primary role or place in, respectively, either the domestic (private) or employment (public) spheres. This particular social condition is examined in more detail in Chapter 7 where we draw attention to the underlying binary distinctions that inform language itself and serve to sustain the gendered public/private structure of communities, institutions, and organizations. However, a central aim of feminist geographies is to take such critical inquiry beyond the public and private spheres and into the complex dynamics that exist between space, place, and culture and that connect "issues of sexuality to those of nationality, imperialism, migration, diaspora and genocide" (Pollock, 1996, p. xii).

Despite, or maybe because of, the tide of globalization that sweeps around us, there can be no doubt that our immediate spaces, our local attachments, remain most significant in our lives. No matter how mobile we might be as individuals, most of us live out our existence in a particular home, neighbourhood, town or region, places that are themselves bounded by the frontiers of a nation-state (McDowell, 2004). These spaces are not biologically determined but culturally given. They each have some level of spatial constraint within them: divisions around class, ethnicity, religion, and, of course, gender (see Massey, Allen, and Sarre, 2005). Such spatial entities not only provide us with an environment within which to act out our individuality and thereby reinforce our sense of belonging, they emphasize gender in obvious and subtle ways.

Over history, as villages became towns and towns became cities, so was confirmed the gender binary at a macro level. The city park, for example, may be a place for young mothers to take their children during the day. After dark, however, the same park becomes a different place—more masculine, dangerous, and threatening. The home can be both a haven of rest and tranquility, or it may be a prison cell, and a violent one at that, for some, especially for women (Dobash and Dobash, 1992). Places of work remain sites where women have to negotiate their femininity amid an invariably dominant masculinist discourse or culture, while men

become a problematical gender when they work with young children or in female-dominated professions (for discussion, see Simpson, 2004).

In many cities, especially in the urban sprawls that surround them, space can become highly contested. Street gangs dominate areas of many **conurbations**, attempting to establish their hegemony over distinct territories, increasingly using firearms to do so. These gangs are invariably male dominated while females play a supporting role or enter only under risk (see Vigil, 2002). An equally powerful gender division, albeit a less physically violent one, can operate in the business centres of cities—those professional, white-collar office blocks that apparently contribute so much to maintaining the social cohesion and wealth of a nation-state. And a cursory examination of any large town or city will reveal the mosaic of cultural and ethnic settlements that constitute it, and the related gender expressions within such spaces.

So in critically reflecting upon the concept of community, we can see there are few communities, if any, that are not marked by specific pockets of social, ethnic, cultural, and economic diversity, together with distinct gender divisions. In recognition of these dynamics, feminist geographers claim it is important to go beyond the appearance of unified communities and into their contested realms, to delve below what we might perceive to be their singular cultural expression in order to expose the dynamic relationships that actually sustain and envelope them.

> The spatial . . . can be seen as constructed out of the multiplicity of social relations across all spatial scales, from the global reach of finance

conurbation

A vast urban area resulting from the merging of individual towns or cities that have grown in population and in size.

and telecommunications, through the geography of the tentacles of national political power, to the social relations within the town, settlement, the household and the workplace. It is a way of thinking in terms of the ever-shifting geometry of social/power relations, and it forces into view the real multiplicities of space-time. (Massey, 2004, p. 4)

The Instability of Space, Time, and Community

We have to move beyond a conception of time, space, and locale as being stable and predetermined. As Melucci (1996b) argues, there are multiple dimensions to space-time, including the social, the inner, the cyclical, and the simultaneous. Therefore, we should not, in a quest for personal equilibrium, seek to impose upon our worlds the linear time of the social world and allow it to dominate our very being and our perception of reality. We have to recognize that behind the visible expression of social relations lies a more sophisticated and complex dynamic, entwined within formations and negotiations around gender identity in particular. For example, research by Laurie et al. (1999) reveals how young British South Asian Muslim women performed the most "appropriate femininity" depending on which sites they were in at the time. The home, the street, and the school all have different codes of behaviour, and these young women understood that. Consequently, they were involved in "strategically managing such expectations, and even subverting them" (Dwyer, 2004, p. 132), shifting almost seamlessly between orthodox Islamic behaviour and expressions of self in one site, to explicit "Western" discourses of identity in another. Such "space-time work," as it is played out in our expressions of identity, not only exposes the myth of space as unified and non-political but also the emotional consequences of moving "our selves" from one

space-time to another, particularly across cultural and social boundaries.

Space is not static. It is under pressure from numerous forces—the environment itself, decay, new building, population shifts, migration, demographic changes, economic forces. We might place all such forces under the heading of "globalization," but globalization is not the whole story, only the most recent version. Historically, gendered and contested space is not new. Indeed, it is likely to have been a factor in the movement and demise of peoples and cultures since the dawn of humankind. Such shifts are never within the control of any power bloc, no matter what its hegemonic dynamic might be. So this reminds us that we all live in an unstable place and that our spatial reality is never constant, fixed, determined. As Massey points out, "all attempts to institute horizons, to establish boundaries, to secure the identity of places, can in this sense therefore be seen to be attempts to stabilize the meaning of particular envelopes of space-time" (2004, p. 5).

But what is the driver for this stability, and how does it relate to our sense of (gender) identity? The driver is the very contingency at the heart of our selves. Precisely because we have to learn the rules, codes, and performances of sexuality and gender (they are not given to us biologically), so environment (space and place) becomes key. For, in Goffmanesque terms (see Chapter 1), the place and locale become the stages, the theatrical setting for both the expression of our selves and, consequently, the space within which we receive validation of our identity and very existence. Remove our place, our cultural home, and we face the instability at the heart of our existence. Space-time has no cultural essence within it. Only we, as humans, can attempt to impose one. We do so primarily through the cultural meanings that we attach to places, boundaries, and space. Through history, we can see how vehemently, violently, people will resist attempts to dispose them from their locales, from their cultural spaces. This is not merely territory that individuals and groups seek to hold on to; it is their very sense of identity. When Hitler spoke to the Germanic masses in the late 1930s, urging them to join him in his expansionist dream/nightmare, he did so primarily through recourse to a single discourse, one which he fully understood would reach into their very sense of self—the apparent unifying ideal of Aryan identity.

However, what is being described here, in terms of place and gender, is a masculinist perception of community and space. It is a maleist way of thinking and organizing space and place that exists within the **paradigm** of community as ultimately, if not necessarily, defensive and counter-positional (Massey, 2004; McDowell, 2004; Rose, 1993). In this gendered perception, identity is something to be constructed through exclusion, opposition, positioning. Feminist geographers argue that the desire for **existential** and ontological security manifests itself in a male-dominated society through the formation of space and place as dominance, reinforced through socio-political boundaries. For example, both industrial and post-industrial male-dominated work has become largely defined through organizations that operate to fairly rigid timetables with limited flexibility for the employee. Consequently, individuals, families and communities become organized around male-defined work patterns; the working day and the working week. Not only does this model reside within a masculinist subjectivity of reality, it is at odds with the actuality of personal identities, which are increasingly multiple, fluid, contingent, changing, and relational in the post- or late modern age. Indeed, Giddens (1992) goes so far as to suggest that a particular condition of "high modernity'" is the separation of time from space, with the "when" marker of social ordering and conduct no longer connected to

paradigm
A set of concepts, views, and assumptions that acts as a standard framework within which scientists interpret particular phenomena.

existential
Pertaining to human existence and to the "meaning of life."

the "where" marker. In other words, our relationship to the social and to others is increasingly and precisely ordered around a global time system, not around the peculiarities of place (see also Giddens, 1990).

Much as we might think so, none of us inhabits a singular, neatly identifiable, unchanging community. And any attempt to impose such (e.g., through armed struggle, revolution, social isolation and retreat, hegemonic forces, violence), merely flies in the face of this reality. As Chantal Mouffe (1988) puts it,

> We do not belong] to only one community, defined empirically and even geographically . . . unified by a single idea of the common good [. . .] We are in fact always multiple and contradictory subjects, inhabitants of a diversity of communities (as many, really, as the social relations in which we participate and the subject-positions they define), constructed by a variety of discourses and precariously and temporarily sutured at the intersection of those positions. (Mouffe, 1988, p. 44, quoted in Massey, 2004, p. 7)

Mouffe is challenging us to rethink time and place as ultimately relational, never constant. The masculine paradigm imposed on communities, space-time, is an attempt, therefore, to get our bearings, to control the "unutterable" confusion at the heart of the social (Laclau, 1990). For example, if we ask a person "Who are you?" they will inevitably answer in terms of place and community. That is, they will reflect on their being and its relationship to clearly identifiable, if not universal, markers. For example, they will give a name and that name will be gendered, culturally identifiable, and have a place and nationality associated with it.

Part of the process of acquiring an identity is to be materially visible to others, and such materializing takes place in spaces, locales, and communities that appear fixed and that therefore reinforce the self. We do not answer the identity question by saying "I am nothing, no one, just a multi-layered, discursive subject who occupies space only transiently." We seek to name, place, and position ourselves very clearly. We do this not just to answer the question, but to "resolve" our own existential dilemmas, which continue regardless of how strong and potent our sense of being might be. Ultimately, our identities remain unstable, but our quest for identity constantly demands an ontological "answer." Therefore, our visible and acceptable location in a particular space and place can mollify this sense of insecurity and contingency, if only temporarily.

A Retreat to Nationhood

Nationhood is an immensely powerful marker of self-identity and one that people can feel compelled to "protect" at all cost. Perhaps this is not surprising given that our place of birth appears to give us at least some solid basis upon which to build our adult identity; that is, we are born American, Canadian, Indian, Chinese, or whatever, and that geopolitical label somehow becomes who and what we are. Thereafter we are defined under those terms. Nationhood provides a strong underlying theme to our identity. We may travel around the world, relocate anywhere, learn new languages, even change our citizenship, but do we ever fully stop being our original nationality? One only has to look at the many "Chinatowns" around the world, and the ways in which, for example, the Irish, the British, and the Afro-Caribbeans congregate within their own national "communities" whatever county they may be living in (see, for examples, Benton and Gomez, 2011, Benson, 2011).

But nationhood in the postmodern age is also something of an illusion. We may feel drawn to it but it is not unchanging, it is not immune from the effects of globalization; nationhood is as contingent as every other aspect of our sense of self. Indeed, some commentators argue that it is precisely because of the threat to individual cultures, and thereby individual identities, posited by the homogeneity of globalization that we are now seeing the emergence of "culture wars," whereby many people retreat to ethnocentricity and nationalism in order to reinforce their ontological status in a world that appears to be experiencing cultural convergence (Lindner and Hawkins, 2012; Machida, 2012). This might explain, perhaps, why sporting events become powerful arenas for reinforcing national identity, albeit if only for a brief moment in time. Witness, for example, the phenomenon of a World Cup football tournament: 32 teams from around the world competing to win a football trophy. Well, that is what appears to be happening, but a closer look reveals the contestations and reinforcements of place and community that inhabit tournaments such as these.

Nationalities, and accompanying nationalisms, become celebrated at the Olympics, the World Cup, and similar global media events. Flag waving, anthem singing—the multitude of diverse cultural expressions that purport to symbolize and signify a nation and its people—become exaggerated and heightened. The major and minor nations of sport can occupy global television space for a limited time, and during this moment they can exhibit their territorial markers of cultural identity. But take a closer look at the audience and participants, and what do you see? You see every possible race and ethnicity in among those spectators and their teams; you see not singular but blended nationalities.

You will see Japanese and Chinese supporting the German football team; black, brown, and white faces supporting the Brazilians; African women cheering on the French. The artificiality of it all is further emphasized through the participants themselves. The English team is managed by an Italian; the Australian team, by a Dutchman; the Ghanaian team, by a Serb. And let us not forget the white player born in Scotland who plays for Trinidad and Tobago, and the black player born in Spain who plays for Holland. What we are seeing here is the artificiality of space and time that exists behind the constructed notion of community as fixed and determined. Ultimately, the realities of human interaction and interconnectedness, which have been unceasingly occurring over millennia but accelerated now in the age of globalization, undermine our belief in any unified presence—even, or especially, that of nationhood.

Nationhood has always carried within it the capacity for contestation. Indeed, one might argue that without nationality the world would never have suffered the seemingly endless imperialist projects it has done (Said, 1993). But, as Said argues, the authority and binary oppositions that sustained the nationalist and imperialist enterprise are being replaced by a new authority:

> New alignments made across borders, types, nations, and essences are rapidly coming into view, and it is those new alignments that now provoke and challenge the fundamentally static notion of *identity* that has been the core of cultural thought during the era of imperialism. (1993, p. xxviii, original emphasis).

We may well yearn to be defined as a member of a nation-state or nationality, that is, a citizen, but none of us can claim a universal "we" with those who live in our communities. For example, what does it mean to be Canadian in a country with such a diverse, if not at

TABLE 4.1   Origins of Ethnic Minorities in Canada (%)

British	28
French	23
Other European	15
Aboriginal	2
Other (mostly Asian, African, Arab)	6
Mixed	26

Source: US Census Bureau 2010
Searching for the "authentic Canadian."

times divided, population? Who are the "true" Canadians? Indeed, can any particular ethnic or racial group lay claim to this authenticity? Moreover, what particular cultural signifiers are brought into play by those who seek to reinforce such a national identity? (See, for discussion, Edwardson, 2008.)

We might also ask the same questions of the Americans. Are they represented by a white fraternity of hegemonically powerful (male) citizens (Nelson, 1998)? Are they an Asian, Hispanic, black, Native American, or European people? What will they be in the future? Are they mostly immigrants with no roots save those put down in very recent history? Is their history a project of individualism and masculinist self-interest based around self-accepted core belief systems (see Rotundo, 1993)? As is shown in Table 4.2, in actuality, Americans are a dispersed people of diverse cultural expressions who nevertheless yearn for an increasingly elusive unitary identity, a melting pot of people undergoing constant and seismic shifts in their demography and racial identities (Said, 1993; Schaefer, 2010; see also Goldin, 1999, for discussion). And just who is the citizen that claims legal and ontological association with the nation-state? Is this identity of citizenship neutral, or does it come already invested with disparities of gender, sexuality, race, class, and ethnicity? Clearly it does,

TABLE 4.2   US Census Population Projections

	2010	2050
Whites (includes "some other race")	79.5%	74.0%
Non-Hispanic Whites	64.7	46.3
Hispanics/Latinos (of any race)	16.0	30.2
African Americans	12.9	13.0
Asian Americans	4.6	7.8
Overall population change	301 million	439 million

Source: www.cia.gov/library/publications/the-world-factbook/fields/2075.html
The American ethnic melting pot.

in which case we need to recognize processes of inclusion and exclusion, not least around gender, which can easily be overlooked when we consider nationhood, citizenship, and belonging (see, for overview, Munday, 2009; also see Thacker, 2003).

Global events such as the soccer World Cup and the Olympic Games are, then, merely a momentary retreat to an apparently unified, and therefore discernibly safer, more secure, and more knowable identity. We cheer on "our" team, but the "our" is in fact an illusion. The community it purports to represent is a fiction within our imaginations. We give this illusion credence and merit simply because doing so enables us to feel alike with others—and be distinguished from those who are not "like us." But this so-called community remains a transient association/distinction, reinforced periodically and only then through the plastic spectacles of the mass media. The results of the sporting contest are not so important. Indeed, they are quickly forgotten by all but the avid enthusiast. The rest of us leave the utopian bounded space temporarily inhabited for the duration of the tournament or the time our team is in it, and re-inhabit, knowingly or otherwise, the multicultural, multi-gendered, multi-sexual complex and non-unitary world that increasingly and self-evidently signifies our place, our community, in the postmodern age.

The next section of this chapter examines the significance of what we call "our community" or "our culture" and the various political meanings these notions can take on.

MULTICULTURALISM AND GENDER

We live in a world of diverse and multiple cultures although not necessarily equal ones. Some are clearly more privileged than others; some are more valued and respected than others. Yet culture is important to each of us: it informs our identity in ways we barely recognize. In the age of globalization, with its pressures toward cultural homogeneity, individual cultures continue to provide us with a powerful sense of belonging. The challenge, then, is to find ways of living together harmoniously and under some larger cultural value system while maintaining our individual cultural identity and association. *Multiculturalism* is the term often used to denote this process.

Culture is a term that has become part of our everyday language. Our popular media tend to associate it with collective forms of expression, such as music, food, art, dress, poetry, and storytelling. For sociologists, culture is a space in which we locate ourselves or find ourselves located and which becomes validated through belief and value systems, ethical codes, moral and political standpoints, style and taste, social practices, epistemic knowledge, habits, and expectations. Taken together, these cultural signifiers reinforce, if not impose upon us, a perception of reality of the world and its peoples, and our place within it. We generally tend to perceive culture as vital to our ability to be and become an ontologically grounded subject, for without it we often see our place within our social and familial group, and even our sense of place within humanity, as being at risk of dissolution.

What is implied in this notion of culture is difference, separation, and uniqueness, but also togetherness. We bond with others but in so doing immediately reinforce our separation, and our differences from those whom we perceive as being outside "our culture." Our identities exist and are largely validated in a relational context; knowing who or what I am requires me to know who or what I am not. But in the age of globalization, with the rapid and constant movement of people across cultural and political boundaries, the rise of urbanization and mega-cities, the instantaneous flow of information, and the contingency of the postmodern, how do we perceive differences and identity? How do we reconcile the desire to form a stable, unified, culturally bounded and secure self with the recognition that identity can also be multiple, fragmentary, and fluid?

Before beginning any discussion as to the influence and impact of multiculturalism on gender identity, it is necessary to clarify the meaning of multiculturalism and set it in context. The term *multiculturalism* has become highly controversial. It purports to encourage mutual respect, societal solidarity, and social justice among people of diverse backgrounds, all learning to live together and thereby contributing to an ongoing and beneficial social order (Vertovec and Wessendorf, 2010). However, it is also a term that is politicized, contested, and laden with ideological projections and ethnic group

investments. These power dynamics reflect its amorphous character and, consequently, its capacity to influence both political debates and individual subjectivities. Multiculturalism can be seen as a political aim or objective, a policy directive, a social and cultural aspiration, and/or the "reality" of modern urban life in the age of globalization. It has become associated with racialized groups, immigration, **diaspora**, and large metropolitan urban centres. Other terms that by association attach themselves to multiculturalism include *ethnicity, post-colonial, Third World, advantaged, disadvantaged, social mobility, cross-cultural, intercultural, trans-cultural,* and *ethno-cultural.*

> **diaspora**
> A group of people who have left their original homeland to settle in different parts of the world but who still share a sense of having a common culture.

Some commentators are increasingly drawn to the term *diversity* rather than to *multiculturalism*, largely because *diversity* seems to speak simultaneously of both exclusion and inclusion, of socially differentiated groups, of individual identity representations. The term *diversity*, furthermore, implies neutrality and relativism and, therefore, carries less political meaning than the term *multiculturalism*, which, on the other hand, suggests a complex if not unstable mixture of assimilation and difference. *Diversity* also speaks to a multitude of subject positions and orientations, including those connecting to sexuality, race, religion, and disability, although some critics have suggested including other disadvantaged groups into the multicultural debate, such as lesbian, gay, bisexual, and transgendered individuals from both black and white communities (Moodley, 2007; Moodley and Curling, 2006).

In addition to its unclear definition, multiculturalism is further problematic because it lacks a coherent, consistent theory (Willet, 1998). Indeed, it can be argued that multiculturalism is not so much a sociological theory as a social movement. However, some scholars do attempt to place multiculturalism within a theoretical paradigm. For example, Parekh (2006) defines *multiculturalism* as a perspective that is composed of a creative interplay of

> . . . cultural embeddness of human beings, the inescapability and desirability of cultural diversity and intercultural dialogue, and the internal plurality of each culture . . . to illuminate the insights and expose the limitations of others and create . . . a vital in-between space, a kind of immanent transcendentalism, from which to arrive at a less culture-bound vision of human life and a radically critical perspective. (pp. 338–9)

This "less culture-bound vision of human life" fits with the postmodern view of the self as able to refashion itself and to exit the rigid boundaries set by society and culture. This view is very different from the way in which many theorists have confined the debates about multiculturalism strictly within an ethnic minority perspective, thus limiting its meaning to the racial and ethnic domains (for example, Parekh, 2006; Tapp, 2000).

The conversations and discussions around the concept *multiculturalism* often appear scripted and constructed but are paragraphed through a drama of political, national, racial, cultural, and ethnic differences and identities. For example, in the US there is talk of integration or of the "melting pot" philosophy (Appiah, 2005; Gutmann, 1994). In Canada, the term *mosaic society* is used to signify a situation where all cultures co-exist to form a national identity (Kymlicka, 1995, 1999). In Britain, some commentators refer to the "salad bowl" scenario, where individual identities are independently part of a dynamic and inclusive national identity (Modood, 1992, 1993). Such terms have arisen

over recent decades, and often in response to tensions between social groups, requiring government agencies and communities to somehow address the inherent and persistent issues at the very heart of multicultural societies.

In their discursive capacity, such terminologies as *melting pot* and *salad bowl* can construct a particular relationship between individuals and groups, between agencies and communities, between religions and between nation-states. However, while perhaps providing a linguistic framework from which to promote the concept and ideal of multiculturalism, these terms can serve to conceal divisions between the dominant culture and the "other." For example, writing from a Canadian perspective, Walcott (2003), raises the issue of the power relations within this kind of multiculturalism. He argues that multiculturalism serves to unify the nation-state as an "imagined community" (Andersen, 1983) of tolerant persons who are accepting of other people, thus making multiculturalism a point of national pride. However, this process does not call into question the continued hegemony of English and French Canadians. Zizek (1997) adopts a similarly critical standpoint:

> Multiculturalism is a disavowed, inverted, self-referential form of racism, a "racism with a distance"—it "respects" the Other's identity, conceiving the Other as a self-enclosed, "authentic" community towards which he, the multiculturalist, maintains a distance rendered possible by his privileged universal position. (p. 22)

Irrespective of whether one uses the term *melting pot, mosaic,* or *salad bowl,* the assumption that cultures are self-enclosed systems tends to essentialize the idea of difference. By so doing, this view also nullifies the hope of commonality among diverse peoples. Furthermore, if society's constituent ingredients, such as gender, race, class, culture, ethnicity, sexual orientation, and disability, "carry with them material consequences for those who are included within or excluded from, them" (Bulmer and Solomos, 1996, p. 781), then the unaddressed tensions of multiculturalism can be expected to lead to more racism, homophobia, cultural isolation, and other hegemonic practices.

Thus, the belief that a society is multicultural tends to conceal distinct and possibly intractable material and social inequalities, all reinforced through differences of language and knowledge. Even though multiculturalism implies social mobility within and across ethnic groups and accommodation of difference, no society is fully multicultural in that there is a *total* absence of any hierarchy of differentiation between minorities and dominant groups. As Paul Sniderman (2007) puts it,

> By arguing that groups in society should be allowed to live according to their beliefs and customs, we are encouraging people to see themselves as different from one another. And not just a little bit different, but fundamentally different. So it fosters a them-and-us attitude. (2007; also Sniderman and Hagendoorn, 2007)

In addition, multiculturalism gets enlisted into particular disciplines, which themselves are associated with certain truth regimes, dominant and subordinate discourses, subjectivities, and so-called realities. Upadhya (2002), for example, writes this:

> Many anthropologists thought that multiculturalism vulgarises the key anthropological idea of cultural relativism by essentialising cultural difference. Multiculturalism also appeared to posit equality among cultures—a premise that neglected relations of hierarchy and domination among different societies. (p. 172; see also Roseberry, 1989)

By becoming a "natural" category, much like the way "race" and "gender" have traditionally been perceived as natural or biological

categories, the category "culture" is sometimes instrumentalized as a way of masking, and therefore legitimizing, certain relations of dominance. By placing all cultures at the same level, the concept of multiculturalism tends to ignore the fact that some cultures occupy dominant positions due to particular historical factors, such as conquest, occupation, and domination. For example, Aboriginal Canadian culture and white Canadian culture differ not just in terms of value and belief systems, rituals, and collective practices but also in terms of the different positions of power they occupy. To reduce cultural difference to a question of different ways of understanding the world is to ignore the power dynamics that inform the ways in which cultures interact with one another.

Similarly, the notion that cultural conflict can be resolved through greater understanding between cultures tends to also ignore the economic, social, and political tensions that underpin cultural conflicts. In Britain during the 1960s to the 1980s the idea of multiculturalism was focused on cross-cultural knowledge, respect for other cultures and religions, and the acquisition of skills and competencies so as to work and communicate across cultures. For example, it was once presumed that if people learned about the food, music, and fashion from other cultures—colloquially known as the "3 S's" (samosas, steel bands, and saris)—they would become "multi-culturally experienced" and be ready for cross-cultural engagements (Moodley, 1999). As Bhandar writes, "[c]ultural practices and traditions, festivals, dance, music, food, and clothing have all been embraced within a multiculturalism that not only tolerates difference but celebrates it in the form of commodification and consumption" (2009, p. 321). This celebration of difference not only reduces cultures considered to be "different" to mere commodities to be consumed but also detracts from the inequalities that exist between cultures. Another example is the way "cultural sensitivity" is often rated high on the list of social-skill requirements for social workers, health practitioners, and educators in multicultural Western societies such as Canada. This tends to suggest that marginalized communities suffer as the result of "cultural insensitivity" rather than as the result of economic and social injustice. The economic blindness of multiculturalism has also often been criticized. Other critics have gone further by arguing that the "culturalizing" of difference prevents processes of collective resistance to domination:

> If a society is conceived as made of several communities with very distinct cultural aspirations, then the possibility of resisting big capital will be the lowest. Further, multiculturalism, by constructing communities which are necessarily fragmented, with a minimum level of agreement across them, if at all, is not able to offer a resistance that classes and class blocs can muster. (Rodriguez, 2002, p. 116)

While multiculturalism appears to reflect and promote the plurality and diversity of postmodern democracy, the concept of multiculturalism is not without contradictions. Writing from an epistemological and philosophical position, Melzer, Weinberger, and Zinman (1998) sum up some of its problems as follows:

> Multiculturalism: it is a movement that radicalises and Nietzscheanizes the liberal ideal of tolerance—thus turning that ideal against liberalism—by tending to deny the possibility of universal truth as well as of non-oppressive power and by seeking, through this very denial, a comprehensive redistribution, not so much of wealth as of self-esteem, and not so much to individuals as to various marginalised groups. (p. 4, cited in Siegel, 2007)

So, is multiculturalism an unattainable utopia or even an undesirable aim? Well despite the many powerful critiques of multiculturalism,

some commentators go so far as to suggest that "we are all multiculturalists now" (Kivisto, 2012), basing part of their conclusion on what they see as the "minority rights revolution" (Skretny, 2002) seen to be gathering pace over the past few decades:

> . . . those proclaiming the death of multiculturalism might appear to be capturing the current zeitgeist. However, what they fail to appreciate is the fact that on two levels the ground has shifted in favour of the ongoing viability of a politics of identity. First, the legislative and judicial landscape has changed, providing venues for outsiders to gain entrée into the mainstream in ways that quite simply were not possible before the middle of the past century. Second, the culture has changed in ways that are conducive to multiculturalism, with those in the centres of culture increasingly embracing the virtues of diversity. . . . Put simply, there are political and cultural structures in place that will serve to sustain the demands made by stigmatized groups for recognition and respect, and to the extent that this is true, then we *really* are all multiculturalists now. (Kivisto, 2012, p. 20, original emphasis)

To summarize, multiculturalism can be understood as a moral project, the aim of which is to promote equality and social cohesion based on mutual recognition and respect. As a result, multiculturalism may be seen to be an entirely laudable aim and in keeping with liberal agendas for social justice for all peoples, whatever their race, nationality, or creed. However, claiming to be multicultural will not remove the underlying inequalities that exist between social groups, nor completely dissipate fear and ignorance between individuals and communities. The complicated if not problematic character of multiculturalism is further revealed when we examine how gender and sexual identity are configured within and across a multicultural environment. This we now discuss in the following section.

Gendered Multiculturalism

In many ways, multiculturalism connects profoundly with gender identity, providing a raft of opportunities for reinforcing the gendered self appropriating particular cultural signifiers or markers. However, as we will see, multiculturalism is never benign. It carries the potential to disrupt, change, and reinforce the status quo. We should not presume, therefore, that a multicultural society is the best possible social model in all circumstances.

In her article "Is Multiculturalism Bad for Women?" (1999), Susan Okin takes a radical feminist stance to critique the Western liberal engagement with multiculturalism. She argues that under certain conditions multiculturalism can be anti-feminist, if not against women's interests generally. Okin claims there are fundamental inconsistencies and conflicts between a commitment to gender equality and a desire to respect and accommodate the customs and practices of minority cultures (also Fisher, 2004). As Susan Okin (1999) says,

> Most cultures are suffused with practices and ideologies concerning gender. Suppose, then, that a culture endorses and facilitates the control of men over women in various ways (even if informally, in the private sphere of domestic life). Suppose, too, that there are fairly clear disparities in power between the sexes, such that the more powerful, male members are those who are generally in a position to determine and articulate the group's beliefs, practices, and interests. Under such conditions, groups' rights are potentially, and in many cases actually, antifeminist. They substantially limit the capacities of women and girls of that culture to live with human dignity equal to that of men and boys, and live as freely chosen lives as they can. (p. 12)

Okin argues that the rarefaction of ethnic cultures, through particular policy directives, has permitted and extended the suffering of ethnic minority women. She cites the French government's accommodation of polygamy in the 1980s, a policy initiative seen to respect the immigrant and French-born Muslim communities and their culture. What was not realized or acknowledged at the time were the difficulties and pressures such a practice, now reinforced through French government policy, placed on women in particular communities. Similarly, she offers clitoridectomy (i.e., female circumcision), "marriage by capture," and forced child marriage as examples of misogynistic, patriarchal cultural practices that are tolerated under the rubric of multiculturalism but that would not be tolerated within wider society. She also discusses the notion of "cultural defense," used, for example in some US criminal cases, where a kind of "my culture made me do it" defence is evoked. Okin cites the case of a Chinese immigrant man in New York who battered his wife to death for infidelity. The defendant raised cultural defence in his plea and got a reduction in his sentencing.

Okin's article has been criticized by a number of scholars. Writing in the same book, and by way of a commentary of the Okin chapter, Homi Bhabha (1999) says that Okin's "version of liberal feminism shares something of the patronizing and stereotyping attitudes of the patriarchal perspective" (Bhabha, 1999, p. 82). Likewise, Ranjoo Seodu Herr (2004) offers a strong attack of Okin's position by maintaining that practices such as female circumcision, forced child marriage, and polygamy are in fact rare occurrences among immigrant communities. Herr argues that such practices are pervasive and pathological and therefore should be classified and understood as sexual and physical abuse, wife battery, or rape. In other words, these are criminal acts that, in mainstream Western society, would be attributed to individuals rather than to the whole of Western culture.

In the debates about so-called honour killings or the controversies about the veil in France, the UK, and Quebec, tensions are heightened by the sensitivities that often accompany questions that are perceived as pertaining to cultural and religious differences. Often, the debates are presented in the media in a way that pits multiculturalist agendas against feminist ones. Some critics have taken the feminist side, warning against the dangers of adopting a relativistic if not apolitical position with regard to different cultural expressions, especially those that can be seen to impinge on the lives and liberties of individuals, men or women. For example, Linda Fisher (2004) poses the problem in dualistic terms: how can we come to recognize the legitimacy of (multi)cultural self-definitions and identities, within a perspective of tolerance, without tolerating practices that could be construed as oppressive and harmful to women?

The notion of "tolerance" that is often used in multicultural debates is itself problematic (Brown, 2006; Bhandar, 2009). In other words, who tolerates whom? According to Wendy Brown, tolerance is a "discourse of power" that goes back to the beginning of European modernity when it was used to pacify religious tensions and control persecutions. Today, she argues, tolerance reveals the failure of liberalism and egalitarianism and reinforces religious, sexual, and cultural norms. Tolerance has the effect of demonizing those who are perceived as culturally different, and at times as dangerous "others." It involves a one-way rather than a reciprocal relationship in the sense that Western culture, as a universal norm, is seen as tolerant while other cultures are placed in a position of being tolerated or not (Bannerji, 2000).

In this respect, multiculturalism often has the effect of producing and reproducing ethnic and cultural categories that are part of a larger project of controlling those deemed "different" (Bhandar, 2009; Bannerji, 2000; Volpp, 2001; Grewal, 2005). This is apparent, for example, in the ways in which patriarchal practices regarded

as "cultural" (such as honour killings) are portrayed in the media. The cultures from which these practices are assumed to originate become the object of a judgmental gaze that perpetuates colonial and neo-colonial myths of civilizational "backwardness" and the idea that women need to be rescued from these traditional and patriarchal cultures (Chatterjee, 1989; McClintock, 1995; Basu, 1995; Bannerji, 2000; Grewal, 2005; Razak, 2008).

Western culture, by contrast, is assumed to be the measuring rod of civilizational progress, gender equality, and democratic rights. Moral responsibility is then posited outside and above cultures that are perceived as separate and self-enclosed systems. Fisher's (2004) response to Okin's argument exemplifies such a conception of "culture" as self-enclosed:

> Perhaps as the outsider we can never grasp the interiority of such cultural knowledge as someone from within that culture. At any rate, such appraisals are arguably our shared philosophical and moral responsibilities—and we are all too familiar with the potential consequences, in a variety of historical and cultural contexts, of not saying something. (pp. 117–8)

But are cultures self-enclosed systems where one can only be an outsider or insider? And are we not all part of the same culture the moment we interact with each other? The way in which multiculturalism defines culture is itself problematic. Bhandar argues that the concept of culture underlying multiculturalism is part of a "totalizing and normalizing project" that has its roots in nineteenth-century industrial liberal societies. As she explains, "Culture is not conceived of as discrete sets of practices that vary from collective to collective but, rather, is an embodiment of a way of life and being (Bhandar, 2009, p. 325).

Such vision of culture as unitary and static is designed to perpetuate a unitary notion of the nation-state. Some even argue that fixed notions of culture suit both the minority and majority cultural patriarchal agendas. Giving the example of Canadian multiculturalism, Bannerji argues that "[i]t suits the Canadian state just as much as it suits the elite in the communities to leave intact these traditions and rituals of power" (Bannerji, 2000, p. 167). In addition to being in line with traditionalist ideologies, this notion of culture as unchanging is also in direct opposition to our fluid, non-unified, and dialogical postmodern condition, which we discussed in Chapter 2.

Furthermore, to regard feminism as antagonistic to multiculturalism is to assume that patriarchy is a permanent fixture of cultures. Thus, this debate could easily overlook the many forms that patriarchy can take when cultures are transplanted in new settings and when they come in contact with other cultures. Many critics have therefore stressed the importance of looking at culture not as pre-given but as an ideological formation and have exposed the patriarchal structures and relations of power that go into the making of culture in our societies (see Bannerji, 2000). For example, Sarah Song (2005) examines "cultural defence" cases in the US and uncovers the ways in which they are underpinned by larger patriarchal structures that have little to do with ethnic cultures. She cites the case of the Chinese immigrant who murdered his adulterous wife, also discussed by Okin. Yet Song's argument is very different from Okin's. For Song, cultural gender norms of male honour were in this case accommodated by already existing patriarchal and sexist practices within the US legal system. She explains that in the case of American men brought to court for crimes of violence against their female partner, special circumstances based on so-called emotional disturbance are often granted if it is judged that the violent crime was provoked by the female partner's infidelity. She goes on to offer her own interpretation of the cultural defence argument in the Chinese immigrant's court case mentioned above:

Although the defence stressed the cultural differences in the ways that an American and Chinese man might respond to adultery, there is an underlying intercultural congruence in the gender norms at work: a man's violent retaliation against his female partner's infidelity is a reasonable response, whether committed out of honor, passion, or emotional disturbance. (Song, 2005, p. 481)

Song argues that cultural defence fits into the same patriarchal laws that condone violence against women, although it uses different arguments. Therefore, cultural defence cases have little to do with minority cultural norms but more with the patriarchal norms that regulate mainstream and other cultures. Song also gives the example of a woman from the Santa Clara Pueblo indigenous tribe in the US who married outside her group and whose children were consequently denied membership in the tribe. The fact that her lawsuit was unsuccessful was, according to Song, the outcome of both the Santa Clara Pueblo cultural norms but also the pressure the US state exercised on indigenous groups to restrict their membership in order to maintain a distinct cultural and political identity. As Song argues, "intercultural interactions may provoke a hardening of hierarchies within minority groups," including gender hierarchies (p. 476). Thus, gender norms pertaining to the mainstream (Western) culture reinforce and perpetuate sexist and patriarchal practices within minority cultural groups (see for discussion Bannerji, 2000). Since patriarchy can infiltrate many cultures at a time, multiculturalism could often signify multiplied forms of oppression for women.

Once again, we can see that the idea of cultures as separate or unified wholes represents a myth and that this myth is often used to conceal the inequalities and hierarchical divisions that exist between cultures and between genders. This is one of the key intersections between multiculturalism and gender. Not all the sources of minority women's oppression stem from their culture. Yet the result of "culturalizing" their oppression often results in more oppression. Furthermore, putting "other cultures" on trial can sometimes lead to a situation whereby the role of the state and state institutions in perpetuating gender inequalities is overlooked (Bannerji, 2000; Song, 2005). For example, some of the oppressive practices that subject the female body to normative ideals of beauty in mainstream Western culture (such as breast enlargement, facelifts, and labiaplasty) do not receive the same amount of criticism from the public as practices associated with minority women's cultural forms of oppression, such as female circumcision. This situation could easily result in normalizing and making acceptable the patriarchal and oppressive practices of the majority culture (Song, 2005).

Clearly, questions about cultural difference and gender can have tremendous consequences on the ways in which we see our world and ourselves. Such questions continue to resonate today—not just in Western societies but in all societies where the traditional confronts the liberal, the modern confronts the postmodern, and cultural differences attempt to negotiate an ameliorated path that values difference without compromising issues of social justice. In the midst of this vortex are individual men and women, often caught up in cultural dynamics not of their choosing but that come to impinge directly, and often oppressively, upon them. Multiculturalism, then, appears a helpful term, if not a reasonable aspiration. In many other ways, however, the term remains highly problematic.

THE IMPACT OF GLOBALIZATION ON GENDER AND IDENTITY

If multiculturalism tends to emphasize separateness and differences between cultures, globalization, on the other hand, is based on the idea of connectedness between cultures. This does not make globalization a less problematic or less ideological concept, for, as we will see, it also presupposes unequal relationships of power. It is precisely these economic but also social, cultural, and political dynamics that have had a profound impact on gender at all levels of society but in particular in areas such as labour, employment, and caregiving.

Powerful as it is, globalization is a difficult concept to define and an even trickier one to intellectually analyze. Part of the problem is that globalization doesn't stand alone; it is irrevocably connected to other equally contested but powerful concepts such as the information society, postmodernism, electronic colonialism, cultural globalization, and the new world information and communication order (see, for discussion, McPhail, 2006; Held et al., 1999; Hutton and Giddens, 2000; Castells, 1998, 2004). Held et al. (1999) put it this way:

> [Globalization] lacks precise definition. Indeed, globalization is in danger of becoming, if it has not already become, the cliché of our times: the big idea which encompasses everything from global financial markets to the Internet but which delivers little substantive insight into the contemporary human condition. (p. 1)

We certainly see the point being made by Held et al. but would disagree with its failure to provide insights into the human condition. As we go on to describe in this section, globalization does reveal much about one key aspect of us—our identity. But first, let us attempt to define this concept.

Simply put, the concept of globalization exposes the interconnectedness of humanity in the late modern or postmodern age (Galbraith, 2002). Through myriad technological innovations, increasing migrations, and universally recognizable cultural icons, globalization has turned the world into a village, or, more accurately, into a rapidly expanding urban town, maybe to become a "mega city" (Doyle, 2006). Globalization changes, reduces, displaces, and sometimes obliterates traditional cultures and associated forms of communicating, relating, and behaving. Globalization has no single agenda, however; it just is. Globalization is what we, as interconnected individuals, experience it as, or make of it; it is as unpredictable and unmanageable as it is inevitable. It is ridden with ambiguities, complexities, and disorders, and chaotic, unimagined consequences (Urry, 2005a, 2005b). We might be able to determine its past, but it is impossible to determine its future direction. Indeed, globalization reveals the porous character of all cultures that we discussed in the previous section, as well as of individual identities. Globalization can place certain cultures and values under siege, promote other cultures worldwide, disrupt our ontological security, question our belief systems, and yet provide each of us with a sense of place and community, not least through its communicative Internet capacities (for overview, see Cavanagh, 2009).

Throughout history, people have tended to live localized existences. If they moved at all, and many didn't, they moved slowly, over time, as did their thinking and understanding of themselves and their world. This produced a state of ontological security insomuch as these localized worlds seemed just that—the entire world, relatively predictable, permanent, unchanging, and unchangeable, to be trusted and relied upon. People were born, lived, married, reproduced, and died in small, rural, often relatively isolated communities. Even the cities of the Industrial Revolution that arose in Europe in the nineteenth century especially remained somewhat isolated conurbations, out of direct influence or contact with similar conurbations elsewhere, and certainly those situated in other regions of the world. All of this has now changed—and dramatically—to produce in turn the "age of migration" and mobility (Ki-moon, 2007). Indeed, as the United Nations predicted, August 2008 was the moment when, for the first time in history, the world's urban population exceeded the rural total (Doyle, 2007) (see Figure 4.1).

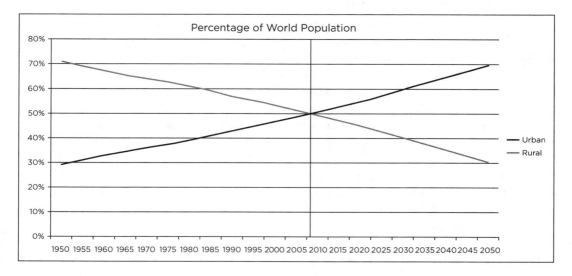

FIGURE 4.1   **Percentage of World that Is Rural or Urban**
The rise of the mega city.

Source: Taylorluker/Wikipedia. Data Source: United Nations, World Urbanization Prospects: The 2007 Revision Population Database http://esa.un.org/unup/p2k0data.asp

To be sure, there has always been movement between peoples and interactions with other cultures, and this dynamic has historically been a powerful force for change, but globalization has speeded up this process, and to incomprehensible levels. To give just one example, during the 1970s China averaged about 200,000 foreign visitors a year. By 2006, that number had risen to 50 million. While in the 1970s few Chinese spoke English, today it is estimated that 20 million Chinese a year are learning English (Callero, 2008). Even just 30 years ago, China and its 1 billion people were relatively isolated, far removed from the experience of globalization. Today, China is central to globalization; in the process, the lives of Chinese, and people around the world, are being dramatically changed, transforming the very core of their sense of self. As Castells puts it, "our world, and our lives, are being shaped by the conflicting trends of globalization and identity" (2004, p. 1; also Galbraith, 2002).

Transformational Effects of Globalization on the Individual

Castells is directing our attention to a key aspect of globalization—its power to transform us as individuals. If you have access to a computer, to a mobile phone, to the Internet, or to a television, a radio, or a cinema, then you are effectively plugged into globalization. If you work for a multinational corporation, or even a national one, then you are directly working within globalization. If you travel abroad at all, plan to live abroad, or even accept this as a possibility for yourself, then you are contributing to the global movement of people. If you are learning English as a second language, or desire to, then you are attempting to speak the current dominant language of globalization. And if you ever watch worldwide sporting events or buy the records of a global pop star, then you are buying into just some of the iconic symbols of globalization.

It is difficult to remain outside the reach of globalization. For sure, some people manage it, but they are effectively isolated either by choice (e.g., monks living in remote parts of the countryside) or force (e.g., prisoners in solitary confinement). For the remainder of us, globalization continues to produce within us identity effects over which we have little direct control.

From our discussion of globalization it would seem appropriate to assume that globalization somehow channels our identity into its own, often rather limiting, definitions and cultural expressions. For example, we might be tempted to declare that globalization not only results in billions of us eating the same burgers and working in the same types of organizations but also imposes a dominant logic of rationalization upon individuals and societies to the extent that we are all caught in the "iron cage" of reality (Ritzer, 1993). However, is it really that simple, that deterministic? Obviously not, for identity work has numerous dimensions to it and globalization connects, in some way, with them all. Castells (2004, p. 8), for example, suggests three primary forms of identity building that are at work in all individuals/subjects at some point in their lives but that are especially influenced by the processes of globalization in "high modernity" (Giddens, 1992):

1. *Legitimizing identity*: This term refers to the power of institutions, nation-states, and associated political and religious ideologies to regulate and dominate us. We become legitimate in social terms by following the dominant cultural codes of our society. These apparatuses produce the civil society, but in so doing come to inform our very sense of self.

2. *Resistance identity*: This term describes the process of collective action or social movements in society that aim to challenge and transform political or other social agendas.

Such collective resistance can be based around any sense of alienation or opposition to the status quo and might arise, for example, from ethnic, religious, sexual, gender, class, or cultural identities: in other words, any collective but minority identity that might feel threatened and marginalized by wider society. Examples of resistance identity range from the Occupy movements to the Arab Spring, all of which have been largely facilitated by the use of global media networks, including the Internet, Twitter, and Facebook.

3. *Project identity*: This arises for individuals when they experience the direct effects of social transformation as a change in their own subjectivity and sense of reality. The collective may be the power force for change, but it is made up of individuals; therefore, the project of the collective becomes, in effect, a project of identity work for the individual. Feminism may be an abstract term for many, but its effect has been to transform the lives and expectations of millions of women, and in very direct ways. In the same way, movements such as trade unionism, anti-capitalism, and environmentalism have become part of a "project identity" shared by millions across the globe.

As we stated in our definition of globalization, at its core is the drive to network, to communicate, to share, to inform. This process cannot be experienced without effect on the individual. What we see, what we read, what we hear, all have a bearing on what we say; and what we say is, as we have described above, pivotal to our presentation and understanding of ourselves. Through the network society, which now transcends all cultures, globalization is transforming communities, making them virtually unrecognizable from what they were just three or four decades ago. But these communities are made up of individuals. It is they who are changing; their very sense of self is being transformed through the forces of globalization (Callero, 2008, for overview).

In terms of the three forms of identity building described by Castells, globalization impacts all of them, but in different ways. It changes the nature of the relationship between the nation-state and the individual, most often but not always by unsettling the power of the nation-state to be a key arbiter of our identity. An example would be the way in which we become less linked to a particular geographical place, country, or culture, and more global in our experience, awareness, and cultural identification. Globalization pressures us to integrate with others, even if we actually desire acute separation.

Not unrealistically, many people fear these forces. They perceive a "clash of civilizations" with themselves caught up at the very centre of it (Fukuyama, 2007). They see their identity under threat by globalization and, therefore, resort to active resistance against its "architects." This is reflected for example in the French government's concern to promote the French language worldwide, and thereby challenge what they see as the English language hegemony embedded within globalization. Others fear that these forces could become totalitarian forms of power. An example here would be the acts of violence by some French people against McDonald's restaurants.

Finally, globalization forces many of us to seek solace in identity projects which might reinforce our sense of self when faced with all the complexity and confusion that globalization brings with it. Such projects include retreating to closed communities and resorting to religious fundamentalism, to extremist ideologies, and to political/personal standpoints that individuals hope will secure them to the ground as the globalization wave sweeps over them.

In other words, if identity work was ever a neutral project, it certainly isn't now in the age of globalization. And this exposes the real tension in globalization, which is between it and the individual; for globalization suggests uniformity, sameness, even the end of history and, consequently, of all those ideologies and dominant narratives that have been historically powerful in our communities, in our selves (Fukuyama, 1993). What this may usher in, many of us feel, is an acute loss of identity, of distinction, of difference. And difference is crucial to identity work. To mark ourselves as individuals, often literally, is to make a statement about our selves and others. We are saying "This is me, I am identifiable, I am unique; I am someone who can be recognized—recognize me." Globalization appears to threaten this uniqueness that we all desire. So, in an ironic if not perverse way, the individual is now rendered centre stage with globalization. Identity work becomes more serious, more political, more contested, more urgent. As Giddens (1992) suggests,

> the more tradition loses its hold, and the more daily life is reconstituted in terms of the dialectic interplay of the local and the global, the more individuals are forced to negotiate lifestyle choices among a diversity of options. . . . Reflexively organized life-planning . . . becomes a central feature of the structuring of self-identity. (p. 5)

As the world increasingly appears to take on the characteristics of a concrete urban township, swept with migratory pressures, so individuals increasingly seek a place within it that is identifiably theirs. Identity work takes on a very new meaning in the age of globalization, for while we may be faced with all the choices of identity presentation that mass consumerism can muster, we are also forced to resort to such life-planning precisely because our local space feels pressured into nonexistence by global forces.

The multiplicity and contingency already inherent in masculinities and femininities does seem even more destabilized in the age of

globalization. Gender remains the bedrock of our sense of self, but just what is this gender we yearn to hold on to? Just what does it mean to be a man or a woman in the twenty-first century? Of course, we cannot answer such questions with any accuracy, precisely because the diversities and differences that pre-exist in the categories "man" and "woman" preclude doing so. But recent research in this area does present some intriguing observations, as we shall now see.

The Effects of Globalization on Men

Globalization has certainly impacted on men, although in precisely what ways is open to some debate. If we posit globalization as largely emerging from the post-war impetus for technological and economic advancement of the 1950s and through subsequent decades to the present day, we can also see that this period marked the beginnings of profound changes for men in terms of work, employment, education, family, and relationships. As we explore in this section, some researchers suggest that globalization can be linked to a larger male crisis while others argue that globalization actually reinforces male dominance.

First, let us examine the issue of a male crisis. Is it the case that pressures of globalization have rendered men's identity less secure? Certainly, many researchers consider this to be so. For example, feminist writer Susan Faludi (1999) suggests that modern men have lost their sense of manhood over the past few decades. A combination of post-industrialization, the demise of the male-breadwinner family, the feminization of work, challenges to traditional expressions of masculinity, and the success of feminism and the women's movement in putting women's needs at the forefront of political agendas have combined to render men "stiffed": unable to adapt and increasingly able to respond only negatively through depression, social isolation, even suicide (see also, Farrell, 1993; Horrocks, 1994). Such analyses have tended to play well with the media and those politicians concerned to address the "problem of men and boys" from a popularist position, but they fail to explore the differences among men while presenting their case simplistically (see Whitehead, 2002, for discussion).

Sally Robinson, by contrast, makes a persuasive case for recognizing that American expressions of white masculinity, for example, may well be in some state of crisis, while also warning that notions of victimhood and powerlessness in men are as much symbolic as they are real, though no less powerful for that, not least in their ability to "impose a certain narrative logic on an event or, more nebulously, a social trend or cultural formation" (2000, p. 11). In this case, we need to be aware that talking up the idea of a male crisis can render it into the hands of politicians and others as something real that demands popularist action by them.

Pro-feminist theorist Michael Kimmel (1995b, also 2006) also makes the case against notions of contemporary male crisis. He argues that the very essence of masculinity as a socially acceptable expression of being a man is historically imbued with ideas of men in retreat (from women and feminization), of men emasculated, of men in emotional crisis, and of men existentially lost or seeking to prove themselves through various tests of manhood. In this case, the current male crisis thesis is merely a continuation of an age-long discourse about men and their masculinity.

Ultimately, the notion of a masculinity crisis may have some material, physical, and psychological basis for and in many males (Clare, 2000), but it would be a mistake to assume a cohesive link between it and globalization. It would also be wrong to envisage men as a unified, singular group who are all "in crisis," for that is not the case at all. There are as many differences between men as there are between women and men. To be sure, the women's movement and feminism

have presented challenges to men to which men must respond. Attempting to ignore or downplay the issues raised by feminists is not going to help men adapt to the new gender reality now seen to be emerging in many locales worldwide. Such responses by men will be diverse and unpredictable, ranging from active, maybe even violent, resistance to feminism specifically and to women's empowerment generally; psychological retreat and social isolation by some males; and perhaps depression in those unable to accept the absence of a clearly defined, traditional male role underpinned by patriarchal values. Such responses are not confined to the West but are apparent now worldwide (see, for examples, Novikova et al., 2004; Ashwin and Lytkina, 2006). Such developments are clearly reinforced in their negativity by the serious gender gap, in favour of women, now appearing in education across all levels and in many advanced and developing countries (see, for examples, Berliner, 2004; Connolly, 2007; also Chapter 9). At the same time, there is ample evidence to show that many men are indeed welcoming the new, more liberating forms of masculinity now accompanying aspects of globalization and defined in the feminist project (see Whitehead, 2002, 2011; Messner, 1997; Connell, 2005; Anderson, 2011; also Chapter 11).

We must also remember that many men have a vested interest in globalization, in particular in the power and authority they derive from the opportunities it offers them. Bob Connell argues that the condition of globalization requires us to explore large-scale structures in order to better understand the "world gender order" and the "globalizing masculinities" it is promoting through its **hegemonic agencies**: for example, multinational corporations, global finance markets, and such masculinist institutions as feed off or serve to sustain these agencies. For Connell, globalization is not necessarily undermining men's identity work; rather, it is itself being sustained by "the structure of relationships that interconnect the gender regimes of institutions, and the gender orders of local society, on a world scale" (1998, p. 7; also 2006). Connell makes the case that globalization can be seen to be implicated in a hegemonic process of male domination with new forms of global masculinities, including a "transnational business masculinity" (Connell and Wood, 2005), emerging out of the practices of the ". . . flexible, calculative, egocentric masculinity of the fast capitalist entrepreneur" (Connell, 1998, p. 17).

However, in a recent reappraisal of the effects of globalization on gender relations, Connell (2005, p. 1806) takes a more optimistic view, pointing out that since "the issue of gender equality was placed on the policy agenda by women," there has been a global response to such issues, which has brought about not only a wave of critical gender research by both women and men, but has created an impulse for change toward gender justice at all levels: from the national to the institutional, from the cultural to the individual.

hegemonic agencies

The means (whether economic, political, social, or cultural) through which a dominant group is able to sustain and reinforce its position of power within society.

The Effects of Globalization on Women

The relationship between women's identity and globalization is equally complex if not equally contested among theorists and researchers. In broad terms, it can be argued that feminism and the women's movement have actually benefited directly from globalization or, more precisely, from the technologies and systems that now enable diverse women's voices to be heard around the world. However, as we will see in this chapter, globalization can also objectify, control,

and subject women to new and more overpowering forms of domination.

There are many positive effects of globalization on women. For example, the massification of further and higher education is now a worldwide phenomena. This phenomena is directly leading to increasing numbers of women achieving a level of education that enables them in some cases to make clear lifestyle choices, especially in respect of their autonomy from their family and from patriarchal social structures. In addition, worldwide travel and immigration are similarly challenging age-old patriarchal values and cultures as women, especially middle-class women, become exposed to more flexible cultural values in terms of sexuality, motherhood, employment, and relationships. The rise in service-sector industries around the world, moreover, has opened up a new space for women to progress both economically and socially. And finally, the use of the Internet is, itself, directly implicated in the reshaping of social relations, both intimate and casual, worldwide.

At the same time, evidence shows that the economic and social pressures that accompany globalization can have a particularly adverse effect on women's lives. As life becomes more materialistic and competitive, inequalities persist if not strengthen, and inequalities against women and girls are particularly persistent worldwide (see Judd and Harriet, 2007). New forms of inequalities appear as women enter the globalized market forces and as the international workforce becomes more feminized. For example, the concept of "women's multiple roles" is now a familiar one with feminists such as Hochschild (1989, 1997) and Franks (1999) showing how women are often trapped in a situation of having to work the first shift at work, the second at home, in large part due to the economic pressures that accompany global consumerist and work practices. Slavery has a long history, but globalization is now presenting it in a particularly vicious form through the global sexual exploitation and trafficking of women and children (see Malarek, 2004; Baker and Williamson, 2006, for examples). Indeed, many writers argue that the capitalist economic imperative at the heart of globalization is fundamentally exploitative especially of women and of those from certain class backgrounds or racial and ethnic origins (see, for example, Mukherjee, 2004; Veneracion-Rallonza, 2004). Females are more likely to be living with HIV/AIDS than are males. Men's violence toward women continues and, in fact, is increasing in many different locales (see Hearn, 1998), meaning women are certainly no safer in the age of globalization than they were in past times. Indeed, women may be less safe due in part to both the breakdown of civil society in some countries and to the glorification of male-on-female violence often promoted through the global media (see Kimmel, 2006, for examples).

Globalization affects women mainly through the gendered division of labour. Globalized economies rely heavily on the migration of female workers from the less developed nations of the South and East to the global cities situated mainly (but not exclusively) in the North and West. The five main migratory movements are from Eastern to Western Europe; from Mexico and central and South America to the United States; from North Africa to Southern Europe; from South Asia to the Persian Gulf; and from the Philippines to Hong Kong, North America, Europe, and Israel (Zlotnik, 2003; Devi, Widding Isaksen, and Hochschild, 2010). The sectors of the economy that are socially undervalued are the ones that attract female migrants, including the services, the hotel industry, tourism, catering, nursing and health care, as well as small industries, such as textiles (Anderson, 2000).

Many activities are made invisible by the fact that they are not recognized as employment and are instead classified as help or support, as in the examples of domestic helpers, caregivers,

and home helpers (Augustin, 2007). The role of foreign caregivers in the affluent cities of the "Global North" (Sassen, 2007) is to respond to the needs of mainly the professional classes. In Japan, for example, foreign caregivers are a vital form of support for what has been described as a "super aged society" (Ito, 2010). In some cases, as in the case of the Japanese caregivers program or the live-in caregivers programs introduced in Canada in 1992, the "exportation" of foreign workers (who are predominantly female) are organized by states. For example, Indonesia sent about 700,000 migrant workers abroad in 2007, 80 per cent of whom were women. The majority of them found employment as domestic workers in Saudi Arabia, Malaysia, Singapore, Taiwan, and Hong Kong (Hirano as quoted in Ito, 2009).

Most of these women who work as caregivers are usually educated and qualified women who are expected to sacrifice their personal lives, often by leaving their children behind, for the benefit of the community. They are sometimes praised by their communities, but are also at times the curse and envy of those who see them as more successful or who think they have transgressed the cultural gender norms by becoming more autonomous (Devi, Widding Isaksen, and Hochschild, 2010). However, their newly acquired autonomy as breadwinners often hides more painful realities. Cases of abuse by employment agencies and by employers are not uncommon (Fudge, 2011; Chuang, 2010; Ehrenreich and Hochschild, 2004).

Clearly, women's increasing participation in the global economy is having profound effects on the way they construct their agency and their sense of identity. The fact that many have to leave their children behind in the care of a mother or a relative for long periods has led to transformation in the way motherhood is understood. Defying gender norms, in particular the image of the "good mother," can lead to feelings of guilt among women migrants (Anderson 2000; Devi, Widding

Isaksen and Hochschild, 2010). However, these women are also able to navigate across many constructs of womanhood and motherhood at the same time and reconstruct a new "selfhood" (Aguilar 1999). It is more difficult, however, to ascertain the presence of agency when it comes to women working in the sex industry, where the line between autonomy and exploitation is a fine one. Nevertheless, whether they are caregivers or sex workers, the growing number of women who leave the global South to work in the global North represents a vital economic force. They are a valuable source of income for the families they have left at home and a source of relatively cheap labour for the families and individuals who employ them. The states that sometimes organize their migration and the banks that deal with their money transfer also benefit from their work. Yet, to see migrant women workers as primarily victims of economic exploitation would be to consider only one aspect of the ways in which they engage with the complexities of globalization. The increasing participation of women in the global economy will in the future undoubtedly reveal more ways in which gender identities can be renegotiated when women and men move across borders (see, for discussion, Bernstein, 2009; Manderson and Jolly, 1997).

So, as Connell (2005), among others, accurately observes, globalization comes with mixed blessings so far as gender is concerned. It would be unrealistic to wholly condemn it and, similarly, to unreservedly and uncritically welcome it. As academics and researchers into the sociological and psychological dimensions of life, what we must do first is recognize and then try to understand the impact of globalization on our identity and sense of agency in the world.

SUMMARY

The age of globalization is a time of movement, change, technological innovation, and rapid transference of knowledge. Each of us is caught up in this vortex, no matter where we live. Even the most remote communities are touched now by the forces of globalization. All it takes is a computer and Internet access to be connected with billions of people. Globalization is, indeed, humanity's greatest ever social experiment, and it is likely to be some time yet before we can stand back from it all and see the results. But, for sure, gender and sexual identity work is affected heavily in this process. Globalization, probably more than any other single dynamic, is reshaping gender relations and influencing masculinity and femininity, and what it means to be a man or woman, in a multitude of ways. For some this is a moment of great opportunity while for others the effects of globalization are highly disturbing. One way to mitigate the unsettling effects of globalization is by feeling connected to the local, to the immediate, be it our local community or our national identity. But as we have seen in this chapter, even nationhood and place are contested, fluid, and invested with change and mythology.

Similarly, the way we have come to conceptualize "culture" has become heavily invested with ideological and political meanings. Our discussion of multiculturalism and gender has revealed the ways in which fixed notions of culture are sometimes used to create or reinforce existing divisions and social hierarchies between social groups and between genders. Perhaps one of the important challenges of feminism today is to understand and deconstruct the essentialized meanings that have crystallized around the idea of culture, nation, and difference.

Another challenge for those wanting to understand the gendered nature of the world we live in is to assess the impact of globalization on gender identity. Globalization and all that comes with it have not removed ethnic conflict and racial discrimination. Nor has globalization empowered all women in all countries. So while we can say that the age of globalization has brought change and movement, challenging the traditional and culturally fixed, opening up opportunities for billions, both women and men, globalization has failed to remove inequality. Indeed, in many instances it has heightened it.

And, as we now explore in the next chapter, into this political turbulence surrounding our gender identity, we can add some other potent ingredients: religion and sexuality.

CASE STUDY

Tina and her Malay boyfriend enter the Italian restaurant in Kuala Lumpur. While watching the Malay dancers performing, they order two Australian fillet steaks with French fries. They chat about her work as an English teacher in the Canadian university that has a franchise in the city and about his work as a businessperson in one of the thriving international business corporations. Tina is Canadian, born in Toronto. She has travelled around the world and, after graduating, has worked as an international volunteer in Brazil and Botswana. She has a degree in English and a teaching qualification. Three years ago, aged 27, she took the teaching job in Kuala Lumpur. Apart from English, Tina also speaks French, Italian, and a little Mandarin. She is currently doing a semi-distance learning British MBA in Education through a university in Thailand.

When Tina and her boyfriend talk about their future together, they do consider that perhaps they would like to settle down, perhaps even get married, although both know that their lifestyles make it difficult to make plans. He is only in Kuala Lumpur for a limited time as his company is thinking of relocating him in Singapore in the near future.

Tina's parents are quite traditional; they are strongly Catholic and talk about steady relationships and having a settled lifestyle, which for them means marriage, children, and permanence. Tina loves the freedom that comes with living abroad in a foreign

country, sampling different cultures, meeting new people. She has no desire to have children. She still sees herself as Catholic but "non-practising." Her boyfriend was born into a Muslim family, and, like Tina, sees himself as "non-practising."

Tina's boyfriend senses that Tina has other aspects to her character, but doesn't question too much. In fact, Tina has been having a relationship with one of her students for some months now. This student is a woman, aged 19. Tina finds that this relationship gives her a different type of satisfaction and fulfilment than the one she has with her boyfriend. Her girlfriend is Chinese, born in Malaysia, and from a Buddhist family. Tina and her girlfriend have to be careful when they are out and around Kuala Lumpur, although most observers would not imagine them to be lovers.

Tina tries not to think too much about her future—there are so many options open to her. But one option she is not considering is returning home to live the sort of female identity expected of her by her family and their traditional culture.

DISCUSSION QUESTIONS

1. What do you consider to be the main influences on Tina's gender identity: place/nationhood, culture, or globalization?

2. In what ways is Tina challenging her parents' traditional culture and value system?

3. How is Tina exercising power in this glo-
    balized lifestyle of hers, and how is glo-
    balization determining her lifestyle?
4. What knowledge does Tina have, and
    what skills has Tina developed in order to
    access opportunities in globalization?

5. In which ways does Tina's socio-economic
    background impact her sense of agency
    in the globalized world?

QUESTIONS FOR REVIEW AND DISCUSSION

1. To what extent is place important in your
    own sense of gender identity, and why?
2. How might national identity be seen, his-
    torically, as being more about the reinforce-
    ment of male identity rather than of female
    identity?
3. What does "culture" mean for you?
4. What are the main critiques of multicultur-
    alism when it comes to gender issues?

5. Make a list of those groups of people whom
    you think would be least likely to be con-
    nected to globalization—and give your
    reasons.
6. How is globalization having a different effect
    on the gender identities of women and men
    (give examples)?

Chapter 5

Contradictory Discourses: Religion and Spirituality, Sex and Sexuality

▲ Religions sometimes have a problem with difference.
Source: © Michael Dwyer/Alamy

Learning Objectives

At the end of this chapter you will be able to:

- Appreciate the power of religion to inform gender identity.
- Explore the gendered character of religion.
- Differentiate between religion and spiritual belief.
- Recognize the intersectionality of sex, gender, and sexuality.
- Recognize the non-biological character of sex and sexuality.
- Understand issues around LGBT identities and rights.
- Appreciate the plurality of sexual identities.
- Connect religious ideologies with traditional gender and sexual values.

OVERVIEW

This chapter examines two important and contradictory discourses of the twenty-first century—religion and sexuality—and how they inform gender. We have chosen to explore these two topics together in order to highlight some of the tensions that lie at the heart of our postmodern and diverse society. Historically speaking, religion and sexuality have never sat together comfortably. In today's world, they still represent antagonistic forces, as is demonstrated by debates on, for example, contraception, abortion, and same-sex marriages. A large part of the resistance to the idea of sexual diversity, sexual freedom, same-sex relationships, and transgender originates from religious arguments. As we will discuss, although religions in today's world are changing, they still support dominant patriarchal structures that are responsible for maintaining social structures based on hegemonic definitions of not only couples and families, but also nations, ethnic groups, and communities. However, religion needs to be differentiated from the less ideological and more private notion of spirituality. As we will discuss, to think in terms of spirituality rather

than religion can allow us to rethink the relationships between the private and the public selves engaged in the act of understanding the meaning of our existence. Sex and sexualities is also a domain that combines the private and the public aspects of our selves. While they might appear to be private and individual matters, they are invested with political agendas that often rely on male/female gender binaries that perpetuate ideological forms of social control. However, as we discussed in our section on queer theory (Chapter 3), the emergence of subversive sexualities have destabilized traditional notions of who we are and opened up the possibility freer forms of sexual expression, especially for women. Today, it is difficult to address the questions of sex and sexualities without referring to the growing body of writing on intersexed, bi-gendered, and transgendered identities. All these forms of gender and sexualities are part of who we are in the twenty-first century. As we will see, these new discourses are particularly important because they contribute to moving our thinking toward a more plural and less dichotomous way of understanding our identities.

HOW RELIGION AND SPIRITUAL BELIEF INFORM OUR SENSE OF IDENTITY

As we discussed in Chapter 2, by the late 1990s many sociologists were turning to the concept of postmodernity to understand not just social changes in the West but worldwide. They drew on postmodernist theory to explain why those ideologies that sustained modernism appeared much less credible at the end of the twentieth century. The world was seen as becoming more fragmented, diverse, contingent, and discontinuous,

and the belief systems of the twentieth century were no longer holding true in the way they used to (Harvey, 1991; Lyotard, 1985).

Meta-narratives, or ideologies, can exist and arise anywhere and in any organizational and social setting, but they are especially visible in religion. Religious ideologies have, through history, been the most enduring, the most persuasive, and arguably the most powerful in terms of informing our identity and sense of belonging (Daly, 1985; also Althusser, 2000; Giddens, 1992; Nawal El Saadawi, 1997). Political and social ideologies such as Marxism, socialism, imperialism, monarchism, and nationalism may not have entirely disappeared, but they no longer play to such a wide and dutiful audience. And postmodernism suggests a similar demise in respect of religion (Harvey, 1991).

Indeed, the world is becoming **secular**, that is, most societies are now organized around economic not religious imperatives, and those religions that exist do so as part of a community of religions, each expected to recognize and pay respect to the others. The diversity and difference that gets celebrated in the postmodern age matches well the pursuit of (materialistic) individualism, which is fundamental to and sustains globalization. One can realistically speculate that, across the world, most people now spend much more of their non-work time in shopping malls or on the Internet than in synagogues, temples, churches, or mosques.

On the other hand, since the beginning of this century religion has shown yet again just how ideologically powerful and discursively conditioning it is; that is, religion continues to carry powerful markers of identity for millions of people, notably through specific language, text, and teaching. Certainly the demise of religion has not happened, at least not to the extent predicted by theorists such as Marx, Weber, and Durkheim (see Table 5.1). If anything, there is a "resurgence of religious belief and conviction" (Giddens, 1992) at least in some cultures and communities. Whether it is within Christianity, Hinduism, Islam, or Judaism, a minority radical fundamentalism has emerged that clearly has the aim of re-enforcing religious orthodoxy; such fundamentalism has been accompanied by an increasing intolerance of difference and critique. In the US, the last two decades of the twentieth century witnessed the emergence of the "megachurch" in American Protestant religion, attracting an average of at least 2000 attendees per week. Most of these megachurches are associated with evangelical and

secular
Not bound by religious rule.

conservative Protestant denominations, with only 10 per cent being affiliated with one of the mainline denominations (Ellingson, 2008).

What is emerging is a polarization of religious belief in many developed countries, including Canada, where a third of the population

TABLE 5.1   National Attitudes Toward Religion

Question: "Is religion very important to you personally?"	
Percentage that answer Yes:	
US	59
Canada	30
Russia	14
Pakistan	91
Brazil	77
Mexico	57
Japan	12
Spain	18
Korea	25
Nigeria	92
Kenya	85
S. Africa	87
Philippines	88
India	92
France	11
Britain	18
Italy	27
Germany	21

Note 1: Questions on the personal importance of religion were not permitted in China and considered too sensitive to ask in Egypt, Jordan, and Lebanon.

Note 2: The global survey showed that wealthier nations tend to place less importance on religion—with the exception of the United States.

Source: 2002 and 2007 Pew Global Attitudes Project (www.pewglobal.org).

Religion shows itself to be resilient in some countries but much less so in others.

avidly follow a religious belief, a third do not, and a third constitute the "ambivalent middle," that is, they claim some religious association but do not practise it (Bibby, 2011).

The aim of this section is not to place a judgment or value on any religious claim; we will leave that to others. Our concern is, first, to try to understand how the promotion of religious discourse or ideology undermines and/or reinforces our pursuit of (gender) identity; and second, to suggest that the tension between modernism and postmodernism, and now played out in some religions, reflects our continuing desire for a spiritually informed **ontology** of the self.

ontology

A branch of philosophy that deals with matters pertaining to being and existence.

Religion and the Self

Both radical and moderate proponents of all religions make the same claim: the claim to truth, the claim to certainty. Major religions, or "world faiths" (King, 2006), do not thrive merely by spreading doubt but by offering to alleviate it. They exist precisely in order to promote particular ideologies and dominant discourses, invariably cultivated around specific historical

contingency

The notion that human experience depends on particular circumstances and contexts that affect its meaning.

agnosticism

A philosophical doctrine that claims that knowing the answer to any particular question with absolute certainty is unattainable. The term also refers to the belief that it is not possible to know whether there is god or whether there is no god.

texts. Their aim is to inform, if not shape, minds, behaviours, and self-identity. In that respect, most religions would seem to be in complete opposition to the fundamental condition apparent in this postmodern age: the condition of **contingency** and the overwhelming evidence of global difference and diversity that accompanies the postmodern age and arises from it. Some consider the only major faith that has contingency at its heart is Buddhism, which is one reason, perhaps, why it is spreading so rapidly from the East to the West; with over 1.5 million adherents, Buddhism is now America's fourth largest religion (Lampman, 2006). Buddhism sits in a unique position between the gods of modernism on the one hand, and the **agnosticism** promoted by a consumerist-driven global economy on the other (Pfeil, 2000; Norberg-Hodge, 2000; also Cupitt, 1985).

Some people have also adapted religious faith to the multiple and diverse realities of our world by combining different religions into one faith. For example, Jewish Buddhism has many followers in the world, including the acclaimed Canadian singer, poet, and writer Leonard Cohen. Such religious **syncretism** is not new; its history is in fact almost as long as the history of religions. For example, historians have recorded that it was not uncommon to see some Jewish communities in eight-century North Africa practise syncretic forms of Judaism that incorporated Islamic practices (Stora, 2006). Today, religious syncretism is common in places that have historically drawn people from diverse religious backgrounds, such as the Caribbean and parts of Africa. In our global cities, religions are still regarded as a distinct feature pertaining to differentiated groups. However, with the growing trend of relationships and marriages between people from different cultures and religions, practising more than one form of religious belief or ritual will become more common.

If religions can be stretched to accommodate the global and diverse world we live in, they are nevertheless not gender neutral, as they are mostly devised and led by men. Although some religions have allowed female priests to perform ritual practices, religions generally promote male, not female, authority. As such they exist in a masculinist paradigm that, at the very least, serves to render the female as separate and, at the very worst, to render the female as "unclean" and inferior in every respect (Daly, 1985; see, for overview, Meade and Wiesner-Hanks, 2006; Ferree, Lorber, and Hess, 1999; Seidler, 1994). So the project of religion could be argued as being much more than simply the promotion of dominant discourses of "truth" about, for example, morality; religions are also implicated in a larger hegemonic project that seeks to elevate men socially, politically, and economically. Consequently, in religious discourse, women's and men's identities are already considered given. That is, gender identities are understood to be rooted in a stable, unchangeable gender binary, itself informed by a conservative understanding of embodied gender difference. This discourse seeks to maintain a gender power status quo over time, through history, consistently and in resistance to wider political, social, and economical transformations, especially those that might lead to the personal and political empowerment of women.

In other words, religions have already decided on what constitutes the gender and sexual identities of men and women; such identities are embedded for all time and for all to access in their respective scriptures. Those who read, learn, believe, and promote such readings are, willingly or not, co-opted into a larger hegemonic project around gender power. From this, many feminists argue that religions are fundamentally patriarchal and, indeed, that they exist not so much to provide spiritual succour to the needy but to "validate" a patriarchal condition

syncretism

The process of combining beliefs or practices from distinct schools of thought or religious traditions.

that oppresses women and reinforces their economic, social, and individual marginalization across all spheres of society and to the material benefit of men (Daly, 1985). As Kate Millett argues, one of the devices used to exercise this power over women is to position the female as sexually "impure" and in need of protection from her own innate desires, with men similarly requiring protection from the impurity that is inherent in women's sexual being:

> Patriarchy has God on its side. One of its most effective agents of control is the powerfully expeditious character of its doctrines as to the nature and origin of the female and the attribution to her alone of the dangers and evils it imputes to sexuality.... Patriarchal religion and ethics tend to lump the female and sex together as if the whole burden of the onus and stigma it attaches to sex were the fault of the female alone.... This mythical version of the female as the cause of human suffering, knowledge, and sin is still the foundation of sexual attitudes, for it represents the most crucial argument of the patriarchal tradition in the West. (Millett, 2005, pp. 51–2)

So while female identity is pre-presumed and promoted by religion to be "other," alien, and shameful, by contrast men are offered a powerful vehicle for the enforcement of male privilege and power. Men's gender identity within religious discourse validates a traditional understanding of masculinity and maleness as being strong, rational, consistent, authoritarian, and pure of heart so long as men resist the temptations posited by the female. Indeed, men as a gender group are seen as being nearer to God, closer to reason, which is why most religions have historically offered men the opportunity to be leaders (see, for discussion Cadge, 2005a, 2005b). It is little wonder, then, that many consider the rise in religious fundamentalism to be a direct attempt by men to "stall the gender revolution," which is itself considered largely a consequence of globalization and the postmodern age (Hutton and Giddens, 2000, p. 27).

However, as we have discussed in Chapter 2, power is never simply one way; there are always mediations, counter-forces, resistances. It would be a mistake to take Millett's persuasive argument as evidence of an unchanging, unchangeable, patriarchal condition. Naomi Sakr offers evidence of change in respect of Iran: under pressure from the spreading women's movement, Ayatollah Khamenei, the arch-conservative leader of the Islamic Republic, was forced to say that Islam rejects any differences between men and women in their "development of the spirit and intellect, and also in the field of social activity" (Sakr, 2004, p. 20). Many Muslim women in America are especially active and organized in challenging Muslim stereotypes in the wider community and in resisting gender traditions within Islam, for example, by promoting and leading mixed-gender gatherings for the *jum'ah* or Friday prayer (Haddad, Smith, and Moore, 2006).

The notion of a Muslim feminist might appear an oxymoron to many people in the West, especially given the heightened visibility of radical Islamism post-9/11, yet there is no doubt that increasing numbers of women, and men, around the world have adopted this personal/political identity. For example, the emergence of Islamic feminism, Muslim feminism, and secular feminism in the Middle East and elsewhere is evidence of the globalizing power and potential of the (pro)feminist discourse (see, for example, Karam, 1998; Eisenstein, 2004; Ahmed, 1998; Sakr, 2004). Similarly, we can see how critical discussions

of men and masculinities, inspired by feminism, now engage with numerous cultural and geographic sites worldwide (see, for example, Lenz et al., 2007; Ouzgane, 2006a; Whitehead, 2006a). Such identity-informing discourses of gender and (pro)feminism are apparent not only within Islam (Gerami, 2006; Ouzgane, 2006a; Talhami, 1996), but also in Buddhism (Cadge, 2004; Banks Findly, 2000; Gross, 1993), Christianity (Schneiders, 2004; Russell, 1993), Judaism (Kaplan and Ben-Ari, 2006; Misra and Rich, 2003), Mormonism (Mihelich and Storrs, 2003), and Hinduism (Robinson, 1999). (For an overview, see also Armstrong, Haddad, and Esposito, 2002; Sharma and Young, 1998).

So it is simplistic and reductionist to claim that religions unilaterally and irrevocably impose their ideologies of conservative gender identity upon the passive consciousnesses of the masses. Many millions of women draw on their respective religion for support, for validation, and for a sense of gender identity. But this does not mean they are all blind to the inequalities within their religion. Indeed, the writers identified above are just some of those who draw on the theoretical and intellectual basis of their respective religions precisely in order to attack male privilege and misogynistic practices, using for, example, the Quran, "to show that the discourse of equality between men and women *is* valid, with Islam" (Karam, 1998, p. 11, original emphasis).

Women's relationship with patriarchal-based religions is never going to be easy so long as such religions continue to promote a particular masculinist discourse. But this does not mean that women cannot elicit a strong sense of gender identity from religions, whichever they may be. Indeed, one could argue that feminist postmodernism has offered precisely the conditions and platform for women activists in, for example, Muslim, Hindu, Catholic, and Buddhist countries to voice their presence and political aims, and far beyond the privileged confines of the more secular West. This was the hope raised by Linda Nicholson in her case for a feminist postmodernism:

> In general, postmodern-feminist theory would be pragmatic and fallibilistic. It would tailor its methods and categories to the specific task in hand, using multiple categories when appropriate and forswearing the metaphysical comfort of a single feminist method or feminist epistemology. (1999, p. 114)

Despite many theoretical differences, feminists such as Millett, Sakr, Kamar, and Nicholson are not so far apart politically. They each point to evidence of a patriarchal condition within religion. But they also provide evidence to show that gender identity is never simply and irrevocably the imposed condition of a patriarchal ideology devised and promoted by men for the benefit of men.

At the same time, religion continues to speak to and of men in the context of privileged male power, and we can expect many men to continue to resist, often violently, women's potential emancipation within a religious paradigm and cultural setting. Religion offers men, especially those men who might otherwise experience social, economic, and political marginalization, a powerful means for self-validation, purposeful action, and self/social elevation. In addition, religion is often used to reinforce relationships of power between men and women as well as between adults and children, especially in those religious groups led by charismatic men (Martin, Zablocki, and Van Gunten, 2012). Cases of child abuse and violence against women committed in the name of religion are a clear indication that religion continues to reinforce a traditional, reactionary, and at times violent model of masculinity. Still, many people are reluctant to turn away from such a model, which they find comforting and secure in a world that is increasingly neither of these.

Spirituality and the Self

We might define religion as the social organization and cultural expression of our inner spiritual quest. That spiritual quest is a yearning for something better, something stronger, something more permanent than we are, a protective, potentially benign and beneficial force for moral closure and certitude within our lives. In order to achieve this, religions aim to provide us with a clearly defined truth system reinforced through ideological and/or discursive systems, invariably enforced through hegemonic conditions and associated prohibitions. As we have explored above, it is not too difficult to deconstruct such belief systems and critique their powerful, sometimes oppressive effects upon states, communities, and individuals. And in this respect, all religions are complicit in a hegemonic contest. They are searching, if not competing, for souls or, at the very least, for the identities of those who would worship. For only through such enlisting of the self, the individual, can religion be sustained. The belief systems must be believed; otherwise they are absolutely and forever reduced to the incredible, the unbelievable, the forgotten, and the powerless, in which case they will eventually be consigned to history.

Religions may change—some may even go out of fashion—but the overall power of religion and the answer as to why it continues to carry so much sway over individuals is contained both in the social and the ontological. That is, many cultures, if not societies and states, are enabled and sustained through religion. They only exist in the way they do because of the larger religious identities that underpin them; for example, would, could Israel and Iran exist without Judaism and Islam, respectively? To be born an Israeli or an Iranian, while itself not guaranteeing membership of a religion, is likely to do precisely that for most of us. Most people are "born a religion" rather than intellectually and rationally selecting one. But there is a force at work here beyond the socially and culturally explicit, and at this point we are into the spiritual realm.

Spirituality refers directly and irrefutably to the **metaphysical** world, that is, it transcends science, logic, rationality, evidence, intellectual critique. Spirituality is a sense, a feeling, an intuition. It can never be more or less than that. But can we trust it? The answer is that we do not have to; we just have to suspend disbelief and our desire for knowing and knowledge. At that point, trust is not the issue, for our sense and intuition of "something outside this world, beyond us" and contained within our subjectivity is all we have and all we need.

metaphysical

Relates to matters or preoccupations that are outside everyday human experience, such as the meaning of existence, the nature of reality, or the existence of a god.

We might even go so far as to consider that God is not spiritual, but is "a humanly constructed ideal" (Cupitt, 1986, p. 270) and, therefore, enlisted into the religious manifestos and hegemonic project of religious discourse. So the spiritual is not necessarily a belief in God or in any religious deity. On the contrary, the spiritual could be said to go much deeper than religion itself and into our very ontological sense of being in the world. The ontological quest, that is, a search for a sense of continuity and being in the world, is common across humanity and across cultures. Yet whatever one's theoretical premise and position on identity as a concept, it appears evident that identity exists in a world that is neither secure nor linear. But religion itself is subject to such forces of unpredictable change that it, too, succumbs over time to cultural transformations and new imperatives.

So what have we left? What else, if not religion, can we rely upon in order to alleviate the existential questions that continue to haunt us?

Some people have used philosophical ways of addressing the question of human existence. For example, existentialist philosophers such as Jean-Paul Sartre and Albert Camus have attempted to replace the idea of God with that of an individual capable of exercising agency and giving some meaning to his/her existence.

Still, for the majority of people, religion and spirituality continue to be a significant aspect of identity. Just so long as we accept the premise, or even the remotest possibility, of a metaphysical world, then our spiritual yearnings can be met. They can ameliorate the otherwise overpowering fear of the emptiness and vacancy that we, as embodied, physically impermanent individuals, otherwise exist within (Giddens, 1991). For this reason, if no other, it is difficult to envisage a conclusion to the spiritual quest within humanity. Whatever the rise or demise of individual religions, whatever the fundamentalist turn of an epoch, or the pressing of the globalization agenda, the spiritual will likely remain. To be sure, this spiritual quest may appear unorthodox if not bizarre to those who do not share it, and many may consider it a delusion, corrupted by ideology and reduced to insignificance by the lack of evidence to prove its existence (see, for example, Dawkins, 2007). For others, however, their spiritual quest remains sufficient in itself in providing an ontological anchor within a world riven by insecurities, impermanence, and unpredictable if not often incomprehensible events.

These questions remain, however: Can the spiritual provide an alternative to a dominant gender discourse or ideology? Can the spiritual even be a (meta)physical place of resistance to those masculinist ideologies that have through history corrupted the major religions? The answers to these questions are unclear, for the spiritual, by its very essence, can be anything we, as individuals, choose it to be. It is only ever, and no more, an expression of our senses and feelings. But these intuitions cannot be said to be in any way pure and uncorrupted by the social. Our imaginings arise from our knowledge, and our knowledge, like our subjectivity, arises from that which we have come into contact with. We, the "I," are no more sovereign for having achieved some sense of satisfaction in terms of our spiritual quest. As Lacan puts it, "it is the world of words that creates the world of things" (Lacan, 1989, p. 66; see also Meredith, 2005). And if we have to name and describe our spirituality, then we can only do so through language.

So we should recognize the power of the spiritual to reside in its ability to speak directly to the individual in a highly personal way, and, therefore, in its capacity to alleviate the existential anxieties and ontological questions that configure all identity work. In other words, the sense of the spiritual is precious to each person and it is enough that the individual trusts his or her sense of it. The spiritual provides emotional comfort, psychological security, and a strong sense that there is more to this life than we can merely see around us.

What the spiritual cannot do is resolve the epistemological dilemmas and contestations that inevitably arise from a world made real only through language, through symbols, and through text. In a world that is speeded up, discontinuous, fragmented, multiple, and disturbing if not threatening, the spiritual is arguably a place we can retreat to, although it is no less gendered for that.

To conclude this section, it seems that the particularity of religion and spirituality is that they engage both the personal and the political aspects of our experiences. Religion does so collectively, while spirituality appeals more to our individual sense of subjectivity. Similarly, sex and sexuality are experiences that we consider as part of our private lives. However, as we will see in the next section, they are also highly invested with ideological and political meanings. In that respect, sex and sexualities, like religion and spirituality, are private and individual experiences that also belong to the realm of collective constructions of identity.

The spiritual and the sexual also co-exist within us.
Source: © Paul Patterson

INTERSECTING SEX, SEXUALITY, AND GENDER?

Whatever our sense of being a gendered individual, it comes heavily laden with ideas and attitudes around sex and sexuality. We may try to separate our sex from our sexuality and our gender from both, but ultimately it is impossible. These three constructs intersect and configure our consciousness and subconscious in powerful and subtle ways. They form a compelling political matrix within us, one that never entirely disappears and always, therefore, influences our subjectivity, practices, social performance, and sense of self. We are never simply gendered; we are always something more in terms of having a sexuality, existing within a male and female binary, and expressing our selves through normative codes of masculinity and femininity. Yet much of the theorizing of sex, sexuality, and gender has positioned them as separate variables with discrete attributes. Psychologists have tended to view sex and gender especially as part of an unchanging dichotomy; the normative alignment that configures them and the sexualities that arise from them are not so much understood as socially given ideologies or discourses, but assumed to be deep, natural roots that nourish and ground our very personhood through a biologically fixed process (see Valocchi, 2005, for discussion).

However, contemporary sociological and psychoanalytical theories critically question these binaries; by applying contemporary empirical research and theory, such binaries are taken apart, dissected, and revealed not as biological givens, but exposed as socially mediated discourses. Queer theory (see Chapter 3), for example, deconstructs sex, sexuality, and gender, by showing how individuals can and do enact gender performances outside of traditional ideas of what it means to be a man or a woman (see Bettie, 2003; Rupp and Taylor, 2003; Schippers, 2000; Seidman, 2003).

Intersectionality theory, discussed in Chapter 3, in respect of race is also useful for understanding how gender, sex, and sexuality are relational concepts and practices, for example, in the way that female gender is seen by society to relate to and thereby inform particular sex acts and female sexuality (for overview, see Phoenix, 2006; Yuvall-Davis, 2006; Brah and Phoenix, 2004). This relationality is, as we have emphasized, neither predictable nor tidy. It is messy in that it always gets expressed as identity but within particular powerful matrixes. One such matrix concerns normative heterosexuality, or as Rich (1983) puts it, "compulsory heterosexuality" (see also Connell, 1995, for discussion). In this respect, whatever our gender or sex identity as male or female, many societies consider it deviant to express this other than as straight sex/sexuality. The social codes that privilege compulsory heterosexuality are reinforced often by state legislation that explicitly labels gay sex as illegitimate and therefore criminal (Tepperman, 2009). However, as Table 5.2 indicates, there appears to be a global trend toward greater acceptance of sexual difference.

From a sociological position, sex and sex characteristics (primary and secondary sex features of male and female bodies) provide a template from which we can get a deeper understanding of the social and ideological workings of society. History and culture engrave their representations and interpretations on the individual's subjectivity. This is not a biological process but a social one and nowhere is such history and culture more powerful and persuasive than when it emerges out of the sex/sexuality/gender matrix. A subject's sense of self may well takes its cue from the anatomical construction of the body, but this should not be understood exclusively in terms of a biological impulse. Nor is it the case that individuals are "passive dupes of socialization" (Pattman, 2005, p. 498) inasmuch as they blindly follow

TABLE 5.2   Becoming More Tolerant?

Question: "Should homosexuality be accepted?"

Percentage that answer Yes (by country):

	2002	2007	2011
US	51	49	60
France	77	83	86
Britain	74	71	81
Germany	83	81	87
Spain	—	82	91

Source: 2001, 2007, and 2011 Pew Global Attitudes Surveys (www.pewglobal.org).
Homosexuality gathers greater acceptance and tolerance.

the "sex roles" that society offers to them (see Connell, 1987, for discussion). We, our identities, are always more than a predictable outcome of either biology or society.

The work of Judith Butler, which we explore in depth in Chapters 2 and 3, has been arguably the most influential in terms of helping us recognize how gender, sex, and sexuality are inseparable as discursive practices (Butler, 1990). Butler's concept of the discursively constituted gendered subject, arising out of the multiple, fluid, political arenas that surround the sexed body, enables us to discount both biological and socially constructed ideological inevitabilities. Rather, sex, sexuality, and gender can be understood as part of the performative actions of an ungrounded discursive subject, one that is in search of ontological grounding through social association. From this perspective, the subsequent practices of gender signification that we all engage in draw heavily on historic and culturally specific discourses of sex and sexuality in order to legitimize themselves, and us, as ontologically grounded individuals.

Recognizing the complexities of sex, sexuality, and gender identity allows us to reject sex and sexual stereotypes and instead understand more fully the relationship between the body, sex, sexual orientation, and gender identity. For example, the transgendered, bigendered, transsexual, or sex/gender-different person creates a complex gender identity matrix within which old gender categories collapse and new ones are constructed and reconstructed. Indeed, as we argue in this book, the simple binary modalities of sex, gender, and sexuality are becoming less and less relevant to the gendered realities of contemporary everyday life (Cahill, 1998). The sex categories of male and female are undoubtedly deeply embedded in specific social and cultural practices of what it is to be male or female, but no individual is born with a gendered sense of femininity or masculinity. These have to be learned.

Understanding Multiple Possibilities of Identity: Intersexed, Bigendered, and Transgendered

Outside of academia, gender roles and identities tend to be correlated with sex differences; i.e., masculinity is significantly more likely to be the gender identification endorsed by a male, while femininity is significantly more likely to be the gender identification endorsed by a female (see Uzzell and Horne, 2006). Although there is a general consensus among scholars that gender is socially constructed, too often they have relied on sex as its initiating point (Dozier, 2005), thus limiting the myriad possibilities for a more complex and dynamic permutation of sex, sexuality, gender, and desire. Throughout this book we have shown that in reflecting on both the theories and the practices of gender it is critical to understand the multiple notions of identity and the intersections and interconnections between the various aspects of a person's sense of self. Such multiplicities are especially apparent when we explore the complexities of intersexed, bigendered, and transgendered identities (see, also Kaufmann, 2010).

In relation to sex, sexuality, and gender identity, we are fortunate to have plenty of literature on lesbian, gay, bisexual, **transgendered**, **transsexual**, intersexed, and **sex-reassigned** people, as well as an excellent canon of work on femininity and masculinity. While this literature problematizes the polarized and dichotomous way in which we have theorized and researched sex, sexuality, and gender, it has also engaged us with new visions of identity development and creative performances of the self.

Dozier (2005), for example, attempts to clarify the relationship between sex, gender, and sexual orientation through interviews with transsexual and transgendered people, who are in a unique position of experiencing social interaction as both women and men. Dozier shows how the social expression of a gender relies on the behaviour and appearance of the performer as male or female:

> Doing gender, then, does not simply involve performing appropriate masculinity or femininity

transgendered

A general term that describes individuals who experience their gender identity as being different from what society expects from their current physical sex characteristics.

transsexual

Describes individuals who desire to adopt the opposite sex from the one they were born with. The term also refers to persons having undergone surgical procedures (sex reassignment surgery) and/or hormone therapy.

sex-reassigned

Describes people having undergone sex reassignment surgery.

based on sex category. Doing gender involves a balance of both doing sex and performing masculinity and femininity. When there is no confusion or ambiguity in the sex performance, individuals are able to have more diverse expressions of masculinity and femininity. This balance between behavior and appearance in expressing gender helps explain the changing behavior of FTMs [female-to-male transgendered people] as they transition as well as the presence of men and women with a diversity of gendered behaviors and display. (2005, p. 314)

Another way of describing this process is that individuals are "trying on" gender and sexuality, almost by way of experimentation (Williams, 2009). While individuals are not totally free to engage in *any* sexual practice or gender performance, not least because of the prohibitions that might operate in their society and culture, as people mature and age they are more likely to experiment sexually and in terms of their gender identity. Practices and performances they may not have considered as teenagers become more acceptable to them as they age. All this reinforces the understanding that sex, gender, and sexuality are intersectional identities that relate strongly to each other within an individual's identity but that are not fixed or predictable. In this case, what is considered normal in society, in terms of sex and sexuality, becomes open to question and maybe only for the individual to decide. However, as Table 5.3 shows, LGBT (lesbian, gay, bisexual, and transgendered) rights continue to be a politically sensitive and contested issue for many "developed" countries.

Perhaps the most powerful examples of how intersexed individuals can become part of the "normality" of society is in Southeast Asia. In Thailand, *kathoey* (euphemistically referred to as "ladyboys") are highly visible and not solely confined to the margins of society. Research

TABLE 5.3   Comparison of LGBT Rights in Canada, US (across all states), UK, Brazil, China and Japan

	Canada	US	UK	Brazil	China	Japan
Same-sex sexual activity legal	yes	yes	yes	yes	yes	yes
Equal age of consent	yes	no	yes	yes	yes	yes
Anti-discrimination employment laws	yes	no	yes	yes	yes	no
Same-sex marriage allowed	yes	no	yes	yes	no	no
Right to legal gender change	yes	no	yes	yes	yes	yes
Access to IVF for lesbians	yes	yes	yes	yes	yes	yes
Adoption by same-sex couples	yes	no	yes	yes	no	no

Equality continues to be unequally spread across countries.

by Jackson, for example (Jackson, 2004; also Jackson and Sullivan, 2000; 2001), reveals that one of the reasons for this is that in Southeast Asia the gender binary does not operate in such a powerful and compelling way as it does in the West. In other words, there is less attachment to the idea of polarization in terms of straight–gay, male–female. The consequences of this are interesting for understanding gender identity and sexuality.

For example, it is only recently that the term *gay* became more common in Southeast Asia as a way of describing MSM: "men who have sex with men." For many Asians, *gay* is not appropriate because MSM may be straight or gay. The fact of the sex act does not immediately confer on Thai or Southeast Asian men the label "gay." Likewise, the *kathoey* of Thailand indicate the existence of a "third sex," one that while receiving some approbation from elements of Thai society is much more readily accepted than it would be in, say, many European countries (Morris, 1994).

This is not to say that Thailand and other parts of Asia are some mythical gay paradise but that there is a high degree of tolerance toward different, indeed alternative, expressions of sex and sexuality, and gender identity

(Jackson, 2004; also Sinnott, 2004). One of the key reasons for this is that many parts of Southeast Asian culture, especially Thailand, have developed outside exposure to the normative assumptions around homosexuality and gender binaries that now configure Western thought. So we need to be careful when looking at gender identity and sexuality, and to avoid, if we can, falling into a monocultural gaze. That is, we can too readily assume that the modes of thinking that permeate the society we may have been raised in are equally operative and accepted elsewhere in the world.

According to Cahill (1998), many of the issues about the construction of gender identity for transgendered people parallel the social control issues that have historically been faced by women/girls and men who are perceived as effeminate. The transgendered and bigendered person breaks the perception of a presumed relationship between corporeal form, attributed/birth-assigned sex, and social performance. Indeed, if we add the dimensions of desire and age/life stages to the sex-gender-sexuality constellation, we begin to see the complexity, fluidity, and sexual creativity of gender identity. But first let us consider the constellations of sex, sexuality, and gender.

Understanding the Complexity of the Sex-Sexuality-Gender Constellation

Sex, gender, and sexuality can be understood as constituted in **constellations**—sex-gender-sexuality (Youdell, 2005), or as a **conflation**—sex/gender/sexuality (Carr, 2005). Therefore, they are neither causal nor linear in the way they interact and interrelate with each other. For example, in the expression and practices of individuals' sexual orientations and gender performances, the permutations of the sex-gender-sexuality constellation are much more complex than early research into these concepts suggested. For example, Deborah Youdell (2005) explored the relationships between sex, gender, and sexuality through an ethnographic study of girls, aged 15 to 16, in a South London secondary school. In this study, students' day-to-day practices of sex, sexuality, and gender (including bodily deportment, physical games, linguistic accounts, and uses of clothing, hairstyles, and accessories) were examined to show how they were the cause of the discursive constitution of students' subjectivities. While Youdell's study found that schools are crucial contributors in constructing gendered and sexual subjects, just as many other researchers have found (see Castro-Vázquez and Kishi, 2003; Renolds, 2000, Walkerdine, 1990; Segal, 2001), Youdell's study demonstrated the complexity of the sex-gender-sexuality constellation. This complexity, in turn, opens up possibilities for shifting our thinking beyond the linear paradigms of gender, culture, class, and age as intersections of gender identity. For example, in Youdell's study, some of the girls deployed

> a sophisticated sexuality/identity politics inclusive of gay, lesbian, bisexual, . . . queer . . . "real" hetero-femininity to impose a categorical frame and short circuit the performances excess of these practices. Refusing categorization might leave any sex-gender-sexuality constituted inaccessible . . . (and) . . . unsettles the usual terms of the heterosexual matrix. (Youdell, 2005, pp. 266–7)

In other words, those individuals whose sexualities do not fit established ideas of heterosexuality but who at the same time resist defining themselves as gay, lesbian, or bisexual need a voice through which they can articulate their opposition and their sense of self. In this sense, the currently changing and contested notions of masculinity and femininity circle the debate of sexuality and make possible new configurations of resistance to the technologies of sex, which have traditionally attempted to fix gender identity to the individual (Burkitt, 1998). In refusing categorization, for example by performing their identity as a bigendered person, individuals not only assert their power to be who they want to be, but also disrupt the political power of the social world to apply labels and stereotypes.

Another study that offers interesting possibilities to think about the sex, sexuality, and gender complexity is one by Carr (2005), who studied the childhood and adolescent narratives of 32 women who were grouped into four gender/sexual status combinations ("lesbian/bisexual butch," "straight butch," "lesbian/bisexual femme," and "straight femme"). The women's gender and sexual statuses appeared to affect the ways they understood and spoke about sex, gender, and sexuality and their distinctions and connections: sex/gender distinctions and

constellation

A group of items, individuals, ideas, or characteristics that are related.

conflation

The blending or fusion of different things (such as words or ideas) so as to form a whole.

sex/gender, gender/sexual, and sex/sexual conflations. Carr's study suggests that stage of the life cycle, gender, and sexual status may influence how sex, gender, and sexuality merge and connect for the individual. For example, a large minority of women recalled wanting to be boys (sex) in order to do the things that boys got to do (gender). This may be a testament to the relative powerlessness of children. Carr argues that for some women who choose masculinity, the rejection of femininity may be an acceptance of gender/sexual conflation, or a more conscious rejection of the principle of consistency that conflates the two. Thus, it seems that in acknowledging the constellation or conflation of sex, sexuality, and gender, we can get a more sophisticated and deeper insight of gender identity theory but also a greater understanding of our own sex, of sexual and gender expressions and practices, and of their relationship to multiple identities.

Understanding How Discourses of Gender Influence Sex Acts and Desire

Doing gender involves a balance of both doing sex and performing masculinity, femininity, or gender ambiguity. The sexual act and associated desire cannot be completely separated from our engagement with discourses of gender; these, in turn, are influenced by our social positioning as male, female, or gender nonconforming. Sex acts are not simply the expression of "natural" behaviour, but are heavily mediated by the social values and cultures we inhabit. What might be considered normal, legitimate sexual behaviour in one social context can be heavily proscribed and thereby rendered illegitimate in another. And such values change over time and become visible or covert across particular social spaces. For example, the practice of "gay sex" is not new to society any more than are homosexual identities, but whereas the concept of the

"sodomite" might have had currency in early Western civilization as signifying an "alternative" sexual identity, today it would generally be considered a pejorative label. Another example would be sadomasochism. While in many cultures such sexual practices might be considered "deviant" and rendered invisible, the reality is that sadomasochism operates throughout many countries in the form of a "sexual subculture," one that cuts across gay, straight, and bisexual identities and traditional notions of female and male sexuality. Indeed, some research indicates that as many as 10 per cent of the US adult population engages in some type of sadomasochistic activity (Moser and Kleinplatz, 2006; also Guidroz, 2008).

We can also see how globalization is disrupting traditional sexual behaviours across most societies. This is apparent for both men and women, although one might argue that the loosening of previously strictly monitored sex codes for women is one of the most important consequences of the emergence of a postmodern condition (for overview, see Harding, 1998).

All this suggests that sexual orientation is not fixed within a person but, rather, can change in response to different life circumstances. Many hitherto straight men and women can, and do, find themselves experimenting with same-sex liaisons. Likewise, gay men and lesbian women often engage in opposite-sex activities. Increasing numbers of straight men and women operate across gender boundaries in their public and private lives, a process we can identify as bigendering. How do we label such individuals? Or do we need to? Rather than attempt to apply unsatisfactory if not limiting and naive language labels, it would seem better to just accept the fluidity of sexuality and gender. Sexual desire is not preconditioned in the brain but conditional upon the world around us. For example, sexual orientations are based not exclusively on the desire and attraction of the object but also on the gendered meanings created in sexual and romantic interaction and language.

According to Adam (2000), gays and lesbians have always been about more than just sex or the homosexual/heterosexual binary or the assertion of an essential sexuality. Rather, the category "gay" has been an elaborated discourse around the potential for emotional involvement and relationships, and also about families. Sexual orientation can be seen as contingent and dynamic, depending on both the perceived sex of the individual and the gender organization of the relationship (Dozier, 2005). For example, research into men who place themselves inside and outside sexual identity categories shows that many find gay identity to be a horizon of increased possibilities (Adam, 2000). For women, on the other hand, sexual behaviour, identity, and desire are not highly intercorrelated and this has implications for new ways of conceptualizing sexual orientation. Furthermore, the multifaceted nature of sexual orientation has implications for conceptualizing sexual activity and sexual desire for women (Rothblum, 2000). In her study, Rothblum found that in the US, the concept of "sex" is closely linked to genital intercourse. When women were asked about their first "sex" experience, they counted the first time they had sexual intercourse with a man, even if that experience was not particularly sexual for them and even if they had prior experiences that were quite arousing and led to orgasm. In this way, these women were attempting to separate their own sexual desire and arousal from what they recognized as dominant social interpretations of sexual experience. In contrast, and in the same study, lesbians and bisexuals said that sex between women allows for a greater variety of sexual expression, exactly because it is not focused on sexual intercourse.

Clearly the overemphasis on sex, says Rothblum, ignores the reality that women have related passionately and emotionally to other women all their lives. She argues that sexual behaviour is only one dimension of women's sexuality and not highly correlated with sexual desire, attraction, and sexual orientation. We also see this lack of correlation in Schleifer's (2006) study of five gay female-to-male transgendered people (gay FTMs: women who become men and who then form erotic relationships with other men). The study explored how the transgendered individuals relied upon and reproduced distinctions between sex, gender, and sexuality in order to make sense of their bodies, their feelings, and their interactions. For Schleifer's participants, sex, gender, and sexuality were produced and reinforced as distinct and real but mutually constituted through a range of interlocking material, discursive, and interactional practices. In examining the interview data of the five gay FTMs, Schleifer found that their discursive and interactional practices were a clear attempt to make themselves intelligible to themselves and to others socially, culturally, and politically (see also Broad, 2002). In other words, the women were engaged not just in sexual practices, but in a personal and political attempt to explore and understand the sex of their bodies; the distinctions between sex, gender, and sexual orientations; and the fluidity of the sex act.

Since Schleifer's five gay FTMs lacked penises and retained many female sex characteristics, they appeared to be unacceptable as sexual partners for some male-born gay men. It is also not unusual for many FTMs to also experience the sex act as an erotic interacting that constitutes itself outside gender and sexual orientation. In other words, sexual intercourse is physically experienced as a female.

Could bodily sex and gender identity therefore constitute the sexuality of interacting erotic partners? Schleifer thinks they do, suggesting that the interviewees were able to reinforce their maleness, their masculinity, and their identity as gay men through erotic interactions that in turn serve to reify sex and gender. However, sexual orientation is multifaceted and future research needs to address this complexity. For example, in research with sexually abused boys/men, some researchers state that they have to struggle with the issue of sexual orientation since being victimized sexually does not necessarily mean being gay (see, for example, Forouzan and Van Gijseghem, 2004; Hopper, 2005; Tremblay and Turcotte, 2005).

Sexual orientation, then, is not a natural precondition of our particular gender. It is always forecasted through the prohibitions and possibilities expressed and understood in the social/cultural space in which we live. Such spaces are, themselves, neither fixed nor pre-determined. They are forever in a state of flux, especially in the age of globalization and media communication, such as the Internet. The desire to be a mature feminine woman or masculine man expresses itself, significantly, through the dominant heterosexual culture that seeks to define just what *feminine* and *masculine* mean. The starting point, at least in Western societies, remains the heterosexual paradigm, and it is this that continues to present the myth that straight is right and all else is not quite so right. But homosexuality, through whatever particular gay or lesbian formation, does exist, in which case it always has the capacity to unsettle or "panic gender" (Butler, 1988, p. 248). At this point, we can see how the very act of being and becoming a man or woman is also, in part, "a repudiation of homosexual attachments" (p. 248), for the identifications of man and woman are not sexually neutral; they come heavily laden with heterosexual assumptions. But despite their power to persuade, such ideologies or dominant discourses can never fully foreclose our identity possibilities; they can never determine our sense of sexuality nor totally prescribe the

sex acts we might choose to engage in as social individuals.

SUMMARY

This chapter has examined two volatile and political dimensions to our gender identity: religion and sexuality. Why are these volatile and contested? Because the first, religion, is invested with so much statement, hope, ideology, history, myth, and defensiveness. In other words, there is, in the world today, a cacophony around religion; it is noisy, loud and, in many instances, accompanied by violence, fear, and oppression. So what it is not is neutral, and certainly not so when it comes to looking at gender identity. None of the main religions can claim to have come to a place of gender equality in their understandings or basic philosophies. Yet when we look at sexuality, we see the very opposite. We have silence, invisibility, and distance. Sure, sexuality is all around us, but it is hardly spoken out loud. It is rendered secret, hidden, and, consequently, posited as dangerous and fearful. All the world's religions have played their own part in bringing about this situation. Clearly, religion and sexuality are uneasy bedfellows, and have been throughout history.

It is as if religion just cannot accommodate the fundamental aspects of human nature, especially female sexuality, homosexuality, and transsexuality. It cannot easily accept diverse ways of being a sexual being outside of the gender binary. Religion seems to immediately come into tension with the diverse postmodern world of globalization and the idea of sexual diversity that has become part of our lives. How do we address this paradox? Well, as we have seen, for millions the answer is a recourse to spirituality—minus the adherence to an orthodox religious code.

However, sexuality too has its normative codes and ways of controlling the human body to make it fit social norms and expectations. As we have discussed, this normative process operates mainly by establishing a male/female binary that pervades the ways in which sexuality is understood in our society. The emergence of subversive sexualities and transgender movements have questioned the male/female binary and made us rethink the ways in which we experience our bodies. Once again, we become aware that our body is social and political as much as it is biological. Above all, the body is part of a social project made of codes of behaviour and ideological meanings that give us a sense of an identity. Subversive sexualities and gender identities also remind us that the social norms and conventions that control our bodies can be undone and that identities or sexualities are far from being static. In other words, if ideology can change the way we perceive our bodies, we can also change these perceptions by undoing the work of ideology. This is our focus in Chapter 6: Gender Movements and Media Representations, which is the next and final chapter of Part Two, The Politics of Gender Identity. We turn to the ways in which the work of ideology and power can be undone by looking at the history of gender movements and the role of the media.

CASE STUDY

Father Thomas takes his car every day to work in a Centre for Mental Health that offers counselling to Catholic priests. The centre is situated outside Ottawa and is run by the Catholic Church. Father Thomas was appointed there as a psychologist after he completed his Ph.D. at the University of Alberta five years ago. Although moving to Ottawa was rather daunting at first, Father Thomas settled down rapidly in a suburb not far from his work. Father Thomas is used to moving around the world. Originally from Chennai in India, he joined the priesthood at a very young age and started working as a priest in the city of Bangalore in his early twenties. He then started to teach psychology in a Catholic college in the South of India before moving to Canada to do his Ph.D.

Father Thomas enjoys meeting people and has always been interested in new experiences and new ideas. At university, he had many friends with whom he sometimes spent the whole night discussing matters regarding spirituality, God, and human existence. Being a priest has never stood in the way of his desire to discover and engage with the world until recently. Two years ago, Father Thomas fell in love with Jeremy, a psychology lecturer whom he met at a conference. Jeremy is a professor of psychology at the University of Ottawa. Father Thomas and Jeremy have had to keep their relationship secret, especially when Jeremy is staying with Father Thomas. This has caused much tension as Father Thomas is by nature an outgoing person, and he feels that they cannot go on hiding their relationship from the world. He knows that the law in Ontario would allow them to get married; yet, to do so, Father Thomas would need to renounce the priesthood. The implications are huge: if he renounces his priesthood, he will not be able to continue to work at the Catholic centre. Securing another job before his work permit expires might not be easy. If he is unable to get another job, he will have to leave Canada, and Jeremy, behind. So far, the letters of application that Father Thomas has sent to potential employers have remained unsuccessful.

Jeremy, on the other hand, is comfortable about keeping the relationship secret, distant, and noncommittal. He does not want Father Thomas to give up his job, the priesthood, or his right to reside in Canada. Jeremy says that he loves Father Thomas very much and would like the relationship to last, yet he does not want to get married. Father Thomas cannot understand Jeremy's attitude. He feels that Jeremy does not really care for him. At the same time, he knows he cannot do without Jeremy. Falling in love with Jeremy has made him discover his sexuality and has given him a new understanding of himself. Deep down, he realizes that, over the past two years, he has been having doubts about his faith. Because his religious convictions are not as strong as they used to be, Father Thomas feels that he cannot go on being a priest.

For the past two months, Father Thomas has been having difficulties sleeping at night. Every day, Father Thomas goes to work, and,

although he has always been enthusiastic about his job, he is now feeling totally unmotivated and disheartened. His mind is constantly preoccupied with his thoughts about Jeremy and his desire to live his life freely and openly.

DISCUSSION QUESTIONS

1. Compare and contrast Father Thomas's and Jeremy's approaches to understanding their relationship and their sexuality.
2. What is the place of spirituality in Father Thomas's life, and how does it relate to his desire to engage in the world?
3. What is stopping Father Thomas from successfully resisting the dominant religious value system and following his own desires?
4. How is the relationship between Father Thomas and Jeremy affected by culture, by nation/place, and by globalization?
5. What advice would you give Father Thomas?

QUESTIONS FOR REVIEW AND DISCUSSION

1. In what ways might same-sex relationships not disrupt the gender binary of masculinity and femininity?
2. What is the difference between religion and spirituality?
3. Why have mass religions become dominated by men?
4. Where do you feel you are situated on the sexual binary of straight to gay?
5. Explain "the constellations of sex-sexuality-gender."

6. Are there instances when you feel pressurized by social norms to perform a certain gender or a particular sexuality?
7. Do you think society is becoming more open to LGBT identities and rights? Give examples.
8. What are the big issues facing religions today in terms of sexual expression and LGBT rights?

Chapter 6
Gender Movements and Media Representations

▲ *The media provide us with a window into our own identity.*

Source: © Janine Wiedel Photolibrary/Alamy

Learning Objectives

At the end of this chapter you will be able to:

■ Understand how past and present gender and social movements have contributed to individual and collective identities.

■ Establish important differences between the various men's movements and the women's movement.

■ Critically examine media representations of gender in the context of social, economic, and political changes around the world.

■ Reflect on the portrayal of women in the media historically.

■ Critically understand the power of the media as it influences gender identity.

■ Appreciate the ways in which the media support masculine and feminine hierarchies.

OVERVIEW

In the previous two chapters, we discussed the ways in which gender identity is shaped by dominant discourses of race, culture, nation, religion, and sexuality. However, individuals and groups are not just the passive recipients of social conditioning. History has shown that social movements and collective forms of resistance have also contributed to transforming the world we live in. This chapter examines the ways in which gender movements and the media represent two important influences on our sense of identity. Gender movements and the media also arguably represent two contradictory aspects of resistance to gender norms. While gender movements presuppose a desire to challenge the gender status quo and restructure the social fabric so that more equality between the genders is achieved, the media are often seen to be doing just the opposite. Both illustrate a contradictory trend in our society: while our world seems to have become more conscious of gender issues than ever before, it is still largely reliant on the idea of gender binaries, which are often reinforced in the media.

Normative representations of the body still abound in the media, whether in fashion magazines, on advertising billboards, on TV advertisements, or in movies. In this respect, gender movements and the media seem to illustrate what Foucault has described as the paradoxical co-existence of power and resistance (Foucault, 2003, p. 95). Foucault's argument is that "power is exercised only over free subjects, and only insofar as they are 'free'" and that "individual or collective subjects . . . are faced with a field of possibilities in which several kinds of conduct, several ways of reacting and modes of behavior are available . . ." (Foucault, 2003, p. 139). In other words, that there is not one but many ways of reacting to power

means that systems of domination do not totally control our behaviours and responses. For example, resistance to gender norms can take a variety of forms, ranging from cross-dressing, street protesting, lobbying, poetry writing, or even friendship. Furthermore, the fact that power and resistance are part of a relationship means that they can be present at the same time. As Foucault argues, ". . . there is not a face-to-face confrontation of power and freedom as mutually exclusive facts (freedom disappearing everywhere power is exercised) but a much more complicated interplay" (Foucault, 2003, p. 139).

Since power is based on an interactive relationship between oppressive systems of power and oppressed individuals and groups, it is dynamic and never remains the same. For example, although gender oppression is deeply rooted in social structures and has been so for a long time, such oppression has evolved over centuries as a result of social changes (demographic, cultural, economic, etc.) but also due to individual and collective forms of resistance and political action. As we will discuss in this chapter, resistance to gender norms and oppression has been an important aspect of the individual and collective struggles for justice, freedom, and democracy in the twentieth and twenty-first centuries. How do the media fit into this trend? As we will see, the role of the media is a contradictory one. While media representations reinforce gender stereotypes and hierarchies, the spread of the global media, and especially online social networking sites, has become an important way in which social movements and ideas are circulating around the world. To use Foucault's terms, it is from this contradictory movement between power and freedom that social transformation can happen.

HOW GENDER MOVEMENTS HELP TRANSFORM THE INDIVIDUAL

Politics may be personal, but it is also collective. Indeed, political action operates most effectively when it is organized and coherent, and has clear aims and objectives. But such political groupings won't survive for long unless they can reach out to individual subjectivities. In other words, the political message takes hold at that point when individuals come to invest something of themselves in the political action and no longer maintain an emotional distance from it. Therefore, the most powerful form of political action is that which connects to the individual's very sense of identity, and can articulate and represent the individual's concerns, felt experiences, and subjective view of the world (see Mouffe, 1995; Taylor and Whittier, 1992; also Fominaya, 2010a, 2010b, for overview). This communal association provides a powerful identity adhesive that generates a sense of unity between the individual and the group, a relationship strongly reinforced through a shared sense of collective agency and political solidarity (see Howell and Mulligan, 2005; Hunt and Benford, 2004; Krook and Childs, 2010; Polletta and Jasper, 2001; Snow, 2001).

The 1960s witnessed the emergence of such forms of political action—social movements. Ranging from localized, sometimes spontaneous protests by small groups of otherwise disparate individuals, to single-issue organizations unaligned with major political parties, such movements began to change the political landscape, especially in Western democracies. The student protests of 1968 that occurred in France especially, but also in other Western countries, were highly significant in themselves, not least because they shook the paternalistic, traditional foundations of many governments. Similarly, the sixties witnessed the emergence of the Civil Rights movement in the US, a movement that was to have a profound and lasting effect upon the political consciousness of that nation and others (see, for example, Ling and Monteith, 2004). But these 1960s movements were not the end. In many respects, this period of sometimes violent, mostly passive, collective action outgrew its New Left roots to spread its discursive message into wider society (see Freeman, 1983; Melucci, 1980, 1989, for discussion). At its core, the message being learned was that organized protest action by cohesive groups can and does bring about change in governments and society. Specifically, strategic political struggle, especially the nonviolent kind, can topple authoritarian regimes, force business corporations to change their practices, and undermine vested interests wherever they might be situated (Zunes, Kurtz, and Asher, 1999).

Since the 1960s, social movements—local, national, and global—have come to play a major role in influencing, educating, and co-opting governments, corporations, political parties, and, not least, individuals, to their agenda. Indeed, it is not unreasonable to claim that a "movement society" has emerged as a consequence (Neidhardt and Rucht, 1991; Porta and Diani, 1999; Grey and Sawer, 2008). However, this is no ordinary society, for it exists beyond national borders, maintains only fleeting alliances, may espouse conflicting ideologies, yet carries the power to bring unexpected but deep transformations in each of us. As Melucci writes,

> Contemporary movements are prophets of the present. What they possess is not the force of the apparatus but the power of the word. They announce the commencement of change; not, however, a change in the distant future but one that is already a presence. They force the power out into the open and give it shape and a face. They speak a language that seems to be entirely their own, but they say something that transcends their particularity and speaks to us all. (Melucci, 1996a, p. 1)

Whether it be the so-called Arab Spring—triggering recent regime change across the Middle East and arising mostly via online social networks—or the quiet but persistent nonviolent resistance to the Burmese military junta inspired by Aung San Suu Kyi, contemporary movements are as apparent today as they have ever been. These movements that speak to us as groups with common preoccupations, aspirations, and political agendas also give us a sense of collective identity. By offering us new ways of understanding ourselves, they not only have the capacity to change societies they can also shape who we are as both groups and individuals.

Gender Movements: The Self and the Collective

Whatever their agenda, politics, or basis for mobilization, social movements can only exist as a direct consequence of the declared intent and actions of individuals (see Grey and Sawer, 2008; Kuumba, 2001). Unlike major political parties and governments, which invariably seem several steps removed from our lived reality and, therefore with whom we often have a distant if not ambiguous relationship, social movements must, by definition, connect to our lived reality in a persuasive and particular way. As Melucci states, their power lies in their ability to speak to the individual, and in significant numbers. Social movements must arise out of the collective concerns of individuals, for without the determination and persistence of the individual to produce the movement, so the movement will wither away. But this process is not only about the political life of the movement, it is very much about the collective identity of those individuals who associate themselves with it. So how might we understand identity as a collective expression?

As we have discussed, identity operates both as association and as separation. That is, it signals who we are, and who we are not. In our presentation of self, so we declare our affinities

and our distinctions. Therefore, identity construction actually requires us to engage in social bonding, participation with others, and identification with similarly minded individuals, a process that simultaneously serves to distinguish us from others while forming a collective identity. These are the actions whereby the self is validated through its relationships with, and distinctions from, other selves. It is the means by which our identity is produced and, crucially, ontologically reinforced. As Porta and Diani (1999) argue, "collective action cannot occur in the absence of a 'we' characterized by common traits and a specific solidarity" (1999, p. 87). Of course, such solidarity as exists is not necessarily permanent, but nevertheless, in expressing one's self as a member of a "we," so the self achieves a sense of unification and purposefulness. The collective signals what it is for and what it is against, and in so doing defines both friends and adversaries for its members.

The being and becoming of the self is never undertaken in solitude. The self requires continuous external validation of its existence and only other selves can offer such. The social movement can provide some of this necessary validation and in a way that can be supportive, trusting, empathetic, and powerful. The self projects its own values onto the social movement and experiences that projection in return as a confirmation of its existence and rightfulness. This might be understood as an intersubjective moment between subjects, or, in Lacanian terms, as the mirrored reflection of the self in the social world, where the subject (child) comes to learn of its existence and relationship to, and difference from, others by gazing upon, reflecting upon its image in a mirror (Lacan, 1989).

We can see, then, a potent mix of individual identity work and collective, or subcultural, identity work operating within the social movement (see Gongaware, 2012, for examples). This identity work is enabled and practised through the memory and narratives that individuals enlist in order to reinforce association, harmony, moral standpoints, and emotional connection with other members (Glass, 2009). In other words, individuals, through their own narratives and engagement, reify the social movement, contribute to a collective memory, and help make it valid and important to both themselves and, potentially, to others. An additional element that operates within any social movement and that adds validation to the members' sense of self is action.

The social movement must, by its own terms of existence, be about change, agendas, projects, transformation, challenge, disruption, and resistance—the expression of power (see Krook and Childs, 2010). The social movement is not neutral, nor is it benign. It exists as a political force and in so doing presents the individual with an attractive proposition. It offers a positive, active, and affirmative definition of the self. So the individual is not merely a member of a movement or collective; indeed, individuals are active participants in the possible transformation of society and, quite likely, of themselves. At this point, we can see that the notion of collective identity transcends the structure/agency dichotomy. The structure *is* the agency, the agent *is* the structure. One exists simultaneously with and within the other. The relationship must be reciprocal, negotiated, and positive. Importantly, it can always be foreclosed by either party. As Snow (2001) puts it,

> . . . discussions of the concept [of collective identity] invariably suggest that its essence resides in a shared sense of "one-ness" or "we-ness" anchored in real or imagined shared attributes and experiences among those who comprise the collectivity and in relation or contrast to one or more actual or imagined sets of others. Embedded within the shared sense of we is a corresponding sense of collective agency. . . . Thus, it can be argued that collective identity is constituted by a shared and interactive sense of "we-ness" and collective agency. (quoted in Fominaya, 2010a, p. 395)

The social movement is, then, more than a political vehicle for change. It is a network of otherwise loosely associated individuals, each of whom has an emotional and identity investment in the movement's continued existence. The collective identity that emerges is reinforced through the symbolically expressed values and meanings of the movement, and emotionally experienced via the generation of intimacies and trust that can arise between individual members as they proceed on a predetermined course of political action (Cohen and Brodie, 2007; Howell and Mulligan, 2005; Krook and Childs, 2010).

The Women's Movement: Activating the Potential for a New Femininity

Arguably one of the most powerful and longlasting of all social movements arising during the 1960s, if not the twentieth century, was the

Never allow anyone to tell you who you are.

Source: www.feministfatale.com. November 1973 cover of Ms Magazine, penned by Marie Severin

women's movement (see Banaszak, 2006; Grey and Sawer, 2009; Rosen, 2001; also Zemlinskaya, 2010, for overview). Women struggling for equality and expressing their resistance to men's dominance and oppression is not a new phenomenon, indeed, the struggle has a long history (Evans, 1980; Freeman, 1975). But the contemporary women's movement of the late twentieth century emerged into an altogether new place. Often operating in tandem and association with gay/lesbian liberation movements, the women's movement presented itself on numerous political fronts, challenging male dominance and patriarchal conditions across both the public and private spheres and directly within the political landscape (Ryan, 1992; also Melucci, 1996a). The women's movement adopted a nonviolent, sometimes passive approach but did not shrink from direct action, often in the face of intimidation and sometimes real, deadly violence by men (see Grey and Sawer, 2009; Roseneil, 1995; Rupp and Taylor, 1999; Taylor and Whittier, 1992).

Women's resistance against patriarchal power in the world has rarely been an isolated or independent struggle in the sense that women have often fought for their rights as part of a larger struggle against poverty and social discrimination. This is particularly true in places where women took part in larger collective struggles, such as trade unionism and anti-racist and anti-colonial resistance. For example, in South Africa, women's resistance against colonialism can be traced back as far as 1913 when women's groups organized passive resistance against the state's racist laws (Benson, 1985, p. 33). In the US, the role of women in the civil rights movement has been key in promoting both the anti-racist and black feminist struggles (see for discussion Brooks, 2008; Collier-Thomas and Franklin, 2001; Frystak, 2010; McGuire, 2010). Women have also played an important role in anti-colonial struggles in places like Algeria, Zimbabwe,

and South Africa. In Palestine, political activism has led many women outside the path of traditional society and into the political arena, thus creating conditions that led them to challenge traditional gender roles (see, for discussion, Augustin, 1993; Rubenberg, 2001; Kassem, 2011).

In other instances, the women's movement allied itself with the labour movement or the anti-racist movement to address the demands of working-class women. For example, in 1995, a group of women from Quebec marched 200 kilometres to present the government with a series of demands for access to employment, equal pay, higher education, and access to services for immigrant women. This march was followed by the "For Bread and Roses" march in Ottawa the following year, which was a march against poverty that ended with the largest women's demonstration in the history of Canada. The success of these marches eventually led to the organization of the World March of Women that took place on International Women's Day in 2000 in over 150 countries and ended at the United Nations on 17 October 2000 (Luxton, 2001, p. 63). All these examples illustrate that women's movements in the world have seldom occurred in a vacuum and have often been linked to other struggles, particularly working-class and anti-racist struggles.

At an academic level, the women's movement reinforced its political message of emancipation and equality with an intellectual rigour as women began to examine, through numerous lenses—not least the social and psychological—the conditions of their existence, gender power, meanings of femininity, the plurality of women, and the commonalities as well as the differences among women (see, for example, Antrobus, 2004; Chodorow, 1978; Cobbie, 2004; Friedan, 1974; de Beauvoir, 1953; Gilligan, 1982; Walby, 1986; Butler, 1990). As feminist theory, this intellectual examination was initially associated most strongly with women's studies. However, from its originally isolated and marginalized place in universities, feminist theory now occupies a highly respected position in academia and is increasingly utilized within very diverse subject disciplines and fields.

This dynamic mix of the intellectual, the personal, and the political, really distinguishes feminism and the women's movement from other social movements. For, more than any other social movement before or since, the women's movement speaks directly of identity—the identity of women, both individually and as a collective (Castells, 2004):

> The women's movement affirms another kind of freedom: no longer a freedom from want but the freedom to want; no longer a struggle for equality but a struggle for difference; *no longer a freedom to act but the freedom to be.* (Melucci, 1996a, p. 135, our emphasis)

We can see, from the 1960s onward, numerous examples of groups of women taking political action against states, corporations, and identifiable groups of men in order to transform society, bring about gender justice, highlight gender inequality and stratification, and challenge male oppression and violence (see, for example, Antrobus, 2004; Cohen and Brodie, 2007; Heywood, 2006; Mountjoy, 2008; Saurer, Lanzinger, and Frysak, 2006). The women's movement may not have a universal political manifesto nor be able to facilitate direct contact among all its members and, indeed, the movement belies the idea of a political group at all. It is, rather, a loose amalgamation of like-minded women, sharing similar concerns, experiencing similar public and private situations, and with the desire and motivation to change things. And for these reasons it appears particularly powerful. Just how powerful is evident in these three narratives, all quoted in Porta and Diani (1999, pp. 83–4):

After Greenham I realized how in fact I was putting myself down on occasions. Simply because there were men around I wasn't verbalizing my thoughts enough. I wasn't coming forward . . . the men were dominating, and I was allowing them to dominate me. (Carola Addington, Greenham Common camper, UK, quoted in Roseneil, 1995, p. 146)

It's made me stronger. I think it's made me really clear about who I am . . . I almost feel my life has a theme. It's not just like I'm this little ant out there living and working with other ants on the anthill. There are things that I care really, really deeply about, and that sort of infuses my whole life with meaning. And I've retained that, and I think I always will. (Radical feminist activist, Columbus, Ohio, US, quoted in Whittier, 1995, p. 95)

Until two years ago, I was a woman who belonged to a man. Then I met women of the collective, and slowly I have acquired the ability to develop new and different relationships with people. Today, I feel myself to be equal in my relationship with this man and in my relationships with the women of the collective. (Martina, member of a women's collective, Milan, Italy, quoted in Bianchi and Mormino, 1984, p. 160)

I was once a "just" in everything: "just" a mother, "just" a wife, "just" me. But since finding out about the feminist movement: the history behind it, the women who fought so valiantly for my sorry ass it has moved me to wake up from my apathetic state; take up the flag and live my life in any other way than "just." Growing up, my mother expected me to marry a well-off man have children and be looked after and I didn't argue, I knew no other way to view my life. But now I see it so very differently. (Rose, mature student on UK sociology degree; comment offered in email communication with the authors)

As Porta and Diani go on to argue, such stories are about identity. They highlight the relationship between the self and the collective, the individual and society (see also, Castells, 2004). The women are voicing a feminist consciousness, an awakening of their (political) self, a potentially liberating moment when they no longer feel confined by the malestream discourse that largely configures society and once, apparently, configured them. It can be argued that the women's movement did not politicize these women, for they were already politicized by virtue of being women in a male-dominated social system. What the women's movement did was give them an understanding of their politicization as women, a voice to express this new awareness, and a political project from which to sustain it. The women's movement activated the potential for a new identity for millions of women around the world and did so through the power of the collective (see, for example, Al-Ali, 2000; Alexeyeff, 2009; Edwards, 2008; Fabian, 2009; Gelb, 2003; Isbester, 2001; Johnson, 2009; Kuumba, 2001; Mariscotti, 2008; Martyn, 2005; Raegin, 1995).

The Women's Movement as an Epistemic Community

But not all women who are concerned for gender justice seek to be radical feminists or political activists. Indeed, as Table 6.1 reveals, most women may not claim a feminist consciousness at all, yet do have a desire for equality and freedom to express themselves as women unfettered by gender stereotypes. A central pillar of the women's movement's political ethos is its claim to be able to speak to and for such women, all women, whatever their colour, ethnicity, sexuality, class, religion, nationality, or place in the world. But how can one single social movement, feminism, claim to represent the interests of half the world's population? It can do this through the concept of an epistemic (knowledge) community of feminists/women.

> Feminists worldwide . . . , despite our numerous disagreements, share a commitment to

modifying and helping to eliminate power differentials based on gender. Some feminists may disagree with that way of describing the above matter; feminists may argue about what "gender" means and what "power" means, and how these differentials have come about. Yet there is broad agreement to a set of values, and it is this commitment, I am suggesting, that makes feminists, as a group, worldwide, an epistemic community. (Assiter, 1996, p. 83)

TABLE 6.1   Perceptions of women in the US today

Opportunities to succeed in life compared to those of your mother

Better 77%
Worse 18%

Overall status of women compared to 25 years ago (among women)

Better 82%
Worse 4%

Has the women's movement made your life better? (among women)

	2009	1999	1983
Yes	69%	48%	25%
No	27	40	65

By age	
18–35	75%
36–44	80
45–64	70
65+	47
Total	69

By education	
High School or less	59%
Some college	76
College grad+	78

TABLE 6.1   (continued)

Do you consider yourself a feminist or not? (among women)

	2009	1999	1992
Yes	24%	26%	21%
No	70	69	63

Calling someone a feminist is . . . (among women)

	2009
A compliment	12%
An insult	17
Neutral	64

"A feminist is someone who believes in social, political, and economic equality of the sexes." Do you think of yourself as a feminist or not? (among women)

Yes	65%
No	32

Is there still a strong need for a women's movement? (among women)

	2009	1992
Yes	48%	57%
No	45	35

Source: CBS News Poll (2009). "Poll: Women's Movement Worthwhile," www.cbsnews.com/2100-500160_162-965224.html

A number of feminists, for example, Sandra Harding (1991), Dorothy Smith (1988), and Nancy Hartsock (1983), take the concept of a feminist epistemic community even further. They claim that women as a whole are a gender community and one that occupies a unique place in the social world. This community of women exists through one key commonality, which is their particular feminine knowledge or subjectivity. However, they reject claims that this is reductionist or biologically determined. Rather, it is a knowledge and relationship to the world based on women's lived lives as female subjects in a gendered world. For "standpoint theorists" such as Harding, Smith, and Hartsock, it is precisely this women's knowledge that provides feminism's empirical and theoretical basis, its political frame of reference, and the motivation to continue the feminist project (see also Stanley and Wise, 1993; Ramazanoglu and Holland, 2005). Indeed, ". . . a culture's best beliefs—what it calls knowledge—are socially situated. The distinctive features of women's situation in a gender-stratified society are being used as resources in the new feminist research" (Harding, 1991, p. 119).

The discussions as to the validity of any claim for an epistemic community of feminists and the concept of a universal female "standpoint" or group representation based on a unique, gendered subjectivity continue within academia (see, for example, Francis, 2002; Squires, 2001). Yet whatever the arguments, there can be little doubt that feminism is a social movement based on some shared values, beliefs, and political positions within the gender category of women. Moreover, the reasons for this social movement to exist remain as pertinent as ever (see Rossi, 2004). These observations do not lesson many feminists' counterclaims for recognizing differences and diversity among women, but they do help explain why the feminist project remains so potent to this day even though many women do lament the current "loss of urgency" that now exists within the women's movement itself (see, for example, Epstein, 2001).

The Diversity of the Women's Movement

One force that has helped revitalize the women's movement is the growing awareness of diversity. The recognition that not all women occupy the same position in society and that some women are more privileged than others led to a rethinking of what the category "woman" means. If we consider issues of race and class, for example, then it is no longer possible to take for granted that all women are oppressed in the same way or that women cannot oppress other women. For example, some of the early feminists in Canada who fought for gender equality, such as Nellie McClung, Louise McKinney, and Emily Murphy, were directly involved in implementing government policies intended to control working-class and Aboriginal women. As well, these early feminists helped put in place the **eugenic** policy of forced sterilization on women considered to be "unfit to have children" that was introduced in Alberta in 1928 and continued until 1972 (Grekul, 2008). This example clearly shows that "woman" as a category is riddled with internal splits and conflicting interests that make the idea of a homogeneous women's movement highly problematic.

As we discussed in Chapter 3, women's gender oppression is intersected with other social hierarchies based on parameters such as race, class, sexuality, ability, and age. These parameters affect both the ways in which women experience domination and the ways in which they respond to it. Many writings by black feminists, such as bell hooks, Audre Lorde, Alice Walker, and others, critique the ethnocentric and classist perspective present in the feminist movement in the West. Alice Walker even coined the term "womanism" to distance herself from "feminism," which she saw as a concept embedded in the history of white domination. What this body of writing, which emerged in the 1980s, emphasized is the importance for racialized women to be able to speak for themselves rather than let white women speak for them (see hooks, 1998).

In many respects, this new awareness (commonly referred to as "third-wave feminism") combined the postmodern idea of diversity and fluidity with the critique of race to formulate what is regarded today as one of the most

eugenic

Relates to "Eugenics," an early twentieth-century movement that claimed that human species could be improved through gene selection and advocated that certain individuals and groups with so-called undesirable genetic traits were to be discouraged from reproducing. This movement is now regarded as promoting discriminatory practices that violate human rights.

significant directions in contemporary feminism. It is not limited to the Western world. Women in other parts of the world have also challenged the basic assumptions of white feminism. For example, in the 1980s black women in South Africa were fighting for rights taken for granted in the Western world, such as the right to vote. The fact that this right was denied not only to black women but also to black men made their struggle different from women's struggle in Western democracies. For the Egyptian writer Nawal El Sa'adawi, the main difference between the women's movement in the West and ones outside the West is that "politicized feminists of the third world . . . make feminism a political issue" (as quoted in Beall, Hassim, and Todes, 1989, p. 34). So it can be argued that feminists of colour helped make feminism more of a political issue by intersecting it with race and class. Today, transnational and global feminism has taken on the role of implementing the critique of white Western feminism by developing a global network to combat the combined effects of gender, class, and race oppression (see, for discussion, Marx Ferree and Tripp, 2006; Mohanty, 2003; Lee and Shaw, 2011; Román-Odio and Sierra, 2011).

The Men's Movements: Responses to Feminism

Since the emergence of the women's movement in the 1970s, men have responded in various ways to the standpoints, theories, and challenges put forward by feminists. These have ranged from those that might broadly be identified as "pro-feminist" men, insomuch as they are groups who are supportive of feminism and feminist agendas, to strongly anti-feminist groups, such as the American-based Christian Promise Keepers, the UK men's movement, and the mythopoetic men's movement (see Allen, 2002; Magnuson, 2007; Newton, 2005; Whitehead, 2002, for overview; also Clatterbaugh, 1990; Messner, 1997; Zemlinskaya, 2010, for overview).

More recently, especially in the UK, men's groups have emerged that, while not always positioning themselves as directly anti-feminist, certainly adopt a stance of resistance to the continuation of what they see as the "feminization of society" and the "miscarriages of justice" that, they argue, arise for men as a consequence. An example would be the Fathers-4-Justice group in the UK. The political activities of such groups of men may well be based around single issues, in this case the legal right of divorced fathers to continue to have contact with their children, but they often veer off toward a more confrontational stance in respect of feminism specifically and the women's movement more broadly. Indeed, some examples of such men's groups are explicitly and vehemently anti-feminist and clearly express the aim of carrying out a backlash against feminism and against women's rights generally (see, for discussion, Flood, 2004; Magnuson, 2007).

There are further important differences between the various men's movements and the women's movement. First of all, the men's movements are not born of a history of discrimination, disadvantage, and oppression by the opposite gender. So it would be unreasonable if not ridiculous to claim that men have been the historic victims of women's ideological and material power, while this claim clearly can and is made by many women against men.

Second, while the effects of globalization and related dynamics are clearly having an adverse impact on the lives of many men, men retain greater levels of power and authority than do women, certainly across the political, business, military, and religious domains (see Connell, 2003; Whitehead and Barrett, 2001). As a result, the need for the women's movement and for feminism has not lessened in the past 50 years; rather, the political direction has adopted a global perspective and orientation. Third, the intellectual underpinnings to feminism are certainly very different to those of the men's movement. The pro-feminist men's groups directly and explicitly associate themselves within the paradigm of critical gender theory and therefore both draw on and add to the rich and sophisticated intellectual heritage that now informs feminism (see Jardine and Smith, 1987; also Whitehead, 2006a, for examples). By contrast, the anti-feminist-oriented men's movements have signally failed to provide any cohesive intellectual rationale for their standpoint, resorting instead to incomprehensible notions of man as a "wounded warrior," now suffering under the "psychic pain" of having to rebuild their mythical masculine project in the face of women's resurgent power (see, for example, Bly, 1990; see Messner, 1997; Kimmel, 1995a, for analysis and discussion).

While such men's movements can be very different in terms of their political agendas, they all have one thing in common and that is they are responding to feminism, either positively or negatively. In that respect, the conditions and consequences of identity work that arise for those women who engage with feminism and the women's movement arise precisely in the same way for men, whatever their political standpoint vis-à-vis feminism. That is, the collective provides both a platform for political positions and standpoints while also providing a means by which the individual can attain some stronger sense of purpose and position within wider society.

HOW MEDIA REPRESENTATIONS INFLUENCE OUR SENSE OF SELF

If globalization is recognized as a force for unprecedented social, economic, and environmental change around the world, then it is equally true that one of the primary facilitators of globalization is the mass media. Today, one can travel most anywhere around the world yet never be far from the representational icons that inhabit this media, including international sports stars, movie stars, and pop stars. Indeed, it is an interesting experience to be travelling a dusty, potholed, largely deserted road in a remote part of Southeast Asia, as one of us has done, and happen upon the face of David Beckham beaming down from a billboard, promoting a particular brand of motor oil. And this promotion is directed at local people, who, as "consumers," would seem otherwise quite disenfranchised—geographically, economically, and culturally—from the globalization experience. Yet when talking to most anyone in this region, it is invariably only necessary to say one word—*Manchester*—and people react as if they are, indeed, directly plugged into the global phenomenon. They respond with avid enthusiasm to connect Manchester with United, thereby demonstrating their membership in the global community. And this is not just a male response for one often gets a similar reaction from women also.

But it is not the particular knowledge or context, in this example soccer, that is important in this social moment, so much as the opportunity such mutual recognition offers both parties to connect across cultural and geographical spaces. For by mutually recognizing global iconic symbols—and there are many of them now (e.g., Justin Bieber)—there is the sense that each party, despite their different cultural backgrounds and locations, is linked to some universal network of humankind. In smiling with recognition, the Gambian, Thai, Mongolian, or Chilean is effectively saying, "I am part of the global experience. I may live here, far from the West, but I can connect with you, a Westerner. I may inhabit a different cultural space, but I am also a global citizen with some global knowledge."

The Media's Power

The past 60 years have been witness to an unprecedented growth in global media communications, now accelerating to light speed through the force of the Internet. As a result, we are entitled to consider the power of the media to dictate or influence our sense of identity (see Gauntlett, 2008; Harper, 2009). Is it the case that the "culture industry," so presciently named and first critiqued by Horkheimer and Adorno in 1947, contains the conditions of our subordination to an overwhelming (capitalist) ideological force, one that reduces our individuality to an endless quest for mindless consumerism? Or are we more sophisticated practitioners of identity work than such a thesis suggests? Are we, as Fisk (1989a, 1989b) argues, quite capable of imposing multiple meanings and interpretations on media texts, symbols, and representations, in the process subverting or reinventing the primary meaning intended by the media/advertiser, and for our own material benefit (see also Gauntlett, 2002, for discussion)?

This question is central to cultural studies and, therefore, to critical explorations of not only gender, but also of race, class, religion, and ethnicity (see Hall, 1997; Hall and du Gay, 1996; Dines and Humez, 1995; Gauntlett, 2002; Jhally, 2006; Shirane, 2008). For in asking whether the media has the power to invent us in its own imagery or whether it is simply another tool we, as individuals, take up and deploy in order to make sense of and validate our own selfhood, so we are exploring the key dimensions to identity itself, in particular the limitations to our identity and the range of its possibilities. Kellner puts it this way:

> . . . the [. . .] products of media culture provide materials out of which we forge our very identities; our sense of selfhood; our notion of what it means to be male or female; our sense of class, of ethnicity and race, of nationality, of sexuality, of "us" and "them." Media images help shape our view of the world and our deepest values: what we consider good or bad, positive or negative, moral or evil. (1995, p. 5)

Ultimately, there is no clear and definitive empirical model that we can use to determine whether the media dictates or whether we direct. The sheer multiplicity of cultural norms and expressions, and not least identities themselves, preclude any final answer, so all becomes analysis, supported by subjective interpretation and political standpoint.

To give an example: all countries in the Far East now appear to have absorbed many of the cultural icons and associated symbols of globalization, but in so doing they are also engaged in reinforcing gender and ethnic stereotypes, not least through Western imagery, while at the same time attempting to retain their unique and "authentic" oriental essence. Many parts of Southeast Asia (e.g., Thailand, Taiwan, Hong Kong, Singapore, Malaysia) are, typically, festooned with countless advertising billboards. But the most cursory examination of such advertising reveals an overwhelming tendency by the advertisers to use light-skinned, Western-looking men and women to promote their products. Indeed, it is an accepted reality in countries such as Thailand that products and services are most effectively promoted when the models used, male or female, are of mixed race origin. This may directly correspond with research that shows the persistent relationship between skin colour and social capital, especially for certain ethnic groups of women—with lighter skin colour evidently improving such women's chances for educational attainment, higher incomes, and higher spousal status (see, for example, Hunter, 2002). Similarly, skin whitening products are now extremely popular in many Asian, African, and Far East countries, although women appear to be the main consumers, not men. But is the advertising merely reflecting a social condition that is already present, or is the social conditioning an effect of the advertising? (See Adel, deBruin, and Nowak, 2010; Mackie, 2011.)

This debate is further complicated when we consider the power of the Internet and an associated technology, the mobile phone, to shape identities, reinforce stereotypes, challenge conventions, explore new modes of being, and validate one's sense of self or indeed undermine it. For example, without question some of the Internet's most successful sites have been those promoting either pornography or social networking (e.g., Facebook and Twitter). Pornographic websites invariably portray the human body in a functional state whereby its objectification is for the pleasure of the consumer/observer. In this respect, sexuality is quickly reduced to the crude, predictable, sensational, even at times the brutal and abusive. The likes of Facebook and Twitter offer a very different experience for the consumer. By being part of a social network, individuals have the opportunity to achieve some sense of validation of their identity, with having friends and contacts as signs that they are important, worthwhile, of value and carrying some social status or level of prestige within their peer group. Social networking sites become a new form of community for the participant, one that can appear to contain many of the benefits of being in a "real-life" community: association, communication, validation, contact, human empathy, emotional comfort, and subjective reinforcement of the self and its value system. At the same time, cellphone text messaging, Twittering, and even blogging can be abusive, bullying, intimidating, and emotionally hurtful to the recipient.

We can conclude that the media (and the businesses that employ them) are not necessarily challenging (gender and racial) stereotypes and similar negative social values; on the contrary, media often appear to be reinforcing stereotypes and profiting in the process. But should we be surprised? For are not the media solely staffed and directed by individuals who are themselves, in post-structuralist terms at least, discursive subjects? In which case, it would be unreasonable if not unrealistic to expect the media to have the intent or capacity to operate outside the very discourses that inhabit the rest of us. But this observation leads us into another issue, and that is the sheer multiplicity of discourses that now exist around gender identity. As we now discuss, while clearly having the capacity if not intent to reinforce gender stereotypes and negative representations of ethnicity and selfhood, the media also have the power to challenge those very stereotypes.

The Media's Influence on Cultural Representations of the Feminine

A fundamental political agenda within feminism has been the struggle to resist media-determined and -imposed "realities and truths" about femininity, whether they be concerned with women's sexuality, beauty, physicality, age, maternalism, work, or leisure possibilities, mothering, or intellect and reason (see, for discussion, Dines and Humez, 1995; Byerly and Ross, 2006; van Zoonen, 1994; Creedon, 1994; hooks, 2006). However, there are very different perspectives within feminism on this matter, and they cover the gamut of debates concerning contemporary media influence, imagery, power, and intent. These positions range from the radical feminist, anti-pornographic standpoint powerfully articulated by Andrea Dworkin (1981), to the queer theorist, cyberspace analysis developed by Wendy Harcourt (1999). Within the feminist

theoretical range, writers such as Germaine Greer (1999), Susie Orbach (1998), Barbara Creed (1993), and Naomi Wolf (1991) have produced writings that have clearly exposed the media's profound but often negative influence both on individual women's self-image and esteem, and on wider cultural representations of the feminine.

The portrayal of women in the media has, however, changed dramatically over the past five or so decades, while yet retaining conventional, if not patriarchal, notions of womanhood in many contexts. For example, Jean Kilbourne, writing in 1989 about how women are portrayed in advertising, states this:

> The aspect of advertising most in need of analysis and change is the portrayal of women. Scientific studies and the most casual viewing yield the same conclusion: Women are shown almost exclusively as housewives or sex objects [. . .] The real tragedy is that many women internalize these stereotypes and learn their "limitations," thus establishing a self-fulfilling prophecy. (from Kilbourne, 1995, pp. 122, 125; also see Adel, deBruin, and Nowak, 2010; Pipher and Kilbourne, 2000)

In her documentary, *Killing Us Softly 4*, Kilbourne defines advertising as follows:

> Advertising does sell products of course; but it also sells a great deal more than products. It sells values, it sells images, concepts of love and sexuality, of romance and success, and perhaps more importantly of normalcy. To a great extent, advertising tells us who we are and who we should be. (Kilbourne, 2000)

Kilbourne also states that the situation is getting worse with more money being spent on advertising than ever before and with new technological advances that can digitally enhance the female body to fit the unrealistic norms of fashion and modelling. The impact of advertising often translates into problems related to physical perception, obsession with thinness, eating disorders, and low self-esteem, particularly among teenage girls who try to conform to standards of beauty, normalcy, and desirability. Kilbourne also highlights the subtext of violence against women and rape fantasy that are present in advertisements that feature women's dismembered bodies or focus on particular body parts.

In contrast, David Gauntlett seems to offer a more optimistic take on the gendered dimensions of the media:

> In the past ten or fifteen years, things have changed considerably [. . .] Movie producers are wary of having women as screaming victims, and have realized that kick-ass heroines do better business. Advertisers have by now realized that audiences will only laugh at images of the pretty housewife, and have reacted by showing women how to be sexy at work instead. (2002, p. 57)

Gauntlett was making this point over a decade ago but if we look at contemporary "kick-ass heroines" in the media, there are plenty about and their number is increasing (Meslow, 2012). Women action heroines are evident today in popular television series (including *Buffy the Vampire Slayer, Hit and Miss, The Killing, Homeland*, and *Covert Affairs*) and in movies (e.g., *Mr and Mrs Smith, Underworld: Awakening, The Girl With the Dragon Tattoo*, and *The Hunger Games*).

However, one could argue that that being "sexy at work" is not a great improvement from being "sexy at home." In all cases, the main message sent by advertisers is that what matters the most is the way a woman looks and her capacity to attract men. This is often done by promoting competition between women, removing the possibility of female solidarity, and encouraging women to be passive (Kilbourne, 2000).

Whereas younger women tend to be glamorized and offered the "kick-ass heroine" roles

referred to by Gauntlett, older women (aged 50 plus) are invariably portrayed as servants (usually ethnic minorities); feisty grandmothers; self-sacrificing, stressed mothers; or manipulative and rich dowagers (Rosselson, 2006). In Hollywood, Bollywood, and the Hong Kong film industries, research shows that the portrayals of older women continue to be limited to stereotypes, especially regarding older women's needs and sexual desires (Griffiths, 2011). In this respect, clearly, the media have yet to catch up with the changing identities of older women, not least as powerfully represented by international superstars such as Madonna, Meryl Streep, Jane Fonda, Helen Mirren, and Kylie Minogue.

Of course, the essential driver within the media, whatever the portrayal of women might be in a particular context, is the search for profit. So it should be no surprise when the media do adapt to, and seek to reflect, changing social trends and values, including representations of womanhood. After all, that is their business. From this, we might conclude that the media are not concerned with a political agenda, but only with profit, and are, therefore, apolitical. But is this necessarily the case?

The feminist position is that the media are male dominated and adhere to a masculine value system. Feminists persuasively argue that the media are based around not only a masculinist view of the world, but also rely for their survival on corporate advertising revenue. And such corporations are, themselves, part of what Connell (2006) identifies as "networked institutions of a global gender order." So the mass global media may not speak of a particular and universal political position but would appear to speak a masculinist and, therefore, political discourse—if not by intent, at least by inclination and culture (see also, Macdonald, 1995; Kaplan, 2000; Thornham, 1999).

But, as we indicated earlier, the growth of the mass media over the past five decades has thrown up some interesting paradoxes, especially around portrayals of women and contradictory expressions of femininity. For example, how would we analyze contemporary international female pop superstars such as Beyoncé, Christina Aguilera, Lady Gaga, and Adele? Are they inspirational feminist role models for millions of young, and not so young, women, as many would suggest, or are they merely female pawns manipulated by a male-dominated, sexist industry? (See, for discussion, Gauntlett, 2002; Lloyd, 1993; also Fisk, 1989b).

Whatever one's position on this question, there can be little doubt that such women have caught the public imagination in terms of their capacity to act as (feminist) role models for a new generation of women. In their sexualized, raunchy, but confident display, in the lyrics of their songs, and in their private lives, the first female pop music artists to signal this shift toward a more explicitly assertive and sexualized femininity were the UK girl band of the 1990s, the Spice Girls. They came to exemplify a new type of femininity and not surprisingly they were quickly followed by a swathe of similar bands and artists, including Destiny's Child, Britney Spears, Salt-N-Pepa, Pussycat Dolls, and Katy Perry. These women speak of a very different type of femininity than that exemplified by earlier generations of women stars, those such as Doris Day, Brenda Lee, Connie Francis, Dinah Shore, Katharine Hepburn, or even Marilyn Monroe:

> The impact of the Spice Girls . . . was to provide a new twist to the feminist discourse of power and subjectivity. By telling their fans that feminism is necessary and fun . . . that girls should challenge rather than accept traditional constraints . . . they sold the 1990s as "a girl's world" and presented the "future as female." (Whiteley, 2000, pp. 216–17, quoted in Gauntlett, 2002, p. 218)

A similar case can be made for television programs such as *Sex in the City*, which began to push at the boundaries surrounding conventional notions of female sexuality, and movies such as *Alien*, *Kill Bill*, and *Crouching Tiger, Hidden Dragon*, which signalled what is now a clear trend toward portraying women as "action chicks"—tough action heroines who are more than a match for any man (see, for discussion, Inness, 2004).

On the negative side, however, what positive impact on young girls' subjectivity and self-esteem can possibly be achieved through reading the majority of those magazines that are aimed at women and teenage girls? Magazines such as *Cosmopolitan*, *BUST*, *Seventeen*, and *Glamour* may well promote a more liberal agenda regarding aspects of female sexuality, but they are depressingly conventional in their obsession with fashion, diet, and how to catch and keep a man, all issues that directly connect to feminist debates regarding media representations of women's (lack of) self-esteem and "need" for validation as female through the male gaze (Gamman and Marshment, 1988; Hermes, 1995; Gauntlett, 2002; also Anderson and Mosbacher, 1997; Cole and Daniel, 2005).

The movie industry has long objectified women, although, again, we can observe different patterns emerging over recent decades. Haskell's (1987) study of women in film from the 1920s to the modern day reveals that while there were shifts in the dominant portrayal of women, the move was from "reverence to rape," culminating in an even more masculinist based, harsher objectification of the female in modern popular culture. One might argue that the Internet and the pornographic sites available on it have indeed heightened this harsher objectification of the female.

A more emancipatory, and more recent, change is noted by Sakr (2004), who applies a Muslim feminist analysis to understand the effects of the popular media on the subjectivities and identities of Middle Eastern women. Her conclusion is that while many gender boundaries are reinforced through the media, many more are crossed and dismantled, the result being that patriarchal ideologies become insecure or rendered dysfunctional in many places, thereby empowering women to new and liberating expressions of femininity (see Al-Ali, 2000).

The Media's Representations of the Masculine

The contradictions and paradoxes apparent in contemporary media representations of women are equally visible in those of men. As with femininities, masculinities are intricately bound up with the gendered discourses, both dominant and subordinate, which circulate within the social web. This is not a new phenomena, however; indeed, it has endured as long as humans have. But what is new, at least particular to the last 100 years, is the speed by which new discourses of masculinity have emerged, come into fashion, gone out of fashion, or disappeared altogether (Tosh, 2004; Mangan and Walvin, 1991; also Whitehead, 2002).

To be sure, the mass media are a major factor here. The antics of men on television programs like *Big Brother* and *The Bachelor* and in movies such as *Fast and Furious*, *The Hangover*, and *Never Back Down* and expressed by pop stars such as Jay-Z and Eminem in the US, Drake in Canada, and Robbie Williams in the UK are simultaneously representative of wider social mores, but also contain some originality or novelty in that they are a media spectacle and performance (see Gauntlett, 2008). Therefore, in viewing such behaviours, many men, particularly those of a similar class, ethnicity, or generation, may well receive them as acceptable expressions of contemporary masculinity for themselves. In this way so does the media transmit gender discourses, but without actually having any control over their appropriation by individuals. We could argue, therefore, that the

media should be more responsible and sensitive to what they portray as "acceptable" male behaviour, given that certain expressions of masculinity can be so socially damaging. But this then takes us into the realms of subjective morality, multiple ways of knowing and being, freedom of expression, and culture, factors further problematized by the elitist character of the media itself. In other words, who are the media to judge what is an acceptable masculine discourse in the postmodern age? Indeed, would we wish the media to have this power and responsibility over us?

Of course, the same case can be made against the media in respect of how it transmits representations of the feminine. But there is a difference. The male, the masculine, men—they all represent a globally dominant gender insomuch as men do control most if not all the regimes of power that enable globalization to function, if not exist. This is precisely the point made by, among others, Connell and Kimmel. Similarly, feminists have successfully argued that women, by virtue of their location within a historic gender order, are more exposed, more vulnerable, and more marginalized than males. This situation is, we would argue, fluid and not determined, not least because the media do have the capacity to assist in redressing the gender power balance, notably by offering more positive social constructions not only of women, but also of gay men, an example being the US television program *Queer Eye for the Straight Guy* (later simply called *Queer Eye*), which ran from 2003 to 2007 (see Kylo-Patrick, 2006; Pullen, 2007, for discussion). But generally, we can deduce that so long as men remain controllers of the media, they will likely perpetuate, not transform, the media's masculinist representation of the feminine.

To give an example, the movies have long used dominant male types as lead stars, while women have, mostly, played subordinate positions to the male, thereby reinforcing the stereotype of women as lesser than men within most social locations. So we should be aware that representations of the masculine in the media do exist within a very different power frame than that of the feminine. This is not to suggest that women are helpless victims of a male-dominated media, but that they are, as women, mostly outside the masculinist culture and male logic that prevails in this corporate setting. And it is precisely this reality that serves to render women more vulnerable than men to representational marginalization (see, for discussion, Thornham, 1999; Kaplan, 2000; Tasker, 1998; Macdonald, 1995).

However, despite any prevailing masculine logic within the mass media, it is also evident that media representations of masculinity do not remain constant over time but respond to larger social shifts (see Craig, 1992, for discussion). This is especially apparent in the film industry. For example, the John Wayne character, an exemplar, in the West, of 1950s masculinity—quiet, stoical, rugged, emotionally illiterate, dutiful, violent when provoked, but chivalrous if not gentlemanly toward women—is hard to find in contemporary cinema. Over the past few decades, Wayne's almost Victorian masculine persona has been usurped by the James Bond model of masculinity—sophisticated, technologically adept, very violent, an explicit sexual predator, unapologetic, and apparently invulnerable. It is a masculine style that works well enough on modern audiences, which is one reason why it has been emulated by Tom Cruise in his *Mission Impossible* series, although given more physicality, emotionality, and technological skilfulness in the process.

In the 1940s and 1950s, audiences were turning out in millions to see the benign, gentlemanly, considerate but ultimately tough masculinity portrayed by film stars such as Humphrey Bogart, Cary Grant, James Cagney, Jimmy Stewart, Gary Cooper, Spencer Tracy, and Clark Gable. In many respects, the masculine discourse

these film stars represented was highly traditional, very conservative, strongly Christian, family oriented, and paternalistic. Even if they were bad guys, they portrayed an inner goodness that could be reached by the "right woman." What these men were not was emotionally literate, reflexive, weak, vulnerable, or feminine. Their masculinity was readily definable and, consequently, highly accessible and acceptable to audiences of the time. And, of course, they were all white (Carby, 1998; Cohan, 1997; Miller, 2009).

In the 1960s and 1970s, however, the male image in film started to change. A new and interesting ambiguity emerged, with the likes of Marlon Brando, Dirk Bogarde, Peter O'Toole, Tom Courtney, James Dean, Laurence Harvey, and Woody Allen taking us toward the postmodern era and explicitly into the deeper and more ambivalent realms of masculine identity, especially around sexuality and class. These male movie stars frequently portrayed characters exhibiting a more unsettled, less assured masculinity; these men didn't always succeed in relationships, were emotionally troubled, perhaps socially clumsy, and often insecure in their sexuality.

Contemporary male film stars of the postmodern age (say from the 1980s onward) offer an altogether more complex model of masculinity, indeed not just one model but many. The likes of Brad Pitt, Johnny Depp, Jude Law, Jake Gyllenhaal, Morgan Freeman, Leonardo DiCaprio, Hugh Grant, Steve Martin, Will Smith, and Denzel Washington cannot be neatly compartmentalized within one type of masculinity that is singular in its ethnicity, sexuality, class, or cultural representation. These actors offer us a window into the multiplicity of modern masculine identities, and yet also signal the persistence of the old cinematic formulae. Their screen personas quite often demonstrate that modern man is flawed, even weak at times, unable to cope with the vicissitudes of life. However, he invariably wins out in the end, usually through some violent means, although not without undergoing some intense masculine self-analysis in the process and at the cost of personal, intimate relationships. (For further discussion, see Clayden, 2005; Powrie, Davies, and Babington, 2004; Berger, Wallis, and Watson, 1995; Benyon, 2001; Hatty, 2000, West, 2012).

However, despite the persistence of the "male hero," the media appears increasingly confident at exposing the contradictory and diverse characteristics of male gender and sexuality and, by doing so, at presenting a more authentic performance for global consumption. The highly acclaimed US television series *The Sopranos* owed much of its success to the fact that the leading male characters were portrayed not simply as violent and aggressive but also as complex failures in terms of their relationships, their family lives, and their capacity for human empathy and emotionality. *Wallander*, the more recent television detective series from the UK, similarly shows a male lead character in emotional turmoil, if not decline, and this despite his success at solving complex crimes; *House* is another example. The cult US television crime series *The Wire* certainly succeeded in breaching the conventional boundaries of masculine identity performance and did so across diverse racial, ethnic, professional, sexual, and social spaces. Indeed, so successful was this series that it has spawned its own particular sociological research focus with international academic conferences and universities, such as Harvard, dedicating space and time to deconstructing the importance and power of the series, not least in terms of gender identity presentations (Wilson and Chadda, 2010).

Finally, a word on men's magazines; what can we perceive to be happening within men's identities from a critical analysis of magazines such as *Loaded* (UK), FHM, *Maxim*, *Esquire*, GQ, and EBONY? Again, the views of researchers in this area are mixed if not contradictory. Several major studies of men's magazines undertaken over the past decade indicate that changes are afoot within modern man, perhaps toward a more enlightened form of maleness, but that, as within film, more traditional if not toxic models persist (Benwell, 2003; Gauntlett, 2008; Nixon, 1996; Pendergast, 2000). For example, Nixon (1996) and Pendergast (2000) suggest that new male identities containing more meaningful visions of masculinity, and across all ethnic groups, are indicated within men's magazines, and that such shifts reflect both the dynamics of popular culture and new societal roles for men. By contrast, Edwards (1997) accepts that perceptions of masculinity and male sexuality have shifted, but argues that the gendered politics behind masculinity have actually changed little, a condition reinforced by the avid commercialism of the genre. Jackson, Stevenson, and Brooks (2001, 2006) acknowledge that men's magazines have "opened up" a space and opportunity for men to reflect on aspects of themselves that they had previously repressed, but warn against reading any such changes as part of a linear movement toward a new egalitarian male identity. Ultimately, what drives and maintains the existence of such magazines is not an emancipatory agenda vis-à-vis male–female relationships, but commercial imperatives (see also, Benwell, 2003; Collins, Hagenauser, and Heller, 2004; Crewe, 2003; Earle, 2009).

Again, as with the movies, television, and pop music, we can see contradictory elements at work in magazines. On the one hand men's and women's magazines can and do provide negative imagery that is based on stereotype, misinformation, lack of knowledge, and incomplete understanding. Such magazines can too readily be partial, judgmental, negative, and concerned only with profit not with empowerment. At the same time, the magazines also reflect trends in society and in that respect they are, as with all aspects of the media, a window into wider social consciousness.

SUMMARY

In exploring the capacity of social movements and the media to influence and reinforce our sense of gender identity, we have actually examined two of the most powerful mediums in the world today: social movements and the media.

To what extent do social movements shape our lives and gender identities? Well, we have shown in this chapter that they are immensely important, and have become more so since the end of World War II. Feminism is such a movement, and certainly without its enormous impact on academic and intellectual thought, it is doubtful a book titled *Gender and Identity* could even be contemplated, never mind written. While some may consider feminism to now have little resonance in their lives, for others its influence is vital and growing. Feminism is now part of the wider global gender movement toward liberalization and emancipation of all people from restrictive gender and sexual stereotypes. And there is no doubt that the gender movement is now more powerful than ever—providing a global political space for those who seek to live outside the restrictions of patriarchal and compulsory heterosexual discourses—both women and men and those who align themselves with LGBT rights especially. Consequently, the critical study of gender and feminism is now having an impact in those regions of the world that hitherto remained isolated from such movements and are becoming increasingly political, vocal, and influential as a result.

Second, what is the media's impact on us? Well, in many ways gender and other social movements now require the oxygen of the media to thrive and indeed use it increasingly effectively. This is to be expected given that the media has become, during the past 100 years, arguably the single biggest creator, shaper, promoter, and

destroyer of iconic identities. Indeed, it would be impossible to imagine our world without television, newspapers, cinema, books, video games, magazines, and, of course, the Internet and all that goes into it, not least blogs and numerous social networking sites. The many and varied channels of communication that constitute the media bring sights, sounds, spectacle, information, knowledge, and both explicit and implicit messages directly into our homes and working lives—24/7. Of course, the debate continues as to what extent the media shape or reflect that which is already out there, but the reality is that few of us are immune to the media's influence.

As we have seen, any critical analysis of the media, whether it be focused on television, movies, magazines, or popular music, needs to take both a historical and balanced overview. The media both reflects society and comes to inform it; it is never simply one or the other. No individual is solely constructed by his or her exposure to particular messages contained in media channels. Individuals change and have some capacity to create themselves in different ways, just like society itself. Similarly, the media is subject to change also. The debate is to what extent the media is influencing society or merely reflecting it. The added variable is, of course, the Internet. And it might be argued that one impact of the Internet is to democratize the media. That is, so long as we have access to a computer, then we can individually participate in the act of media production: social networking, website creation, blogging, tweeting, texting, and emailing. All of this is enhanced communication and it functions primarily at the micro (individual) level but with the power to feed out such communications to countless millions. Just how this will in turn come to influence gender identity remains to be seen, although influence it certainly will.

Social movements and the media actually need each other; they sustain each other but not in a neutral way. Both are highly political: not only the explicit political character of the social movement, but also the often less apparent political character of the media. It would be tempting to see the individual man and woman as merely corks bobbing around on this sea of influence. We prefer to recognize that both the social (gender) movement and the media are made up of people just like us—people with genders, sexualities, and numerous aspects to their identity. People sometimes feel secure and certain in who they are, and sometimes just the opposite. In the final analysis, there is no single group of individuals unaffected by this unpredictable power play of social movements and media. We are all in it together.

CASE STUDY

In the beginning it was a game, a matter of fun. But it changed quickly. And once the game changed, so too did Matt. He had always enjoyed spending time exploring the Internet, meeting new friends through the social networking sites, and, more recently, posting videos of himself on YouTube. Occasionally, after work, Matt sat in front of his computer sending out these videos, imagining they would enter cyberspace, be picked up by random souls, then disappear forever. Most did precisely this, except his last video. This was his most ambitious and audacious yet. Although only four minutes long, the YouTube video was powerful. It showed Matt talking solemnly yet frankly about suicide—his own. It was not a rant, not an outpouring of emotion, simply him going through the reasons why he should continue to live or why he should end his life soon. Most who watched it felt drawn to Matt, compelled to know more about him, anxious for him. His matter-of-fact, stoical reappraisal of his life struck a chord.

Matt is a 38-year-old single male, living alone in a small town in Pennsylvania. He works in the local library, has no girlfriend, has a basic education, and his friendship group consists mostly of people he's met online. He has never travelled outside of the US.

For some time, Matt has been feeling depressed over his social situation. He's always found it difficult to make friends, especially female friends, but recently he's begun to feel especially lonely. Then he made the video.

The video went viral. Within a few days, over 20,000 people around the world had viewed it; within a week, the number was up to 250,000, and then over a million. The local radio and newspapers quickly arrived on Matt's doorstep, followed by the big media networks. Matt suddenly found himself propelled into the spotlight. They wanted to know: Would he kill himself? Would he do it soon? How would he kill himself? Where? And, especially, they wanted to know if he would make a video of his suicide.

But that was not the only response to the video. The media approach appeared hard and, to some extent, ugly. Matt felt it to be false and manipulative. The journalists and media folk didn't care about him at all; they only purported to care. There was no sincerity in their desire to know more about him. But others also contacted Matt—people like him—lonely, single males especially. These people did apparently care. They cared because they were like Matt, or thought they were. Within a short time Matt had found himself taking on a very new identity—as a member of a loose collective of males who had contemplated suicide, were unsatisfied with their lives, and felt disenfranchised from society. These males were of different ages and ethnic groups, but all had two things in common—they were single, they were socially marginalized, and they were men.

Matt no longer contemplates suicide. But he still does YouTube videos and he has a steady stream of viewers. He also has a website and a new social networking site on which he has developed his thoughts about the plight of modern man. He is still without a girlfriend, but he is happier than before. Now he feels he has some purpose in life. Now he feels useful and valuable. Now he feels connected. He feels more like the man he wanted to be when he was a boy.

DISCUSSION QUESTIONS

1. Why might Matt be finding it difficult to connect with women?
2. In what ways is Matt's new sense of self political?
3. How has Matt both benefited from and been used by the media?
4. How has the experience changed Matt's sense of masculinity?
5. What are the key elements of the collective identity that Matt now connects with?
6. How might the actions of Matt following the video be construed as reinforcing a particular political movement?

QUESTIONS FOR REVIEW AND DISCUSSION

1. How and why might women find membership in feminist political movements empowering?

2. What are the factors that might militate against the possibility of a feminist epistemic community (a sisterhood of women)? What are the factors that might reinforce it?

3. Explain how individual identity might be reinforced through membership of a collective social movement.

4. Consider some male and female cinematic icons of the twenty-first century—in what ways do their cinematic personas reinforce or challenge gender stereotypes?

5. Do you think the media influence who we are as individuals (our gender identity), or do the media draw on representations that are already present in society (and in us)?

6. Give examples of how the media enable the gender movement and examples of how they undermine it.

7. Some commentators consider that men are now increasingly portrayed in the media as hopeless cases—emotionally dysfunctional, manipulated by assertive and confident women, and therefore increasingly marginalized. Do you agree or not? Give your reasons.

8. What does feminism as a gender movement mean to you personally? Does it have resonance in your life or not? How has feminism influenced your life today, and how might it influence your life in the future?

9. Do you think the Internet is having a positive, negative, or neutral affect on gender and sexual identities? Give your reasons.

Part Three

The Practices of Gender Identity

Chapter 7

Public and Private Selves and Gender Relations

▲ *Our friends can powerfully reinforce who we want to be.*
Source: © David Grossman/Alamy

Learning Objectives

At the end of this chapter you will be able to:

- Understand how gender relations are enacted in public and private spheres.
- Critically examine the sexual division of labour and its political and economic consequences.
- Critically reflect on how the discourses of love, intimacy, and relationships are experienced through public and private spheres.
- Understand how gender intersects with friendship, bonding, trust, and association.
- Appreciate the role of class, sexuality, race, ethnicity, age, and culture in the private world of love, intimacy, feelings, and emotions.

OVERVIEW

As we have discussed in Part Two, it is clear that, as a social structure, gender defines and controls our interactions with others. This is done mainly through the male/female binary and its capacity to infiltrate both the public and private spheres of our lives. Gender informs our identities, whether cultural, national, religious, sexual, or other. In Part Three we now examine the ways that gender affects our lives on a day-to-day basis, starting from personal relationships; then on to leisure time; followed by the more public realms of education, health, and employment; and finally into those social areas that can readily cut across both the public and the private, notably war, crime, and violence. Throughout Part Three our central focus will be on the ways that gender identities are informed by our daily interactions with others and with institutions but also by our attempts to challenge existing structures and create alternative ways of being.

In this chapter, we examine the public and private spheres that help structure our lives, validate our sense of self, reinforce our place in society, and serve to confirm our gender identity. In particular, we explore the world of the intimate and the emotional, especially love, relationships, friendships, and association. These realms of our being are incredibly vulnerable to change and disruption, and to disappointment. We often have idealistic if not unrealistic expectations of our relationships and friendships, even our more casual associations. But they are very important to our sense of individuality and self-esteem. They provide us with ontological nourishment and in so doing substantiate our identity and feeling of being part of a community. The ways in which the intimate and the emotional play out in our lives and across the public and private spheres often serve to be the most crucial to us in terms of providing security and stability, but in a context that is always vulnerable to unexpected change.

THE PUBLIC SELF VERSUS THE PRIVATE SELF

We all live compartmentalized lives. That is, we exist in numerous social spaces and arenas. Some are clearly distinguishable (e.g., work, family, community), while others are more fluid (e.g., relationships and friendships). These spaces help define us and our sense of reality (Baumeister, 1986). They are powerful not least because they provide us with immediate, strong, and persuasive identity associations. While these spheres are not so absolute and fixed as they might appear, there is a sense that we have both a public and private self; that is, we operate in a public world of work, but also exist in a private world of intimate relationships. Indeed,

many of us work hard to maintain such a separation in our daily lives, engaging in practices that might appear distinct but in fact coalesce to create the sense of us as unified, holistic beings. However, as we now go on to explore, the public and private are not neutral spaces with distinct neutral practices, for they are heavily caught up in the political gender dynamics that exist in all societies and communities (see Hekman, 2004; Freeman, 1987).

One of the most powerful critiques to emerge out of feminist thought concerns the social stratification arising from the particular conditions prevailing within the public and private spheres (Landes, 1998; Pateman, 1979). Feminists such as Rosemary Crompton and pro-feminist writers such as Jeff Hearn have argued strongly that patriarchy draws breath and sustenance in large part from women's continued placement in the private, domestic sphere, leaving men with the space, time, and opportunity to occupy powerful positions across the public world of work (Crompton and Mann, 1994; Hearn, 1992), a condition that we examine next.

The Sexual Division of Labour

This division, understood by feminists as a sexual division of labour (see Tong, 1994, for discussion), posits that women's work and, therefore, women themselves are of less value and importance than men and men's work (see Brown, 2006; Jenkins, 2004). From this, some Marxist feminists have argued that women constitute a distinct social class involved in a particular aspect of (re)productive work and that they should, therefore, receive payment for such by the state (for example, Boje and Leira, 2000; Costa and James, 1972; Edmond and Fleming, 1975).

While there has been much contention within feminism as to the usefulness of a "wages for housework" policy, this Marxist feminist position does make a powerful statement about the relationship of women to systems of production, not only capitalist but also socialist. Indeed, one can trace the history of the public/private divide and the associated sexual division of labour through various ideological and political doctrines from contemporary social democracy back through liberalism, Protestantism, and on to ancient Greece (Mann, 1994; Hearn, 1992; O'Brien, 1983). As Hearn argues, this arrangement may appear historically as a "natural order of things," but it has a direct material and therefore political consequence for women:

> "Men" and "women," and the "public" and "private," are as they are in a balanced complementary. Similarly, the private and the public domains are seen as separate realms, and division between

them as given. This approach takes many forms: philosophical, political, economic, sociobiological, and so on. It is clearly represented in the works of Plato and Aristotle, as elaborate, and sometimes contradictory, rationales are provided for keeping women out of public life. (1992, p. 30)

Feminist perspectives highlight this continuing gender differentiation between men and women, a social division that appears to advantage men at the expense of women, leaving women in low-level work, outside the realms of political power, economically disadvantaged, reliant on men for their security, tied to the home, and juggling multiple roles as employee, carer, and housewife (Franks, 1999). The case might be made that women's biological condition as the conceivers and bearers of children is at the root of the public/private division, ensuring that as a gender they remain removed from or at least disadvantaged in relationship to the world of full-time paid employment and, consequently, to material security and political and economic power. However, this thinking takes us into the realms of socio-biology and the reactionary position of those who would seek to maintain an existing gender order in favour of men—e.g., the notion that men and women are biologically different to the extent that any attempts to tamper with this arrangement merely fly in the face of nature, reason, and reality. In other words, men are leaders in the public sphere because it is in their masculine character to be so while women are carers in the private one because it is in their feminine character to be so (see Horrell et al., 2008).

This argument may appear simplistic and anachronistic to readers of this book, but the argument remains influential to this day. Recent developments have exposed the illusion behind any continuing adherence to a so-called natural public and private divide. For example, in many societies, the male-breadwinner family is rapidly becoming history (Creighton, 1999); in many instances, females have overtaken males in educational achievement; women are more visible at the highest levels across many fields of employment; and increasing numbers of men are becoming househusbands since global unemployment affects both genders. Similarly, to suggest that men cannot, by virtue of their gender, be carers or homeworkers is no longer a valid idea (see Bettio and Verashchagina, 2008; Birch, Le, and Miller, 2009; Lenz, Ullrich, and Fersch, 2007).Yet what is significant is that professions that are "feminized," such as primary-school teaching or caregiving, still suffer from lower prestige and a lower economic status.

Gendered Dualisms Sustaining the Public and Private Spheres

But the ideology behind a distinct public and private sphere goes deeper than employment, family, and educational statistics. Such a division is historically constructed and, therefore, as Genevieve Lloyd (1984) argues, embedded in our very thought processes and in language itself:

> From the beginning of philosophical thought, femaleness was symbolically associated with what Reason supposedly left behind—the dark powers of the earth goddesses, immersion in unknown forces associated with mysterious female powers. (1984, p. 2, quoted in Whitehead, 2002, p. 175)

So when we engage with conventional dualisms such as rationality/irrationality, hard/soft, intimacy/distance, and emotion/reason, we are touching on the deeper assumptions that sustain the dichotomy of masculinity/femininity. It is out of this thinking that politicized definitions of maleness and femaleness have emerged over history as well as distinctions of public (male) and private (female) gendered time, space, orientation, work, and emotional spheres (see Akerlof

and Kranton, 2010; Germon, 2009; Pateman, 1979). To be sure, such definitions may now be under question in many societies, but as Lloyd and others have argued, so long as they remain located in language, philosophy, and theology, so they will continue to be able to reinforce a public and private divide, and an associated sexual division of labour.

But the gendered separation and distinctions that continue to sustain the public and private spheres are more than a social stratification; they go deeper than philosophy and theology, and are more far reaching in their effects than language itself. For the notion of a public and private dualism touches our very sense of who we are as gendered beings. This dichotomy fundamentally informs our gender identity.

Dichotomized Identity

Feminists have long struggled with the implications of their own critical take on the public and private. Once we argue that women's work is undervalued and somehow demeaning, are we not merely pandering to the very stereotypes and gendered assumptions that sustain gender divisions and a dichotomized identity? As Tong points out,

> Any woman whose *identity* is that of a wife and mother is likely to become either angry or depressed if after investing years of blood, sweat, tears, and toil in becoming and being a wife and mother, she is told that "wifing" and "mothering" are merely roles, and problematic ones at that. It is one thing to tell a woman she should change her hairstyle; it is quite another to tell her she should get a more meaningful identity (1994: 33, original emphasis)

Tong is supporting the point made by Elshtain (1981), who argues that mothering is far more than merely a job and that to compare it to a job is to pander to "malestream" (O'Brien, 1983) perspectives and values (see also Jagger, 1983).

Yet this has been one of the core debates within liberal feminism: that women should get out of the home, unlock themselves from the domestic sphere, and compete with men on an equal basis in the world of paid employment. In other words, women should become more like men or at least pursue such activities until both women and men become androgynous, both genders expressing a mix of the masculine and feminine to the point that gender is no longer a social divide or a real distinction (see Akerlof and Kranton, 2010; Germon, 2009; Friedan, 1974, 1981; also Eisenstein, 1986; Heilbrun, 1973, for discussion). A similar argument can be made in respect of how we understand reproductive labour. It cannot be claimed that women are the primary gender in terms of reproduction on the basis of the historical public/private divide; both men and women are active and implicated in this process and not just in terms of conception.

As Rosemary Crompton puts it, we have to recognize the contributions of both men and women and across both spheres:

> Our understanding of *men's* work cannot be grasped adequately unless women's contribution in both the public and private spheres is also taken into account. Work carried out in both is essential to the reproduction of society . . . it is obvious that the relationship of interdependence between the public and private spheres is not fixed and immutable, but in continual flux. (1994, p. 135, original emphasis)

What appears to be happening across many societies is a transformation of the traditional public/private dichotomy, at least in terms of how it gets played out in work and labour. From Scandinavia to Singapore, Brazil to Israel, governments are grappling with a multitude of demographic and social changes, some arising from globalization, some a product of the information society, and some indicative of a post-modernization of economic and social life. There

is evidence of a direct challenge to the social/gender order that sustained and was sustained by the traditional public and private divide (see, for example, Chant, 1991; Barraclough and Faison, 2009; Eviota, 1992; Esteve et al., 2012).

A re-ordering is taking place that is challenging the traditional gender codes previously reinforced through the public and private spheres. We are seeing a general decline in the rates of marriage; increasing numbers of divorces; increases in cohabitation; women postponing motherhood or deciding not to have children at all; women becoming financially independent; an increase in single-parent families; a general move toward single lifestyles for both sexes; a massive rise in the number of dual-income families; moves by women into traditional male-dominated industries and professions and, likewise, by men into female-dominated ones; and more fluid models of family life and relationships generally, as illustrated in Figure 7.1.

If we add in all the evidence, which points to paid work increasingly taking place in the home setting via the Internet, and to an eroding of the traditional times for work and leisure, then it is clear that notions of a public and private divide, at least an economically invested one, don't hold true in quite the way they used to. Variables such as class, race, age, and ethnicity also affect traditional notions of private and public. We no longer live in quite the ordered place we once did. And as the dichotomy breaks down, so too do the many gender stereotypes that accompanied it.

So does this mean that the public and private spheres, and what they signify for our sense of self, no longer hold true, no longer have the capacity to define our gender identity? Well, not quite. As we reveal in this part of the book, i.e., Part Three, the gendered character of domains such as work, leisure, professions, religion, intimacy, and crime, to mention just a few, remains evident. Precisely what the gendered expression

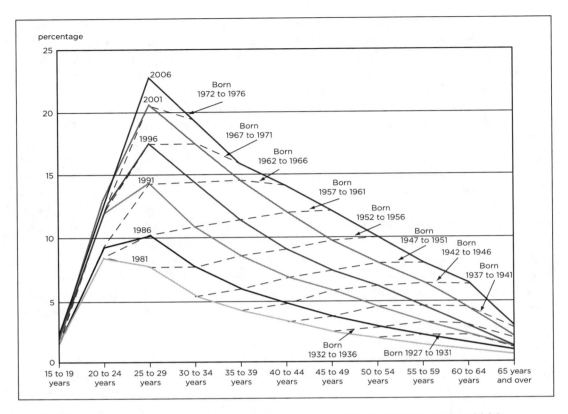

FIGURE 7.1   **Proportion of Persons Living in Common-Law Unions, Canada, 1981 to 2006**

Note: Refers to population in private households.

Sources: Statistics Canada, Report on the Demographic Situation in Canada, 2005; and 2006, Catalogue no. 91-209-X, Figure 6.2, p. 71.

might be does appear to change over time and space, but the expression persists in having a gendered dimension to it.

So society is not close to the state of androgyny advocated by some liberal feminists back in the 1970s, although we do suggest in the final chapter of this book that definitions of masculinity and femininity are changing—at times blurring and at other times becoming more accentuated. We predict that these definitions will be subject to further significant change as the impact of globalization becomes more apparent. It does not follow, however, that definitions of femininity and masculinity are changing to such an extent that distinctions are meaningless,

any more than are the particular gender power arrangements behind those distinctions being dismantled in every cultural site.

Public Personas

The operation of a public and private divide works through and into our very identity, to the point at which we feel both public and private in our selves. We exhibit a public persona, one that we hope reflects the discursive conditions around it. Therefore, any confidence we may feel is a direct consequence of how practised we are in our presentation of gender identity and to what extent this presentation is accepted by the culture, community, and society we exist in. But such practice is not done knowingly, although it can be. More likely the practice of our gender identity is the performative repetition of language, bodily movement, dress, and style that persuades others to recognize, accept, and validate us. In some highly sensitive social conditions, for example those cultural spaces that adopt highly negative responses to LGBT identities and to nontraditional sexual relationships, it is vital we get this identity work right. This public self is no more grounded and fixed than any other aspect of our being, but it is felt and it is therefore important to who we think we are or seek to be. As we explore in this chapter, this public persona is quite clearly bodily in its expression—clothes, attire, hairstyle, makeup. It is also circumstantial in that it will necessarily reflect the local setting in which we are placed. So, for example, if one is working in a very masculinist profession or industry one can expect some pressure to conform to the malestream discourses that configure it. Similarly, if one is located in a female-dominated setting, then there will be related expectations and conditions regarding how one presents oneself to others. This is true for both men and women.

What is at work here is the "gendered eye" or, more accurately, the "male eye." It is, as Bourdieu argues, highly persuasive in influencing our actions:

> The social world functions (to a greater of lesser extent, depending on the field) as a market in symbolic goods, dominated by the masculine vision: for women, as has been noted, to be is to be perceived, and perceived by the male eye or an eye informed by masculine categories. . . . To be "feminine" means essentially to avoid all the properties and practices that can function as signs of manliness. (2001, p. 99)

For women, for example, wearing makeup, covering oneself with a veil, and wearing revealing clothes could be interpreted as performances

of the feminine that relate to the dominant (male) gaze. The veil, for example, whether it is the Christian bridal veil or the Muslim hijab/burka, can be seen as reinforcing the concept of the female as a mythical, sensual subject (see, for discussion, Alvi, Hoodfar, and McDonough, 2003; Ask and Tjomsland, 1998; Bullock, 2002; El Guindi, 1999; MacMaster, 2009). Another way of looking at these performances would be to see them as a joint male/female agreement that the female body is tempting. In any case, what these performances do is claim a feminine presence and identity and unmistakably mark the female body as not male (see, for discussion, Krook and Childs, 2010).

What such performances do not do is challenge the male eye; women are acceding to it, but apparently willingly not least because in so doing they are confirming their gender identity and having that confirmation returned by others. Indeed, the women who may well receive some condemnation from those around them are those who break ranks in the gender order, that is, the women who disrupt the gender binary, who appear ambiguous or contrary in their gender identity and behaviour: the sharp-suited chief executive who pays a nanny to look after her children; the housewife who leaves her husband, and her children, to go and live with another man; the schoolgirl who never learns or adopts the dominant social codes/discourses of the (feminine) school playground and ends up being socially excluded by her peers; and especially the transgendered individual who may be identified as a male by society but who seeks to transpose herself into the female sex/gender category, legally, sexually, and socially.

Private Personas

To what extent we as individuals internalize these discourses is impossible to quantify, but internalize them we do. They come to be us. Indeed, it is through this internalization that we acquire the sense of the core of our being. The reality may be a contingent, fluid, discursive self, but that is not what we want to be told. We aspire to something much more permanent and settled. In fact, the very notion of "settling down," a powerful discourse in its own right, suggests we have reached a phase of being constant in ourselves, one that is mature, content, no longer searching for an elusive other, wherever or whoever that might be.

So we have this private persona to recognize as well as the public one. Of course, like all dualisms it is open to question and critique, and we are not suggesting that there operates within us some mind-body distinction. We do, however, argue that if there is an external eye with the power to influence our behaviour and inform our sense of gender identity in the process, then that external eye cannot function without its equivalent internal manifestation. For we are private in so many ways—private in our wish to separate from others; private in our thoughts and imaginations; private in our dreams and nightmares; private in our desires and hates; private in our fears and certainties. There is much about each of us that never gets revealed, at least to most of those around us. Even in the most intimate of relationships, there is always that sense of sustained individuality, something beyond the relationship itself: the knowledge that, in the final reckoning, one is on one's own.

But much as we might like to imagine this private persona as somehow at the core of us and, therefore, removed from the world around us, it isn't. This private person is merely, we suggest, our minds at work, recording, assimilating, expressing. And what do our minds record and express precisely? Well, they record and express what they know, and what they have received in whatever form it has been transmitted from the social setting. Each of us is severely limited in knowledge, for the simple reason that most knowledge has never come to us. It may be close

by, physically, but unless we have absorbed it then it may as well be light years off.

And that is the reality, indeed the irony, of our private persona; it is not private at all. Whatever we feel, whatever we think, however we see ourselves, it is highly likely that precisely such thoughts, feelings, and perceptions are being held by others, and have been held by others. We are never alone in our thoughts any more than we are alone in our gender identity; our thoughts are never exclusively ours—they have been thought before. We remain, then, publicly and privately, social beings (see Baumeister, 1986; Hekman, 2004).

THE POWER OF LOVE, INTIMACY, AND RELATIONSHIPS

Arguably the most profound experiences of our lives occur in the realms of the intimate. Our sexual, gendered, emotive self realizes itself, its identity, in our close relationships with others. In no other area of our lives is our identity quite so exposed, quite so vulnerable as in this very private space wherein we feel and express love and engage in intimate, sexual relationships. Our experiences of love, intimacy, and relationships can and do change us. They can elevate us to heights of joy and delight, or plunge us into the deepest grief and despair. But we cannot avoid them. No one can evade these feelings for they can come to us at any time in our lives, any place we are situated in, and unexpectedly. In the most far-reaching of ways they can validate or unsettle our sense of self, reinforce or disrupt our persona.

Love, intimacy, and relationships cut through the public and private spheres, indeed each and every cultural space that appears otherwise to structure and secure our being and experience of life. Love, intimacy, and relationships are never predicted, never scripted, and never manageable; they are dynamic and uncertain, contingent in the extreme. They can seriously disrupt, even erode, whatever cultural and social boundaries exist around us. We can fall in love at work, feel a lack of intimacy in our home life, seek and find relationships anywhere. Add in the technological dimension to modern living—email, Internet, webcams, chat rooms, mobile phones—and suddenly all our conventional notions of love, intimacy, and relationships are overturned. We find there are no boundaries, only experiences (see Ben-Ze'ev, 2004; Gackenbach, 2007; Ray, 2007).

But despite these profound social transformations occurring across societies and within each of us, some things do appear to remain the same. One of these is what we term the "love discourse," which has not changed much over the centuries, although it may have possibilities for serious change in the not too distant future.

The Love Discourse as a Quest for Identity

Love is, of course, a powerful emotion and one that can emerge in many aspects of our lives—with our parents, our children, our friends, our siblings, even our pets. But it is the romantic and sexual dimension to the love discourse that defines it and makes it unique within the range of love experiences we may be open to (see Cowburn, 2003; Dilman, 1998; Lindberg, 2008).

The love discourse is the belief in a romantic and intimate utopia, a time/place we will come to inhabit with another human being whom we regard as our soulmate. This partner is more than just a lover, for he/she is "the one" whom we perceive as making our life meaningful or perfect; the one we see ourselves as meant to be with in an exclusive relationship that surpasses all others (Whitehead, 2006c, 2012). The love discourse also has another side to it, but that is connected to this socially and culturally constructed yearning and desire for a lifetime partner. This side of the love discourse concerns the value our society

places on faithfulness, monogamy, trust, and intimacy in a relationship.

The love discourse is firmly embedded in Western society in the postmodern age. It has become "enshrined in the expectations of Western societies" (Evans, 2003; also Bauman, 2004). It has become almost a right, a requirement for our contentment, a demand we place on ourselves and on others especially on those we love. We associate being in love with personal fulfilment and happiness, rarely stopping to question the problematic dimensions and elusiveness of this romantic ideal.

There seems to be no escape from the love discourse. It is constantly expressed in all aspects of the media and underpins many of our assumptions about love, intimacy, and relationships. It is told and retold through fairy tales, romantic fiction, film, pop songs, television dramas, art, soap operas, magazines—indeed it appears in each and every aspect of the media, and through both formal and informal language and communication. This love discourse is passed down through generations and is imposed on children, young people, men and women virtually across the adult age spectrum in all cultures (Rowe, 2007). We have idealized and elevated pure romantic love to the point that it is almost a secular religion (Beck and Beck-Gernsheim, 1995). Consequently, to be a non-believer in the utopian ideal of a perfect love that lasts a lifetime is to be relegated to some awkward place in society, a place for "the cynical, the lonely, the disillusioned" (Whitehead, 2006c, 2012).

The love discourse serves to reinforce and validate the notion of a traditional, life time relationship, usually one invested in through marriage. We have to ask ourselves, then, why the love discourse continues to be so powerful across so many cultures and societies, and why it has, so far, maintained is omnipresence in society in spite of the massive changes in how we live as sexual beings (see also Evans, 2003; Bauman, 2004).

For one of the most obvious conditions of the postmodern, global era is a breakdown in traditional relationships. We are moving in and out of relationships with increasing frequency. We are experimenting with new intimate "arrangements" that require only limited commitment but that serve to provide us with sexual and emotional satisfaction (Roseneil, 2006). Our sexual lives are commonly beginning younger and continuing longer and with more partners. As Figure 7.2 indicates, marriage is on the decline in most if not all modern industrialized states while divorce rates are rising. Cohabitation and single lifestyles are now common experiences for increasing numbers of people. Marriage, when do we venture into it, is no longer for life; it is only for as long as the love lasts.

Figure 7.2 and Figure 7.3 offer only a very broad insight into what is happening with regard to marriage and divorce worldwide. What is not revealed, for example, is the surge in the number of divorces over the past decade in fast-developing countries such as China, Taiwan, Thailand, Singapore, Brazil, Dubai, and India. While often, as in the case of India, this increase is from a relatively low base, the impact on a country's socio-economic base and culture is, nevertheless, profound (see, for example, Wang and Zhou, 2010). Similarly, there are often differences within a particular country that are not easily explained by statistics. For example, the Canadian province of Quebec now has such a low marriage rate, high divorce rate, and incidence of children born out of wedlock that it is being labelled the "world's first post-marriage society" (Ozipko, 2010). In the US, African-American marriage rates, especially for black middle-class women, have so significantly declined that some researchers speculate whether "marriage is now only for white people?" (Banks, 2011).

All the evidence, both qualitative and quantitative, shows that finding love, and holding onto it, is increasingly difficult. We can readily find ourselves in a relationship, but rarely do we come across that holy grail of so-called perfect

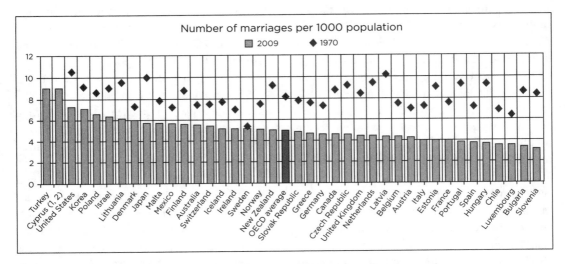

FIGURE 7.2   The Decline in Crude Marriage Rates between 1970 and 2009

Note: Data refers to 2008 for Cyprus, Iceland, and Turkey; 2007 for the United States, Japan, New Zealand, Korea, the United Kingdom, Australia, Ireland, Mexico, Canada, and EU; 2006 for Israel and Chile.

Source: OECD (2011) OECD Family Database www.oecd.org/social/family/database www.oecd.org/dataoecd/4/19/40321815.pdf

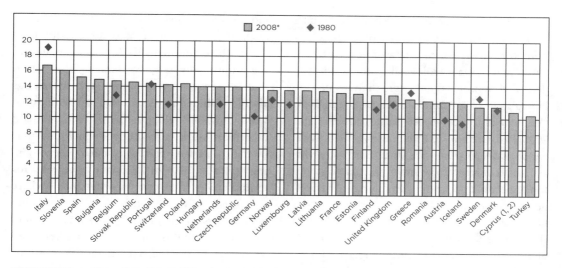

FIGURE 7.3   **Mean Duration of Marriage to Divorce, 1980 and 2008**

Note: Countries are ranked in descending order of mean duration from marriage to divorce in 2008. Data refers to 2007 for Italy, Belgium, Portugal, the United Kingdom, and Greece; 2006 for France.

Source: OECD (2011) OECD Family Database www.oecd.org/social/family/database www.oecd.org/dataoecd/4/19/40321815.pdf

love. So what is the force behind this constant quest for love? One answer is that it is, in fact, a quest for identity:

> The fundamental theme behind marriage is not just the social structure of our lives; it is also increasingly a matter of *identity*. This is the aspect revealed particularly by psychological studies of marriage: in seeking an exchange on many levels with our partner we are also seeking ourselves. . . . We mirror ourselves in the other, and our image of a You is also an idealized image of I. (Beck and Beck-Gernsheim, 1995, p. 51, original emphasis)

For some critics, the condition of being in love is a search for oneself that is achieved through a dialogue with others:

> Being in love is the search for one's own destiny . . . a search for one's own self, to the very bottom. This is achieved through the other person, in dialogue with her, in the encounter where each person seeks recognition in the other. (Alberoni, 1983; quoted in Beck and Beck-Gernsheim, 1995, p. 51)

This gender identity we seek to confirm through love is itself amorphous, changing, unpredictable, and subject to countless variables within the social environment. If our identity is grounded at all, it is only loosely. The discursive self is just that, a discursive construct—contingent and fluid. So what, or whom, is it we actually love? Is it perhaps an illusion, an illusion of self that we construct in order to give meaning and validation to our own desire for identity? We have an idealized image of the other, but contained in that image is our own reflection. From this we might reasonably conclude that our investment in the love discourse is as much if not more an investment in self (Bauman, 2004; also Whitehead, 2003a, 2012).

Intimacy and the Gender Binary

The realm of emotion and its expression through love, relationships, and intimacy is one infested with numerous gender stereotypes. While these may have some basis in reality for many individuals, they cannot possibly accurately reflect the full complexity and diversity of human expressiveness. There are no biological conditions that inform men and women's emotionality: "men are not biologically programmed to deny their emotions" any more than women are biologically programmed to engage with them (Whitehead, 2002; see also Bersani and Phillips, 2008; Podimattam, 2004; Jamieson, 1998). What we do have, however, are dominant social discourses that surround gender and that can give the appearance of arising from some "natural" gender condition.

As we discussed earlier, a consequence of the historic ordering and gendering of the public and private spheres is that women have come to assume and be identified as the gender imbued with natural caring and maternal instincts. This association of the feminine with nurturing goes beyond the realms of parenting, domesticity, and caring practices; it emerges in our notions of love and expressions of intimacy. Women have come to be seen as the guardians of love. Much more than men, women are expected to champion the cause of love, have a natural ability to express deep emotional connections, and a natural instinct for desiring deep love and intimacy in their relationships. Women are expected to protect love from the intrusions of male instrumentalism, infidelity, and selfishness, and insist on its purity and worthiness (also Jamieson, 1998; Kureishi, 1998).

By contrast, men can have a problematic relationship to love and especially to intimacy. As masculine subjects they appear less able to "let go" in a relationship. Whereas women are expected to be reflective and sensitive to feelings and emotions, men are expected to perform a masculinity that is distant, rational, imbued with reason and instrumentality, and largely unreflective of its actions (Kerfoot, 2001).

This is one reason why the concept of and claim to "natural emotional intelligence" is invariably applied to women, and much more rarely to men. This notion, has, in turn, inspired many gender stereotypes, not least that of the emotionally dysfunctional male and the emotionally reflexive female. The notion that women are more emotional than men has also contributed to render women's "emotional work" invisible (Hochschild, 1983). Unpaid emotional work involves producing emotions both inside the private sphere when raising children, and in the public sphere in, for example, so-called caring professions—where caring is traditionally regarded as a feminine attribute—such as nursing or primary-school teaching. Since this form of labour is regarded as natural to women, such labour is taken for granted and is unrecognized in capitalist economies. Consequently, some of the lower paid jobs are in the care industry.

If femininity is associated with emotions, masculinity is often configured around (emotional) control, power, superiority, and self-management (Whitehead, 2002; for example see Rogers, 2005). This pursuit of control by the masculine subject renders masculinity always vulnerable to rejection and feelings of loss of control, a consequence being that masculinity becomes imbued with deep insecurities that are difficult to acknowledge by the masculine subject, i.e., males. This makes trust and intimacy problematic for the reason that these very expressive emotions require us to trust in another, to let go and be in the moment, to engage with intimacy for its own sake and not for any purpose other than to be and to feel. To give and receive love we have to trust, not only in love of the other but in the intention and ability of the other to give and receive our love in return (Misztal, 1998). Importantly, as Jonathon Rutherford's narrative of love illustrates, before we can truly love another we have to come to terms with our selves, with our very own gender identity, and for many men especially, this can be highly problematic:

That is the nature of love—the desire to achieve a sense of completeness through unity with another. Only when men fall in love with women, they fall in love with that part of themselves that is missing. . . . Men have colluded in a masquerade of silence around their emotional dependency on women, their loud self-assurance, nothing more than a brittle patina. In truth, men are unsure what to do about themselves and what to do about women. (1999, pp. 12–13)

The pursuit of heterosexual romantic love is an attempt to overcome the inherent sense of isolation and exclusion that exists at the core of our identity, yet the very fact of the continued existence of a masculine-feminine binary suggests that men and women can never symbolically be fully reconciled as one. The binary exists in order to confirm and maintain a hierarchical separation of the sexes through the social web. This masculine-feminine binary has no other purpose than to identify the sexes as socially distinct, but in so doing it informs and partly constructs the social web, not least through the public and private dichotomy. So male and female come to inhabit very different subjectivities—the male informed by masculine codes and behaviours, the female, by feminine ones (Seidler, 1997; Middleton, 1992). Of course, these distinctions are never total, never absolute. These are porous and amenable areas of identity, and subject to individual interpretation and action. But they do create a divide that goes on to permeate the social web and inform our very concept of gender identity—the divide between men and women. And nowhere is this divide more vivid than in the socially and culturally constructed realm of love, intimacy, and relationships. Not for nothing are gender relationships colloquially referred to as the "sex war."

So in learning to be masculine, males must recognize what is deemed to be feminine but only so as to avoid expressing it. Men are socially and culturally identified through their exclusion of the feminine, women mostly through their exclusion of the masculine. However, this corresponds to a problematic relationship to love and intimacy, for love is, in discursive terms, invested with the feminine, not the masculine. Indeed, emotional expression has been seen, historically, as corresponding very closely to the feminine. But more than that, emotional expression has been discursively associated with madness, hysteria, danger, risk, and lack of control (Lloyd, 1984). This, in turn, reinforces the separation of male and female as the feminine comes to reflect the emotional and the mysterious, the unmanageable, the illogical. Consequently, for many men, emotional intimacy can be seen as an expression of something unfathomable and inexpressible to them, and therefore potentially threatening to their sense of maleness (Bologh, 1990). Rather than engaging with intimacy genuinely, for its own sake and on its own terms, men often project an instrumental intimacy that serves to protect their inner vulnerability as masculine subjects. According to Kerfoot (2001),

> Masculinity gives the appearance of providing masculine subjects with the knowledge of how to respond, and of how to manage—rather than experience—intimate situations. In consequence, emotional intimacy remains ever on the horizon for masculine subjects, who are ever guarding against its possibility. (p. 237)

In recognizing the distinct discursive patterns weaving their way through masculinities and femininities, so we can understand a little better why many men, as masculine subjects, may well find intimacy problematic and are uneasy when expressing their emotional selves, either to other men, to women, or reflectively to themselves. For to do so is to pull at the gender binary, to disrupt it, to unsettle the distinctions that make gender real to them, to you and I, but that we, as social animals, have structured our world around (see Bersani and Phillips, 2008; Podimattam, 2004).

Relationships as Feminized Discourse

Relationships require an emotional and usually practical investment; that is, they necessitate commitment, can only really survive within a culture of trust, and are mostly entered into with high expectations of a positive emotional response. Unlike friendships, which we discuss later in the chapter, relationships are time-consuming. And this is just one of the facets that makes them increasingly problematic in the postmodern age of hectic lifestyles, multiple roles and responsibilities, and unsettled boundaries around work, leisure, home, and office. Our frantic, increasingly pressured and individualistic lifestyles take their toll on us; in addition, we experience guilt at the limited time we give to those with whom we emotionally connect (see Hirsch and Wardlow, 2006; Noller and Feeney, 2006).

There is, however, an important compensatory factor at work here. The very fact of our fast-moving, full-to-the-brim lifestyle is itself a powerful confirmation of our identity, of our existence. Our overflowing diary, our constantly ringing mobile phone, the full email inbox, the need to constantly update our online presence (e.g., Facebook), the incessant chatter around us: all of these confirm our ontological place in the world. Not many of us are suited for a solitary existence. We seek out busy lives, not in order to be busy for its own sake but because being busy fills any empty spaces, potentially threatening spaces, in our heads. The fact we don't have time to think means we don't have to. Our full diaries take care of that (see also Bauman, 2004; Firestone, Firestone, and Catlett, 2006).

But in among all this busyness and absorption in everyday living is the constant desire we have for closeness with others. We invariably yearn for a deeper, more profound communication with another self, something beyond the superficial, the mere friendship, and the simply casual. This need can only really be ameliorated in a relationship. It need not be sexual, but it must be intimate. It must reach into our very sense of who we are, and validate it in a powerful and fulfilling way.

It is often assumed that men and women do relationships very differently, that they have different emotional and gender resources to draw on when committing to a relationship. Such assumptions are not new—they have probably been around as long as love has. But it is possible to see some changes in relationships and how we approach them. Anthony Giddens suggests that a characteristic of the late modern age is an increasing desire for a "pure relationship" (1992, 1993), which he defines as a search for emotional and personal satisfaction; the pursuit of personal happiness, fulfilment and contentment through one's devotion and commitment to another. We will make what Giddens terms an "effort bargain" in order to sustain our relationships, but ultimately they are demanding, they don't succeed without effort, and, as we note above, there are many variables that impact on and lessen our capacity for applying such effort. So the commitment we give is qualified and so, therefore, is the way in which we construct love. For in the event that such happiness disappears, then so too does the relationship. This pureness we seek is, then, highly fragile. We commit, but only to the degree that we get a return on that commitment (see also Bauman, 2004, for discussion). As we indicated earlier, the idea of marriage is transforming today in the sense that it might not necessarily be "for life" as in the Christian tradition, but more "for love" according to what our postmodern society and culture construct as love (see Hirsch and Wardlow, 2006; Schaef, 1989).

Is this an emergent masculinist, instrumental approach to relationships? Yes, in a way, although we could argue that love and relationships have always contained an instrumental, functional dimension. People have always fallen in love, but usually not until they have ticked off some important mental boxes first. How many of us actually undertake some rational evaluation of this "pure love" of ours before we commit to it? Both men and women do this. At the same time, there is no evidence to show that the pursuit of love has lessened. On the contrary, our status as individuals can be powerfully elevated in the attainment and successful pursuit of love. So love, as a feminized discourse, continues its dominance through the postmodern age, albeit subject to the particular conditions and effects of globalization and new technology, e.g., Internet dating agencies, email, global travel, and communication systems (see, for discussion, Ben-Ze'ev, 2004; Gackenbach, 2007; Ray, 2007).

FRIENDSHIP AND ASSOCIATION AS ENABLERS OF IDENTITY

The process of individualizing our selves, becoming a socially inscribed and accepted person in both particular and multiple cultural locations cannot wholly take place without association with others (see Allan, 1989; Epstein, 2006). In order to "know" who we are and to develop our self-identity, we must first recognize that we are part of society; and such recognition is triggered by the gaze of the other. It cannot originate from within us as there is nothing socially predicted within us that exists prior to our entry into the social world at birth. That gaze of the other may be a welcoming acceptance into a social space, or it may be a rejection. But the very process of the gaze upon us is to have the attention of others, and we in turn gaze upon them and so attend to their identity validation needs. From a **Lacanian** perspective, we might envisage this as a constant ontological desire for wholeness, arising from the lack and absence of anything

> **Lacanian**
>
> Relates to the ideas developed by the French psychoanalyst Jacques Lacan (1901–81), who reinterpreted Freud's theories and paid particular attention to the importance of language in shaping the human psyche. Lacan is also known for having written about the role of the gaze and its impact on human psychological development (see our discussion in Chapter 1).

fundamental and essential at the root of our self-identity (Lacan, 1989).

We mostly seek to avoid feelings of loneliness, isolation, and social exclusion for they can be disquieting, unsettling, and uncomfortable experiences, certainly if we are subject to them for any length of time, and without choice. So in being and becoming an individual we are seeking to gratify the desire for acceptance that is within us. According to Hegel, this is a process of negation; that is, by seeking association, bonding, and friendships, so we are addressing our need for belonging—we are satisfying our existential hunger. To desire the gaze and appreciation of the other is a desire for recognition of our selves, and to a great extent we spend much of our lives in the overt or covert pursuit of precisely this recognition. However, as much as we wish for recognition of our uniqueness as individuals, we have to negotiate this in respect of our universality, our social presence. We are never just individuals for we are also embedded in the formation of society itself and are, thus, social beings (Jenkins, 1996). In **Hegelian** terms,

> **Hegelian**
>
> Relates to the ideas and the followers of the German philosopher Georg Wilhelm Friedrich Hegel (1770–1831), who is known for having theorized human consciousness, the role of the mind and ideas, and the influence of society and history as forces that involve contradictory movements.

it is out of this complex but dynamic arrangement of the particular within the universal that our identity emerges, with association being the fulcrum enabling this process (see Hruschka, 2010; Sarup, 1993).

The Importance of Sex and Gender to Association and Trust

Association can be described, then, as the enjoining of the individual to the universal. But it is the particular within the universal that makes this association important, vital even. So we do not simply link with the universal, we link with that which appears to have similarity to us, and which in turn reinforces us. Indeed, many of us may seek to distance ourselves from the universal precisely because of its threatening anonymity. The larger the mass of selves around us, the greater our feeling of being alone.

Cities, for example, can be experienced as soulless places, vast areas of human habitation where no one feels any association with anyone. The universality of the city is too great to provide our necessary identification. We need something smaller, a unit that we can identify with and thereby have that identification returned to us, validated, ideally in a positive and constructive manner. This is why all cities become constructed around areas of distinct religious, professional, class, sexual, ethnic, social, and cultural particularity. These may be identified as communities or they can be much smaller, looser, and fluid social and private spaces/arrangements that provide individuals with a sense of the collective, if not solidarity (Habermas, 1992; Mulhall and Swift, 1992).

Such groups, locations, and collectives will have boundaries, sometimes physical, always cultural, often racial and ethnic (Jenkins, 1996). People gravitate to those who are like them or who at least can offer the likelihood of achieving some ontological grounding through acceptance into a distinct social and cultural space

or category. However, this is not simply about preferences for types of food, expressions of language, dress codes, or familial connections; it goes much deeper. It is about trust (see, for discussion, Sztompka, 1999; Hardin, 2006; Nooteboom, 2002). The excitement and diversity that may be offered via multicultural expressions and lifestyles in a cosmopolitan city can be compelling, but only so long as we can retreat to those local, personal, accessible, secure and trusted, often gendered associations when we feel the need (see, for example, Simmons, 1995). As Misztal puts it,

> Ontological security, as the most important psychological need, is founded upon the formation of trust relationships, and centres initially on parents, members of the family and friends. Without the development of this basic trust, people may experience persistent existential anxiety, and a lack of confidence in the continuity of their self-identity and the constancy of their environment. (1996, p. 91; see also Giddens, 1990, 1992)

So we can recognize trust to be a necessary precondition both of social cohesion and our identity work. But where does this trust come from, and how does it connect with association? Trust is the counterbalance to danger, risk, and uncertainty. We may have some sense that we live in "risk societies" (Beck, 1992), and that risk and danger are ever present in our lives (Giddens, 1990), but so long as certain fundamentals remain constant—i.e., that there remain key aspects of the social that we can rely on—so the unstable and fragmented world appears not so insecure. As a result, we can perceive the importance of sex and gender to trust and, thereby, to association. For whatever happens around us and to us, the basic order of all communities, collectives, and societies remains the sex/gender distinction.

Within the universal, or the wider social world, there are countless opportunities for association: family, work, leisure, nationality, religion, sexuality, education. They exist in and across both the public and private spheres. However, such associations always come with a sex/gender connotation. There is, in the final analysis, no escape from the sex/gender binary that configures the social spaces within which we engage in this identity work. As we have argued, gender identifications are primary. They exist as a distinct dualism in all communities, groups, and social categories. They do not determine our identity, but they do influence our perceptions of our possibilities and they do enable us to understand our boundaries as social actors. Our social class, racial identity, religion, sexuality, nationality, and ethnicity are similarly formed, expressed, and reinforced through association, but they are layered upon what most people perceive to be the most natural and unchanging aspect of their being—their sex/gender identity. We can travel around the world, we can enter any community, institution, or cultural space, and the one thing we take with us that is most visible, indeed that consistently marks us wherever we are, is our identification as male or female. The exceptions to this rule are those transgendered individuals who have deliberately sought to move across the gender binary and therefore bestride it, and those who deliberately present themselves as androgynous.

There is, then, a fundamental, apparently essential, dynamic at work within all associations. It is sex/gender: the identification and separation of male and female, man and woman. We must, in the final analysis, trust something. To trust nothing is ontologically intolerable. We may not trust individuals, communities, or collectives, but we can, paradoxically, trust that which is anonymous. We can trust the gender binary. We can trust that there are men and women in the world. And from this we can begin to construct some social order for our selves and give meaning to our existence.

The gender binary serves its purpose as a core social building block. It validates us as gender beings, it tells us we are male or female, and it provides us with a framework for constructing our lives through association—beginning, for most of us, with mother, father, maybe sister, brother, aunt, uncle, and so on. Even those who seek to operate outside the sex identification first imposed upon them, for example transsexuals, must inevitably negotiate any emergent, contra identity in association with the sex/gender distinction. Its omnipresence remains, for the most part, inviolable, the result being that no associations can ignore it or exist outside it. Indeed many—e.g., male and female bondings and networks—exist and are sustained through it.

Bonding as a Reinforcement of Relationships

Association in itself, however, can offer us only limited existential comfort, there has to be more. There has to be a reinforcement of our relationship to others, especially to the community, team, group, or collective, and this invariably comes about through practices of bonding. Such practices may be formal gender-specific rituals that declare the individual to have undergone rites of passage into adulthood, such as boys being circumcised as part of their religious code. They can be informal group activities wherein a stranger is declared to be "one of us," for example, gang initiation rites, Masonic Lodge ceremonies, and the hazing rituals enacted by students in some US and Canadian colleges. They can be socially and legally inscribed events, such as the coming of age of 18-year-olds. Or they can be those moments when we share humour, cultural signifiers, and language codes with others. Bonding practices may, as well, be organized activities specifically designed to reinforce team and work culture identities. They could be unpredicted, dynamic situations affecting relatively large numbers of people and resulting in those people feeling a strong sense of connection and associa-tion with each other, for example, sharing emo-tions of fear and anguish, or joy and pleasure. So we can bond with those who, like us, survived a plane crash, just as we can bond with those of us attending, say, a rock concert.

The opportunities for bonding with oth-ers are many and can arise in work and orga-nizational sites, during leisure activities, or in family settings, predictably or without warning. They may be formally constructed and overtly political, or spontaneous and unforeseen. The bonding experience can be short-lived, e.g., the few hours spent attending a hockey game or football match with other supporters, or longer lasting, e.g., a marriage, friendship, or partner-ship. In all instances, the bonding moments and activities reinforce our solidarity with others, whether they be friends, family, or strangers. In whatever manner they occur, such bonding moments are vital both for sustaining social networks and for confirming our place in the world. Invariably, however, they become medi-ated by factors such as class, age, culture, and gender, in which case they often operate within a political context in that they serve to include some and exclude others.

In Intimate Relationships

Many intimate relationships rely heavily on the unique bonding experience that comes when the couple engage in sexual activity together. Sexual expression, of all types, is not simply about phys-ical desire; it has a strong identity-reinforcing component, not least through its capacity to generate intimacy between individuals through the practice of sex (see Plummer, 1995; Simon, 1996; Beasley, 2005).

Similarly, we can see that the increased incidences of fathers attending the birth of their child is a bonding mechanism that purports to reinforce the nuclear family unit, perhaps as an unconscious response to its continued demise.

Birthing can be, then, a celebration of the fam-ily and its new member, a rite of passage into parenthood for both parents, and a validation of both parents' adult gender identity.

Among Young Males

Extensive research has been conducted on the rites of passage of young males (see, for exam-ple, Gilmore, 1990; Majors, 2002). These reveal that the meanings ascribed to masculinity are varied and multiple, but inevitably result in the social and cultural separation of the male and female. Gilmore adopts a post-Freudian per-spective to argue that young boys' public rites of passage serve to alleviate the contradictions of distance and desire they feel toward their mother. The rites-of-passage rituals reinforce both masculine identity and a distinction from women and femininity, thereby producing adult masculinity. However, as Haywood and Mac an Ghaill (2003) argue, the boys "become men," not through a natural process but through a distinct and ordered arrangement laden with imagery, symbolism, and cultural specificity. Haywood and Mac an Ghaill go on to critically question the notion of a "ubiquitous male" by examining three cultural and national contexts: the Masai warriors of Tanzania and Kenya, the milita-rized culture that informs Israeli society, and the working-class masculinities in Mexico City. Haywood and Mac an Ghaill conclude that male bonding rituals, such as fraternal rites of passage, are not so much a necessary social requirement for producing a man but, rather, socially medi-ated attempts to present the male as a unitary, natural individual and therefore distinct from the female:

> . . . these cross-cultural studies demonstrate that masculinity and femininity are not reducible to two discrete biological categories [in fact] there appear to be more differences amongst men as a social group than there are between men and

women. . . . Within various cultural contexts a number of competing masculinities are visible that are arranged within historically contingent value systems. (2003, p. 92)

So we should be wary of assuming that male bonding rituals are necessary in order to maintain the purity of masculinity and thereby elicit so-called proper manhood in young males. Rather, such practices are inevitably infused with political, class, race, sexual, and cultural factors that purport to present the male and female as naturally different. In other words, the rituals serve to (en)gender the identity of individuals in a particular social context; they do not arise as an inevitable social validation of natural gender differences. At the same time, the absence of a positive role model for many young people, especially disenfranchised males, can itself be highly problematic for their social and individual identity, leading many academics to argue for specific rites-of-passage programs led by educationalists/mentors (Majors, 2002).

As Identity-Forming Behaviour

In postmodern cultures, where dominant sexual and gender values/identities are undergoing some revision (see Adkins, 2002; Simon, 1996; also Weeks, 2000), the examples and incidences of female and male bonding processes are increasingly diverse yet not always considered socially acceptable. Examples might be young women whose femininity is expressed precisely through rejection of conventional codes of feminine behaviour, or those male adolescents who seek the badge of social acceptance with their male peers by engaging in anti-social activities (see, for discussion, Winlow, 2001; Macdonald, 2001).

Such behaviours may be forms of resistance to external and familial pressures, social conditions, and/or economic and cultural marginalization (Willis, 1990). Always, however, the

individual is expressing him- or herself, through the bonding process, as an active member of a group or collective. The fact that this may, in some instances, involve binge drinking, sexual promiscuity, graffiti writing, or even violence does nothing to lessen its potential as identity-forming behaviour (Hussain and Bagguley, 2005). So-called male bonding can involve sexist and homophobic language, college fraternity misogynistic initiation rites, sexual harassment, random violence, or even the predetermined rape and physical abuse of women and men. In condemning such acts, we can better understand them if we see them not as testosterone laden and, therefore, "natural" behaviours of men, but as socially mediated expressions of (often group) masculinity designed to reinforce what remains, at its core, a contingent and fragile sense of maleness (see, for examples, Messner, 1992; Lyman, 1995; May, 1998; Kimmel and Mahler, 2003; Parry and Malcolm, 2004; Johnson and Meinhof, 1997; Quinn, 2002; Pascoe, 2005; Bandyopadhaya, 2006).

Dominant and subordinate expressions of masculinities and femininities are often in tension with each other; it is impossible to predict just how they may get reformed in different cultural places over time. What we can be sure of is that gender discourses, as languages and practices, will continue to be infused with expressions of class, culture, sexuality, and ethnicity to produce distinct representations of masculinity and femininity in particular locals. The specific processes of bonding that may occur in various gender groups or collectives are pivotal to how such representations come to be reinforced and made visible across society. In this way, gender-bonding processes and rituals may not only sustain the distinction of male and female, they can work to exclude those who do not appear as part of, or wish to conform to, the group or collective identity. Gender-bonding activities are, then, heavily political in that they are infused with both inclusionary and exclusionary characteristics and intentions.

The Significance of Friendship to the Formation of Identity

Our connections with others may be mere associations, they may be reinforced through bonding processes, and they may have a love or sexual dimension, but they are arguably most enduring and sustainable through friendship. Friendship can have a purity to it that is untrammelled by expectations of sex, money, or social status. It can merely "be" in this otherwise confusing, contingent, and changeable world. Friendship may also, of course, come with particular material expectations or hopes, which indicate the strength and particularity of friendship as well as its fluidity and adaptability. Our friendships may be developed however, whenever, wherever, and with whomever we want (see Allan, 1989; Grunebaum, 2003; Hruschka, 2010). At the same time, friendships can be powerful in confirming our sense of having a gender identity. Our friendships may be singular or multiple, informal or networked, but they always come with a strong identity dimension or potential.

Stereotypes of Male and Female Friendships

Yet despite their adaptability, some of the most enduring gender stereotypes relate to friendships. That is, women are perceived as being able to generate long-lasting intimate friendships with each other while men are perceived to be emotionally inexpressive, shallow, and fearful of intimacy with other men. Men are also seen as being largely incapable of sustaining platonic friendships with women (Swain, 1992; see for discussion, Messner, 2001; Whitehead, 2002; Walker, 1994; Nardi, 1992).

Yet if we take this notion of friendship a bit further, and into the concept of loyalty, then something rather different emerges. Stereotypically, women can be perceived as potentially disloyal to each other—competitive, jealous, underhanded, and hostile, especially when vying for the attention of men (Pahl, 2000; Coward, 1993). Men, stereotypically, are seen to have a capacity for great loyalty with each other, especially if such loyalty occurs within male-dominated organizational sites, e.g., criminal gangs, army regiments, the police, male prisons, schools and universities, and sports clubs (see for example, Fielding, 1994; Sim, 1994; Sabo et al., 2001; Mirande, 1997). Men are generally and stereotypically perceived to be loyal to their comrades, especially in the face of adversity. Examples of men's loyalty abound in films and literature, ranging from the legend of Merlin to movies such as *The Godfather* and *The Deer Hunter*. Men may not wish to display intimacy to each other, but they stay loyal to their friends no matter what. Even nonconforming authors, such as the British novelist E.M. Forster, whose gay sexuality and anti-establishment ideas marked him as an ardent critic of Victorian morality, subscribed to the idea of loyalty to friends: "I hate the idea of causes, and if I had to choose between betraying my country and betraying my friends, I hope I should have the guts to betray my country" (Forster, 1939; quoted in Pahl, 2000, p. 41).

The concept of loyalty that is often co-opted into the dominant discourses of masculinities is, then, a loyalty that seeks to sustain male friendships, male bonding, and maleness. It becomes a loyalty to the gender group of men. It may appear specific to an individual, group, or collective but the underlying message is that "real men are there for their buddies."

Friendship is, then, a slippery, contested, and variably understood concept within dominant ideas around gender; this warns us to be wary of assuming a fixed truth behind the stereotypes. For example, Pahl's research reveals that while there appear to be differences in men's and women's friendships, which define men as "instrumental and task-orientated" and women as "affective and socio-emotionally orientated" (2000, p. 122), the longer a friendship lasts and the older the individuals become, so is it more likely that any gender differences will diminish (see also, Adams, 1994).

Differences in Friendship Due to Sexual Orientation, Ethnicity, and Class

We should also be sensitive to differences accruing out of sexual orientation, ethnicity, and class. Nardi, for example, argues that friendship is central to gay men's sense of self, to their social networks, and to the "reproduction of gay community and political identity" (1999, p. 9; also 1992). Allan's (1998) research into friendship and class revealed the importance of language and terminology and its specific deployment as a way of reinforcing solidarity with one's friends. Mirande's research suggests cultural differences between Anglo and Latino culture, showing that loyalty and male friendships are a "highly valued quality amongst Latinos" (1999, p. 86). Simmons, meanwhile, underlines the importance of ethnicity, especially in white-dominated societies, as a factor in reinforcing black men's friendships:

> The fact is, men need the company of each other as much as women need the company of other women or men need the company of women. Men need to shoot the breeze, talk shit, chase women and run the jungle together. More to the point, Black men need to reaffirm their worth in this place that is constantly denying that worth—and such affirmation can only come from other Black men. (1995, p. 360; see also Franklin, 1992)

Even though this statement can sound essentialist and stereotypical, it points to the importance of friendship as a way of retrieving a sense of self-worth. Research into women's friendships similarly reveals the underlying political/personal tensions and issues behind friendship and identity. Some feminist researchers have argued that women's friendships with women are carried out within a patriarchal culture that attempts to position women in sexual categories, enforce notions of maternalism upon them, and increase their economic dependency on men (O'Connor, 1992; Schneider and Gould, 1987; Oliker, 1992). From this it might be argued that women's friendships are, then, a necessary defence against patriarchal conditions, requiring women to be mutually dependent on each other in the face of male dominance. Consequently, women become adept at networking and "attending to each other's welfare" (Pahl, 2000, p. 127) as a means to alleviate the material and emotional conditions arising from their social marginalization and possible lack of agency as women.

Friendships, whether they are between men and women, women and women, or men and men, and however mediated they may be by variables of class, sexuality, race, ethnicity, age, and culture, operate within the realm of identity formation. That is, they have the capacity to appease the marginalization, isolation, and rejection of any individual in most any social setting while also reinforcing individuality and connection to the universal. At the very least, friends "'may help to confirm the fine-tuning of emerging identities" (Pahl, 2000, p. 39). We may have just one friend in this world of over seven billion individuals, but that one friend is enough to strengthen and validate our sense of who we are. Networks of friends have the added benefit of enabling us to operate on difference social spheres—we can move between groups and collectives quite effortlessly, guided and facilitated by our friendship networks. Clearly, in many instances, such networks can have a positive material effect for us, e.g., the individuals we meet in such networks may be able to help us into employment, assist us in business endeavours or increase our social status. Or the network may simply be made up of individuals who are, like us perhaps, culturally distinctive and therefore perceived as different by wider society. In this case, the friendship network may provide a protection against potential exploitation, discrimination and isolation. Examples would be the friendship networks that sex workers often build up with each other, and those friendship networks established by isolated communities living in otherwise impersonal cities. Precisely this process is revealed in research undertaken by Ross (2012) on the "outdoor brothel culture" of transsexual sex workers in Vancouver, which shows the degree to which informal friendship networks can sustain individuals who are socially marginalized and harassed by the authorities and wider community.

Friendships may also become more common in the postmodern age, in that they connect very strongly with a "subtext of difference, individuality and individualism" and the particular conditions of technological communication now at our disposal (Whitehead, 2000, p. 159). In this age of hectic lifestyles, serial sexual relationships, extended family networks, and the constant movement of people across geographical and cultural boundaries, friendships can appear a given, a constant. They can be relied upon when much else cannot. Because friendships are adaptable and flexible, so can they accommodate change and diversity. Friendships are less demanding than relationships, which invariably become accompanied by the love discourse; friends are not required nor expected to

Foucauldian

Relates to the theories developed by the French post-structuralist philosopher Michel Foucault (1926–84), who is known for his analysis of knowledge and discourse as interconnected systems that work to support relationships of power within society and create an individual's identity (see our discussion in Chapter 2).

invest the sort of deep and lasting intimate commitment required in a love relationship. Rather, friendships can be entered into with varying degrees of closeness and intimacy.

Indeed, in the age of the Internet we only need have access to email and we can be friends with most anyone, most anywhere, which underlines friendship's capacity to sustain one's "place in the world" while at the same time providing an opportunity for personal exploration. For, as Steve Garlick's **Foucauldian** examination of the concept of friendship concludes, ". . . we can uncover a notion of friendship as a work of art that reconciles us with our finitude . . . through the beauty of friendship, one may face up to the limits of the self and transgress them in an experience of freedom" (2002, p. 16).

SUMMARY

In this chapter, we have explored some dimensions of our gender identity that often get overlooked in common-sense accounts and reflections of who we are. First, we live compartmentalized lives, where the daily practices of doing gender emerge as very different depending on where we are, whom we are with, and the prevailing social expectations operating in these different spaces. Second, the dynamics surrounding love and intimacy, in terms of relationships, are today highly potent if not problematic, for millions of people. We are investing a lot of ourselves in finding love, but we are also finding love hard to keep. Indeed, with increasing numbers of us living out our lives as single people, albeit surrounded by a multitude of others, the work and effort involved to get into and hold onto a relationship has probably never been greater; while the Internet does render relationships more accessible and immediate, it also has the capacity to render them more tenuous. And finally, we have explored the power of friendship to provide us with a strong sense of who we are and what our place is in the world. Friendships are fluid and hopefully flexible, but they are not the same as a relationship that is invested in trust, love, and hope.

Much of this chapter has been taken up with exploring the private world of love and intimacy, feelings and emotions. Continuing the theme of practising gender identity, the next chapter continues with the duality of public and private but examines these divisions in what is their most widely understood manifestation: family and work.

CASE STUDY

By the age of 24, Paul was married; by the age of 43 he and his wife had two teenage children, two good incomes, and a delightful house just outside London. From childhood through to his early forties, Paul's life was patterned and predictable. He graduated from Lancaster University with a degree in economics, immediately got a job with a major drug company, and quickly climbed the corporate ladder to become one of its directors. His wife was a part-time teacher. Paul looked and played the part of a London businessman. He wore suits to work, jeans on Saturdays, and on Sundays played golf at the Royal Wimbledon club. His wife died of cancer at 44, the same age as Paul. He looks back now with deep sadness but avoids assuming this was the start of his life change; maybe it was just coincidence.

But Paul's life did change, as he did. Two years after his wife died, Paul began the long legal and medical process to change his sex. He called himself Elle and began growing his hair long and wearing skirts. His employers were very supportive and put no pressure on him to resign. His children found it difficult to adjust but they loved their father nevertheless. After eight years of medical and hormonal treatment, and psychological assessment, the British legal system eventually accepted that Paul, now aged 54, had transgendered into Elle. She had a new passport to prove

it. Elle went to Thailand to undergo gender-reassignment surgery. That surgery cost her just $4000, and was performed by a specialist surgeon in a Bangkok private hospital.

Elle lost a lot of friends during this time. They knew Paul, but didn't want to know Elle. For them, the gender identity adjustment to accept Elle was just too hard to make. Elle's father had died when she was a teenager but her mother was still alive. She supported her now daughter, although she still called her Paul. Elle's younger brother, Tim, never spoke to her again. While in Thailand for the operation, Elle met Som, who was a nurse in the hospital, and 20 years younger than Elle. They became close friends and kept in contact after Elle returned to the UK.

Elle took early retirement at 57, twelve months after the operation for full gender reassignment. Although she loved the UK she now felt out of place there. It was not her home in the way it had once been. Her children were now leading independent lives, and she no longer had the same circle of friends. In fact, she had few friends. She no longer played golf at Royal Wimbledon. She never wore a suit. Elle not only needed to change her gender identity, she realized she needed to change her whole life. She and Som had become lovers. The age difference did not matter, nor did the fact of their sex. Elle and

Som had become a "same-sex" couple, and in Thailand Elle was seen as a "Tom" (a masculine woman), while Som was seen as a "Dee" (a feminine woman). Tom and Dee couples are common in Thailand, so Elle and Som just fit into this new gender/sexual category. They were lovers, they lived together in Bangkok, and they had all the closeness and intimacy of any couple anywhere.

Elle is now more content than she has ever been. The change of gender identity was not so sudden as it appears, for she had feelings of femininity long before her wife died. But she was in a role as a man and it worked for much of her life. Then it no longer applied. In Thailand she can be accepted for the woman she is. She has a new friendship group, lots of activities, a new Internet business to run, and a young woman who loves her very much indeed.

DISCUSSION QUESTIONS

1. Is Elle a lesbian, or is she in a heterosexual relationship?
2. Can Elle ever make the full transition to being a woman?
3. What are Toms and Dees?
4. What legal and medical processes must Elle have gone through to become a woman?
5. How was Elle's first life, as Paul, reinforced through the public and private divide?
6. Give examples of how friendships both supported and stood in the way of Elle's gender identity transition.
7. What role does Som now play in Elle's life?

QUESTIONS FOR REVIEW AND DISCUSSION

1. How is your own life divided into the public and the private?
2. Do you consider "happily ever after" to be a realistic possibility in your own current intimate relationship—or for an intimate relationship in the future?
3. How do friendship groups reinforce your own gender identity?
4. What is meant by the term "love discourse"?
5. How does the sexual division of labour reinforce gender divisions, and which gender do you consider most benefits, materially, from this arrangement?
6. Do you find it easier to bond with members of the opposite sex, or members of your own sex? And why?
7. Why and how is the public-private divide breaking down in postmodern societies?
8. Why are friendships easier to maintain than relationships?
9. Why is it difficult to turn an ended relationship into a friendship?

Chapter 8

Identities at Work, Identities at Home

▲ *How you manage the public and the private is up to you.*
Source: © Maartje van Caspel/iStockphoto

Learning Objectives

At the end of this chapter you will be able to:

- Appreciate the ways in which parents/guardians influence gender-role identities.
- Understand the role that family cultural constructions of masculine and feminine play in the development of gender values, gender stereotyping, and gender identity.
- Critically examine the complex and subtle ways that parents/guardians model and transmit the gender norms and values that form the schema of gender identity.
- Understand how work, division of labour, and employment patterns establish particular constructions of masculinity and femininity.
- Critically reflect on how work and organizational cultures are imbued with dominant forms of patriarchal and masculine value systems.
- Critically examine leadership styles and professional identities that posit males as "natural" occupiers of these roles, statuses, and identities.

OVERVIEW

Chapter 7 has shown us that both our private and public lives are informed by gender conventions, scripts, and hierarchical structures. This process starts in early childhood and from our first interactions with others: namely those who parent us and those who are parented with us, our siblings. Thus, the family, in any form and shape, has a crucial role to play in shaping our gender identity. As we discussed in Chapter 2, the theories developed by psychoanalysts such as Freud, Jung, and Irigaray have highlighted our first relationships as crucial stages in the process of learning what it means to be a "boy" or a "girl." However, while psychoanalytical theory deals with the symbolic meanings associated with the child's attachment to the mother and, to a lesser extent, the father, it does not really consider that these relationships are part of a larger socially constructed institution: the family. Neither marriage nor the family is "natural": both are institutions influenced by socio-historical and economic factors. Family households are primarily economic units supported by discursive and cultural frameworks within which religion has often played an important ideological part in offering a moral justification and legitimization of particular types of family. As part of the larger fabric of our society,

the family is inevitably embedded in historically constructed gender discourses that regulate certain hierarchical gender structures. As we will discuss, marriage and the family are largely constructed through certain gender scripts, which we learn very early even though we often come to challenge them or reflect on them critically later on in our lives.

This does not mean, however, that these institutions are unchanging or that we ourselves arrive at adulthood already fixed in our gender identity as a consequence of family influence. If we are capable of learning gender scripts, we are also capable of unlearning them. As we extend our interactions with the world beyond the family and into the realm of work, management, and organization, gender scripts become more complex and also more dynamic. So we have included in this chapter a discussion of the private areas occupied by the family and parenting alongside the public world of work, management, and organization precisely in order to emphasize the commonalities between them. Since these are inseparable aspects of our identity, we have chosen to explore them in one chapter with the aim of highlighting the continuity that connects our private lives (family and relationships) to our public lives (work, management, and organization).

PARENTING AND THE FAMILY: INFORMING OUR GENDER IDENTITY

We never stop learning or practising gender identity. It is a process that begins in the cradle and ends when we do. No matter what our life stage is, we are always, to some degree, engaged in adjusting, adapting, and reinventing our presentation of self as a gendered being. Learning to

be male or female is a central component of our emergent identity. And for most of us, the most influential variable in this process is our family, especially our parents.

The family, both its members and associated domestic cultural experiences, is fundamental not only to our gender identity, but to the gendered social responses (Leaper et al., 1998) and gender **schemata** (Bussey and Bandura, 1999), which we inculcate and internalize as unchangeable, natural elements of our being. Indeed, as Bronstein (2006) puts it, we become "educated" about gender-role behaviour and identity primarily through our parents (see Ajeto, 2009; Hollway, 2006; Ranson, 2010). Through the course of everyday social interaction within the family environment, so children internalize parental messages regarding gender-appropriate behaviour, attitudes, and performances (Abrahamy et al., 2003). Inevitably, this is a powerful and political process—powerful because such learning never fully leaves us, and political because in being taught how to be male or female so we learn a conditioned response to the world around us.

The combined power and influence of parents/guardians and wider family culture cannot be overstated or underestimated. The family and especially our parents are the crucible within which our initial gender values and attitudes to society are forged. Children are born innocent of gender and sexual identity, but such innocence is soon lost, making way for increasingly sophisticated social behaviours and responses. All this is part of our desire for being and becoming a socially accepted and recognizable person. But, as children, we have little or no control over this process. We must accept the realities around us and learn from them. Thus, we take on and repeat, through endless practice, those discourses of gender identity that are at our disposal in the familial setting. Indeed, inevitably we are expected to do so. This is the learned process that the vast majority of children, whatever their culture and ethnicity, go through.

Via various processes, such as gender role-modelling, early childhood play (often with gender-stereotyped toys), and other familial interactions, individuals observe, engage with, and internalize family cultural and parental messages regarding appropriate performances of masculinity and femininity. As children age,

> **schemata**
>
> A psychological term that refers to a mental pattern or a way of thinking that we have internalized and that influences the way we perceive and acquire new knowledge.

so in both direct and indirect ways are they in constant (re)negotiation with their family and parental cultures to claim or reclaim their gendered identities. However, the sheer power of these external forces is overwhelming to children in their formative years. Bronstein (2006) suggests that the frequency and quality of parent and child interaction, the time and activities that parents spend with daughters versus with sons, and the degree to which they support or restrict particular forms of behaviours in different situations all eventually lead to establishing gender-role identities. This is a subtle, often unrecognized, but nevertheless potent identity formulating process that each child goes through. Furthermore, Bronstein argues that although some parents, in an attempt to counterbalance traditional gender-role expectations, may offer gender-neutral or even cross-gender toys for their children, the unconscious or indirect messages of gender identity are difficult if not impossible to monitor, change, and modify. This statement corresponds with recent research that shows that while most parents feel it is wrong to treat boys and girls differently, nearly nine in ten believe parents do so. For example, mothers are twice as likely to be critical of their daughters than of their sons, and more likely to attribute positive personality traits to their sons than to their daughters (*The Independent*, 2010; see also Van Leeuwen, 1990; Ranson, 2010). But none of this is predictable. For no two families are identical, no two childhood experiences alike in every way. Difference is all around us, not least in the formations and dynamics of contemporary family life.

Different Families, Different Lives

In the postmodern, globalized age, the very multiplicity of families seems to be increasing. Whereas once the nuclear and traditional model held sway, this is no longer the case. A 2012 survey undertaken in the UK revealed there were 35 different types of families (Netmums, 2012). In the UK, more children are now born to single parents than are born into traditional nuclear families; furthermore the latest data reveals 45 per cent of all births in the UK to be outside of marriage, compared to just 10 per cent in the late 1970s (Thirst, 2011). Similar trends are apparent around the world: Canada shows an increase from 5 per cent (1970) to 25 per cent (2008). In 2008 the US had 39 per cent of births outside of marriage, while France, Norway, Sweden, Iceland, and Mexico all recorded over 50 per cent of births outside of marriage (OECD, 2011). The region with the highest rates is Latin America (between 55 per cent and 74 per cent). Rates in Asia are much lower with the exception of the Philippines at 37 per cent (Social Trends Institute, 2012).

There are, of course, regional, class, and religious differences that affect the ways that individuals view marriage and family. However, one could safely state that in any country where high percentages of women are in paid employment and education, then the demise of the nuclear family is increasingly marked. What is also in decline is the male-breadwinner family, with statistics showing that 40 per cent of American women are now the main breadwinners for their families (Thomas, 2012), and American women professionals forecast to be earning more than their male peers by 2024 (Leonard, 2010).

Consequently, the male breadwinner–nuclear family model is losing its hegemony across most industrialized countries (also Creighton, 1999; Crompton, 1999). What we have is increasing diversity and cultural pluralism among families, and not just in the West. The very same trends are now wholly apparent in all developed and developing countries. Some commentators may regret the passing of the traditional model, replaced as it now is with no single dominant family type. But perhaps with this change comes an opening up, a loosening of related traditional gender expectations, and a widening of gender aspirations. Single-parent families, extended families, househusbands, dual- and single-income families, gay and lesbian parents—all of these are part of the postmodern family reality, and each may bring with it a different set of gender values. While the consequences of having multiple family models within a single society are not predictable, clearly the various permutations that families organize into can and will have a direct impact on a child's gender identity formation. And all of this raises important questions as to just what impact such key variables may have. For example, is it the case that children from single-parent families present a gender-role socialization that is markedly different from children of extended or nuclear families? Do the various roles that parents adopt in a family setting have a predictable impact on a child's developing gender identity? What influence does a family's socio-economic circumstances have on a child's gender development? And with more children now being born to lesbian, gay, and bisexual parents, what are the issues for such children and what are their perspectives on marriage and relationships? (See, for example, Goldberg and Kuvalanka, 2012.)

Kulik (2005) found that family status and cultural/familial definitions of masculine and feminine attributes do affect children's self-perception of their gender identity; these attributes in turn are informed by parents' socio-economic levels, employment circumstances, marital status, and cultural history. However, in terms of family sex-role characteristics, Kulik's research shows a significant decline in gender-stereotyped behaviour across most family groups over recent years, whether they are single or nuclear. In other words, there is no longer a clear distinction between attributes that were once stereotyped and socially categorized as feminine or masculine across family roles, i.e., domestic chores as feminine and technical chores as masculine.

Research conducted by Katz (1987) indicates that socio-economic effects are highly influential determinants, especially for older children, with marital status and parental employment being especially powerful influences on the gender identity development of preschool children. Two-parent families with lower socio-economic levels and with mothers who are not employed outside the home appear to be associated with more traditional gender stereotypes. Katz (1987) concludes that parents with such attitudes, who are themselves more gender stereotyped or who employ more gender-stereotyped socialization techniques, have children with more highly stereotyped gender identities. By contrast, single-parent families, whether led by the mother or father, and gay-parent families can often offer children more contemporary, liberal models of non-stereotyped gendered behaviour, whatever the family's socio-economic circumstances (see Brooks, 2006; Bond, 2010; Coles, 2009; Ellingsaeter and Leira, 2006; Goldberg and Kuvalanka, 2012).

Research shows that gender-stereotype behaviour persists in many family settings but may shift in emphasis through different life stages and in response to changing life circumstances. Perkins and Demeis's (1996) study, for example, suggests that for many men, a reduced sense of responsibility with regards to gender equity emerges as they go through their later teenage years. Furthermore, the study indicates that this lower sense of domestic and parenting responsibility, in comparison to that of women, is reinforced, regardless of their marital status, once men become parents. Clearly, the results of this research do not support any notion that

the largely female burden of the "second shift" (working at home after the day employment) is disappearing for young adults once they are parents. This suggests that residual gender attitudes, inculcated as children, may re-emerge even stronger as individuals become parents faced with complex interactional pressures to adopt more traditional gender roles. Although this finding was unequivocal in Perkins and Demeis's research, longitudinal research is needed to reveal changes in behaviour and attitudes for men and women as they actually make the transition to parenthood and as their children age.

While the research by Kultz, discussed above, suggests a more positive shift in gender-role behaviour within families, clearly there are many families in which the gender stereotyping of household chores is the central nucleus by which gender identity is defined and reinforced. For example, in some cultures and societies, women's household work is extremely domesticated: women are confined to the home and its extended family arrangements; very little or no public outings are permitted; they are not allowed to leave the buildings; and the courtyard becomes their place of refuge and social habitat. Although in these arrangements younger girls are often allowed outside these confining limits, e.g., to attend school and play with friends, such freedoms can be curtailed as girls reach puberty and, subsequently, womanhood (see, for discussion, Abel and Pearson, 1989; El-Azhary Sonobol, 2003; Shahidian, 2002; Warren and Lengel, 2005).

Clearly, gender overlaps and intersects with other discourses of identity that are dominant within a family setting, e.g., race, sexuality, social class, and religion. Research by Hill (2002) confirms this. Hill conducted in-depth interviews with a non-random sample of 35 African-American parents (25 mothers and 10 fathers; 21 middle-class and 14 lower-income parents) to explore the gender identity development of children. Social class, religiosity, homophobia, and religious funda-mentalism were a number of issues that the study explored. Hill found family structure and class sta-tus affected the organization of gender within the family. The middle classes were more conscious of gender equity and subsequent gender-role behav-iours than the lower-income parents. However, for all social class groups the greatest contradiction for women, between their gender ideology, equal-ity, and gender identity development, occurred in the actual practice of day-to-day lived experience. In other words, the family, and especially parent-ing duties, became a setting wherein a traditional gender divide or the sexual division of labour was reinforced for women. Likewise, in Raffaelli and Ontai's (2004) research into Latino families, while male and female respondents described different experiences of household activities, socialization of gender-typed behaviour, and freedom to pur-sue social activities or gain access to privileges, female respondents in all cases were the ones who reported more limits and curtailment in their lives than did male respondents.

Such processes are also reinforced by the heavy sense of responsibility that men and women can feel as parents. This is especially so for women, who often internalize feelings of guilt and shame at not being "good enough mothers" (Winnicott, 1973). Mothering exists within a powerful gender ideology/discourse, reinforced through a social gaze that has clearly established definitions and markers of what it means to be a good mother. All mothers, across the world, to some extent operate under this social scrutiny, a scrutiny that is invariably most critical when it comes from other mothers (May, 2008; Gazso, 2012; see Sutherland, 2010, for overview).

The Power of Parents to Influence Gender Behaviour

Through children's crucial early formative years, the power of parents/guardians to establish the parameters and definitions of "normal gender

behaviour" is immense. For example, play activi-ties and the toys associated with play are, to some degree, governed and controlled by parents. But as we examine below, there are many other ways this process of influencing gender identity is undertaken by family members, especially par-ents, and done so both overtly and subtly.

By Encouraging Gender-Stereotyped Behaviour

Wood, Desmarais, and Gugula (2002) con-ducted a study in which they examined gender-role socialization as a function of parenting experience in an actual toy/play situation and as a function of adults' perceptions of typically gender-stereotyped children's toys. The study involved 48 children (24 boys and 24 girls), who played with 3 adults—either their own mother or father, plus a matched mother or father of another child, plus a matched man or woman who was not a parent. The study examined the amount of time the children and adults played with gender-specific toys, adults' categorization of toys into gender categories, and adults' desir-ability ratings of gender-specific toys. The results revealed that regardless of how parents sorted toys into stereotypical gender categories, when playing with boys, adults encouraged interaction with masculine toys. However, when it came to girls' play there was much greater flexibility as to the kinds of toys that were played with. Wood, Desmarais, and Gugula found that parents were more likely to offer girls stereotyped boys' toys, such as cars, lorries, carpentry tools, toy guns, etc., but boys were not directly or overtly exposed to dolls, kitchen sets, nursing toys, etc.

The fear of gay and queer conscious-ness appears to be an agency for such parental responses. Certainly, in terms of sexual identi-ties, judging from the research, it seems that irrespective of social class, parents tend to be more encouraging of their children when they are engaged in gender-stereotyped rather than in cross-gender behaviour. For example, boys are more likely than girls to be taught to avoid feminine-type behaviours and punished for gender-role transgression. Always, the underlying concern in such families seems to be to develop the correct sexual/gender orientation of the child (Albanesi, 2010; Gallagher and Smith, 1999; Leaper et al., 1995; McCreary, 1994). Such research illustrates how dominant expressions of masculinity become apparent through many boys' lives, internalized by the child as natural and normal. Despite the liberalization of sexual attitudes in many parts of the world and across many cultures, many parents continue to fear their male child becoming gay and expressing so-called queer behaviours.

Through Modelling

Parents may also influence their child's gender development through **modelling**, that is, by presenting specific gender roles and values that serve to reinforce feminine attitudes in girls and masculine attitudes in boys (Leaper, 2002). Parents can do this in both direct, overt and indirect, subtle ways. Direct ways include the verbal transmission of cultural gender norms, such as telling sons that boys don't cry and telling daughters that it is unladylike to swear. Direct ways also include dictating to their children what types of clothing they must wear, how they should express their bodily language, and how they should interact with other children and adults of the same or opposite sex (Bronstein, 2006). In a more subtle form of modelling, children pick up the different frequencies of fathers' and mothers' everyday unconscious behaviour as examples of what constitutes "appropriate" gender practice (Lindsey and Caldera, 2006; see also (Belsky et al., 1995; DeSalvo and Zurcher, 1984). Indirect messages are transmitted in the complex and subtle ways parents relate to each other and to the child. What the child connects with over time is the particular prototype being

> **modelling**
>
> Following the example of usually older and influential individuals, such as parents, teachers, and other role models.

modelled by the parents and which in turn the child comes to unconsciously emulate. Research confirming that modelling influences the development of gender identity in families rather than biology, justifies the claim by contemporary sociologists and psychologists that gender is "not hard-wired" into the brains of men and women, but is "flexible, malleable and changeable" (Fine, 2010).

In mirroring parental gender patterns, children are not merely reflecting back parental attitudes of gender identity but also building up a *schemata of gender identity* through this reflection (Liben and Signorella, 1987). This **schema** invariably becomes the dominant model that stays with children, in some form or another and in varying degrees of influence, throughout their lives. It can be challenged and changed in adult life, but this relies on contradictory external influences, perhaps education and/or relationship experiences, coming to impact on the subjectivity of adults and forcing them to re-evaluate and perhaps critically reflect on the gender values presented by their parents. In this way, so is individual subjectivity constituted through the power of parental modelling, although one cannot claim it will remain unchanged in adulthood in every instance. Indeed, according to Katz (1987) by middle childhood, parental behaviours become less influential. Katz suggests that this may be the result of a ceiling effect occurring

> **schema**
>
> A mental pattern or a way of thinking that we have internalized and that influences the way we perceive and acquire new knowledge.

with the growing child so that by early adolescence child-related gender behaviours become discounted and rejected, possibly to be replaced by social pressure from peer groups and other external influences, such as the media.

While Katz's observations may account for some patterns of adjusting gender behaviour in a growing child, the research by Arditti et al. (1991) indicates the persistence of parent-informed gender values and performances and particularly their specificity to the parent's gender. They examined the effect of perceptions of mothers' and fathers' parenting behaviour on their college-aged daughter's gender identity development. Perceptions of mothers' parenting were generally more strongly related to their daughters' gender-role development than were perceptions of fathers' parenting. They argue that this may be due to the same-sex influence, which is hypothesized in the literature to be stronger than the influence of the opposite-sex parent. The mother-daughter relationship is characterized by warmth and physical closeness whereby mothers encourage nurturance and interpersonal skills such as sharing and reflective communication. While some studies indicate that mothers tend to be more restrictive of daughters than sons, girls typically are more closely supervised in play and have less freedom to explore than boys, which may have the effect of bringing daughters closer to mothers. In contrast to mothers, Arditti et al. argue that fathers generally are more restrictive of boys than of girls, and their restrictiveness is often related to specific expectations of masculine behaviour concerned with achievement, competition, and mastery (also see Block, 1984; Lindsey and Mize, 2001).

Through Storytelling

Another way in which modelling is proffered by parents is through stories—the narrative construction that goes into family and cultural storytelling. Skillman and Fiese (2000) conducted research with 120 US families and their four-year-old children from the following backgrounds: white (91 per cent), black (4 per cent), Hispanic (2 per cent), and Asian (2 per cent). Parents were asked to tell their children stories about their own childhood. Fathers told stories with stronger autonomy themes than did mothers, and sons were more likely to hear stories with themes of autonomy than were daughters. Traditional gender-typed parents told stories with stronger achievement themes to their sons, and nontraditional gender-typed parents told stories with stronger achievement themes to their daughters. The authors examined the relationship between story theme, parent gender type, and child behaviour and found that higher levels of externalizing behaviours were found in boys whose fathers endorsed strong masculine attitudes, and higher levels of internalizing behaviours were found in girls whose mothers told stories with strong affiliation themes. Clearly family storytelling and the gendered voices of a parent's childhood play a critical role in shaping a child's own constructs of masculine and feminine identity (see Blakemore, Berenbaum, and Liben, 2008; Leccardi and Ruspini, 2006; Leydesdorff, Passerini, and Thompson, 1996).

By Acting as Gatekeepers

Finally, Leaper (2002) suggests a more direct form of gender influence may occur as a result of parents acting as *gatekeepers* of their children's experiences and through their differential treatment of daughters and sons. Leaper highlights four ways (with examples) in which this happens:

- *Through direct instruction or guided participation.* Examples include a father teaching a son how to throw a ball or a mother teaching a daughter how to change a baby's diaper.
- *Through the type of expectations that a parent imposes on a child.* For example, parents

may convey gender-stereotyped expectations that science and mathematics are difficult for girls or that boys do not exhibit emotion or appear "weak."

• *Through the types of opportunities parents provide or encourage.* For example, feminine-stereotyped toys tend to emphasize practising affiliative behaviours (e.g., feeding a baby doll), whereas masculine-stereotyped toys are more likely to induce instrumental behaviours (e.g., constructing a tower of blocks or competing in sports).

• *Through the way parents monitor and manage their children's activities.* For example, parents may place more overall restrictions on daughters than on sons, or they may monitor certain behaviours more closely in one gender than the other (see Leaper, 2002, for full discussion; also see Blakemore, Berenbaum, and Liben, 2008; Bussey and Bandura, 1999; Rogoff, 1990; Huston, 1985; Leaper, 2000a; Lytton and Romney, 1991; Lott and Maluso, 1993).

The family is often lauded by politicians as the being the building block of society, that is, a primary component in the continued effective functioning and maintenance of the social order (see Silva and Smart, 1999, for discussion). Certainly, the family can be seen as this, but neither is the family predictable or value-free. The family—or, more precisely, the parents/guardians who constitute the central framework for a child's sense of security and place in the world—is a political arena as much as it is a social one. The family is also a very fluid term and only the individual within a family can truly define its parameters. In prescribing and proscribing gender-specific behaviours for a child, parents contribute to the continuation of a particular gender order, or at the very least reinforce a series of gender and sexual assumptions/expectations. In many instances, and in many cultures, this attempt to

teach gender identity, and sexuality, to a child is explicit and unapologetic, reinforced as it is through physical and emotional sanction and penalty. In other cultures and settings, a similar socialization process goes on but not in such an overt or direct way. But whatever the intent of such socialization, ultimately the child becomes an adult and thereby perhaps begins to connect with and take on alternative perspectives, values, discourses. Often this process results in the child leaving the parents behind, that is, coming to exist in an intellectual and cultural space that the parent cannot recognize, accept, or connect with. This may, in fact, be one of the consequences of globalization—specifically the rapid transference of contesting cultural values and attitudes across hitherto fixed borders. As a result, we can expect formations of gender identity to continue to emerge through family and parental influence, while also seeing increasing instances where traditional gender and sexual values become challenged and renegotiated by the maturing child.

THE IMPACT OF WORK, ORGANIZATIONS, AND MANAGEMENT ON FORMATIONS OF SELF

The social arena that is paid employment appears to have been gendered through history, in that the public world of work seems always to have been socially, symbolically, and materially associated and identified with men and maleness (Alvesson and Billing, 2009; Hearn, 1992; Thomas, Mills, and Mills, 2004). Correspondingly, most men come to invest much of their masculine subjectivity in their work role, in their career. However, we should not slip into the mistaken assumption, exemplified in **functionalist social theory** (see, for example, Parsons, 1951), that this relationship of men to paid work is essential to the continued order of society. With women now occupying nearly 50 per cent or more of all jobs in countries

functionalist social theory

A social theory that sees the different institutions that make up society as a coherent and interconnected system that works toward ensuring that society as a whole functions in an orderly manner (see our discussion in Chapter 1).

such as the US, Japan, Canada, Sweden, France, Australia, Netherlands, Germany, and the UK—and this percentage is rising—no case can be made that paid work is the natural habit of the male, as Table 8.1 reveals.

TABLE 8.1 Women's Share of the Labour Force (by Country), 1975–2010

Country	1975	2010
Canada	37%	48%
UK	39	50
US	41	48
Germany	38	52
Netherlands	31	46
Sweden	39	51
Australia	32	48
Italy	28	43
France	41	49
Japan	32	46

Source: http://research.stlouisfed.org/fred2/series

post-Fordist

Relates to the period following Fordism, a system of industrial manufacturing based on mass production that was characteristic of the beginning of the twentieth century and that takes its name from Henry Ford, the owner of the Ford Motor Company. In contrast to Fordism, post-Fordism is defined by aspects characteristic of the latter part of the twentieth century, such as the use of information technology, the development of specialized markets, and the feminization of labour.

What we can see, since the 1950s especially, is this tearing apart of the male-dominated world of work, with the emergence of women into paid employment, and especially into many of the occupations previously assumed to be the preserve of men. But this change has not come about because men desired it, nor indeed simply because feminists fought for it. Rather, it was largely the emergence of a post-industrial, serviced-based economy in the West, together with its **post-Fordist** work systems (see, for discussion, Hancock and Tyler, 2001; Edgell, 2005; also Kumar, 1995) that opened the doors for women into mass paid employment. These changes, as part of the larger globalization process, gathered momentum through the 1960s and 1970s, and continue to this present day (Castells, 2004; Friedman, 1994). They have brought profound change in how we order our lives, our relationships, and our families. Such issues as arise from these transformations have powerful economic and material dimensions and implications, ranging from the changed expectations and aspirations of women, especially regarding marriage (Musick, Brand, and Davis, 2012); the demise of the nuclear, male-breadwinner family (Crompton, 1999); and our apparent devotion to consumerism (see Ransome, 2005). Many of these shifts are explored elsewhere in this book and in every case bring the reader back to that arguably most significant aspect of such transformations—their impact on formations of self, especially gender identity.

However, as this chapter discusses, the gendered identity dimensions of paid work are not as straightforward as might be assumed. That is, with women increasingly in employment, we might assume that the liberal feminist agenda, particularly of women attaining equal status with men in employment, has been achieved. But this is not the case. As we will discuss, the gendered aspects of work go beyond the issue of a critical mass of women in employment (Kanter,

1977, 1993), and into the very culture and work systems within management and organizations, proceeding to inform both the subliminal and overt gendered values that arise with notions of leadership and professionalism (see Ely, Foldy, and Scully, 2003).

Work and the Crisis of Masculinity

To gauge the importance of work to gender identity, especially men's identity, one need look no further than the notion of a "crisis of masculinity." In the 1950s, American sociologists such as Hacker (1957) and Hartley (1959) were signalling some profound changes in work and family life, with implications for men's sense of masculinity. They suggested that the changing post-war work patterns emerging in the West were combining with wider social and gender shifts to render traditional sex roles redundant. This debate came to inform not only feminist theory, especially liberal feminist agendas, but also the emergent sociology of men and masculinities. Pro-feminist theorists, such as Pleck (1976) and David and Brannon (1976), developed male sex-role theory, a central tenet of which was that new forms of work and family life were resulting in "male gender-role strain," at least in those men unwilling or unable to forsake traditional roles for modern ones (Pleck, 2005; see also Chapter 1).

The research by Pleck and other gender-role theorists was important in signalling that masculinity was neither fixed nor inevitable, but contingent on constantly changing social, economic, and cultural factors. This discussion was to set the tone for the debate that emerged in the 1980s and 1990s concerning a crisis of masculinity: in particular, the argument that men have a deep psychological need to express their innate manliness and have it validated by other men, and that the public world of work has, hitherto, provided such a space and opportunity. However, with male-dominated manufacturing industries in decline, male unemployment increasing, and women generally preferred by employers for the new service industry jobs, men can no longer turn to the arena of paid work for validation of their inner masculinity, thus setting the conditions for a male crisis (Hodson, 1984; Faludi, 1999; Horrocks, 1994; Bly, 1990; see for discussion, Whitehead, 2002, 2006a; also Clare, 2000).

Discounting such a crisis thesis, from the late 1970s onward British writers such as Tolson (1977), Willis (1977), Hearn (1992), and Morgan (1992) contributed to a more nuanced investigation into men's relationship to paid work. Their research revealed the relationship to be neither straightforward nor predictable in that it can serve to reinforce patriarchal capitalist values/systems while also undermining men's sense of selfhood; moreover, their research revealed that any examination of men and work needs to be cognizant of underpinning class, sexual, age, and ethnic variations. In other words, men may well engage with work as a means to achieve a stronger sense of masculine self, but such engagement was never entirely within their control anyway. As Tolson (1977) describes it,

> And though it becomes the basis for the whole of his adult life, a man's personal commitment to work, is by no means unproblematic. It is equally important to recognize that, because of the way it is socially organized, the experience of work poses a constant threat to masculinity.
>
> Here again we return to the central ambivalent structure to masculine identity: although it is a man's destiny, work is simultaneously an overwhelming disappointment. In capitalist societies, with their highly developed divisions of labour and the ever-widening split between work and home, masculine expectations can only be maintained at the price of psychological unity. At work, a man's gender identity is no longer complete—it is slowly and inexorably split apart. (p. 48) (see also, Cotter, 2004; Julia, 2000; Puchert, Gärtner, and Höyng, 2005)

Tolson's point is reinforced in this age of seemingly endless work intensifications and dramatic changes in employment patterns, all of which appear to be a particular condition of globalization and emergent new knowledge economies (Rifkin, 2004; Beck, 2000). As a result, men's identity association with work is not only insecure but, in some instances, potentially psychologically hazardous (see, for discussion, Casey, 1995; Sennett, 1998; Gorz, 1999; Forrester, 1999).

Of course, the same argument can be made in respect of women and paid work: that is, that too close an association of self to paid work is highly risky not least because employment is always undertaken in the shadow of unemployment and, in modern capitalist states, is now subject to the pressures of target-driven, appraisal-based, performative work cultures (see Dent and Whitehead, 2001). Moreover, Tolson's argument that work and home exist in separation, while now not entirely accurate given modern technology and the increased incidence of working from home, does draw attention to a

We all switch identities constantly, although mostly we don't realize it.

Source: © Betsy Streeter/CartoonStock

further issue in respect of women and work, that is, multiple roles. There is now overwhelming evidence to show that one of the consequences of women's emergence into mass paid employment has been the demands placed upon them to continue to perform both traditional "female" duties in the private sphere (e.g., child care, domestic work) while also now undertaking full-time paid employment (see Cotter, 2004; Franks, 1999; Hochschild, 1989; Puchert, Gärtner, and Höyng, 2005; Hood, 1993).

Clearly, many men continue to be unwilling to share the dual burdens of housework and paid work more equitably. This suggests that women find it easier to enter and perform in traditional masculine spheres than men do in feminine ones. We might conclude, therefore, that as a general indicator masculine identity is more brittle and fragile than feminine identity, that is, more easily threatened at an ontological level. Alternatively, on an instrumental level, many men may simply be unwilling to give up their identity association with paid employment because they recognize that to do so would reduce their social power as a gender group and their individual economic independence. In other words, men are unwilling to assume the conditions that have historically informed women's lived experience.

How Organizational Life Influences Gender Identity

One may conclude that there have always been organizations in some form or another, from the ideologically laden religious to the geographically, familial-based tribal. However, work organizations seem to have assumed a particular cultural and identity form from the 1950s onward, with many emerging in the latter part of the twentieth century as internationally recognizable corporate cultural brands (see, for discussion, Deal and Kennedy, 2000; Kunda, 1992; Parker, 2000). Indeed, as globalization has picked up momentum, this desire by organizations to have a clear identity marker—a "We"—has assumed even greater intensity (see Webb, 2006, for discussion; also Casey, 1995; du Gay, 1996). But what of the workers themselves? How might their sense of self relate to an organization's culture and expression of identity?

First, let us take the point that work organizations are not gender neutral but, rather, are imbued with a masculine ethos, discourse, or rationality that serves to posit men as their "natural" occupants, thereby reinforcing a culture of masculinism (see, for discussion, Roper, 1994; Collinson and Hearn, 1996; Mills and Tancred, 1992; Cheng, 1996; Ely et al., 2003). From a Marxist or socialist feminist perspective, we can understand industry and organizations as sites wherein men hold and exercise (patriarchal) power, and get a conception of themselves as so-called real men (see, for example, Cockburn, 1983; also Crompton and Mann, 1994; Nicholson, 1996). Similarly, no organization exists outside of its social, cultural, and economic location; as a result, organizations are invariably inculcated not just with gender differentiations, but susceptible to the same discourses and experiences of sexuality, violence, stress, and discrimination that circulate in wider society (see, for discussion, Hearn and Parkin, 2001; Hearn, et al., 1989; Lewis and Simpson, 2010).

Max Weber (2001 [1930]), one of the earliest and most influential theorists of organizations, argued that organizations are not only central to the capitalist system but in order to meet their ends, they function through an "iron cage" of bureaucratic rationality—a calculative, instrumental reason that operates outside of emotion, empathy, intimacy, superstition, and tradition and largely in the realm of impersonal practice (see Morrison, 2001, for overview). Even though organizations rely on personal interactions between employers, many operate as impersonal places where only efficiency and profitability

matter. Ritzer, a contemporary social theorist, likens this obsession with rationalization and technocracy to an emergent "**McDonaldization** of society" (Ritzer, 1993). For him, this process occurs when an organization or culture is run with the rational, instrumental, and apparently dehumanized efficiency of a fast-food restaurant, where service is standardized, where quantity and rapidity prevail over quality, and where employees can easily be replaced, not least by technology.

> **McDonaldization**
>
> A term coined by the sociologist George Ritzer in *The McDonaldization of Society* to describe the way the principles of fast-food restaurants such McDonald's—such as efficiency, quantity, and uniformity—have entered other aspects of our society and our culture.

One can see here the relationship between a particular notion of masculinity and organizational culture (Morgan, 1992); that is, men, as perceived instrumental, rational, non-emotional beings, come to be the dominant and representative gender of organizations worldwide. Men occupy the public sphere of work and thereby come to create organizations that in turn mirror dominant notions of masculinity; men create organizations in their own image. In so doing, men in organizations have the opportunity to receive confirmation of their status as men in the social world, and validation of their inner sense of masculinity (Roper, 1994).

However, whatever powerful cultural and deterministic iron cage may have once existed in organizations seems less apparent and secure today, as do the men in them (see Roper, 1994). We now have plenty of evidence that organizations and their members can be irrational, emotional, chaotic, illogical, unpredictable, and dysfunctional (Lewis and Simpson, 2010; Parker, 2000; Knights and Willmott, 1999; Ackroyd and Thompson, 1999; Fineman, 1993; Gabriel, et al.,

2000). The power and control dynamics that circulate within organizations are endlessly subject to contestation, to resistance, and to countless contingent variables (Jermier, Knights, and Nord, 1994; Gabriel, 1999). Even if they once could, men can no longer look to organizations for confirmation of their perceived status as men, any more than they can for validation of themselves as natural technocratic, rational, reasoned beings (Wajcman, 1991; Seidler, 1997). As a result, we have to seek a less deterministic theory to understand how organizations relate to gender identity.

Post-structuralist analysis, especially Foucauldian notions of the discursive subject, alerts us to the subtleties of power, points of disruption and discontinuity, and moments of resistance within organizations. All of this suggests that work cultures do not simply and irrevocably colonize subjectivities and identities to the extent that workers' blindly and unknowingly internalize such organizational value systems (Nicholson, 1996; McKinlay and Starkey, 1998; see Willmott and O'Doherty, 2001; Jackson and Carter, 2007, for overview). Rather, a dynamic relationship is seen to operate between the discourses of organizational culture, and the discourses that inform or are available to the self (Parker, 2000; Knights and Willmott, 1999; Webb, 2006). This perspective tells us that organizations have no existence outside their membership; there is no ontological reality to any organization (Knights and Willmott, 2012). Rather, it is the cultural identity markers of the workers themselves that ultimately determine an organization's culture (Jackson and Carter, 2007; Hofstede and Hofstede, 2004; for overview see Kenny, Whittle, and Willmott, 2011).

Women in Management

One of the most significant changes to take place in management over the past two decades has been the rise of the woman senior manager.

Globally, women now occupy over 20 per cent of senior management posts, up from less than 10 per cent in the early 1990s. Russia has the highest percentage of women in senior management at 45 per cent while the Philippines has the highest representation of women in all management positions at 56 per cent (Whitehead, 2013). Countries such as Canada, Thailand, Poland, Italy, Malaysia, China, and Taiwan all have over 25 per cent representation (Grant Thornton International Business Report, 2012).

As a result, given that many organizations now have what Kanter (1977) described as a necessary "critical mass" of women managers who could bring about gendered cultural change—that is, over 15 per cent—we might reasonably expect such organizations to be feminine in expression, in values, and in culture. However, there is little evidence that this happening (Fletcher, 1999; Itzin and Newman, 1995; Whitehead, 2013). Particular organizations may have a majority of women as senior managers, but this does not necessarily translate into a feminine work culture. Fletcher suggests that while contemporary organizations may place a rhetorical value on those so-called feminine human resource management practices that emphasize emotional intelligence and relational behaviour, in reality such behaviours get "disappeared," primarily because they are in tension with the more dominant, harder-edged, competitive, and instrumentalist work culture (see Legge, 2005, for overview). More globally, it is often racialized men and women who occupy the area of so-called softer labour markets, such as catering, telemarketing, and the caring professions. In the global North, these forms of labour tend to be relegated to migrant men and women.

As we discuss next, a further reason that gendered cultural change is not keeping pace with the increase in women in management positions might be that women, as they move up the management ladder, learn to take on some masculine discourses as part of their professional presentation of self. Such women successfully operate within both the feminine and masculine spheres, and therefore do not need to, nor seek to, privilege the feminine over the masculine. However, as Gherardi (1995) notes, this can create a "schizogenic" condition for some women as they attempt to straddle the psychological boundaries of the masculine and the feminine in competitive, highly stressful, masculinist work organizations. This may be why many women senior managers leave corporate cultures in order to set up as self-employed entrepreneurs (see Marshall, 1995).

Organizations may not simply colonize, create, and control gender identity in any overpowering and deterministic fashion, but they do continue to function within a particular masculinist paradigm. At a general level, organizations speak of, reinforce, and operate in accordance with masculine values, not feminine ones, for example, emphasizing discourses of competition, selfishness, careerism, instrumentality, rationality, devotion to work, and so on (Hearn and Collinson, 2001). This gender dimension may reflect the bureaucratic "iron cage" described by Weber when referring to the impersonal nature of organizations that are run according to the rule of efficiency. By claiming to be rational and efficient, organizations also perform a masculine sense of scientific rationality, what Lyotard refers to as pseudo-scientific performativity (1994; see also Dent and Whitehead, 2001), and, more generally, what Foucault describes as the discursive conditions of power (1978, 1980).

Whatever the means by which organizations function, we should recognize that while they do not determine gender identity, they do have the capacity to inform and reinforce it (Ely, Foldy, and Scully, 2003; Gherardi and Poggio, 2007; Holmes, 2006). Our sense of self is porous and therefore open to the cultural practices, as discourses, that circulate those organizational sites within which most of us spend much of our daily lives. At the same time, organizations do not exist outside the subjectivities and identities of their members. From this, we can understand organizations to be as fluid, complex, changeable, persuasive, and unpredictable as the people who inhabit them.

Management and Masculinities

While individual organizations may be numerically dominated by women or by men, or in numerical gender balance, the organizational space that has historically been accepted as the province of the male is management. In the mid-1990s, (pro)feminist scholars such as Kerfoot and Knights (1993) and Collinson and Hearn (2001[1993]) exposed the "man in management" and in so doing opened the way for what was to become a comprehensive examination of how different expressions and practices of masculinity become accepted as the "way we do things around here" in numerous managerial sites.

As the research shows, such discourses not only come to inform managements, they percolate through the organization itself, embedding themselves in the organization's culture and ethos, and influencing the perceptions and subjectivities of the workforce (for overview, see Knights and Willmott, 2006; 2007; Rees, 2003). So we should recognize management's capacity to set the tone for organizational culture without necessarily determining it. Managements are at the sharp edge of organizational practice insomuch as they are perceived to be powerful; indeed, one might assume that individuals would not go into management as a career move unless they believed they would have power to change things and make effective decisions. For many men, promotion into management would appear, then, to resolve many of their existential dilemmas as masculine subjects. That is, being the manager speaks to a particular masculine discursive mix of power, control, rationality, agency, self-actualization, instrumentality, and purposefulness (Whitehead, 2003b, 2006b; Kerfoot and Whitehead, 1998); they are men and they are managers, a relationship that appears seamless and symmetrical.

But management can also be seen to be a risky business, full of uncertainties, contingencies, stresses, and insecurities (Casey, 1995). In the age of globalization, rapid movements of capital, and audit-obsessed post-Fordist work systems, the manager is pressured and exposed like never before (Watson and Harris, 1999; Watson, 2000; Power, 1997; Misztal, 2001). Managers may write five-year plans but can never present them with any degree of confidence that they will become reality. Indeed, for many, five-*week* plans might appear ambitious. So what issues emerge here for the man and the woman who invest a strong sense of gender identity in their position as purposeful, powerful manager?

For individual men, management, as with work generally, can both reinforce and disrupt their sense of masculinity. While it appears to offer an ontological grounding attributed through (gender) status, being the manager can extract a heavy toll on individuals unprepared for, or unable to meet, its demands (Casey, 1995). Yet, as a gender group, men do have a stronger discursive association with the realm of management than do women—and for four reasons:

1. The discourses of management closely correspond with or emulate discourses of masculinity.
2. Management has historically been seen to be a place of men.
3. Managements remain significantly dominated by men, not by women (Teather, 2006).
4. The work intensification of management that has taken place over the past few decades places expectations on managers to put work above all else, including family.

Indeed, managers are expected, required, to put in the hours, to be present, to be visible.

Therefore this culture of "presenteeism" in management corresponds with a sexual division of labour that places the man firmly in the public sphere, not the private one. All these factors reinforce men's identification with management, both as individual men and as a gender in cultural contexts (see, for example, de Four and Williams, 2002; Kimoto, 2005).

So what of women: how might they fit into this male-dominated world of management? Well, when they can overcome whatever glass or cellophane ceilings may exist (David and Woodward, 1997; see Purcell, MacArthur, and Samblanet, 2010, for overview), when they can pass the gaze of men managers who may recruit in their own image (Collinson, Collinson, and Knights, 1990), and when they can accept that they will likely work more hours yet possibly earn a fifth less than their male counterparts (Institute of Directors, 2006), then women are clearly very capable if not comfortable in management. Importantly, women are just as likely as men to achieve some gender identity confirmation of themselves as powerful actors by occupying a senior management position. Indeed, because there are relatively fewer women than men in management in most organizations, one can see that being a women manager has the potential to be a highly seductive ontological reinforcement of self (see, for discussion, Whitehead, 2001a).

There are many reasons why women become or seek to be managers, but we should not assume they enter this realm unaware of gender differences. Despite the media-inspired notion that feminism is dead (Hall and Rodriguez, 2003), research continues to show that women do recognize the persistence of gender inequalities in many areas of life, not least in work, in management, and in organizations (see, for example, Aronson, 2003). By contrast, this reflexive recognition appears to be absent in many if not most men managers (Whitehead, 2001b). A possible reason for this is that dominant expressions of masculinity are reinforced through management, while traditional expressions of femininity are not. So when women go into management, they are learning to exist as women in a male world, maintaining a feminine presence and identity while also practising a masculine one (see Alvesson and Billing, 2009). This is the ontological accomplishment that makes management both a highly seductive arena for women and a potentially problematic one.

In summary, it is important to recognize that masculinist cultures can and do persist in organizations even while those organizations may have a numerical predominance of women managers. Largely this is because such masculinities, as daily practices, connect strongly and historically with dominant organizational cultures and thereby become the accepted ways of behaving for managers. In this way, so too is the relationship between management and masculinity sustained while being rendered hidden and invisible, not least to managers themselves (Whitehead, 2013).

The Gendered Evolution of Leaders and Professionals

As with *manager*, the labels *leader* and *professional* have an acute gendered history, one that has powerfully and persuasively posited males as "natural" occupiers of these roles, statuses, and identities (Witz, 1992; Crompton, 1987; Davies, 1996; Collard and Reynolds, 2004). Partly this has come about because of the gendered public and private spheres and the sexual division of labour that has reinforced them. But there is also the argument that men have used their presence in the public sphere to deliberately exclude women as leaders and professionals in organizations, thereby reinforcing a patriarchal condition (Witz, 1992). This exercise of male power has been evident across the organizational spectrum, incorporating religions and their leaders, unions

and their leaders, political parties and their leaders, and most professions, even those numerically dominated by women and perceived to be feminine in orientation and values, for example, education and health (see, for discussion, Ledwith and Colgan, 1996; Barry, Dent, and O'Neill, 2003). A commonality of all these white, male-dominated groups has been their ability to exclude, through both covert and overt systems of occupational closure, those whom they perceive do not belong—a *de facto* condition if such professional and organizational groupings are to have a distinct (gender) identification and to claim the right to exercise and reinforce it in their own interests as a power group.

Precisely because of the assumptions and actualities of power that serve to enforce their status and legitimacy, we can argue that leadership and professional roles are the most influential across the public and organizational spheres. The exclusivity, autonomy, trust, and expert knowledge base that define a professional also provide a foundation upon which powerful gender discourses can emerge. Likewise, conventional notions of good leadership as being imbued with hard-headed rationality, aggressiveness, determination, ruthlessness, and single-mindedness to the exclusion of all else and others suggest masculinity, not femininity (see Painter-Morland and Werhane, 2010, for overview).

So, for example, we can see how a masculinist culture and associated languages, values, and practices come to be reinforced and privileged in professions dominated by men, including, for example, politics, accountancy, architecture, engineering, the armed forces, the police, the judiciary (see, for discussion, Anthony, 2001; Holmes, 2006). In turn, such a culture serves to validate the gender identities of those males who come to occupy these roles and positions. The man and his professional identification are synergistically positioned and self-sustaining, each thereby acquiring an unquestioned legitimacy. The surgeon, the policeman, the politician, the judge, the doctor, the architect, the company director, the leader of the armed forces, the police superintendent, and the president of the United States signal, in gender terms, men and masculine behaviours.

But the reality is that at the outset of the twenty-first century we have now moved into an era when such assumptions no longer hold true in quite the way they did. To be sure, women are still outnumbered by men in most positions of power and authority, especially at the highest level senior management and leadership positions (typically by a ratio of 5 to 1 globally), and there is a dearth of black, Latino, and Asian women running major corporations. However, the gender barriers that once kept women from the boardroom, from government, and from the professions are breaking down and are being challenged. For example, despite the fact that Switzerland was the last European country to introduce universal suffrage (1991), in 2010 Swiss women took control of the country's government, outnumbering men in its Cabinet (Waterfield, 2010). Similarly, in Canada, which has historically been slow in seeing women move into male-dominated professions, women now represent 36 per cent of the legal profession (30 per cent in the US) and are increasingly visible in medicine, chemistry, business, engineering, and dentistry (Kay and Gordon, 2008; Magocsi, 1999). South Korea has the highest percentage of women CEOs in the world (30 per cent), followed by China, Thailand, Brazil, and Russia. In 2012, the chief executive officers of PepsiCo, Yahoo, Morgan Stanley, DuPont, Kraft Foods, eBay, IBM, London Stock Exchange, Tesco.com, Hewlett-Packard, Western Union, Siebert, Xerox, Avon, Pearson, Sempra, and Sara Lee were all women.

In many places around the world, women are moving into powerful leadership and professional roles. Former political figures like Indira Gandhi, Margaret Thatcher, Eva Peron, Mary McAleese, and Benazir Bhutto and current ones such as Hillary Clinton, Australian prime minister Julia Gillard, German chancellor Angela Merkel, Indian president Pratibha Patil, Bangledeshi prime minister Hasina Wajed, and Brazilian president Dilma Rousseff have left their marks on the international political scene—although not all of them are known for having promoted gender equality. On the contrary, some would even argue that, in some cases, female politicians are as capable as male politicians when it comes to promoting masculinistic and patriarchal ideologies and policies. In a sense, both men and women are part of the political culture of masculinity that prevails in the world, and the gender of the politicians that implement this ideology is sometimes of little consequence.

However, the situation of women has indeed evolved around the world with regard to access to professions that had previously been exclusively male territories. The idea that the surgeon or the politician must, by definition, be a man is now unthinkable. This perception is not simply a politically correct response to gender issues; it is an acknowledgement of the work realities that exist at this point in history (see Coughlin, Wingard, and Hollihan, 2005).

So we can perceive an interesting shift in gender identities here, and one that is different for men than for women. First, men can no longer assume a right, by virtue of their gender, to be seen as natural leaders, managers, or professionals. They may have been able to claim this in the past but not today. Second, women have relatively more possibilities for occupying leadership and professional positions, and increasingly they are taking them, though not without male resistance in some quarters. In the process, women are exhibiting this interesting mix of the traditionally masculine and feminine, something that is beyond the subjectivities, perhaps even capabilities, of most men.

Not only does this suggest a weakening of male power—at least in the way that Marxist feminists, for example, have theorized it—it also indicates that gender identity is never fixed and determined in an individual. Rather, we can see that gender identity is constantly subject to change and adjustment by individuals, not least through the practices and discourses that envelope the public sphere of paid employment. At the moment it would appear that women are more willing and capable of making such adjustments, although we should not rule out this possibility in men, at least in the future. So work and its organizations have not lost any of their capacity to provide us with a social space for practising, performing, and validating our gender identity; they have just lost some of their capacity to do that almost exclusively for males. It is into this highly fluid and increasingly gender-ambivalent work setting that men and women now enter. However, they enter a space that is also subdivided by hierarchical divisions of class, race, and other differentiating categories. As gender categories shift, others may get reinforced. At times, new categories could even appear and re-enact the masculinistic scripts of gender difference.

SUMMARY

Family life is changing, yet it also remains at the core of society and community. All of us, or at least most of us, come from some type of family unit, although no longer can we assume it to be the nuclear model. Does this matter or not? Well, as we have discussed in this chapter, it does matter, not least because in learning our gender, discovering what it means to be a male or female, we inevitably take our cue from those nearest to us—and that usually means parents and siblings. As a result, the family, whatever its particular manifestation in the twenty-first

century, loses none of its power to influence who we are and who we can be. All of us seek direction, mentors, social indicators, cultural codes, and barriers. Without them, life is just too fluid, too contingent, too random and insecure. Family provides us with such a framework. However, for many of us this framework can be an iron cage—inflexible, hard, risky to challenge—just too fixed. We may see through the iron bars of our own heritage and family experience and out into the more open and diverse global world around us, but we cannot easily become a part of it, at least not without risking opprobrium from community and family and ontological uncertainty as we step away from the familiar, reinforced, and known of our upbringing into something altogether quite different and unpredictable.

The one place that we can test out alternative gender performances is at work and in organizations. Women can, and increasingly do, become masculinized leaders and managers, every bit as ruthless, instrumental, and rational as any iconic male leader. You walk into any hospital in Canada, the US, or the UK and ask to see a doctor or surgeon, and you are almost as likely to see a woman as a man. Your local politician is as increasingly likely to wear a skirt as a suit. Correspondingly, men can become carers, nurses, teachers in kindergarten schools, and social workers, and increasingly they do. This particular gender transition, however, is much less common with men. It is as if the feminine arena still holds many uncertainties and threats for most men. They are not so comfortable with it, even if they are comfortable with accepting gender equality at work. They just want to keep the feminine at a distance, not have it become who they are. The irony is the feminine is within them, within all men. But they don't like to engage it.

How we each negotiate and experience family and work is, in the final analysis, the story of our lives. Families may not ultimately define us, but they come pretty close to it. Work and professional identities may not be all we are, but for most of our adult life it does feel like it. Negotiating these tensions occupies most of us for most of our adult life. Moreover, it is a negotiation heavily invested with gender identity assumptions and parameters.

CASE STUDY

Su lives and works in one of the most Westernized, and prosperous, nations on earth—Singapore. She is one of the 4.5 million citizens of this island state, which lies at the southern tip of the Malaysian peninsula. Aged 27, Su has benefited from the high standard of education that Singapore offers. After six years of continuous study, two years ago she graduated from the National University of Singapore with both a BA and MBA in business and management. She now works as a manager for an international insurance company and is responsible for a team of 10, mostly males.

Su is used to the expectations placed on her as the eldest daughter. She knows that she will have to repay the sacrifices her parents have made to ensure she gets the best possible education. Already, Su has visited major European cities, New York, Australia, and Japan. She is a Chinese Singaporean woman, but she is also very much a global citizen. She knows many languages; her education is the very best; her expectations for the future, high.

Like her colleagues and most other Singaporeans of her class and education, Su works long hours, usually putting in not fewer than 70 hours per week. She lives comfortably, however, and will soon be able to put down the deposit on her own high-class condominium. She drives a new Honda 4x4, and is saving up for a second trip to Europe next year.

The long hours of Singapore's work culture do make it difficult for Su to find a partner, and she is also concerned that any man she dates meet the approval of her family. This means he should be more educated than her, or at least as educated. Unfortunately, the trend in Singapore now mirrors that of the West, with more women than men graduating from university. This puts a premium on suitable men for Su. The fact that Su often doesn't leave her office till 8:00 p.m., and catches up with paperwork over the weekend, doesn't leave her much time for socializing. She did start dating a Western man, an American, a little older than her, who was working in Singapore for a year. But she never had enough confidence to take him home to meet her family, so the relationship eventually came to an end. She knows her parents expect her to marry a Chinese man, not a Westerner. For Su, her high level of education has moved her up to into the realm of the elite middle class of Singaporean society. She has independence, financial security, and good prospects. But this comes at the price of little leisure time and long work hours.

There is also a second issue and it is one that Su is now beginning to recognize as she moves up the career ladder. It is that as a woman she is expected to be subservient to male managers in her organization. This fact also puts her off having a relationship with any of them. So Su finds herself in a very different place to that which her mother occupied when she was 27. By that age her mother already had two children, Su and her brother, and had been married for eight years. She lived her life solely for her family, and never did paid work. Neither of her parents went to university, although her father is a successful businessman. For Su, such options are not available, or have passed her by. She has the world at her feet, but as things are at the moment, she will be walking alone.

DISCUSSION QUESTIONS

1. What different identities can you see operating in Su's life?
2. How are the traditional, modern, and the postmodern impacting Su's life?
3. Why has education been so important to Su in forming her gender identity?
4. What gender barriers remain for Su to overcome if she is to have freedom of choice in her life?
5. How is Su demonstrating masculine characteristics, and how is she demonstrating feminine ones?
6. What sacrifices would Su have to make in order to have the same family life as her mother?
7. To what extent does Su's experience resonate with your own?

QUESTIONS FOR REVIEW AND DISCUSSION

1. Explain the notion that organizations have no ontological identity.
2. To what extent is management still the privileged arena of men?
3. Who were the iconic leaders of the twentieth century? How many of them were women? Which ones do you think changed the world and in which ways?
4. Why is the male family-breadwinner model in decline across all developed and developing nations?
5. Do you think that men can adjust to a new reality that requires them to invest more time in family life (i.e., as househusbands and carers) than as full-time paid workers? What will men have to give up to take on these nurturing roles?
6. Do you believe that family life is in decline or just changing? Give evidence to support your position.
7. What anecdotal or personal evidence do you have to support or question the idea that mothers and fathers react differently to male and female children?
8. In what ways do women continue to be disadvantaged at work and in organizations?

Chapter 9
Education and Schooling, Sport and Leisure

▲ *What goes into a young mind is likely to stay there, long after it has been forgotten.*
Source: © Jo Unruh/iStockphoto

Learning Objectives

At the end of this chapter you will be able to:

- Understand how education influences gender identity and gender relations.
- Critically examine how school experiences engage culture, class, and race in shaping gender identities.
- Appreciate how sport and leisure are not gender-neutral arenas.
- Critically reflect on how sport evolves into a primary site for the reproduction of gender identity, specifically hegemonic expressions of masculinity.
- Understand and appreciate how the concept of "leisure society" and "leisure industry" become primary sites for the development of gender identity and the discursive self.

OVERVIEW

Outside the home, schooling, sport, and leisure are three key activities that play a role in our socialization and, therefore, in the acquisition of gender norms. Education is one of the areas that has seen the most dynamic patterns of gender change in the past 50 years. The growing number of women entering further and higher education and their relative success has altered the traditional notions of what education means and how it influences us. Similarly, sport is no longer the exclusively male domain it used to be, while leisure has not only become a major industry but recognized as the time when we can be most ourselves. Education, sport, and leisure are therefore important areas that continue to shape children's and young adults' sense of self-esteem in significant ways. While these spaces are becoming more inclusive, however, they also continue to perpetuate significant markers of difference. Normative discourses based on class, race, and sexuality are often learned in the classroom, on the playground, or on the playing fields, either explicitly or in more covert but still pervasive ways. As the gendering of our identities is becoming an increasingly complex process in the postmodern era, so too are the ways in which education, leisure, and sport provide ideological support for old and new gender roles. As with previous topics, this chapter examines both the emancipatory and controlling influence of education, leisure, and sport, in addition to considering intersecting factors of difference that add complexity to the ways in which gendered selves are acquired outside the home environment.

EDUCATION AND SCHOOLING: POWERFUL INFLUENCES ON SELF-ACTUALIZATION

There are particular areas of social activity that have always been and remain heavily invested with both opportunity for, and/or control over, the development of cultural and social norms and values, human potential, and, consequently, identity. Such areas are inevitably political, and none more so than education. Indeed, when contending theorists offer contrasting perspectives on the aims, philosophies, and practices of education, one can see most vividly the competing positions and standpoints. And only rarely is there agreement between (see Peters, 1998). In amongst this confusion of differing perspectives, policies, and theories lies the vital issue of identity; for education is one of the most powerful indicators of, and influences upon, social class, social mobility, professional and work identifications, and relationship and friendship networks—indeed for the very self-actualization of the individual. For most of us, our experiences within the educational arena are a compelling influence on our sense of self, our intersubjective processes and experiences, and our expectations and possibilities for future identity development. This applies not just to the young child in the primary- or secondary-school setting, but equally so to the mature student at college or university. At every level, from the micro (individual) to the macro (social), education is undoubtedly one of the most powerful determinants of our possibilities as human agents. Indeed, in the highly competitive global age of the knowledge economy, there is overwhelming evidence to show that advancing educational opportunity for all, and especially for women, has the most impact on the social well-being and economic development of a nation-state and its peoples (Agostinone-Wilson, 2010; World Bank, 2007, 2012; Walby et al., 2006; Cohen and Bloom, 2005).

Theorizing Education

The range of perspectives on schooling and education is vast. The early writings of Marxist theoreticians Bowles and Gintis (1976), for example, posit education as a site for reproducing labour power in capitalist societies, not least through the ideological effectiveness of the "hidden curriculum," which serves to dissipate social resistance (see also, Hill et al., 1999). Later perspectives include the postmodernist position of, for example, Stronach and Maclure (1997), and Usher and Edwards (1994), which we examine below. The more deterministic views of education focus on the role of schools in preparing students for their future roles as workers. Schools deliver the curriculum but also teach us implicit values, such as conformity, competitiveness, and obedience to authority. These are not part of the students' textbooks or lessons, or the set of rules they are presented with, but are acquired more implicitly through their daily interactions in classrooms, on playgrounds, and in other school settings (see Wotherspoon, 1998; Bowles and Gintis, 1976; Dreeben, 1968; Jackson, 1968).

So having access to education does not necessarily simply mean being given opportunities for personal development. School is also the place where we are introduced to the relationships of dominance and subordination that prevail in the wider economic and social spheres. Education systems can shape individuals whereby they internalize a dominant value system, for example, ideas of national identity, specific cultural ways of behaving, obedience to authority, and especially stereotypes of sexuality and gender. As schoolchildren, we also assimilate the value of external rewards, such as grades and qualifications, in the same way, later in life,

we receive paycheques and promotions (Aulette and Wittner, 2012 [2009], p. 167).

In this respect, school mirrors the world of work and employment. A study carried out in a New York high school in 1975 showed that while some personality traits—such as perseverance, dependability, consistency, identification with the school, punctuality, predictability, and tactfulness—were regarded as valuable and rewarded by the school system, others—such as creativity, aggressiveness, and independence—were penalized. Interestingly, these same traits correspond to the ones disapproved or approved of by work supervisors (Bowles and Gintis, 1976, pp. 137–38). In some cases, the project of producing docile and efficient citizens colludes with other authoritarian ideologies, such as colonialism. In Canada, for example, the boarding and residential schools set up in the nineteenth century for children of Aboriginal ancestry and operating until the 1960s illustrate, often in tragic ways, the role of education in assimilating individuals within a hierarchical social structure and ensuring their future compliance with an unequal and racialized society. The highly regimented, controlled, and often abusive regime of these schools was in many respects part of a disciplining project in line with the colonial ideology of subordination and cultural assimilation (see for discussion Wotherspoon, 1998; Kirkness and Bowman, 1992).

While some critics have highlighted the role of schools in disciplining individuals and preparing them for the workplace, others contend that education is not without emancipatory possibilities for individuals. Usher and Edwards (1994) argue that education in the postmodern moment offers "tangible" prospects of resistance, "even though it might not result in the emancipatory utopia posited by modernity" (p. 224). Between these standpoints is the structural-functionalist position of Parsons and Durkheim (see Chapter 1), who see schools as key sites for the transmission of general values, specialized skills, and the development of a socially responsible individual who functions effectively and in a contributory fashion to the collective.

A number of theorists have offered studies that appear to chart a path through the maze that emerges from attempting to understand the combined effects of educational systems, action, and pedagogy on individual subjectivities: that is, between ideological inculcation and individualistic disposition. Bourdieu's influential analysis of the relationship between education and social (cultural) capital might be placed in this context (Bourdieu and Passeron, 1998; see Wildhagen, 2010, for overview), especially his concept of **habitus**, which has been extensively used as a theoretical device to understand how social and class relations are reproduced and how such might be resisted, as least through the reflexive capacity of the social actor (see Reay et al., 2005). Similarly, Willis's study (1977) into the dynamic if not corrosive relationship of working-class boys to their schooling and education, although claiming a neo-Marxist perspective, can be interpreted as a failure of the (capitalist) education system to determine the subjectivities and behaviour of these young males. This ethnographic study carried out among non-academic working-class boys in UK schools examines the transition from school to work and highlights some of the complex ways in which these boys interact with dominant ideological structures. The objective of Willis's study, conducted mainly through interviews with school boys, is to discover "how working class kids get working class jobs" (Willis, 1977, p. 1). For Willis, the answer does not lie in one single explanation but rather in the complex cultural forms that surround working-class "lads." For despite the efforts of the educational system, the young men in Willis's study ultimately rejected its promise, not least because they came to see through, or penetrate, the structural ideological apparatus it otherwise concealed.

> **habitus**
> A set of attitudes and ideas that members of a particular social class have acquired through socialization and that manifests itself, consciously or unconsciously, through particular dispositions, such as our taste for food, books, music, cinema, etc. Also relates to aspects of our culture or social class that we express through particular attitudes and values and through our body language and that we have acquired, consciously or unconsciously, through socialization.

A constant theme through all readings on education aims and philosophy is the issue of potential—that is, the role of education to function as an effective vehicle to promote human potential and empowerment outside of structural constraints and influences. This liberal perspective, typified by the writings of John Dewey, Paulo Freire, Ivan Illich, and Jean Piaget, is one with which many contemporary educationalists would concur, often in the face of whatever political and policy agenda might be washing over them at the time (see, for overview, Noddings, 2011; Spring, 2007).

Ultimately, and whatever their standpoint, most educational theorists have to address the question of power—that is, is the power of education invested in the state, in dominant social groups and classes, in business and commerce, in the teacher/educator, or in the individualized and developing subjectivities of the learners themselves. For sure, there is a lot of power exercised and offered in the whole educational process. A Marxist position, exemplified by Hill et al. (2003) and Rikowski (1997) would take power as structural and ideologically framed within the prevailing social (capitalist) apparatus, with learners having only limited capacity to resist. Similarly, neo-Marxist writer Andre Gorz (1999) argues that the contemporary educational system reduces the individual's power and self-esteem by "investing all its efforts in integrating people into a society of workers" (p. 69) whose sense of identity subsequently relates only to their possible employability. By contrast, Foucault (1994) offers a more agentic, if complex, but certainly less deterministic interpretation of (education and) power:

> Take, for example, an educational institution: the disposal of its space, the meticulous regulations that govern its internal life, the different activities that are organized there, the diverse persons who live there or meet one another, each with his own function, his well-defined character—all these things constitute a block of capacity-communication-power. (p. 358)

According to Foucault (1994), institutions such as schools are part of a larger power structure:

> This is not to deny the importance of institutions (e.g. schools) in the establishment of power relations but, rather, to suggest that one must analyze institutions from the standpoint of power relations, rather than vice versa, and that the fundamental point of anchorage of the relationships, even if they are embedded and crystallized in an institution, is to be found outside the institution. (p. 343)

So rather than seeing power as simply a product of (educational) institutions, a Foucauldian analysis takes the school as a site for the expression, moderation, practice, and resistance of powers already circulating in wider society. Such an analysis will expose the dominant discursive conditions under which the educational process and related policies and practices operate while recognizing its contingency. From this, we may, as Ball (1994) argues, adopt a poststructuralist perspective and critically consider the discursive shifts in education over recent decades—notably from a paternalistic model of education practice to one imbued with entrepreneurial, **performative** characteristics and grounded in a **neo-liberalist** agenda (also Ball, 2003; Blackmore, 2005; Whitehead, 1999), while recognizing that no single agency is in total control of this process.

But as with all the social arenas explored in this book, education also comes with a gendered character and constitution. Over recent decades, numerous feminist theorists have critically explored the gendered constitution of education in all its manifestations—for example, the management and organization of education, the gendered curriculum, and the gendered classroom. In the process, such theorists have drawn attention to the prevailing masculinist paradigm at the heart of educational practices and systems (Connell, 2000; Kerfoot and Whitehead, 1998; Kerfoot, Prichard, and Whitehead, 2000; Weiner, 1994; Connolly, 2004; Skelton, 2001; Davies, 1989; Francis, 2000; Mac an Ghaill, 1994). Such discussions draw on a range of theoretical paradigms within the genre of feminist theory, from social constructionist through to postmodern

---

performative

A term originating from the work of the French philosopher and sociologist Jacques Lyotard to describe an aspect of postmodernity that is the preference for scientific knowledge over subjective knowledge. It has been since adopted by organizational theorists to explain the trend in organizations to measure and quantify every aspect of employee performance (e.g., targets, assessment, appraisal).

---

neo-liberalist

One who espouses economic liberalization from state intervention and promotes free-market principles and practices across both the public and private sectors, for example, the privatization of state-owned enterprises (energy), the deregulation of markets (finance), and the introduction of private sector methods in the public services (education).

and post-structuralist. However, as we now discuss, they all serve to illustrate how gendered expectations of practice and identity can be both reinforced and challenged within the school and educational system, in so doing eliciting diverse expressions of identity work in learners.

Schooling the Girls

When feminist sociologists turned their attention to schooling and education, mostly from the 1970s onward, they did so recognizing several long-standing conditions. First, education is not now, nor likely ever has been, gender neutral: it comes ready invested in dominant discourses/ideologies around gender and sexuality that play themselves out in all educational sites. Second, educational opportunity had, historically, gone to boys, not girls, with females underachieving and under-represented at all educational levels, especially university. Third, educational organization policy and practice remained under the control of men. Fourth, the relationship between education and the continuing gender inequalities in society required analyzing from a feminist standpoint if a new discourse of equality was to be developed across all education sectors.

Feminists such as Weiner (1994), Walkerdine (1989), Jones and Mahony (1989), Spender (1981), and Acker (1994) linked, through their research, educational processes and continuing gender inequalities. But they also suggested ways of eradicating such differences through a variety of strategies, all aimed at establishing an equal-opportunities culture and agenda in schools, not least by developing a non-discriminatory (feminist) pedagogy and curriculum (see, for example, Weiner, 1994). Their central thesis was that a core aim of education, at least in a secularized social-democratic society, should be to promote equity and equality, in which case the schooling and the curriculum must be arranged so as to meet this aim, thereby challenging bigotry, sexism, and discrimination in all forms (also Troyna, 1989).

Whatever these feminists' theoretical standpoints were, and they did vary, they were grounded in a feminist **praxis**, wherein the theory informed the development of subsequent (educational) practice. Their studies highlighted the gendered practices in classrooms, the masculine character of the curriculum, racial and sexual harassment and bullying, the dominance of the heterosexual paradigm in schools, gender differentiations in academic and vocational subjects, and the intersections of race, class, and gender across educational cultures (Francis and Skelton, 2001, 2005; Arnot and Mac an Ghaill, 2006, for overview). The underlying theme in most feminist educational research, certainly during the 1970s and 1980s, was that the continued marginalization, stereotyping, and disenfranchisement of women and girls in schools, colleges and universities should not and could not be allowed to continue (see also Skelton and Frances, 2009).

> **praxis**
> A theoretical idea or concept translated into practice.

Political Changes Affecting Education

However, at the same time as such feminist research was beginning to have an impact on the consciousness and practices of teachers and educators, significant political changes were occurring in many Western societies. The emergence of a new-right, market ideology in public services—neo-liberalism—brought a distinct managerialist imperative to the culture and organization of education, sweeping aside decades of public service provision where control of education had been largely in the hands of the teachers (Gerwitz, 2002). The UK was one of the first Western nations to begin this move towards the marketization of education, although many others soon followed. Led by Conservative Party leader and Prime Minister, Margaret Thatcher, the changes began in the early 1980s. Various policies, notably the 1988 Education Reform Act (which introduced the national curriculum into England and Wales and encouraged schools to promote open enrolment), and the 1992 Further and Higher Education Act (which released colleges and polytechnics from the control of local education authorities), provided a greater emphasis on performance, access, measurement, audit, and the role of government in education. Now, for possibly the first time in the history of (UK) education, the major stakeholders were no longer the teachers and educators (the professionals), but the government and, to a somewhat lesser extent, industry, parents, and pupils (see, for analysis, Jones, 2002; Tomlinson, 2001; Whitty, 2002).

The new rhetoric was about educational choice, effectiveness, and accountability in an increasingly competitive global knowledge economy (Handy, 1995). This rhetoric has since taken hold in most developed and developing countries as they too seek to secure their economic standing in the insecure global economy and judge the imposition of private sector managerialist practices in education to be a means of improving their national educational performance (see, for discussion, Maringe and Foskett, 2010; Lingard and Ozga, 2006). In the UK, and elsewhere around the world, the emergent middle classes, those with the necessary social and economic capital at their disposal, took advantage of these changes to promote the educational opportunity of their sons and daughters, often by transferring their children from so-called failing state schools to those higher up the performance indicator ladder or into the independent school sector.

However, the market did not work for everyone. Many of the underlying tensions in Western society, e.g., the demise of manufacturing industries, an emergent "underclass" (Murray and Phillips, 2001), and, not least, acute social divisions around class and race continued and,

indeed, were likely exacerbated by the policy transformations arising from the introduction of a quasi-market in education (Alexiadou and Brock, 1999). Nevertheless, a transformation in gender relations was apparent, beginning with noticeable improvements in girls' performances in schools. From being at the rear of educational achievement for decades, girls were now seen to be moving to the front of the class.

> Cultural, demographic and labour market changes have clearly influenced the way students and teachers think about the schooling of girls and boys such that few now consider girls' education to be less important. In fact high scoring female students are proving attractive to schools in the competitive climate of the 1990s, and it is poorly behaved and low achieving boys who appear to be the subjects of greatest concern. (Arnot, David, and Weiner, 1999 p. 162)

A Transformation in Female Educational Attainment

The "gender gap" (Arnot, David, and Weiner, 1999) that had hitherto existed prior to the 1990s was, in North America, the UK, and elsewhere, shifting. Girls were emerging as the gender most likely to succeed in education, and at all levels. To be sure, the academic results always needed to be interpreted with both eyes on other variables, not least those concerning race, disability, ethnicity, sexuality, religion, income, culture, and class (see, for discussion, Jackson et al., 2010). But the signs were unmistakable.

As Arnot, David, and Weiner (1999) argue, the reasons for this transformation in female attainment are complex, but no doubt they result from the changes in educational legislation described plus the acceptance of equal opportunities, and thereby liberal feminist ideas, across most advanced industrial societies; and the opportunities afforded to women in the new post-Fordist, post-industrial, service-sector oriented workplace. However, this is not to say that gender stereotypes have disappeared completely and that girls' academic success is synonymous with gender equality. Although girls are succeeding academically, their self-concept and self-confidence are still affected by their status as "girls." Surveys of schoolchildren in the US, for example, show that teenage girls are more likely than boys to see themselves as "not as smart" and "not good enough" and that this tendency increases as they move from elementary to middle and secondary school. Race and ethnicity intersect with gender in the case of Latinas whose self-esteem drops lower than that of white and African-American girls (Orenstein, 2002). Furthermore, research in US schools shows that girls tend to perceive themselves to be better in English than in mathematics, even if their results were comparable to boys. This has of course direct consequences for their choice of future studies and career (Correll, 2001). Another area where the gender stereotypes persist is in vocational education. Women still outnumber men in vocational courses such as cosmetology, child care, and health aide, and are under-represented in vocational training such as plumbing, welding, and carpentry (Aulette and Wittner, 2012 [2009], p. 151). This clearly points to the intersection of class and gender and more precisely to the fact that gender binaries persist in certain professions.

But perhaps the most significant change has come about not in schools, but in universities: a powerful and influential location for the transformation of one's sense of self. Until recently there was an equal balance of men and women in universities in most Western countries. In 1994, in the UK for example, the ratio of male to female students at first degree level was 50-50; however, by 2004, 58 per cent of first-year UK undergraduates were women. In 2003 there was an increase in women full-timers of more than 103 000, compared with an increase

of only 36 850 in men (HESA, 2004; also Brown and Hesketh, 2004). By end of the twentieth century, the biggest student increase across most UK universities was with females, not males, to the extent that British women aged 20 to 34 are now more likely to have a degree than men (Swinford and Warren, 2010). In the UK, across a range of degree subjects the ratio of women to men applicants now exceeds four to one (Brown and Hesketh, 2004). Indeed, it is expected that by 2015, 72 per cent of all British graduates will be women (Vincent-Lancrin, 2008).

The evidence for women "exploiting the meritocratic ethos of competitive elite education" (Arnot, David, and Weiner, 1999, p. 108) is now significant. And the transformation continues. A recent study in East Germany revealed a "mass female exodus since 1991" to Western Germany and an emergent demographic crisis. This is due to an increasing polarization between educated women and poorly educated, jobless men. The proportion of East German women with degrees is now 31 per cent, compared to just 20 per cent of men. As one East German academic put it, "the clever girls are leaving the East German working-class boys behind" (Connolly, 2007). During the 1990s, women accounted for 100 per cent of enrolment growth in German universities and 60 per cent in French universities. In Hungary, the percentage of women graduates is currently 64 per cent, expected to increase to 73 per cent by 2020. In Sweden, the percentage of women graduates is set to increase from 63 per cent in 2005, to 76 per cent by 2020 (Vincent-Lancrin, 2008). Overall, across the EU, since 2000, women have filled 6 million of the 8 million jobs created and now account for 59 per cent of all EU graduates (CEO, 2008).

This trend is not confined to the UK and other parts of Europe. In the US, there are now 2 million more women than men in college. In some Canadian universities women are the majority in nine out of ten faculties. In Australia, women now account for 55.7 per cent of all university students, and in the past two decades have moved from 44 per cent to 58 per cent of the total workforce (FAHCSIA, 2010). In some Caribbean countries, up to 75 per cent of the student body is female. In Thailand, more women than men are now enrolled in tertiary-level education (75 per cent versus 60 per cent). More women than men in Singapore are graduating from local universities (over 60 per cent in some subjects), and women now make up nearly 50 per cent of the workforce. Across Asia (including the Middle East), women earn 43 per cent of first university degrees in math and computer science (NITRD, 2009). In Japan and Korea, in 2005, 49 per cent of graduates were women, and this figure is expected to rise to 54 per cent and 56 per cent, respectively, by 2020 (Vincent-Lancrin, 2008).

Nevertheless, differences persist in higher education. For example, in the US, if women outnumber men in elementary, middle, and secondary schools, men outnumber women in the higher ranks of university positions such as associate professors and professors. Male professors also outnumber women in disciplines such as physical sciences, political sciences, computer science, business, and law (see Aulette and Wittner, 2012 [2009]). In higher education positions, women also tend to occupy part-time and temporary positions and to advance in rank more slowly than men (see Aulette and Wittner, 2012 [2009]; Spade, 2001). A recent report revealed that far more young women scientists in the UK leave academia than young men scientists. While more women than men embarking on a PhD want to pursue careers as researchers in industry or academia, this number goes down significantly as they advance into their studies (Rice, 2012). The masculine culture that prevails in academia (also known as the "old boys' network") but also in industry and business is one of the many obstacles that women are still facing in today's world.

This reminds us that, even though change is happening, gender stereotypes and power relationships based on gender can persist, both in the lower and higher strata of the social structure.

Education's Impact on Other Roles

As would be expected, some of the advancements that women have made educationally are now beginning to impact correspondingly upon their economic, work and social roles, and general upward social mobility. Recent research by Oxford University (Swinford and Warren, 2010) that analyzed official surveys of up to 25 000 UK households (married and unmarried couples) over the past four decades revealed the following:

1. In 1968–69 only 4 per cent of women aged 16–60 (520 000 people) earned more than their husbands or boyfriends. In 2006–07, the last year for which figures were available, the proportion had risen to 19 per cent, or 2.7 million women.
2. Some 44 per cent of British women now earn at least the same amount as their husbands and boyfriends.

Separate research in the UK confirms this trend. British women aged 22–29 now earn 1.7 per cent more than men of the same age who are in full-time work. Overall, and more than 40 years since the introduction of equal pay legislation in the UK, the gender gap in pay has fallen to 10.2 per cent in 2010, down from 12.02 per cent in 2009. To put this in perspective, in 1971 men were on average paid 36.5 per cent more than women (O'Grady, 2010).

The emergence of women into the professions is significant. In the UK, 63 per cent of solicitors aged 30 or under are female. More than half of new medical students are already women and they are set to overtake men in many areas of medicine within a decade. At present, in the UK, women account for 40 per cent of all doctors and 28 per cent of consultants (Smith, 2010).

A similar trend is apparent in North America. Government statistics in the US show that by 2024, if current trends continue, American women professionals will overtake their male peers in average earnings. Indeed, 35 per cent of American women in professional dual-income homes are now earning more than their husbands/partners. That proportion was only 28 per cent in 2005 (Leonard, 2010).

One of the biggest success stories in education since the late 1990s has concerned black women. In the US, the black middle classes are rising in number. In the 2000s, 40 per cent of black families in the US had an income above $50 000; 55 per cent, above $35 000 (US Census Bureau, 2011). This enlargement of the black middle class appears to be largely driven by black women's success in higher education and work. Black women now outnumber black men enrolled in graduate schools by a ratio of over two to one. On average, black women who are married are likely to be better educated and earn more than their spouses, and among black people, women occupy 60 per cent of professional and managerial jobs, often earning more than their black male peers. The result is that the black middle class in the US is predominantly female, while the black poor are disproportionately male (Banks, 2011).

However, this does not mean that equal pay has now been attained for all women. Recent figures show that pay differences between men and women still exist. For example, although, as we have just discussed, much progress has been achieved, figures show that, as an average across the full-time job market, Canadian women earn 79 per cent of what men do, compared to 80 per cent for women in the US, 77 per cent for German women, and 68 per cent for Japanese women (The Conference Board of Canada, 2009, as quoted in Aulette and Wittner, 2012 [2009], p. 178). Also, race and ethnicity affect the gender gap. In the US, for example, white men tend to hold better paid jobs compared to men

from other ethnic categories and compared to all women (National Center for Education Statistics, 2008, as quoted in Aulette and Wittner, 2012 [2009], p. 179). In addition to the gender gap, one has also to consider the fact that women are more likely than men to work part-time or do temporary jobs. As we have seen, there might be instances when women in full-time (and usually qualified) employment earn as much or sometimes more than men, yet these figures often leave out the women in part-time, temporary, and often precarious employment (see for discussion, Rose and Hartmann, 2004; Mishel, Bernstein, and Allegretto, 2005; Aulette and Wittner, 2012 [2009]).

Even though inequalities between men and women remain, relative changes have been taking place among the younger generation of women in the West, but also in other places around the world such as Asia and Southeast Asia. These changes are being driven by educational change and the rise in the number of women attending university, getting degrees, and leaving to begin careers in the professions. The implications for women's and girls' gender identity are profound. Education is no longer an arena the majority of females enter into with no expectations beyond leaving school early, getting married, and having children (Francis, 1998; Reay, 2001). As Reay (2001) puts it,

> Over the last two decades femininity has moved from being equated with poor academic performance to a position at the beginning of the twenty-first century where it is viewed as coterminous with high achievement. While research in the 1970s and 80s found that female pupils avoided displays of cleverness because they felt boys would then find them unattractive, today many girls articulate a confidence in female educational abilities. (p. 156)

The dominant feminine discourse that emerges with these dramatic and relatively rapid educational, economic, and social changes signals independence, multiple relationships, a globalized perspective, sexual expressiveness, confidence, attainment, and a declining adherence to a traditional feminine value system that promotes marriage, life-long partnerships, dependence on a male breadwinner, and motherhood. In short, what emerges is a distinct feminine cultural capital that has more in common with a masculine value system than with a traditionally feminine one.

But there is more than one femininity, just as there is more than one masculinity. And, as with masculinities, discourses of femininity often exist as multiple and paradoxical expressions of identity, not least within teenage schoolgirls (for overview, see Jackson et al., 2010). Reay's research (2001), for example, also shows that working-class girls often reject contemporary femininities of the type expressed by more middle-class girls, instead adopting discourses of traditional femininity as a reinforcement of their particular social, gender, sexual, and cultural identity. Yet these same girls also show a reluctance to lose the sense of feminine individuality and assertive self-expression that exists now in society. Research by Shain (2003) and Laurie et al. (1999) into Muslim and Asian girls' experiences of schooling similarly reveals the diversity of femininities that ethnic minority girls utilize, often in quite an agentic fashion, that is, shifting in a sophisticated manner between contrasting femininities coterminous with particular subject positions, including friend, sister, daughter, pupil, etc. While Francis's research into primary- and secondary-school pupils illustrates the fundamental identity shift that has occurred in many girls in respect of how they view and relate to education and schooling, work opportunities, marriage, and parenting, not only in an increased desire for living an economically independent life, but also in their lingering adherence to more traditional expressions of femininity (Francis, 1998, 2000).

What appears not to have changed significantly for most girls, at least at school level, is the dominance of the heterosexual paradigm, the discourse of compulsory heterosexuality. Francis's research supports that of, for example, Holland et al. (1998) and Kehily (2001, 2002; see also Rasmussen, 2005) to show that despite an increased fluidity and diversity around expressions of femininity, most girls remain highly limited in their range of sexual codes. Whereas girls may be less inclined toward homophobia than boys and young men, girls do consider their sexual reputation to be most significant and influential in their construction of self-identity as an emergent woman. Most girls' desire to maintain a heterosexual presence at school and an "unsullied" sexual reputation is not only a reflection of female peer group pressure and an acquiescence to the ubiquitous male gaze, but a continuing and a strong association with the ideal of a romantic, monogamous (heterosexual) love relationship.

The range of research into femininities in schools, colleges, and universities shows that girls and women are not necessarily compliant in the act of identity construction, yet neither are they fully agentic. The discourse of education achievement that femininity now confidently associates with is always mediated by other factors, including race, disability, sexuality, and, especially, class. The neo-liberalist agenda of the early 1990s, which is now apparent worldwide, did not set out to promote a liberal feminist agenda. However, in many respects, and as feminist researchers such as Arnot, David, and Weiner show, that has been an outcome. The overwhelming educational achievements of girls and women, worldwide, are evidence of that. This transformation is dramatically expanding the discursive range of feminine identities. However, at the same time, discourses of masculinity have not changed so significantly. Indeed, as we now discuss, many researchers argue that the positive association of femininity to educational achievement has served to reinforce an anti-educational discourse in many males.

Schooling the Boys

During much of the twentieth century, few seemed interested in the issue of girls' generally disadvantaged position with regard to education, other than feminists. However, when the wheel turned and the educational underachievement of boys arose as an issue, it triggered what has been described as a "moral panic" across society and not just in the UK but worldwide (Epstein, 1998; Lingard and Douglas, 1999; Kenway, 1995). Clearly, many politicians and educationalists were more than just a little uneasy with the implications of girls' educational success. For one thing, it completely squashed any stereotypes or simplistic assumptions about males' "innate" superiority over females, either educationally or in any other capacity. Second, it raised the issue of how to address the social and educational needs of a growing band of "disadvantaged," potentially "unemployable" males. Third, it threatened to derail the neo-liberalist agenda of constantly applying performative measures of "improvement, quality, and effectiveness" to schools, colleges, and universities (see Ball, 2008, for overview).

But the debate also served to reinforce the myths contained in the gender binary, that is, that one gender group is fundamentally different from the other, with such differences functionally acted out in society via contrasting sex roles/performances; for the research shows a range of differences, in terms of educational achievement, within each gender group. Although gender can to some degree be considered a predictor of academic achievement, other factors, such as poverty, disability, race, and class, are equally influential. While there is now an international concern about boys and

schooling, it is important to recognize cultural and national differences. For example, there is evidence to show that a "racialized discourse" operates in many educational arenas that serves to posit black boys as a "big lump of rebellious phallocentric underachievers" (Sewell, 1999, p. 111; also Majors, 2002; Archer, 2003). Indeed, educational and pedagogic processes in all countries are mediated by various historical and contemporary influences, for example, colonialism, nationhood (Parry, 2000; Beckles and Shepherd, 2007), religion (Wright, 2003), and culture (Alexander, 2001).

The Relationship between Education and Masculinity

What the so-called educational crisis for boys has done is throw a spotlight on the relationship between formations of masculinity and education. Importantly, we can now see more clearly how male identity work is undertaken in schools and colleges and how this intersubjective process informs males' attitudes to schooling. It is not the case that boys, any more than girls, are biologically programmed to succeed or fail in schools. A host of variables come into play, some of which are in the remit of the school, college, or university (e.g., teaching methods; curriculum content and design; subject offer; classroom organization; staff training, skill, and expertise; pupil/student behaviour management), and many of which are not (see Martino, Kehler, Weaver-Hightower, 2009).

As we have emphasized in this book, identity work is a dynamic, variable and unpredictable process within each individual. It is not simply constituted by external, ideological, structural factors, nor is it only a matter of choice: a fully agentic action undertaken by knowing subjects. Schools do not constitute either males' or females' identities in any deterministic manner, though some schools may try to. What we do have are dominant and subordinate discourses circulating within schools and similar sites. Such discourses originate not only from the school members themselves, but also arise from the social and cultural environment within which the school is situated. It is how these discourses become constituted as performances of masculinity that reveals the relationship between boys' (under)achievements and education.

An early study into this gender identity arrangement in schools, undertaken by Mac an Ghaill (1994), exposed not only the ways in which young male students "learnt the heterosexual codes of behaviour that marked their rite of passage into manhood" (p. 53), but also highlighted how dominant discourses of masculinity identity corresponded with students' social, racial, and educational position. Mac an Ghaill (1994) identified four student groups, each distinguished by the particular narratives, as masculine identities expressed by their members:

> I have summarized these in the following terms: that of the Macho Lads' "survival against authoritarianism," the Academic Achievers' "ladders of social mobility," the New Enterprisers' "making something of your life,", and the Real Englishmen's "looking for real experiences." These links were further displayed by the students' differential participation in and celebration of form and informal school rituals, through which masculine subjectivities are constructed and lived out, such as attendance at prize-giving and involvement in the playground smoking gang. (p. 56)

Mac an Ghaill's research reveals both alienation and association between different student groups and the school, and the discursive positions adopted by students. In all cases the students are utilizing the school setting to formulate a sense of themselves as accepted males/youths although clearly the school is not in control of this process, even though it is powerfully influential. In Goffman's terms, the school is the scene, the setting for the presentation and performance of self, although it also establishes many of the parameters under which this action is undertaken. Similarly, Price's research into African-American males and schooling reveals how young men's expressions of masculinity become reified through the power relations that exist with both their peers and the institution, with some students adapting their model of self so as to connect with teachers, and others choosing to adopt a more confrontational model of masculinity to challenge teachers. As Price (2006) contends, these contrasting versions of "racialized masculinity . . . may not define their identities as working-class, African American men," but they are an aspect of their social identity and sense of self (p. 273; see also Archer, 2006; Alexander, 2006).

One of the tensions within boys' masculinity work is the unrelenting pressure on them to "prove their manhood every second" (Martino and Meyenn, 2001). Unsurprisingly, the school then becomes a key testing ground for maleness and differing forms of masculinity. But boyhood is not an innocent time of play and pleasure. It may be this for many, some of the time, but for many more it can also be a brutal, violent, deeply disturbing period. Most boys' experiences of growing up, both in and outside the school environment, are interspersed with fear, threat, anxiety, insecurity, bullying, and violence (Mills, 2001). The learning that occurs in the school setting often has little to do with the formal curriculum. Indeed, the way boys learn to be men is more a consequence of experiences outside the classroom than inside it (Frosh et al., 2002; Seidler, 2006).

The Consequences of a Male Anti-Education Culture

The unfortunate consequence of many boys' distancing themselves from educational attainment is that it increases their chances of being jobless, getting into crime and ending up in prison, and getting trapped in an economic and social male underclass. Black men especially are vulnerable to finding themselves not only consigned to the bottom of the social ladder, but in prison (Banks, 2011). Indeed, whether they are white or black, Canadian, British, American, Russian, or French, the reality is that uneducated, virtually unemployable men are an emerging social problem:

> Overlooked by society, irrelevant to employers, unwanted by women who can raise families on benefits without their help, the man who has no work or a series of part-time jobs is a problem. A lot of these women describe the real fathers of their children as "useless" or worse. The men have no role. (Cavendish, 2010)

At the same time that we might despair at the emergence of a male underclass, we should not underestimate the level of sophistication that is required of young people in their journey to a complete sense of manhood or womanhood. Educationalists may consider they are promoting the good of society, and the opportunity of the individual, through their skilful development and management of teaching and learning, but the objective is often lost on the individual child. For these children, a much greater and more pressing concern is to be accepted as a male or female and to be recognized, not least by their peers, as a valid individual, a future man or woman. For many children, just learning how to survive in their immediate social/peer group is a major challenge and one that occupies much of their time and attention. For this requires the subject (boy and girl) to engage with and relate to those dominant discourses that serve to facilitate this identity work in their particular social arena, and disregard those discourses that do not. Such dominant discourses may well relate to wider gender myths in society, especially around sexuality and culture (Segal, 2001; Gilbert and

Gilbert, 1998); but for the child the important task is not so much to critically evaluate these discourses as to distinguish between those that will secure their acceptance in their peer community and those that will unsettle or disrupt it. It is this dangerous and dynamic mixture of differentiation and accommodation that each child must learn to negotiate. And the school setting is a most vivid and powerful arena for this process (see, for example, Farrell, 2011).

The turn in the educational tide from female disadvantage to, now, international concerns over boys' underachievement clearly resonates with a widespread anti-education culture in young males. This culture is real and it is potent. And its potency results from how it corresponds to many boys' desire to position themselves as valid, powerful, independent, and competing masculine subjects. As recent research reveals (Cassen and Kingdon, 2007; also Grace et al., 2010; Farrell, 2011), it is not simply the case that all young males, of whatever class or ethnic origin, are anti-education. What is apparent from this and similar research is the power of an anti-educational discourse to infect the subjectivities of many boys, and in so doing inform their sense of masculine identity (Epstein, 2006). No doubt such a discourse has always been apparent, to some degree, in boys' compulsory education. However, this discourse can now be seen as clearly linked with an anti-female stance. That is, many boys seek to distance themselves from a discourse that corresponds with femininity; and educational achievement now has that connection, at least in their imaginings.

Again, the relational character of the gender binary and differential formations of masculinity and femininity impact identities. As the research by Cassen and Kingdon (2007) shows, in the UK white working-class boys are the worst performers in school, although overall the educational performance of Caribbean boys is poorer. However, when one factors in issues of poverty and class, then the white boys from low-income families fare worst of all groups. But not all white and black working-class boys seek to emulate this discourse. Very many are keen to achieve at school. The difficulty arises from peer pressure and wider social influences, which results in pro-education boys being placed in real tension between competing discursive positions, for example, being identified as marginal and "uncool," as "nerds," by their peers. When young males label their more studious male peers as "wimps" or "nerds," they are not simply imposing a signifier of difference: they are imposing a signifier that implies a reduced masculinity, a social marginalization, and an unwelcome association with femininity (Farrell, 2011). Culture, class, and race all intersect to influence the extent and depth to which such a discourse gets taken up by the boys, which in turn results in an anti-educational male culture (also Archer, 2003; Connolly, 2004; Majors, 2002; Grace et al., 2010). This is the situation in the UK, but elsewhere around the world identical processes are occurring (Parry, 2000; Lesko, 2000; Lopez, 2002).

None of this provides easy answers for governments, parents, educationalists, or the pupils themselves. But at least by appreciating and understanding the ways that gender identity work comes to inform educational, and life, chances, then so we move a little closer to redressing disadvantage and ensuring equity in the system.

HOW SPORT AND LEISURE INFLUENCE GENDER IDENTITY

Among the range of practices of gender identity available to us, we can see that some are more heavily oriented toward one gender than another. For example, as we discussed earlier, the family setting is significantly laden with discourses around maternalism and associated expressions of femininity, while the educational environment has, at least up until relatively recently,

Sport is not just a physical activity: it is also a statement of identity.

Source: © Michael Steele/Getty Images

been more strongly associated with males and masculine accomplishments. Another example of a particular weighting in respect of discursive gender orientation is in the areas of sport and leisure. These arenas of social activity have long been associated with maleness, masculinities, men; they have provided, through history, a cultural space in which men might demonstrate their physicality, competitiveness, distinctiveness, social status, and particular expression of manliness (Deem, 1986; Talbot and Wimbush, 1989; Theberge, 1987; Messner and Sabo, 1990; Green, Hebron, and Woodward, 1990; Wearing, 1998).

Importantly, such arenas have long offered men a clear separation from the realm of femininity, femaleness, and women. Indeed, feminist research shows how women have been and continue to be marginalized if not, in many instances, rendered invisible in these spaces (for overview, see Scraton and Flintoff, 2002; Henderson et al., 1989; Blackshaw, 2003; Aitchinson, 2003). By being invested with masculinist discourses, sport and leisure have come to reinforce the gender polarization that differentiates masculinity from femininity, men from women, while providing a gendered space in which men may achieve some material advantage and sense of power over women and each other, and an ontological grounding as masculine subjects.

Recognizing such, we can see several important gendered factors operating within these arenas. First, sport and leisure are not gender neutral. As we will discuss, they have over time come to be seen as the primary province of the male. Second, sport and leisure are relatively privileged social spaces insomuch as access to them requires the individual to have the capacity to exercise a degree of freedom, cultural and economic capital, choice, and agency (see, for example, Urry, 2002; MacClancy, 1996). Third, it can be argued that the opportunity to partake in leisure, free-time activities, which might include sports, enhances individuals' physical and emotional well-being, in which case those who are excluded from this opportunity may well experience health problems as a consequence (McGillivray, 2006). Fourth, sport especially is a social activity that serves to reinforce what might be described as a hegemonic expression of masculinity, in which case it can be co-opted into the prevailing gender order or patriarchal condition on behalf of men, thereby reinforcing gender stereotypes and the material marginalization of women (Messner and Sabo, 1990). Finally, all practices of gender identity are, to some degree, invested with socializing roles. These may not necessarily be universally accepted roles, but they can, certainly within sport and leisure, be strongly associated with

males and therefore used to reinforce male bonding and fraternities through masculinist, potentially violent, misogynistic, homophobic ritual and practice, and acceptance of rape and abuse of women (see, for example, Messner, 1992; Hughson, 2007; Hall and Winlow, 2006; Kreager, 2007).

But as we go on to discuss, sport and leisure are not now, if they ever were, the exclusive province of men. Women occupy both spaces and do so increasingly in a visible and assertive fashion. This raises interesting questions in respect of not only shifting forms of femininity, but also how women's involvement in sport and leisure serves to challenge prevailing masculine codes and stereotypes.

Sport and Our Sense of Self

The centrality of sport in society is self-evident. It is blazoned across the media in every country of the world, while sporting heroes are increasingly global icons, touching the lives of billions of people. One might surmise from this that the whole world has a love affair with sport. Indeed, for many, sport has replaced religion as their most important, socially binding value system (Mangan, 2000).

But sport is not only about physical prowess and individual or team performances in an arena; sport is a powerful and persuasive indicator of society itself, highlighting the social divisions that inhabit it and the distinct historical and political spaces that constitute it (see, for example, Bale and Cronin, 2003). But to understand this significance of sport to our lives and sense of self, we must first apply a critical gaze. As Sage (1990) puts it, "A critical sociological perspective invites us to step back from thinking about sport as merely a place of personal achievement and entertainment and study sport as a cultural practice embedded in political, economic, and ideological formations" (p. 110).

A critical examination of sport reveals its power not so much in its entertainment value, but in the messages and signifiers it circulates about the nature of reality. As Sage goes on to argue, sport is never entirely value-free but is inculcated with ideologies and dominant discourses about the way society is, or should be. In a global capitalist economy, then, it is of little surprise that sport has been co-opted by governments, nation-states, agencies, corporations, and individuals as a powerful metaphor for success in life. For a central message within sport is that winning counts above all else and that "losing is for losers" (Sage, 1990, p. 54). This reinforcing of the win-at-all-costs ethos has certainly been heightened by the professionalization of sport that has occurred over the past four or five decades, which is further exemplified in the examples of corruption and drug abuse that now configure many sports (see, for examples, Wilson, 2000; Pound, 2004).

A Site for Expressions of Masculinity

Sport does, then, purport to make powerful statements about us, both as members of communities and as individuals, and one such key message concerns our gender. For sport is a primary site for the reproduction of gender identity, specifically hegemonic and dominant expressions of masculinity (Messner and Sabo, 1990; McKay, Messner, and Sabo, 2000). Sporting performance is, for men, an opportunity to practise, reproduce, and reinforce not only socially acceptable and privileged discourses of masculinity, but also a sense of power, a power that is invested in the very embodiment of the masculine self:

> to learn how to be a male is to learn to project a physical presence that speaks of latent power . . . sport is empowering for many young males precisely because it teaches us how to use our bodies to produce effects and because it teaches us how to achieve power through practiced combinations of force and skill. (Whitson, 2006, p. 307; also Connell, 1983)

Sport has historically privileged masculine expressions, values, and identities; it has elevated the male body over the female, maleness over femaleness. This was as apparent in the gladiator arenas of ancient Rome as it has been on the playing fields of British public schools such as Harrow, Eton, and Rugby, or, indeed, in the emergence of the modern Olympics themselves (Mangan, 2000; Mangan and Walvin, 1987; Sage, 1990). This gendering of sport serves to encourage and validate not only the association of men and masculinity with sport, but also the masculinist culture that pervades sporting institutions: from professional sports teams through to the gendered representations of sport in the media (Creedon, 1994). Importantly, for many feminists, "forms of sport have served to naturalize men's power and privilege over women" (Messner and Sabo, 1990, p. 2), to the extent that sport has lost whatever gender neutrality it ever had to become, for many, quite simply, "a fundamentally sexist institution that is male dominated and masculine in orientation" (Theberge, 1987a, p. 342; see also Theberge, 1987b; Scraton and Flintoff, 2002 Hargreaves, 1994).

The masculine discourses that configure sport speak of conflict, competition, domination, supremacy, and heterosexual conquest. Much less is sport about benign and friendly participation, or play for the benefit of all regardless of gender and sexuality (see Dufur and Linford, 2010, for overview). To be successful in sport, certainly at the highest professional level, now requires a degree of single-minded determination and focus that is almost beyond human capability. This may, indeed, be the reason why so many men and women in sport are drawn into a drug-enhanced performance culture and suffer sports-related injuries, their mental determination not being matched by their physicality. All this suggests the term "female athlete" to be "almost an oxymoron—to the extent that one is a woman, one cannot excel at sports; to the extent that one excels at sports, one cannot be a woman" (McKay, Messner, and Sabo, 2000, p. xiii).

The Gendered Gaze Is Slowly Changing

But despite the gendered constraints and culture of masculinism that continue to bedevil sport (Messner, 2002), women, globally, are excelling and increasingly competing. Female sporting icons such as Serena and Venus Williams, Caroline Wozniacki, Danica Patrick, Kim Yu-Na, Paula Creamer, and Hayley Wickenheiser are representative of a new type of female athlete: women who successfully challenge male athletes for their place in the public eye and for their share of the professional purse (Heywood and Dworkin, 2003; Allred, 2003). In China, a new breed of super-sportswomen has emerged, overtaking their male counterparts in public esteem and media visibility (Jinxia, 2002; Hong and Mangan, 2002), while women's soccer is now one of the fastest growing sports worldwide (Hong and Mangan, 2003). Clearly, women too can invest a sense of identity in the sporting arena, not only as spectators but also as participants at the highest competitive levels.

Some of this change has come about through direct affirmative action to challenge women's discrimination in sport. For example, in the US, concern with females' absence from sport and the prevalence of masculinist attitudes in sport were spurs to introduce legal interventions, such as Title IX. This federal statute, enacted in 1972, prohibits sex discrimination in education institutions and in their program and activities that receive federal funding. In the four decades since Title IX became law, sporting opportunities for girls and women in the US have changed dramatically, as the statistics below reveal.

Between 1972 and 2007, female participation in US high school sports rose from 294 015 participants to 3 665 367 participants—a 1246 per cent increase. Male athletic participation rose from

3 021 807 to 4 320 103 during the same time period. As a percentage of the total high school population, female athletes rose from around 5 per cent to over 35 per cent in the period from 1971 to 1999, while male athletic participation remained relatively stable at around 50 per cent (from Dufur and Linford, 2010; also from Stevenson, 2007).

So where legal interventions are enacted to combat sex discrimination, positive change occurs that dramatically increases the likelihood of girls' and women's participation in sport. But is this a new phenomenon? And what does it suggest about women's gender identity? Feminist research has shown that while women's sporting activities have traditionally been trivialized and marginalized by men, women's involvement in sport is not new but goes back through history. For centuries women have played sports and have done so competitively and professionally (Smith, 1999; Guttmann, 2004). However, the growth in popularity of women's sports means that a greater attention is now being turned to the challenges that women athletes face as they pursue a sporting career and a recognition that their sporting achievements are, if anything, more significant than those of men if only because of the institutionalized gender discrimination that women athletes have to overcome on their path to success (Smith, 1999; Allred, 2003; see, also, Cohen, 1993). These factors, coupled with a greater interest in women's sports globally and the emergence of more women sports participants, means that the gendered gaze on sport is slowly, but inevitably, changing.

"Female athlete" is no longer an oxymoron but a reality with an increasingly visible presence in the public eye. Additionally, numerous indicators show that female participation in sports can significantly enhance girls' and women's self-esteem, confidence, and sense of identity; they also show that those girls who play sports are less likely to experience the more negative and potentially damaging pitfalls of adolescence (Zimmerman, 1999).

So women now occupy the sporting arena in an increasingly visible and potent way. The female body becomes, in its contemporary athletic manifestations, a challenge to and resistance against the gender dualism that has long configured the male body as symbolic of power and dominance, and the female body as frail and subservient (Dowling, 2001; Choi, 2000; Bordo, 1993). We appear to be at a point in history when new forms of femaleness, underpinned by a self-evident feminine muscularity, are emerging into the public consciousness, aided no doubt by the performances of highly visible female athletes around the world (Allred, 2003; Scraton and Flintoff, 2002; Smith, 2003).

But female involvement in sport is not just having a positive effect on the minds of women and girls through the emergence of new female role models and a physically confident femininity. The re-gendered messages that are transmitted here can have an equally beneficial effect on the masculine psyche. Males can no longer consider sport to be their exclusive domain. They might, but the reality suggests otherwise. Sport will continue to offer men a space within which to act out, through their physicality, a sense of muscular masculine embodied identity with strong heterosexual overtones, but they will do so increasingly with women alongside them. This could provide men with the opportunity to shift their own sense of masculine expression toward a gender identity that does not get its ontological validation through feeling superior to women and other men. In other words, women's successful and highly visible participation in sport has the power to redefine sport away from its previously unchallenged male, heterosexual association, thereby helping males to reject hypermasculinity (both in and out of sport) as a legitimate, worthy, and attainable way of being a man (Wheaton and Tomlinson, 1998).

Leisure and Our Sense of Self

Our free time, which is when can be most ourselves, is precious. In our hectic, increasingly competitive world, time is under pressure; the time for work becomes, for many, oppressively intensified and expanded while the time for rest, recuperation, and leisure gets squeezed into an ever-shrinking space. Those in paid work are too often starved of leisure, while those without paid work have plenty of free time but few of the material resources with which to fully enjoy it. Given this tension between our work time and our free time, it can be of little surprise that the study of leisure reveals it to be heavily inculcated with various power formations, with quality leisure time becoming, arguably, more valuable than money itself (see, for discussion, Pieper and Malsbary, 1998; see also Aitchinson, 2003).

The concept of a "leisure society" and a "leisure industry" to service it first emerged in the late 1970s and early 1980s (see, for example, Parker, 1976; Rojek, 1985; Veal, 1987). Driven and supported by the then emergent "technological revolution," leisure was to become both a vehicle for economic change and development, and an opportunity for the actualization of human potential (see, for overview, Rojek, 1995). However, some writers took a less optimistic view. Clarke and Critcher (1985) argued that the underlying capitalist imperative and logic at the heart of leisure, both as personal space and as an industry, reduced it to an expression of unequal class and social power relations. Feminists pointed out that leisure time was heavily gendered in favour of men, with women of all classes being subjected to a "time famine" that arose not only as a consequence of women's multiple roles (Hochschild, 1989, 1997; Franks, 1999; Deem, 1982, 1986; Sullivan, 2000) but also due to men's capacity to exercise power over leisure, both as free time in the family setting and as an industry (see, for discussion, Talbot and Wimbush, 1989; Green, Hebron, and Woodward, 1990; Henderson et al., 1989; Wearing, 1998; Blackshaw, 2003).

Such studies reveal our gender identity to be significantly affected and curtailed, not only by spatial considerations but also by temporal ones. For example, the public and private divisions are built around a gendered time differential while the organization of work and leisure exists for the most part within an inflexible linear time framework, which can seriously disadvantage women (see, for discussion, Adam, 1990; Young, 1988; Davies, 1990; Knights and Odih, 1995; see Whitehead, 2002, for overview). The reality of leisure for many women is that they have little of it, locked as many are into low-paid work, demanding child-rearing and caring roles, and often restrictive cultural gender expectations (see Wearing, 1998; Green, Hebron, and Woodward, 1990, for overview). What becomes clear is that leisure, as free time, is not equally available to everyone. It becomes a material resource to be used and deployed, sold and purchased, experienced, under certain conditions, and within distinct power regimes circulating class, race, and gender (Thompson, 1967; Gorz, 1985; Wearing, 1998). And one of the most persuasive and enduring of these regimes is masculinism (Brittan, 1989):

> Masculinism is, then, the point at which dominant forms of masculinity and heterosexuality meet ideological dynamics, and in the process become reified and legitimized as privileged, unquestioned accounts of gender difference and reality. As an ideology, masculinism can be seen to be threaded across both the public and private spheres . . . (Whitehead, 2002, p. 97)

Leisure is particularly vulnerable to the ideology or dominant discourse of masculinism, for leisure time cannot be enjoyed fully without a high degree of choice and agency. And such agency is often subject to gender pressures and expectations, that is, who can or should do what, when, and where. Many leisure environments remain male dominated and, as such, operate within a particular masculinist gaze that overtly or covertly marginalizes and stereotypes women. Moreover, as research into Americans' work and leisure time reveals (see Table 9.1), men are less likely to experience the pressures of having to undertake multiple roles across both the public and private spheres, mostly because they are unwilling to do so. Moreover, the fact of men's larger average disposable incomes versus those of women means men are more likely to have both the time and the money to experience and enjoy quality leisure time.

Yet despite the gender inequalities that persist within leisure, there can be no doubt that it has all the capacities to provide women, as well as men, with gender identity validation and to do so, increasingly, over many life stages. In post-structuralist terms, the individual, man or woman, as a discursively based subject, can achieve a powerful ontological grounding through the experience and practice of leisure activities. We may, as individuals, have a judgment as to the value, worth, and benefit of certain such activities (see, for example, West, 2002; Hall and Winlow, 2006), but we cannot deny their capacity to inform our sense of self as man or woman.

Leisure can offer perhaps an even a greater sense of self-actualization and personal achievement than work can, precisely because it is a time to be most ourselves. The element of choice that configures leisure means it becomes a space/time within which we can experiment with alternative codes of behaviour without necessarily experiencing high risk—unless we choose to. We can move, mentally and physically, beyond the boundaries of gender codes and regulations or at least expand them to our benefit. In the age

TABLE 9.1   Americans' Work and Leisure Time, 2010

	Men	Women
Working time (full-time employment)	Men work 8.2 hours a day on average.	Women work 7.8 hours a day on average.
Household contribution (daily)	64% of men spend some time on household activities. Men spend an average of 2.1 hours on household activities. 20% of men do housework. 41% of men do food preparation.	84% of women spend some time on household activities. Women spend an average of 2.6 hours on household activities. 49% of women do housework. 68% of women do food preparation.
Leisure and sport activities (daily)	Men spend 5.8 hours in leisure activity (mostly watching TV). 22% of men participate in sport or exercise. Men spend 1.9 hours in sport or exercise.	Women spend 5.1 hours in leisure activity (mostly watching TV). 16% of women participate in sport or exercise. Women spend 1.3 hours in sport or exercise.
Child-care activities (daily)		
• Households with children under 6	Men spend 1.3 hours providing primary care.	Women spend 2.53 hours providing primary care.
• Households with children under 18	Men spend 0.87 hours providing primary care.	Women spend 1.7 hours providing primary care.

Source: US Department of Labor (Bureau of Labor Statistics, 2011), www.bls.gov/news.release/atus.nr0.htm

of cyberspace and the Internet and the fantasy worlds that can arise from them, such expanding is, quite literally, at our fingertips (Fine, 2003). Moreover, we can undertake such activities with others, those like us, thereby reinforcing both our sense of individuality and our sense of belonging to a particular group or community. As some commentators have noted, the Internet, especially as a "leisure-orientated technology," has become humanity's biggest social experiment, with results unforeseeable but potentially powerful and dramatic in terms of social and political change (see, for example, Head, 2010; also Albarran and Goff, 2000, for overview). So despite the presence of powerful ideologies or dominant discourses upon leisure, it is not simply reducible to an arena of social control. To be

sure, leisure can and often does reinforce gender differentiation and damaging expressions of masculinity, especially, but it is also more than that. As with sport, leisure is potentially a most powerful conduit for our gender identity validation, providing a space/time when we may well attempt to "be" someone else, or to reinforce who we think we are.

SUMMARY

As globalization has taken hold around the world, so has education undergone many changes. Politicians recognize that educational achievement brings with it skill and knowledge advancement within the population, thereby helping the nation-state to compete in an increasingly intense global market economy, one that puts a premium on knowledge and educational achievement. From this emerges the possibility of cultural capital or knowledge capital for societies and individuals.

However, as this chapter has shown, this process contains strong gender dynamics and conditions, with girls and women now overtaking boys and men in the educational stakes. The results are complex, with more women achieving at university and leading independent lives—and now with the likelihood in some cases of earning more than men of their own age group. But as we have seen, these changes cannot be interpreted at face value. Stereotypes and inequalities often persist when it comes to the ways girls and boys perceive their success, and the ways they choose their future studies and future careers. Men also are achieving, as they have in the past, but many millions are not, which raises serious issues in respect of an emergent male (uneducated and unemployable) underclass. Correspondingly, we can see the emergence of a middle class of female who is likely to live a very different lifestyle than that of her mother and grandmother. Already we see this change in many countries around the world. Its implications for gender identity and for male-female relationships are significant.

Yet while we can see educational opportunities arising for females and females taking up such opportunities, other aspects of everyday life remain heavily gendered in favour of boys and men. Leisure—i.e., free time—is one such area. With women in relationships often taking on multiple roles (mother, housewife, and breadwinner), their leisure time is heavily restricted. To be sure, more men are househusbands and are doing their share of housework and caring roles in the family but still not to the extent that women are. So this is one area where equal opportunities for women still have some way to go. It is also one reason why many middle-class educated women increasingly avoid marriage in favour of long-term, informal relationships with men: it gives them freedom from the gender restrictions that all too often accompany marriage.

Finally to sport: again we can see how male attitudes and culture continue to define sport although the barriers are being taken down. More women than ever are involved in sport, both professionally and informally. This in turn serves to challenge the stereotype of females as non-physical or non-athletic and thereby opens up the likelihood of the emergence of different, more assertive expressions of feminine identity.

CASE STUDY

Michael is aged 16. He lives in London, Ontario, and attends a public school. His father is an accountant for an insurance company, and his mother works as a hospital nurse. Michael is the only child in his family. Up until 18 months ago, Michael's progress through the Canadian education system had been almost perfect. He was consistently achieving the highest grades in his class, had a 100 per cent attendance record, and was receiving exemplary school reports. He was also a gifted musician (piano) and accomplished sportsman (hockey). He never missed a piano lesson or a hockey practice. Then Michael started to change. He dropped out of music classes, started to be increasingly argumentative with his parents, and spent more time alone in his bedroom on the computer. At first his parents just accepted this as part of his adolescent journey, but after Michael's attitude became increasingly aggressive they sought help from the guidance counsellor at his school.

Michael had several sessions with his guidance counsellor and shared some of his problems with her. He explained how the adolescent males in the school were formed into various subgroups or social cliques. These groups had adopted labels such as "nerds," "emos," "normals," "outcasts," "jocks," "superheroes," and "cools." Michael gave her a full account of his experiences within these groups. When Michael first moved into this age group, at 14, he find himself labelled a nerd by his peers, with a subsequent loss of social status to the point that he felt himself to be at risk of being labelled an "outcast" and therefore basically without any friends at school—not part of the male adolescent subculture at all. This was when his behaviour started to change at home. Michael was essentially reacting to the very real threat of becoming an outcast among his peers, and he knew this was because of his academic accomplishments. However, he managed to redress this situation and in time become a "jock." Now he spends less time on his homework and more of his free time with his male friends, especially via Internet social networks; and he also spends a lot of his time in sport— he has moved up his peer group hierarchy by becoming a very good hockey player. This earns him a lot of respect and admiration, not only with his male peers but also with the girls in his year. Michael now feels much more comfortable and secure in his peer group, although his academic results have deteriorated and he rarely talks much with his parents.

The guidance counsellor had a session with Michael and his parents; this has helped his parents understand and appreciate why Michael has become more rebellious and reclusive at home. However, despite knowing the reasons, they feel at a loss to know what they can do to improve the situation. As the guidance counsellor put it, "It seems that Michael is now totally immersed in finding his own male identity among his peers, and this is taking precedent over his studies and even his family relationships." Still, Michael's parents do not know what to do to help him.

DISCUSSION QUESTIONS

1. Give examples of when and where you have witnessed a situation such as Michael's in your own experience of school.
2. Do you agree with the psychologist's summary?
3. How are education, sport, and leisure interacting to influence Michael's journey into male adulthood?
4. Is Michael now secure or insecure in his masculine identity? Give your reasons.
5. Why are the males forming into these subgroups? Can you give examples, from your experience, where females do the same?
6. What can the teachers do to challenge the formation of these male subgroups? And if they do not challenge them, then how should they relate to them?

QUESTIONS FOR REVIEW AND DISCUSSION

1. To what extent do you think educational achievement has become closely associated with an assertive feminine performance of identity? What are the educational obstacles women are still facing?

2. How might schools help underachieving males to become more focused on their studies and more confident in their adolescent masculinity?

3. Give examples of how leisure continues to be gendered.

4. Do you consider sport to still be dominated by male values and a masculine culture, or is it now open fully to girls and women?

5. How might you measure the continuing dominance of men in sport? For example, who are the current top 20 earners in international sport, and how many of these are women?

6. How do women's multiple roles impact the quality of their leisure time?

7. Give examples from your own personal experience of how women are changing in terms of their career, relationship, and lifestyle aspirations. How much of this change do you feel has been due to educational attainment?

8. How can society avoid the expansion of a male underclass?

Chapter 10

The Body: Impacts of Violence and Aging

▲ *Resort to violence and lose the argument: ideas are infinitely more powerful than weapons.*
Source: © REUTERS/Stringer

Learning Objectives

At the end of this chapter you will be able to:

- Appreciate and understand how sex and gender identities are configured and expressed through the body.
- Reflect on the constraints and possibilities of the body and the gender power effects that circulate around it.
- Understand and critically reflect on the gendered relationship between violence, war, and crime.
- Critically examine the issue of male violence and masculinities.
- Understand how gender identity, masculinities, and femininities are affected by aging.

OVERVIEW

Many of our experiences, if not all, are constructed through our bodies. Although it is a physical and material entity, the body is also in many ways social, political, symbolic, and representational. The human body can have different meanings assigned to it, depending on whether a doctor, a sculptor, a body builder, or a fashion designer is looking at it. In other words, the body is far more than simply organic and physical: it is social, cultural, and political. Above all, part of society's project is to make the body productive through normalizing and disciplining effects, for example, to try and ensure the body contributes to and reflects prevailing social values and beliefs (Foucault, 1977 [1975]; see also Butler, 1993). Even though a body is made to appear "fixed" and "real" through dominant cultural codes and discourses (for example, humans have historically been defined as either male or female), the body can constitute and reconstitute itself in the sense that it is in a dynamic relationship with the world around it and with other bodies (Spinoza, 1951; Deleuze, 1997). As part of a social and symbolic system of power, the body is at the same time a space of control onto which social norms are imposed, as well as a space of freedom and liberation since we are also capable of freeing the body from these norms. In this respect, the body can make and unmake itself (Deleuze, 1997) and, by doing so, can make and unmake our identities.

In our postmodern world, highly influenced as it is by media and advertising, the body has become a potent site for the representation of gender and sexuality. Such imagery can have a powerful influence on the perception we have of ourselves and our embodied possibilities.

A large part of the feminist movement of the 1960s and 1970s was dedicated to freeing the female body from the gendered and patriarchal representations as exemplified in the struggle for legal access to abortion and the challenges of gendered stereotypes of the "perfect" female body. Similarly, the gay and lesbian movement has been involved in a struggle to free the body from hegemonic and heteronormative definitions of sexuality, in the same way anti-racist and disability movements continue to battle for the acceptance of bodies regarded as different. In this era of diversity, the body has become a contentious space where struggles for equality, for acceptance of difference, and against normativity are being fought. Whether it is the sexualized bodies of women, the subversive bodies of transgendered people, the traumatized bodies of soldiers, or the aging bodies of men and women in the aging societies of the world, the body remains a powerful marker of difference. As we will discuss, the body is a signifier of class, race, gender, sexuality, and (dis)ability and often is co-opted into relationships of dominance and subjugation.

We begin by examining theories about the body and the process of embodiment in order to understand the complex ways in which our bodies are represented and the impact of body imagery on our sense of gender identity. We then turn to the specific issue of violence and focus on masculinity and its embodiments, especially through crime and war, before turning to a discussion of aging as a process that alters traditional cultural constructions of the so-called perfect body and potentially challenges gender norms and identities.

BODIES AND GENDERED IDENTITY

Our sex and gender identities are ultimately configured and expressed in the most apparent and persuasive manner through our bodies (Butler, 2011; Merleau-Ponty, 1962; Thapan, 1997; Young, 1990). It is through our bodily presentation of self that we primarily achieve recognition and acceptance as a gendered being: man or woman. Yet while this embodied presentation is compulsive, it is not without its contradictions and tensions. Bodies are visible and therefore open to judgment and evaluation. In fact, one might argue that bodies are commodified in that some body shapes, sizes, colours, and presentations are more valued than others (see, for discussion, Ford, 2008). This is the reality of gender embodiment and we are all caught up in it.

Our physical presence appears as a sexed being, and therefore socially prescribed in a particularly gendered way to the social eye. There seems no escape from this. It is, as in Foucault's panoptic gaze (1979), an ever-present mechanism of external conditioning or control from which we have only limited respite. We enter this world as embodied beings, emerging within a body that mostly, although not in every case, appears to conscribe to the sex–gender dualism; that is, the body is either self-evidently male or female. From that point on, our lives will be lived out within or in relation to this condition. Is this a social effect or a biological one? Most likely it is a mix of both. But which comes first: the biological, material, and physical body coming to inform our actions and behaviours, or the cultural, social, contingent world doing likewise?

Many feminist theorists draw on Foucauldian theory to argue that even our sexed body is prescribed through social prerogatives; the terms *male* and *female* being so imbued with naturalizing codes and taboos that they are fully corrupted by the panoptic gaze of the social and its attendant needs for identity validation (Butler, 1993). As Butler puts it,

> In this sense, then, "sex" not only functions as a norm, but is part of a regulatory practice that produces the bodies it governs. . . . In other words, "sex" is an ideal construct which is forcibly materialized through time. It is not a simple fact or static condition of a body . . . (p. 2)

Butler's work in this area has produced a persuasive argument, but her ideas are also contentious. This privileging of social conditions while marginalizing the fact of our physicality and its attendant hormones, etc., seems to dismiss the biologically responsive aspects of our behaviour (see Butler, 2011; Clare, 2000; Thapan, 1997; see also Roberts, 2002, for discussion). Most sociologists would probably take the middle ground, and see our sex as biological and our gender as its cultural expression (see, for discussion, Beasley, 2005). However, whatever the reality of this for each individual, ultimately our physical presence is denoted through the social web; how we see our selves largely depends on how we are seen, and the first and most powerful expression of that visibility is our body. Our skin colour, our size, our shape, our posture, our movements, our dress, the adornments we place upon us: these are the most persuasive indicators, signifiers, of who we are or appear to be. They, above all else, portray our gender identity to others. Among these variables we have some choice; with other aspects, we have little or none.

---

panoptic

Foucauldian term to describe how every person is constantly subject to the gaze and scrutiny of others—the all-seeing eye. Uses metaphor of the panopticon (Jeremy Bentham's design for a nineteenth-century prison) to show how we can never know when we are being watched or when we are seen, only that we are.

This, then, is the reality of gender body work. The multiple, varied, nuanced, and often subconscious acts of identity construction, presentation, and performance are all engaged in one aim: to show ourselves as convincingly masculine or feminine, or ambiguous.

A Complex Body

Clearly, the body is a complex and contested site, a place we cannot escape from and which is signalled as a sexed/gendered entity from birth, yet also a site upon which we can fasten and fashion expressions of our selves to some extent at our discretion. Moreover, the body is a place that, in our imaginings at least, appears constant, given, continuous. We wake up with it and we go to bed with it. Our body accompanies us on our life journey. Love it or hate it, there is no escape from it or from the social and cultural indicators that mark it through time.

Whatever assumptions we hold about the fixedness of our bodies and yearnings we have for permanence and settlement within our selves, such notions and desires are inevitably compromised by an essential fact—that our bodies are fragile, impermanent, changing. We can no more control our own bodies than we can control those around us. To be sure, we can impose upon our bodies a regime that bodies are forced to adapt to—for example, diet, exercise, medication, stress, rest—but ultimately our bodies slip out of our grasp. We grow old, we grow infirm, we age, we mature, and our bodies tire. Our bodies inevitably succumb, no matter how much we might attempt to slow or even reverse this state.

Yet would we have any gender identity without our body? Is it not the case that our body's very materiality signifies, in the most profound way, our core identity as male or female? Certainly it would appear so. However, given the contingency of the body, what does this suggest regarding our sense of being, or sense of embodiment as gender subjects? Just how secure am I

in this body of mine, and how secure can I ever be? What is the relationship between my gender subjectivity and my physicality? What does my body say about me? What do I want it to say? We may have the agency to inscribe upon our body all manner of gender signifiers, but is it not the panoptic gaze of the other upon our body that ultimately labels, categorizes, or maybe even determines its, and our, possibilities?

These and similar questions clearly illustrate how central the body is to examinations of identity, whether such engagements draw on sociological and/or psychological theories. Yet somehow the body has long remained off-limits to much critical inquiry; it appears elusive, laden with taboos, stereotypically assumed, apparent yet hidden (Shilling, 1993; Frank, 1991; Scott and Morgan, 1993; Witz, 2000). This is especially so of the male body, which looms large in the social conscience and public discourses, not least through its phallic overtones and associated implications of material and political power. Manhood, as an act of identity, is primarily performed on and expressed through a male body. This embodied identity work of males contains within it the assumed presence of male genitalia as its ultimate validation of masculinity/manhood (see Schrock and Schwalbe, 2009; also Vaccaro, 2011, for overview). However, such omnipresence has only served to conceal its inherent fragility and attendant anxieties (see, for examples and discussion, Whitehead, 2002; Goldstein, 1997; Connell, 1983, 2003; Jefferson, 1998; Haywood and Mac an Ghaill, 2003). Therefore, to understand the body, both male and female, and its relationship to our gender identity, we must first deconstruct its social and cultural attire.

Designer Bodies

To what extent are our bodies given and fixed, and to what extent can we "design" them? Certainly the research into contemporary beauty work around the body suggests a degree of agency and choice (see Kwan and Trautner, 2009, for overview). Many individuals go to great lengths to appear attractive to others. And there are good reasons for doing so, for the research also reveals that perceptions of beautiful people are generally positive and can lead to significant social and economic advantages for those deemed attractive (Kwan and Trautner, 2009).

However, our body does not just appear through happenstance, nor does it appear solely through design. Likewise, our gender is not the product of our body, any more than our body is the inevitable outcome of our gender. Rather, we have here a dynamic relationship between the prescriptions of gender possibilities that circulate society at any one time and the endless reforming of such prescriptions by the individual, the subject (Bordo, 1993, 1995). The body is the site where these dynamics encounter each other and come to invest themselves in our sense of identity, in the most visible and apparently permanent manner—our embodiment as gendered beings (Giddens, 1992; also Budgeon, 2003). But, as we have already indicated, any apparent readings of the body need to be treated with caution. What we see is not necessarily reality. As Foucault puts it, "Nothing in man [sic]—not even his body—is sufficiently stable to serve as the basis for self-recognition or for understanding other men [sic]" (quoted in Butler 2004, p. 105; also Foucault, 1984).

Drawing on Foucauldian concepts and ideas, Judith Butler refers to the "normative" forms of gender that surround us, notably through the discursive signifiers and metaphors that signal "how the gendered world ought to be" (Butler, 2004, p. 99). But, as Butler (2004) illustrates, such signals are open to disruption, to subversion, to question, and to deconstruction:

> If one thinks that one sees a man dressed as a woman or woman dressed as a man, then one takes the first term of each of those perceptions as the "reality" of gender: the gender that is introduced through the simile lacks "reality," and is taken to constitute an illusory appearance. . . . We think we know what the reality is, and take the secondary appearance to be mere artifice, play, falsehood, and illusion. (p. 100)

Gender differences have never been fixed. There are many examples in history of people who have explored the ambiguity and the illusory appearance of gender. In nineteenth-century France and Britain, the fashionable middle-class dandies' preoccupation with clothes and feminized manners marked them as different, or even eccentric at times, while it was fashionable for middle-class educated women, such as Virginia Woolf or George Sand, to transgress gender boundaries by smoking cigarettes and wearing men's clothes. In today's world, where it is no longer scandalous for women to wear pants, a man wearing a dress would still be regarded as transgressive. In our postmodern cities, where women are generally considered to be more emancipated and independent than in the past, most children's clothes retailers still have very distinct boys' and girls' sections. Each section has its own markers of gender difference: usually hearts, flowers, or peace signs for girls' clothes; and trucks, cars, and trains for boys' clothes. There are, however, signs this is tentatively shifting to more unisex displays, at least in some major stores in cities such as London (Topping, 2012).

Our gaze upon the body of an individual is a gaze that seeks, needs, desires confirmation, not confusion. Our gaze looks to find an answer to the question "Who/what is this?" We have a desire to know the other, for in knowing the other so we are, somehow, knowing ourselves; we can place ourselves in relation to them. When the other appears unknowable in terms of gender and sexuality, our own gender identity becomes distressed and put under question. Our social and cultural reference points are removed, and the assumptions of gender identity are undermined. Dressing or presenting the body in a contra-gender fashion is, as Butler notes, an act of resistance to the dualism of male and female, and, importantly, to the gender and sexual power regimes that arise from it. At the same time, while contra-gender fashion and display is a point of resistance to gender dualisms, precisely by being a resistance so it serves to confirm the continued dominance of the gender dualism and the compulsion societies have toward heterosexual normalizing codes and bodily presentations.

But much as we may seek confirmation, the reality is we cannot assume anything about the bodies of others. The bodies of transsexual, transgendered, and intersexed persons are an obvious example of this. This ambiguity in gender and sex embodiment is exemplified by the "ladyboys" or *kathoeys* of Thailand; the *hijras* of India; the *bichas* of South America; the *xaniths* of the Middle East; and the *mahus* of Polynesia. Bodies that appear as male bodies but have "women's souls" (Costa and Matzner, 2007) express themselves most persuasively as feminine, but we cannot gaze upon them and somehow withhold or ignore the knowledge that their "sex," or at least in most cases their genitalia, is male. In the same way, babies born with ambiguous genitals that are seen as neither male nor female have traditionally been considered a threat and subjected to gender interventions such as surgery. Guidotto argues that it is the "fear of hybrid bodies" and the potentially bisexual nature of the intersexed person that generates society's need to intervene through the medical institution (Guidotto, 2007; also Kessler, 1998; Hird, 2003). Ambiguous bodies confuse us. And such confusion is unsettling; some might consider it threatening, even dangerous—and it is, at least to the dominant dualistically placed discourses of gender signification that surround us, and that feminist theorists such as Butler seek to

undermine and question (Kulik, 1997; see also van Esterik, 2000, for discussion).

In effect, and as Foucault argues, we can never trust any body we are gazing upon; we can never assume anything of the other through their appearance; we cannot truly know someone through their embodied presentation of self (see also Halberstam, 2005). Yet gender demands this assumption of us, for without it we cannot maintain the social web around which it is woven. If all is open to question, what can we trust? What can we assume as given? What can we rely upon? Each and every questioning of the body becomes a subversion of the normative gender categories and assumptions that surround us and inculcate our very subjectivity. In feminist terms, such subversions are to be welcomed in that they undermine the power of all the (masculinist) rules, regulations, codes, orthodoxies, taboos, and power regimes that have over time come to legitimize and sustain a particular gender and (hetero) sexual "reality" (Connell, 2003; Jones and Pugh, 2005). For feminists in particular, any disruption to such a reality is not only to be welcomed; it is indeed part of the feminist project toward gender and social justice (see, for example, Price and Shildrick, 1999). And a key first step in this political process toward social and individual enlightenment is to recognize that "people come in bewildering sexual varieties" (Fausto-Sterling, 2000a, p. 19; also 2000b). Indeed, when it comes to (sexual) bodies, ambiguity and variety is the norm, not the exception.

The research of sociologists such as Butler and biologists such as Fausto-Sterling alerts us to both the constraints and possibilities contained in the body and the gender power effects that circulate around it—indeed that in the final analysis render it gendered in constitution. Yet for most people the body is a given. Most individuals are less concerned with disrupting dominant notions of gender identity with their bodies than they are with reinforcing their sense of gender identity through it. Dress, jewellery, hairstyle, makeup, muscle tone, posture, and, increasingly, surgical enhancement, are part of the body construction and physical presentation menu available to increasing numbers of people. There is now, perhaps more than ever, an intense scrutiny upon the body, both male and female. Driven by the public's apparently insatiable voyeuristic gaze, the media dwell upon the body, endlessly pouring over its possibilities, its limitations, its physical performances, and its functions.

Our bodies are increasingly precious vessels that we seek to protect, to control, to fashion, to sculpt in an image of whom/what we desire to be. For many of us, this has become an obsessive compulsion generating a vast industry devoted to meeting our psychological desire for physical perfection. Indeed, it is largely through our bodily presentation of self and preoccupation with physical appearance that the contemporary narcissism epidemic now visible in many societies, but especially apparent in the West, becomes manifest (Twenge and Campbell, 2009).

Four decades of feminism critique of the objectified (female) physique have failed to quell this obsession with the sexed/gendered body (see, for examples, Young, 1990; Chapkis, 1986). Indeed, if anything, the body is now more open, judged, and exposed than ever before. Certainly we seem to desire it more, not less. From the nude and sexually explicit chat rooms increasingly inhabited by teenagers worldwide to popularist celebrity culture within which famous bodies are exposed and demeaned, from the proliferation of porn and sexualized images in mainstream culture, to our obsession with dieting and exercise: so we maintain an unremitting gaze upon our bodies and upon those of others. Often this is a pejorative gaze, a critical scrutiny of such physical representations of self. Today, globalization takes the body and displays it for universal consumption, not least through the Internet. Web-based dating sites have mushroomed in the past decade

and they operate primarily through the display of bodies to others, our physical attributes being scrutinized for consumption by possible future lovers. Children are exposed to sexually explicit and normative body images at every turn, reinforcing the objectification of the female body especially (see, for example, Bell, 2007) although young men are also increasingly pressured in this way. We see a body and we place it in a category, we compartmentalize it, we assess its value and worth, we require it to occupy a social box in our imaginations, we assess it against what we consider to be "normal." This labelling and distinguishing of bodies is part of the powerful objectification of the self to which we are all victim, illustrating that our body self-image is a fragile construct at best.

The body is, therefore, not neutral but, rather, heavily political, occupying stereotypical imaginings, possibilities, and limitations. For example, studies on the effect of negative perceptions of fatness, particularly on women, have highlighted the insidious ways in which discourses of exclusion and normativity are operating in Western societies. The conceptualization of fatness as a disease, illness, or epidemic with global impact, which has been referred to by the World Health Organization as "globesity" (WHO, 2000, 2003), has resulted in anti-fat attitudes that have had major consequences on women's self-image (Rice, 2007). Media coverage and schools in particular have contributed to stigmatizing those who are perceived as "fat" and as not fitting into prescribed norms of what it means to be healthy, successful, feminine, attractive, and upwardly mobile (see Rice, 2007; Bordo, 1993; LeBesco, 2004). According to Carla Rice,

[a]mid escalating anti-fat attitudes over the past thirty years, weight has emerged as a major marker of social status in western countries. Consequences of body size standards and stereotypes are especially exacting and far-reaching for

girls and women, who encounter frequent evaluation of physical appearance and difference as part of their social experience of gender. (Rice, 2007, p. 158)

Among other findings, Rice's study of 81 Canadian women between the ages of 20 and 45 from a variety of backgrounds revealed a relationship between gender identity and body size. As she observes, "gender identities frequently became fixed in a negative direction by devaluation of women's size differences" (Rice, 2007, p. 168). Some participants saw themselves as unfeminine because of "fat" but also saw themselves disqualified at school from tomboy identities because of "boys' aggressive challenges to big girls' physical abilities and strength" (2007, p. 168). One of the consequences of gendered size norms is the violence women often inflict on their bodies through strict dieting, which often results in eating disorders like bulimia and anorexia. Furthermore, anti-fat prejudice seldom stands alone and is often combined with other body hierarchies based on gender, race, ethnicity, or (dis)ability. The ethnicity of the body—e.g., white, black, Asian, Latino—is already heavily invested with political meanings (see, for examples, Monaghan, 2005; Grogan and Richards, 2002; Drummond, 2005; Frost, 2005; Ford, 2008). For racialized women who are already perceived as being outside the dominant constructions of femininity, weight reinforces the stereotype of "deviant womanhood" (see Beauboeuf-LaFondant, 2003).

Therefore, bodies come ready invested with statements about power, potential, and prowess. We are increasingly judgmental about bodies, especially those that may be consigned as "ugly," "unfashionable," "infirm," or "different." Our own gender identity may well be fragile but through our relationship with the body so we seek to construct an apparently unchanging symbol of our selves to others. And many of us work hard at this task. Male bodies may be invested with

an Adonis complex, whereby men are obsessively engaged in the "the pursuit of muscle" as a definer of their masculine identity and male prowess (Pope, Phillips, and Olivardia, 2000; also Klein, 1990). Many female bodies increasingly follow such a pathway of physical enhancement, in the process blurring the boundaries of masculinity and femininity, signifying perhaps a new female masculinity in the process (Halberstam, 1998; also Kwan and Trautner, 2009).

Both male and female bodies may appear to confirm the dominant codes of gender and sexuality around them, or to disrupt and question the same; however, they can also be seen to be increasingly subjected to measures of performance and assessment and systems of surveillance, not least through what Giddens (1992) refers to as the reflexive project of self-identity (Ball, 2005; Budgeon, 2003). We do not own our bodies so much as we display them for approval to others. Our bodies become commodified via the catwalks of Milan and Paris—the sublime and sensual strutting of the "perfect" physicality of the male and female models perhaps serving to undermine our own body self-image.

Ultimately, we have little or no control over our bodies; we may have them for life, but they are not ours to do with as we will. We have not designed them, nor have they been designed for us. Moreover, we do not have total agency to expend on our bodies. There are numerous social and cultural conditions and possibilities that always surround us and that we are forced to pay attention to. For example, our bodies can be subject to abuse, to violence, to isolation, to contempt. We may succumb to explicit pathological body conditions, such as anorexia nervosa, perhaps signalling, through our self-imposed decaying physicality, our disgust with the world and acting as a statement of resistance to it (see MacSween, 1995). As beggars on the streets of any city will tell us, our bodies can also be ruthlessly ignored, consigned to an invisible, marginalized space among the masses. And as most physically disabled people will testify, certain bodies can be feared, rejected, misunderstood, overlooked, and misrepresented. The policy of forced sterilization (of mostly women from working-class and Aboriginal background) that was implemented in Alberta, Canada, from 1928 to 1972 is one of the many examples of such violence on bodies regarded as unworthy to reproduce (see Grekul, 2008).

We have limited control over how others see us and over the judgments they duly make about our physical presentation of self. Factors of class, race, ethnicity, and age all intersect with gender and our general embodiment to form an apparently composite identity of us in the eyes of the gazer. But this is no objective gaze. Indeed, it is totally subjective—based on cultural interpretation and whatever dominant discourses around the body may be circulating in a society at any given time. Within this subjective assessment, some bodies are seen as repulsive; others, as attractive and compelling. Our gendered selves inhabit sexed bodies upon which are already inscribed codes and regulations of sexuality, class, race, and gender presentation and practice (see, for example, Carby, 1998). As the next section of this chapter develops, far from being part of a process functional for social coherence, the codes and regulations that are inscribed upon our bodies can be interpreted as part of a hegemonic process arising from masculinist ideologies and power regimes (see Watson, 2000). Violence, crime, and war are the expression of such relationships of power and dominance that lie at the core of our social organization and that are largely regulated through gender hierarchies.

THE GENDERED FACE OF VIOLENCE, CRIME, AND WAR

As Bob Dylan, in his inimitable way, tells us: "Democracy don't rule the world, you better get this in your head; this world is ruled by violence, but I guess that's better left unsaid" (*Union Sundown*).

While nicely and ironically summarizing the axiom that the world is a violent place, although some parts are more so than others (see Table 10.1), Dylan omitted to mention, as do most other writers and commentators on violence (see, for example, Wydra, 2008), that it is men who do the vast majority of the assaulting, maiming, torturing, and slaughtering. There are, of course, historical, sociological, and political reasons why some societies are more violent than others. Some of them are related to factors other than gender, such as poverty, social inequalities, organized crime, and political instability, often resulting from the impact of colonial, neo-colonial, and imperialist domination as is the case in many parts of Africa, the Caribbean, and South America. Furthermore, one needs to consider that some countries that have a relatively low homicide rate and appear to be peaceful places can also engage in other forms of violence, such as military occupation, police brutality, and warfare. Having said that, whether it is perpetrated by individuals, groups, or states, violence is overwhelmingly a gendered, masculine act performed by males. Indeed, men commit almost 100 per cent of all violent crime, make up approximately 90 per cent of the prison population in most developed countries, are more likely to be the victim of violence, and have a homicide rate that is 400 per cent higher than the rate for females (Maguire, 2009; also DeKeseredy and Schwartz, 2004; Evans and Wallace, 2008). Despite the recent moral panic over apparent increases in girls' violence, there is "scant evidence to show that girls are committing more violence; indeed, most of the evidence that exists is to the contrary" (Irwin and Chesney-Lind, 2008, p. 851).

Of course, once we notice this connection between men and violent acts then it strikes us as a given, to the point that the relationship of men

TABLE 10.1   "World Murder Map": Top 20 National Homicide Rates per 100 000 Population, 2011

1. Honduras	82.1
2. El Salvador	66.0
3. Cote d'Ivoire	56.9
4. Jamaica	52.1
5. Venezuela	49.0
6. Belize	41.7
7. Guatemala	41.4
8. US Virgin Islands	39.2
9. St. Kitts and Nevis	38.2
10. Zambia	38.0
11. Uganda	36.3
12. Malawi	36.0
13. Trinidad and Tobago	35.2
14. South Africa	33.8
15. Lesotho	33.6
16. Colombia	33.4
17. Congo	30.8
18. Central African Republic	29.3
19. Bahamas	28.0
20. Puerto Rico	26.2

Other Countries by Comparison:

Afghanistan	2.4
Mexico	18.1
Iraq	2.0
Israel	2.1
Japan	0.5
United Kingdom	1.2
United States	5.0
Russia	11.2
Canada	1.8
Spain	0.9

Note: UN data collected between 2008 and 2010 from 207 countries and based on homicide rate per 100,000 population.

Source: United Nations Office on Drugs and Crime (UNODC). 2011 Global Study on Homicide. www.unodc.org/unodc/en/data-and-analysis/statistics/crime/global-study-on-homicide-2011.html

to violence, crime, and war seems so embedded and self-evident that it is sorely tempting to dismiss these problematic, frequently horrific acts as simply the product of men's nature. If that is the case, society must endure such realities for as long as men exist as a gender group. Violence is what men do. They do it to strangers and they do it to those they love. Indeed, the fact is that if you are a woman living with a man you are at much more risk of violence from that man (intimate partner violence) that you are from a male stranger: "the safest place for men is the home, the home is, by contrast, the least safest place for women" (Edwards, 1989, p. 214; also Hearn, 1998; Dobash and Dobash, 1992; Archer, 1994; see Bergen and Logue, 2009, for overview).

The hard truth is that violence and its associated realms, crime and war, appear compulsive for many males and have appeared so through history, to the point that any violence we fear inevitably comes from the male image, not the female one. In other words, if someone wakes in the middle of the night hearing noises in the home, that person generally does not fear the female intruder armed with a gun or knife. This overwhelming link between men and aggression has led some scientists to suggest there is an evolutionary tribal male warrior instinct operating within males, closely linked to the male sex drive (Vugt, 2012). Such a biologically deterministic explanation for the complexities yet persistence of male violence can be attractive for it suggests there is little we can do to change men—they are aggressive by nature so society must accept and suffer it. But as we have shown very clearly in this book and further explore next in respect of violence, masculinity is not biology and biology is not destiny any more than it constitutes some solid and unwavering biological foundation upon which our gender identity is constructed. Violence is a learned trait. Men have to be taught how to kill and maim. They have to be socially conditioned to consider some people less than human; e.g., ethnic, racial, and religious groups whom they can then "justify" killing and torturing because they are "sub-human" or just different. Warriors are not born, they are made as army training camps around the world recognize. The child who comes out of the womb is not hard-wired to be a rapist, a serial killer, a torturer; he becomes that through the social experiences he is subjected to from childhood onward.

Within many masculine cultures and value systems, male aggression is not considered problematic; indeed, it is actually lauded. Criminal gangs, the armed forces, militaristic and totalitarian societies are where we are most likely to witness and experience "toxic masculinity" (Pascal and Dedman, 2011): that is, aggressive male behaviour that is fundamentally corrosive to society and to individuals, including those who perform it; such behaviour continues to be expressed by, indeed attracts to it, males of all ages, cultures, ethnicities, and social statuses.

No country or culture is immune from these violent acts of men. In the past 12 months at time of writing, individual men, acting apparently without accomplices, have gone on inexplicable killing rampages against their own citizens in countries as diverse as Norway, the UK, the US, and China. Such killings reveal a depressing similarity in that they are committed by males and carried out randomly and largely without warning. And yet still the question remains as to why it is always men who develop grudges against society and then go out and kill strangers and innocents en masse apparently as a way of alleviating their inner anger and angst.

One particularly gendered act of violence is rape by men of women and other men. Whether this is planned (as in the rape camps of Bosnia during the 1990s war in former Yugoslavia) or simply opportunistic, the sheer global incidence of rape suggests that toxic masculinity is not easily eradicated from the minds of men (see Table 10.2).

TABLE 10.2 Officially Recorded Incidence of Male–Female Rape, 2009

United States	28.6
United Kingdom	24.1
Lesotho	91.6
New Zealand	30.9
Trinidad and Tobago	58.4
Sweden	53.2
Iceland	21.6
Belgium	26.3
Zimbabwe	25.6
Canada	1.5
Switzerland	8.1
South Africa	121.16*

Note: Comparative data per 100,000 population.

*2001 rate. In 2007, 36 190 cases of rape were officially reported in South Africa. However, the South Africa Medical Research Council considers this accounts for no more than one out of nine cases. Estimates of the total number of rapes in South Africa each year range from 500 000 to 1 000 000, putting the incidence of male–female rape at above 200 per 100 000.

Sources: UNODC (United Nations Office on Drugs and Crime: statistics on rape at the national level, number of police-recorded offences, www.unodc.org/documents/data-and-analysis/Crime-statistics/Sexual_violence_sv_against_children_and_rape.xls+data+on+rape&cd=9&hl=en&ct=clnk

www.rape.co.za/index.php?option=com_content&task=view&id=875

Beyond a critical scrutiny of men and masculinity, we can see that society itself is born out of violence, is often sustained through violence, and is subject to periodic eruptions of violence, both socially organized as war and randomly perpetrated as individual crimes. As Bryan Turner (2003) suggests, a culture of violence appears to be at the very heart of our existence and has almost spiritualistic overtones. Most societies have needed to defend themselves at various points in their history, invariably from the violence of others—those others almost always being men. And in defending ourselves, so we too turn to violence, and invariably we turn to men, to young men, to perform that violence on our behalf and for our benefit and protection. We call them the armed forces, the police. Violence envelops us all, as actuality or as threat. Indeed, there is unlikely to be anyone reading this who has not been the subject of men's violence, men's crimes, or men's wars.

This is not to say that women are incapable of violence, crime, and war. But the armies of the world are organized by, led by, sustained by, and thrive on men. Criminal gangs are overwhelmingly male and prison populations are overwhelmingly male while the incidence of men's violence dwarfs that of women's violence (Bowker, 1998; Kimmel, 2000). Women who are violent are usually defending themselves from the violence of men, not simply emulating male performances of violence out of sheer aggression (Irwin and Chesney-Lind, 2008). One might reasonably conclude, then, that without men there would be no violence, leading some feminists to declare that only through women's separation from men can women's physical and emotional safety be guaranteed (see, for example, Dworkin, 2006).

"Explaining" the Violent Acts of Men

So does this take us back to nature, to the popularly held belief that men are naturally aggressive and often actually enjoy expressing that aggression either through individual acts of violence or through organized violence, e.g., in the armed forces or in criminal gangs? Is men's violence the consequence of their biology, in particular their testosterone levels? A social constructivist would certainly answer that men's violence is the result of social patterns learned early in childhood, perhaps due to a lack of social connectedness together with emotional deprivation—a process of isolation and emotional dysfunctionality that becomes reinforced in adult life (see, for example, Rojas, 2012).

But what about the testosterone effect? How influential is the male sex hormone on men's violence? As Jeff Hearn (1998) reveals, much research has shown a correlation between higher levels of testosterone—the male (androgen) hormone—and violent crimes: men who commit violent crimes have been found to have higher levels than other convicts (Dabbs et al., 1987; Ehrenkranz, Bliss, and Sheard, 1974). Surges in testosterone can arise from intensive competition between men, for example, participating in sporting contests (Elias, 1981; Mazure and Lamb, 1980). As well, men who committed violent crimes at a younger age have been found to have high testosterone levels (Kreuz and Rose, 1972), and some animal studies similarly show a relationship between surges in testosterone and males' struggles for dominance over territory and access to sexual partners.

But, as Hearn points out, to posit men's violence as a consequence of testosterone fails to explain why women, who also have testosterone, are much less violent than men; why many men with high levels of testosterone are not violent; why many men with low levels are violent; and similarly, why many prepubertal boys, with very little testosterone, are seriously aggressive or violent. This argument is supported by Clare (2000), who examines much of the research in this area:

> What these studies really show is a *correlation* between levels of aggression and levels of testosterone. There is more than one explanation for such a correlation. Yes, indeed, raised levels of testosterone might cause aggression. But, likewise, increased levels of aggressive behaviour might *cause* higher levels of testosterone. And, then again, neither might *cause* the other. And there is little consistency in the findings. For every study that reports a positive correlation between this or that aggressive or antisocial behaviour and testosterone, there is another which fails to find such a link. (p. 22, original emphasis; also Rose and Rose, 2000)

Numerous studies show that the incidence of male violence in societies can go up and it can go down (Hatty, 2000), independent of the unchanging levels of testosterone in men. For example, fascism erupted as a dominant racist ideology in Europe and Japan in the 1930s, leading to the horrors of World War II. The Italians had the Black Shirts of Mussolini; the Japanese, the *Bushido* culture of "never surrender"; and the Germans, the Nazis' Aryan race ethos. For a relatively brief period up until 1945 and the end of the war, these otherwise different cultures encouraged a similar, violent, militaristic, and racist form of masculinity. Yet within a few decades that particular discourse had lessened significantly, to the point that while it has not disappeared entirely it is no longer dominant in any of those previously hypermasculinist, violent societies.

Much crime and violence is socially and culturally validated and spatially and economically related, which reveals that "violent crime is concentrated in specific areas of large cities and that some individuals suffer repeat victimization" (Hatty, 2000, p. 4). If you are a young, African-American male living in a specific area of a large North American city, then you are at high risk of experiencing violence from other males. Indeed Kimmel (2000, p. 246) goes further to point out that "young American men are the most violent in the industrialized world." The incidence of violent crime on women continues to arise around the world, while testosterone levels do not (Cain and Howe, 2008; Hatty, 2000; Hearn, 1998; Dobash et al., 2000). And, importantly, men who have been violent can learn not to be, while nonaggressive men who associate with violent groups can become violent themselves (Hearn, 1998; Hatty, 2000; Bowker, 1998; Ray, 2011).

Hearn (1998) summarizes the dilemmas and variables around gender and violence very succinctly:

1. Violence can be understood as a biological or social fact.
2. Violence can be constructed as part of the inherent "badness" of people or an exception to the inherent "goodness" of people.
3. Violence can be something taken on by individuals from the social or something placed upon individuals by the social.
4. Violence can be expressive of internal needs or instrumental to achieve external needs.
5. Violence of one party, in this context particular men, can be considered as separate from or in relation to the violence or potential violence of others.
6. Violence can be a means of maintaining social structures or of disrupting social structures. (p. 20)

There are a multitude of explanations for men's violence and the gendered character of violence, but the most persuasive take us beyond the biological and into the realms of the social: into culture, into value systems, into practices of learning and association, and into the realities of male domination that exist in both organized and covert ways across most societies. For example, there are distinct "cultural scripts" around violence (Waldron, 2009), operating in particular social spaces and offering a gendered template that individuals, both male and female, can find very hard to resist. Such scripts are especially powerful in closed organizational sites, such as prisons (Sabo et al., 2001). They are also apparent in schools (Majors and Bilson, 1992; see Waldron, 2009, for overview) and reinforced in male youth cultures generally (Hogeveen, 2007). Gendered scripts concerning violence and aggression will not be followed by everyone in precisely the same way; however, individuals in such settings recognize the scripts, understand them, and have to negotiate and accommodate them. What they cannot do is ignore them.

There is nothing inevitable, evolutionary, or compulsively Darwinian about men's violence (Rose and Rose, 2000; Archer, 1994). However, violence is clearly not only a consequence of social factors; biological influences do play their part, making any distinct and absolute statement about all male violence being a product of nature or nurture largely sterile. It is an outcome of the dynamic of both, although not in any clear or predictable way either socially or individually. But what is clear is that violence, and its expressions in crime and war, is less a consequence of men's essential gender identity and more a powerful masculine performance engaged in by men as an attempted validation of their manhood. Therefore, whatever the precise causes of men's violence, the reality is that the association between men and violence goes deep into the male psyche, becoming a powerful expression of men's very sense of themselves as gendered beings. As we discuss below, the masculine cultures of crime and war not only validate many men's identities, they also serve to reinforce both the gendered polarization of male and female and the very material power base that validates men's sense of themselves as "superior" to women. This leads on to an interesting hypothesis that we now conclude this section with.

Historically, male violence appears to have always been present in society. But is the world becoming less violent? Is there some underlying civilizing process at work in contemporary society, a theory posited by sociologist Norbert Elias (1969) over 40 years ago? Well, statistics on violence can be ambiguous. As Pinker (2012) tells us, while 55 million people were killed during World War II, far more deaths proportionate to the population at the time occurred during the An Lushan revolt in eighth century China, the Mongol conquests of the thirteenth century, and the Mideast and Atlantic slave trade. At this point in the twenty-first century, approximately 1.6 million people die as a consequence of violence each year. Given the increasing world population, then, is violence actually on the decline as Pinker suggests? And is this a consequence of some larger feminization of society, something we discuss in Chapter 11? If so, then perhaps we should

be concerned at the increasing trend in many societies for unnatural selection: choosing boys over girls. As Hvistendahl (2011) shows, there is now an increase in sex-selective abortions in many parts of the developed and developing world, but especially in Asia, leading to a current global deficit of 160 million women. Given that a "world full of men" is, from the historical evidence thus far, likely to lead to more not less violence, then this raises some profound moral questions, as Basu (2012) notes:

> (There is) a counterpart to the Asian son preference; the intense *daughter* preference of many North American parents who seek to select the sex of a birth or a conception. . . . If we accept the grave consequences of a world full of surplus men and the presumed intrinsic violence of American life, then we should in fact be encouraging sex selection in the United States (and in Asia as well), as long as the selected births are female! (p. 173, original emphasis)

Crime as a Validation of Masculinity

First, it is important to recognize that what counts as crime and criminal is largely defined through social values and cultural imperatives, and these change over time. So all crime cannot simply and irrevocably be linked with bad and evil; rather, crime reflects social judgments prevailing across society at a particular period in history. That said, crime is clearly gendered, that is, it, like violence, is committed overwhelmingly by men. As a result, we must address whether there is something innate in men that inclines them toward acts of crime. Well, as we have discussed above, the suggestion that men's testosterone is the culprit just doesn't hold up. So why is it that, as a gender group, men are much more likely to be criminals, to be an active part of a criminal subculture, to commit crimes than women? This question leads, somewhat inevitably, to a feminist analysis of crime and criminology (see Moore, 2007, for overview).

One suggestion is that hegemonic masculinity (see Chapter 1) offers men a powerful and seductive pattern of behaviours that exist in a hierarchical relationship to subordinate expressions of masculinity (Connell, 1987, 2003). Men's power is, in this analysis, always contested and always in a state of being produced and reproduced. From this perspective, we might perceive men's crimes to be a direct consequence of this constant hegemonic contest between men for position, status, and material and social power. The fact that such contestation may well lead to individual men losing power—i.e., through being imprisoned or even killed—does not lessen the power of hegemonic masculinity as a persuader of men's behaviour, not least because it so closely connects to what many see to be men's core characteristics: "unemotional, independent, non-nurturing, violent and dispassionate (whilst at the same time being, on occasion, inappropriately passionate)" (Collier, 1998, p. 18; also Messerschmidt, 1993; Newburn and Stanko, 1994; see Hearn, 2006, for discussion).

So hegemonic masculinity offers us a theoretical model with which to understand men and criminality, but, as Collier points out, it fails to address the question of behavioural differences among men that may exist in time, in place, and over life courses; it does not account for the non-aggressive characteristics of men, and it posits within all men an essential, biological desire for contestation (see also for discussion, Whitehead, 2002; Jefferson, 2006; Connell and Messerschmidt, 2005). As Collier (2000) points out,

> What is actually being discussed in accounts of (hegemonic) masculinity and crime is, in effect, a range of popular ideologies of what constitute ideal or actual characteristics of "being a man" . . . [the concept of] . . . Hegemonic

masculinity imposes an a priori theoretical/conceptual framework on the psychological complexity of men's behaviour. (pp. 21–2)

Hegemonic masculinity cannot explain the range of social and psychological variables that induce individual men to criminality. To be sure, there is a socialization process at work with many men that creates the conditions for potential acts of crime and violence (Bandura, 1973; Goldstein, 1989). We can see such processes operating within society, in particular cultural settings, and, not least, in the prison system itself (Sabo et al., 2001). Membership in a street gang or mafia group is compelling if not irresistible for many men who find themselves socially connected, spatially, economically and culturally, with such groups (Winlow, 2001; see also Giordano, 2010). But the question remains, "How, and why, do men choose particular actions, to 'become' particular kinds of men?" (Collier, 2000, p. 17; Jefferson, 2006; Walklate, 1995).

To give an example, we may well read in tomorrow's newspaper of another serial killer on the loose. At some point in the future that serial killer will, hopefully, be arrested, charged, and imprisoned. It is all too likely that the serial killer will be a white, middle-aged male (Hatty, 2000). But why did this man become a serial killer? What set of circumstances and conditions triggered this action in him but did not have the same effect in women, black men, younger men, older men? What psychological changes took place in this man that resulted in his committing a series of premeditated acts of murderous violence on strangers? How did he go from being your friendly neighbour to being your worst nightmare?

It may be that the man, himself, was a victim of violent crime and abuse by men as a child, these experiences triggering a psychological disorder that resulted in his repeating these actions as an adult. In this case, the crimes are a direct consequence of learned or reproduced behaviour (Bandura, 1977; Goldstein, 1989; see Hearn, 1998, for overview). This follows Campbell's point that "violence seems to beget violence, rather than decrease it" (1993, p. 8; quoted in Hearn, 1998, p. 26). The more men are violent to each other and to women, the greater the likelihood men will do violence to each other and to women.

But there is more to crime than the act itself. Many criminologists argue that the criminal justice system, the framing and enacting of law, the prison system, police work, the very institutional systems of the judiciary, if not the state, are all gendered in that they are overwhelmingly conditional upon the presence of men as victims, aggressors, participants, and enforcers (see, for example, Walklate, 1995; Sabo et al., 2001; see Collier, 1998, for overview).

To put it another way, crime arises out of and exists within a masculinist culture that privileges particular expressions of masculinity and maleness. These expressions may not be identical—they may in fact be in tension with each other—but they are part of a gendered system that offers men a sense of themselves as masculine subjects. However, masculinity, as a concept, because of its multiplicity and contingency, can only tell us so much about this process. Rather, we suggest that the culture of masculinism that exists in many parts of society, especially in crime and the judicial system, provides arenas for the validation of men as embodied beings in search of ontological grounding. So crime becomes another arena for the practice and validation of men as masculine subjects. This perspective in no way addresses all the issues and variables that exist in relation of men to crime, nor, indeed, of women to crime, but it does alert us to the relationship of men's identity to crime and criminology.

From a feminist post-structuralist perspective, the male body—man—and the female body—woman—are constituted in discourse and, as such, become gendered subjects by inculcating the practices of gender signification that are at their disposal (see Chapter 2). These can be varied, reflect local and larger cultures, and are often in contestation with each other. For example, imagine the male youth living on the periphery of inner city gang culture. He may have a desire to go to college and get a job, not get involved in crime at all, but jobs are scarce, and going to college keeps him without money and without the social connection of his male peers, most of whom are involved in the local gang. He is faced therefore with two powerful discourses, either of which can validate him as an individual (a man) but only one of which offers an immediate sense of power with his male associates. First is the discourse of "be a good citizen, be patient, make sacrifices, and follow the recommended path toward paid employment via education and learning." Second is the discourse of "be a man, join the gang, enjoy local power and male esteem immediately, and have money in your pocket." The pressure to take up the latter discourse is immense. How many males could resist it in such circumstances?

This ontological process of being and becoming (a man or a woman) requires discursive environments for its enaction and validation. In the example above, the discursive environment is the inner city, the local gang culture, the prevailing codes of masculinity and manhood. For a middle-class youth raised in a prosperous suburb by middle-class parents, both of whom went to university themselves and became professionals, the discursive choices are very different indeed. For this youth, it would be almost unthinkable for him to get into inner city gang culture. He is much more likely to follow the "good citizen" discursive pathway to male validation.

Clearly, crime, and all its attendant settings, does provide a powerful discursive environment for many young men, whether through an LA street gang, a Colombian drug cartel, the Russian or Italian mafia, London's East End Boys, or the

Jamaican Yardies. In such environments, the relationship of men to crime is already established. It is already apparent in society, in the judicial system, in the state, on the street via discourses that reinforce it. The discourses surrounding crime only requires individual men to engage with them. But why should men engage in crime in this way but not women? We would suggest it is because the discourses at work here are already gendered in society, and already speak a gendered language; they reinforce a masculinist culture to which many men will gravitate. This process is reinforced through our voyeuristic obsession with violence and crime. Crime and the violent acts of men sell books, sell newspapers, and sell films. Hollywood constantly produces films that rely on portrayals of men's violence to attract an audience. It is no coincidence that what many consider to be the greatest work of American literature, written by Truman Capote, was based on the factual account of the brutal murder of a Kansas family by two young men in 1959, and their subsequent execution for that crime (1966). The sad truth is that, for most of us, the crimes of men hold a fascination and a strong entertainment value.

One might conclude that until we can change society into a model that glorifies nurturing, compassion, love, passiveness, and empathy—e.g., a model that speaks of traditional notions of femininity/women more than it does of violence/men—then the relationship of men to crime will continue. However, much as this scenario might benefit all humanity, as we now discuss, there remain powerful symbols within society that reinforce, often in seemingly positive ways, the relationship of men to violence.

War and Combat and the Myth of the Male Warrior Hero

Many would argue that all wars are criminal acts, not least because they result in crimes against humanity, in which case there can be no justification for them. However, we would suggest that war is very different than crime in respect of what war signals about gender identity, and about men and masculinities in particular (see Amy, 2010; Sjoberg and Via, 2010).

One of the persistent themes within discourses, ideologies, and models of male gender identity is the notion of a "heroic male project" (Whitehead, 2002; see also Beynon, 2002; Jackson, 1990; Low, 1993; Lash, 1995). Such a model is an expression of masculinity that is somehow hyper-masculine to the extent that it overwhelms and controls all around it, compulsively attracts both men and women to it, and is elevated in society as an iconic and glorified expression of (heterosexual) manliness. This is male power at its most raw and overt, a masculinity that thrives on the myth of potency and, by implication, the relative disempowerment or perceived vulnerability of women and the marginalization of the feminine, both in women and in men. The heroic male project can emerge in any social space, but it is invariably enabled by the presence of a male hero.

The male hero has existed as a model or exemplar of masculinity throughout history and is now a fundamental part of global culture and the media (see, for examples, Donald, 2001; Mellen, 1977; Dawson, 1994). The male hero can be any colour, creed, class, or religion. He may be a gentleman or he may be a scoundrel. He may be communist (Che Guevara), imperialist (Napoleon), capitalist (Churchill), or simply a rebel (Geronimo). Invariably, he portrays most effectively masculinity-as-action (Beynon, 2002). He is not passive, docile, or idle; he is not a coward. He is brave, resolute, imbued with courage and physical and mental fortitude, but also comradely (Low, 1993; Rutherford, 1997). The male hero model lives in both fact and fiction, thriving across the history books and the cinematic screen. He is in our hopes and imaginations, our aspirations and fears. If a country doesn't have one, then it must invent him and then ensure his continuation in the cultural discourse through song, statue, education, and myth (Lash, 1995; see, for example, Adams, 2008).

As we discuss in this book, both male and female identities draw heavily on socially enabled models or truth signifiers about men and women. These truth signifiers may not be apparent in every individual, but they are powerful symbolic expressions to which we feel compulsively drawn. Such truth signifiers are heavily invested in fantasy, myth, imagination, and fiction (see, for example, Bly, 1990), in which case they can only persist so long as they have a social space in which to be presented as possibilities, as real. One powerful truth signifier for males is the man as hero, especially the warrior hero.

War and combat offer many things but are especially powerful as a social space, an opportunity for men to become heroes if only in their own imaginations (Dawson, 1994; Lash, 1995). War reinforces the gender dualism through its very clear statement about men as potential warrior heroes within societies, and women as dutiful supporters of this role (McCarthy, 1994; Low, 1993; Tosh, 1991; Beynon, 2002). Importantly, war provides a powerful statement about men becoming men, or, more likely, boys becoming men: a vehicle for enacting and validating their masculinity (Kinsella, 2007; Adams, 2008). War and combat are, then, important sites for continuing the traditional masculine project, that is, man as maker, enforcer, architect, and, if need be, destroyer of his environment. At the same time, and as Ferguson (2004) argues, combat can traumatize identity, violate it, render it helpless amidst the insane logic of death and destruction:

> In combat identity is lost; surrendered to impenetrable processes which can be ascribed a meaning only at the cost of denying their real/unreal character . . . the solidarity and self-composure of the ego are washed away in combat, so that "experience" itself becomes clouded . . . combat is not configured as an experience, it is, rather, an episode of unreality. (pp. 21–2, original emphasis)

So are war and combat only ever about men and their masculine identities? No, for as Moser and Clark (2001) argue, women and their femininities are fully implicated in war as soldiers, prisoners, refugees, activists, jailers, and suicide bombers. Historically, as partners, wives, mothers, lovers, and sisters, women around the world tend to experience war primarily as victims not perpetrators (Cockburn, 2007; see Riley, 2008, for overview). However, the fact that more women are now engaged directly as combatants in many armies suggests that the relationship of women to combat may be intensifying. As Eisenstein (2007) puts it, "sometimes it looks like women are becoming more like men; if being militarized is the same as being masculinised" (p. 2). Certainly, as is shown in Table 10.3, one of the unlikely consequences of feminism and women's liberation over the past few decades has been to offer women the opportunity to engage in male ways of being, a military career being one of them.

TABLE 10.3   Women in the Military

Canada
Women represent 17% of the armed forces and serve in all branches including onboard submarines. Women have commanded large military units and warships.
Women can serve in combat (Capt. Nichola Goddard was the first Canadian female soldier to die in active combat on the front line, Afghanistan, 2006).

TABLE 10.3   (continued)

United States

There are approximately 215 000 women on active duty. They constitute 14.5% of the armed forces.

Women have access to 95% of military jobs (excluding on board submarines).

Women can now serve close to front lines but not in combat.

United Kingdom

Women serve in all branches of the armed forces excluding on board submarines.

Women have access to 71% of British Army jobs and 96% of Royal Air Force jobs, including fighter pilot.

Women are excluded from direct close-quarters contact with the enemy.

Israel

Only country to have compulsory military service for both males and females (18–49).

Women represent a third of all Israeli Defence Forces.

There has been a 40% increase in the number of women career soldiers in past 10 years.

Women have access to 90% of all military jobs, including fighter pilot.

Women are excluded from serving on board submarines.

China

Has the highest number of women in the military of any nation.

Women (18–49) can be conscripted into the military.

Women are now fighter-jet pilots, anti-terror special forces members, and amphibious reconnaissance troops.

Women in Combat Roles

At September 2011, the countries that allow women "in close combat roles" defined as "engaging with the enemy while being exposed to hostile fire and possibility of direct physical contact with hostile forces," are Canada, Denmark, Finland, France, Germany, Israel, the Netherlands, Norway, Poland, Romania, Sweden, and Australia. Countries where women have flown combat missions as fighter pilots include Britain, Pakistan, Serbia, South Africa, and the US.

Sources:

www.china.org.cn/features/60years/2009-10/01/content_18640458.htm

www.indiandefencereview.com/spotlight/Women-in-the-Armed-Forces.html

www.cbc.ca/news/background/military-international/

www.womensmemorial.org/PDFs/StatsonWIM.pdf

www.mod.uk/DefenceInternet/FactSheets/PersonnelFactsheets/WomenInTheArmedForces.htm

www.npr.org/2012/02/13/146802589/foreign-policy-women-on-the-front-lines

www.mfa.gov.il/MFA/Israel+beyond+politics/Integration_women_in_IDF-March_2009

www.npr.org/2012/02/13/146802589/foreign-policy-women-on-the-front-lines

Whether more women join the military or not, in the final reckoning, war can, we suggest, only be a possibility for so long as there is a male militaristic culture to glorify it and men prepared to sacrifice themselves in its name. Women have not produced armies that consist solely of women; that are led by women; that commit acts of organized violence against women, children, and men; that deliberately strive to kill, enslave, and subjugate millions. These acts have been the acts of men. To be sure, women have actively participated in wars and revolutions and likely will continue to do so (see Oakley, 1972; Knauss, 1987). But the bureaucratic, militaristic, organizational culture that makes war a possibility is masculinist at its very core (see also Hearn and Parkin, 2001; Morgan, 2006; Jeffrey, 2007; also Riley 2008).

Whether we are caught up in a global conflagration as in a world war or a national conflict such as in Iraq and Afghanistan, or simply happen to be in the wrong place at the wrong time when a suicide bomber detonates, war and conflict are a continuing part of our daily reality in some form or another. All of us—men, women, and children—are potential victims of war. Indeed, one of the tragic hallmarks of modern warfare is the increased toll on civilians, with non-combatants now more likely to be slaughtered than the soldiers themselves, as the following figures attest:

- World War I: Civilian death toll, 10 per cent
- World War II: Civilian death toll, 50 per cent
- Vietnam War: Civilian death toll, 70 per cent
- Iraq War: Civilian death toll, 90 per cent (Pilger, 2010)

As Morgan (2006) notes, all societies have called upon men to fight, to be prepared to kill, to commit acts of violence on men, women, and children, and to do so in the name of, variously, God, freedom, democracy, justice, and peace. Fed by an endless supply of technologically advanced weaponry and masculinist ideology, men today are as prepared to kill, torture, and maim as ever men were who lived in the so-called dark ages and primitive cultures of world history:

> Of all the sites where masculinities are constructed, reproduced, and deployed, those associated with war and the military are some of the most direct. Despite far-reaching political, social and technological changes, the warrior still seems to be a key symbol of masculinity . . . combat and the military experience separate men from women while binding men to men. It is a separation that reaches deep into a man's sense of identity and self. (Morgan, 2006, pp. 444–5)

Men are not born warriors, however, and they are not born violent or warlike. Neither are they born natural soldiers. What turns a man into a soldier, in effect into a death machine, is the masculinist, bureaucratic, militaristic culture of the armed forces (Jeffrey, 2007; Barrett, 2001; Armitage, 2003; Adams, 2008)—a culture that is, in turn, enabled, glorified, and validated by society itself, not least through the myth of the male warrior hero. Such a culture is enforced by the boundedness and spatial representation (Morgan, 2006) of the military camps, military training, military ranks, uniforms, and drilled body posture of the soldier as warrior. It is through these discursive mechanisms that a particular male gender identity is generated and reified. This identity exists in traditional, powerful, if not mythical, separation from the feminine, from other men. As such, it continues to be a conduit through which many men voluntarily if not eagerly pass on their way to manhood. This leads us to a sad but inescapable conclusion: that if men did not go to war, there would be no war.

How Aging Alters Our Sense of Gender

The overwhelming and unremitting relationship of men to violence, crime, and war, and the damage and pain this relationship causes to others and to themselves, suggest the male body to be a potentially dangerous entity.

But are we trapped inside a man's or woman's body? Or do our bodies also offer us the possibility for subverting the norms that bind (Butler, 1993), thereby creating our selves as an embodied work of art through particular technologies of self (Foucault, 1988)? Can we, as individuals, challenge and resist the larger social pressure to conform to dominant ways of being a woman or a man? Such questions appear to demand an either/or response. However, the reality is that the sheer multiplicity of gazes upon the body— i.e., who is seeing what through what social eye and assumptions—means there is no singular condition of the body, only endless possibilities. Some such possibilities may be within our control, at least in the virtual world of cyberbodies and cyberspace (Featherstone and Burrows, 1996). Other possibilities are not. The power of the gaze upon the body does lie in its omnipresence, but the sheer multiplicity of gazes, especially in the postmodern world, means there is no absolute and final description of any body, only singular interpretations, none of which are entirely neutral in their appraisal and viewing.

While we cannot predict all the gazes or their interpretations on us, we can be fairly sure of one thing: as we physically age so do people see us differently. The aging body is the most visible indicator of the contingent reality to our sense of embodied self. Aging has become, in the Western world at least, something of an anathema. We are distressed by it, and many of us seek to avoid it or certainly curtail its more unsettling aspects. Globalization, and the consumerist culture that accompanies it, does not appear to celebrate old age, old bodies. On the contrary,

We grow old, but we don't stop needing others.

Source: © Carrie Boretz/Corbis

old age, at least in the West, becomes the state to avoid, a condition to defend oneself from, a truth we cannot fully embrace and accept. In the consumerist hierarchies that now globally circulate around the body, old, infirm, and distressed bodies are at the bottom, while youthful, fit, firm, and explicitly sexually attractive bodies are at the top. Ultimately, over time, we each experience the slow but irreducible reduction of our bodies in terms of their social status. Even in the East, where old age has long been held in esteem and respect, the pressures of the globalized consumerist culture on the body appear to be shifting perceptions of aging and of the elderly toward a celebration of youth above all else.

Recognizing this, both masculinities and femininities are clearly affected by aging. Our gender identity is always, to some extent, a condition of our age, our point in our life course. As our age increases, so too does our sense of gender alter, become reconstituted. As individuals, we may not always, or ever, fully reflect on this condition, but it is ever with us (Arber and Ginn, 1995; Arber, Davidson, and Ginn, 2003). Old age is also one of those social areas heavily laden with stereotypes: dominant social and cultural notions about health, sexuality, independence, love, and desire (see, for examples, Browne, 1998; Chambers, 2005; Gullette, 2011; Jones and Pugh, 2005). Old lives are, as Chambers puts, all too often hidden lives, concealed from the public gaze, compartmentalized, assumed, dismissed. Why is this so, given that old age is something all of us, if we live long enough, will experience?

In addressing this issue in respect of "older men as invisible men in contemporary society," Thompson (1994, p. 1) suggests that one of the reasons is that aging in men suggests a negation of masculinity. As men age they somehow, at least in the public imagination, become slightly more feminine, in need of protection and care, helpless, and, therefore, invisible as masculine beings. This assumption may explain why there has been relatively little research undertaken into the masculinities of older men while research into the masculinities of young and younger men is relatively plentiful (see, for examples, Seidler, 2006; Frosh, Phoenix, and Pattman, 2002). This is not to negate the importance of research into younger masculinities, but it has seemed as if masculinity is assumed to be a condition of youthfulness and vigour, not of old age. Certainly, there is evidence to suggest that declining health in aging men further undermines dominant norms of masculinity: symbolically, socially, and in individual men's sense of maleness (see, for discussion, Sabo and Gordon, 1995; Courtney, 2006). However, some men might be more affected than others since maleness and old age do not stand alone and are intersected by factors such as race, ethnicity, and social background. For example, even as they age, more economically advantaged men tend to live longer lives than less economically advantaged men. Canada Pension Plan records that higher earnings for men aged 45 to 64 are associated with lower mortality rates at older ages (McMullin, 2004, p. 246).

Can the same be said of femininity? How is the femininity of older women perceived? Are women affected by old age in the same way as men are? The stereotype of the older woman is of someone who is no longer sexually active, a woman who, having gone through menopause, is disinterested in sexual adventures and in having children, and who no longer seeks pleasure and satisfaction through sexualized love and child-bearing. The older woman has, in the past at least, been seen as someone more settled, the eternal granny who is always there to wipe a brow, expressing her femininity through a steady and benign maternalism, which she selflessly directs toward her now maturing children and grandchildren (see Bell, 1986; Gannon, 1990; Rosenthal, 1990).

Increasingly, such stereotypes are being dismantled. Spurred on by the burgeoning anti-aging industries, successful aging is now an aspiration, if not expectation, of millions. Older women and men, aged 50 and over, are now recognized by both sexual health organizations and dating agencies to be increasingly sexually active, romantically adventurous groups. Those older women and men with the necessary economic, social, and cultural capital are now more likely to expend it on seeking love and romance, on worldwide travel, and on acquiring new skills and knowledge than on settling for invisible retirement (Whitehead, 2012, also Calasanti and King, 2005). As well, increasing numbers of older women, certainly in their fifties, some even in their sixties, are now using new medical technology (e.g., IVF treatment) to give birth to children (see, for example, Bernard, 2000; Catan, 2007; Onyx, Leonard, and Reed, 1999).

The drive for individualism that accompanies the postmodern, globalized era appears to be surfacing in the lives of older people especially. The opportunity to delay the onset of old age or even to reinvent what it means to be elderly is increasingly apparent. In centuries past, 50- and 60-year-olds were clearly the elderly. Now 60 is only middle age. Today, at least in developed countries, centenarians (people aged 100 and over) are the fastest growing part of the population, projected to rise from 72 000 currently to over 1 million by 2050 in the US alone (*The Centenarian*, 2011).

For those with the material and cultural resources at their disposal, growing old no longer holds out the same definitions, or limitations, of gender identity it did to their ancestors. Growing old always comes with risks, especially around health and poverty, and ultimately we all die, but worldwide demographics show the growth of aging, economically independent populations in all modern industrialized countries. This trend is accompanied by the growth of a class of (predominantly migrant) workers specialized in caring for the elderly in the developed nations of the world. For example, Japan has one of the most rapidly aging populations with 21 per cent of the population aged over 65 projected to rise to almost 40 per cent by 2050. Consequently, long-term care for the elderly has become a priority in Japan to the extent that state-organized programs have been set up for migrant care workers (especially Thai and Philippine workers) to provide care in hospitals and long-term care institutions (Ito, 2010, pp. 137–8). Of course, not everyone has the means to afford care, which raises the question of who constitutes the growing economically independent and aging population of the world. Nevertheless, there is no doubt that this population is growing. We can assume, therefore, that such populations of older people with economic power will push back the boundaries of gender identity for a particular category of people, reconfiguring the relationship of the body with age and, to some extent, challenging the stereotypes of enfeebled masculinity and selfless, maternalistic femininity that have, hitherto, informed our assumptions of what lies in store for us as we get older. Whatever new practices of gender identity surface within the "young elderly" and "very elderly" (Thompson, 1994), one can assume that the drive and motivator will be, for most, to maintain and extend over their life course a youthful definition of masculinity or femininity in their embodied expression of self—a definition, however, contingent on economic and social privilege.

SUMMARY

In this chapter we have examined the ways the physical presence of the male is constructed in different symbolic ways than that of the female—the former connects to a (mythical) phallic symbolism of strength, hardness, and control, while the latter connects to a more nuanced and emotively engaged construction of being in the world. These are not biologically inevitable but culturally given—we learn to emulate and appreciate these differences from early childhood. However, this is not to say that we always or solely inhabit the masculine or the feminine in our embodied sense of being. The fact is, we all move between the two realms at different times. But the warrior, the soldier, the gangster, and those associated with these social arenas will inevitably be required to practise and reinforce masculinist, not feminist, ways of being a person. They exist and operate in a social space that encourages, indeed demands, particular hegemonic masculine codes of behaviour from its participants.

Two of the most obvious, but often least discussed, aspects of society and individuality are violence and the body. Out of these two arenas, gender differentiations emerge. They do so through distinct performances of masculinity and femininity, reinforced, all too often, through those embodied acts of aggression that we all engage in at times, or at least experience. Such acts of aggression are most apparent in the (mostly male) acts of crime and war. However, violence and passivity are both ultimately about identity work, which is something we are all required to engage in every moment of our waking lives. It matters not whether we are male or female, black or white, rich or poor; the truth is, none of us exists as a disembodied actor. We all have a physical presence, whether we choose to enact that presence as a soldier or gangster, or as a nurse or social worker.

The body is, then, a site upon which are written for us numerous gender and sexual codes and aspirations. It is not a gender-neutral place, which is the main reason we invest a lot of hope and effort, and material resources, in maintaining or enhancing our body image. Our body is us—or at least appears to be. But the body remains vulnerable to decay, to illness, to accident, to aging, and, of course, to the violence of others. If life is uncertain at its core, then that uncertainty and insecurity is manifest most notably in the body itself—a physical entity that remains, much to our ontological unease, outside our ultimate control.

CASE STUDY

Frank is 89 years old. A recent widower, he now lives alone by the coast in the north of England. Most people who pass by Frank's smartly painted bungalow and see him attending to his trimmed and attractive garden couldn't imagine Frank as anything other than an old-age pensioner. But the truth is, Frank has had a fascinating life. He was placed in an orphanage when he was just 9 years old. He left the orphanage when he was 16 to join the British Royal Navy. Frank subsequently went with the Royal Navy to every corner of the world, and saw active service in many places during World War II. He was a fit young man, a superb swimmer, and the Royal Navy trained him for underwater rescue missions, especially learning to dive to release sailors trapped in submerged vessels. Frank won't talk much about this aspect of his war experiences, but he saved many lives. Even so, it was always a disturbing experience to come across men he couldn't rescue—those dead or dying of wounds.

At the end of the war, Frank left the Royal Navy to go into business. By then he was married. Within a few years he was a father. But the business failed; Frank was a good man in an organization like the Navy, but not so good at running an independent operation. He liked and needed direction and structure to his life, so he joined the prison service. Frank relished his role and he stayed in the prison service until retirement. He was tough, very firm, but sympathetic to the prisoners, having himself been institutionalized, in one form or another, most of his life.

Unfortunately, Frank found it difficult to be the sympathetic and empathetic father at home. His three children all became estranged from him when they became adults. Frank's style of discipline was just too austere; he had experienced regular physical punishment as a child and consequently applied it to his own children, often in a very aggressive way. His wife left him when he was 50; she had tired of his unpredictable and often violent eruptions. Frank remarried some years later, but his second wife became very ill and disabled, and eventually Frank had to nurse her full-time, although he continued to do occasional gardening jobs for a little extra money.

Frank has remained physically strong throughout his life. Even today, apart from his gardening, he keeps mentally and physically active by walking, looking after his home, and driving a car. Frank has always taken pride in being physically independent, although if he were honest he'd reflect that his weakness was not so much physical strength as emotional stability. He cannot handle stress nor is he good in social situations. But at 89 he does pretty well for himself, even though he is, as a widower, often very lonely.

To alleviate his loneliness, Frank has a visitor. It is a woman who used to help nurse his wife part-time. She comes once a week to Frank's house. Frank looks forward to her visits very much indeed. In fact, often she is the only person he really has a conversation with from one visit to the next. He will go to a lot of trouble to prepare for her visit, baking homemade cakes and scones. Then they sit in his lounge drinking tea and chatting. Afterward they go to the bedroom where she will help Frank to relax through sexual massage. Frank pays her a little money each visit.

Frank's life is nearing its end, but he has no regrets, other than the fact that he rarely, if ever, sees his children. Even though he divorced his first wife, and she died just a few years ago, he always loved her; she was his soulmate. He has a picture of her over his fireplace and often he will talk to her. She is still very present in his life. For Frank, the most important thing is to keep going, not to give up, and to keep active. He may not have many friends left now, a negligible social life, and his family is estranged from him, but in many respects he feels lucky.

DISCUSSION QUESTIONS

1. In what ways has Frank's sense of masculinity been reinforced through embodied identity work?
2. How has Frank managed his aging process in order to retain his sense of manhood?
3. What appear to be the threats to Frank's ongoing sense of himself as a man?
4. How has Frank's masculinity come to be validated through institutional life?
5. What might we presume to be the trigger points for Frank's violence when he was younger?
6. Consider how violence, crime, war, and aging embodiment have, in different ways and at different times in his life, manifest themselves in Frank's identity work.

QUESTIONS FOR REVIEW AND DISCUSSION

1. Consider how you do your own embodied identity work. How has this identity work changed as you got older?

2. How do you feel about your body? How would you like to improve it if you could?

3. If women do violence, are they, then, emulating a male performance? Give reasons for your answer.

4. How can society change the pattern of ongoing male violence?

5. Do research on the Internet to find out the sorts of crimes that women are mostly imprisoned for in your country. What are men mostly imprisoned for?

6. Consider how war differentially impacts women and men.

7. How old do you hope to be when you die? In what ways do you think your sexuality and gender will be different when you are 80 than what it is today?

8. Describe ways in which males reinforce their identity through "manhood body acts." Then compare these with the ways in which females reinforce their identity through "female body acts."

Part Four

New Directions in Gender Identity

Chapter 11

The Contingent Self in the Postmodern, Globalized Age

▲ *Are you a postmodern person?*

Source: © Peter Frank/Corbis   Source: © Tassh/Shutterstock

Learning Objectives

At the end of this chapter you will be able to:

- Understand how gender identities are changing in the postmodern, globalized age.
- Critically examine the gender consequences of migration and diaspora.
- Appreciate and understand how cyberspace and the virtual world engage the discursive gendered subject through fact, fiction, and fantasy.
- Reflect on and understand the concepts of postmodern woman and postmodern man.
- Critically examine how postmodern man and postmodern woman have shifted our sense of traditional, conservative, modernist understandings of gender identity.

OVERVIEW

As this book has demonstrated, the primary realization to emerge from any sociologically informed examination of gender identity is that it is contingent, malleable, and multiple. Gender identity is not fixed and settled through a lifetime or even irrevocably rooted within a powerful, ideologically overwhelming social structure. Gender identity is ultimately conditional upon external factors—culture and environment. It is relational to the social setting within which it seeks to emerge and become validated, and social settings change. Indeed, in today's world they change rapidly and profoundly. Whatever biological or psyche impulses work within us, they play only a relatively minor role in our cultural presentation and identity work. Women are not the same the world over, and neither are men. Women have not been the same throughout history, and neither have men. There is diversity and difference all around us. Such individualism remains our strength, and the ultimate reminder of our uniqueness and distinctiveness.

But when gender identity is explored in the contemporary era, a second powerful theme emerges: globalization. It is, arguably, the most important condition of the last half-century, influencing everything from global warming to global media, and global wealth to global poverty. No country or community is, today, totally isolated from the rest of the world. Whoever we are and wherever we live, we are increasingly likely to meet strangers, to mix with other ethnic groups, and to be exposed to alternative cultures. These strangers will appear as men and women, but we cannot assume they will think and act as we do. They will be gendered individuals for sure, but their expression of gender identity will not necessarily match

or reinforce our own. We may decide to ignore such differences, but the very fact of their existence only serves to remind us of our own contingency and relational place in the world. Whatever one's view as to the political and economic conditions sustaining and arising from globalization, there can be little doubt that globalization is having an increasing effect on our sense of who we are or who we might become. The force of globalization meets the contingent character of our being and suddenly all is open to question, if not doubt. Importantly, the gender and sexual stereotypes that once appeared as truths about men and women, femininity and masculinity are vulnerable; they stand exposed for what they are, which is convenient myths we use to reinforce our particular, localized perspective on reality.

In this final part of the book, we consider how gender identities are responding to these two conditions: globalization and the contingency of self. We explore four new directions within gender identity apparent at this point in history. The first refers to the diaspora effect: the movement and displacement, both intellectual and physical, of people across social and cultural spaces. The second considers the ways that humans are responding to the advanced technology now at their disposal, especially how people are using such technology to reinvent themselves in cyberspace. The final two sections of this chapter explore the emergence of postmodern man and postmodern woman. As we discuss, this postmodern gender identity is illustrated by the mixing of masculinity and femininity within the sexes, the blurring of sexual boundaries, and, ultimately, the breaking down of traditional codes of gender.

THE GENDERED CONDITIONS OF MIGRATION AND DIASPORA

Diaspora, the movement of people from their ancestral or established homelands, is not a new phenomenon. Indeed, it has been a characteristic of human existence throughout history. Nor is diaspora a specific regional or cultural phenomenon; it has been recorded across the Middle East, Asia, Africa, Europe, Australasia, and the Americas. Whether it has been the consequence of war, persecution, famine, pestilence, or simply a desire for new pastures, diaspora has been elementary to the human condition ever since modern humans walked out of Africa some 100 000 years ago (Braziel, 2008; Cohen, 2008).

Over recent decades, **migration** has become increasingly apparent and increasingly fraught with political, economic, and social consequences (see Esman, 2009, for overview). Today, approximately 200 million people, 3 per cent of

> **migration**
> The mass movement of people from one locality or country of residence to another.

the world's population, are involved in migration, mostly from undeveloped to developed countries (see Table 11.1). In developed countries, permanent migration is now at an annual rate of 10 per cent. Added to this number are the millions of internal migrants within individual countries. For example, the World Bank estimates that in China alone there are 130 million internal migrants (World Bank, 2010).

Diaspora is a phenomenon that affects most every country and all peoples, from the poorest to the richest and from the rural to the urban. Indeed, the United Nations Secretary General, Ban Ki-moon, has named this the "migration age" and identified it as the "second stage of globalisation" (2007). In addition to people

TABLE 11.1   Diaspora: Major Movements and Destinations in 2005 (Based on Government Data Accurate at 2009)

Country	Numbers	Top Destination
Armenia	812 700	Russia
Bangladesh	4 885 704	United States
Brazil	1 135 060	Japan
China	7 258 833	US
El Salvador	1 128 701	US
India	9 987 129	United Arab Emirates
Mexico	11 502 616	US
Morocco	2 718 665	France
Philippines	3 361 405	US
Poland	2 316 405	US
Romania	1 244 052	Israel
Serbia	2 298 352	Germany
Syria	480 708	Saudi Arabia
Tunisia	623 221	France

Source: www.migrationinformation.org/Feature/display.cfm?ID=748

escaping economic deprivation and/or climate change, included in this migratory dynamic are enslaved and sex-trafficked peoples; forced migrants; retirees; international students; adventure travellers; the educated, skilled, and professional classes; international marriage migrants; and individuals and families from diverse cultural and ethnic backgrounds. All are in search of new (better) life opportunities and experiences. It is not possible, therefore, to identify a single symbol of the diaspora; it encapsulates a multitude of motivations, peoples, and nations. Moreover, despite the often negative political rhetoric that surrounds immigration, especially in developed countries, the reality is that diasporas have always been, and certainly are today, important "agents of development," making major contributions to the prosperity of many nations (Agunias, 2009).

But migration in the age of globalization is rather different to that which went on in previous centuries. For example, one of the drivers of contemporary migration is the media and the new technology surrounding it. People around the world can now tune into the television and view programs from other countries, especially from the West. Such programs can have a powerful influence on how people perceive other, more distant cultures and their relative attraction. For example, Chen (2012) shows in her research into Taiwanese sojourners in America that notions of the American dream are highly potent and can be a key factor in Taiwanese choosing to study and live in the US. However, for the sojourners, the idea of the American dream is often symbolized in television series, such as *Dynasty*, *Dallas*, and *Baywatch*, programs they may have watched over many years. Once actually living in America, the Taiwanese come to realize the image has very little relationship to the reality.

Whatever their social origin and motives for migration, such groups of people are growing in number and political significance around the world (see Table 11.2). Their presence in a new host country may be welcome or not, but it cannot be ignored. Not only do such peoples face the challenge of building new and better lives, they must manage their very sense of self, their identity work, in negotiation with the various cultural domains that exist in their new home (Brah, 1996). They must try to re-establish and reproduce their culture and practices, but in strategic negotiation with the host or dominant culture in which they become settled. This itself is a major challenge, especially for those migrants who are facing exclusion and racism. This process not only involves learning new languages, it involves learning new cultures, and at times it requires some level of assimilation. But the migration of people does not conclude at a specific point in time: in the age of globalization migration is continuing relentlessly, and with each new wave of immigrants so does a group or community's cultural identity change while at the same time retaining a core essence of difference. This process has the consequence of creating a

TABLE 11.2   Annual Flows of Foreign Population: Top Receiving Countries (2006)

Country	Number of legal immigrants arriving in 2006 (trend since 2000)
1. United States	1 266 000 (increasing)
2. Spain	802 000 (increasing)
3. Germany	558 000 (decreasing)
4. United Kingdom	451 000 (increasing)
5. Japan	325 000 (no change)
6. Korea	314 000 (increasing)
7. Canada	251 000 (no change)
8. Turkey	191 000 (increasing)
9. Italy	181 000 (decreasing)
10. Australia	180 000 (increasing)

Source: OECD 2008 and www.canadaimmigrants.com

contingent, potentially unsettled, diasporic-informed identity within those same individuals and communities (Agnew, 2005; Braziel, 2008; De Tona, 2004; Brah, 1996; also Gilroy, 1993).

Gendering the Diaspora

Studies into diaspora and migration have increasingly been applying a feminist analysis, recognizing that the gender identity of the diasporic individual is very likely to be crucially affected by the political, social, economic, and cultural framework of the host society (Kostovicova and Prestreshi, 2003; Derne, 2002; Huang, Teo, and Yeoh, 2000; Popoviciu, Haywood, and Mac an Ghaill, 2006; Rostami-Povey, 2007; Siu, 2005; Yeoh and Huang, 2000; see Nawyn, 2010, for overview). Such studies reveal not only the dynamic constitution of diasporic identity, but also the very non-essentialist character of gender itself. As Huang, Teo, and Yeoh (2000) put it,

> The concepts of diaspora and diasporic identities provide for a less essentialised and more historically and analytically informed framework to understand not only the large and complex range of (trans)migrant movements that is taking place today, but also the ability to challenge our current conceptualizations of culture, place and identity as closed, fixed, and unchanging. (p. 392)

The dynamics of diaspora ultimately affect everyone: the multiple diasporic communities existing in any given location, and ultimately all members of the host community, even those who might otherwise feel distant from this phenomenon (Brah, 1996; Durham, 2004). One can see this in the multicultural and multi-ethnic cities in the West, with their multiple diasporas and increasing cosmopolitanism, and in the slow but persistent movement of diasporic individuals out of the metropolis and to new locations. As a diasporic community experiences acculturation, assimilation, and integration, so does that community's sense and expression of identity change

subtly. This process results in the emergence of modified discourses around gender, sex, race, class, and so on, especially in the younger, less traditionally minded members of the diasporic group (Nawyn, 2010).

But people do not simply find new expressions of gender identity once they arrive in a new geopolitical location. They bring with them the dominant discourses of gender that have hitherto informed their sense of being women and men. Research undertaken by Yeoh and Huang (2000) into migrant women from the Philippines, Indonesia, and Sri Lanka, who arrived in Singapore to work as domestic workers, clearly shows that notions of gender underlie migrant women's (re)negotiations of self. These in turn influence their attitudes and responses to the host culture. Thus, dominant gender discourses of the diasporic individual are retained within their local community, but always this process exists in relation to the host culture and therefore is susceptible to ultimately significant transformation. Huang, Teo, and Yeoh (2000) cite Anthias's call for the need to recognize the "gender of the diaspora" so as to acknowledge the different "ways in which men and women of the diaspora are inserted into the social relations of the country of settlement, within their own self-defined 'diasporic communities' and within the transnational networks of the diaspora across national borders" (Anthias, 1998, p. 527).

While the socio-cultural heritage of communities provides the holdfast for any diasporic identity, men and women negotiate their own individual gender identities within the possibilities and limitations of that history. For example, Yeoh and Huang (2000) suggest that

> Women must constantly negotiate new, and sometimes unexpected twists and turns on their diasporic journeys. . . . Their sense of identity is tied up in one way or another, with their roles as dutiful, even sacrificial, female family members,

whether as daughters, sisters, mothers, or wives, and almost never with the larger framework of the global capitalist stage within which their diasporic journey take place. (p. 428)

Mulki Al-Sharmani (2006) in her study of Somali diasporic women in Cairo, asserts that through their diasporic experiences "women are engaging in new forms of activism to establish lives with more security, better future opportunities, and more dignity for their families and themselves" (p. 55). Similarly, Gammage's (2004) research into gendered patterns of migration in Haiti suggest that women have participated in changing the financial architecture and political landscape, have contributed to the feminization of agriculture, and are emerging at the forefront of a nationalist movement to secure land rights and redistribute wealth to the countryside. For some of the women and men in this cultural setting, the traditional roles seem to have been reversed and challenged, thus making way for a differently gendered life experience.

The Yeoh and Huang and the Al-Sharmani analyses appear to offer different interpretations of the issues facing women and men situated within a diasporic condition, but they are very similar in one respect. That is, the issues of gender that diasporic women face are always connected, in some way, to dominant gender values and associated practices of masculinity. The desire of diasporic women to renew their lives and opportunities is often in tension with the retained traditional, conservative values of the diasporic men as well as the patriarchal values of mainstream society. Thus, the diasporic condition not only reveals the impact of the migrant communities upon the host culture, it also highlights the often less apparent impact of such movements upon the lives of individuals within family and local settings.

Derne (2002) asserts that "men are attracted to transnational celebrations of masculinity that strengthen male dominance. But they respond to transnational challenges to existing gender arrangements by reconstituting local gender hierarchies" (p. 161). Furthermore, Derne notes that men tend to identify public cosmopolitan spaces as masculine preserves, while focusing on domestic and religious spaces as the fundamental sites of their national identity, for which they hold women ultimately responsible in terms of maintenance and care.

However, such masculine values do not go necessarily go unchallenged in the emergent gender regime of the diaspora. Derne (2002) offers this vignette as evidence:

> A couple who emigrated to the United States several years ago [did so] with one dream—to become citizens. Through [sic] much tape and years of study they were hopeful. Then one day the husband rushed into the kitchen with the long awaited good news, "Lizzy!" he shouted, "At last we are Americans!" "Fine," replied the wife, tying her apron around him. "Now you wash the dishes." (p. 159)

This example might appear to demonstrate that women in the United States enjoy more gender equality than in other parts of the world. Yet a closer look at the lives of migrant women reveals a more complex situation as migrant women are suppressed both as migrants and as women. An example is that of undocumented immigrants who, in some cases, are unable to report domestic violence abuses to the police for fear of being deported. In this respect, migration often creates a situation whereby gender equality is compounded with other issues involving citizenship.

However, the fact that gender and migration often collude to create more marginalization for migrant women does not mean that there is no possibility for change. As De Tona (2004) argues, women in their collective narrative and practices create spaces and opportunities for transforming diasporic identities, thus offering possibilities of further change for the diaspora's future generations. But male dominance often travels with the migrant community and can find itself lauded once again in the diasporic conditions of the new life. Rostami-Povey (2007), for example, reveals how Afghan women, who migrated to Iran and Pakistan, were in constant battle, in their diasporic condition, between social, political, economic, ethnic, cultural, and gender forces. Nevertheless, despite marginalization and exile the Afghan women were successful in reshaping their gender identities. They challenged imperialist representations of themselves while seeking freedom from hierarchical and patriarchal domination, thereby establishing their individual gender identities largely free from male, ethnic, and religious domination. Indeed, Rostami-Povey's research shows that many Afghan women were not passive victims of male domination, religion, and tradition but active in their construction of a new ontologically grounded diasporic identity.

An effective way to explore and better appreciate the experiences of disadvantaged diasporic populations is through the lens of intersectionality, as discussed in Chapter 3. This approach requires an examination of race, class, and gender. It effectively "probes beneath the single identity to discover how other identities contribute to a situated disadvantage" (Hsiung and Nichol, 2010, p. 8). Using this approach, Hsiung and Nichol reveal how female foreign domestic workers (FDWs) in Canada experience discrimination, harassment, and marginalization while being increasingly sought after by Canadian middle-class professionals to take on the role of "woman of the house," work that includes emotional labour, thereby freeing their employers from these responsibilities.

Sexuality and the Diaspora

Intersectionality is also especially useful to help unpick the complex dynamics that occur when individuals from diverse cultures meet, embark on relationships, and perhaps enjoin through marriage. This is the moment when "sexuality meets globalisation" (Erker, 2011), and it is a powerful force behind, and major consequence of, the diaspora. International marriage migrants make up an increasingly important part of some countries' wealth and social fabric. In parts of Thailand, for example, the incidence of marriage and settlement between Western men and Thai women is such that it has created towns and villages in the country that are demographically dominated and economically reliant on such partnerships. One such village in a rural part of Northeast Thailand now has 200 German and Swiss husbands out of 500 families (Erker, 2011). Across most of Asia there has been a marked increase in international marriage over recent decades. According to Jones and Shen (2008), the percentage of international marriages among all marriages in 2005 was 32 per cent in Taiwan, 17 per cent in Singapore, and 14 per cent in South Korea (Kim, 2010). Not only in Asia but also in Australasia, in Western Europe, and in North America communities and social networks are emerging that largely consist of international marriage migrants. Such relationships require sensitive negotiation not only regarding gender and sexuality but also ethnicity, nationality, and citizenship. Understanding this dynamic requires more than simply seeing it as an extension of patriarchal conditions or the global political economy; the agency of both the women and the men involved in such relationships needs to be recognized along with the economic and cultural dynamics occurring at the local level and especially in more marginalized communities (see Kim, 2010, for discussion).

Examples of how the diaspora adversely affects already marginalized and **racialized** communities becomes apparent when we look at the situation of Aboriginals, hill tribes, First Nations, indigenous peoples, American Indians, and Inuit in South America, China,

racialized

Assigned to a specific racial category on the basis of aspects such as skin colour, facial features, or religion.

Australasia, the US, Canada, and Southeast Asia. Globalization and the diaspora combine to have a profound and far-reaching effect on such peoples (Hall and Fenlon, 2009; Kirmayer and Valaskakis, 2009; Haig-Brown, 2009). These communities often have high incidences of depression, alcohol and drug abuse, high unemployment, and low educational attainment. Social isolation, low levels of political power, and racial discrimination quickly lead to economic marginalization and a multitude of health issues. In terms of diaspora, what is emerging in many instances is an exodus of younger people, especially women, from such communities, a process that serves to further aggravate the community's economic and social marginalization. For example, in Northern Thailand it is now common to visit a hill tribe village (Akha, Karen, Mon, Lisu) to find that very few women of child-bearing age remain. They have moved to Bangkok to find work, leaving behind their young children, single men, and grandparents. Such migration is not confined to indigenous women, but it is increasingly marked as such. Consequently, the very future of these communities is placed under question.

The age of migration is certainly upon us, offering new opportunities and new challenges; however, the movement of people across social, political, and cultural borders is not new. In fact, it has gone on for many millennia, frequently as a desperate flight for survival, often as forced migration such as slavery. Countries such as the US, Canada, and the UK are just three that are largely constituted out of, and have benefited from, diasporic conditions occurring over hundreds of years. Certainly such countries cannot

claim to be populated by a culturally or demographically dominant host, one that can trace it roots to a time before the diaspora. Similarly, Celtic ethnic groups, such as the Irish, Scottish, and Welsh, and African ethnic groups, such as the Bantu, Ashanti, and Kikuyu, are to be found now around the world, as are Jews, Christians, Buddhists, Hindus, and Muslims (Amrith, 2011; Erikson, 2007; Leung et al., 2009; Palriwala and Uberoi, 2008).

But in among this ever-evolving mix of people is self-identity, notably our sense of being men and women. People rarely embark on migration in order to have their sense of gender challenged and reconstituted. But this is one of the consequences of migration in the age of globalized diaspora. We suggest that the speeding up and expansion of migration will inevitably result in reformed femininities and masculinities in peoples, cultures, and communities that have, hitherto, largely felt immune from such pressures. This process is not one that is simply confined to the diasporic group—it inevitably impacts everyone, both the host community and the immigrants. The second stage of globalization—that is, the mass and increasingly rapid migration of peoples—is only just beginning. It may be largely driven by economic need and material desire, but its greatest impact will be on who we think we are.

CYBERSPACE: CHANGING HOW WE LEARN TO BE WHO WE ARE

In a multitude of ways, technology is at the heart of globalization and, consequently, is a key factor facilitating the globalized diaspora. But we do not necessarily have to travel around the world or relocate to another country to experience the effects of technology on our sense of self. As we now discuss in this section, we can readily experiment with new forms of identity sitting in front of our computers at home.

It has been called the day when "virtual communities" (Rheingold, 2000) came of age—1 June 2007. That was the day "the Swedish virtual world Entropia Universe announced its partnership with CRD, an offshoot of the Beijing municipality, to build a virtual universe able to handle 7 million users at any one moment" (Keegan, 2007). This make-believe world, inhabited solely by avatars (on-screen characters constructed out of the user's imagination), now has a population greater than many countries. Indeed, the registered population of online communities such as Second Life and Blue Mars is now greater than that of the US and Europe combined (Keegan, 2010).

In the past five years there has been an explosion in the proliferation and use of online virtual realities with communities such as Stardoll, Onverse, SmallWorlds, Active Worlds, and Twinity attracting hundreds of millions of users—communities with very different aims, user profiles, and interests. Alongside the virtual world is the online social networking phenomenon, that is, the world of Facebook, Twitter, and Myspace. Facebook alone, launched only in 2006, now has over 1 billion active users every month, or one in seven of the world's population (Kiss, 2012). *Social Media Today* estimates that 41.6 per cent of the US population has a Facebook account (Wells, 2010).

Teenagers alive today were born into a world absent of online social networking and virtual worlds; those same teens, certainly if they live in a developed or developing nation, are now likely to be avid and accomplished users. For increasing numbers of people, the virtual world—their online social community—has displaced their real one in terms of time involvement, emotional importance, and, we would suggest, ontological security. It is highly likely that you, the reader of this book, have an online social networking account. You may already be an enthusiastic participant in some virtual world.

It is worth reflecting on the extent to which this involvement with the virtual is displacing your involvement with the real (see Liebowitz, 2007; Martinez Alemán and Wartman, 2009).

Although only early in the twenty-first century, we can see most clearly that the world of cyberspace has the capacity to inform, if not shape, human identity and our sense of self. At the very least, it will surely provide many millions with a sense of community, association, comfort, and belonging. Indeed, it already is doing so. The virtual world is seductive for a number of reasons. It not only allows us to live out parallel existences online, largely removed from the discomforts and challenges of real-life human interaction, it enables us to feel ontologically grounded—connected to others through some online community. Cyberspace may be virtual, but for the discursive subject it will appear seductively real, allowing people to move between numerous subject positions, all the while exploring, searching, discovering, and challenging, playing with their sense of who they really are.

Yet while this holds out fascinating prospects for humankind, the truth is we do not fully understand that which has been unleashed, in just a few short years, by the Internet. We are only now beginning to get some indication of its more unpredictable potential, such as in the case of WikiLeaks. The World Wide Web is the most profound social experiment ever in the history of humankind. And it is controlled by no single entity. Eric Schmidt, the chief executive of Google, recently raised precisely this concern:

> The internet is the first thing that humanity has built that humanity doesn't understand, the largest experiment in anarchy we've ever had. . . . When the internet publicity began, I remember being struck by how much the world was not the way we thought it was, that there was infinite variation in how people viewed the world. (Taylor, 2010)

As Schmidt saw for himself, the Internet exposes the multiplicity, variability, and endless subjectivity at the heart of the human species. The 7 billion inhabitants, and rising, of this world are all different. And that diversity is vividly exposed, if not multiplied, in cyberspace (Christensen, Jansson, and Christensen, 2011; Liebowitz, 2007).

Clearly, technological change is now so rampant and rapid that it's become impossible to predict with either accuracy or confidence its precise directions or its consequences for humans. What is certain is that the combined drivers of global capitalism, human ingenuity, economic necessity, and human desire and curiosity are taking us to a new (dis)embodied world—the virtual one of cyberspace. With over a quarter of the world's population now regularly online, we can see that the Internet is changing social structures; it is changing the ways we communicate, the ways we interact, and the ways we present ourselves. Indeed, it is changing how we learn to be who we are—how to be male and female.

In response to this, feminist writers such as Donna Haraway (1991), Jenny Wolmark (1999), and Rosi Braidotti (2002) have begun to chart the beginnings of a new critical gender perspective: cyber theory.

Theorizing Cyberspace

Cyber theory can be understood as an offspring of post-structuralist and postmodernist theories insomuch as it attempts to understand, in the new cyber age, how individuals might turn to or

cyborg

A creature that combines human and non-human features (such as Frankenstein, for example). According to Haraway, the cyborg represents the ultimate symbiosis between nature and technology that challenges the traditional boundaries of what it means to be human.

be turned into embodied, technologically connected subjects (new identities) in their search for a momentary ontological security. Cyber theory recognizes quite clearly the multiple and therefore potentially discordant dimensions to our identity; our non-unitary and fragmented subjectivity; and the nomadic experience of being and becoming an individual. In an age when the persuasive narratives of religious and political ideology no longer persuade and convince in quite the way they did, we are, Rosi Braidotti (2002) argues, ontologically cast adrift, swept along on a tide of technological change that simultaneously attracts and appalls:

> . . . the current fascination with monstrous, mutant or hybrid others expresses both a deep anxiety about the fast rate of transformation of identities and also the poverty of the social imaginary and our inability to cope creatively with the on-going transformations. (p. 5)

However, Braidotti is not especially pessimistic about this new human condition but keen to develop a feminist, materialist philosophy through it, one rooted in a "plea for different forms of thinking about and representing the body" (p. 5), which, as a consequence, recognizes the new possibilities for (gender) identity construction while retaining a feminist standpoint. In this respect, Braidotti's contribution to cyber theory aligns itself with the work of Haraway, who also uses cyber theory to understand, first, the ways in which male dominance is enacted and experienced through science and technology; and second, seeks to challenge that domination through the opening up of new possibilities of living and acting as embodied gendered subjects. Haraway introduces the concept of the "**cyborg** monster" to make her point:

> [the cyborg monster is] a hybrid of machine and organism, a creature of social reality as well as a creature of fiction. (1991, p. 149)

[Cyborg monsters] make very problematic the statuses of man or woman, human, artefact, member of a race, individual identity, or body (ref). [they promise] to help redefine the pleasures and politics of embodiment and feminist writing [through a new "political language"]. (1989, pp. 201–02)

The concepts of the **nomad** and the cyborg link very closely together in cyber theory; each is trapped in an endless process of becoming, never actually being settled in any one place or fixed in any one identity. The subjectivity of the cyborg, like the nomad, is never stable, never steady, and never complete. It increasingly searches for meaning and connectedness through the countless interactions at its disposal in the technologically driven social world, for example, computer games, email, Internet sex, online dating, virtual messaging, and the displaced but compelling "otherness" of science fiction, television, and cinema. Haraway sees the cyborg as an unsettled and dispersed entity—a **chimera**—formed not from one identity but many, a cluster of performatively enacted discursive associations that, together, script themselves upon the body. The nomadic cyborg has no centre, no sovereign subjectivity. But what it does have is the desire to be. Technological innovation, in particular the pleasures and boundless possibilities for virtual identity construction that it offers, momentarily satisfies the cyborg's desire for being and becoming someone, something.

But the cyborg has the option to achieve a more direct sense of a new material embodiment by recourse to advanced science and technology, for example, breast implants, artificial (titanium) limbs and joints, pacemakers, artificial heart valves, artificial teeth, face transplants, coloured contact lenses, penis enhancers, sexual surgery, hair transplants, Botox injections, and body-building drugs such as steroids. In a very

> **nomad**
> A person or a group of people with no fixed residence who move from one place to another. This concept was used by critics such as Braidotti to describe the postmodern condition.

> **chimera**
> A creature made up of parts taken from different animals.

real, physical, and materialist way, our embodied (gender) identity can be manicured, manufactured, and manipulated, according to the recommendations of the manufacturer. This process is potentially further reinforced through our ability to present ourselves as anyone, any identity, within the fluid temporal and spatial conditions of cyberspace.

So where, in all this, is the potential for liberating individuals, especially women, from dominating discourses of gender or, indeed, from the culture of masculinism to which many men gravitate in their ontological quest for masculine identity? Certainly, not all cyberspace "realities" contain emancipatory messages. For example, recently the British Board of Film Classification felt forced to ban the video game *Manhunt 2* because of its "unrelenting focus on the brutal slaying of prostitutes and pimps" (Johnson, 2007). In 2008, Thailand banned the *Grand Theft Auto* series after a young man killed a taxi driver and claimed it was due to playing *Grand Theft Auto*. Video games that depict any Nazi image or are judged to promote racist propaganda have been banned in Germany, while any video rated at R18+ is banned in Australia. Similar bans have recently come into force in Switzerland and Venezuela. Clearly, the debate as to the potential of such games to influence males' masculine identity, particularly their violent inclinations, is likely to intensify.

Reproducing/Disrupting Gender Identity in Cyberspace

Many cyber theorists argue that the gender binary upon which gender differences rest can be fundamentally disrupted or overturned through new technology, in which case space and opportunity is created for a thorough blurring if not dismantling of gender identity from its previously considered natural roots of femininity and masculinity. While recognizing the gendered constitution of science and new technology, writers such as Davis (1995) and Negrin (2002) argue that cosmetic surgery, for example, may be a "strategy which enables women to exercise a degree of control over their lives" (p. 21). Wolmark (1999) makes the case that the disruptive conditions of postmodernity explode within the new cyberspace reality, thereby calling into question just what it means to be a man and a woman in an age increasingly represented through cyborg identities and cyberspace temporal conditions:

> The metaphors of the cyborg and cyberspace seem particularly relevant to the times we are living in: they signify the temporal, spatial and cultural shifts and dislocations of postmodernism, while also operating as a means of understanding those same shifts and dislocations. They allow us to explore the new critical contours of postmodernity, in which alternative constructions of difference and identity become possible. (p. 9)

Empirical studies into how participants in online environments actually present, reinforce, and act out gender and sexual identities reveal varied practices. Gender identities get swapped, resisted, stereotypically reinforced, challenged, and fundamentally altered (Armentor-Cota, 2011). From this we can see that while gender identity is ultimately relational to a wider social structure, once that social structure is removed, replaced in this instance by a cyberworld, then gender operates in a much more fluid and unpredictable way.

Virtual realities or MUDs (text-based multi-user virtual reality environments) (Bruckman, 1993) offer endless possibilities for self-reinvention, not least as a gender being. As Turkle (1997) argues, this action corresponds with the postmodern persona, where individuals can pick and mix their online identity. They can be someone online they could never be in real life. The woman user, for example, can become the macho-male gangster; the man can present himself as a young virginal woman; the older user can take decades off his or her real age; the younger user can, conversely, add years; black users can become white, white users can become black, and so on. Gender swapping online has become commonplace—most users do it at some point. Women often adopt male identities in order to avoid sexual harassment; men may adopt female identities as a safe experiment in being "the other" (see, for examples, Samp et al., 2003; Roberts and Parks, 1999).

However, despite the opportunity to present themselves as an unconventional gender identity, most online participants actually remain within the gender binary system (Roberts and Parks, 1999). Very few participants go so far as to create their own gender (Danet, 1998), although this may change as more and more people immerse themselves in and experiment with their virtual selves.

Pseudonyms are also deployed extensively online, often to present an alternative gender identity or to mask one. Again, this practice both reinforces gender fluidity and can challenge it although as Armentor-Cota (2011) suggests, more research is needed to better understand the particular processes and motivations at work here.

Post-structuralist, qualitative research by Kelly et al. (2006) looked at how young girls in Vancouver, Canada, learned about issues of femininity online through participation in community forums. The research reveals the multiplicity of femininities used by women and girls: how some femininities are strategically deployed to resist male dominance online; how some are used to reinforce hyper-feminine identities; and how some femininities are deliberately used as expressions of rebellion against conventional femininity and ideologies of gender subordination (Armentor-Cota, 2011).

A study in the Netherlands by Valkenburg et al. (2005) found that boys and girls often revert to stereotypical hegemonic performances of masculinity and femininity online: the girls in order to appear more beautiful and older than they are; the boys in order to appear more macho and tougher.

In virtual worlds such as Second Life, the medium for communication and personal expression is the avatar. While this medium is theoretically open to any form of social construction and representation, research shows that most users tend to create avatars that have stereotypical masculine and feminine appearances (Dumitrica and Gaden, 2009; Heider, 2009). Many avatars also "objectify women and marginalize sexual minorities" (Armentor-Cota, 2011; also Brookey and Cannon, 2009).

Cyberspace is not only a playground wherein we may perform contra-indicated gender identities or indeed reinforce gender and sexual stereotypes; it also has the potential to act as a community for those who might otherwise be socially marginalized and stigmatized. Research by Hill (2005) into transgendered individuals living in Toronto, Canada, certainly shows how the Internet, and online communities, can provide support for such people, thereby reducing feelings of alienation and social isolation.

Theoretically, the world of cyberspace offers us infinite opportunities for virtual recreation and presentation of alternative, different, maybe empowering expressions of gender and sexual identity. It is a site where we can be

anything, anyone, and in that respect we are limited only by our imaginations. But being ultimately a human-based environment, cyberspace inevitably operates alongside a social (language and bodily) structure that contains strong and persuasive discourses, most of which serve to replicate the gender binary. The avatars of Second Life do not have a life of their own. They are merely on-screen representations, behind which sits a very human operator. Ultimately, the subjectivity of the user gets translated into the actions of the avatar, or the social interactions on Facebook. And subjectivities are already gendered long before they reach cyberspace.

Yet precisely because science and technology appear beyond the final control of any group or individual, and therefore may be seen as rampant and uncontrollable, their potential as a liberating force in respect of gender identity is that they can totally and utterly destroy the boundaries upon which femininity and masculinity are expressed through the body. Old differences can be erased, new differences created; the gender binary can cease to exist or at least cease to have the centrality it did. Within cyberspace, all is possible. And once all is possible within cyberspace so, eventually, may all become possible in real time. The seepage between cyberspace and the material world is the point at which gender identity potentially dissolves into a multitude of imagined, and subsequently enacted, possibilities, although to what extent these actions of an ontologically driven cyber self will disrupt or merely reinforce gender identities remain to be seen.

It is in this realm of the unreal that cyber wo/man gets created: a postmodern blend of the masculine and feminine, operating within a virtual universe but very powerfully making a statement about what it might mean to be male or female in the twenty-first century.

POSTMODERN MAN: REFLECTING THE FEMININE

In this section, we explore the possibilities of men changing: in particular, we look at the evidence for the emergence of postmodern men and masculinities. By "postmodern man," we mean a presentation of masculinity that does not neatly fit within, or represent, those dominant discourses of masculinity highly visible, especially in the West, during the last two centuries. Postmodern man is not only comfortable exhibiting femininity, both as physical display and style, he also rejects traditional ways of being a man. By adopting styles that blend the masculine and feminine in an active and individualistic manner while still retaining a male, possibly heterosexual essence, postmodern man reflects the multiplicity and fluidity of gender identity in the postmodern age.

A key aspect of postmodern man's being is a rejection of previously dominant discourses around masculinity. Such discourses are powerfully illustrated in the descriptor "hegemonic masculinity." While we recognize the term's limitations as a sociological concept and have explored this at length in previous chapters, it is useful as a label to describe a way of being a man that is in direct opposition to femininity and any feminine-masculine display. In its most overt form, hegemonic masculinity is homophobic, misogynistic, emotionally dysfunctional, and celebrates unreflective macho behaviour. The hegemonic masculine man of the twentieth century, regardless almost of his class or culture, was overtly heterosexual, the head of the household and the family breadwinner, devoting most of his life to career and employment and having strong opinions and principles that he was prepared to enforce aggressively if necessary. The culture of compulsory heterosexuality in which this type of male lived his life as a man was both powerful and persuasive. It did not allow for much deviance from this masculine norm;

indeed, it carried many social, economic, and cultural penalties if such norms were breached or disregarded.

Whatever the psychological uncertainties and insecurities going on in the minds of the millions of men who reverted to such forms of masculinity, hegemonic masculinity strives hard to present itself as "natural." Consequently, masculine subjects who undertake such performances in order to appear "manly"—i.e., have themselves socially validated as men—inevitably have to function several steps removed from femininity. That is, femininity, and all the characteristics that affirm it, becomes the "other," which must always remain outside the discursive repertoire of the hegemonic masculine man.

For much of the twentieth century, if not before, such behaviours and performances of men as hegemonic masculinity had currency and credibility and were generally taken as the way men were. Of course, not all men were like this. That is not the point. The point is that such expressions of masculinity were deemed acceptable and, for the most part, went unchallenged. In many cultures and environments, they were actively celebrated, and in many cultural settings they still are. However, there is now clear evidence of new expressions of masculinity in many societies that do not draw on hegemonic masculine principles. Indeed, these new ways of being a man are in direct opposition to traditional macho male performances. It is these emergent male performances, which we group together under the heading "postmodern man," that we now examine.

The Metrosexual

In November 1994 an article titled "Here Come the Mirror Men" appeared in the major British daily newspaper, *The Independent*. Written by Mark Simpson (1994), this article introduced the concept of "metrosexual man" into contemporary urban language. Promoted and developed further by Simpson (2002, 2003, 2005), Marian Salzman (see, for example, O'Reilly et al., 2005), and Marc van Bree (2004), metrosexual man suggests a fascinating shift in presentations of masculine/male identity. It signals a re-orientation of (some) men's behaviour away from an avid pursuit of (hegemonic) macho masculinity to something altogether softer, feminine, and narcissistic. *Metrosexual* describes a man in touch with his emotions, reflective and expressive, concerned with his appearance, comfortable in both straight and gay culture, and certainly not homophobic (see also Coad, 2008). Not surprisingly, the media have played long and hard with this concept, in particular seeking out exemplars of metrosexual masculinity (e.g., David Beckham, Jude Law, Brad Pitt, Barak Obama, Chris Martin, Prince, A-Rod, Dominic Monaghan, David Navarro, Ian Thorpe) and comparing them with the more traditional, if increasingly perceived as dated, (retro)models of manliness (see, for discussion, Wikipedia, 2011).

From an academic perspective it is relatively easy to dismiss the concept of metrosexual man as yet another empirically weak, media-inspired gender stereotype to place alongside "new men." And to be sure, marketers such as Marion Salzman have been quick to move the debate along by identifying even more contemporary shifts in masculinity, for example, offering us the "ubersexual" (O'Reilly, Matathia, Simpson, 2005), claiming this term more accurately describes the "straight version" of metrosexual man. In response to this, Simpson points out that marketers have long tried to "straighten out" his original metrosexual man, perhaps in order to make it more appealing to potential corporate clients by playing down any feminine or gay orientation, when in fact his original definition of the term remained sexually ambiguous by intent:

> Some, including Simpson and Armistead Maupin, have suggested that behind this marketing-speak there was something rather simpler going on:

a homophobic attempt to stop the metrosexual being so "gay." Or as Salzman herself put it proudly, the ubersexual, unlike the metrosexual "doesn't invite questions about his sexuality." (Wikipedia, 2007)

This debate as to who, what, and why metrosexual man is has since been engaged in enthusiastically by journalists and media around the world, with numerous newspaper articles bemoaning, disbelieving, welcoming, or sometimes just expressing confusion over whether or not metrosexual man actually exists and, if so, whether women and/or gay man are attracted to him (see, for example, Harris, 2005; Innes, 2004; Ellen, 2007a, 2007b; Kane, 2012).

However, behind the media hype lies an interesting academic question, one that persists in any inquiry into gender identity: Are men changing, and if so how and why? To be sure, one can perceive some substance behind the concept of metrosexual man. This term may appeal to marketers and social trendspotters especially, but it also indicates important shifts in dominant discourses of masculinity. As Simpson is keen to point out,

> Contrary to most of the skin-deep coverage of the past two years, metrosexuality is not about going to spas and wearing flip flops, nor is it essentially "girly" or "feminine"—unless you think that narcissism and self-centredness are essentially feminine qualities. Metrosexuality, do I really have to spell it out, is mediated masculinity. Mediated masculinity that has replaced the "real" thing. This is why I described the metrosexual as a collector of fantasies about the male sold to him by the media. Those fantasies can be butch ones as well as faux fairy ones. Or both. (Simpson, 2005)

The real or retro (traditional) masculinity that Simpson refers to is, in part, a perception that he holds about men, or men of a certain era, class, sexuality, culture, age. Similarly, his metrosexual man concept also arises from his subjective interpretation of shifts in men and masculinity at this point in history. But his perception cannot be simply discounted on the basis that it is subjective, for behind the term lies an interesting and emergent discourse around men and their possibilities. Importantly, the term also relates to shifts in discourses of femininity.

Metrosexual man is, according to Simpson, engaged in exhibiting a "mediated masculinity." From a sociological perspective, such a masculinity might be seen to occupy a social or discursive space between what Connell has described as hegemonic masculinity (see Chapter 2) on one hand, and a more emotional masculinity, illustrative perhaps of something we can loosely describe as "gay masculinities" (Nardi, 2000), on the other. However, in attempting to understand these gender dynamics we must first accept that these terms are problematic in themselves, even if they remain useful at a simplistically descriptive level. The intellectual critique of the concept of hegemonic masculinity is now well established (see Chapter 1), while Nardi (2000) makes the case that "gay men exhibit a multiplicity of ways of 'doing' masculinity that can best be described by the plural form 'masculinities'" (p. 1). The difficulty we have, then, is that in accepting all these qualifications, and they are certainly justified, we are left with such multiplicity that it becomes almost impossible to clearly identify a fixed and explicit performance of masculinity. That is why Simpson's term, *metrosexual man*, helps not just the media and therefore the general public to understand and make sense of wider social change around gender identity, but is also helpful to people like us who are interested in understanding gender and identity.

In trying to understand different formations of gender identity we must, inevitably, label them. As researchers, we cannot continue to circle this plurality and thereby leave the terminologies to be constructed only by the media. There are, in fact, good examples of gender researchers effectively applying labels to different performances or discourses of masculinity (see, for example, Mac an Ghaill, 1994; Collinson and Hearn, 2001[1993]; Heasley, 2005). The fact that *metrosexual man* is not an academic term does not diminish its veracity or usefulness. However, we are then entitled to ask questions concerning the origin of this new formation of masculinity, and the possibilities that metrosexual man offers for changes in gender identities and relationships.

The evidence suggested by the metrosexual discourse in terms of reformed perceptions and values around manliness and masculinity indicates that new, more liberal forms of masculine subjectivity are taking root in some men across some societies. Such a discourse corresponds well with many feminist agendas, not least an increased male desire to strike a better work/life balance and a willingness to assume more responsibility for home and child-care duties (O'Reilly et al., 2005). At the very least, it is a discourse that offers a point of resistance to homophobic, and likely racist, expressions of masculinity, in which case it should be welcomed for these reasons alone.

Some might argue that what we have here are merely surface expressions of masculinity and that beneath this layer little changes. That is, the male media icons who are labelled metrosexual are themselves influential and materially privileged men, a fact that does little to redress gender injustices and conditions of global gender inequality and oppression. Similarly, metrosexual man may comfortably occupy some cultural borderland between compulsory heterosexuality and gayness, but in many societies to even suggest that one has gay or lesbian inclinations is to invite opprobrium at best and a violent response at worst. However, a counter to this argument is that the incidence of metrosexuality cannot be simply and only sustained through a relatively small number of male superstars. There has to be something more substantial that is reaching out into the lives and gender subjectivities of millions of men. And academic research, when combined with that undertaken by marketing research organizations such as RSCG, clearly indicates there is:

> After the get-rich-quick, work-all-hours, wild frontier days of the 1990s, the signs are that American men [. . .] are embracing their feminine sides and putting the last decade of the 20th century firmly behind them [our] study reveals that while fame, wealth and desirability still appeal to the American man, his most highly prized aspirations are friendship, growing old with the woman he loves, and having happy, healthy children. (Euro RSCG Worldwide, 2003a, see also 2003b)
>
> The most important shift in masculinity is that there is less avoidance of femininity and the emergence of a segment of men who have embraced customs and attitudes once deemed the province of women. (Alzheimer, 2003)
>
> We [gender scholars] all knew that the homophobic, sexist and violent form of masculinity . . . *could* change, but since scholars started studying it seriously in the late 1980s, it had not. This book is significant because I show that things are now finally beginning to change. [My premise] is that the esteemed versions of masculinity among university-attending men are changing [to a more inclusive masculinity]. (Anderson, 2011, p. 5, original emphasis)

So where does this more liberal discourse originate from? One perspective would see metrosexual man as simply a commodified gender stereotype that is produced and redistributed via the media and subsequently consumed by the public to the financial benefit of international business (Yaksich, 2005). In other words, sophisticated marketing techniques identify, reify, and distribute this masculine performance for profit. For Yaksich, the commodification of identity and culture goes hand-in-hand with the conditions and requirements of the consumerist-driven postmodern age, with the media-inspired rise of metrosexual man as merely evidence of this (also Featherstone, 1991).

However, such theories serve to reduce all lifestyles that have some marketable aspect, including gay and lesbian (see, also Chasin, 2000), into presentations for consumption. Such lifestyles, therefore, become part of a hegemonic process whereby identity performances and individuality become assimilated into the demands and needs of a larger, more powerful group, e.g., international corporations. This perspective is firmly located within the oppressive ideological apparatus identified by Althusser (see Chapter 1), that is, that individual and group agency are virtually invisible with social change and therefore individual identities, being ultimately mediated by dominant power blocks.

An alternative, more agentic perspective would argue that it is the feminist discourse of the past four to five decades and, at a more general level, new expressions of and expectations around femininity that have assisted in the birth of metrosexual man. In other words, this discourse of masculinity, increasingly significant and noticeable as it is, is as much a response by men to changes in women's subjectivity and accompanying lifestyles as it is a response to men's desire for more liberal, and liberating, ways of being a male. So metrosexual man emerges as part of the condition of globalization described earlier, to be sure with consumerist overtones, but arising in the first instance as a reaction and response to new, more assertive, and powerful expressions of womanhood. This process has been further facilitated by the increased acceptance of gay culture, as evidenced through particular media representations, for example television programs such as *Queer Eye for the Straight Guy* and *Queer as Folk* (see, for discussion, Kylo-Patrick, 2006). This is not to suggest that images of metrosexual man are not vulnerable to being hijacked by corporate marketing techniques; clearly they are. But it does suggest that behind the corporate-speak there exists a significant shift in masculine subjectivity and one that is not simply an unreflective response to media conditioning but a reaction to much deeper and profound cultural movements within gender identities and subjectivities. As some analysts put it,

> The overall reduction in men's gender role conservatism over the past 30 years [partly] results from expansions in women's educational and labor force experiences and the discourse of the 1970s feminist movement. (Ciabattari, 2001, p. 14; see also, Brewster and Padavic, 2000; Twenge and Zucker, 1999)

What we are seeing, in effect, are increasing numbers of men responding to new lifestyle opportunities, to feminist discourses, and to the demise of traditional masculine role models, all combining under the conditions of globalization.

Herbivorous Males (the "Grass Eaters")

Not all the evidence for postmodern man comes from the West. There is an even more striking and explicit example of this new masculinity in Asia, especially Japan and South Korea but also surfacing in major cities in China, Thailand, and Taiwan as well as Singapore and Hong Kong. Also known as a "girly man" (Ojo-man) or "generation xx," the herbivorous male of Asia represents a type of masculinity that is heavily shaped by femininity, yet still retains a heterosexual identity. These men are not gay. They have been described as "metrosexuals without the testosterone," and certainly they appear to disregard the characteristics of the traditional Asian male, that is, a stoical, fierce, dedicated salaryman in pursuit of "fast cars, career success, designer labels and trophy women" (Parry, 2009; also Turnbull, 2009; Maliangkay, 2010; Morioka, 2008; Otake, 2009; Ushikubo, 2008). In appearance, the herbivorous male performs femininity by plucking his eyebrows; wearing long, wavy hair; using foundation and lip gloss; and generally appearing as sensitive, soft, polite, and passive. One Japanese company, WishRoom, has even produced a brand of bra for such men, while a range of products, from weaker beer to skirts and lacy tops, some of them pink, are now available and being heavily marketed to this group of males. Despite this explicit association with the feminine, the herbivorous male retains an ultimately masculine, not feminine, gender presence. This blending of the masculine and

Source: http://www.asianart.com/exhibitions/museum/7.html   Source: © Payless Images/Shutterstock

feminine corresponds with what we are seeing in Western metrosexual males, who are increasingly comfortable utilizing feminine lifestyles without feeling their heterosexuality is compromised as a result (Hannah, 2012).

The herbivorous male (so named because such males are seen to lack the "carnivorous instincts" of more traditional Asian men) has been an emerging trend in Asia for a decade now. Originally inspired by Chinese, Japanese, and especially South Korean male pop stars such as Rain, actors such as Lee Jun Ki and Bae Yong-joon, and soccer star Ahn Jung-Hwan, the herbivorous man, while having a stronger appeal to younger men, is challenging commonly held ideas around masculinity. Importantly, this new expression of masculinity is seen by many to be more comfortable with gender equality, with women's rising power in Asian societies, and with ambivalent sexual orientation. In short, it is a masculine display that undermines hegemonic masculine ideals; not only does it render machismo passé, it highlights many Asian women's disillusionment with traditional male roles/behaviours while also signalling a growing desire in Asian men for a less militaristic and corporate lifestyle:

> Today's students, after all, are less likely to find much appeal in the macho type that for decades dominated popular entertainment. Those tough men usually had no chance of going to university and/or leading normal quiet lives. Instead, they were forced to show their grit as soldiers, gangsters, or policemen, often sorting out differences through violent means, while appearing fragile only in their inability to express their feelings in words. Although they were able to protect and financially support their love interests, they could not care less about the myriad social pressures on women. (Maliangkay, 2010, p. 2)

The extent to which the herbivorous male type has taken hold in Asian countries and emerged as a distinct expression of adult masculinity is underlined by estimates that claim up to two-thirds of Japanese men aged 20 to 34 are in this demographic category or show "herbivorous tendencies" (Ushikubo, 2010). According to research into this group, over half are unmarried, only 20 per cent are in relationships with women, and 30 per cent have never had a sexual partner (Yamada, 2009, quoted in Parry, 2009). The herbivorous male is, then, more than a marketing cliché but represents a significant shift in the way the current younger generation of Japanese males feel about their gender identity and relationship to traditional Japanese masculine culture:

> Japanese men from the baby boomer generation were typically aggressive and proactive when it came to romance and sex. But as a result of growing up during Japan's troubled economy in the 1990s, their children's generation was not as assertive and goal-orientated. Their outlook came, in part, from seeing their father's model of masculinity falter even as Japanese women gained more lifestyle options. (Neill, 2009)

One self-described Japanese herbivore male, Junichoro Hori, describes his approach to life and emphasizes that this goes beyond looks and attitudes to sex: "Some guys still try to be manly and try to be like strong and stuff, but you know personally I'm not afraid to show my vulnerability because being vulnerable or being sensitive is not a weakness" (25-year-old herbivore male quoted in Neill, 2009).

This general passivity of the herbivore male extends also to his sex life, or lack of it. Research indicates that many completely eschew sexual relations altogether, leading commentators to be particularly concerned at the ongoing decline in the Japanese birthrate:

> I've had lots of female friends that I am attracted to, but you weigh up the risks and benefits and come

to the conclusion that things are best left as they are. I'm lucky to work in an industry where there's no stigma attached to being single and no pressure to get involved with someone . . . (30-year-old herbivore male quoted in McCurry, 2009)

I am worried that herbivorous boys are the future of Japan, as young Japanese men become more timid and more averse to taking risks, it will affect the energy and vitality of the society. For a country like Japan, which already has a shrinking population, this is a disaster. (Yamada, quoted in Parry, 2009)

Some Japanese sociologists argue that the economic problems in Japan, especially since the early 1990s, have been a major trigger for this emergence of a more passive and timid, less macho type of male. The suggestion is that the decline of traditional male roles, the emergence of women in positions of power, and men's heightened job insecurity all combine with the lack of desire for a "salaryman" existence and the more distant, corporate-oriented masculinity that it demands (Gill, 2003). The result is a very different, indeed overtly and unashamedly feminine masculinity. This new generation of men strongly decline to slot into either of the "two dominant Japanese male groups of the past century: soldiers and their peacetime offspring, corporate warriors" (McCurry, 2009).

This analysis of the Japanese herbivore male appears to have some currency. Yet at the same time it fails to fully explain why the same gender identity phenomenon is now occurring in Korea and across large swaths of Asia, especially Southeast Asia. The economic downturn in Japan is not mirrored in quite the same way in Korea, and certainly not in China and Taiwan. However, one common factor is the pressure on Asian men to be providers, to get married, to have children, to follow a corporate lifestyle, and generally to adhere to the strict social and cultural roles that have traditionally signified

proper Asian men. As research into changing men in the West revealed some decades ago, the inflexibility of such male roles can lead to damaging consequences for those men who cannot fulfill them (see Whitehead, 2002, for discussion), and this is clearly the case in Asia:

To this day, however friendly and good-looking a man may be, he is still judged by the degree to which he provides for his family's well-being and what is printed on his business card. This may help explain why, in 2006, the suicide rate of Korean men was more than double that of women. I surmise that Korea's kkonminan [herbivore males] provide a hint that men, experiencing disillusionment with their traditional personas are reacting, to a degree, by shunning conformity and embracing a style that makes them feel better about themselves. (Maliangkay, 2009, p. 2)

We can call the herbivore man a new fashion in masculinity, and that may be accurate. Certainly, it can be seen as a discursively based change in that the discourse of what it means to be a man in Southeast Asia is altering to reflect the new gender reality as experienced by a younger generation of males. And discourses have viral properties; that is, they are readily and easily transmitted across societies and cultures, especially in the age of the Internet, which means they can and do go in and out of fashion. However, so long as the conditions for change are similar, as they are across urban Asia, then we can hypothesize that increasing numbers of younger Asian men will similarly eschew traditional masculine appearances and the lifestyles that accompany them in favour of a more feminine, less assertive, and certainly less aggressive masculine performance.

So, in summary, just how strong a shift is this toward the postmodern man? Well, the evidence is there both in the Western metrosexual and in the Eastern herbivorous male to suggest that something quite profound is occurring in men's gender identity. This may be more apparent in the younger generation, and it does also have class and economic factors attached to it, but it is a global change and, therefore, an aspect of globalization.

What is especially significant is the way that such men are comfortable embracing and expressing femininity, or discourses that have long been associated with women. Not only is there no resistance to femininity by these men, it is actually privileged. The fact that there are millions of such men, none of whom profess to be gay or transsexual, is a key factor that highlights the discursive property of masculinity, and of gender identity generally. The metrosexual and the herbivorous male are engaging with those practices of gender signification now at their disposal in their respective social settings; these practices are increasingly acceptable within societies that have traditionally been highly inflexible about gender roles, indeed negatively judgmental toward the feminine, especially in males.

Whatever their long-term future and even though they remain minoritized discourses, the metrosexual and herbivorous male confirm that masculinity and femininity are not singular, not predicted, not protected. They exist in a dynamic relationship with the social and cultural forces that influence, if not serve to configure, identity in each of its many manifestations. Masculinities are, by their very multiplicity, only what we, as ontological subjects, present them as, and how others present them to us. There is no biological reason why men cannot change, and the boundaries of such change are neither fixed nor limited. A persistent characteristic of femininities and masculinities is their relationality, which works through the dynamics of the social network. One of the most powerful of these dynamics is clearly the media, so we should not be surprised if men come to exhibit alternative ways of being

a man just so long as such expressions comply with particular cultural and social values and appear as generally acceptable ways of performing masculinity in given locales.

At the same time, we cannot simply dismiss metrosexual man and herbivorous males as largely media and marketing constructs. Indeed, the evidence from Asia and the West is that companies have been flummoxed by the emergence of this male type and now avidly try to understand it and, of course, market to it. Capitalism has not directly or intentionally created postmodern man, but he is with us anyway.

Postmodern man, we suggest, is indicative of important shifts in the masculine identity of men of a certain class and culture; as such, it is an emergent gender discourse that offers insights into the simultaneously powerful but amorphous character of masculine expression. This is not to say that the intuitive and expressive feminized performances of postmodern man are completely unique to men at this point in time. Clearly, there have always been men of all sexualities who presented themselves in such a way and who located their masculine ontology in such discourses, not least the narcissistic. The difference is that postmodern man indicates an emergent powerful, potentially dominant discourse in masculinity, one that completely rejects what have long been the characteristics of traditional, dominant, hegemonic masculinity.

In Table 11.3, we summarize the main indicators of postmodern man and his masculinity performance.

POSTMODERN WOMAN: REFLECTING THE MASCULINE

If the evidence for postmodern man is increasingly apparent, the same can be said many times over for "postmodern woman." The similarities between these two identities are interesting, as are the differences.

TABLE 11.3   Postmodern Man and his Masculinity

Primary Indicators

Supportive of women's rights and gender equality

Supportive of LGBT rights

If heterosexual, does not feel threatened by gay/lesbian sexualities

Anti-racist

Liberal-minded, open to alternative cultural expressions

Reflective, able to recognize and express his emotions positively

Negotiates and shares household duties with partner (may be househusband)

Negotiates and shares child-care duties with partner

Pro-choice (abortion and birth control)

Approaches intimate relationships from the standpoint of equality and equity

Masculinity not threatened by partners with higher professional status or earning power

Concerned with personal health, fitness, grooming, and appearance

Is comfortable working for women and having women bosses

Does not consider men superior to women

Secondary Indicators

College/university educated

Seeks personal improvement (physically and intellectually)

Ambitious but also aims for a good work–life balance

Not avidly following any single religion but possibly spiritual

Can articulate his thoughts and feelings

Not prone to outbursts of aggression or violence

Comfortable with new technology

Uses online social networks

Considers himself a global citizen—not overly nationalistic

Has developed emotional bonds and friendship networks with men (straight and gay)

Note: Postmodern men will match all of the primary indicators and a majority of the secondary indicators.

As we have suggested above, postmodern man can be interpreted as a consequence, a reaction to the changing roles and identities of women in the age of globalization. Indeed, as we have shown, it is impossible to ignore femininity and women's new ontologies when examining postmodern man. He has come to be who he is not independently of women/femininity, but very much as a consequence of dramatic and profound changes in the old gender order; changes outside any person or group's direct control. Postmodern man may well exhibit, at times, a rather stereotypical and traditional expression of femininity—passive, soft, gentle, wrapped in pink with long flowing hair—but it is still femininity and recognized as such globally. In this respect he both reinforces the gender binary while also unsettling it. As we go on to discuss, there seems no escape from this binary; it remains with us so long as male and female are seen as separate entities in society.

Our point here is that postmodern man did not come first; postmodern woman did. She is the marker of change in society and across cultures. Postmodern man is a reaction to something already happening in society, which began long before the metrosexual and herbivore male first started experimenting with makeup and skin cream. Postmodern man moves the gender boundaries, specifically male performances and ways of being, into the realms of the imagined female, and in so doing he dramatically undermines macho male behaviour and renders it passé. To be sure, this process is very much ongoing and no one can predict precisely how it will transpire across different societies, but it is happening and worldwide.

This brings us to postmodern woman. She is, in many ways, the unlikely, unbidden, and unassuming architect of postmodern man. It is she who arrived on the gender scene first, probably toward the latter third of the twentieth century. Her momentum is still gathering pace and she has, we suggest, much further to go.

If postmodern man moves into the realms of the feminine (historically, a fearful ontological journey for many straight men), then postmodern woman moves similarly into the realms of the masculine. She does so with confidence and lack of regret, and in great number. Like postmodern man, she may not see herself at the frontier of a new gender order, but that is where she has arrived. To be sure, many women were there long before her, not least the feminists of the early part of the twentieth century. The point is, however, that she is now there in such number as to be unmistakable. She cannot be dismissed as an aberration, a one-off, a temporary blip in men's ongoing saga of self-proclaimed supremacy.

Before we go on to actually describe postmodern woman, it is worth examining the feminist theories and perspectives surrounding female masculinities, not least because female masculinities are what postmodern woman expresses and constructs in her own inimitable way.

Female Masculinities

One of the most interesting paradoxes evident in much feminist theory is the assumed relationship between men and masculinities, and between women and femininities. It is as if only men are seen as capable of "doing" masculinity while only women are capable of a "natural" performance of femininity. This raises interesting questions about the persistent power of the discourses around femininity and masculinity and the assumption we continue to make about the relationship between gender identity and biologically differentiated bodies. As Ranita Chatterjee puts it, "Why do we [feminist theorists] insist on, or at least act like we believe in, an inherently natural bond between masculinity and biologically male bodies" (Chatterjee, 2007)? Chatterjee argues that there has been a "failure" both in and outside academia to consider "female masculinity" even though there has been a sustained critique by feminists upon essentialist notions of an inherent masculinity in men. One feminist theorist who has, however, drawn attention to and developed a persuasive analysis of the concept and performance of a female masculinity is Judith Halberstam. She argues (1998) that the lack of any serious exploration of female masculinity reflects, first, a deep reluctance in Western society to accept "ambiguously gendered bodies" into social situations, and second, is a consequence of men's "protectionist attitude" toward masculinity:

> Such an attitude has been bolstered by a more general disbelief in female masculinity. I can only describe such disbelief in terms of a failure in a collective imagination: in other words, female-born people have been making convincing and

powerful assaults on the coherence of a male masculinity for well over a hundred years: what prevents these assaults from taking hold and accomplishing the diminution of the bonds between masculinity and men? (p. 15)

During the course of writing this book we spoke to colleagues and friends about the possibilities and instances of women performing masculinity, of behaving, in some ways, like men. The overwhelming response was "of course" women can behave like men and increasingly, to the concern of many feminists, appear to be doing so (see, for discussion, Dougary, 2007). Indeed, many people indicated some surprise that we should assume that women cannot do masculinities. Halberstam (1998) experienced identical responses during the course of writing her book:

> People tend to nod and say, "Yes, of course, female masculinity," as if this is a concept they have grown up with and use every day. In actual fact, there is remarkably little written about masculinity in women, and this culture generally evinces considerable anxiety about even the prospect of manly women. (p. xi)

There are several issues that are evidenced in this conundrum. First, as academic researchers we should not assume that all knowledge arises with us. Often, we are merely the fulcrum, a conduit for the articulation of knowledges already out there. Many scientists may produce new knowledge but as sociologists it is more likely that we merely record, evidence, deconstruct, and analyze that which is common currency as discourse in communities and society. We may be academics, trained researchers, but we should not laud ourselves too highly, nor fail to recognize the sophistication of the gendered subject, male and female, as it goes about its identity work within an increasingly complex social milieu.

The second issue in this conundrum is that the sheer strength and persistence of the association of men to masculinities can be seen to privilege men and marginalize women. Men, as masculine subjects, have an identity and power investment in maintaining an uncorrupted version of masculinity, one that validates it and them as a means and opportunity to achieve some inner gendered identity, an apparently coherent but ultimately mythical maleness that stands untainted by the "other," be it gayness or femininity. Once we remove and challenge this connection, where does that leave men? What can they be if not masculine? What is the male if not a masculine subject? So long as masculinity is commonly assumed to contain some deep, psychological connection to the male body, then so can the male body, through its ontological pursuit of being, legitimately desire its fulfillment as a masculine subject, as a man. But this is a social process, not a biologically determined one.

Our third point is that the gendered binary traps us all, in our thinking and in our practices. No amount of skilful and adept intellectual and ontological movement between the male and female can entirely remove the binary. It resists its own demise with an impressive resilience. To begin a separation of men to masculinity by showing how women can and increasingly do perform female masculinities is, however, to subvert conventions around gender identity, to open up new, sometimes threatening, sometimes liberating spaces for alternative gender performances. To even posit the notion of a female masculinity is to blur if not destabilize traditional gender norms, values, and codes. However, "gender blending" (Devor, 1989) can only take us so far; there are limits to the extent the male/female dualism can be deconstructed. In this case, we are still left with the questions as to what constitutes a man, and what constitutes a woman. These questions require an answer for every individual, and not just in the present time but in the future, for they arise not from some overarching power play of patriarchal intent, but from our given desire for ontological validation.

Our fourth and final point is to emphasize the political possibilities, variations, and limitations of female masculinity. This point, as with the others above, arises primarily from Halberstam's writings, so we consider it appropriate that we allow her words to state it:

> Within a lesbian context, female masculinity has been situated as the place where patriarchy goes to work on the female psyche and reproduces misogyny within femaleness. . . . Sometimes female masculinity coincides with the excesses of male supremacy, and sometimes it codifies a unique form of social rebellion: often female masculinity is the sign of sexual alterity, but occasionally it marks heterosexual variation; sometimes female masculinity marks the place of pathology, and every now and then it represents the healthful alternative to what are considered the histrionics of conventional femininities. (1998, p. 9)

Halberstam is alerting us to the diverse and relational ways in which female masculinity might be performed and the potential consequences of such performances for the individual, communities, societies, and any existing gender order. Our own term, *postmodern woman*, is offered as an identity marker to illustrate a similar occurrence of corresponding, sometimes contradictory discourses of gender within a female subject. Our intention is to take Halberstam's notion of a female masculinity and reify it as a distinct expression of gender identity for some women, not an identity that is necessarily located in a specific sexuality—e.g., lesbian—but one that represents a significant shift in how many women are constructing and expressing their sense of femininity. The postmodern woman is, we suggest, becoming a powerful identity marker for many women. In the same way that one might distinguish a masculine identity performance that could be labelled "metrosexual" or "herbivorous male" so we are attempting to

identify a relational performance in women, one that we term *postmodern woman*.

Identifying Postmodern Woman

Even though a diversity of different ways of being woman exists in today's world, postmodern woman illustrates, for us, a distinct set of gender discourses that are taken up by increasing numbers of female subjects in their pursuit of an alternative feminine-oriented ontology. That is, these are women who are, for various reasons, comfortable with exhibiting a gender performance that draws on what have been understood until recently as distinctly masculine ways of being in and relating to the world. We accept Halberstam's point that individual women have, through history, engaged with a female masculinity, an identity performance not inevitably or stereotypically tied to a lesbian identity; however, we suggest that the wider social changes arising out of globalization especially are opening up new avenues for women to express themselves as female/masculine subjects.

So, at an ontological level, postmodern woman exists within the gender binary but disrupts its essentialist message by virtue of operating across its female-masculine boundaries. She does so through a performative discursivity within everyday situations and multiple subject positions. For example, postmodern woman may be seen at senior levels within organizations, in professions, in positions of power, influence, and leadership—many if not most of which were once the exclusive realm of the male. Now women are in such places and in increasing numbers, not just in traditional feminine professions but represented across the public and private sectors of work. Postmodern woman may well have chosen to devote her life to her career, not to marriage, children, domesticity, or any of the traditional modes of female expression that were the province and aspiration of her female ancestors. This is not because she is not attracted to men—indeed, she may well seek a satisfying and exclusive love relationship with a male partner—but she is not going to sacrifice her education or her economic and emotional independence in order to achieve and hold on to such a relationship. Similarly, the notion of marriage, which now appears to be in terminal decline in most developed and developing countries (ONS, 2011), will not appeal to her for she recognizes that her love interest may well change as she does.

Postmodern woman is not in any way compromising her sense of femininity; rather, she is expanding the boundaries and definitions of what it means to be a woman. In this way she is engaged in an agentic process of liberating herself from traditional codes of femininity while severely undermining the given association of men to masculinity. In Foucauldian terms, she is cultivating her sense of identity in a sophisticated manner, as a work of art, always within a discursive framework but expressive also of cognitive decisions she has made regarding her lifestyle and aspirations. She can clearly see her life choices before her, and they may or may not include having children, getting married, settling down to domestic routine, or turning away from the realization of her potential in her chosen career and profession. Just because postmodern woman chooses to be child-free and career-oriented in no way negates her sense of being a feminine woman (Gillespie, 2003). In a way it matters little whether postmodern woman is bi, lesbian, or straight, for the realm of sexuality is one in which she is likely to experiment anyway even if in so doing she appears at times to be pandering to "raunch culture" and male sexist stereotypes (Levy, 2006). Perhaps she just relishes the freedom to behave in a masculine way or maybe she senses that traditional feminine values are part of a historical social intent to impose a strict sexual compartmentalization upon women. For some women, especially

younger ones, trying on gender, experimenting with masculinity and femininity, is also part and parcel of their desire to find out who they are. They do so via an intersectional process that draws on various identity elements, including race, ethnicity, and class. From this we should not assume that the process of trying on gender is wholly or ultimately emancipatory in every instance (see Williams, 2009, for discussion), although clearly it operates outside of the rigid sexual/gender codes that operated so persuasively for most women throughout the nineteenth and twentieth centuries.

As with postmodern man, the conditions of globalization have provided the means and opportunity for postmodern woman to come into existence worldwide, have provided the setting within which she tries out various identities, and have associated new and expanded meanings on the identity "woman." The specific changes that have opened up opportunities for a number of generally middle-class professional women include the massification of further and higher education; the shift from industrial to post-industrial work; the demise of the male-breadwinner nuclear family; the ready availability of numerous forms of contraception; new technology and forms of mass communication, including global travel; the breaking down of previously dominant sexual codes for women; post-Fordist work patterns and an associated increase in meritocratic work cultures; and the increased pressure for and evidence of equal-opportunities legislation across the public and private spheres. Subjectively and politically, these changes reflect and reinforce the discourse of feminism that was established in the 1970s in the West.

As Connell (2005) notes, such dynamics, as conditions and consequences of globalization, are shifting the political landscape around gender, with many men now around the world "engaged in gender reforms," perhaps even moving such a process toward a hegemonic agenda for gender equity.

However, as Connell also warns, we should not infer from all these changes that women are now in some utopian place of democratic gender justice. We are far from that. In many countries, including some of the most economically prosperous, women continue to face major structural and cultural barriers in their path toward new expressions of feminine identity (see, for examples, Fujioika, 2007; Mesure, 2006; Bennett, 2007). In too many societies there are those who adopt a conservative approach to gender roles, if not a fundamental, occasionally violent, resistance to women's emancipation and to more liberal expressions of masculinity.

However, what is also apparent is that the period from the 1960s, essentially the past 50 years, has ushered in profound and far-reaching changes in how gender identity, most specifically forms of femininity, can be expressed by educated middle-class women, especially. In the 1960s, for example, only a relatively small number of Western women went to university, chose not to get married and have children, or if they did have children then did so outside of wedlock, remained single and/or in serial monogamous relationships, devoted themselves to a career, went on to post-graduate study, and generally operated outside the dominant gender (female) codes that prevailed at the time. Now, at the early stages of the twenty-first century, millions of women worldwide are living out urbanized, individualized, existences in precisely these ways and in so doing are engaging in alternative subject positions in their constructions of self. As a result, they are reforming, intentionally or otherwise, the dominant meanings attached to the identity "woman" (see for examples, Nielson, 2004; Gillespie, 2003; Wongruang, 2007).

The feminist project is not disabled by the emergence of postmodern woman; indeed, her presence in numerous social and cultural sites only strengthens the feminist agenda, which must be to encourage the broadening of lifestyle choices and identity aspirations for increasing numbers of women, whatever their class, race, ethnicity, religion, or culture. At the same time, and as Halberstam so powerfully argues, we cannot continue to ignore the evidence before us that clearly shows that masculine performances are not the exclusive property of men. Women, too, can perform what have historically been seen as masculine modes of being, whether as a singularity of purpose in pursuit of a professional career, as a reluctance to commit to a monogamous life-long relationship, as family breadwinner, or operating in a competitive and individualistic manner as a senior executive in a multinational corporation. Millions of women, worldwide, are now actively engaged in precisely such roles, not simply trying on a new gender but actually living it out daily.

In Table 11.4, we list the key indicators of postmodern women and their femininity.

TABLE 11.4   Postmodern Woman and her Femininity

Primary Indicators
Supports women's rights for gender equality (although may or may not consider herself feminist)
Supports LGBT rights
Anti-racist
Pro-choice (abortion and birth control)
If heterosexual, does not feel threatened by gay/lesbian sexuality

TABLE 11.4   (continued)

Liberal-minded, open to alternative cultural expressions

Sexually confident and self-aware (to what extent is age dependent)

Prepared to seek sexual pleasure with a series of partners

Is comfortable being single or in a relationship

Would consider having children outside of a relationship

Would delay having children until her education/career is established or not at all

Seeks self-improvement (physically and intellectually)

Does not strictly adhere to traditional gender value systems

Would seek a love relationship, not merely a functional one

Would not marry for social aspirational reasons but for love

Has strong appreciation of herself and the sort of lifestyle and relationships she wants

Does not consider the identities of wife and mother to solely define her

Considers men no more than her equal, not her superiors

Secondary Indicators

College/university educated

Considers herself middle-class and upwardly socially mobile

Financially independent or striving for it

Career orientated and ambitious

Professional status and/or self-employed (businesswoman)

Not avidly following any single religion but considers herself spiritual

Comfortable with new technology

Uses online social networks

Considers herself a global citizen—not overly nationalistic

Lives an individualistic city/urban lifestyle

Note: Postmodern woman will have all of the primary indicators and a majority of the secondary ones.

SUMMARY

So what of the future? What are the indicators of gender identity in the twenty-first century? As we conclude, each of these globalized expressions of identity corresponds to new and alternative gender formations. This places them in some opposition to those traditional ways of being male and female that largely configured the modern age. Yet traditional, conservative, modernist understandings of gender identity have certainly not disappeared; it is just that they now stand increasingly in stark contrast to, if not tension with, these more fluid and potentially emancipatory ways of being female or male. Importantly, for those who seek to research and understand more fully contemporary conditions of gender identity and its many new, emergent directions, exploring the four very different but related social dynamics that we examined in this chapter is a good place to start.

We consider the diasporic, cyber wo/man, postmodern man, and postmodern woman to be clear markers of ontological being for increasing numbers of individuals. Emerging out of these movements is the concept of bigender, and this may well become a more socially acceptable and therefore more prominent expression of gender identity as the century progresses. The bigendered person (see Chapter 3) may be socially identified as male or female but consciously or unconsciously adopts different gender behaviour depending on the social role that person is in at the time. Imagine such a person as transgendered but more fluid and flexible. Both postmodern man and postmodern woman take us into the realm of bigender and into, perhaps, a more explicit example of the Foucauldian concept of identity work as art. In addition, it seems to us that cyberspace identities (e.g., the avatar) and the multiple, politicized, multicultural intersected self (explored in Chapter 2) will both become increasingly apparent, and increasingly important, although all remain conditional upon globalization and its attendant characteristics.

In terms of theoretical research, the tensions between those who favour the notion of a fixed, innate, sovereign identity and those who recognize that no self exists before society will likely disappear. Certainly for us, as for many others, the contest is over. The post-structuralists have the edge. There is no predictability in the self, nor is there any true, authentic self to be found through painstaking psychological archaeology or analysis. We are each products of our social history and environment. As David Brooks (2007), in his discussion of Douglas Hofstadter's

(2007) book, puts it, "you may be a flaming liberal in New York, but it's likely you'd be a flaming conservative if you grew up in Wyoming" (p. 11).

Accepting, then, the reality of a non-unitary self in the age of globalization, the future suggests a significant if not potentially radical reforming of gender identities. This is likely to come about through (1) the blurring, if not dismantling, of discursive boundaries between male and female; (2) narrative confusion between social and technological representations of a gendered self; and (3) a political and ontological blending of previously distinct, if contradictory, cultural markers of gender identity. For those uneasy with or fearful of such confused identity blurring, then retreat to the more traditional expressions of self is likely to prove increasingly attractive, although increasingly marginal.

Whatever the particular consequences and outcomes for communities and individuals, no doubt these expressions of identity will continue to connect in multiple ways with those political arenas discussed in this book. Likewise, they will come to be practised in the many social and cultural sites examined also. But any predictions remain tentative. The rapidity and unpredictability of current social change ultimately unsettles all promises and expectations. What will not change, however, is our eternal desire to be: the never-ending ontological quest for identity. This will continue to exist for so long as we do.

CASE STUDY

It was in her final year at university when Dee started to realize she might have a problem with men. Up until then, she'd had boyfriends, some serious, but nothing that she considered to be a big relationship. And anyway, she had

her law school studies to concentrate on. At 23 years of age, life was good. She had lots of friends, mostly female students like herself, and her family was supportive; in fact her mother was a powerful and positive female role model for her, and Dee was bristling with confidence as a result.

Her last love, Paul, had seemed so perfect for her—good-looking, intelligent, sexy, and interested in her and her needs. For the first few months Dee and Paul hung out together a lot and with friends. In fact, Dee had actually taken Paul home to meet her family at the end of the spring semester. There had been times when Paul had seemed rather distant, even a little angry, although about what he never revealed. Also, he could be a bit of a jock, especially around his friends. Dee didn't appreciate it when Paul acted this way, although she knew enough about young college males to understand the pressures on him to act like this at times.

So why the man problem now? Dee wasn't sure, but she sensed it was something to do with her; the guys she was attracted to were good-looking, with lots of social credibility. And these guys seemed to like her. But relationships never lasted. She thought the one with Paul might last, but after six months they split. It seemed to Dee that Paul always wanted to be in control. He never seemed keen to talk about their relationship or his feelings. He would talk for hours about sport and stuff, but not about his emotions. If he didn't get his own way he would sulk or get angry.

The only person that Dee could really open up with was her mother. She was such a strong woman—very much her own person. Dee thought her mom was a feminist; she always looked out for the well-being of women, especially. Dee wasn't so keen herself on the feminist label; it just didn't seem to fit her own personality or outlook on life. At the same time, Dee certainly wanted equality in a relationship and she expected it in her career. She didn't see herself as beneath any man. Her mom always told her to look out for herself, to be her own woman, and that she could do anything she set her mind on. This was the way Dee was living her life. She could see her pathway unfolding before her: degree, grad school, law school, and eventually attorney in a top city law firm. She wanted children, although marriage was less important to her. But right now, and for the next decade, Dee had plans for herself.

But what about the men? Surely all this didn't mean she would have to be on her own? Was she being selfish in putting herself first? Maybe the men she'd met so far just weren't comfortable with a woman like her? She hoped that wasn't the case. She liked men, and she wanted their companionship. But just what compromises would she have to make to keep one?

In her more pessimistic moments of reflection, Dee doubted whether there would be any soulmate for her, no true love in her life. In those moments she blamed herself and wondered what she had to do to be a woman who could keep a man. But then at other times she looked around her, saw all these young women, just like her, just as determined, ambitious, and independent as she was, and she realized the problem was not with her, it was with the men.

DISCUSSION QUESTIONS

1. Is Dee a feminist, and, if so, how would you describe her type of feminism?
2. How would you summarize Dee's problems with men?
3. If you are a woman, can you recognize Dee's difficulties with her boyfriends? If

you are a man, do you recognize Paul's behaviour?

4. In what respects is Dee a postmodern woman?

5. Is Paul a postmodern man? Give your reasons.

6. What do you think are the main influences on Dee's sense of femininity and approach to womanhood?

7. What do you think are the main influences on Paul's sense of masculinity and approach to manhood?

QUESTIONS FOR REVIEW AND DISCUSSION

1. Give examples of the diaspora effect occurring in your own community or in your family.

2. In what ways might diaspora have gendered aspects and consequences?

3. Do you consider Facebook and similar social networking sites to be improving human communication and interaction, or detracting from them? Give your reasons.

4. Would you use the Internet for dating? Give your reasons. If you have used the Internet for dating, describe some of your experiences.

5. Do you know of any males who might be considered postmodern? How would you describe their masculine identity?

6. Do you know of any females who might be considered postmodern? How would you describe their feminine identity?

7. Do you consider your gender identity performance and outlook to be traditional or postmodern? Give your reasons.

8. Explore the argument that postmodern gender identities are simply a consequence of global capitalism and media and are, therefore, not under the control or agency of the individual.

9. What inhibits men from trying on femininity in the way that women try on masculinity?

10. Is the future female? Give your reasons.

GLOSSARY

a priori Describes an idea or a knowledge that already exists in our mind before we make a judgment and does not depend on experience to be validated.

agentic Capable of making choices and exercising free will.

agnosticism A philosophical doctrine that claims that knowing the answer to any particular question with absolute certainty is unattainable. The term also refers to the belief that it is not possible to know whether there is god or whether there is no god.

amorphous Having no definite shape, structure, or pattern.

anima A term coined by Carl Gustav Jung to describe the female side of personality, which he believed is present in both men and women.

animus A term coined by Carl Gustav Jung to describe the male side of personality, which he believed is present in both men and women.

archetype A symbol or pattern that is found in cultural representations, such as in mythology, literature, folk stories, dreams, art, and religion, and is believed to be the same across cultures, across historical times, and across geographical places.

ascription of gender The process by which individuals are identified as male or female at birth.

biological sex roles The roles men and women perform based on their biology (for example, being a mother or a father).

black feminism A feminist approach that focuses on the question of race and the interconnection between sexism, racism, and class domination.

chimera A creature made up of parts taken from different animals.

compulsory heterosexual paradigm The ideas and values that are promoted by society through institutions such as the law, the media, and religion in order to impose heterosexuality as the norm.

conflation The blending or fusion of different things (such as words or ideas) so as to form a whole.

constellation A group of items, individuals, ideas, or characteristics that are related.

contingency The notion that human experience depends on particular circumstances and contexts that affect its meaning.

conurbation A vast urban area resulting from the merging of individual towns or cities that have grown in population and in size.

cyborg A creature that combines human and non-human features (such as Frankenstein, for example). According to Haraway, the cyborg represents the ultimate symbiosis between nature and technology that challenges the traditional boundaries of what it means to be human.

deconstruction A method of analysis that aims to highlight the contradictions inherent in language and reality.

diaspora A group of people who have left their original homeland to settle in different parts of the world but who still share a sense of having a common culture.

discourse A Foucauldian concept that refers to both language and practice. These languages and practices, as discourses, are the means by which subjects become individuals in society. So, for Foucault, all individuals are primarily discursive subjects.

Electra complex A phrase coined by Carl Gustav Jung using the Greek myth to refer to what he saw as an unconscious desire in young girls to sexually desire their fathers and compete with their mothers.

Enlightenment project   A way of seeing the world based on ideas that emerged in seventeenth- and eighteenth-century Europe and have continued to influence Western thinking, namely the belief in rationality, logic, science, objectivity, and progress.

epistemic   Relating to knowledge and ways of knowing.

epistemic unity   The process by which individuals can be members of a specific social group (e.g., women), and by having a unified experience (as women) share one single way of knowing and understanding the world.

epistemological   Pertaining to the study of the ways in which society and individuals understand the world and the nature and limitations of the knowledge they produce about it.

essentialism   The belief that individuals, groups, or cultures are shaped by some fixed and unchanging (essential) characteristics and properties that define who or what they are.

eugenic   Relates to "Eugenics," an early twentieth-century movement that claimed that human species could be improved through gene selection and advocated that certain individuals and groups with so-called undesirable genetic traits were to be discouraged from reproducing. This movement is now regarded as promoting discriminatory practices that violate human rights.

existential   Pertaining to human existence and to the "meaning of life."

false consciousness   Being unaware of and unable to recognise one's own repression and subjection to ideological conditions.

Foucauldian   Relates to the theories developed by the French post-structuralist philosopher Michel Foucault (1926–84), who is known for his analysis of knowledge and discourse as interconnected systems that work to support relationships of power within society and create an individual's identity (see our discussion in Chapter 2).

functionalist social theory   A social theory that sees the different institutions that make up society as a coherent and interconnected system that works toward ensuring that society as a whole functions in an orderly manner (see our discussion in Chapter 1).

gender   The social expression of our sex identity. So whereas "male" and "female" can be understood as biological identities, our gender is the cultural presentation of such sex identity in the social world, e.g., our individual balance, combination, and performance of femininity and masculinity.

gendered binary   The way in which society divides individuals into men and women as distinct and opposite categories.

Gramscian hegemony   The situation whereby, according to Antonio Gramsci, the ruling class uses language, culture, and ideology (such as the media) to make its dominant position look "normal" and "natural" to the larger population.

habitus   A set of attitudes and ideas that members of a particular social class have acquired through socialization and that manifests itself, consciously or unconsciously, through particular dispositions, such as our taste for food, books, music, cinema, etc. Also relates to aspects of our culture or social class that we express through particular attitudes and values and through our body language and that we have acquired, consciously or unconsciously, through socialization.

Hegelian   Relates to the ideas and the followers of the German philosopher Georg Wilhelm Friedrich Hegel (1770–1831), who is known for having theorized human consciousness, the role of the mind and ideas, and the influence of society and history as forces that involve contradictory movements.

Hegelian dialectic of spirit   A theory developed by Georg Wilhelm Friedrich Hegel about the capacity for the human spirit to achieve self-awareness and freedom by being able to resolve contradictions and reconcile opposites.

hegemonic agencies   The means (whether economic, political, social, or cultural) through which a dominant group is able to sustain and reinforce its position of power within society.

hegemonic masculinity   A form of male behaviour and expression of male identity that seeks to reinforce men's power and patriarchal values. Based on characteristics such as competition, ambition, self-reliance, physical strength, aggression, and homophobia.

hegemony The dominant position occupied by certain groups of people, certain ideas, and certain social norms over others.

hybridity The situation that results from the mixing of two or more languages, cultures, or identities.

ideological apparatus The institutions (such as the school, the state, the church) that are responsible for spreading the ideas, values, and norms of a dominant social class.

intersexed individuals Individuals whose genitals are not immediately recognizable as either male (penis) or female (vagina).

intersubjectivity The process by which our understanding of the world is influenced by our engagement with others.

juridico-discursive model of power A macro perspective of power that considers a combination of state apparatuses (e.g., laws and legal system) and cultural norms to enable certain individuals and groups to dominate others.

Lacanian Relates to the ideas developed by the French psychoanalyst Jacques Lacan (1901–81), who reinterpreted Freud's theories and paid particular attention to the importance of language in shaping the human psyche. Lacan is also known for having written about the role of the gaze and its impact on human psychological development (see our discussion in Chapter 1).

liberal feminists Feminists who advocate the need for more opportunities for women as individuals rather than a total transformation of the social system responsible for gender inequalities.

"malestream" perspective A variation of the word *mainstream* that describes the way in which the dominant point of view in society is often the male point of view, although it is not attributed as such.

Marxist feminism A feminist approach that sees women's oppression as part of the larger capitalist and imperialistic inequalities that underpin society.

masculine ontology The desire by males/men to be recognized and accepted and to have their masculine identity validated in the social world.

McDonaldization A term coined by the sociologist George Ritzer in *The McDonaldization of Society* to describe the way the principles of fast-food restaurants such McDonald's—such as efficiency, quantity, and uniformity—have entered other aspects of our society and our culture.

meta-narrative A broad and overarching model or story that serves to explain the way society works. Can also be linked to the concept of ideology.

metaphysical Relates to matters or preoccupations that are outside everyday human experience, such as the meaning of existence, the nature of reality, or the existence of a god.

migration The mass movement of people from one locality or country of residence to another.

mimicry A process that involves imitating or reproducing an existing and usually dominant discourse, behaviour, or attitude.

misogynistic An attitude that consists of mistrusting, disliking, or hating women.

modelling Following the example of usually older and influential individuals, such as parents, teachers, and other role models.

mythopoetic Literally meaning myth-making.

neo-liberalist One who espouses economic liberalization from state intervention and promotes free-market principles and practices across both the public and private sectors, for example, the privatization of state-owned enterprises (energy), the deregulation of markets (finance), and the introduction of private sector methods in the public services (education).

nihilistic Considers human existence as being without inherent meaning or purpose.

object-relations approach A psychoanalytical approach that focuses on the way in which individuals internalize the reality around them and create representations of objects and people in their mind.

nomad A person or a group of people with no fixed residence who move from one place to another. This concept was used by critics such as Braidotti to describe the postmodern condition.

Oedipus complex A phrase coined by the psychoanalyst Sigmund Freud using the Greek myth to describe what he saw as an unconscious desire in young boys to sexually relate to their mothers and to kill and/or compete against their fathers.

ontological Pertaining to the study of the nature and the meaning of existence.

ontology A branch of philosophy that deals with matters pertaining to being and existence.

orthodoxy The act of conforming to an idea, doctrine, or opinion believed to be the truth.

panoptic Foucauldian term to describe how every person is constantly subject to the gaze and scrutiny of others—the all-seeing eye. Uses metaphor of the panopticon (Jeremy Bentham's design for a nineteenth-century prison) to show how we can never know when we are being watched or when we are seen, only that we are.

paradigm A set of concepts, views, and assumptions that acts as a standard framework within which scientists interpret particular phenomena.

performative A term originating from the work of the French philosopher and sociologist Jacques Lyotard to describe an aspect of postmodernity that is the preference for scientific knowledge over subjective knowledge. It has been since adopted by organizational theorists to explain the trend in organizations to measure and quantify every aspect of employee performance (e.g., targets, assessment, appraisal).

performativity The process by which individuals and groups draw on and repeat particular discourses (behaviour, language, dress, and other verbal or non-verbal markers) in their everyday behaviour, thereby reinforcing their sense of (gender) identity.

positivism The belief that society, like the natural world, can be explained through scientific observation and experimentation.

post-colonial feminism A feminist approach that sees women's liberation as dependent on the process of decolonization from Western forms of domination inherited from colonialism.

post-Fordist Relates to the period following Fordism, a system of industrial manufacturing based on mass production that was characteristic of the beginning of the twentieth century and that takes its name from Henry Ford, the owner of the Ford Motor Company. In contrast to Fordism, post-Fordism is defined by aspects characteristic of the latter part of the twentieth century, such as the use of information technology, the development of specialized markets, and the feminization of labour.

praxis A theoretical idea or concept translated into practice.

racialized Assigned to a specific racial category on the basis of aspects such as skin colour, facial features, or religion.

radical feminists Feminists who consider patriarchy and sexual domination as the root causes of women's oppression.

reflexive production The signs and meanings that are created when individuals reflect on how they relate to society and each other.

role performance The process by which individuals are expected to display particular behaviours in society depending on their social position.

schema/schemata A psychological term that refers to a mental pattern or a way of thinking that we have internalized and that influences the way we perceive and acquire new knowledge.

secular Not bound by religious rule.

sex-reassigned Describes people having undergone sex reassignment surgery.

sex-role theory A theory of gender that focuses on the physical and biological differences between men and women as the basis for understanding the different roles they perform in society.

simulacra Images or representations that produce a simulation of reality without bearing any relationship to it.

social constructionism A perspective that considers the roles we perform in society as the result of the social or cultural factors that influence our behaviour.

social mores The customs and values of a given society.

socialist feminists Feminists who consider women's oppression as the result of both patriarchy and class inequalities.

socio-symbolic order The system of social rules, norms, and representations that organize and control society.

structural functionalism A sociological perspective that views society as a set of coherent parts that work together to create social order and equilibrium.

subaltern   Refers to a person or a class of individuals occupying an inferior and subordinate position in society.

subjectivity   Our individual understanding of the world around us and our engagement with it.

subject position   The particular position or status that we acquire through the act of expressing ourselves. Individuals may use many different (discursive) subject positions depending on the social situation they are in at the time.

symbolic interactionism   A sociological perspective that sees the self as being constructed through face-to-face interactions with others and the use of symbols in social communication.

syncretism   The process of combining beliefs or practices from distinct schools of thought or religious traditions.

total institution   An institution (e.g., the army, a prison, the police, etc.) where individuals are under the total control of an authority and subjected to a powerful organizational system and dominant singular culture.

transgendered   A general term that describes individuals who experience their gender identity as being different from what society expects from their current physical sex characteristics.

transsexual   Describes individuals who desire to adopt the opposite sex from the one they were born with. The term also refers to persons having undergone surgical procedures (sex reassignment surgery) and/or hormone therapy.

REFERENCES

Abel, E.K., & Pearson, M.L. (1989). *Across cultures: The spectrum of women's lives*. New York: Gordon and Breach.

Abel, S., deBruin, M., & Nowak, A. (Eds.). (2009). *Women, advertising and representation: Beyond familiar paradigms*. New York: Hampton Press.

Abrahamy, M., Finkelson, E.B., Lydon, C., & Murray, K. (2003). Caregivers' socialization of gender roles in a children's museum. *Perspectives in Psychology*, 6, 19–24.

Acker, J. (2006). Inequality regimes: Gender, class and race in organizations. *Gender & Society*, 20, 441–61.

Acker, S. (1994). *Gendered education*. Buckingham, UK: Open University Press.

Ackroyd, S., & Thompson, P. (1999). *Organizational misbehaviour*. London: Sage.

Adam, B. (1990). *Time and social theory*. Cambridge: Polity.

Adam, B.D. (1995). *The rise of a gay and lesbian movement*. New York: Twayne.

Adam, B.D. (2000). Love and sex in constructing identity among men who have sex with men. *International Journal of Sexuality and Gender Studies*, 5(4), 325–39.

Adams, J.R. (2008). *Male armor: The soldier-hero in contemporary American culture*. Charlottesville: University of Virginia Press.

Adams, M. (2006). Hybridizing habitus and reflexivity: Towards an understanding of contemporary identity? *Sociology*, 40, 511–28.

Adams, R.G. (1994). Older men's friendship patterns. In E.H. Thompson, Jr (Ed.), *Older men's lives*. Thousand Oaks, CA: Sage.

Adams, T., & Duncan, A. (2003). *The feminist case: Jung, aesthetics and creative process*. London: Karnac Books.

Adkins, L. (2001). Risk culture, self-reflexivity and the making of sexual hierarchies. *Body & Society*, 7(1), 35–55.

Adkins, L. (2002). *Revisions: Gender and sexuality in late modernity*. Buckingham, UK: Open University Press.

Adu-Poku, S. (2001). Envisioning (black) male feminism: A cross-cultural perspective. *Journal of Gender Studies*, 10(2), 157–67.

Agnew, V. (Ed). (2005). *Diaspora, memory, and identity: A search for home*. Toronto: University of Toronto Press.

Agostinone-Wilson, F. (2010). *Marxism and education beyond identity: Sexuality and schooling*. New York: Palgrave Macmillan.

Agustin, L.M. (2007). *Sex at the margins: Migration, labour markets and the rescue industry*. New York, NY: Zed Press.

Ahmed, L. (1992). *Women and gender in Islam*. New Haven, CT: Yale University Press.

Ahmed, S. (1998). *Differences that matter: Feminist theory and postmodernism*. Cambridge, UK: Cambridge University Press.

Ahmed, S. (2004). Declarations of whiteness: The non-performativity of anti-racism. *Borderlands*, 3(2), 1–16.

Aitchinson, C. (2003). *Gender and leisure: A social-cultural nexus*. London: Routledge.

Ajeto, D.M. (2009). *A soul has no gender: Love and acceptance through the eyes of a mother of sexual and gender minority children*. Rotterdam: Sense.

Akerlof, G.A., & Kranton, R.E. (2010). *Identity economics: How our identities shape our work, wages, and well-being*. Princeton, NJ: Princeton University Press.

Al-Ali, N. (2000). *Secularism, gender and the state in the Middle East: The Egyptian women's movement*. Cambridge: Cambridge University Press.

Albanesi, H.P. (2010). *Gender and sexual agency: How young people make choices about sex*. Lanham, MD: Lexington Books.

Albarran, A.B., & Goff, D.H. (2000). *Understanding the web: Social, political and economic dimensions of the Internet*. Ames: Iowa State University Press.

Alberoni, R. (1983). *Falling in love*. New York: Random House.

Alderman, G. (1985). Explaining Racism. *Political Studies, 33*, 129–35.

Alexander, B.K. (2006). Passing, cultural performance, and individual agency: Performative reflections on black masculine identity. In S.M. Whitehead (Ed.), *Men and masculinities: Critical concepts in sociology* (Vol. IV). London: Routledge.

Alexander, J. (1994). *Fin de siècle social theory: Relativism, reduction and the problem of reason*. London: Verso.

Alexander, R.J. (2001). *Culture and pedagogy: International comparisons of primary education*. New York: Blackwell.

Alexeyeff, K. (2009). *Dancing from the heart: Movement, gender, and Cook Islands globalization*. Honolulu: University of Hawaii Press.

Alexiadou, N., & Brock, C. (1999). *Education as a commodity*. Suffolk, UK: Catt Educational.

Allan, G. (1989). *Friendship: Developing a sociological perspective*. Hemel Hempstead, UK: Harvester Wheatsheaf.

Allan, G. (1998). Friendship and the private sphere. In R.G. Adams & G.A. Allan (Eds.), *Placing friendship in context*. Cambridge: Cambridge University Press.

Allen, L.D. (2002). *Rise up, o men of God: The men and religion forward movement and promise keepers*. Macon, GA: Mercer University Press.

Allred, A.P. (2003). *Atta girl: A celebration of women in sports*. New York: Wish.

Al-Sharmani, M. (2006). Living transnationally: Somali diasporic women in Cairo *International*. *Migration, 44*(1), 55–77.

Althusser, L. (1971). *Lenin and philosophy and other essays*. London: New Left Books.

Althusser, L. (1984). *Essays on ideology*. London: Verso Books.

Althusser, L. (2000). Ideology interpellates individuals as subjects. In P. du Gay, J. Evans, & P. Redman (Eds.), *Identity: A reader*. London: Sage.

Alvesson, M., & Billing, Y.D. (2009). *Understanding gender and organizations*. Los Angeles: Sage.

Alvi, S.S., Hoodfar, H., & McDonough, S. (Eds.). (2003). *The Muslim veil in North America: issues and debates*. Toronto: Women's Press.

Alzheimer, L. (2003, June 22). *Metrosexuals: The future of men?* Euro RSCG.

Amrith, S.S. (2011). *Migration and diaspora in modern Asia*. Cambridge, NY: Cambridge University Press.

Amy, L.E. (2010). *The wars we inherit: Military life, gender violence, and memory*. Philadelphia: Temple University Press.

Anderson, B. (2000). *Doing the dirty work? The global politics of domestic labour*. London: Zed Books.

Anderson, D.C., & Mosbacher, M. (Eds.). (1997). *British women today: A qualitative survey of the images of women in British magazines*. London: Social Affairs Unit.

Anthias, F. (1998). Evaluating "diaspora": Beyond ethnicity? *Sociology, 32*(3), 557–80.

Anthony, K.H. (2001). *Designing for diversity: Gender, race and ethnicity in the architectural profession*. Illinois: University of Illinois Press.

Antrobus, P. (2004). *The global women's movement: Origins, issues and strategies*. London: Zed Books.

Anzaldúa, G. (1987). La conciencia de la mestiza/ Towards a new consciousness. *Borderlands/ La Frontera*. San Francisco: Aunt Lute Books, 99–113.

Appiah, A. (1985). *Assertion and conditionals*. Cambridge, UK: Cambridge University Press.

Appiah, A. (1986). *For truth in semantics*. Oxford, UK: Blackwell Publishing.

Appiah, K.A. (2005). *The ethics of identity*. Princeton, NJ: Princeton University Press.

Arber, S., Davidson, K., & Ginn, J. (2003). *Gender and ageing*. Buckingham, UK: Open University Press.

Arber, S., & Ginn, J. (1995). *Connecting gender and ageing: A sociological approach*. Buckingham, UK: Open University Press.

Archer, J. (Ed.). (1994). *Male violence*. London: Routledge.

Archer, L. (2003). *Race, masculinity and schooling: Muslim boys and education*. Buckingham, UK: Open University Press.

Archer, L. (2006). 'Muslim brothers, black lads, traditional Asians': British Muslim young men's constructions of race, religion and masculinity. In S.M. Whitehead (Ed.), *Men and masculinities: Critical concepts in sociology* (Vol. IV). London: Routledge.

Arditti, J.A., Godwin, D.D., & Scanzoni, J. (1991). Perceptions of parenting behavior and young women's gender role traits and preferences. *Sex Roles, 25*(3), 195–221.

Armentor-Cota, J. (2011). Multiple perspectives on the influence of gender in online interactions. *Sociology Compass, 5*(1), 23–36.

Armitage, J. (2003). Militarized bodies: An introduction. *Body & Society, 9* (4), 1–12.

Armstrong, K., Yazbeck Haddad, Y., & Esposito, J. (Eds.). (2002). *Daughters of Abraham: feminist thought in Judaism, Christianity and Islam*. Tallahassee, FL: University Press of Florida.

Arnot, M., David, M., & Weiner, G. (1999). *Closing the Gender Gap: Post-war Education and Social Change*. Cambridge: Polity.

Arnot, M., & Mac an Ghaill, M. (Eds.). (2006). *The Routledge/Falmer reader in gender and education*. London: Routledge/Falmer.

Aronson, P. (2003). Feminists or "postfeminists"? Young women's attitudes towards feminism and gender relations. *Gender & Society, 17*(6), 903–22.

Asche, A., & Fine, M. (Eds.). (1988). *Women with disabilities: Essays in psychology, culture, and politics*. Philadelphia: Temple University Press.

Ashwin, S., & Lytkina, T. (2006). Men in crisis in Russia: The role of domestic marginalization. In S.M. Whitehead (Ed.), *Men and masculinities: Critical concepts in sociology* (Vol. IV). London: Routledge.

Ask, K., & Tjomsland, M. (Eds.). (1998). *Women and Islamization: contemporary dimensions of discourse on gender relations*. Oxford: Berg.

Assiter, A. (1996). *Enlightened women: Modernist feminism in a post-modern age*. London: Routledge.

Augustin, E. (Ed.). (1993). *Palestinian women: Identity and experience*. London: Zed Books.

Aulette, J.R., & Wittner, J. (2012). *Gendered worlds*. New York: Oxford University Press.

Bailly, L. (2009). *Lacan: A beginner's guide*. Oxford: Oneworld.

Baker, L., & Williamson, C. (2006). *Sex trafficking: The global market in women and children*. London: Worth Publications.

Bal, M. (1999). *Narratology: Introduction to the theory of narrative*. Toronto, ON: University of Toronto Press.

Bale, J., & Cronin, M. (2003). *Sport and colonialism*. London: Berg.

Ball, K. (2005). Organization, surveillance and the body: Towards a politics of resistance. *Organization, 12*(1), 89–108.

Ball, S.J. (1994). Education reform: A critical and post-structuralist approach. Buckingham, UK: Open University Press.

Ball, S.J. (2003). The teacher's soul and the terrors of performativity. *Journal of Education Policy, 18*(2), 215–28.

Ball, S.J. (2008). *The education debate*. Bristol: The Policy Press.

Banaszak, L.A. (Ed.). (2006). *The US women's movement in global perspective*. Lanham, MD: Rowman & Littlefield.

Bandura, A. (1973). *Aggression: A social learning analysis*. Englewood Cliffs, NJ: Prentice-Hall.

Bandura, A. (1977). *Social learning theory*. New York: General Learning Press.

Bandyopadhaya, M. (2006). Competing masculinities in a prison. *Men and Masculinities, 9*(2), 186–203.

Banks Findly, E. (Ed.). (2000). *Women's Buddhism, Buddhism's women: Tradition, revision, renewal.* Boston: Wisdom.

Bannerji, H. (1995). *Thinking through: Essays on feminism, Marxism and anti-racism.* Toronto: Women's Press.

Bannerji, H. (2000). *The dark side of the nation: Essays on multiculturalism, nationalism and gender.* Toronto: Canadian Scholars' Press.

Barbieri, N.B. (1999). Psychoanalytic contributions to the study of gender issues. *Canadian Journal of Psychiatry, 44*(1), 72–6.

Bargh, J.A. (2006). What have we been priming all these years? On the development, mechanisms, and ecology of nonconscious social behavior. *European Journal of Social Psychology, 36*, 147–68.

Barnard, I. (1999). Queer race. *Social Semiotics, 9*(2), 199–212.

Barraclough, R., & Faison, E. (2009). *Gender and labour in Korea and Japan: Sexing class.* Milton Park, UK: Routledge.

Barrett, F.J. (2001). The organizational construction of hegemonic masculinity: The case of the US navy. In S.M. Whitehead & F.J. Barrett (Eds.), *The Masculinities Reader.* Cambridge: Polity.

Barrett, M. (1980). *Women's oppression today: Problems in Marxist feminist analysis.* London: Verso.

Barrett, M. (1991). *The politics of truth.* Cambridge: Polity.

Barry, J., Dent, M., & O'Neil, M. (Eds.). (2003). *Gender, professionalism and managerial change: An international perspective.* London: Routledge.

Bart, P. (1977). The mermaid and the minotaur: A fishy story that's part bull. *Contemporary Psychology, 22*, 147–52.

Basow, S.A., & Heckelman, L. (1980). *Sex-role stereotypes: Traditions and alternatives.* Monterey, CA: Brooks/Cole.

Basu, A. (1995). *The challenge of local feminisms: Women's movements in global perspective.* Boulder, CO: Westview Press.

Baudrillard, J. (1983). *Simulations.* New York: Semiotext(e).

Bauman, R. (2004). *A world of others' words: Cross-cultural perspectives on intertextuality.* Malden, MA: Blackwell.

Bauman, Z. (1991). *Modernity and ambivalence.* Cambridge: Polity.

Bauman, Z. (1997). *Postmodernity and its discontents.* Cambridge: Polity.

Bauman, Z. (2003). *Liquid love: On the frailty of human bonds.* Cambridge: Polity.

Baumeister, R.F. (Ed.). (1986). *Public self and private self.* New York: Springer-Verlag.

Beall, J., Hassim, S., & Todes, A. (1989). 'A bit on the side'? Gender struggles in the politics of transformation in South Africa. *Feminist Review, 33*, 30–56.

Beasley, C. (2005). *Gender and sexuality: Critical theories, critical thinkers.* London: Sage.

Beauboeuf-LaFondant, T. (2003). Strong and large black women? Exploring the relationship between deviant womanhood and weight. *Gender and Society, 17*(1), 111–21.

Beck, U. (1992). *Risk society.* London: Sage.

Beck, U. (1994). The reinvention of politics: Towards a theory of reflexive modernization. In U. Beck, A. Giddens, & S. Lash (Eds.), *Reflexive modernization.* Cambridge: Polity Press.

Beck, U. (2000). *The brave new world of work.* Cambridge: Polity.

Beck, U., & Beck-Gernsheim, E. (1995). *The normal chaos of love.* Cambridge: Polity.

Beck, U., Giddens, A., & Lash, S. (1995). *Reflexive modernization: Politics, tradition and aesthetics in the modern social order.* Cambridge: Polity.

Beckles, H. McD., & Shepherd, V.A. (2007). *Freedoms won: Caribbean emancipations, ethnicities and nationhood.* Cambridge: Cambridge University Press.

Beemyn, B., & Eliason, M. (1996). *Queer studies: A lesbian, gay, bisexual & transgendered anthology.* New York: New York University Press.

Bell, D. (1975). *The coming of post-industrial society.* New York: BasicBooks.

Bell, M.J. (1986). *Women as elders: The feminist politics of aging.* New York: Harrington Park Press.

Bell, R. (2007, January 30). Love in the time of phone porn. *The Guardian Education.*

Bell, V. (1999). *Feminist Imagination.* London: Sage.

Belsky, J., Crnic, K., & Gable, S. (1995). The determinants of co-parenting in families with toddler boys: Spousal differences and daily hassles. *Child Development, 66*, 629–42.

Bem, S.L. (1974). The measurement of psychological androgyny. *Journal of Consulting and Clinical Psychology, 42*, 155–62.

Beneviste, E. (2000). *Problems in general linguistics.* Miami: Miami University Press.

Benhabib, S. (1997). Strange multiplicities: The politics of identity and difference in a global context. *Macalester International, 4*(1), 8.

Bennett, N. (2007, March 12). A post-feminist age? Think again. *The Guardian.* Retrieved from http://commentisfree.guardian.co.uk/ natalie_bennett/2007/03/building_feminist_ walls.html

Benson, M. (1985). *The struggle for a birthright.* London: IDAF (International Defense and Aid Fund for Southern Africa).

Benwell, B. (Ed.). (2003). *Masculinity and men's lifestyle magazines.* Oxford: Blackwell.

Benyon, J. (2002). *Masculinities and Culture.* Buckingham, UK: Open University Press.

Ben-Ze'ev, A. (2004). *Love online: Emotions on the Internet.* Cambridge, NY: Cambridge University Press.

Bergen, R.K., & Logue, M.A. (2009). Intimate partner violence during pregnancy: What does the research tell us? *Sociology Compass, 3*(2), 196–216.

Berger, M., Wallis, B., & Watson, S. (Eds.). (1995). *Constructing masculinity.* London: Routledge.

Bergner, G. (2005). *Taboo subjects: Race, sex and psychoanalysis.* Minneapolis: University of Minnesota Press.

Berliner, W. (2004, May 18). Where have all the young men gone? *The Guardian* [Higher education supplement], pp. 18–19.

Bernard, M., Davies, V.H., Machin, L., & Phillips, J. (Eds.). (2000). *Women ageing: Changing identities, challenging myths.* London: Routledge.

Bernstein, R. (2009). *The East, the West and sex: A history of erotic encounters.* New York: Knopf.

Berry, J.W. (1980). Acculturation as varieties of adaptation. In A.M. Padilla (Ed.), *Acculturation: Theory, models and some new findings.* Boulder, CO: Westview.

Berry, J.W. (1997). Immigration, acculturation, and adaptation. *Applied Psychology: An International Review, 46*, 5–68.

Berry, J.W. (2001). A psychology of immigration. *Journal of Social Issues, 57*, 615–31.

Bersani, L., & Phillips, A. (2008). *Intimacies.* Chicago: University of Chicago Press.

Bettie, J. (2003). *Women without class: Girls, race, and identity.* Berkeley: University of California Press.

Bettio, F., & Verashchagina, A. (Eds.). (2008). *Frontiers in the economics of gender.* London: Routledge.

Bhabha, H. (1987). What does the black man want? *New Formations, 1*, 118–24.

Bhabha, H. (1990). *Nation and narration.* London: Routledge.

Bhabha, H. (1994). *The location of culture.* London: Routledge.

Bhabha, H.K. (1999). Liberalism's sacred cow. In J. Cohn, M. Howard, & M.C. Nussbaum (Eds.), *Is multiculturalism bad for women?* Princeton, NJ: Princeton University Press.

Bhandar, B. (2009). The ties that bind: Multiculturalism and secularism reconsidered. *Journal of Law and Society, 36*(3), 301–26.

Bianchi, M., & Mormino, M. (1984). Militanti de se stesse. Il movimento delle donne a Milano. In A. Melucci (Ed.), *Altri Codici.* Bologna: Il Mulino.

Birch, B.C. (2007). Impairment as a condition in Biblical scholarship: A response. In H. Avalos, S. Melcher, & J. Schipper (Eds.), *This abled body: Rethinking disabilities in Biblical studies.* Atlanta: Society of Biblical Literature.

Birch, E., Le, A.T., & Miller, P. (2009). *Teamwork and gender at home: The household division of time.* London: Palgrave MacMillan.

Blackmore, J. (2005). The emperor has no clothes: Professionalism, performativity and educational leadership in high-risk postmodern times. In J. Collard & C. Reynolds (Eds.), *Leadership, gender, and culture in education.* Buckingham, UK: Open University Press.

Blackshaw, T. (2003). *Leisure life: Myth, modernity and masculinity.* London: Routledge.

Blakemore J.E.O., Berenbaum, S.A., & Liben, L.S. (2008). *Gender development.* New York: Psychology Press.

Blee, K.M., & Tickamyer, A.R. (1995). Racial differences in men's attitudes about women's gender roles. *Journal of Marriage and the Family*, *57*(1), 21–30.

Block, J. (1984). *Sex role identity and ego development*. San Francisco: Jossey-Bass.

Blumer, H., & Kuhn, M. (1991). Symbolic interactionism. In J.H. Turner (Ed.), *The structure of sociological theory* (5th Edn). Belmont: Wadsworth.

Bly, R. (1990). *Iron John*. New York: Addison-Wesley.

Boer, I.E. (2003). After Orientalism : Critical entanglements, productive looks. Amsterdam: Rodopi.

Bogue, R. (1996). *Deleuze and Guattari*. London: Routledge.

Boje, T.P., & Leira, A. (Eds.). (2000). *Gender, welfare state, and the market: Towards a new division of labour*. New York: Routledge.

Bologh, R.W. (1990). *Love or greatness: Max Weber and masculine thinking—a feminist inquiry*. London: Unwin Hyman.

Bond, M.H. (Ed.). (2010). *The Oxford handbook of Chinese psychology*. New York: Oxford University Press.

Bonnett, B. (2002). Constructions of whiteness in European and American anti-racism. In R.D. Torres, L.F. Miron, & J.X. Inda (Eds.), *Race, identity and citizenship*: *A reader*. London: Blackwell.

Bordo, S. (1993). Feminism, Foucault and the politics of the body. In C. Ramazanoglu (Ed.), *Up against Foucault*. London: Routledge.

Bordo, S. (1995). *Unbearable weight*. Berkeley, CA: University of California Press.

Boseley, S. (2009, June 3). The future is female—how women are transforming face of the health service. *The Guardian*. Retrieved from www.guardian.co.uk/society/2009/jun/03/women-doctors-nhs-medicine-review

Bourdieu, P. (1979). *Distinction: A social critique of the judgement of taste*. London: Routledge.

Bourdieu, P. (1984). *Distinction: A social critique of the judgement of taste*. London: Routledge.

Bourdieu, P. (1990). *The logic of practice*. Cambridge: Polity.

Bourdieu, P. (2001). *Masculine domination* (R. Nice, Trans.). Cambridge: Polity.

Bourdieu, P., & Passeron, J.-C. (1998). *Reproduction in education, society and culture* (2nd Edn). London: Sage.

Bowker, L.H. (Ed.). (1998). *Masculinities and violence*. Thousand Oaks, CA: Sage.

Bowles, S., & Gintis, H. (1976). *Schooling in capitalist America*. RKP: London.

Brah, A. (1996). *Cartographies of diaspora: Contesting identities*. London: Routledge.

Brah, A., & Phoenix, A. (2004). Ain't I a woman? Revisiting intersectionality. *International Journal of Women's Studies*, *5*, 75–86.

Braidotti, R. (2002). *Metamorphoses: Towards a materialist theory of becoming*. Cambridge: Polity.

Braziel, J.E. (2008). *Diaspora: An introduction*. Malden, MA: Blackwell.

Brenda S.A., Yeoh, B.S.A., & Huang, S. (2000). "Home" and "away": Foreign domestic workers and negotiations of diasporic identity in Singapore. *Women's Studies International Forum*, *23*(4), 413–29.

Brewster, K.L., & Padavic, I. (2000). Change in gender ideology, 1977–1996: The contributions of intracohort change and population turnover. *Journal of Marriage and the Family*, *62*, 47–87.

Brittan, A. (1989). *Masculinity and power*. Oxford: Basil Blackwell.

Broad, K.L. (2002). GLB+T? Gender/sexuality movements and transgender collective identity (de)constructions. *International Journal of Sexuality and Gender Studies*, *7*(4), 241–64.

Bronstein, P. (2006). The family environment: Where gender role socialization begins. In J. Worell & C.D. Goodheart (Eds.), *Handbook of girl's and women's psychological health*. New York: Oxford University Press.

Brookey, R.A., & Cannon, K.L. (2009). Sex lives in second life. *Critical Studies in Media Communication*, *26*(2), 145–64.

Brooks, A. (2006). *Gendered work in Asian cities: The new economy and changing labour markets*. Aldershot, England: Ashgate.

Brooks, D. (2007, July 21). A partnership of minds. *Bangkok Post*, p. 11.

Brooks, P.E. (2008). *Boycotts, buses, and passes: Black women's resistance in the US South and South Africa*. Amherst: University of Massachusetts Press.

Brouwer, J. (2002). Multiculturalism as a modern and an indigenous concept in India. In K. Deb (Ed.), *Mapping multiculturalism*. New Delhi: Rawat.

Brown, J. (2006). *Sex segregation and inequality in the modern labour market*. Bristol, UK: Policy Press.

Brown, P., & Hesketh, A. (2004). *The mismanagement of talent: Employability and jobs in the knowledge economy*. Buckingham, UK: Open University Press.

Brown, W. (1991). Feminist hesitation, postmodern exposures, differences. *Journal of Feminist Critical Studies*, 3(1), 63–83.

Browne, C.V. (1998). *Women, feminism, and aging*. New York: Springer.

Buchanan, I., & Colebrook, C. (Eds.). (2000). *Deleuze and feminist theory*. Edinburgh: Edinburgh University Press.

Budgeon, S. (2003). Identity as embodied event. *Body & Society*, 9(1), 35–55.

Buhle, M.J. (1998). *Feminism and its discontents: A century of struggle with psychoanalysis*. Cambridge, MA: Harvard University Press.

Bullock, K. (2002). *Rethinking Muslim women and the veil: Challenging historical and modern stereotypes*. Herndon, VA: International Institute of Islamic Thought.

Bulmer, M., & Solomos, J. (1996). Introduction: race, ethnicity and the curriculum. *Ethnic and Racial Studies*, 19, 777–88.

Burkitt, I. (1998). Sexuality and gender identity: From a discursive to a relational analysis. *The Sociological Review*, 46(3), 483–504.

Burr, V. (2003). *Social constructionism* (2nd Edn). London: Routledge.

Busby, C. (2000). *The performance of gender: An anthropology of everyday life in a South Indian fishing village*. London: Athlone Press.

Bussey, K., & Bandura, A. (1999). Social cognitive theory of gender development and differentiation. *Psychological Review*, 106, 676–713.

Butler, C.S. (2003). *Structure and function: A guide to three major structural-functional theories*. Amsterdam: J. Benjamins.

Butler, J. (1990). *Gender trouble: Feminism and the subversion of identity*. New York: Routledge.

Butler, J. (1993). *Bodies that matter: On the discursive limits of sex*. London: Routledge.

Butler, J. (1999). Performativity's social magic. In R. Shusterman (Ed.), *Bourdieu: A critical reader*. Oxford: Blackwell.

Butler, J. (2011). *Bodies that matter: On the discursive limits of sex*. New York: Routledge.

Butler, J., & Scott, J.W. (Eds.). (1992). *Feminists theorize the political*. New York: Routledge.

Byerly, C.M., & Ross, K. (2006). *Women and media: A critical introduction*. Oxford: Blackwell.

Byrne, B. (2000). Reciting the self: Narrative representations of the self in qualitative interviews. *Feminist Theory*, 4(1), 29–49.

Byrne, B. (2003). In search of a "good mix": "race," class, gender and practices of mothering. *Sociology*, 40(6), 1001–17.

Cadge, W. (2004). Gendered religious organizations: The case of Theravada Buddhism in America. *Gender and Society*, 18(6), 777–93.

Cadge, W. (2005a). Lesbian, gay and bisexual Buddhist practitioners. In E. Gray & S. Thumma (Eds.), *Gay religion*. Walnut Creek, CA: AltaMira Press.

Cadge, W. (2005b). Reconciling congregations bridging gay and straight communities. In E. Gray & S. Thumma (Eds.), *Gay religion*. Walnut Creek, CA: AltaMira Press.

Cahill, C. (1998). Nancy, Sean and Birdie Jo: Contested convictions of gender. *Journal of Gender Studies*, 7(3), 307–17.

Cain, M., & Howe, A. (Eds.). (2008). *Women, crime and social harm: Towards a criminology for the global age*. Oxford: Hart Publishing.

Calasanti, T., & King, N. (2005). Firming the floppy penis: Age, class and gender relations in the lives of older men. *Men and Masculinities*, 8(1), 3–23.

Callero, P.L. (2008). The globalization of self: Role and identity transformation from above and below. *Sociology Compass*, 2(2), 1972–88.

Campbell, A. (1993). *Out of control: Men, women and aggression*. London: Pandora.

Campbell, J. (2000). *Arguing with phallus: Feminist, queer, and postcolonial theory: A psychoanalytic contribution*. London: Zed Books.

Campbell, K. (2004). *Jacques Lacan and feminist epistemology*. New York: Routledge.

Capote, T. (1966). *In cold blood*. New York: Random House.

Carby, H.V. (1998). *Race men*. Cambridge: Harvard University Press.

Carr, C.L. (2005). Tomboyism or lesbianism? Beyond sex/gender/sexual conflation. *Sex Roles, 53*(1/2), 119–31.

Carrigan, T., Connell, R.W., & Lee, J. (1987). Hard and heavy: Toward a new sociology of masculinity. In M. Kaufman (Ed.), *Beyond patriarchy: Essays by men on pleasure, power, and change*. Toronto: Oxford University Press.

Carter, T.R., Williams, B., Juby, H.L., & Buckley, T.R. (2005). Racial identity as mediator of the relationship between gender role conflict and severity of psychological symptoms in black, Latino, and Asian men. *Sex Roles, 53*(7/8), 473–87.

Case, S. (2009). *Feminist and queer performance: Critical strategies*. Basingstoke, UK: Palgrave Macmillan.

Casey, C. (1995). *Work, self and society: After industrialism*. London: Routledge.

Cassen, R., & Kingdon, G. (2007). *Tackling low educational achievement*. York, UK: Joseph Rowntree Foundation.

Castells, M. (1998). *End of millennium*. London: Blackwell.

Castells, M. (2004). *The power of identity* (2nd Edn). London: Blackwell.

Castro-Vázquez, G., & Kishi, I. (2003). Masculinities and sexuality: The case of a Japanese top ranking senior high school. *Journal of Gender Studies, 12*(1), 21–33.

Castro-Vázquez, G., & Kishi, I. (2003). "Nemureru ko wo okosu mono dearu": Learning about sex at a top ranking Japanese senior high school. *Sexualities, 5*(4), 465–86.

Catan, T. (2007, January 29). World's oldest mum seeks younger man to help with twins. *The Australian*.

Cavanagh, A. (2009). From culture to connection: Internet community studies. *Sociology Compass, 3*(1), 1–15.

Cavendish, C. (2010). Useless, jobless men—the blight of our age. *The Times*. Retrieved from http://www.timesonline.co.uk/tol/comment/columnists/camilla_cavendish/article7138520.ece

The Centre for Social Justice (2012). Never in Britain's history has family breakdown hit such heights. Retrieved from http://www.centreforsocialjustice.org.uk/default.asp?

Chambers, P. (2005). *Older widows and the life course: Multiple narratives of hidden lives*. London: Ashgate.

Chandler, E. (2010). Sidewalk stories: The troubling task of identification. *Disability Studies Quarterly, 30*(3/4). Retrieved from http://dsq-sds.org/article/view/1293/1329

Chant, S. (1991). *Women and survival in Mexican cities: Perspectives on gender, labour markets, and low-income households*. Manchester, UK: Manchester University Press.

Chapkis, W. (1986). *Beauty secrets*. London: Women's Press.

Charles, H. (1992). Whiteness: The relevance of politically colouring the "non". In H. Hinds, A. Phoenix, & J. Stacey (Eds.), *Working out: New directions for women's studies*. London: Falmer Press.

Chasin, A. (2000). *Selling out: The gay and lesbian movement goes to market*. New York: St. Martin's Press.

Chatterjee, R. (2007). Charlotte Dacre's nymphomaniacs and demon lovers: Teaching female masculinities. In B. Knights (Ed.), *Masculinities in text and teaching*. London: Palgrave Macmillan.

Cheng, C. (Ed.). (1996). *Masculinities in organizations*. Thousand Oaks, CA: Sage.

Chetwynd, J., & Hartnett, O. (1977). *The sex role system: Psychological and sociological perspectives*. London: Routledge & K. Paul.

Chodorow, N. (1978 [1999]). *The reproduction of mothering: Psychoanalysis and the sociology of gender*. Berkeley: University of California Press.

Chodorow, N. (1998). *Feminism and psychoanalytic theory*. Cambridge: Polity Press.

Choi, P.Y. (2000). *Femininity and the physically active woman*. London: Routledge.

Christensen, M., Jansson, A., & Christensen, C. (Eds.). (2011). *Online territories: Globalization, mediated practice, and social space*. New York: Peter Lang.

Chuang, J.A. (2010). Achieving accountability for migrant domestic worker abuse. *North Carolina Law Review, 88*, 1627.

Ciabattari, T. (2001). Changes in men's conservative gender ideologies: Cohort and period influences. *Gender & Society, 15*(4), 574–91.

Clare, A. (2000). *On men: Masculinity in crisis*. London: Chatto & Windus.

Clare, E. (1999). *Exile and pride: Disability, queerness and liberation*. Cambridge, MA: South End Press.

Clarke, J., & Critcher, C. (1985). *The devil makes work: Leisure in capitalist Britain*. London: Macmillan.

Clatterbaugh, K. (1990). *Contemporary perspectives on masculinity: Men, women, and politics in contemporary society*. Boulder, CO: Westview Press.

Coad, D. (2008). *The metrosexual: Gender, sexuality, and sport*. Albany, NY: SUNY Press.

Cobble, D.S. (2004). *The other women's movement: Workplace justice and social rights in modern America*. Princeton, NJ: Princeton University Press.

Cockburn, C. (1983). *Brothers: Male dominance and technological change*. London: Pluto Press.

Cockburn, C. (2007). *From where we stand: War, women's activism and feminist analysis*. London: Zed Books.

Cohen, G.L. (Ed.). (1993). *Women in sport: Issues and controversies*. New York: Sage.

Cohen, J.E., & Bloom, D.E. (2005). Cultivating minds. *Finance and Development, 42*(2). Retrieved from www.imf.org/external/pubs

Cohen, J.H., & Sirkeci, I. (2011). *Cultures of migration: The global nature of contemporary mobility*. Dallas: University of Texas Press.

Cohen, M.G., & Brodie, J. (Eds.). (2007). *Remapping gender in the new global order*. London: Routledge.

Cole, E., & Daniel, J.H. (Eds.). (2005). *Featuring females: Feminist analyses of media*. Washington: American Psychological Association.

Coles, R.L. (2009). *The best kept secret: Single black fathers*. Lanham, MD: Rowman & Littlefield.

Collard, J., & Reynold, C. (2004). *Leadership, gender and culture in education: Male and female perspectives*. Buckingham, UK: Open University Press.

Collier, R. (1998). *Masculinities, crime and criminology: Men, heterosexuality and the criminal(ised) other*. London: Sage.

Collier-Thomas, B., & Franklin, V.P. (Eds.). (2001). *Sisters in the struggle: African-American women in the civil rights–black power movement*. New York: New York University Press.

Collins, M.A., Hagenauer, G., & Heller, S. (2004). *Men's adventure magazines in postwar America: The Rich Oberg collection*. Koln, Germany: Taschen.

Collinson, D., & Hearn, J. (1996). *Men as managers, managers as men*. London: Sage.

Collinson, D., & Hearn, J. (2001 [1993]). Naming men as men: Implications for work, organization and management. In S.M. Whitehead & F.J. Barrett (Eds.), *The masculinities reader*. Cambridge: Polity.

Collinson, D., Knights, D., & Collinson, M. (1990). *Managing to discriminate*. New York: Routledge.

Connell, R.W. (1983). *Which way is up? Essays on class, sex and culture*. Sydney: Allen & Unwin.

Connell, R.W. (1987). *Gender and power*. Cambridge: Polity.

Connell, R.W. (1994). Psychoanalysis on masculinity. In H. Brod & M. Kaufman (Eds.), *Theorizing masculinities*. Thousand Oaks, CA: Sage.

Connell, R.W. (1995 [2003]). *Masculinities*. Cambridge: Polity Press.

Connell, R.W. (1998). Masculinities and globalization. *Men and Masculinities, 1*(1), 3–23.

Connell, R.W. (2000). *The men and the boys*. Cambridge: Polity.

Connell, R.W. (2005). Change among the gatekeepers: Men, masculinities, and gender equality in the global arena. *Signs: Journal of Women in Culture and Society, 30*(3), 1801–25.

Connell, R.W. (2006). Masculinities and globalization. In: S.M. Whitehead (Ed.), *Men and masculinities: Critical concepts in sociology* (Vol. 1). London: Routledge.

Connell, R.W., & Messerschmidt, J.W. (2005). Hegemonic masculinity: Rethinking the concept. *Gender & Society, 19*(6), 829–59.

Connell, R.W., & Wood, J. (2005). Globalization and Business Masculinities. *Men and Masculinities, 7*(4), 347–64.

Connolly, K. (2007, June 1). Educated women leave East German men behind. *The Guardian.*

Connolly, P. (2004). *Boys and schooling in the early years.* London: Routledge/Falmer.

Connor, D.J. (2008). *Urban narratives: Portraits in progress: Life at the intersections of learning disability, race and social class.* New York: Peter Lang.

Corber, R.J., & Valocchi, S. (Eds.). (2003). *Queer studies: An interdisciplinary reader.* Oxford: Blackwell.

Cornell, D.L. (1992). Gender, sex and equivalent rights. In J. Butler & J.W. Scott (Eds.), *Feminists theorize the political.* Thousand Oaks, CA: Sage.

Cornell, S.E., & Hartmann, D. (2006). *Ethnicity and race: Making identities in a changing world.* Thousand Oaks, CA: Pine Forge Press.

Correll, S. (2001). Gender and the career choice process. *American Journal of Sociology, 106*(6), 1691–730.

Costa, L.M., & Matzner, A.J. (2007). *Male bodies, women's souls: Personal narratives of Thailand's transgendered youth.* New York: Haworth Press.

Costa, M.D., & James, S. (1972). *The power of women and the subversion of the community.* Bristol: Falling Wall Press.

Cotter, A.M. (2004). *Gender injustice: An international comparative analysis of equality in employment.* Aldershot, UK: Ashgate.

Coughlin, L., Wingard, E., & Hollihan, K. (Eds.). (2005). *Enlightened power: How women are transforming the practice of leadership.* New York: Pfeiffer Wiley.

Courtney, W.H. (2006). Constructions of masculinity and their influence on men's well-being: A theory of gender and health. In S. Whitehead (Ed.), *Men and masculinities: Critical concepts in sociology* (Vol. 3). London: Routledge.

Coward, R. (1993). *Our treacherous hearts: Why women let men get their way.* London: Faber & Faber.

Cowburn, L. (2003). *Love* (1st Edn). Milwaukee, WI: Marquette University Press.

Craib, I. (2001). *Psychoanalysis: A critical introduction.* Cambridge: Polity.

Craig, S. (Ed.). (1992). *Men, masculinity and the media.* New York: Sage.

Creed, B. (1993). *The monstrous-feminine: Film, feminism, psychoanalysis.* New York: Routledge.

Creedon, P.J. (1994). *Women, media and sport: Challenging gender values.* London: Sage.

Creighton, C. (1999). The rise and decline of the "male breadwinner family" in Britain. *Cambridge Journal of Economics, 23,* 519–41.

Crenshaw, K. (1989). Demarginalizing the intersection of race and sex: A black feminist critique of antidiscrimination doctrine, feminist theory and antiracist politics. *University of Chicago Legal Forum.*

Crewe, B. (2003). *Representing men: Cultural production and producers in the men's magazine market.* Oxford: Berg.

Crompton, R. (1987). Gender, status and professionalism. *Sociology, 21,* 413–28.

Crompton, R. (1994). Women and the "service class." In R. Crompton & M. Mann (Eds.), *Gender and Stratification.* Cambridge: Polity.

Crompton, R., & Mann, M. (1994). *Gender and stratification.* Cambridge: Polity.

Cudd, A.E., & Andreasen, R.O. (Eds.). (2005). *Feminist theory: A philosophical anthology.* Oxford: Blackwell.

Cupitt, D. (1985). *The sea of faith: Christianity in change.* London: BBC.

Dabbs, J.M., Frady, R.L., Carr, T.S., & Besch, N.F. (1987). Saliva testosterone and criminal violence in young adult prison inmates. *Psychosomatic Medicine, 49,* 174–82.

Daly, M. (1978). *Gyn/ecology: The metaethics of radical feminism.* Boston: Boston Beacon Press.

Daly, M. (1985). *Church and the second sex.* Boston: Beacon.

Danet, B. (1998). Text as mask: Gender, play, and performance on the Internet. In S.G. Jones (Ed.), *Cybersociety 2.0: Revisiting computer-mediated communication and community.* Thousand Oaks, CA: Sage.

D'Angelo, R., & Douglas, H. (2008). *Race and ethnicity: Taking sides: Clashing views of race and ethnicity*. New York: McGraw-Hill.

David, D.S., & Brannon, R. (Eds.). (1976). *The male sex role*. London: Addison-Wesley.

David, M. (2002). From Keighley to Keele: Personal reflections on a circuitous journey through education, family, feminism and policy sociology. *British Journal of Sociology of Education, 23*(2), 249–69.

David, M. (2003). *Personal and political: Feminism, sociology and family lives*. Stoke-on-Trent, UK: Trentham Books.

David, M., & Woodward, D. (1997). *Negotiating the glass ceiling: Careers of senior women in the academic world*. London: Routledge.

Davies, B. (1989). *Frogs and snails and feminist tails*. London: Allen & Unwin.

Davies, B. (2000). *A body of writing: 1990–1999*. New York: AltaMira Press.

Davies, B. (Ed.). (2008). *Judith Butler in conversation: Analysing the texts and talk of everyday life*. New York: Routledge.

Davies, B., & Banks, C. (1995). The gender trap: A feminist poststructuralist analysis of primary school children's talk about gender. In J. Holland & M. Blair (with S. Sheldon) (Eds.), *Debates and issues in feminist research and pedagogy*. Clevedon, UK: Multilingual Matters.

Davies, D. (1996). The sociology of professions and the profession of gender. *Sociology, 30*(4), 661–78.

Davies, K. (1990). *Women, time and the weaving of the strands of everyday life*. Aldershot, UK: Avebury.

Davis, K. (1995). *Reshaping the female body: The dilemma of cosmetic surgery*. New York: Routledge.

Davis, K., Leijenaar, M., & Oldersma, J. (Eds.). (1991). *The gender of power*. London: Sage.

Dawkins, R. (2007) *The God delusion*. London: Black Swan.

Dawson, G. (1994). *Soldier heroes: British adventure, empire and the imagining of masculinity*. London: Routledge.

Dayal, S. (2007). *Resisting modernity: Counternarratives of nation and masculinity in pre-independence India*. Newcastle, UK: Cambridge Scholars.

Deal, T.E., & Kennedy, A.A. (2000). *Corporate cultures*. New York: Perseus Books.

de Beauvoir, S. (1973 [1954]). *The second sex* (E.M. Parshley, Trans. & Ed.). New York: Vintage.

Deem, R. (1982). Women, leisure and inequality. *Leisure Studies, 1*, 29–46.

Deem, R. (1986). *All work and no play*. Milton Keynes, UK: Open University Press.

Deem, R. (1996). Border territories: A journey through sociology, education and women's studies. *British Journal of Sociology of Education, 7*(1), 5–19.

de Four, L.C., & Williams, G. (2002). *Gender management: Cases from the Caribbean*. Kingston: I. Randle.

De Francisco, V.P., & Palczewski, C.H. (2007). *Communicating gender diversity: A critical approach*. Los Angeles: Sage.

Degado, R., & Stefancic, J. (Eds.). (2001). Critical race theory: An introduction. New York: York University Press.

DeKeseredy, W.S., & Schwartz, M.D. (2004). Separation/divorce sexual assault: The current state of social scientific knowledge. *Aggression and Violent Behavior, 9*(6), 675–91.

Deleuze, G. (1997). Desire and pleasure. In A. Davidson (Ed.), *Foucault and his Interlocutors*. Chicago: University of Chicago Press.

Deleuze, G., & Guattari, F. (1977). *Anti-Oedipus* (R. Hurley, M. Seem, & H.R. Lane, Trans.). Minneapolis: University of Minnesota Press.

Deleuze, G., & Guattari, F. (1988 [1980]). *A thousand plateaus* (B. Massumi, Trans.). London: Athlone.

Demetriou, D.Z. (2001). Connell's concept of hegemonic masculinity: A critique. *Theory and Society, 30*(3), 337–61.

Dent, M., & Whitehead, S. (Eds.). (2001). *Managing professional identities: Knowledge, performativity and the "new" professional*. London: Routledge.

Denzin, N.K. (2001). *Interpretive interactionism*. (2nd Edn). Thousand Oaks, CA: Sage.

Derne, S. (2002). Globalization and the reconstitution of local gender arrangements. *Men and Masculinities, 5*(2), 144–64.

Derrida, J. (1967 [1972]). *Of grammatology*. London: John Hopkins University Press.

Derrida, J. (1990). Some statements and truisms about neologisms, newisms, positisms, parasitisms, and other small seismisms (A. Tomiche, Trans.). In D. Carroll (Ed.), *The states of "theory": History, art, and critical discourse*. New York: Columbia University Press.

DeSalvo, F.J., & Zurcher, L.A. (1984). Defensive and supportive parental communication in a discipline situation. *Journal of Psychology, 117*, 7–17.

Desmarais, S., Gugula, S., & Wood, E. (2002). The impact of parenting experience on gender stereotyped toy play of children. *Sex Roles, 47*, 39–49.

de Spinoza, B. (1951). On the improvement of understanding/The Ethics/Correspondence. (R.H.M. Elwes, Trans.). New York: Dover.

De Tona, C. (2004). "I remember when years ago in Italy": Nine Italian women in Dublin tell the diaspora. *Women's Studies International Forum, 27*, 315–34.

Devi, U.S., Widding Isaksen, L., & Hochschild, A.R. (2010). La crise mondiale du care: Point de vue de la mère et de l'enfant (Veronique Perry, Trans.). In J. Falquet, H. Hirata, D. Kergoat, B. Labari, N. Le Feuvre, & F. Sow (Eds.), *Le sexe de la mondialisation: Genre, classe, race et nouvelle division du travail*. Paris: Les Presses de Science Po.

Devor, H. (1989). *Gender blending: Confronting the limits of a duality*. Indiana: Indiana University Press.

Dewey, J. (1953). *Democracy and education: An introduction to the philosophy of education*. Macmillan: New York.

Dilman, I. (1998). *Love: Its forms, dimensions, and paradoxes*. New York: Palgrave.

Dines, G., & Humez, J.M. (Eds.). (1995). *Gender, race, and class in media: A text reader* (1st Edn). Los Angeles: Sage.

Dinnerstein, D. (1976). *The mermaid and the minotaur: Sexual arrangements and the human malaise*. New York: Harper & Row.

Dobash, R.E., & Dobash, R.P. (1992). *Women, violence and social change*. London: Routledge.

Dobash, R.E., Dobash, R.P, Cavanagh, K., & Lewis, R. (2000). *Changing violent men*. London: Sage.

Dolan, J. (1993). *Presence and desire: Essays on gender, sexuality, performance*. Ann Arbor: University of Michigan Press.

Domash, M., & Seager, J. (2001). *Putting women in place*. New York: Guildford Press.

Donald, R.R. (2001). Masculinity and machismo in Hollywood's war films. In S.M. Whitehead & F.J. Barrett (Eds.), *The masculinities reader*. Cambridge: Polity.

Donaldson, M. (1993). What is hegemonic masculinity? *Theory and Society, 22*, 643–57.

Dougary, G. (2007, September 25). Yes, we are bovvered. *Timesonline*. Retrieved from http://women.timesonline.co.uk/tol/life_and_style/women/article2523264.ece

Dowling, C. (2001). *The frailty myth: Redefining the physical potential of women and girls*. New York: Random House.

Doyle, A. (2006, December 11). In epochal shift, half humanity to become urban. *Reuters*.

Doyle, J. (2007a). Historicising surgery: Gender, sex and the surgical imaginary. *Social Semiotics, 17*(3), 341–59.

Doyle, J. (2007b). Anatomy of the womb: Imag(in) ing reproduction in the discourse of surgery. *Women: A Cultural Review, 17*(3), 310–24.

Dozier, R. (2005). Beards, breasts, and bodies doing sex in a gendered world. *Gender & Society, 19*(3), 297–316.

Dreeben, R. (1968). *On what is learned in school*. Boston: Addison-Wesley.

Dreidger, D., Feika, I., & Batres, E. (Eds.). (1996). *Across borders: Women with disabilities working together*. Charlottetown, PEI: Council of Canadians with Disabilities Gynergy Books.

Driedger, L. (1996). *Multi-ethnic Canada: Identities and inequalities*. New York: Oxford University Press.

Drummond, M.J.N. (2005). Men's bodies: Listening to the voices of young gay men. *Men and Masculinities, 7*(3), 270–90.

Dufur, M.J., & Linford, M.K. (2010). Title IX: Consequences for gender relations in sport. *Sociology Compass, 4*(9), 732–48.

Du Gay, P. (1996). *Consumption and identity at work.* London: Sage.

Dugger, K. (1998). Social location and gender role attitudes: A comparison of black and white women. *Gender & Society, 2*(4), 425–48.

Dumitrica, D., & Gaden, G. (2009). Knee-high boots and six-pack abs: Autoethnographic reflections on gender and technology in Second Life. *Journal of Virtual Worlds Research, 1*(3), 1–23.

Durham, M.G. (2004). Constructing the "new ethnicities": media, sexuality, and diaspora identity in the lives of South Asian immigrant girls. *Critical Studies in Media Communication, 21*(2), 140–61.

Durkheim, E. (1933). *The division of labour in society.* New York: Free Press.

Durkheim, E. (1957). *Professional ethics and civic morals.* London: Routledge & Kegan Paul.

Dworkin, A. (1981). *Pornography: Men possessing women.* New York: The Women's Press.

Dworkin, A. (2006). *Intercourse.* New York: Basic Books.

Dwyer, C. (2004). Feminist geographies: Intersections of space and gender. In A. Rogers & H.A. Viles (Eds.), *The Student's Companion to Geography.* Oxford: Blackwell.

Eagleton, T. (1983). *Literary theory: An introduction.* Oxford: Blackwell.

Eagleton, T. (1987, February 20). Awakening from modernity. *Times Literary Supplement.*

Earle, D.M. (2009). *All man! Hemingway, 1950s men's magazines, and the masculine persona.* Kent, OH: Kent State University Press.

Edgell, S. (2005). *The sociology of work: Continuity and change in paid and unpaid work.* London: Sage.

Edley, N., & Wetherall, M. (1995). *Men in perspective: Practice, power and identity.* London: PrenticeHall/Harvester Wheatsheaf.

Edmond, W., & Fleming, S. (Eds.). (1975). *All work and no pay.* London: Power of Women Collective & Falling Wall Press.

Edwards, L. (2008). *Gender, politics and democracy: Women's suffrage in China.* Stanford, CA: Stanford University Press.

Edwards, S. (1989). *Policing domestic violence.* London: Sage.

Edwards, T. (1997). *Men in the mirror: Men's fashion, masculinity and consumer society.* London: Cassell.

Edwards, T. (1998). Queer fears: Against the cultural turn. *Sexualities, 1*(4), 471–81.

Edwardson, R. (2008). *Canadian content: Culture and the quest for nationhood.* Toronto: University of Toronto Press.

Ehrankranz, J., Bliss, E., & Sheard, M.H. (1974). Plasma testosterone: Correlation with aggressive behaviour and social dominance in men. *Psychosomatic Medicine, 36,* 469–75.

Ehrenreich, B. (1983). *The hearts of men: American dreams and the flight from commitment.* London: Pluto Press.

Ehrenreich, B., & Hotchschild, A.R. (Eds.). (2004). Global woman: Nannies, maids, and sex workers in the new economy. New York: Metropolitan/Owl Books.

Eichenbaum, L., & Orbach, S. (1985). *Understanding women.* Harmonsdworth: Penguin.

Eisenstein, H., & Jardine, A. (1985). *The future of difference.* New Brunswick, NJ: Rutgers University Press.

Eisenstein, Z. (1986). *The radical future of liberal feminism.* Boston: Northeastern University Press.

Eisenstein, Z. (2004) *Against empire: Feminisms, racism and the west.* London: Zed Books.

Eisenstein, Z. (2007). *Sexual decoys: Gender, race and war in imperial democracy.* London: Spinifex Press.

Elam, D. (1994). *Feminism and deconstructionism.* New York: Psychology Press.

El-Azhary Sonbol, A. (2003). *Women of Jordan: Islam, labor, & the law* (1st Edn). Syracuse, NY: Syracuse University Press.

El Guindi, F. (1999). *Veil: Modesty, privacy and resistance.* Oxford: Berg.

Elias, M. (1981). Serum cortisol, testosterone, and testosterone binding globulin response to competitive fighting in human males. *Aggressive Behaviour, 7,* 215–24.

Ellen, B. (2007a, April 29). Facials, manicures, emotional outbursts… Is metrosexual man more of a woman than you? *The Observer.*

Ellen, B. (2007b, May 6). Bemoaning the rise of "metrosexual man." *The Nation*.

Ellingsaeter, A.L., & Leira, A. (Eds.). (2006). *Politicising parenthood in Scandinavia: Gender relations in welfare states*. Bristol: Policy Press.

Ellingson, S. (2008). The rise of megachurches and changes in religious culture: Review article. *Sociology Compass*, 3(1), 16–30.

Elliott, A. (2002). *Psychoanalytic theory: An introduction*. Basingstoke: Palgrave.

El-Saadawi, N. (1997). *The Nawal El-Saadawi reader*. London: Zed Books.

Elshtain, J.B. (1981). *Public man, private woman*. Princeton, NJ: Princeton University Press.

El-Tayeb, F. (2011). *European others: Queering ethnicity in postnational Europe*. Minneapolis: University of Minnesota Press.

Ely, R.J., Scully, M.A., & Foldy, E.G. (Eds.). (2003). *Reader in gender, work and organization*. Oxford: Blackwell.

Epstein, B. (2001). What happened to the women's movement? *Monthly Review*, 53(1). Retrieved from www.monthlyreview.org/0501epstein.htm

Epstein, B. (2006). Real boys don't work: "Underachievement," masculinity and the harassment of "sissies." In S.M. Whitehead (Ed.), *Men and masculinities: Critical concepts in sociology* (Vol. II). Cambridge: Polity.

Epstein, D., Elwood, J., Hey, V., & Maw, J. (Eds.). (1998). *Failing boys? Issues in gender and achievement*. Buckingham, UK: Open University Press.

Erben, M. (Ed.). (1998). *Biography and education: A reader*. London: Falmer Press.

Erikson, T.H. (2007). *Globalization: The key concepts*. Oxford: Berg.

Esman, M.J. (2009). *Diasporas in the contemporary world*. Cambridge: Polity.

European Commission (2007). *Report on equality between women and men—2007*. Luxembourg: European Commission.

Euro RSCG Worldwide (2003a). *Prosumer pulse: The future of men USA*.

Euro RSCG Worldwide (2003b). *Prosumer pulse: The future of men UK*.

Evans, M. (2003). *Love: An unromantic discussion*. Cambridge: Polity.

Evans, S. (1980). *Personal politics: The roots of women's liberation in the civil rights movement and the new left*. New York: Vintage.

Evans, T., & Wallace, P. (2008). A prison within a prison? The masculinity narratives of male prisoners. *Men and masculinities*, 10(4), 484–507.

Eviota, E.U. (1992). *The political economy of gender: Women and the sexual division of labour in the Philippines*. London: Zed Books.

Fabian, K. (2009). *Contemporary women's movements in Hungary: Globalization, democracy, and gender equality*. Washington, DC: Woodrow Wilson Press.

FAHCSIA. (2010). *Review of the equal opportunity for women in the workplace act 1999 consultation report*. Retrieved from http://www.fahcsia.gov.au/sa/women/pubs/general/eowa_kpmg_rpt/Documents/EOWW_Act_Consultation_rpt.pdf

Faludi, S. (1999). *Stiffed: The betrayal of modern man*. London: Chatto & Windus.

Fanon, F. (1963). *The wretched of the Earth* (C. Farrington, Trans.). New York: Grove Press.

Fanon, F. (1965). *A dying colonialism* (H. Chevalier, Trans.). New York: Grove Press.

Fanon, F. (1967). *Towards the African revolution: Political essays* (H. Chevalier, Trans.). New York: Monthly Review Press.

Fanon, F. (1968). *The wretched of the earth*. Harmondsworth, UK: Penguin Books.

Fanon, F. (1986 [1968]). *Black skin, white masks* (C. Lam Markmann, Trans.). London: Pluto Press.

Farrell, W. (1993). *The myth of male power: Why men are the disposable sex*. New York: Simon & Schuster.

Fast, I. (1998). Developments in gender identity: The original matrix. In N. Burke (Ed.), *Gender and envy*. London: Routledge.

Fausto-Sterling, A. (2000). *Sexing the body: Gender politics and the construction of sexuality* (1st Edn). New York: Basic Books.

Featherstone, M. (1991). *Consumer culture and postmodernism*. London: Sage.

Featherstone, M., & Burrows, R. (Eds.). (1996). *Cyberspace/cyberbodies/cyberpunk*. London: Sage.

Fein, R. (1978). Research on fathering: Social policy and an emergent perspective. *Journal of Social Issues*, 1(34), 122–35.

Ferber, A.L. (1998). *White man falling: Race, gender, and white supremacy.* Lanham, MD: Rowman & Littlefield.

Ferguson, H. (2004). The sublime and the subliminal: Modern identities and the aesthetics of combat. *Theory, Culture & Society, 31*(3), 1–33.

Ferree, M.M., Lorber, J., & Hess, B.B. (Eds.). (1999). *Revisioning gender.* New York: Sage.

Fielding, N. (1994). Cop canteen culture. In T. Newburn & E.A. Stanko (Eds.), *Just boys doing business? Men, masculinities and crime.* London: Routledge.

Fiese, B.H., & Skillman, G. (2000). Gender differences in family stories: Moderating influence of parent gender role and child gender. *Sex Roles, 43*(5/6), 267–83.

Fine, C. (2010). *Delusions of gender: How our minds, society, and neurosexism create difference.* New York: W.W. Norton.

Fine, G.A. (2003). *Shared fantasy: Role playing games as social worlds.* Chicago: University of Chicago Press.

Fine, M. (1994). Working the hyphens: Reinventing the self and other in qualitative research. In N. Denzin & Y. Lincoln (Eds.), *Handbook of qualitative research* (pp. 70–82). Newbury Park, CA: Sage.

Fine, M., & Kuriloff, P. (2006). Forging and performing masculine identities within social spaces: Boys and men negotiating the crucible of dominant cultural representations at the intersection of class, race, ethnicity, and sexuality. *Men and Masculinities, 8*(3), 257–61.

Fineman, S. (Ed.). (1993). *Emotion in organization.* London: Sage.

Firestone, R.W., Firestone, L.A., & Catlett, J. (2006). *Sex and love in intimate relationships.* Washington, DC: American Psychological Association.

Fisher, L. (2004). State of the art: Multiculturalism, gender and cultural identities. *European Journal of Women's Studies, 11*(1), 111–19.

Fisk, J. (1989a). *Understanding popular culture.* London: Unwin Hyman.

Fisk, J. (1998b). *Reading the popular.* London: Unwin Hyman.

Flax, J. (1990). Postmodernism and gender relations in feminist theory. In L. Nicholson (Ed.), *Feminism/postmodernism.* London: Routledge.

Fletcher, J.K. (1999). *Disappearing acts: Gender, power and relational practice.* Cambridge, MA: MIT Press.

Flood, M. (2004). Backlash: Angry men's movements. In S.E. Rossi (Ed.), *The battle and backlash rage on.* New York: Xlibris Corps.

Fominaya, C.F. (2010a). Collective identity in social movements: Central concepts and debates. *Sociology Compass, 4*(6), 393–404.

Fominaya, C.F. (2010b). Creating cohesion from diversity: The challenge of collective identity formation in the global justice movement. *Sociological Inquiry, 80*(3), 377–404.

Ford, K.A. (2008). Gazing into a distorted looking glass: Masculinity, femininity, appearance ideals and the black body. *Sociology Compass, 2*(3), 1096–114.

Forouzan, E., & Van Gijseghem, H. (2004). Recension des ecrits sur l'impact des contacts sexuels precoces sur les hommes [Literature review on the impact of early sexual contacts on men]. *Canadian Psychology/Psychologie Canadienne, 15*(1), 59–82.

Forrester, V. (1999). *The Economic Horror.* Cambridge: Polity.

Foucault, M. (1972). *The archeology of knowledge* (S. Smith, Trans.). London: Tavistock.

Foucault, M. (1978). *The History of Sexuality: Volume 1: An Introduction* (R. Hurley, Trans.). Harmondsworth, UK: Penguin.

Foucault, M. (1979). *Discipline and Punish: The Birth of the Prison* (A. Sheridan, Trans.). New York: Vintage Books.

Foucault, M. (1980). *Power/knowledge: Selected interviews and other writings, 1972–1977* (C. Gordon, Ed.). New York: Pantheon Press.

Foucault, M. (1983). The subject and power. In H. Dreyfus & P. Rabinow (Eds.), *Michel Foucault: Beyond structuralism and hermeneutics.* Chicago: University of Chicago Press.

Foucault, M. (1984). Nietzsche, genealogy, history. In P. Rabinow (Ed.), *The Foucault reader.* London: Penguin.

Foucault, M. (1988). Technologies of self. In L.H. Martin, J. Gutman, & P. Hutton (Eds.), *Technologies of the self: A seminar with Michel Foucault*. London: Tavistock.

Foucault, M. (1991). On the genealogy of ethics: An overview of work in progress. In P. Rabinow (Ed.), *The Foucault reader*. London: Penguin.

Foucault, M. (1994). *Power: The essential works* (Vol. 3) (J.D. Faubion, Ed.). London: Allen Lane/Penguin.

Foucault, M. (2000). *Boys, girls and achievement*. London: Routledge/Falmer.

Foucault, M. (2002). Relativism, realism, and feminism: An analysis of some theoretical tensions in research on gender identity. *Journal of Gender Studies, 11*(1), 39–54.

Foucault, M. (2003). *The subject and power: The essential Foucault* (P. Rabinow & N. Rose, Eds.). New York: New Press.

Francis, B. (1998). *Power plays*. Stoke on Trent, UK: Trentham Books.

Francis, B., & Skelton, C. (Eds.). (2001). *Investigating Gender: Contemporary Perspectives in Education*. Buckingham, UK: Open University Press.

Francis, B., & Skelton, C. (Eds.). (2005). *Reassessing gender and achievement: Questioning contemporary key debates*. London: Routledge.

Frank, A.W. (1991). For a sociology of the body: An analytical overview. In M. Featherstone, M. Hepworth, & B.S. Turner (Eds.), *The Body*. London: Sage.

Franklin, C.W., II (1992). "Hey, home-yo, bro": Friendship among black men. In P.M. Nardi (Ed.), *Men's friendships*. Thousand Oaks, CA: Sage.

Franks, S. (1999). *Having none of it: Women, men and the future of work*. London: Granta Books.

Fraser, N. (1989). *Unruly practices: Power, discourse and gender in contemporary social theory*. Oxford: Blackwell.

Freedman, E., & Marshall, J. (2004). *Issues of gender*. New York: Pearson.

Freeman, J. (1975). *The politics of women's liberation*. New York: David McKay.

Freeman, J. (Ed.). (1983). *Social movements in the sixties and seventies*. New York: Longman.

Freud, S. (1912). *Selected papers on hysteria and other psychoneuroses* (A.A. Brill, Trans.). New York: The Journal of Nervous and Mental Disease.

Freud, S. (1937). Analysis terminable and interminable. In S. Freud, *The Standard Edition of the Complete Psychological Works of Sigmund Freud* (Vol. 23). London: Hogarth.

Freud, S. (1974). Some psychical consequences of the anatomical distinction between the sexes. In J. Strachey (Ed. & Trans.), *The Standard Edition of the Complete Psychological Works of Sigmund Freud* (Vol. 19.) London: Hogarth Press.

Freud, S. (1974). *The Standard Edition of the Complete Psychological Works* (Vols. 1–24) (J. Strachey (with Anna Freud), Ed. & Trans.). London: Hogarth.

Freud, S. (1991). *On sexuality: Three essays on the theory of sexuality and other works*. London: Penguin.

Friedan, B. (1974). *The feminine mystique*. New York: Dell.

Friedan, B. (1981). *The second stage*. New York: Summit Books.

Friedman, J. (1994). *Cultural identity and global process*. London: Sage.

Frosh, S., Phoenix, A., & Pattman, R. (2002). *Young masculinities*. London: Palgrave.

Frost, L. (2005). Theorizing the young woman in the body. *Body & Society, 11*(1) 63–85.

Frost, M. (n.d.). Frost's Meditations: Metrosexual. Retrieved from www.martinfrost.ws/htmlfiles/mar2008/metrosexual1.html

Frystak, S. (2010). Our minds on freedom: Women and the struggle for black equality in Louisiana, 1924–1967. Baton Rouge: Louisiana State University Press.

Fudge, J. (2011). Global care chains, employment agencies, and the conundrum of jurisdiction: Decent work for domestic workers in Canada. *Canadian Journal of Women and the Law, 23*(1), 235–64.

Fujioka, C. (2007, June 19). Japanese women lag in boardrooms, politics: Report. *Reuters*.

Fukuyama, F. (1993). *The end of history and the last man*. New York: Penguin.

Fukuyama, F. (2007, August). On the "clash of civilisations." *American interest/global viewpoint.* Tribune Media Services.

Gabriel, Y. (1999). *Organizations in depth: A psychoanalysis of organizations.* London: Sage.

Gabriel, Y., Fineman, S., & Sims, D. (2000). *Organizing and organizations: An Introduction.* London: Sage.

Gackenbach, J. (Ed.). (2007). *Psychology and the Internet: Intrapersonal, interpersonal, and transpersonal implications.* Amsterdam: Academic Press.

Galbraith, K. (Ed.). (2002). *Globalization: Making sense of an integrated world.* New York: Bloomberg Press.

Gallagher, S.K., & Smith, C. (1999). Symbolic traditionalism and pragmatic egalitarianism: Contemporary evangelicals, families, and gender. *Gender and Society, 13,* 211–33.

Gammage, S. (2004). Exercising exit, voice and loyalty: A gender perspective on transnationalism in Haiti. *Development and Change, 35*(4), 743–71.

Gammon, L., & Marshment, M. (Eds.). (1988). *The female gaze: Women as viewers of popular culture.* London: The Women's Press.

Gannon, L.R. (1999). *Women and aging: Transcending the myth.* London: Routledge.

Gannon, M.J., & Pillai, R. (2009). *Understanding global cultures.* Thousand Oaks, CA: Sage.

Garber, L. (2001). *Identity poetics: Race, class, and the lesbian-feminist roots of queer theory.* New York: Columbia University Press.

Garland-Thomson, R. (2005). Feminist disability studies: A review essay. *Signs: Journal of Women in Culture and Society, 30*(2), 1557–87.

Garlick, S. (2002). Melancholic secrets: Gender ambivalence and the unheimlich. *Psychoanalytic Review, 89,* 61–876.

Garlick, S. (2004). The beauty of friendship: Foucault, masculinity and the work of art. *Philosophy and Social Criticism, 28*(5), 558–77.

Gauntlett, D. (2002). *Media, gender and identity: An introduction.* London: Routledge.

Gauntlett, D. (2008). *Media, gender and identity: An introduction* (2nd Edn). London: Routledge.

Geertz, C. (1979). From the Native's point of view: On the nature of anthropological understanding. In P. Rabinow and W.M. Sullivan (Eds.), *Interpretive social science.* Berkeley: University of California Press.

Gelb, J. (2003). *Gender policies in Japan and the United States: Comparing women's movements, rights and politics.* New York: Palgrave Macmillan.

Gerami, S. (2006). Mullahs, martyrs, and men: Conceptualizing masculinity in the Islamic Republic of Iran. In S. Whitehead (Ed.), *Men and masculinities: Critical concepts in sociology* (Vol. 5). London: Routledge.

Gergen, K., & Gergen, M. (1983). Narratives of the self. In T.R. Sarbin & K.E. Scheibe (Eds.), *Studies in social identity.* New York: Praeger.

Gergen, K., & Gergen, M. (1987). Narrative and self as relationship. In L. Berkowitz (Ed.), *Advances in experimental social psychology.* New York: Academic Press.

Gergen, K., & Gergen, M. (1988). Narrative form and the construction of psychological theory. In T.R. Sarbin (Ed.), *The narrative perspective in psychology.* New York: Praeger.

Germon, J. (2009). *Gender: A genealogy of an idea.* New York: Palgrave Macmillan.

Gerontology Research Group (2012). Supercentenarians. Retrieved from www.grg.org/calment.html

Gerschick, T.J. (2000). Towards a theory of disability and gender. *Signs, 25*(4), 1263–9.

Gerson, K. (1985). *Hard Choices.* Berkeley: University of California Press.

Gerwitz, S. (2002). *The managerial school: Post-welfarism and social justice in education.* London: Routledge.

Gherardi, S. (1995). *Gender, symbolism and organizational cultures.* London: Sage.

Gherardi, S., & Poggio, B. (2007). *Gendertelling in organizations: Narratives from male-dominated environments.* Copenhagen: Copenhagen Business School Press DK.

Gibbons, J.L., Hamby, B.A., & Dennis, W.D. (1997). Researching gender-role ideologies internationally and cross-culturally. *Psychology of Women Quarterly, 21*(1), 151–70.

Giddens, A. (1976). *New rules of sociological method*. Cambridge: Polity.

Giddens, A. (1990). *The consequences of modernity*. Cambridge: Polity.

Giddens, A. (1992). *Modernity and self-identity: Self and society in the late modern age*. Cambridge: Polity.

Giddens, A. (1993). *The transformation of intimacy: Love, sexuality and eroticism in modern societies*. Cambridge: Polity.

Gilbert, R., & Gilbert, P. (1998). *Masculinity goes to school*. London: Routledge.

Gillespie, R. (2003). Childfree and feminine: Understanding the gender identity of voluntarily childfree women. *Gender & Society*, *17*(1), 122–36.

Gilligan, C. (1982). *In a different voice*. Cambridge, MA: Harvard University Press.

Gillis, S., Howie, G., & Munford, R. (2007). *Third wave feminism: A critical exploration*. London: Palgrave Macmillan.

Gilmore, D. (1990). *Manhood in the making: Cultural concepts of masculinity*. New Haven, CT: Yale University Press.

Gilroy, P. (1990). The end of anti-racism. *New Community*, *17*(1), 71–83.

Gilroy, P. (1993). *Black Atlantic: Modernity and double consciousness*. London: Verso.

Giordano, P.C. (2010). *Legacies of crime: A follow-up of the children of highly delinquent girls and boys*. New York: Cambridge University Press.

Goering, S. (2002). Beyond the medical model? Disability, formal justice, and the exception for the "profoundly impaired." *Kennedy Institute of Ethics Journal*, *12*(4), 373–88.

Goffman, E. (1971). *Relations in public: Microstudies of the public order*. New York: Basic Books.

Goffman, E. (1972). *Interactions ritual: Essays on face-to-face behaviour*. Harmondsworth, UK: Penguin Books.

Goffman, I. (1959). *The presentation of self in everyday life*. Harmondsworth, UK: Penguin.

Goffman, I. (1961). *Asylums*. Harmondsworth, UK: Penguin.

Golay, A. (2007). Féminisme et postcolonialisme: De Beauvoir, Fanon et la guerre d'Algérie. *International Journal of Francophone Studies*, *10*(3), 407–24.

Goldin, L.R. (Ed.). (1999). *Identities on the move: Transnational processes in North America and the Caribbean basin*. New York: University of Albany Press.

Goldman, J.D., & Goldman, R.J. (1983). Children's perceptions of parents and their roles: A cross-national study of Australia, England, North America and Sweden. *Sex Roles*, *9*(7), 791–812.

Goldstein, J.H. (1989). Beliefs about human aggression. In J. Groebel & R.A. Hinde (Eds.), *Aggression and war: Their biological and social bases*. Cambridge: Cambridge University Press.

Goldstein, L. (Ed.). (1997). *The male body: Features, destinies, exposures*. Michigan: Michigan University Press.

Goodchild, P. (1996). *Deleuze and Guattari: An introduction to the politics of desire*. London: Sage.

Goodley, D., & Lawthom, R. (Eds.). (2005). *Disability and psychology: Critical introductions and reflections*. London: Palgrave.

Gorz, A. (1985). *Paths to paradise*. London: Pluto.

Gorz, A. (1999). *Reclaiming Work: Beyond the work-based society*. Cambridge: Polity.

Gottschalk, L. (2003). Same-sex sexuality and childhood gender non-conformity: A spurious connection. *Journal of Gender Studies*, *12*(1), 35–50.

Graham, S. (2004). It's like one of those puzzles: Conceptualising gender among Bugis. *Journal of Gender Studies*, *13*(2), 107–16.

Gramsci, A. (1971). *Selections from prison notebooks*. London: Lawrence & Wishart.

Green, E., Hebron, S., & Woodward, D. (1990). *Women's leisure, what leisure?* London: Macmillan.

Greer, G. (1999). *The female eunuch*. London: Harper Collins.

Grekul, J. (2008). Sterilization in Alberta, 1928–1972: Gender matters. *Canadian Review of Sociology*, *45*(3), 247–66.

Grewal, I. (2005). Transnational America: Feminisms, diasporas, neoliberalisms. Durham NC: Duke University Press.

Grey, S., & Sawyer, M. (2011). *Women's movements: Flourishing or in abeyance?* London: Routledge.

Griffiths, I.J. (2011, March 28). Older women unhappy over their portrayal in films, survey shows. *The Guardian*. Retrieved from http://www.guardian.co.uk/film/2011/mar/28/women-unhappy-portrayal-films-survey

Grigg, R. (2008). *Lacan, language, and philosophy*. Albany, NY: State University of New York Press.

Grogan, S., & Richards, H. (2002). Body image: Focus groups with boys and men. *Men and Masculinities, 4*(3), 219–32.

Grönvik, L., & Söder, M. (Eds.). (2008). *Intersektionalitet och funktionshinder*. Stockholm: Gleerups.

Gross, R.M. (1993). *Buddhism after patriarchy: A feminist history, analysis, and reconstruction of Buddhism*. New York: State University of New York Press.

Grosz, E. (1990). *Jacques Lacan: A Feminist introduction*. London: Routledge.

Grue, L., & Tafjord Laerum, K. (2002). "Doing motherhood": Some experiences of mothers with physical disabilities. *Disability and Society, 17*(6), 671–83.

Grunebaum, J.O. (2003). *Friendship: Liberty, equality, and utility*. Albany: State University of New York Press.

Gubrium, J., & Holstein, J. (Eds.). (2007). *The handbook of constructionist research*. New York: Guilford.

Guggenbuhl, A. (1997). *Men, power and myths: The quest for male identity* (G.V. Hartman, Trans.). New York: Continuum.

Guidotto, N. (2007). Monsters in the closet: Biopolitics and intersexuality. *Wagadu: A Journal of Transnational Women's and Gender Studies* [Special issue on intersecting gender and disability perspectives in rethinking postcolonial identities], 4, 48–65.

Guidroz, K. (2008). Are you top or bottom? Social science answers for everyday questions about sadomasochism. *Sociology Compass, 2*(6), 1766–82.

Gullette, M.M. (2011). *Agewise: Fighting the ageism in America*. Chicago: University of Chicago Press.

Gutmann, A. (Ed.). (1994). *Multiculturalism*. Princeton, NJ: Princeton University Press.

Guttmann, A. (2004). *Sports: The first five millennia*. Massachusetts: University of Massachusetts Press.

Habermas, J. (1992). *Postmetaphysical thinking*. Cambridge: Polity Press.

Hacker, H.M. (1957). The new burdens of masculinity. *Marriage and Family Living, 3*, 227–33.

Haig-Brown, C. (2009). Decolonizing diaspora: Whose traditional land are we on? *Cultural and Pedagogical Inquiry, 1*(1), 4–21.

Halberstam, J. (1998). *Female masculinity*. Durham, NC: Duke University Press.

Halberstam, J. (2005). *In a queer time and place: Transgender bodies, subcultural lives*. New York: New York University Press.

Hall, E.J., & Rodriguez, M.S. (2003). The myth of postfeminism. *Gender & Society, 17*(6), 878–902.

Hall, T.D., & Fenelon, J.D. (2009). *Indigenous peoples and globalization: Resistance and revitalization*. Boulder, CO: Paradigm Press.

Hall, S. (1985). Signification, representation and ideology: Althusser and the post-structuralist debates. *Critical Studies in Mass Communication, 2*(2).

Hall, S. (1992). The question of cultural identity. In D. Hall & T. Held (Eds.), *Modernity and it's future* (pp. 274–316). Cambridge, UK: Polity Press.

Hall, S. (Ed.) (1997). *Representation: Cultural Representations and Signifying Practices*. London: Sage.

Hall, S. (2000). Who needs "identity"? In S. Hall & P. du Gay (Eds.), *Questions of cultural identity*. London: Sage.

Hall, S., & du Gay, P. (Eds.). (1996). *Questions of cultural identity*. London: Sage.

Hall, S., & Winlow, S. (2006). *Violent night: Urban leisure and contemporary culture*. London: Berg.

Hancock, P., & Tyler, J.T. (2001). *Work, postmodernism and organization: A critical introduction*. London: Sage.

Handy, C.B. (1995). *The empty raincoat: Making sense of the future*. London: Hutchinson.

Hanh, T.N. (1991). *Peace is every step: The path of mindfulness in everyday life*. London: Ebury Press.

Hanson, K., & Joshi, H. (Eds.). (2007). *Millennium cohort study: Second survey*. London: Institute of Education.

Harari, J.V. (Ed.). (1979). *Textual strategies: Perspectives in post-structural criticism*. London: Routledge.

Haraway, D. (1989). A manifesto for cyborgs: Science, technology, and socialist feminism in the 1980s. In E. Weed (Ed.), *Coming to terms*. New York: Routledge.

Haraway, D. (1991). *Simians, cyborgs and women: The reinvention of nature*. New York: Routledge.

Harcourt, W. (Ed.). (2000). *Women @ Internet: Creating new cultures in cyberspace*. London: Zed Books.

Hardin, M. (2002). Altering masculinities: The Spanish conquest and the evolution of the Latin American Machismo. *International Journal of Sexuality and Gender Studies*, 7(1), 1–22.

Hardin, R. (2006). *Trust*. Cambridge: Polity.

Harding, J. (1998). *Sex acts: Practices of femininity and masculinity*. London: Sage.

Harding, S. (1990). Feminism, science, and the anti-Enlightenment critiques. In L. Nicholson (Ed.), *Feminism/postmodernism*. London: Routledge.

Harding, S. (1991). *Whose science? Whose knowledge? Thinking from women's lives*. Ithaca, NY: Cornell University Press.

Harding, S.G. (Ed.). (1993). *The "racial" economy of science: Toward a democratic future*. Bloomington: Indiana University Press.

Hargreaves, J. (1994). *Sporting females: Critical issues in the history and sociology of women's sport*. London: Routledge.

Harper, C. (2007). *Intersex*. New York: Berg.

Harper, S. (2009). *Madness, power and the media: Class, gender and race in popular representations of mental distress*. Houndmills, UK: Palgrave Macmillan.

Harre, R. (1979). *Social being*. Oxford: Blackwell.

Harre, R. (1983). *Personal Being*. Oxford: Blackwell.

Harris, P. (2005, October 23). Metrosexual man bows to red-blooded ubersexuals. *The Observer*.

Harris, R.J., Firestone, J.M., & Vega, W.A. (2005). The interaction of country of origin, acculturation, and gender roles ideology on wife abuse. *Social Science Quarterly*, 86(2), 463–83.

Hartley, R.E. (1959). Sex-role pressures and the socialization of the male child. *Psychological Reports*, 5, 457–68.

Hartsock, N.C.M. (1983). The feminist standpoint: Developing the ground for a specifically feminist historical materialism. In S. Harding & M.B. Hintikka (Eds.), *Discovering reality*. Dordrecht, Netherlands: Reidel.

Hartsock, N.C.M. (1989). Masculinity, heroism, and the making of war. In A. Harris and Y. King (Eds.), *Rocking the ship of state: Toward a feminist peace politics* (pp.133–52). Boulder, CO: Westview.

Harvey, D. (1991). *The condition of postmodernity*. Oxford: Blackwell.

Haskell, M. (1987). *From reverence to rape: The treatment of women in the movies*. Chicago: University of Chicago Press.

Hatty, S.E. (2000). *Masculinities, violence, and culture*. New York: Sage.

Haywood, C., & Mac an Ghaill, M. (2003). *Men and masculinities: Theory, research and social practice*. Buckingham, UK: Open University Press.

Head, T. (2010). *It's your world, so change it: Using the power of the Internet to create social change*. Indianapolis: Pearson Education.

Healey, J.F. (2009). *Race, ethnicity, gender and class: The sociology of group conflict and change*. Thousand Oaks, CA: Pine Forge Press.

Hearn, J. (1987). *The gender of oppression: Men, masculinity and the critique of Marxism*. Brighton: Harvester.

Hearn, J. (1992). *Men in the public eye*. London: Routledge.

Hearn, J. (1998). *The violences of men*. London: Sage.

Hearn, J. (2006). From hegemonic masculinity to the hegemony of men. In S. Whitehead (Ed.), *Men and masculinities: Critical concepts in sociology* (Vol. 1). London: Routledge.

Hearn, J., & Collinson, D. (2001). Naming men as men: Implications for work, organization and management. In S.M. Whitehead and F.J. Barrett (Eds.), *The masculinities reader*. Cambridge: Polity.

Hearn, J., & Parkin, W. (2001). *Gender, sexuality and violence in organizations*. London: Sage.

Hearn, J., Sheppard, D.L., Tancred-Sheriff, P., & Burrell, G. (Eds.). (1989). *The sexuality of organization*. London: Sage.

Heasley, R. (2005). Queer masculinities of straight men: A typology. *Men and Masculinities, 7*(3), 310–20.

Hekman, S.J. (1996). *Feminist interpretations of Michael Foucalt*. University Park, PA: Pennsylvania State Press.

Hekman, S.J. (1999). *The future of differences: Truth and method in feminist theory*. Cambridge: Polity.

Hekman, S.J. (2004). *Private selves, public identities: Reconsidering identity politics*. University Park, PA: Pennsylvania State University Press.

Heilbrun, C.G. (1973). *The promise of androgyny*. New York: Alfred A. Knopf.

Held, D., McGrew, A., Goldblatt, D., & Perraton, J. (1999). *Global transformations: Politics, economics and cutlure*. Cambridge: Polity.

Helms, J.E. (1995). An update of Helms's white and people of color racial identity models. In J.G. Ponterotto, J.M. Casas, L.A. Suzuki, & C.M. Alexander (Eds.), *Handbook of multicultural counseling* (pp. 181–98). Thousand Oaks, CA: Sage.

Henderson, J., Briere, J., & Hartsough, W.R. (1980). Sexism and sex roles in letters of recommendation to graduate training in psychology. *Canadian Psychology, 21*, 75–80.

Henderson, K.A., Bialeschki, M.D., Shaw, S.M., & Freysinger, V. (1989). *A leisure of one's own: A feminist perspective on women's leisure*. London: Spon Press.

Henwood, F. (1994). Engineering difference: Discourses on gender, sexuality and work [Working paper series, No. 3]. London: Innovation Studies, University of East London.

Henwood, K., & Phoenix, A. (1996). "Race" in psychology: Teaching the subject. *Ethnic and Racial Studies, 19*(4), 841–63.

Hermes, J. (1995). *Reading women's magazines: An analysis of everyday media use*. Cambridge: Polity.

Herr, R.S. (2004). A third world feminist defence of multiculturalism. *Social Theory and Practice, 30*(1), 73–92.

Heywood, L., & Drake, J. (1997). *Third wave agenda: Being feminist, doing feminism*. Minneapolis: University of Minnesota Press.

Heywood, L. & Dworkin, S.L. (2003). *Built to win: The female athlete as cultural icon*. Minnesota: University of Minnesota Press.

Heywood, L.L. (2006). *The women's movement today: An encyclopedia of third-wave feminism*. Westport, CT: Greenwood Press.

Hibberd, F.J. (2005). *Unfolding social constructionism*. New York: Springer.

Higher Education Statistics Agency (2004). Students in higher education 2004/2005. Retrieved from http://www.hesa.ac.uk/content/view/2483/251/1/1/

Hill, D., McLaren, P., Cole, M., & Rikowski, G. (Eds.). (1999). *Postmodernism in educational theory*. London: Tuffnell Press.

Hill, L. (2007). *The Cambridge introduction to Jacques Derrida*. Cambridge: Cambridge University Press.

Hill, S.A. (2002). Teaching and doing gender in African American families. *Sex Roles, 47*(11/12), 493–506.

Hill Collins, P. (1990). Black feminist thought: Knowledge, consciousness, and the politics of empowerment. Boston: Unwin Hyman.

Hill Collins, P. (1999). Moving beyond gender: Intersectionality and scientific knowledge. In J. Lorber, M.M. Ferree, & B. Hess (Eds.), *Revisioning gender* (pp. 261–84). Thousand Oaks, CA: Sage.

Hill Collins, P. (2000). *Black feminist thought: Knowledge, consciousness, and the politics of empowerment*. New York: Routledge.

Hillyer, B. (1993). *Feminism and disability*. Norman, OK: University of Oklahoma Press.

Hird, M.J. (2003). Considerations for a psychoanaltyic theory of gender identity and sexual desire: The case of intersex. *Signs: Journal of Women in Culture and Society, 28*(4), 1067–92.

Hird, M.J. (2004). *Sex, gender, and science*. Houndmills: Palgrave Macmillan.

Hirsch, J.S., & Wardlow, H. (Eds.). (2006). *Modern loves: The anthropology of romantic courtships and companionate marriage*. Ann Arbor: University of Michigan Press.

Hoagland, S.L., & Frye, M. (2000). *Feminist interpretations of Mary Daly*. University Park, PA: Pennsylvania State University.

Hochschild, A.R. (1983).The managed heart: Commercialization of human feeling. Berkeley: University of California Press.

Hochschild, A.R. (1989). *The second shift*. New York: Avon Books.

Hochschild, A.R. (1997). *The time bind*. New York: Metropolitan Books.

Hodson, P. (1984). *Men: An investigation into the emotional male*. London: British Broadcasting Corporation.

Hoffman, R.M. (2006). Gender self-definition and gender self-acceptance in women: Intersections with feminist, womanist, and ethnic identities. *Journal of Counseling & Development, 84,* 358–71.

Hofstadter, D.R. (2007). *I am a strange loop*. New York: Basic Books.

Hofstede, G., & Hofstede, G.J. (2004). *Cultures and organizations: Software of the mind*. New York: McGraw Hill.

Hogeveen, B.R. (2007). Youth (and) violence. *Sociology Compass, 1*(2), 463–84.

Holland, J., Ramazanoglu, C., Sharpe, S., & Thompson, R. (1998). *The male in the head: Young people, heterosexuality and power*. London: Tuffnell Press.

Hollway, W. (1984). Gender difference and the production of subjectivity. In J. Henriques, W. Hollway, C. Urwin, C. Venn, & V. Walkerdine (Eds.), *Changing the subject*. London: Methuen.

Hollway, W. (2006). *The capacity to care: Gender and ethical subjectivity*. London: Routledge.

Holmes, J. (2006). *Gendered discourse in the workplace: Constructing gender identity through workplace discourse*. Oxford: Blackwell.

Holmstrom, N. (Ed.). (2003). *The socialist feminist project: A contemporary reader in theory and politics*. New York: Monthly Review Press.

Hong, F., & Mangan, J.A. (2003). *Sport in Asian society: Past and present*. London: Frank Cass.

Hood, J.C. (Ed.). (1993). *Men, work, and family*. Thousand Oaks, CA: Sage.

hooks, b. (1981). *Ain't I a woman: Black women and feminism*. Cambridge, MA: South End Press.

hooks, b. (1998). *Talking back: Thinking feminism, thinking black*. Toronto: Between the Lines.

hooks, b. (2004). *We real cool: Black men and masculinity*. New York: Routledge.

hooks, b. (2006). *Outlaw culture*. New York: Routledge.

Hopper, J. (2005). Sexual abuse of males: Prevalence, possible lasting effects, and resources. Retrieved from http://www.jimhopper.com/male-ab

Horkheimer, M., & Adorno, T.W. (1979). *Dialectic of enlightenment*. London: Verso.

Horney, K. (1973). *Feminine psychology*. New York: WW Norton.

Horrell, S., Johnson, H., & Mosely, P. (Eds.). (2008). *Work, female empowerment and economic development*. London: Routledge.

Horrocks, R. (1994). *Masculinity in crisis: Myths, fantasies and realities*. London: Macmillan.

Howell, J., & Mulligan, D. (2005). *Gender and civil society: Transcending boundaries*. London: Routledge.

Hruschka, D.J. (2010). *Friendship: Development, ecology, and evolution of a relationship*. Berkeley: University of California Press.

Hsiung, P.-C., & Nichol, K. (2010). Policies and experiences of foreign domestic workers in Canada. *Sociology Compass, 4*(9), 766–78.

Huang, S., Teo, P., & Yeoh, B.S.A. (2000). Diasporic subjects and identity negotiations: Women in and from Asia. *Women's Studies International Forum, 23*(4), 391–8.

Huffer, L. (2010). *Mad for Foucault: Rethinking the foundations of queer theory*. New York: Columbia University Press.

Hughson, J. (2007). The boys are back in town: Soccer support and the social reproduction of masculinity. In S. Whitehead (Ed.), *Men and masculinities: Critical concepts in sociology* (Vol. 2). London: Routledge.

Hunt, S., & Benford, R. (2004). Collective identity, solidarity and commitment. In D. Snow, S. Soule, & H. Kriesi (Eds.), *The Blackwell companion to social movements*. Oxford: Blackwell.

Hunter, M.L. (2002). "If you're light you're alright": Light skin colour as social capital for women of color. *Gender & Society, 16*(2),175–93.

Hussain, Y., & Bagguley, P. (2005). Citizenship, ethnicity and identity: British Pakistanis after the 2001 "riots." *Sociology*, *39*(3), 407–25.

Huston, A.C. (1985). The development of sex-typing: Themes from recent research. *Developmental Review*, *5*, 1–17.

Hutton, W., & Giddens, A. (Eds.). (2000). *On the edge: Living with global capitalism*. London: Jonathon Cape.

Illich, I. (1973). *Deschooling society*. Harmondsworth, UK: Penguin.

The Independent (2010). Mothers "more critical of daughters than sons." Retrieved from http://www.independent.co.uk/life-style/health-and-families/features/mothers-more-critical-of-daughters-than-sons-2099187.html

Innes, J. (2004, December 24). Metrosexual man is still a rare species. *The Scotsman*.

Inness, S.A. (2004). *Action chicks: New images of tough women in popular culture*. New York: Palgrave Macmillan.

Institute of Directors. (2006). *Directors rewards survey 2006*. London: IoD.

Irigaray, L. (1977). *This sex which is not one* (C. Porter & C. Burke, Trans.). New York: Cornell University Press.

Irigiray, L. (1985). *The sex which is not one*. Ithaca: Cornell University Press.

Irwin, K., & Chesney-Lind, M. (2008). *Beyond bad girls: Gender, violence and hype*. New York: Routledge.

Isbester, K. (2001). *Still fighting: The Nicaraguan women's movement, 1977–2000*. Pittsburgh, PA: University of Pittsburgh Press.

Ito, R. (2010). Immigration et travail de care dans une société vieillissante: Le cas du Japon. In J. Falquet, H. Hirata, D. Kergoat, & B. Labari (Eds.), *Le sexe de la mondialisation: Genre, classe, race et nouvelle division du travail* (pp.137–50). Paris: Presses de Sciences Po.

Itzin, C., & Newman, J. (Eds.). (1995). *Gender, culture and organizational change*. London: Routledge.

Jackson, C., Paechter, C.F., & Renold, E. (2010). *Girls and education 3–16: Continuing concerns, new agendas*. Maidenhead: McGraw-Hill/Open University Press.

Jackson, N., & Carter, P. (2007). *Rethinking organisational behavior: A poststructuralist framework*. New York: Prentice Hall/Financial Times.

Jackson, P., Stevenson, N., & Brooks, K. (2001). *Making sense of men's magazines*. Cambridge: Polity.

Jackson, P. Stevenson, N., & Brooks, K. (2006). The politics of new men's lifestyle magazines. In S.M. Whitehead (Ed.), *Men and masculinities: Critical concepts in sociology* (Vol. 3). London: Routledge.

Jackson, P.A. (2004). Tolerant but unaccepting: The myth of a Thai "gay paradise." In P.A. Jackson & N.W. Cook (Eds.), *Genders and sexualities in modern Thailand*. Chiang Mai: Silkworm Books.

Jackson, P.A., & Sullivan, G. (Eds.). (2000). *Lady boys, tom boys and rent boys*. Chiang Mai: Silkworm Books.

Jackson, P.A., & Sullivan, G. (Eds.). (2001). *Gay and lesbian Asia: Culture, identity and community*. Binghamton, NY: Harrington Park Press.

Jackson, S. (1990). *Unmasking masculinity: A critical autobiography*. London: Unwin Hyman.

Jacobsen, M.H. (Ed.). (2010). *The contemporary Goffman*. New York: Routledge.

Jacobus, M. (1986). *Reading woman: Essays in feminist criticism*. London: Methuen.

Jagger, A.M. (1983). *Feminist politics and human nature*. Totowa, NJ:Rowman & Allanheld.

Jagger, G. (2008). *Judith Butler: Sexual politics, social change and the power of the performative*. Abingdon, England: Routledge.

Jagose, A. (1997). *Queer theory*. New York: New York Press.

Jagose, A. (1996). *Queer theory: An introduction*. New York: New York University Press.

Jameson, F. (1984). Postmodernism: The cultural logic of late capitalism. *New Left Review*, *146*, 53–92.

Jamieson, L. (1998). *Intimacy: Personal relationships in modern societies*. Cambridge: Polity.

Jardine, A., & Smith, P. (Eds.). (1987). *Men in feminism*. New York: Methuen.

Jefferson, T. (1998). Muscle, "hard men" and "Iron" Mike Tyson: Reflections on desire, anxiety and the embodiment of masculinity. *Body and Society*, 4(1), 77–98.

Jefferson, T. (2002). Subordinating hegemonic masculinity. *Theoretical Criminology*, 6(1), 63–88.

Jefferson, T. (2006). Theorizing masculine subjectivity. In S. Whitehead (Ed.), *Men and masculinities: Critical concepts in sociology*, (Vol. 3). London: Routledge.

Jenkins, R. (1996). *Social Identity*. London: Routledge.

Jenkins, S. (2004). *Gender, place, and the labour market*. Aldershot, UK: Ashgate.

Jermier, J.M., Knights, D., & Nord, W.R. (Eds.). (1994). *Resistance and Power in Organizations*. London: Routledge.

Jhally, S. (2006). *The spectacle of accumulation: Essays in culture, media & politics*. New York: Peter Lang.

Jinpa, G.T. (2000). The foundations of a Buddhist psychology of awakening. In G. Watson, S. Batchelor, & G. Claxton (Eds.), *Psychology of awakening: Buddhism, science and our day-to-day lives*. York Beach, ME: Red Wheel/Weiser.

Jinxia, D. (2002). *Women, sport and society in modern China: Holding up more than half the sky*. London: Frank Cass Publishers.

Johnson, B. (2007, June 20). Escape asylum, stab nurse, kill prostitutes. Not here you won't, say British censors. *The Guardian*.

Johnson, J.E. (2009). *Gender violence in Russia: The politics of feminist intervention*. Bloomington: Indiana University Press.

Johnson, S., & Meinhof, U.H. (Eds.). (1997). *Language and masculinity*. Oxford: Blackwell.

Jones, C., & Mahony, P. (1989). *Learning our lines: Sexuality and social control in education*. London: The Women's Press.

Jones, G., & Shen, H.-H. (2008). International marriage in East and South-East Asia. *Citizenship Studies*, 12(1), 9–25.

Jones, J., & Pugh, S. (2005). Ageing gay men: Lessons from the sociology of embodiment. *Men and Masculinities*, 7(3), 248–60.

Jones, K. (2002). *Education in Britain: 1944 to the present*. Cambridge: Polity.

Judd, T., & Griffey, H. (2007). Discrimination against girls "still deeply entrenched." Retrieved from http://news.independent.co.uk/world/politics/article2542406.ece

Julia, M. (2000). *Constructing gender: Multicultural perspectives in working with women*. Australia: Brooks/Cole.

Jung, C.G. (1982). *Aspects of the feminine*. Princeton, NJ: Princeton University Press.

Juschka, D. (2009). Penetrating the body of the masculine "other": White US masculinity, war and the ritual of "truth." *The CSSR Bulletin*, 38(4), 1–6.

Kanter, R.M. (1977). *Men and women of the corporation*. New York: BasicBooks.

Kaplan, D., & Ben-Ari, E. (2006). Brothers and others in arms: Managing gay identity in combat units of the Israeli army. In S. Whitehead (Ed.), *Men and masculinities: Critical concepts in sociology* (Vol. 5). London: Routledge.

Kaplan, E.A. (Ed.). (2000). *Feminism and film*. Oxford: Oxford University Press.

Karam, A.M. (1998). *Women, Islamisms and the state: Contemporary feminisms in Egypt*. London: Macmillan.

Kassem, F. (2011). Palestinian women: Narrative histories and gendered memory. London: Zed Books.

Katz, P.A. (1987). Variations in family constellation: Effects on gender schemata. In L.S. Liben & M.L. Signorella (Eds.), *Children's gender schemata: New directions for child development*. San Francisco: Jossey-Bass.

Kay, F., & Gorman, E. (2008). Women in the legal profession. *Annual Review of Law and Social Sciences*, 4, 299–332.

Keegan, V. (2007, June 2). Watch out *Second Life*: China launches virtual universe with seven million souls. *The Guardian*. Retrieved from http://technology.guardian.co.uk

Keegan, V. (2010). Virtual worlds: Is this where real life is heading? *The Guardian*. Retrieved from http://www.guardian.co.uk/technology/2010/aug/22/discover-virtual-worlds-revolution

Kehily, M.J. (2001). Issues of gender and sexuality in schools. In B. Francis & C. Skelton (Eds.), *Investigating gender: Contemporary perspectives in education*. Buckingham, UK: Open University Press.

Kehily, M.J. (2002). *Sexuality, gender and schooling: Shifting agendas in social learning*. London: Routledge.

Kellner, D. (1995). Cultural studies, multiculturalism and media culture. In G. Dines & J.M. Humez (Eds.), *Gender, race and class in media: A text-reader*. New York: Sage.

Kelly, D.M., Pomerantz, S., & Currie, D.H. (2006). "No boundaries"? Girls' interactive, online learning about femininities. *Youth & Society*, *38*(1), 3–28.

Kenway, J. (1995). Masculinities in schools: Under siege, on the defensive and under reconstruction. *Discourse*, *16*(1), 59–79.

Kerfoot, D. (2001). The organization of intimacy: Managerialism, masculinity and the masculine subject. In S.M. Whitehead & F.J. Barrett (Eds.), *The masculinities reader*. Cambridge: Polity.

Kerfoot, D., & Knights, D. (1994). Into the realm of the fearful: Power, identity and the gender problematic. In H.L. Radtke & H.J. Stam (Eds.), *Power and gender*. London: Sage.

Kerfoot, D., & Knights, D. (2006 [1993]). Management, masculinity and manipulation: From paternalism to corporate strategy in financial services in Britain. In S.M. Whitehead (Ed.), *Men and masculinities: Critical concepts in sociology* (Vol. II). London: Routledge.

Kerfoot, D., Prichard, C., & Whitehead, S. (Eds.). (2000). Special issue: (En)gendering management: Work, organisation and further education. *Journal of Further and Higher Education*, *24*(2).

Kerfoot, D., & Whitehead, S. (1998). "Boy's own" stuff: Masculinity and the management of further education. *The Sociological Review*, *46*(3), 436–57.

Kessler, S. (1998). *Lessons from the intersexed*. New Brunswick, NJ: Rutgers University Press.

Kilbourne, J. (1989). Beauty… and the beast of advertising. *Media & Values*, Winter, 8–49.

Kilbourne, J. (1995). Beauty and the beast of advertising. In G. Dines & J.M. Humez (Eds.), *Gender, race and class in the media: A text-reader*. New York: Sage.

Kilbourne, J. (2010). *Killing us softly. Advertising's image of women* [DVD]. Media Education Foundation.

Kim, H.J., Arnold, D.H., Fisher, P.H., & Zeljo, A. (2005). Parenting and preschoolers' symptoms as a function of child gender and SES. *Child & Family Behavior Therapy*, *27*(2), 19–25.

Kim, M. (2010). Gender and international marriage migration. *Sociology Compass*, *4*(9), 718–31.

Kimmel, M.S. (Ed.). (1995a). *The politics of manhood*. Philadelphia, PA: Temple University Press.

Kimmel, M.S. (1995b). "Born to Run": Nineteenth century fantasies of masculine retreat and re-creation (or the historical rust on Iron John). In M.S. Kimmel (Ed.), *The politics of manhood*. Philadelphia, PA: Temple University Press.

Kimmel, M.S. (2000). *The gendered society*. New York: Oxford University Press.

Kimmel, M.S. (2006). "Born to Run": Nineteenth century fantasies of masculinie retreat and re-creation (or the historical rust on Iron John). In S.M. Whitehead (Ed.), *Men and masculinities: Critical concepts in sociology*. London: Routledge.

Kimmel, M.S. (2006). Globalization and its (male) contents. In S.M. Whitehead (Ed.), *Men and masculinities: Critical concepts in sociology* (Vol. 1). London: Routledge.

Kimmel, M.S., & Mahler, M. (2003), Adolescent masculinity, homophobia, and violence: Random school shootings, 1982–2001. *American Behavioural Scientist*, *46*(10), 1439–58.

Kimmel, M.S., & Messner, M.A. (Eds.). (1995). *Men's lives* (3rd Ed.). Boston: Allyn and Bacon.

Ki-moon, B. (2007, July 10). We should welcome the dawn of the migration age. *The Guardian*. Retrieved from http://www.guardian.co.uk/commentisfree/2007/jul/10/comment.globalisation

Kimoto, K. (2005). *Gender and Japanese management*. Melbourne: Trans Pacific Press.

King, U.A. (1996). *Religion and gender*. London: Wiley-Blackwell.

Kinsella, H.M. (2007). Understanding a war that is not a war: A review essay. *Journal of Women in Culture and Society*, *33*(1), 209–31.

Kirkness, V.J., & Bowman, S. (1992). *First nations and schools: Triumphs and struggles*. Toronto: Canadian Education Association.

Kirmayer, L.J., & Valaskakis, G.G. (2009). *Healing traditions: The mental health of Aboriginal peoples in Canada*. Vancouver: UBC Press.

Kiss, J. (2012). Facebook hits 1 billion users a month. *The Guardian*. Retrieved from http://www.guardian.co.uk/technology/2012/oct/04/facebook-hits-billion-users-a-month

Kleeman, J.A. (1971). The establishment of core gender identity in normal girls. I. (a) introduction; (b) development of the ego capacity to differentiate. *Archives of Sexual Behavior, 1*(2), 103–16.

Klein, A.M. (1990). Little big man: Hustling, gender narcissism, and bodybuilding subculture. In M.A. Messner & D.F. Sabo (Eds.), *Sport, men, and the gender order*. Champaign, IL: Human Kinetics Books.

Klein, M. (1998). *Early stages of the Oedipus complex*. In N. Burke (Ed.), *Gender and envy*. New York: Routledge.

Knauss, P.R. (1987). *The persistence of patriarchy: Class, gender, and ideology in twentieth century Algeria*. New York: Praeger.

Knights, D., & Odih, P. (1995). "It's about time!" The significance of genderd time for financial services consumption. *Time and Society, 4*(2), 205–31.

Knights, D., & Willmott, H. (1999). *Management lives: Power and identity in work organizations*. London: Sage.

Knights, D., & Willmott, H. (2006). *Introducing organizational behaviour and management*. London: Thomson Learning.

Komarovsky, M. (1950). Functional analysis of sex roles. *American Sociological Review, 15*, 508–16.

Koosed, J., & Schumm, D. (2009). From Superman to super Jesus: Constructions of masculinity and disability on the silver screen. *Disability Studies Quarterly, 29*(2). Retrieved from http://dsq-sds.org/article/view/917/1092

Kostovicova, D., & Prestreshi, A. (2003). Education, gender and religion: Identity transformations among Kosovo Albanians in London. *Journal of Ethnic and Migration Studies, 29*(6), 1079–96.

Kreager, D.A. (2007). Unnecessary roughness? School sports, peer networks, and male adolescent violence. *American Sociological Review, 72*(5), 705–24. Thousand Oaks, CA: Sage.

Kreuz, L., & Rose, R.M. (1972). Assessment of aggressive behaviour and plasma testosterone in a young criminal population. *Psychosomatic Medicine, 34*, 470–1.Kristeva, J. (1984). *Revolution in poetic language*. New York: Columbia University Press.

Kristeva, J. (1986). *The Kristeva reader* (T. Moi, Ed.). Oxford: Blackwell.

Krook, M.L., & Childs, S. (Eds.). (2010). *Women, gender, and politics: A reader*. Oxford: Oxford University Press.

Kroska, A. (2000). Conceptualizing and measuring gender ideology as an identity. *Gender & Society, 14*, 368–94.

Kulik, D. (1998). *Travesti: Sex, gender, and culture among Brazilian transgendered prostitutes*. Chicago: University of Chicago Press.

Kulik, L. (2005). The impact of family status on gender identity and on sex-typing of households. *The Journal of Social Psychology, 145*(3), 299–316.

Kumar, K. (1995). *From post-industrial to post-modern society*. Oxford: Blackwell.

Kunda, G. (1992). *Engineering culture: Control and commitment in a high-tech corporation*. Philadelphia: Temple University Press.

Kureishi, H. (1998). *Intimacy*. London: Faber & Faber.

Kuumba, M.G. (2001). *Gender and social movements*. Walnut Creek, CA: AltaMira Press.

Kwan, S., & Trautner, M.N. (2009). Beauty work: Individual and institutional rewards, the reproduction of gender, and questions of agency. *Sociology Compass, 3*(1), 49–71.

Kylo-Patrick, R.H. (2006). We're here, we're queer — and we're better than you: The representational superiority of gay men to heterosexuals on *Queer eye for the straight guy*. In S. M. Whitehead (Ed.), *Men and masculinities: Critical concepts in sociology* (Vol. III) London: Routledge.

Kymlicka, W. (1995). *Multicultural citizenship: A liberal theory of minority rights*. Oxford: Clarendon Press.

Kymlicka, W. (1999). *Finding our way: Rethinking ethnocultural relations in Canada*. Toronto: Toronto University Press.

Lacan, J. (1977). *Ecrits: A Selection*. London: Tavistock.

Lacan, J. (1989). *Ecrits: A Selection* (A. Sheridan, Trans.). London: Routledge.

Laclau, E. (1990). *New reflections on the revolution of our time*. London: Verso.

Laclau, E., & Mouffe, C. (1990). Post-Marxism without apologies. In E. Laclau (Ed.), *New reflections of the revolution of our time*. London: Verso.

Landes, J.B. (1998). *Feminism, the public and the private*. New York: Oxford University Press.

Lanzetta, B.J. (2005). *Radical wisdom: A feminist mystical theology*. Minneapolis, MN: Fortress Press.

Lapota, H., & Thorne, B. (1978). On the term sex roles. *Signs*, *3*(3), 718–21.

Lash, S. (1995). Reflexivity and its doubles: Structure, aesthetics, community. In U. Beck, A. Giddens, & S. Lash (Eds.), *Reflexive modernization*. Cambridge: Polity.

Lash, S., & Urry, J. (1993). *Economies of signs and space*. London: Sage.

Laurie, N., Dwyer, C., Holloway, S., & Smith, F. (1999). *Geographies of new femininities*. London: Longman. Lawrence, M., Bernstein, J., & Allegretto, S. (2005). *The state of working America, 2004–2005*. ILR Press.

Leaper, C. (2000a). The social construction and socialization of gender. In P.H. Miller & E.K. Scholnick (Eds.), *Toward a feminist developmental psychology*. New York: Routledge.

Leaper, C. (2002). Parenting girls and boys. In M.H. Bornstein (Ed.), *Handbook of parenting: Volume 1: Children and parenting*. London: Lawrence Erlbaum.

Leaper, C., Anderson, K.J., & Sanders, P. (1998). Moderators of gender effects on parents' talk to their children: A meta-analysis. *Developmental Psychology*, *34*, 3–27.

Leaper, C., Leve, L., Strasser, T., & Schwartz, R. (1995) Mother–child communication and sequences: Play activity, child gender, and marital status effects. *Merrill-Palmer Quarterly*, *41*, 307–27.

LeBesco, K. (2004). *Revolting bodies? The struggle to redefine fat identity*. Amherst: University of Massachusetts Press.

Leccardi, C., & Ruspini, E. (2006). *A new youth? Young people, generations and family life*. Aldershot, UK: Ashgate.

Leckey, R., & Brooks, K. (2010). *Queer theory: Law, culture, empire*. New York: Routledge.

Ledwith, S., & Colgan, F. (1996). *Women in organisations*. London: Palgrave Macmillan.

Lee, D., & Newby, H. (1984). *The problem of sociology: An introduction to the discipline*. London: Hutchinson.

Lee, J., & Shaw, S. (2011). *Women worldwide: Transnational feminist perspectives on women*. New York: McGraw-Hill.

Legge, K. (2005). *Human resource management: Rhetorics and realities*. New York: Palgrave Macmillan.

Lemert, C. (1997). *Social things: An introduction to the sociological life*. New York: Rowman & Littlefield.

Lemert, C., & Branaman, A. (Eds.). (1997). *The Goffman reader*. Malden, MA: Blackwell.

Lenz, I., Ullrich, C., & Fersch, B. (Eds.). (2007). *Gender orders unbound: Globalisation, restructuring and reciprocity*. Farmington, MI: Budrich.

Leonard, P. (2010). Expatriate identities in postcolonial organizations: Working whiteness. Farnham, England: Ashgate.

Lesko, N. (Ed.). (2000). *Masculinities at school*. Thousand Oaks, CA: Sage.

Leung, H.H., Hendley, M., Compton, R.W., & Haley, B.D. (Eds.). (2009). *Imagining globalization: Language, identities, and boundaries*. New York: Palgrave Macmillan.

Levy, A. (2006). *Female chauvinist pigs: Women and the rise of raunch culture*. New York: Pocket Books.

Lewis, P., & Simpson, R. (2010). *Revealing and concealing gender: Issues of visibility in organizations*. Basingstoke: Palgrave Macmillan.

Lewis, R. (1996). *Gendering orientalism: Race, femininity and representation*. London: Routledge.

Lewis, R. (2004). *Rethinking orientalism: Women, travel and the Ottoman harem*. London: I.B. Tauris.

Leydesdorff, S., Passerini, L., Thompson, P. (1996). *Gender and memory*. New York: Oxford University Press.

Liben, L.S., & Signorella, M.L. (Eds.), *Children's gender schemata: New directions for child development*. San Francisco: Jossey-Bass.

Liebowitz, J. (2007). *Social networking: The essence of innovation*. Lanham, MD: Scarecrow Press.

Lindberg, C. (2008). *Love: A brief history through Western Christianity*. Malden, MA: Blackwell.

Lindsey, E.W., & Caldera, Y.M. (2006), Mother–father–child triadic interaction and mother–child dyadic interaction: Gender differences within and between contexts. *Sex Roles, 55*(7–8), 511–21.

Lindsay, E.W., & Mize, J. (2001). Contextual differences in parent–child play: Implications for children's gender role development. *Sex Roles, 44*(3–4), 155–76.

Lindsey, L.L. (2004). *Gender roles: A sociological perspective*. New York: Pearson.

Ling, P.J., & Monteith, S. (Eds.). (2004). *Gender and the civil rights movement* (1st Edn). New Brunswick, NJ: Rutgers University Press.

Lingard, B., & Douglas, P. (1999). *Men engaging feminisms: Pro-feminism, backlashes and schooling*. Buckingham, UK: Open University Press.

Lingard, B., & Ozga, J. (2006). *The Routledge/Farmer reader in education policy and politics*. London: Routledge.

Linton, R. (Ed.). (1945). *The science of man in world crisis*. New York: Columbia University Press.

Lloyd, F. (Ed.). (1993). *Deconstructing Madonna*. London: Batsford.

Lloyd, G. (1984). *Man of reason: "Male" and "female" in Western philosophy*. London: Metheun.

Lloyd, M. (2005). *Beyond identity politics: Feminism, power and politics*. London: Sage.

Lock, A., & Strong, T. (2010). *Social constructionism: Sources and stirrings in theory and practice*. Cambridge, UK: Cambridge University Press.

Lofland, J. (1980). Early Goffman: Style, structure, substance, soul. In J. Ditton (Ed.), *The view from Goffman*. London: Macmillan.

Loomba, A. (2005). *Colonialism/postcolonialism* (2nd Edn). Abington, England: Routledge.

Lopata, H.Z., & Thorne, B. (1978). On the term "sex roles." *Signs: Journal of Women in Culture and Society, 3*, 718–21.

Lopez, N. (2002). *Hopeful girls, troubled boys: Race and gender disparity in urban education*. New York: Routledge.

Lorber, J. (1994). *Paradoxes of gender*. London: Yale University Press.

Lorber, J. (2010). *Gender inequality: Feminist theory and politics* (4th Edn). New York: Oxford University Press.

Lott, B., & Maluso, D. (1993). The social learning of gender. In A.E. Beall & R.J. Sternberg (Eds.), *The Psychology of Gender*. New York: Guilford.

Low, G.C.-L. (1993). Histories, narratives and images of imperialism. In E. Carter, J. Donald, & J. Squires (Eds.), *Space and place: Theories of identity and location*. London: Lawrence & Wishart.

Luxton, M. (2001). Feminism as a working class act: Working class feminism and the women's movement in Canada. *Labour/Le Travail, 48*, 63–88.

Lyman, P. (1995). The fraternal bond as a joking relationship: A case study of the role of sexist jokes in male group bonding. In M.S. Kimmel & M.A. Messner (Eds.), *Men's lives*. Boston: Allyn and Bacon.

Lynch, M. (2001). The contingencies of social constructionism. *Economy and Society, 30*(2), 240–54.

Lyotard, J.-F. (1984). *The postmodern condition: A report on knowledge*. Manchester: Manchester University Press.

Lytton, H., & Romney, D.M. (1991). Parents' differential socialization of boys and girls: A meta-analysis. *Psychological Bulletin, 109*, 267–96.

Mac an Ghaill, M. (1994). *The making of men*. Buckingham, UK: OpenUniversity Press.

MacClancy, J. (1996). *Sport, Identity and Ethnicity*. London: Berg.

Macdonald, M. (1995). *Representing women: Myths of femininity in the popular media*. London: Arnold.

Macdonald, N. (2001). *The graffiti subculture: Youth, masculinity and identity in London and New York*. New York: Palgrave.

MacInnes, J. (1998). *The end of masculinity*. Buckingham, UK: Open University Press.

Mackie, V. (2011). *Transcultures: Asia–Pacific media representations of globalization* [Media, culture and social change in Asia series]. New York: Routledge.

MacMaster, N. (2009). *Burning the veil: The Algerian war and the "emancipation" of Muslim women, 1954–62*. Manchester, UK: Manchester University Press.

MacSween, M. (1995). *Anorexic bodies: Feminist and sociological perspectives on anorexia nervosa*. London: Routledge.

Magnuson, E. (2007). *Changing men, transforming culture: Inside the men's movement*. Boulder, CO: Paradigm.

Magocsi, P.R. (1999). *Encyclopedia of Canada's peoples*. Toronto: University of Toronto Press.

Maguire, M., Morgan, R., & Reiner, R. (Eds.). (2012). *The Oxford handbook of criminology*. Oxford: Oxford University Press.

Mahalingam, R. (2007). Beliefs about chastity, machismo, and caste identity: A cultural psychology of gender. *Sex Roles, 56*, 239–49.

Majors, R. (Ed.). (2002). *Educating our black children: New directions and radical approaches*. London: Routledge Falmer.

Majors, R., & Bilson, J.M. (1992). *Cool pose: The dilemmas of black manhood in America*. New York: Lexington Books.

Malarek, V. (2004). *The Natashas: Inside the new global sex trade*. New York: Arcade.

Maliangkay, R. (2010). The effeminacy of male beauty in Korea. *IIAS Newsletter, 55*, 6–7.

Malson, H., Marshall, H., & Woollett, A. (2002). Talking of taste: A discourse analytic exploration of young women's gendered and racialized subjectivities in British urban, multicultural contexts. *Feminism and Psychology,12*, 469–90.

Maltz, D.N., & Boker, R.A. (1982). A cultural approach to male–female miscommunication. In J.J. Gumperz (Ed.), *Language and society identity* (pp.195–217). Cambridge, UK: Cambridge University Press.

Mangan, J.A. (2000). *Making European masculinities: Sport, Europe, gender*. London: Frank Cass.

Mangan, J.A., & Hong, F. (Eds.). (2000). *Freeing the female body: Inspirational icons (sport in the global society)*. London: Frank Cass.

Mangan, J.A., & Walvin, J. (Eds.). (1991). *Manliness and morality: Middle-class masculinity in Britain and America, 1800–1940*. Manchester: Manchester University Press.

Mangan, J.E. (2005). *Trading roles: Gender, ethnicity, and the urban economy of colonial Potosí*. Durham, NC: Duke University Press.

Mann, M. (1994). A crisis in stratification theory? Persons, households/families/lineages, genders, classes and nations. In R. Crompton & M. Mann (Eds.), *Gender and stratification*. Cambridge: Polity.

Manning, P. (1992). *Irving Goffman and modern sociology*. Cambridge: Polity.

Maringe, F., & Foskett, N. (2010). *Globalization and internationalization in higher education: Theoretical, strategic and management perspectives*. New York: Continuum International.

Mariscotti, C. (2008). *Gender and class in the Egyptian women's movement, 1925–1939: Changing perspectives*. Syracuse, NY: Syracuse University Press.

Marks, E., & de Courtivron, I. (Eds.). (1981). *New French feminisms*. Brighton: Harvester.

Marshall, J. (1995). *Women managers moving on: Exploring career and life choices*. London: Routledge.

Martinez Aleman, A.M., & Wartman, K.L. (2009). *Online social networking on campus: Understanding what matters in student culture*. New York: Routledge.

Martino, W., Kehler, M., & Weaver-Hightower, M.B. (2009). *The problem with boys' education: Beyond the backlash*. New York: Routledge.

Martino, W., & Meyenn, B. (Eds.). (2001). *What about the boys? Issues of masculinity in schools*. Buckingham, UK: Open University Press.

Martyn, E. (2005). *The women's movement in post-colonial Indonesia: Gender and nation in a new democracy*. London: Routledge Curzon.

Marx Ferree, M., & Tripp, A.M. (2006). *Global feminism: Transnational women's activism, organizing, and human rights*. New York: New York University Press.

Mason, J. (1996). *Qualitative researching*. Thousand Oaks, CA: Sage.

Massey, D. (2004). *Space, place and gender.* Cambridge: Polity.

Massey, D., Allen, J., & Sarre, P. (Eds.). (2005). *Human geography today.* Cambridge: Polity.

May, A.M. (2008). *The "woman question" and higher education: Perspectives on gender and knowledge production in America.* Northampton, MA: Edward Elgar.

May, L. (1998). *Masculinity and morality.* New York: Cornell University Press.

Mazure, A., & Lamb, T.A. (1980). Testosterone, status and mood in human males. *Hormones and Behaviour, 4,* 236–46.

McCarthy, B. (1994). Warrior values: A socio-historical survey. In J. Archer (Ed.), *Male violence.* London: Routledge.

McClintock, A. (1995). Imperial leather: Race, gender, and sexuality in the colonial contest. London: Routledge.

McClintock, A. (1997). No longer in a future heaven: Gender, race, and nationalism. In A. Mufti & E. Shorat (Eds.), *Dangerous liaisons: Gender, nation and postcolonial perspectives.* Minneapolis: University of Minnesota Press.

McCreary, D.R. (1994). The male role and avoiding femininity. *Sex Roles, 31*(9–10), 517–31.

McCurry, J. (2009, December 27). Japan's "grass eaters" turn their backs on macho ways. *The Guardian.* Retrieved from http://www.guardian.co.uk/world/2009/dec/27/japan-grass-eaters-salaryman-macho

McDowell, L. (2004). *Gender, identity & place: Understanding feminist geographies.* Cambridge: Polity.

McGillivray, M. (2006). *Human well-being: Concept and measurement.* London: Macmillan.

McGuire, A. (2010). Disability, non-disability and the politics of mourning: Re-conceiving the "we." *Disability Studies Quarterly, 30*(3/4). Retrieved from http://dsq-sds.org/article/view/1282

McKay, J, Messner, M.A., & Sabo, D. (Eds.). (2000). *Masculinities, gender relations, and sport.* New York: Sage.

McKinlay, A., & Starkey, K. (Eds.). (1997). *Foucault, management and organization theory.* Thousand Oaks, CA: Sage.

McLeod, J. (2005). Feminists rereading Bourdieu: Old debates and new questions about gender habitus and gender change. *Theory and Research in Education, 3,* 11–30.

McMullin, J. (2004). *Understanding social inequality: Intersections of class, age, gender, ethnicity and race in Canada.* Toronto: Oxford University Press.

McNay, L. (1992). *Foucault and feminism: Power, gender and the self.* Cambridge: Polity

McNay, L. (1994). *Foucault: A critical introduction.* Cambridge: Polity.

McNay, L. (1999). Gender, habitus and the field: Pierre Bourdieu and the limits of reflexivity. *Theory, Culture and Society, 16*(1), 95–117.

McNay, L. (2000). *Gender and agency: Reconfiguring the subject in feminist and social theory.* Cambridge: Polity.

McNay, L. (2003). Agency, anticipation and indeterminacy in feminist theory. *Feminist Theory, 4*(2), 139–48.

McNeill, D. (2009). Japan's Generation XX. *The Independent.* Retrieved from www.independent.co.uk/news/world/asia/japans-generation-xx

McPhail, T.L. (2006). *Global communications.* London: Blackwell.

McQuillan, M., & Willis, I. (Eds.). (2010). *The origins of deconstruction.* Houndmills, UK: Palgrave Macmillan.

Mead, G.H. (1934). *Mind, self and society.* Chicago: University of Chicago Press.

Mead, M. (1934[2001]). *Sex and temperament in three primitive societies.* New York: Harper Perennial.

Meade, T.A., & Wiesner-Hanks, M.E. (Eds.). (2006). *A companion to gender history.* Oxford: Blackwell.

Meekosha, H. (1999). Feminism, disability and the body. In *Feminist perspectives on the body.* Geelong: Deakin University Press.

Meekosha, H. (2004). Drifting down the Gulf Stream: Navigating the cultures of disability studies. *Disability and Society, 19*(7), 721–33.

Meekosha, H. (2005). What the hell are you? An intercategorical analysis of race, ethnicity, gender and disability in the Australian body politic. *Scandinavian Journal of Disability Research, 8*(2–3), 161–76.

Mellen, J. (1977). *Big bad wolves: Masculinity in the American film*. New York: Pantheon.

Melucci, A. (1980). The new social movements: A theoretical approach. *Social Science Information, 19*, 199–226.

Melucci, A. (1989). *Nomads of the present: Social movements and individual needs in contemporary society*. Philadelphia, PA: Philadelphia University Press.

Melucci, A. (1996a). *Challenging codes: Collective action in the information age*. Cambridge: Cambridge University Press.

Melucci, A. (1996b). *The playing self: Person and meaning in the planetary society*. Cambridge: Cambridge University Press.

Melzer A.M., Weinberger, J., & Zinman, M.R. (Eds.). (1998). *Multiculturalism and American democracy*. Lawrence: University Press of Kansas.

Meredith, F. (2005). *Experiencing the postmetaphysical self: Between hermeneutics and deconstruction*. London: Palgrave Macmillan.

Merle, F., Rubin, E., & Sprung, B. (1999). Connecting gender and disability. *WEEA Digest*. WEEA Equity Resource Centre.

Merleau-Ponty, M. (1962). *The phenomenology of perception* (C. Smith, Trans.). New York: Humanities Press.

Messerschmidt, J.W. (1993). *Masculinities and crime: Critique and reconceptualization of theory*. Lanham, MD: Rowman and Littlefield.

Messner, M.A. (1992). *Power at play: Sports and the problem of masculinity*. Boston: Beacon Press.

Messner, M.A. (1997). *Politics of masculinities: Men in movements*. Thousand Oaks, CA: Sage.

Messner, M.A. (2001). Friendship, intimacy, and sexuality. In S.M. Whitehead & F.J. Barrett (Eds.), *The masculinities reader*. Cambridge: Polity.

Messner, M.A. (2002). *Taking the field: Women, men and sports*. Minnesota: University of Minnesota Press.

Messner, M.A., & Sabo, D.F. (Eds.). (1990). *Sport, men and the gender order: Critical feminist perspectives*. Champaign, IL: Human Kinetics.

Mesure, S. (2006, January 10). Business Analysis: City career women find glass ceiling firmly intact on their way to the top. *The Independent* [Online edition].

Michalko, R. (1998). *The mystery of the eye and the shadow of blindness*. Toronto: University of Toronto Press.

Michalko, R. (2002). *The difference that disability makes*. Philadelphia, PA: Temple University Press.

Middleton, P. (1992). *The inward gaze: Masculinity and subjectivity in modern culture*. London: Routledge.

Mihelich, J., & Storrs, D. (2003). Higher education and the negotiated process of hegemony: Embedded resistance among Mormon women. *Gender & Society, 17*(3), 404–22.

Miles, R. (1982). *Racism and migrant labour*. Boston: Routledge & Kegan Paul.

Millen, J. (1990). *Living in the eye of paradox: Gender, post modernism, sociology* (Doctoral dissertation). University of Toronto.

Miller, T. (Ed.). (2009). *The contemporary Hollywood reader*. Abingdon, UK: Routledge.

Millett, K. (2005 [1970]). *Sexual politics*. New York: Doubleday.

Mills, A.J., & Tancred, P. (Eds.). (1992). *Gendering organizational analysis*. London: Sage.

Mills, M. (2001). *Challenging violence in schools: An issue of masculinities*. Buckingham, UK: Open University Press.

Mills, S. (2004). *Discourse: The new critical idiom*. London: Routledge.

Min ha, T.T. (1989). *Woman, native, other: Writing postcoloniality and feminism*. Bloomington: Indiana University Press.

Mirande, A. (1999). *Hombres y machos: Masculinity and Latino culture*. Boulder, CO: Westview Press.

Misra, K., & Rich, M. (2003). *Jewish feminism in Israel: Some contemporary perspectives*. Waltham, MA: Brandeis University Press.

Misztal, B.A. (1996). *Trust in modern societies: The search for the bases of social order*. Cambridge: Polity.

Misztal, B.A. (1998). Memory and trust: Post-communist societies in search for rules for recalling their past. *Political Expressions, 2*(1), 7–30.

Misztal, B.A. (2001). Trusting the professionals: A managerial discourse for uncertain times. In M. Dent & S. Whitehead (Eds.), *Managing professional identities*. London: Routledge.

Mitchell, J. (1971). *Women's estate*. New York: Pantheon Books.

Mitchell, J. (1974). *Psychoanalysis and feminism*. London: Penguin.Modood, T. (1992). *Not easy being British: Colour, culture and citizenship*. Stoke-on-Trent, UK: Trentham Books.

Modood, T. (1993). Muslim views on religious identity and racial equality. *New Community*, *19*(3), 513–19.

Modood, T. (1994). Establishment, multiculturalism, and British citizenship. *Political Quarterly*, *65*(1), 53–73.

Modood, T., Berthoud, R., Lakey, J., Nazroo, J., Smith, P., Viree, S., & Beishon, S. (1997). *Ethnic minorities in Britain: diversity and disadvantage*. London: Policy Studies Institute.

Mohanty, C.T. (1984). Under Western eyes: Feminist scholarship and colonial discourses. *Boundary 2*, *12/13*(3), 333–58.

Mohanty, C.T. (2003). *Feminism without borders: Decolonizing theory, practicing solidarity*. Durham, NC: Duke University Press.

Moi, T. (2004). From femininity to finitude: Freud, Lacan, and feminism, again. *Signs: Journal of Women in Culture and Society*, *29*(3), 841–78.

Molloy, D., Knight, T., & Woodfield, K. (2003). *Diversity in disability: Exploring the interactions between disability, ethnicity, age, gender and sexuality* [DWP research report No. 188]. Leeds, UK: CDS.

Monaghan, L.F. (2005). Big handsome men, bears and others: Virtual constructions of "fat male embodiment." *Body & Society*, *11*(2), 81–111.

Moodley, R. (1999). Challenges and transformation: Counselling in a multicultural context. *International Journal for the Advancement of Counselling*, *21*, 139–52.

Moodley, R. (2007). (Re)placing multiculturalism in counselling and psychotherapy. *British Journal of Guidance and Counselling*, *35*(1), 1–22.

Moodley, R., & Curling, D. (2006). Multiculturalism. In Y. Jackson (Ed.), *Encyclopedia of multicultural psychology*. Thousand Oaks, CA: Sage.

Moodley, R., & Palmer, S. (Eds). (2006). *Race, culture and psychotherapy*. London: Routledge.

Moore, D. (2007). Feminist criminology: Gain, loss and backlash. *Sociology Compass*, *2*(1), 48–61.

Morgan, D.H.J. (1992). *Discovering men*. London: Routledge.

Morgan, D.H.J. (2006). Theater of war: Combat, the military, and masculinities. In S. Whitehead (Ed.), *Men and masculinities: Critical concepts in sociology* (Vol. 2). London: Routledge.

Morioka M. (2008). *Lessons in love for herbivore boys*. Tokyo: Media Factory.

Morris, J. (2001). Impairment and disability: Constructing an ethics of care that promotes human rights. *Hypata*, *16*, 1–16.

Morris, R. (1994). Three sexes and four sexualities: Redressing the discourses on gender and sexuality in contemporary Thailand. *Positions*, *2*(1), 15–43.

Morrison, K. (2001). *Marx, Durkheim, Weber*. London: Sage.

Moser, C., & Kleinplatz, P.J. (2006). Introduction: The state of our knowledge on SM. In P.J. Kleinplatz & C. Moser (Eds.), *Sadomasochism: Powerful pleasures*. Binghampton, NY: Harrington Park Press.

Moser, C.O.N., & Clark, F.C. (2001). *Victims, perpetrators or actors? Gender, armed conflict, and political violence*. New York: Zed Books.

Mottier, V. (2002). Masculine domination: Gender and power in Bourdieu's writings. *Feminist Theory*, *3*(3), 345–59.

Mouffe, C. (1988). Radical democracy: Modern or postmodern? In A. Ross (Ed.), *Universal abandon? The politics of postmodernism*. Minneapolis: University of Minnesota Press.

Mouffe, C. (1995). Democratic politics and the question of identity. In J. Rajchman, (Ed.), *The identity in question*. London: Routledge.

Mountjoy, S. (2008). *The women's rights movement: Moving toward equality*. New York: Chelsea House.

Mukherjee, M. (2004). Women and work in the shadow of globalisation. *Indian Journal of Gender Studies*, *11*(3), 276–90.

Mulhall, S., & Swift, A. (1992). *Liberals and communitarians: An introduction*. Oxford: Blackwell.

Munday, J. (2009). Gendered citizenship. *Sociology Compass, 3*(2), 249–66.

Murray, C., & Phillips, M. (2001). *Underclass + 10.* London: Civitas.

Namaste, V.K. (2005). *Sex change, social change: Reflections on identity, institutions, and imperialism.* Toronto: Women's Press.

Narayan, U. (1997). *Dislocating cultures: Identities, traditions and third world feminism.* London: Routledge.

Nardi, P.M. (Ed.). (1992). *Men's friendships.* Thousand Oaks, CA: Sage.

Nardi, P.M. (Ed.). (1999). *Gay men's friendships: Invincible communities.* Chicago: Chicago University Press.

Nardi, P.M. (Ed.). (2000). "Anything for a sis, Mary": An Introduction to gay masculinities. In P.M. Nardi (Ed.), *Gay masculinities.* Thousand Oaks, CA: Sage.

Natanson, M. (1970). *The journeying self: A study in philosophy and social role.* Reading, MA: Addison Wesley.

National Science Foundation (2012). Science and engineering indicators 2012. Retrieved from http://www.nsf.gov/statistics/seind12/c2/c2h.htm

Nawyn, S.J. (2010). Institutional structures of opportunity in refugee resettlement: Gender, race/ethnicity, and refugee NGOs. *Journal of Sociology and Social Welfare, 37*(1), 149–67.

Negrin, L. (2002). Cosmetic surgery and the eclipse of identity. *Body & Society, 8*(4), 21–42.

Neidhardt, F., & Rucht, D. (1991). The analysis of social movements: The state of the art and some other perspectives for further research. In D. Rucht (Ed.), *Research on social movements: The state of the art in Western Europe and the USA.* Boulder, CO: Westview Press.

Neill, M. (2009). Japan's "herbivore men"—less interested in sex, money. *CNN World.* Retrieved from http://articles.cnn.com/2009-06-05/world/japan.herbivore.men_1_japanese-men-men-and-women-girlfriend?_s=PM:WORLD

Nelson, D.D. (1998). *National manhood: Capitalist citizenship and the imagined fraternity of white men.* Durham, NC: Durham University Press.

Newburn, T., & Stanko, E.A. (Eds.). (1994). *Just boys doing business? Men, masculinities and crime.* London: Routledge.

Newton, J. (2005). *From Panthers to promise keepers: Rethinking the men's movement.* Lanham, MD: Rowman & Littlefield.

Nicholson, L. (Ed.). (1990). *Feminism/postmodernism.* London: Routledge.

Nicholson, L. (1999). *The play of reason: From the modern to the postmodern.* Buckingham, UK: Open University Press.

Nicholson, L., & Fraser, N. (1999). Social criticism without philosophy: An encounter between feminism and postmodernism. In L. Nicholson, *The play of reason: From the modern to the postmodern.* Buckingham, UK: Open University Press.

Nicholson, P. (1996). *Gender, power and organization: A psychological perspective.* London: Routledge.

Nielson, H.B. (2004). Noisy girls: New subjectivities and old gender discourses. *Young: Nordic Journal of Youth Research, 12*(1), 9–30.

Nietzsche, F. (1973). *Beyond good and evil: Prelude to the philosophy of the future* (J. von Gut und Böse, Trans.). Harmondsworth, UK: Penguin.

Nishida, M. (2003). *Slavery and identity: Ethnicity, gender and race in Salvador, Brazil, 1808–1888.* Indiana: University Press.

Nixon, S. (1996). *Hard looks: Masculinities, spectatorship and contemporary consumption.* London: UCL Press.

Nizami, N., & Ahmed, R. (2005). Influence of marital status and sex role orientation on women power. *Journal of the Indian Academy of Applied Psychology, 31*(1/2), 29–36.

Noller, P., & Feeney, J.A. (Eds.). (2006). *Close relationships: Functions, forms and processes.* New York: Psychology Press.

Nooteboom, B. (2002). *Trust: Forms, foundations, functions, failures and figures.* Cheltenham, UK: Edward Elgar.

Norberg-Hodge, H. (2000). Compassion in the age of the global economy. In G. Watson, S. Batchelor, & G. Claxton (Eds.), *The psychology of awakening: Buddhism, science and our day-to-day lives.* York Beach, ME: Red Wheel/Weiser.

Nosek, M., & Hughes, R. (2003). Psychosocial issues of women with physical disabilities: The continuing gender debate. *Rehabilitation Counseling Bulletin, 46*(4), 224–33.

Novikova, I., Pringle, K., Hearn, J., Mueller, U., Oleksy, E., Lattu, E., . . . Tallberg, T. (2004). Men, masculinities and "Europe." In I. Novikova & D. Kambourov (Eds.), *Men in the global world*. Helsinki: Kikimora.

Nussbaum, M. (1999, February 22). The professor of parody. *The New Republic*. Retrieved from http://www.tnr.com/archive/0299/022299/nusbaum022299.html

Oakley, A. (1972) *Sex, gender and society*. London: Temple-Smith.

O'Brien, M. (1983). *The politics of reproduction*. London: Routledge & Kegan Paul.

O'Connor, P. (1992). *Friendships between women: A critical review*. London: Prentice-Hall.

Office of National Statistics (2007). *Marriage rates fall to lowest on record*. London: Office of National Statistics.

O'Grady, S. (2010). Women in their twenties smash glass ceiling to reverse pay gap. *The Independent*. Retrieved from http://www.independent.co.uk/news/business/news/women-in-their-twenties-smash-glass-ceiling-to-reverse-pay-gap-2154836.html

Okin, S.M. (1999). Is multiculturalism bad for women? In J. Cohn, M. Howard, & M.C. Nussbaum (Eds.), *Is multiculturalism bad for women?* Princeton, NJ: Princeton University Press.

O'Leary, T., & Falzon, C. (2010). *Foucault and philosophy*. Malden, MA: Wiley-Blackwell.

Oliker, S.J. (1992). *Best friends and marriage: Exchange among women*. Berkeley: University of California Press.

Olkin, R. (2002). Could you hold the door for me? Including disability in diversity. *Cultural Diversity & Ethnic Minority Psychology*, 8(2), 130–7.

Olsen, T. (1980). *Silences*. London: Virago.

Onyx, J., Leonard, R., & Reed, R. (1999). *Revisioning aging: Empowerment of older women*. New York: P.Lang.

Orbach, S. (1998). *Fat is a feminist issue*. New York: Arrow.

O'Reilly, A., Matathia, I., & Salzman, M. (2005). *The future of men*. New York: Palgrave Macmillan.

Orenstein, P. (2002). Shortchanging girls. In P. Dubeck & D. Dunn (Eds.), *Workplace/women's place* (pp. 38–46). Los Angeles: Roxbury.

Otake, T. (2009, May 10). Blurring the boundaries. *The Japan Times*. Retrieved from http://www.japantimes.co.jp/text/fl20090510x1.html

Ouzgane, L. (Ed.). (2006a). *Islamic Masculinities*. London: Zed Books.

Ouzgane, L. (Ed.). (2006b). The rape continuum: Masculinities in Ben Jelloun's and El Saadawi's works. In S. Whitehead (Ed.), *Men and masculinities: Critical concepts in sociology* (Vol. 5). London: Routledge.

Ozbilgin, M.F., Tsouroufli, M., & Smith, M. (2011). Understanding the interplay of time, gender and professionalism in hospital medicine in the UK. *Social Science*, 71(10), 1588–94.

Ozipko, J. (2010). Is Quebec Canada's California? *TheTRUMPET.com*. Retrieved from http://www.thetrumpet.com/?q=7496.6060.0.0

Pahl, R. (2000). *On friendship*. Cambridge: Polity Press.

Painter-Morland, M., & Werhane, P.H. (2010). *Cutting-edge issues in business ethics*. New York: Springer.

Palmary, I. (2006). Gender, nationalism and ethnic difference: Feminist politics and political psychology? *Feminism & Psychology*, 16(1), 44–51.

Palriwala, R., & Uberoi, P. (Eds.). (2008). *Marriage, migration and gender*. New Delhi: Sage.

Parekh, B. (2006). *Rethinking multiculturalism: Cultural diversity and political theory* (2nd Edn). London: Palgrave Macmillan.

Parker, A., & Sedgwick, E.K. (1995). *Performativity and performance*. New York: Routledge.

Parker, M. (2000). *Organizational culture and identity*. London: Sage.

Parker, S. (1983). *Leisure and work*. London: Unwin Hyman.

Parker, S.R. (1976). *The sociology of leisure*. London: Allen & Unwin.

Parry, M., & Malcolm, D. (2004). England's barmy army: Commercialization, masculinity, and nationalism. *International Review for the Sociology of Sport*, 39(1), 75–94.

Parry, O. (2000). *Male underachievement in high school education: In Jamaica, Barbados and St*

Vincent and the Grenadines. Jamaica: Canoe Press.

Parry, R.L. (2009, November 2). Girly men of Japan just want to have fun. *The Times.*

Parsons, T. (1951). *The social system*. New York: The Free Press.

Pascal, E., & Dedman, A. (2011, November). Presentation on gender and sexuality. *South East Asian Institute for Gender Studies, Payap University, Chiang Mai, Thailand.*

Pascoe, C.J. (2005). "Dude, you're a fag": Adolescent masculinity and the fag discourse. *Sexualities, 8*(3), 329–46.

Pateman, C. (1979). *The problem of political obligation: A critique of liberal theory*. Berkeley: University of California Press.

Patterson, L., Cameron, J.E., & Lalonde, R.N. (1996). The intersection of race and gender: Examining the politics of identity in women's studies. *Canadian Journal of Behavioural Science, 28,* 229–39.

Pattman, R. (2005). "Boys and girls should not be too close": Sexuality, the identities of African boys and girls and HIV/AIDS education. *Sexualities, 8*(4), 497–516.

Pendergast, T. (2000). *Creating the modern man: American magazines and consumer culture 1900–1950*. University of Missouri Press. Columbia, MO: University of Missouri Press.

Perkins, W.H., & Demeis, D.K. (1996). Gender and family effects on the "second-shift" domestic activity of college-educated young adults. *Gender and Society, 10*(1), 78–93.

Person, E.S. (1980). Sexuality as the mainstay of identity: Psychoanalytic perspectives. *Signs, 5*(4), 605–30.

Peters, M.A. (2001). *Poststructuralism, Marxism, and neoliberalism: Between theory and practice*. Maryland: Rowman & Littlefield.

Petersen, A. (1998). *Unmasking the masculine: "Men" and "identity" in a sceptical age*. London: Sage.

Pfeil, F. (2000). Subjects without selves: Contemporary theory accounts for the "I." In G. Watson, S. Batchelor, & G. Claxton (Eds.), *The psychology of awakening: Buddhism, science and our day-to-day lives*. York Beach, ME: Red Wheel/Weiser.

Phillips, A. (2010). *Gender and culture*. Cambridge, UK: Polity.

Phoenix, A. (2006). Editorial. *European Journal of Women's Studies, 13,* 187 –96.

Pieper, J., & Malsbary, G. (1998). *Leisure: The basis of culture*. London: St Augustine's Press.

Pipher, M., & Kilbourne, J. (2000). *Can't buy me love: How advertising changes the way we think and feel*. London: Prentice Hall.

Pirovolakis, E. (2010). *Reading Derrida and Ricoeur: Improbable encounters between deconstruction and hermeneutics*. Albany: State University of New York Press.

Pleck, J.H. (1976). The male sex-role: Problems, definitions, and sources of change. *Journal of Social Issues, 32,* 155–64.

Pleck, J.H. (1981). *The myth of masculinity*. Cambridge, MA: MIT Press.

Pleck, J.H. (1995). The gender role strain paradigm: An update. In R.F. Levant & W.S. Pollack (Eds.), *A new psychology of men*. New York: Basic Books.

Pleck, J.H., & Sawyer, J. (Eds.). (1974). *Men and masculinity*. Englewood Cliffs, NJ: Prentice-Hall.

Plummer, K. (Ed.). (1991). *Symbolic interactions*. Aldershot, England: E.Elgar.

Plummer, K. (1995). *Telling sexual stories: Power, change, and social worlds*. London: Routledge.

Podimattam, F.M. (2004). *Intimacy*. Delhi: Media House.

Polletta, F., & Jasper, J. (2001). Collective identity and social movements. *Annual Review of Sociology, 27*(1), 283–305.

Pollock, G. (Ed.). (1996). *Generations and geographies in the visual arts: Feminist readings*. London: Routledge.

Pope, G.H., Phillips, K.A., & Olivardia, R. (Eds.). (2000). *The Adonis complex: The secret crisis of male body obsession*. New York: Free Press.

Popoviciu, L., Haywood, C., & Ghaill, M.M. (2006). "Migrating Masculinities": The Irish diaspora in Britain. *Irish Studies Review, 14*(2), 169–87.

Porta, D.D., & Diani, M. (1999). *Social movements: An introduction*. Oxford: Blackwell.

Pound, D. (2004). *Inside the Olympics*. London: John Wiley.

Power, M. (1997). *The audit society: The rituals of verification*. Oxford: Oxford University Press.

Powrie, P., Davies, A., & Babington, B. (Eds.). (2004). *The trouble with men: Masculinities in European and Hollywood cinema*. London: Wallflower Press.

Poynting, S., & Donaldson, M. (2005). Snakes and leaders: Hegemonic masculinity in ruling-class boys boarding schools. *Men and masculinities*, 7(4), 325–46.

Prasso, S. (2006). *The Asian mystique: Dragon ladies, geisha girls and our fantasies of the exotic Orient*. New York: Public Affairs.

Predelli, L.N. (2004). Interpreting gender in Islam: A case study of immigrant Muslim women in Oslo, Norway. *Gender & Society*, 18(4), 473–93.

Price, J., & Shildrick, M. (Eds.). (1999). *Feminist theory and the body: A reader*. Edinburgh: Edinburgh University Press.

Price, J.N. (2006). Schooling and racialized masculinities: The diploma, teachers, and peers in the lives of young, African-American men. In S.M. Whitehead, (Ed.), *Men and masculinities: Critical concepts in sociology* (Vol. II). London: Routledge.

Prokos, A., & Padavic, I. (2006). "There oughta be a law against bitches": Masculinity lessons in police academy training. In S.M. Whitehead (Ed.), *Men and masculinities: Critical concepts in sociology* (Vol. II). London: Routledge.

Puchert, R., Gärtner, M., & Höyng, S. (2005). *Work changes gender*. Leverkusen, Germany: Barbara Budrich.

Pullen, C. (2007). *Documenting gay men: Identity and performance in reality television and documentary film*. Jefferson, NC: McFarland & Co.

Purcell, D., MacArthur, K.R., & Samblanet, S. (2010). Gender and the glass ceiling at work. *Sociology Compass*, 4(9), 705–17.

Purvis, T., & Hunt, A. (1993). Discourse, ideology, discourse, ideology, discourse, ideology. *Sociology*, 44(3), 473–99.

Pyke, K.D., & Johnson, D.L. (2003). Asian-American women and racialized femininities: "Doing" gender across cultural worlds. *Gender & Society*, 17(1), 33–53.

Qian, N., Fong, G.S., & Smith, R.J. (2008). *Different worlds of discourse: Transformations of gender and genre in late Qing and early republican China*. Leiden, Holland: Brill.

Quinn, B.A. (2002). Sexual harassment and masculinity: The power and meaning of "girl watching." *Gender & Society*, 16(3), 386–402.

Radtke, H.L., & Stam, H.J. (Eds.). (1994). *Power/gender: Social relations in theory and practice*. London: Sage.

Raffaelli, M., & Ontai, L.L. (2004). Gender socialization in Latino/a families: Results from two retrospective studies. *Sex Roles*, 50(5/6), 287–99.

Rajchman, J. (Ed.). (1995). *The identity in question*. London: Routledge.

Ramazanoglu, C. (Ed.). (1992). *Up against Foucault: Explorations of some tensions between Foucault and feminism*. London: Routledge.

Ramazanoglu, C., & Holland, J. (2005). *Feminist methodology: Challenges and choices*. London: Sage.

Ramesh, R. (2010). More black people jailed in England and Wales proportionally than in US. *The Guardian*. Retrieved from http://www.guardian.co.uk/society/2010/oct/11/black-prison-population-increase-england

Ransome, P. (2005). *Work, consumption and culture: Affluence and social change in the twenty-first century*. London: Sage.

Ranson, G. (2010). *Against the grain: Couples, gender, and the reframing of parenting*. Toronto: University of Toronto Press.

Rasmussen, M.L. (2005). *Becoming subjects: Sexualities and secondary schooling*. New York: Routledge.

Ray, A. (2007). *Naked on the Internet: Hookups, downloads, and cashing in on Internet sexploration*. Emeryville, CA: Seal Press.

Ray, L. (2011). *Violence & society*. Thousand Oaks, CA: Sage.

Razak, S. (2008). *Casting out: The eviction of Muslims from Western law and politics*. Toronto: University of Toronto Press.

Reagin, N.R. (1995). *A German women's movement: Class and gender in Hanover, 1880–1993*. Chapel Hill: University of North Carolina Press.

Reay, D. (2001). The paradox of contemporary femininities in education: Combining fluidity with fixity. In B. Francis & C. Skelton (Eds.), *Investigating gender: Contemporary perspectives in education*. Buckingham, UK: Open University Press.

Reay, D., David, M., & Ball, S. (2005). *Degrees of choice: Social class, race and gender in higher education*. Stoke-on-Trent, UK: Trentham Books.

Rees, B.A. (2003). *The construction of management: Competence and gender issues at work*. Northampton, MA: Edward Elgar.

Renold, E. (2000). "Coming out": Gender, (hetero) sexuality and the primary school. *Gender and Education, 12*(3), 309–26.

Reynolds, L.T., & Herman-Kinney, N.J. (Eds.). (2003). *Handbook of symbolic interactionism*. Walnut Creek, CA: AltaMira Press.

Rheingold, H. (2000). *Virtual communities: Homesteading on the electric frontier Virtual communities: Homesteading on the electric frontier*. Cambridge, MA: MIT Press.

Rice, C. (2007). Becoming "the fat girl": Acquisition of an unfit identity. *Women's Studies International Forum, 30*, 158–74.

Rice, C. (2012, May 24). Why women leave academia and why universities should be worried. *The Guardian*. Retrieved from http://www.guardian.co.uk/higher-education-network/blog/2012/may/24/why-women-leave-academia

Rich, A. (1983). Compulsory heterosexuality and lesbian existence. In A. Snitow, C. Stansell, & S. Thompson (Eds.), *The powers of desire: The politics of sexuality*. New York: Monthly Review Press/New Feminist Library.

Richardson, D., McLaughlin, J., & Casey, M.E. (Eds.). (2006). *Intersections between feminist and queer theory*. Houndmills, UK: Palgrave Macmillan.

Ricoeur, P. (1991). *From text to action: Essays in hermeneutics II*. London: Northwestern University Press.

Ricoeur, P. (1992). *Oneself as another*. Chicago: University of Chicago Press.

Rifkin, J. (2004). *The end of work*. Los Angeles: J.P. Tarcher.

Rikowski, G. (1997). Scorched earth: Prelude to rebuilding Marxist educational theory. *British Journal of Sociology of Education, 18*(4), 551–74.

Riley, R.L. (2008). Women and war: Militarism, bodies, and the practice of gender. *Sociology Compass, 2*(4),1192–208.

Ritzer, G. (1993). *The McDonaldization of society*. Thousand Oaks, CA: Pine Forge Press.

Roberts, C. (2002). "A matter of embodied fact": Sex hormones and the history of bodies. *Feminist Theory, 3*(1), 7–26.

Roberts, L.D., & Parks, M.R. (1999). The social geography of gender-switching in virtual environments on the Internet. *Information, Communication & Society, 2*(4), 521–40.

Robinson, S. (2000). *Marked men: White masculinity in crisis*. New York: Routledge.

Robinson, S.A. (1999). *Tradition and liberation*. New York: St Martin's Press.

Rodrigues, V. (2002). Is there a case for multiculturalism? In K. Deb (Ed.), *Mapping multiculturalism*. New Delhi: Rawat.

Rogers, A. (2005). Chaos to control: Men's magazines and the mastering of intimacy. *Men and Masculinities, 8*(2), 175–94.

Rogoff, B. (1990). *Apprenticeship in thinking: Cognitive development in social context*. New York: Oxford University Press.

Rojek, C. (1985). *Capitalism and leisure theory*. London: Tavistock.

Rojek, C. (1995). *Decentring leisure: Rethinking leisure theory*. London: Sage.

Román-Odio, C., & Sierra, M. (Ed.). (2011). *Transnational borderlands in women's global networks: The making of cultural resistance*. New York: Palgrave Macmillan.

Roper, M. (1994). *Masculinity and British organization man since 1945*. Oxford: Oxford University Press.

Rose, G. (1993). *Feminism and geography*. Cambridge: Polity.

Rose, H., & Rose, S. (2000). *Alas, poor Darwin: Arguments against evolutionary psychology*. London: Jonathon Cape. Rose, J. (1986). *Sexuality in the field of vision*. London: Verso.

Rose, N. (1996). *Inventing ourselves: Psychology, power, and personhood*. Cambridge: Cambridge University Press.

Rose, S., & Hartmann, H. (2004). *Still a man's labor market*. Washington, DC: Institute for Women's Policy Research.

Roseberry, W. (1989). Multiculturalism and the challenge of anthropology. *Social Research, 59*(4), 841–58.

Rosen, R. (2001). *The world split open: How the modern women's movement changed America*. New York: Penguin Putnam.

Roseneil, S. (1995). *Disarming patriarchy: Feminism and political action at Greenham*. Milton Keynes, UK: Open University Press.

Roseneil, S. (2006, October). Queer individualisation: Practices of sociability, sexuality and self in the early twenty-first century. Paper presented at the International Conference on Changing Forms of Intimacy, University of Oslo.

Rosenthal, E.R. (Ed.). (1990). *Women, aging, and ageism*. New York: Harrington Park Press.

Rosselson, R. (2012). Ageing, Ageism and Feature Films. Retrieved from http://oldwomaninfeaturefilms.wordpress.com/

Rossi, S.E. (Ed.). (2004). *The battle and backlash rage on*. New York: Xlibris.

Rostami-Povey, E. (2007). Gender, agency and identity: The case of Afghan women in Afghanistan, Pakistan and Iran. *Journal of Development Studies, 43*(2), 294–311.

Rothblum, E.D. (2000). Sexual orientation and sex in women's lives: Conceptual and methodological issues. *Journal of Social Issues, 56*(2), 193–204.

Rotundo, E.A. (1993). *American manhood: Transformations in masculinity from the revolution to the modern era*. New York: Basic Books.

Rousso, H. (1988). Daughters with disabilities: Defective women or minority women? In M. Fine & A. Asch. (Eds), *Women with disabilities: Essays in psychology, politics and culture* (pp.139–71). Philadelphia: Temple University Press.Rousso, H. (Ed.) (1988). *Disabled, female and proud! Ten stories of women with disabilities*. Boston, MA: Exceptional Parent Press.

Rowe, K.E. (1986). Feminism and fairy tales. In J. Zipes (Ed.), *Don't bet on the prince:Contemporary feminist fairy tales in North America and England* (pp. 209–26). New York: Scholar Press.

Rowe, K.E. (2007). *Feminism and fairy tales*. Retrieved from www.broadviewpress.com/tales/printable/feminism.htm

Rowlands, S. (2002). *Jung: A feminist revision*. Cambridge, UK: Polity.

Rubenberg, C.A. (2001). *Palestinian Women: Patriarchy and resistance in the West Bank*. Boulder, CO: Lynne Rienner.

Rubin, G. (1984). Thinking sex: Notes for a radical theory of the politics of sexuality. In C. Vance (Ed.), *Pleasure and danger: Exploring female sexuality*. London: Routledge.

Rubin, G. (1992). Of catamites and kings: Reflections on butch, gender and boundaries. In J. Nestle (Ed.), *The persistent desire: A femme-butch reader*. Boston: Alyson.

Rupp, L., & Taylor, V. (1999). Feminist identity in an international movement: A collective identity approach to feminism. *Signs, 24*, 363–86.

Rupp, L.J., & Taylor, V. (2003). *Drag queens at the 801 cabaret*. Chicago: Chicago University Press.

Russell, L. (1993). *Church in the round: Feminist interpretation of the church*. Louisville, KY: Westminster John Knox Press.

Rutherford, J. (1997). *Forever England: Reflections on masculinity and empire*. London: Lawrence & Wishart.

Rutherford, J. (1999). *I am no longer myself without you: An anatomy of love*. London: Flamingo.

Ryan, B. (1992). *Feminism and the women's movement: Dynamics of change in social movement's ideology and activism*. New York: Routledge.

Sabo, D., & Gordon, D.F. (Eds.). (1995). *Men's health and illness: Gender, power, and the body*. Thousand Oaks, CA: Sage.

Sabo, D.F., Kupers, T.A., & London, W. (Eds.). (2001). *Prison masculinities*. Philadelphia: Temple University Press.

Sage, G.H. (1990). *Power and ideology in American sport*. Champaign, IL: Human Kinetics.

Said, E.W. (1978). *Orientalism*. London: Routledge & Kegan Paul.

Said, E.W. (1993). *Culture and imperialism*. London: Chatto & Windus.

Said, E.W. (2000). *Reflections on exile and other essays*. Cambridge, MA: Harvard University Press.

Sakr, N. (Ed.). (2004). *Women and media in the Middle East: Power through self-expression.* New York: I.B. Tauris.

Salih, S. (2002). *Judith Butler.* London: Routledge.

Salih, S., & Butler, J. (Eds.). (2004). *The Judith Butler reader.* Malden, MA: Blackwell Publishing.

Samp, J., Wittenburg, E., & Gillett, D. (2003). Presenting and monitoring a gender-defined self on the Internet. *Communication Research Reports, 20*(1), 1–12.

Sanlon, P. (2010). *Plastic people: How queer theory is changing us.* London: Rainbow Book Agencies.

Sarup, M. (1993). *Post-structuralism and postmodernism* (2nd Edn). London: Harvester Wheatsheaf.

Sassen, S. (2007). *Sociology of globalization.* New York: W.W. Norton.

Saurer, E., Lanzinger, M., & Frysak, E. (2006). *Women's movements: Networks and debates in post-communist countries in the 19th and 20th centuries.* Köln, Germany: Böhlau.

Saussure, F. de (1974). *A course in general linguistics.* London: Fontana

Sawicki, J. (1991). *Disciplining Foucault: Feminism, power, and the body.* New York: Routledge.

Schaef, A.W. (1989). *Escape from intimacy: The pseudo-relationship addictions: Untangling the "love" addictions, sex, romance, relationships.* New York: Harper & Row.

Schaefer, R.T. (2010). *Race and ethnicity in the United States* (6th Edn). New York: Prentice Hall.

Scheff, T.J. (2006). *Goffman unbound! A new paradigm for social science.* Boulder, CO: Paradigm.

Schippers, M. (2000). *Rockin' out of the box: Gender maneuvering in alternative hard rock.* New Brunswick, NJ: Princeton University Press.

Schleifer, D. (2006). Make me feel mighty real: Gay female-to-male transgenderists. Negotiating sex, gender, and sexuality. *Sexualities, 9*(1), 57–75.

Schneider, B.E., & Gould, M. (1987). Female sexuality: Looking back into the future. In B.B. Hess & M.M. Ferree (Eds.), *Analyzing gender.* Thousand Oaks, CA: Sage.

Schneiders, S.M. (2004). *Beyond patching: Faith and feminism in the Catholic Church.* Mahwah, NJ: Paulist Press International.

Schrock, D., & Schwalbe, M. (2009). Men, masculinity, and manhood acts. *Annual Review of Sociology, 35,* 277–96.

Schutz, A. (1967). *On phenomenology and social relations.* Chicago: University of Chicago Press.

Schwartz, A. (2010). *Gender and modernity in Central Europe.* Ottawa: University of Ottawa Press.

Scott, S., & Morgan, D. (Eds.). (1993). *Body matters.* London: The Falmer Press.

Scranton, S., & Flintoff, A. (Eds.). (2002). *Gender and sport: A reader.* London: Routledge.

Sedgwick, E.K. (1990). *The epistemology of the closet.* Berkeley: University of California Press.

Segal, A. (2001). Masculinity, school, and self in Sweden and the Netherlands. In S.M. Whitehead & F.J. Barrett (Eds.), *The masculinities reader.* Cambridge: Polity.

Seidler, V.J. (1993). *Unreasonable men: Masculinity and social theory.* London: Routledge.

Seidler, V.J. (1994). *Recovering the self: Morality and social theory.* London: Routledge.

Seidler, V.J. (1997). *Man enough: Embodying masculinities.* London: Sage.

Seidler, V.J. (2006). *Young men and masculinities: Global cultures and intimate lives.* London: Zed Books.

Seidman, S. (1994). Special volume on queer theory. *Sociological Theory, 4*(2).

Seidman, S. (Ed.). (1996). *Queer theory/sociology.* Oxford: Blackwell.

Seidman, S. (2002). *Beyond the closet: The transformation of gay and lesbian life.* New York: Routledge.

Seidman, S. (2003). *The social construction of sexuality.* New York: W.W. Norton.

Sellars, S. (Ed.). (1994). *The Helene Cixous reader.* London: Routledge.

Sennett, R. (1998). *The corrosion of character: The personal consequences of work in the new capitalism.* New York: W.W. Norton.

Settles, I.H. (2006). Use of an intersectional framework to understand black women's racial and gender identities. *Sex Roles, 54,* 589–601.

Sewell, T. (1999). Loose canons: Exploding the myth of the "black macho" lad. In D. Epstein, J.

Elwood, V. Hey, & J. Maw (Eds.), *Failing boys?* Buckingham, UK: Open University Press.

Shahidian, H. (2002). *Women in Iran*. Westport, CT: Greenwood Press.

Shain, F. (2003). *The schooling and identity of Asian girls*. Stoke-on-Trent, UK: Trentham Books.

Sharma, A., & Young, K.K. (Eds.). (1998). *Feminism and world religions*. New York: State University of New York Press.

Shepard, A., & Walker, G. (Eds.). (2009). *Gender and change: Agency, chronology and periodisation*. Chichester, England: Wiley-Blackwell.

Sherry, M. (2007). (Post)colonising disability. *Intersecting Gender and Disability Perspectives in Rethinking Postcolonial Identities, Wagadu, 4*, 10–22.

Shilling, C. (1993). *The body and social theory*. London: Sage.

Shirane, H. (2008). *Envisioning the tale of Genji: Media, gender, and cultural production*. New York: Columbia University Press.

Shotter, J., & Gergen, K.J. (Eds.). (1989). *Texts of identity*. London: Sage.

Showalter, E. (1977). *A literature of their own: British women novelists from Brontë to Lessing*. Princeton, NJ: Princeton University Press.

Shusterman, R. (Ed.). (1999). *Bourdieu: A critical reader*. Oxford: Blackwell.

Siegel H. (2007). Multiculturalism and rationality. *Theory and Research in Education, 5*(2), 203–23.

Siltanen, J., & Doucet, A. (2008). *Gender relations: Intersectionality and beyond*. Toronto: Oxford University Press.

Silva, E.B., & Smart, C. (Eds.). (1999). *The new family?* London: Sage.

Silverman, H.J. (1989). *Derrida and deconstruction*. London: Routledge.

Silverman, M. (1992). *Deconstructing the nation: Immigration, racism and citizenship in modern France*. London: Routledge.

Sim, J. (1994). Tougher than the rest? Men in prison. In T. Newburn & E.A. Stanko (Eds.), *Just boys doing business? Men, masculinities and crime*. London: Routledge.

Simmons, M. (1995). The truth about male friendships. In M.S. Kimmel & M.A. Messner (Eds.), *Men's lives*. Boston: Allyn and Bacon.

Simon, W. (1996). *Postmodern sexualities*. London: Routledge.

Simpson, M. (1994, November 15). Here come the mirror men. *The Independent*.

Simpson, M. (2002, June 22). Meet the metrosexual. Retrieved from www.MarkSimpson.com

Simpson, M. (2003, June 28). Beckham, the virus. Retrieved from www.MarkSimpson.com

Simpson, M. (2005, December). *Metrodaddy v. Ubermummy*. Retrieved from www.MarkSimpson.com

Simpson, R. (2004). Masculinity at work: The experiences of men in female dominated occupations. *Work, Employment and Society, 18*(2), 349–68.

Singh, K., & Agrawal, P. (2007). Perceived sex role and fear of success: A study on urban working women. *Journal of Social Science, 15*(1), 65–9.

Sinnott, M. (2004). *Toms and dees: Transgender identity and female same-sex relationships in Thailand*. Chiang Mai: Silkworm Books.

Siray, M. (2009). *Performance and performativity*. Frankfurt am Main, Germany: P. Lang.

Siu, L. (2005). Queen of the Chinese colony: Gender, nation, and belonging in diaspora. *Anthropological Quarterly, 78*(3), 511–42.

Sjoberg, L., & Via, S. (Eds.). (2010). *Gender, war, and militarism: Feminist perspectives*. Santa Barbara, CA: Praeger.

Skelton, C. (2001). *Schooling the boys: Masculinities and primary education*. Buckingham, UK: Open University Press.

Skelton, C., & Francis, B. (2009). *Feminism and "the Schooling scandal."* New York: Routledge.

Skillman, G., & Fiese, B.H. (2000). Gender differences in family stories: Moderating influence of parent gender role and child gender. *Sex Roles, 43*(5/6), 267–83.

Smit, B., & Fritz, E. (2008). Understanding teacher identity from a symbolic interactionist perspective: Two ethnographic narratives. *South African Journal of Education, 28*, 91–101.

Smith, D. (2009). Categories are not enough. *Gender and Society, 23*(1), 76–80.

Smith, D.E. (1988). *The everyday world as problematic: A feminist sociology*. Milton Keynes, UK: Open University Press.

Smith, G. (2006). *Erving Goffman*. Abingdon, UK: Routledge.

Smith, L. (Ed.). (1999). *Nike is a goddess: The history of women in sports*. New York: Atlantic Monthly Press.

Sniderman, P. (2007, July 3). Identity Crisis. *The Guardian* [Higher education supplement].

Sniderman, P., & Hagendoorn, L. (2007). *When ways of life collide: Multiculturalism and its discontents in the Netherlands*. Princeton, NJ: Princeton University Press.

Snow, D. (2001). Collective identity and expressive forms. *University of California, Irvine eScholarship Repository*. Retrieved from http://repositories.cdlib.org/csd/01-07

Sobsey, D., Gray, S., Wells, D., Pyper, D., & Relmer-Heck, B. (1990). *Sexuality, disability, and abuse: An annotated bibliography*. Edmonton, Alberta: The University of Alberta.

Solomos, J., & Back, L. (1995). *Race, politics, and social change*. New York: Psychology Press.

Song, S. (2005). Majority norms, multiculturalism, and gender equality. *American Political Science Review, 99*(4), 473–89.Spade, J. (2001). Gender and education in the United States. In D. Vannoy (Ed.), *Gender Mosaics: Social Perspectives* (pp. 85–93). Los Angeles: Roxbury.

Speer, S.A. (2001). Participant's orientations, ideology and the ontological status of hegemonic masculinity: A rejoinder to Nigel Edley. *Feminism and Psychology, 11*(1), 141–44.

Spelman, E.V. (1988). *Inessential women: Problems of exclusion in feminist thought*. Boston: Beacon Press.

Spelman, E.V. (1998). *Inessential woman: Problems of exclusion in feminist thought*. Boston: Beacon Press.

Spender, D. (1980). *Man made language*. London: Routledge & Kegan Paul.

Spender, D. (1981). *Men's studies modified*. Oxford: Pergamon Press.

Spivak, G. (1987). French feminism in an international frame. *Yale French Studies, 62*, 154–84.

Spring, J. (2007). *Wheels in the head: Educational philosophies of authority, freedom, and culture from Socrates to human rights*. Mahwah, NJ: Lawrence Erlbaum.

Squires, D. (Ed.). (1993). *Principled positions: Postmodernism and the rediscovery of value*. London: Lawrence & Wishart.

Squires, J. (2001). Representing groups, deconstructing identities. *Feminist Theory, 2*(1), 7–27.

Stanley, L. (1993). On auto/biography in sociology. *Sociology, 27*(1), 41–52.

Stanley, L., & Wise. S. (1993). *Breaking out again: Feminist ontology and epistemology*. London: Routledge.

Steele, T.L. (2005). *Sex, self, and society: The social context of sexuality*. Belmont, CA: Thomson/Wadsworth.

Stephens, D.P., & Phillips, L. (2005). Integrating black feminist thought into conceptual frameworks of African-American adolescent women's sexual scripting processes. *Sexualities, Evolution and Gender, 7*(1), 37–55.

Stets, J.E., & Burke, P.J. (2005). New directions in identity control theory. *Advances in Group Processes, 22*, 43–64.

Stevenson, B. (2007). *Title IX and the evolution of high school sports*. Munich: CESifo.

Stora, B. (2006). *Les trois exils, Juifs d'Algérie*. Paris: Stock.

Stronach, I., & Maclure, M. (1997). *Educational research undone: The postmodern embrace*. Buckingham, UK: Open University Press.

Stryker, S. (2008). *Transgendered history*. New York: Seal Press.

Sullivan, O. (2000). The division of domestic labour: Twenty years of change? *Sociology, 34*(3), 437–56.

Summers, M., (2003). Diasporic brotherhood: Freemasonry and the transnational production of black middle-class masculinity. *Gender & History, 15*(3), 550–74.

Sutherland, J. (2010). Mothering, guilt and shame. *Sociology Compass, 4*(5), 310–21.

Sutherland, S. (Ed.). (1995). *The Macmillan dictionary of psychology*. Basingstoke, UK: Macmillan.

Swain, S.O. (1992). Men's friendships with women: Intimacy, sexual boundaries, and the informant rule. In P.M. Nardi (Ed.), *Men's Friendships*. Thousand Oaks, CA: Sage.

Swarr, A.L., & Nagar, R. (2010). *Critical transnational feminist praxis*. Albany, NY: State University of New York Press.

Swinford, S., & Warren, G. (2010, January 31). Breadwinner wives reign in 44 per cent of homes. *The Sunday Times*, p. 11.

Sztompka, P. (1999). *Trust: A sociological theory*. Cambridge: Cambridge University Press.

Tacey, D.J. (1997). *Remaking men: Jung, spirituality and social change*. London: Routledge.

Talbot, M., & Wimbush, E. (Eds.). (1989). *Relative freedoms*. Milton Keynes, UK: Open University Press.

Talhami, G.H. (1996). *The mobilization of Muslim women in Egypt*. Tallahassee, FL: University Press of Florida.

Tamaoka, K., Lim, H., Miyaoka, Y., & Kiyama, S. (2010). Effects of gender-identity and gender-congruence on levels of politeness among young Japanese and Koreans. *Journal of Asian Pacific Communication, 20*(1), 23–45.

Tapp, R.B. (Ed.). (2000). *Multiculturalism*. New York: Prometheus Books.

Tarrant, S. (2006). *When sex became gender*. New York: Routledge.

Tasker, Y. (1998). *Working girls: Gender and sexuality in popular cinema*. London: Routledge.

Taylor, G. (2010). *The new political sociology: Power, ideology and identity in an age of complexity*. Houndmills, UK: Palgrave Macmillan.

Taylor, V., & Whittier, N. (1992). Collective identity in social movement communities: Lesbian feminist mobilization. In C.M. Mueller & A.D. Morris (Eds.), *Frontiers in Social Movement Theory*. New Haven, CT: Yale University Press.

Teather, D. (2006, October 2). Glass ceiling still blocks women from executive floor. *The Guardian*.

Tengan, T.P.K. (2008). *Native men remade: Gender and nation in contemporary Hawai'i*. Durham, NC: Duke University Press.

Tepperman, L. (2009). *Deviance, crime, and control: Beyond the straight and narrow*. New York: Oxford University Press.

Teubert, W. (2010). *Meaning, discourse and society*. New York: Cambridge University Press.

Thacker, A. (2003). *Moving through modernity: Space and geography in modernism*. Manchester, UK: Manchester University Press.

Thapan, M. (Ed.). (1997). *Embodiment: Essays on gender and identity*. Delhi: Oxford University Press.

Theberge, N. (1987a). A critique of critiques: Radical and feminist writings on sport. *Social Forces, 60*(2), 341–53.

Theberge, N. (1987b). Sport and women's empowerment. *Women's Studies International, 10*(4), 387–93.

Thomas, R., Mills, A.J., Mills, J.H. (2004). *Identity politics at work: Resisting gender, gendering resistance*. New York: Routledge.

Thompson, E.H., Jr (Ed.). (1994). *Older men's lives*. Thousand Oaks, CA: Sage.

Thompson, E.P. (1967). Time, work discipline and industrial capitalism. *Past and Present, 38*, 615–33.

Thompson, N. (2002). Social movements, social justice and social work. *The British Journal of Social Work, 32*(6), 711–22.

Thomson, R. (1997). *Extraordinary bodies: Figuring physical disability in American culture and literature*. New York: Columbia University Press.

Thornham, S. (Ed.). (1999). *Feminist film theory: A reader*. Edinburgh: Edinburgh University Press.

Thorpe, H. (2009). Bourdieu, feminism, and female physical culture: Gender reflexivity and the habitus-field complex. *Sociology of Sport Journal, 26*, 491–515.

Tilley, V. (1997). The terms of the debate: Untangling language about ethnicity and ethnic movements. *Ethnic and Racial Studies, 20*, 497–522.

Titchkosky, T. (2007). *Reading and writing disability differently: The textured life of embodiment*. Toronto: University of Toronto Press.

Tolson, A. (1977). *The limits of masculinity*. London: Tavistock.

Tomlinson, S. (2001). *Education in a post-welfare society*. Buckingham, UK: Open University Press.

Tong, R. (2008). *Feminist thought*. London: Routledge.

Tosh, J. (1991). Domesticity and manliness in the Victorian middle class: The family of Edward

White Benson. In M. Roper & J. Tosh (Eds.), *Manful assertions: Masculinities in Britain since 1800*. London: Routledge.

Tosh, J. (2004). *Manliness and masculinities in nineteenth-century England*. London: Longman.

Traustadottir, R. (2010). Childhood disability, identity and human rights. *Journal of Applied Research in Intellectual Disabilities, 23*(5), 453.

Tremblay, G., & Turcotte, P. (2005). Gender identity construction and sexual orientation in sexually abused males. *International Journal of Men's Health, 4*(2), 131–47.

Troyna, B. (Ed.). (1989). *Racial inequality in education*. London: Routledge.

Turkle, S. (1997). Constructions and reconstructions of self in virtual reality: Playing in the MUDs. In S. Keisler (Ed.), *Culture of the Internet*. Mahwah, NJ: Lawrence Erlbaum.

Turner, B. (2003). Warrior charisma and the spiritualization of violence. *Body & Society, 9*(4), 93–108.

Twenge, J.M., & Zucker, A.N. (1999). What is a feminist? Evaluations and stereotypes in closed- and open-ended responses. *Psychology of Women Quarterly, 23*, 591–605.

Tyson, P. (1990). *Psychoanalytic theories of development: An integration*. New Haven, CT: Yale University Press.

Upadhya, C. (2002). Culture wars: The anthropological debate on multiculturalism. In K. Deb (Ed.), *Mapping multiculturalism*. New Delhi: Rawat.

Urry, J. (2002). *The tourist gaze*. London: Sage.

Urry, J. (2005a). The complexity turn. *Theory, Culture & Society, 22*(5), 1–14.

Urry, J. (2005b). The complexities of the global. *Theory, Culture & Society, 22*(5), 235–54.

Usher, R., & Edwards, R. (1994). *Postmodernism and education*. London: Routledge.

Ushikubo, M. (2008). *The herbivorous "ladylike" men are changing Japan*. Tokyo: Kodansha.

Uzzell, D., & Horne, N. (2006). The influence of biological sex, sexuality and gender role on interpersonal distance. *British Journal of Social Psychology, 45*, 579–97.

Vaccaro, C.A. (2011). Male bodies in manhood acts: The role of body talk and embodied practice in signifying culturally dominant notions of manhood. *Sociology Compass, 5*(1), 65–76.

Valentine, D. (2007). *Imagining transgender: An ethnography of a category*. Durham, NC: Duke University Press.

Valkenburg, P.M., Schouten, A.P., & Peter, J. (2005). Adolescents' identity experiments on the internet. *New Media & Society, 7*(3), 383–402.

Valocchi, S. (2005). Not queer enough: The lessons of queer theory for the sociology of gender and sexuality. *Gender & Society, 19*(6), 750–550.

van Bree , M. (2004). The metrosexual defined. Retrieved from http://mcmvanbree.com/metrosexual.htm

van Dijk, T.A. (2008a). *Discourse and context: A sociocognitive approach*. Cambridge, UK: Cambridge University Press.

van Dijk, T.A. (2008b). *Discourse and power*. Basingstoke, England: Palgrave Macmillan.

van Esterik, P. (2000). *Materializing Thailand*. New York: Berg.

van Leeuwen, M.S. (1990). *Gender & grace: Love, work and parenting in a changing world*. Downers Grove, IL: Intervarsity Press.

van Zoonen, L. (1994). *Feminist media studies*. London: Sage.

Veal, A.J. (1987). *Leisure and the future*. London: Allen & Unwin.

Veneracion-Rallonza, L. (2004). Women and the "post-sovereign" state: A feminist analytic of the state in the age of globalisation. *Gender, Technology and Development, 8*(3), 382–405.

Vigil, J.D. (2002). *A rainbow of gangs: Street subcultures in the mega-city*. Austin: University of Texas Press.

Vincent-Lanrin, S. (2008). Student mobility, internalization of higher education and skilled migration. *World migration report 2008*. International Organization for Migration.

Volpp, Leti (2001). Feminism versus multiculturalism. *Columbia Law Review, 101.5*, 1181–218.

Wajcman, J. (1991). *Feminism confronts technology*. Pennsylvania: Penn State University Press.

Wajcman, J. (1998). *Managing like a man*. Cambridge: Polity.

Walby, S. (1986). *Patriarchy at work*. Cambridge: Polity.

Walby, S., Gottfried, H., Gottschall, K., & Osawa, M. (Eds). (2006). *Gendering the knowledge economy: Comparative perspectives*. London: Macmillan.

Walcott, R. (2003). *Black like who? Writing black Canada*. Toronto: Insomniac Press.

Waldron, L.M. (2009). Cultural approaches to understanding school violence. *Sociology Compass*, *3*(4), 595–615.

Walker, K. (1994). "I'm not friends the way she's friends": Ideological and behavioural constructions of masculinity in men's friendships. *Masculinities*, *2*(2), 38–55.

Walkerdine, V. (1989). *Counting girls out*. London: Virgo.

Walkerdine, V. (1990). *Schoolgirl fictions*. London: Verso.

Walklate, S. (1995). *Gender and crime: An introduction*. Hemel Hempstead: Prentice Hall/Harvester Wheatsheaf.

Wang, Q., & Zhou, Q. (2010). China's divorce and remarriage rates: Trends and regional disparities. *Journal of Divorce & Remarriage*, *51*(4), 257–67.

Warnke, W. (2005). Race, gender and antiessentialist politics. *Signs*, *31*(1), 93–116.

Warren, J.T., & Lengel, L. (Eds.). (2005). *Casting gender: Women and performance in intercultural context*. New York: P. Lang.

Waterfield, B. (2010). Switzerland has women majority cabinet for first time. *The Telegraph*. Retrieved from http://www.telegraph.co.uk/news/worldnews/europe/switzerland/8018776/Switzerland-has-women-majority-cabinet-for-first-time.html.

Waters, M. (1994). *Modern sociological theory*. Thousand Oaks, CA: Sage.

Watson, J. (2000). *Male bodies: Health, culture and identity*. Buckingham, UK: Open University Press.

Watson, T.J. (2000). *In search of management*. London: Thomson Learning.

Watson, T.J., & Harris, P. (1999). *The emergent manager*. London: Sage.

Wearing, B. (1998). *Leisure and feminist theory*. London: Sage.

Webb, J. (2006). *Organizations, identities and the self*. London: Palgrave Macmillan.

Weber, M. (2001 [1930]). *The Protestant ethic and the spirit of capitalism*. London: Routledge.

Weed, E., & Schor, E. (1997). *Feminism meets queer theory*. Bloomington, IN: Indiana University Press.

Weedon, C. (2003). *Feminist practice and poststructuralist theory*. Oxford: Blackwell.

Weeks, J. (2000). *Making sexual history*. Cambridge: Polity.

Weiner, G. (1994). *Feminisms in education: An introduction*. Buckingham, UK: Open University Press.

Weisner, T.S., Garnier, H., & Loucky, J. (1994). Domestic tasks, gender egalitarian values and children's gender typing in conventional and non-conventional families. *Sex Roles*, *30*(1–2), 23–54.

Weitzman, L. (1984). Sex role socialization. In J. Freeman (Ed.), *Women: A feminist perspective*. Palo Alto, CA: Mayfield.

Wells, R. (2010). 41.6 per cent of the US population has a Facebook account. Retrieved from http://socialmediatoday.com/roywells1/158020/416-us-population-has-facebook-account

West, L.A. (2006). Negotiating masculinities in American drinking subcultures. In S. Whitehead, (Ed.), *Men and masculinities: Critical concepts in sociology* (Vol. II). London: Routledge.

Wetherell, M., Taylor, S., & Yates, S.J. (2001). *Discourse theory and practice: A reader*. London: Sage.

Wheaton, B., & Tomlison, A. (1998). The changing gender order in sport? The case of windsurfing subcultures. *Journal of Sport & Social Issues*, *2*(3), 252–74.

Whitehead, S. (1999). From paternalism to entrepreneurialism: The experiences of men managers in UK postcompulsory education. *Discourse*, *20*(1), 57–72.

Whitehead, S. (2000). Masculinity: Shutting out the nasty bits. *Gender, Work and Organization*, *7*(2), 133–37.

Whitehead, S. (2001a). Woman as manager: A seductive ontology. *Gender, Work and Organization*, *8*(1), 84–107.

Whitehead, S. (2001b). Man: The invisible gendered subject? In S.M. Whitehead & F.J. Barrett (Eds.), *The masculinities reader*. Cambridge: Polity.

Whitehead, S. (2003a). *Men, women, love and romance: Under the covers of the bedroom revolution.* London: Vision Paperbacks.

Whitehead, S. (2003b). Identifying the professional manager: Masculinity, professionalism and the search for legitimacy. In J. Barry, M. Dent, & M. O'Neil, (Eds.), *Gender, professionalism, and managerial change: An international perspective.* London: Macmillan.

Whitehead, S.M. (2002). *Men and masculinities: Key themes and new directions.* Cambridge: Polity.

Whitehead, S.M. (2006a). *Men and masculinities: Critical concepts in sociology.* London: Routledge.

Whitehead, S.M. (2006b). Contingent masculinities: Disruptions to "man"agerialist identity. In S.M. Whitehead (Ed.), *Men and masculinities: Critical concepts in sociology* (Vol. II). London: Routledge.

Whitehead, S.M. (2006c, October). "365 times in 3 weeks": The unbearable lightness of online love. Paper presented at the International Conference on Changing Forms of Intimacy, University of Oslo.

Whitehead, S.M. (2013a). *The relationship manifesto.* London: Andrews.

Whitehead, S.M. (2013b). Masculinities in management: Hidden, invisible and persistent. In S. Kumra, R. Simpson, & R. Burke (Eds.), *The Oxford handbook of gender in organizations.* Oxford: Oxford University Press.

Whitehead, S.M., & Barrett, F.J. (Eds.). (2001). *The masculinities reader.* Cambridge: Polity.

Whiteley, S. (2000). *Women and popular music: Sexuality, identity and subjectivity.* London: Routledge.

Whitson, D. (2006). Sport in the social construction of masculinity. In S. Whitehead (Ed.), *Men and masculinities: Critical concepts in sociology.* London: Routledge.

Whittier, N. (1995). *Feminist generations: The persistence of the radical women's movement.* Philadelphia, PA: Temple University Press.

Whittle, S. (2002). *Respect and equality: Transsexual and transgender rights.* London: Cavendish.

Whitty, G. (Ed.). (2002). *Making sense of educational policy.* London: Paul Chapman.

Wildhagen, T. (2010). Capitalizing on culture: How cultural capital shapes educational experiences and outcomes. *Sociology Compass, 4*(7), 519–31.

Willett, C. (1998). *Theorising multiculturalism: A guide to the current debate.* Oxford: Basil Blackwell.

Williams, J. (2005). *Understanding poststructuralism.* Stocksfield, UK: Acumen.

Williams, P.J. (1997). *Seeing a color-blind future: The paradox of race.* London: Virago.

Williams, S.L. (2009). Doing culture with girls like me: Why trying on gender and intersectionality matters. *Sociology Compass, 3*(2), 217–33.

Willis, P. (1977). *Learning to labour.* Farnborough, UK: Saxon House.

Willis, P. (1990). *Common culture.* Buckingham, UK: Open University Press.

Willmott, H., & O'Doherty, D. (2001). Debating labour process theory: The issue of subjectivity and the relevance of poststructuralism. *Sociology, 35*(2), 457–76.

Wilson, W. (2000). *Doping in elite sport: The politics of drugs and the Olympic movement.* Champaign, IL: Human Kinetics.

Wilson, W.J., & Chaddha, A. (2010, September 12). Why we're teaching *The wire* at Harvard. *Washington Post.*

Winlow, S. (2001). *Badfellas: Crime, tradition and new masculinities.* London: Berg.

Winnicott, D.W. (1973). *The child, the family, and the outside world.* Harmondsworth, UK: Penguin Books.

Witz, A. (1992). *Professions and patriarchy.* London: Routledge.

Witz, A. (2000). Whose body matters? Feminist sociology and the corporeal turn in sociology and feminism. *Body & Society, 6*(2), 1–24.

Wolf, N. (1991). *The beauty myth: How images of beauty are used against women.* New York: Vintage.

Wolmark, J. (Ed.). (1999). *Cybersexualities: A reader on feminist theory, cyborgs and cyberspace.* Edinburgh: Edinburgh University Press.

Wongruang, P. (2007, July 18). Studying sex and the city. *Bangkok Post,* p. 14.

Wood, E., Desmarais, S., & Gugula, S. (2002). The impact of parenting experience on gender stereotyped toy play of children. *Sex Roles*, *47*(1/2), 39–49.

Woolf, Virginia. (1929). *A room of one's own.* London: The Hogarth Press.

World Bank (2007). Girls' education. Retrieved from www.worldbank.org/education

World Bank (2011). *Migration and remittances factbook 2011.* Washington, DC: World Bank.

World Bank (2012). *World development report 2012: Gender equality and development.* Washington, DC: World Bank.

World Health Organization (1980). Definition of persons with disabilities.

World Health Organization (2000). Obesity: Preventing and managing the global epidemic. Geneva, Switzeland: WHO.

World Health Organization (2003). Controlling the global obesity epidemic. Geneva, Switzerland: WHO. Retrieved from http://www.who.int/nutrition/topics/obesity/en/index.html

Wotherspoon, T. (1998). *The sociology of education in Canada: Critical perspectives.* Toronto: Oxford University Press.

Wright, A. (2003). *Religion, education and post-modernity.* London: Routledge.

Wydra, H. (2008). The recurrence of violence. *Sociology Compass, 2*(1), 183–4.

Yaksich, M.J. (2005). Consuming queer: The commodification of culture and its effects on social acceptance. *Elements*, Spring, 24–35.

Yamada, M. (2004). *A hope-divided society.* Tokyo: Chikuma Shobo.

Yeoh, B.S.A., & Huang, S. (2000). "Home" and "away": Foreign domestic workers and negotiations of diasporic identity in Singapore. *Women's Studies International Forum, 23*(4), 413–29.

Yim, J.Y., & Mahalingam, R. (2006). Culture, masculinity, and psychological well-being in Punjab, India. *Sex Roles, 55*, 715–24.

Youdell, D. (2005). Sex–gender–sexuality: How sex, gender and sexuality constellations are constituted in secondary schools. *Gender and Education, 17*(3), 249–70.

Young, I.M. (1990). *Throwing like a girl and other essays in feminist philosophy and social theory.* Bloomington, IN: Indiana University Press.

Young, K. (1989). Narrative embodiments: Enclaves of the self in the realm of medicine. In J. Shotter & K.J. Gergen (Eds.), *Texts of identity.* London: Sage.

Young, M. (1988). *The metronome society: Natural rhythms and human timetables.* London: Thames and Hudson.

Yuval-Davis, N. (2006). Intersectionality and feminist politics. *European Journal of Women's Studies, 13*, 193–209.

Zemlinskaya, Y. (2010). Social movements through the gender lens. *Sociology Compass, 4*, 628–41.

Zhong, X. (2000). *Masculinity besieged? Issues of modernity and male subjectivity in Chinese literature of the late twentieth century.* Durham, NC: Duke University Press.

Zimmerman, J. (1999). *Raising our athletic daughters: How sports can build self-esteem and save girls' lives.* New York: Main Street Books.

Zitzelsberger, H. (2005). (In)visibility: Accounts of embodiment of women with physical disabilities and differences. *Disability and Society, 20*(4), 389–403.

Zizek, S. (1997). Multiculturalism, or, the cultural logic of multinational capitalism. *New Left Review, 225*, 28–51.

Zlotnik, H. (2003). The global dimensions of female migration. Retrieved from http://www.migrationinformation.org/feature/display.cfm?ID=109

Zoonen, L. van. (1994). *Feminist media studies.* New York: Sage.

Zunes, S., Kurtz, L.R., & Asher, S.B. (Eds.). (1999). *Nonviolent social movements: A geographical perspective.* London: Blackwell.

INDEX

Deleuze, G. and F. Guattari, 44, 52–53
Derne, S., 270
Derrida, Jacques, 44, 46, 50; *Of Grammatology*, 77
desire: post-structuralism and, 43, 52–53; *see also* sex and sexualities
Destutt de Tracy, Antoine Louis Claude, 17
De Tona, C., 270–71
diaspora, 267–68, 269–72, 292; Aboriginal communities, 271–72; communities, 269, 271; definition, 105, 297; major movements and destinations, 267; men and, 270; reasons for, 268; retention of dominant gender discourses, 269; sexuality and, 271–72; women and, 270; *see also* migration
diaspora effect, 266
difference, 46
difference, theories of, 66–67, 91–92
Difference That Disability Makes, The (Michalko), 85
Dinnerstein, Dorothy, 29
disabilities, people with, 85; gender stereotypes and, 87; in media, 88; psycho-social difficulties of, 87
disability movements, 86
disability theory, 84–88, 91; definitions and, 85; intersection of disability, gender, and sexuality, 88; medical model of disability, 86; moral model of disability, 86; multiple identities and, 88; "people first" language, 84; social model of disability, 86–87
discourse, 44, 48, 75, 297; dominant, 50, 51; of modernity, 58; post-structuralism and, 43, 48–50
discursive subject/self, 33, 48, 49–50, 53, 60, 61, 81, 133, 204
diversity, 105, 266; *see also* multiculturalism
division of labour, gendered, 119
division of labour, sexual, 169–70, 196, 206, 207
divorces, 176
domestic workers, female foreign, 271
Douglass, Frederick, 66
Dozier, R., 134
dualism, sex-gender, 30, 91, 230, 238, 253; resisting, 241, 288
Du Bois, W.E.B., 66
Dugger, K., 73
Durkheim, Émile, 8, 54, 214–15
Dworkin, Andrea, 155
Dylan, Bob, 244
Eagleton, Terry, 55
earnings: aging men and, 257; black women and, 221; gender gap, 220–21; race and ethnicity and, 221
East Germany: females and males in universities in, 219
economy, global: women in, 119, 120
Écrits: A Selection (Lacan), 31
education, 213–14; black women and, 221; boys

and, 223–26; feminist theories of, 216–17; gender binary in, 223; gender dynamics in, 233; gendered character and constitution, 216–17; gender stereotypes in, 219; girls and, 217–22; human potential and, 215; impact on other roles, 220–22; liberal perspectives on, 215; marketization of, 217–18; Marxist perspectives on, 215–16; masculinity and, 223–24; theorizing, 214–17; value of, 232–33; vocational training, 219
educational achievement, 218–20; boys', 223, 225–26; women's, 118, 218, 222, 170
Education Reform Act (UK), 218
Edwards, Tim, 81–82
elderly people: long-term care for, 258
Electra complex, 27, 297–98
Elias, Norbert, 249
Elliott, A., 31, 32
El Saadawi, Nawal, 78, 151
Elshtain, J.B., 170
emotionality, 178, 179
employment. *See* work
Enlightenment project, 54, 58, 59, 298
epistemic, 57, 298
epistemic unity, 55, 298
epistemological, 47, 298
Epistemology of the Closet (Sedgwick), 78
Eros, 30
essentialism, 80, 81, 298
ethnic cleansing, 68
ethnicity, 68–69
eugenic, 151, 298
Euro RSCG Worldwide, 281
events, global media, 102–3, 104
existential, 101, 298
Facebook, 60, 154, 273, 277
false consciousness, 18, 298
Faludi, Susan, 116
families, 192–93, 199, 209, 210; gender and other discourses of identity and, 195–96; gender-role behaviour in, 194–95; male-breadwinner, 116, 169–70, 194, 200, 290; multiplicity of, 194–96; nuclear, 13, 184, 194; single-parent, 171, 194, 195
Fanon, Frantz, 75–76, 78; "Algeria Unveiled", 76; Bhabha on, 77; *Black Skin, White Masks*, 75, 76; *A Dying Colonialism*, 76; *The Wretched of the Earth*, 76
fascism, 248
fashion, 240–41
Fast, I., 29
fathers, 7, 13, 26, 152, 184, 198
Fathers-4-Justice, 152
fatness, 242–43